In memoriam

Lissi Astrup

Depicting the Dead

Aarhus Studies in Mediterranean Antiquity (ASMA)

XI

ASMA is a series which is published approximately once a year by the research programme Classical Antiquity at Aarhus University, Denmark.

The programme includes researchers from various disciplines studying Graeco-Roman Antiquity, such as Classical Archaeology, Classical Philology, Ancient History, the Study of Religion, and Theology.

The objective of the series is to advance the interdisciplinary study of Antiquity by publishing articles, e.g., conference papers, or independent monographs, which among other things reflect the current activities of the programme.

Depicting the Dead

Self-Representation and Commemoration on Roman Sarcophagi with Portraits

Stine Birk

Aarhus University Press |

Depicting the Dead

Cover by Jørgen Sparre

Illustration: Rome, Museo Nazionale Romano, Palazzo Massimo, inv. 126372 (cat. 645)

Typeset with Adobe Garamond

and printed by Narayana Press

Printed in Denmark, 2013

ISBN 978 87 7124 018 4

ISSN 1399 2686

Aarhus University Press

Langelandsgade 177

DK-8200 Aarhus N

www.unipress.dk

International distributors:

Gazelle Book Services Ltd.

White Cross Mills

Hightown, Lancaster, LA1 4XS

United Kingdom

www.gazellebookservices.co.uk

ISD

70 Enterprise Drive, Suite 2

Bristol, CT 06010

USA

www.isdistribution.com

Published with the financial support of

Aarhus University Research Foundation

Elisabeth Munksgaard Fonden

CONTENTS

Acknowledgements

The present monograph is the outcome of years of fascination with sarcophagus reliefs. In 2009 I defended my PhD on third-century Roman sarcophagi at Aarhus University, supervised by Dr. Björn Christian Ewald and Professor Emeritus Niels Hannestad, and this monograph reflects that work in some aspects. The groundwork for the catalogue had at that time been completed, but it has been revised and substantially expanded in the present version. The entire corpus of sarcophagi with portrait figures has been included here, including those from the second and fourth centuries as well as the third. In writing this book a greater focus was put on the portrait figure and issues of the commemoration and representation of individuals. First and foremost, I am grateful to the Carlsberg Foundation for funding my postdoctoral work. It is their financial support that has allowed this study to come to completion. I would like to acknowledge the further financial support towards the cost of this publication that was provided by the Aarhus University Research Foundation and the Elisabeth Munksgaard Foundation.

It would have been impossible to write this book without the support of colleagues, friends, and institutions. In particular, I would like to thank the Danish Institute in Rome, Hoyt Fields at the Hearst Castle, California, Daria Lanzuelo at the German Archaelogical Institute in Rome, the Staatliche Museen, Berlin, the Huntington Art Gallery, San Marino, and the Ny Carlsberg Glyptotek. I am grateful to Katharina Meinecke for useful discussions and for sharing results from her own work on sarcophagi with me, Zahra Newby for reading and commenting on the text, especially chapter 1. I am also grateful to Björn Christian Ewald for reading both early and later versions of the text, Hanne Sigismund Nielsen for discussions of the role of women and for assistance with the inscriptions, and Lea Stirling, who during her time as a visiting professor at Aarhus University was a great inspiration. Furthermore, early versions of chapters were read, critiqued, and significantly improved by my colleague at Aarhus University Birte Poulsen. A special thank you to my friend and colleague Lone Iversen for help with the catalogue and for locating around the world sarcophagi previously unknown to me.

As for the committee of my PhD, I am greatly indebted to Michael Koortbojian and Janet Huskinson, not least for pointing out both the weaknesses and the positive aspects of my study and for fruitful discussion at the defence. They encouraged me to continue work on the material. Special thanks go to Janet Huskinson, who was always ready to discuss the enigmatic world of sarcophagi during her visiting professorship in Aarhus.

My final and most heartfelt thanks are due to a person who has been a rock-solid support throughout the entire process: my husband Troels Myrup Kristensen. He was my constant inspiration and untiring friend during the many troublesome phases of writing this book, and he read and commented on all parts of the manuscript. Without him I would never have finished it.

I have dedicated this book to my beloved grandmother, since a book focusing on commemoration and role models appears to me to be an appropriate dedication to the memory of a woman with admirable virtues. She was my own role model.

Negotiating Identity on Sarcophagi

Best of all seems the Roman custom, which publicly renders to women, as to men, a fitting commemoration after the end of their life.

Plutarch, *On the Bravery of Women*[1]

To be remembered after death was important in Roman society; Roman funerary arts bear witness to the efforts that were made to ensure that the memory of individuals survived.[2] According to Ulpian, monuments (*monumenta*) were erected to preserve memory.[3] In line with this tradition of using monuments to keep the memory of a specific event or person alive, funerary monuments of various kinds were erected all over the Roman Empire.[4] Many still stand today as expressions of the hope for a persisting memory, particularly those made of durable materials, such as brick buildings or marble altars, *stelae*, and sarcophagi.[5] The Roman view was that as long as the monument existed, the memory of the person was maintained, and through the memory the *anima* of the deceased lived on. Passing into oblivion was the worst possible scenario. As such, acts that erased the memory of a person were seen as a disgrace, and inscriptions warn or condemn those who dared to desecrate or reuse a tomb.[6]

Sarcophagi, made for one or at most two individuals, have been preserved in large numbers. Some 15,000 in total survive from the Roman Imperial period, of which it has been estimated that around 6,000 were produced in the city of Rome.[7] The production of sarcophagi

1 Plutarch, *Moralia* III, *On the Bravery of Women* (introduction), trans. Babbitt; Pantell 1992.

2 For the importance of constructing a memory, see Hope 1997; 2003; 2011. On Roman funerary culture in general, see Andreae 1963; Hesberg & Zanker 1987; Hesberg 1992; Koch 1993a; Hope 1997a; Bodel 2008.

3 Ulpian, *Digest,* 11.7.2.6. Though the word *monumentum* is sometimes used to denote funerary monuments (Carroll 2006, 30; 2011, 66), it most likely also refers to other kinds of monuments such as statues erected to commemorate something or someone, and to pieces or collections of writing (Hope 2007, 71).

4 It has been estimated that from the period between Augustus and Constantine only 1.5 % of all burials from Rome have been preserved to the present day (Bodel 2008, 179), which says something about how extensive the production must have been. The idea that the strongest hope for survival was found in fame, and not in the hope for an afterlife, is also expressed in Greek culture, see Nortwick 2008, xiii.

5 As, for example, evident from the phrasing *memoriam perpetuam* on a funerary inscription from Tarragona (*CIL* II 4332).

6 See Carroll 2006, 79-83; 2011. In one instance from Rome, a person named Gaius Annidienus Frequens tried to prevent his tomb from being defiled by passers-by (*ne quis hic urina*), *CIL* VI 3413. Inscriptions that aim to protect the tomb and keep it within the family are frequent in the Eastern Empire, especially on sarcophagi from Asia Minor (see, for example, Reynolds & Roueché in Işik 2007, cat. 178, 179, and 196). Such inscriptions bear evidence of the importance of the tomb in society but also of the fact that despite legislation against it, tombs were neglected or reused by later generations. For phrases threatening any violater of a tomb, see Meinecke 2010, 100 with further literature in note 74.

7 Koch 1993, 59; Rogge, *ASR* IX, 1, 1 (1995) 15. The word sarcophagus is of Greek origin: *sarx*, meaning "flesh", and *phagein*, meaning "to eat". The stone from which the sarcophagus was carved was said to contain enough lime to hasten the decomposition of the body. Pliny in *Natural History* (36.131) writes about sarcophagi as flesh-eaters that consumed every part of the corpse except the teeth. Pliny is, however, talking about a certain type of stone that is only quarried in Assos in Asia Minor (Koch & Sichtermann 1982, 23-5). According to Ward-Perkins the *lapis sarcophagus* from Assos has now been located (1992, 55-60).

emerged at approximately the same time in many parts of the Empire, from Turkey in the East through Athens to Rome in the West.[8] Their popularity was probably to some extent a matter of fashion as inhumation gradually gained ground in funerary traditions otherwise dominated by cremation burial.[9] In Rome, the first relief-adorned sarcophagi date to the Trajanic period,[10] but they were not produced on a major scale before the reign of Hadrian.[11] In the third century, a period in which sarcophagi were almost mass-produced, the types varied from large high-quality sarcophagi to smaller, less ambitious works with an iconographic repertoire that ranged from elaborate mythological scenes to small images of daily life (so-called *vita romana* scenes) or simple decorative schemes.[12] The quality of the production (some mediocre and without full figural decoration, and others of impressive workmanship) indicates that at this time sarcophagi were available to people from different strata of society. Only with difficulty, however, can the social status of the patrons be identified, but in all probability they were situated on a spectrum that ranged from the highest social classes (cat. no. 671 has been interpreted as the sarcophagus of the emperor Balbinus and his wife) to a whole variety of social groups in well-to-do Roman society.[13] In spite of the sometime mediocer quality, a marble sarcophagus must have been costly and therefore would not have been available to the lower social classes.[14]

Sarcophagi use a formulaic language in the scenes that adorn them, and they have often been organised into categories according to the type of motif shown. Apart from the choice of motif, Rome shows two characteristics of sarcophagus production that make the coffins unique as a source of evidence for exploring social change. First, it is continuous from the second to the beginning of the fourth century, whereby the iconography illustrates changes in mentality and the complex interplay between pagan and Christian cultures.[15] Second, it includes a large number of pieces in which a figure was individualised through the application of a portrait.[16] In the other parts of the empire, portraits were rarely carved on sarcophagus reliefs.[17] The very earliest of these

8 For the production outside Rome, see, for example, for Asia Minor: Wiegartz 1965; Heinz 2001; Reynolds & Rouché in Işik 2007; Koch 2010. Dalmatia: Cambi 1998. Attic sarcophagi: Rogge, *ASR* IX, 1, 1 (1995); Ewald 2004; 2011; Oakley, *ASR* IX 1, 3 (2011).

9 The reason for this change in burial fashion is obscure; see Nock 1932; Toynbee 1971, especially 39-42; Brandenburg 1978, 324-26; Morris 1992, 31-69; Bodel 2008; Davies 2011.

10 Brandenburg 1978, 327.

11 Froning 1980, 322-23. Koch (1993, 58, 66) is more specific and estimated the beginning of the major production to be around 110-120 AD. The production of prevailingly Christian sarcophagi continued, evidenced by a few pieces, into the fifth century. For the early sarcophagi and their development, see Junker 2005/6, 164 with further literature. All dates given in this book are AD, unless otherwise stated.

12 This category was established by C. Robert, the founder of the corpus *Die antiken Sarkophagreliefs* (*ASR*), but it is rather problematic. Despite the name, it does not show scenes from real life and should be read metaphorically, like other categories of sarcophagus reliefs. Often non-mythological scenes are depicted that imitate situations that could have taken place in real life, such as people driving in a wagon, hunts, or marriage scenes. For a re-evaluation of the categorisation of mythological images in opposition to genre images, see Giuliani 2003.

13 Huskinson 2002, 12. Ewald suggests that sarcophagi made in Rome had spread to social strata other than the elite (2004, 234). In his earlier book on philosopher sarcophagi, Ewald discusses the social strata of the deceased based on the scarce evidence provided by inscriptions (1999, 116-17). The conclusion finds an inhomogeneous group centred on the higher middle classes, such as, for example, knights, which in the third century was a title achieved either through a military career or through birth. Also Denzey makes a good effort to localise and describe the social class of a girl whose undisturbed sarcophagus with skeleton and grave goods were unearthed in Rome and opened by Lanciani in 1894. The girl was probably of a wealthy freeborn family and Denzey uses the term "middle class" to describe her status (Denzey 2007, 4). See also Fittschen 1975, 15-8 and Bielefeld, *ASR* V 2, 2 (1997) 86-8. Fittschen dismisses the identification of the so-called Balbinus sarcophagus as that of the emperor (1979).

14 On production and costs, see most recently Russell 2011.

15 After the middle of the fourth century they were only carved on a minor scale.

16 The catalogue of this monograph contains 677 entries, which, despite of years of collecting, is not a complete collection but a representative corpus of what I would estimate to be around 90 % of the preserved material. For the catalogue and its premises, see p. 203.

17 There are examples of sarcophagi with portraits from other places as, for example, those found in the production from Aphrodisias, cf. Işik 2007, cat. 6, 101, 103-107, 109-111, 113,

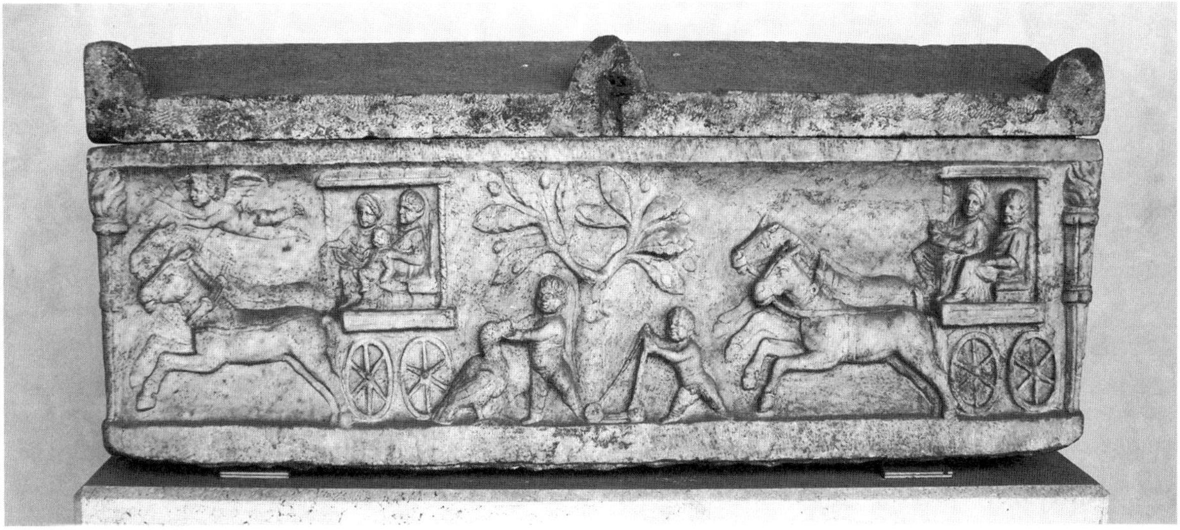

Child sarcophagus (cat. no. 621). Rome, Museo Nazionale Romano, inv. 65199. Photo: Author, courtesy of Soprintendenza Speciale per i Beni Archeologici di Roma. **Fig. 1**

individualised sarcophagi, as far as I know, is a sarcophagus showing parents and a child driving wagons dated around 100 (**Fig. 1**; cat. no. 621).[18] This is an example of the so-called interacting type, in which the portrait figures act in the scene. Another type which was to become very popular is the sarcophagus with a bust portrait, the first example of which is dated to the Trajanic period (cat. no. 257). It shows a bust of a boy carried by cupids and flanked on each side by a griffin and another cupid. The fashion of applying a portrait to the relief decoration did not become widespread before the third century. The continuous production and the fashion for portraits, together with the quantity in which they are preserved, make sarcophagi a valuable source of historical and cultural inquiry, and indeed complementary to the testimony of the literary sources of the period.

Sarcophagus reliefs have been intensively studied since C. Robert founded the corpus *Die antiken Sarkophagreliefs* in 1890, and since then changing approaches have been applied to the material, varying from stylistic analysis and chronology to studies of identity constructions and personal commemoration.[19] Crudely, it can be stated that chronological issues and the problem of identifying myths dominated scholarly discussions of sarcophagi into the 1980s.[20] However, religion and afterlife beliefs symbolised through sarcophagus images and not least the symbolic value of the image were prominent topics of discussion since 1942, when F. Cumont presented his *Recherches sur le symbolisme funéraire des Romains* and D. Nock reviewed this important work.[21] Gradually, an social historical approach gained ground in the studies of sarcophagi with contributions such as P. Blome's *Zur Umgestaltung griechischer Mythen in der römischen Sepulkralkunst* (1978) and *Funerärsymbolische Collagen auf mythologischen Sarkophagreliefs* (1992), K. Fittschen's article on how to interpret Greek myths on Roman sar-

117, 119, 120, 121a, 130, 133, 135, 137, 139, 171, 177-180, and 182. Also Koch & Sichtermann 1982 mention more sarcophagi made outside of Rome often as an imitation of the Roman production: cf. 312, figs. 337-38, 340-42 (North Africa), 317, figs. 350-51 (Dalmatia), and the more characteristic sarcophagi with what could be termed family galleries from Macedonia, cf. 347, 352, figs. 374-75, just to mention a few examples.

18 Amedick, *ASR* I 4 (1991) cat. 190

19 For a review of the earlier scholarship, see the section on chronology below.

20 See, for example, Bovini 1949; Himmelmann-Wildschütz 1974; Andreae 1984. The approach continues to be reflected in the series *Sarkophag-Studien*, edited by G. Koch (see, for example, Amedick & Koch 1998 and Kirchhainer & Koch 2002). For a review of the approach to sarcophagi, see Birk 2010/11.

21 Nock 1946.

cophagi (1992), F. Müller's monograph on the so-called Peleus and Thetis sarcophagus in Villa Albani (1994), D. Grassinger on the meaning of myths on sarcophagi (1994), and finally M. Koortbojian's *Myth, Meaning and Memory on Roman sarcophagi* (1995). In the latter monograph, it was ascertained that sarcophagus imagery should not be interpreted in one way only, as a static visual expression of a specific idea. Instead, it is convincingly argued that they were meaningful on multiple levels.

The present monograph takes its place in this now well-established tradition of seeing sarcophagi as visual statements of deceased individuals that used allegories to plot lives and personal memories against mythological and other idealised narratives.[22] It focuses on the portrait figure of relief-adorned marble sarcophagi made in or in the near vicinity of Rome in the imperial period. This group is often referred to as *stadtrömisch*, which reflects the fact that the field has traditionally been dominated by German scholars.

The aim of this book is twofold: Firstly, it is an exploration of how to *read* Roman sarcophagi, which starts from those with portraits, but which can contribute more broadly to the study of sarcophagi in general. Scholars familiar with the main issues of reading sarcophagi can skip chapter 1's introduction to self-representation and the funerary context since it deals with the some of the basic premises for working with sarcophagi. Secondly, this book investigates gender values as represented through images and how to locate the individual in standardised iconography. Chapter 2, therefore, takes as its point of departure some of the main themes represented on sarcophagi and offers a sociological analysis of them. The importance of social status has played a seminal role in the way the sarcophagi have been interpreted. However, it will be argued that what they express about self-representation, is much more than a statement of status. They give us insights into the formation of an elite culture that expressed itself through new burial forms and are informative about the social experiences of individuals as well as their emotions at times of bereavement and in confronting death. An increased focus on the self and an awareness of the value of remembrance means that sarcophagi were generally made as personal monuments, an aspect of Roman funerary culture that is revelatory of the importance of individuals, as they negotiated their roles and identities in life and death.[23] In the discussion of ideals and self-understanding among Roman citizens, learnedness and the concept of *paideia* has been brought to the fore.[24] In chapter 2, I will explore this topic further through an assessment og the learned figure, together with a discussion of the individualised mythological figure and figures performing rituals.

Although sarcophagi were made for private commemoration, they possessed an aspect of self-representation that was directed outwards. The book is therefore also concerned with the problem of how to understand the relationship between the private and the social aspects of sarcophagus images. As such, I take one sarcophagus to be a manifestation of an individual or singular unity such as a marital couple, whereas a larger sample of sarcophagi reflects the norms and virtues that are prevalent in society. The combination of the micro level (one individual sarcophagus) with the macro level (a larger sample of sarcophagi) allows us to construct a narrative that includes personal as well as social history. It is, unfortunately, mostly impossible for us to address personal aspects or experiences such as profession or ethnicity, but we can discuss what the portrait figure expresses in terms of values, ideals, and morals. Chapter 3 is concerned with this aspect, mostly from the perspective of gender. Here it will be empha-

22 Just to mention some of the most important works to which I will return during my discussions: Blome 1978; 1992; Fittschen 1975a; 1979; 1984; 1992a; Giuliani 1989; Ewald 1998; 1999; 2003; 2004; 2005; Zanker 1999; 2000; 2005; Wrede 2001; Zanker & Ewald 2004; Bielfeldt 2005a; Elsner & Huskinson 2011.

23 Ewald plausibly sees the sarcophagi as a mechanism that "becomes a redemption for death and decay, and a principal means in the fight against the threat of oblivion." (2011, 261). Furthermore, he explains the emergence of sarcophagi during the second century as a consequence of discourses about the self (2011, 261-63). Ewald is in this article mostly concerned with the iconography of Attic sarcophagi, but refers in his general discussion to the "male urban elite of the empire". In the context of studying the use of funerary monuments to nego tiate the identity of the deceased, V. Hope's works on Roman funerary art are also important: Hope 1997; 1998; 2000; 2003.

24 See, for example, Ewald 1998; 1998a; 1999 (reviewed by D'Ambra 2001; Kranz 2001; Raeck 2002; Trimble 2002; Balty 2005); 1999a; 1999b; 2003; 2004; 2005; 2011.

sised how the idealised portraits of men and women conformed to societal norms, and how scenes did not present the world as it was: in the choice of motifs used to represent the deceased, some virtues were accentuated and others were left out. It will be argued, building on important scholarship on sarcophagi by authors such as Koortbojian and P. Zanker, that individualised figures on sarcophagi function as analogies to roles, values, and ideals that were generally accepted in society, and that they allow us to understand the desired virtues and qualities of the deceased.[25] Though the figure types were mostly represented in realistic roles, there are some roles that did conform to the ideal of a living role model and which therefore could only be taken on iconographically, such as, for example, the naked woman so frequently seen in mythological scenes.[26]

As studies of identity and gender have multiplied in the last decade, so have studies of funerary art in a social context. In the repercussions of this, the social significance of sarcophagi has increasingly come into focus, and questions of the relationships between iconography, age, gender, and identity construction have been given particular attention (here especially in chapters 3 and 4). One scholar who has contributed substantially to this field is J. Huskinson, who sees sarcophagi as both mediating certain aspects of human life, and reflecting different roles through which people could negotiate their identity.[27]

The relationship between actual lived experiences and the image represented on sarcophagi has been explored in several studies. In some earlier scholarship scenes imitating everyday life situations were interpreted as symbolising the profession of the deceased, as for example, a bucolic scene on cat. no. 430 (**Fig. 2**) show-

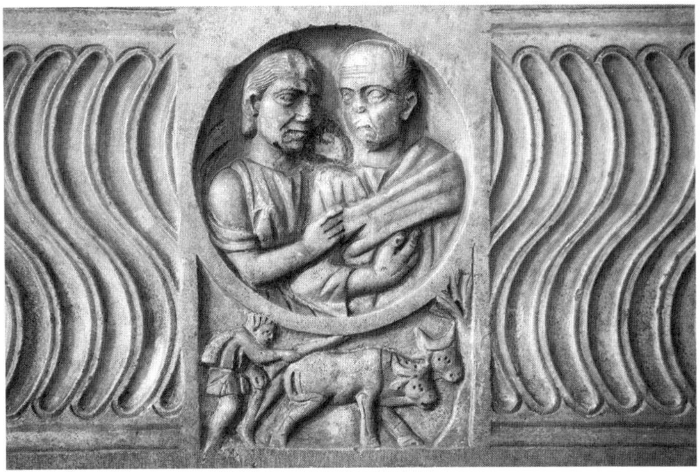

Strigillated sarcophagus with a portrait of a woman and a man (cat. no. 430). Cefalù, S Chiesa di S. Francesco. Photo: Paul Hammann. **Fig. 2**

ing a man who cultivates his land with an ox-drawn plough.[28] More recently, however, several scholars have emphasised the difficulty of approaching individual lives through sarcophagus reliefs and argued that images of everyday life are expressions of societal values and expectations, similar to the function of mythological scenes.[29] Therefore, sarcophagus reliefs tend to say more about the society in which they were produced than about the lives of the men, women, and children they depict. Seen in this light, the reliefs allow us to analyse the *Mentalitätsgeschichte* of a stratum of Roman society in a specific period, since the idealised method of self-representation reflects the value systems and cultural standards of the period in which the reliefs were produced.[30]

The reading of sarcophagus images should take the expectations of the viewer as its starting point, and look at how the images function in relation to acts of commemoration.[31] Still, even the Romans did not believe that memory was simply stored in material objects. Memory and remembrance are rather less stable enti-

25 The idea of analogies in sarcophagus imagery was developed by Koortbojian (1995), who discusses the importance of analogies on sarcophagi and the complexity implied in the relationship between the imagery and the dead (see especially pp. 1-9; reviewed by Elsner 1996); Zanker in Zanker & Ewald 2004.

26 Olson writes that "female nudity or undress was associated with prostitution and sexual license; the lowest women were those whose display of their bodies marked them as sexually available" (2008, 95).

27 Huskinson 1993; 1996, especially 104 (reviewed by Ghilardi 1996; Koch 1997; Bartman 1999; Koortbojian 1999; Ewald 1999c) 1999; 2002, particularly 29; 2005; 2007; 2007a; 2008.

28 Tusa 1995 [1957], 27-8. Also Whitehead (1984) approached the profession of the deceased through sarcophagus images, but as already Marrou (1938, 197-207) and later Ewald (1999, 111) acknowledge iconography on sarcophagi seldom addresses profession.

29 Huskinson 2002, 11-2; Bielefelt 2005a and latest Lorenz 2011.

30 Ewald 2004, 230.

31 Zanker 1999; 2000; Huskinson 2002, 21-2.

ties evoked by, for example, social practice, rituals, and customs.[32] In recent years agency theory, with a focus on the individual, has influenced the way funerary culture is studied and the wishes, actions, and demands of individuals have gained more importance in the social analysis of sarcophagi.[33] The approach taken here oscillates between the traditional approach that assumes funerary culture can be indicative, though not a direct reflection, of the norms and values of the society in which they were produced, and the acknowledgement of the agency of the individual. The sarcophagus is therefore seen as a monument that creates a space for acts of mourning, as it is a means of self-representation. The viewer-centric approach to the visual decoration of sarcophagi reflects a wish to understand them beyond their expressions of social status. A consequence is that sarcophagus images become multi-layered, meaning that they were able to fulfil the diverse needs of people by offering interpretations that could be adapted according to the individual visiting the tomb.[34] This flexibility in the reading of scenes is one of the great advantages of sarcophagi, and it may help to explain why they became such a popular medium for *post-mortem* self-representation. On the other hand, there may have been a limit to this degree of readability and a general consensus as to what qualities specific images conveyed; a total fluidity in the meaning of the scenes would have obstructed the possibility of constructing an ideal identity, which was after all one of the main purposes in erecting a commemorative monument.

When discussing these issues, the third century will often stand as a focal point of reference, since in this period one may speak of a 'portrait boom' on sarcophagi. The portrait figure helps us to read the images, since it focuses the viewer's attention on a particular figure or episode.[35] The figure makes it explicit which virtues and qualities the patron wanted to be remembered for. Many of these constructions of personal identity and social ideals are particularly clear in the third century, but the methodology involved in reading sarcophagus images also holds lessons for the study of both the earlier and later production.

Portraits on Sarcophagi

A characteristic feature of the production undertaken in Rome is, as previously mentioned, the great number of sarcophagi on which one or more of the figures were individualised through the application of a portrait. This means that a variety of idealised and mythological figures were given an individual value by means of portrait features.[36] In the context of using sarcophagus images as expressions of identity, the portrait added an extra dimension to this mode of self-representation, an idea evolved and unravelled by several leading scholars and most recently by Zanker, B.C. Ewald, and Z. Newby.[37] By combining a portrait with the body of an ideal figure, the virtues and qualities of that figure were transferred to the identity of the deceased.

The use of portraits on sarcophagi should be understood as a continuation of the Roman tradition of using portraits to represent individuals in diverse social contexts. Portraits could be used for public and political purposes, in sanctuaries, to show patronage, or in honorific contexts which include tombs. Whereas the public display focused on status and career, the private use is about defining oneself in relation to the family and to preserve memory. Carving portrait on funerary monuments in Rome was a continuing phenomenon from the first century BC into the fourth century.[38] The use of portraits in the funerary sphere were not limited to sarcophagi; funerary altars, marble couches with reclining figures, statues, urns, and reliefs could all include depictions of the person they were meant to

32 Robinson 2010, especially 92.

33 For example, Dobres & Robb 2000.

34 An approach, for example, taken by Zanker & Ewald 2004 (reviewed by Hallett 2005; Huskinson 2005a).

35 Newby 2011, 224.

36 For this phenomenon within Roman mythological sculpture in general, see Wrede 1981.

37 Zanker & Ewald 2004, especially 179, 185-88; Newby 2011. Furthermore the issue is briefly summarised in Stewart 2008, 70-6. For earlier studies of the same tradition some of the most important contributions are Brandenburg 1967; Fittschen 1970a; 1979; Schauenburg 1980; Wrede 1981, though he is not only concerned with sarcophagi; Koch & Sichtermann 1982, 607-14. See also chapter 1.

38 Stewart 2003, 92. The role of ancestor masks is likely to be rather small in second- and third-century funerary culture (Stewart 2003, 83). On ancestors masks, see Flower 1996 (reviewed by Saller 1998).

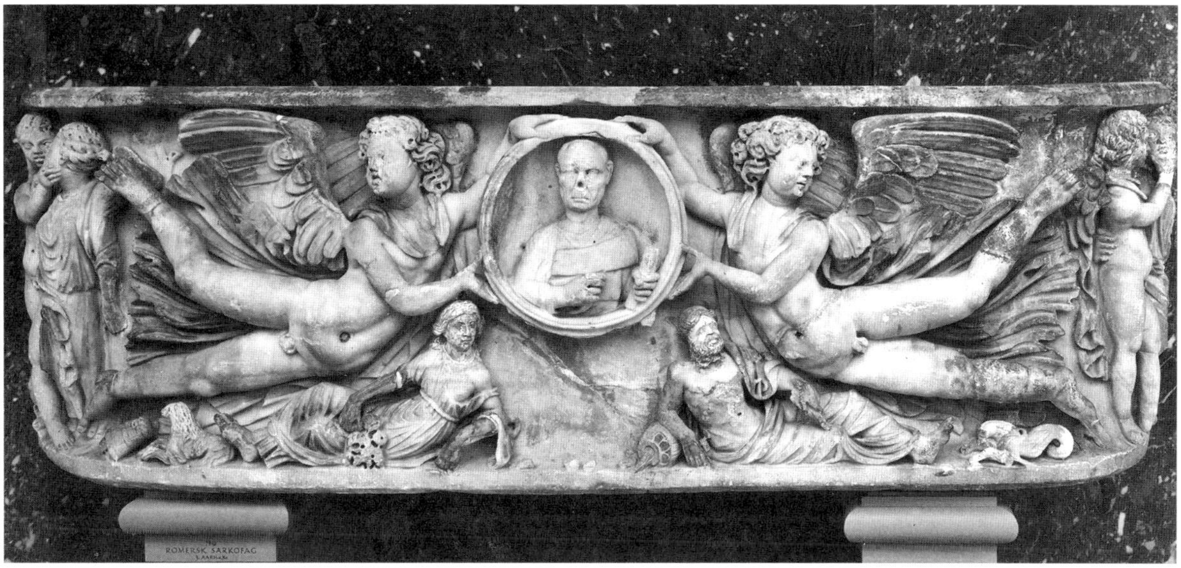

Detail of clipeus sarcophagus with two flying cupids. Eros and Psyche are shown on the short ends, and Tellus and Oceanus are depicted beneath the cupids (cat. no. 68). Copenhagen, Ny Carlsberg Glyptotek, inv. 1890. Photo: Ny Carlsberg Glyptotek. **Fig. 3**

commemorate.[39] While altars, statues, and reliefs with portraits were also produced in the previous centuries, the third century is characterised by the new fashion of having a sarcophagus with a portrait.

In contrast to the modern portrait, Roman portrait seldom express emotions, moods, or psychological states. Rather than being an actual likeness, they were self-representational statements of the deceased that symbolise the person in order to preserve his or her memory. That the portrait symbolises the deceased, instead of imitating his or her facial features, means that it becomes 'an image of a portrait'.[40] The fact that sarcophagus portraits were not true likenesses of individual people, intended to express the inner self of that person, means that we find sarcophagi that have been reused without alteration of the portrait features.

39 For *kline*-monuments see Wrede 1977, 395-431. For funerary altars, see Boschung 1987; Kleiner 1987. For the significance of the portrait on diverse types of Roman monuments, including funerary sculpture, see Stewart 2003, 83-90. For the different uses of portraits in Roman statuary and reliefs, see Fejfer 2008.

40 On the discussion of the portrait as an expression of an ideal or a likeness, see Massner 1982, 1-5 with further references; Huskinson 1998, 130-34. However, some believe that Roman portraits by their very nature seek to convey information about the personality of a human being, Wood 1986, ix.

Such a symbolic representation of the person seems to have been sufficient to individualise the portrait figure in order to preserve the memory of a person. When portraits use standard expressions, more influenced by the style of the period in which they were carved (the period face) than by the personality of the portrait subject, they cannot be read in order to understand the personalities of those they represent. Instead identity markers such as age and sex can be recognised, and a fairly large number of portraits on sarcophagi shows signs of age.[41] However, more specific determination of age is difficult, except for in those cases where it is mentioned in the inscription, because the portraits are idealised and thus used the appearance of the face, including signs of age, to negotiate an ideal identity.

The repertory of idealised and allegorical figures that could be carved on sarcophagi is extensive but, as we will see, only a small proportion of them were used by the deceased for self-representation through the application of a portrait. Portraits can be distinguished from idealised heads by the time-specific hairstyle, expressions of realism (**Fig. 3**; cat. no. 68), and by non-idealised facial features approaching the style of the current period face (**Fig. 4**; detail of cat. no. 641). Furthermore, traces

41 Examples are cat. nos. 7, 71, 130, 142, 364, and 430.

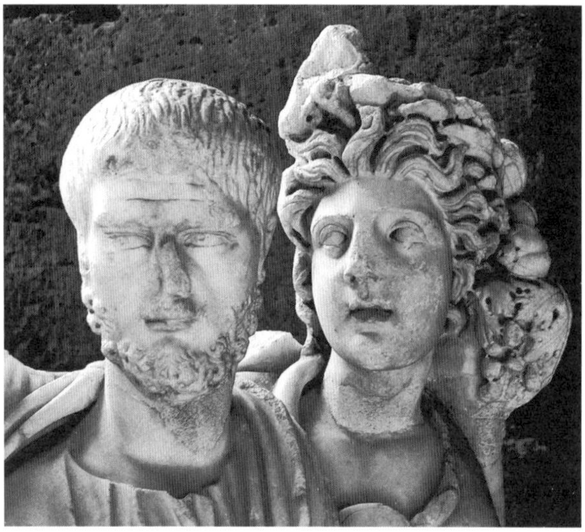

Fig. 4 *Detail of the man in the marriage scene on the right end of the so-called Brother sarcophagus (cat. no. 641). Naples, Museo Nazionale, inv. 6603. Photo: Author, courtesy of the Soprintendenza Speciale per i Beni Archeologici di Napoli e Pompei.*

of tool marks can often be observed on the surface of a portrait, which give it a more rough expression than the faces of idealised figures (**Fig.** 5; cat. no. 645). Apart from the portraits, sarcophagus reliefs rarely show visible traces of tool marks, and the skin of idealised figures is as a general rule polished or at least smooth. Leaving tool marks on the portrait adds an additional dimension to the lifelike appearance of the face and emphasises the fact that what we are looking at is the image of an individual person. It was necessary to distinguish portraits from generic heads, because the idealised body type used for self-representation did not make such a differentiation in itself. The same body types could be used for generic heads and for portraits.

Portraits on sarcophagi appear most commonly on a bust carved on the lid or in a *clipeus* on the frontal relief supported by garlands, seasonal personifications, cupids, or *victoriae*.[42] Another popular place is on a full-length figure. Sometimes these figures are interacting in a narrative scene, a design with one continuous scene covering the full length of the relief. At other times the figure appears on non-narrative types of sarcophagi, defined by the fact that the portrait figure, instead of interacting with the other figures, is framed by, for example, columns (dividing the frontal relief into several sections) or an imitation of a *parapetasma*, or it is carved on panels on strigillated sarcophagi.[43] In rare instances portrait figures are found on the end reliefs (cat. no. 114) and small portrait figures can be found in places such as in a mandorla on strigillated sarcophagi.[44]

Determining the sex of a portrait figure can some-

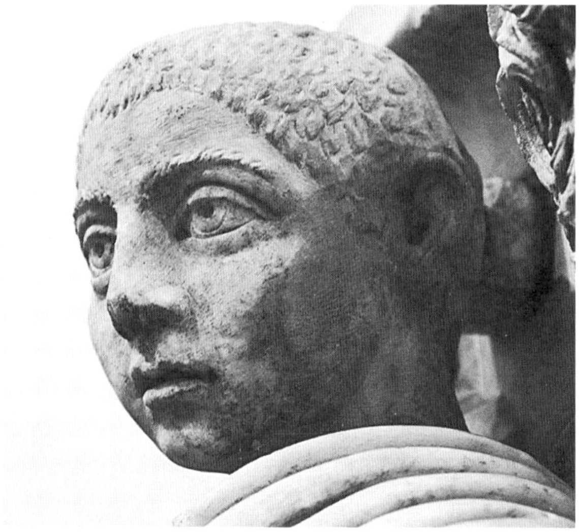

Fig. 5 *Detail of the boy on the left end of the so-called Acilia sarcophagus (cat. no. 645). Rome, Museo Nazionale Romano, Palazzo Massimo, inv. 126372. Photo: Author, courtesy of Soprintendenza Speciale per i Beni Archeologici di Roma.*

42 I use the term *clipeus* for all the circular frames that enclose one or more busts.

43 'Strigillated' refers to the ornamentation on the two panels on the front of that sarcophagus (for the term, see Baratta 2007, 192, note 1). These sarcophagi are adorned with curved profiles with rounded ends that run from top to bottom of the relief. This type of decoration started in the late second and continued into the fourth century. These sarcophagi have not had a volume dedicated to them in the corpus *ASR*, and is rarely studied together as a group. A study of this group, however, will be published in a forthcoming book by J. Huskinson.

44 Examples are: a strigillated sarcophagus from Musei Vaticani, Cortile del Belvedere, inv. 111 with a learned figure with a blank portrait in a mandorla (Addendum A1), a similar piece in S. Paolo a Ripa, Pisa with a couple with blank portraits in a *mandorla* (cat. no. 662), and another strigillated sarcophagus in Cliveden with a lion-deer group at each end and a learned woman with a portrait in the mandorla (cat. no. 135).

times be difficult. Because of the size of such figures, the facial features are not always carved in detail, and sometimes the state of preservation makes the face difficult to read. However, the hairstyle often reveals the sex, and through this feature sex determination becomes reliable. We assume that with sculptures in the round, the hairstyle of sarcophagus portraits follows the fashion of the period set by the imperial family. On sarcophagi it often occurs that the head was left blank, which means that it remained roughly carved and never received portrait features. In such cases it is more problematic to decide if a sarcophagus was carved for a man or a woman, since the blank portraits also have a roughly carved hairstyle. Based on the appearance of this roughly carved hairstyle, it can be conjectured that if a portrait were prepared for a woman, it would have hair that continued to a point below the ears; if for a man, it would have a short hairstyle. It is, however, not always that simple, because the bound hair of female figures sometimes meant that the roughly carved hair did not protrude below the ears. On the lid of cat. no. 50 is a bust with a blank portrait (**Fig. 90**). The unfinished portrait bust has a short hairstyle, but the inscription mentions a girl's name. In such cases, I trust the inscription more than the roughly carved hairstyle. After all, the sarcophagus was in the end used for a girl. The fact that also a roughly carved head prepared for a man could be re-carved with a portrait of a woman, and vice versa (see, for example, **Fig.** 77; cat. no. 246), makes such sex determination difficult. This means that it is not always easy to know from the roughly carved figure if the iconography of the sarcophagus was meant to commemorate a man or a woman. But then we can bring the appearance of the bust into discussion: though busts could be carved fairly generically with no special indication of either sex, a bust in combination with a blank portrait can often be used to establish the sex of a figure.

From a workshop perspective, the generic bust meant that the sarcophagus could be purchased for either a man or a woman. This 'asexual' appearance of the bust should be considered in a discussion about gender in Roman society, because it means that similar iconographic schemata could be used for both men and women. I will return to this issue in the following chapters. If nothing directly suggests the contrary, I have categorised the heads with roughly carved long hair as female, whereas the blank portraits with a short hairstyle have been categorised as male. The full-length figures are easier to categorise as either male or female than a bust. The long dress is considered female (often a *chiton* and a *palla*), whereas the short dress is male (often a tunic and a *pallium* or a toga), and the naked or semi-naked mythological figures often provide the answer immediately by the exposed genitals.

Chronology

Portraits on sarcophagi are used to establish a development of style and chronology, given that they represent a better tool for dating than the *motivgeschichtliche* approach.[45] There are problems involved in this methodology, however, and a few historiographical remarks are necessary here in order to underline some of the premises for the present study.

G. Rodenwaldt was almost a founding father of the scientific study of sarcophagi. His 1936 article "Zur Kunstgeschichte der Jahre 220 bis 270" became seminal to all subsequent works in this field of study.[46] Rodenwaldt suggested a chronological sequence for some of the most famous sarcophagi, taking the Mattei I lion hunt sarcophagus as his point of reference (**Fig. 59**; cat. no. 508). This sarcophagus has played an important role in the following discussion on sarcophagus chronology, starting when B. Andreae suggested a new stylistic development that deviated from Rodenwaldt's.[47] Among other things, for example, he altered

45 Koch 1993, 49. For a discussion on the potential of the portrait for dating a sarcophagus and the implications of later periods' engagement with sarcophagi, see Birk 2010/11.

46 Other important works by Rodenwaldt on sarcophagi are: 1935; 1943; 1944. F. Matz (1958) continues this approach in his discussion on the Badminton sarcophagus. See also the monograph of Hanfmann (1951) on the seasonal sarcophagus from Dumbarton Oaks, Himmelmann-Wildschütz 1973; 1974, and Fittschen 1969, 1970; 1971; 1972 (an important review of Wegner's contribution to the *ASR* corpus *Die Musensarkophage* from 1966 in which the chronology of many sarcophagi is reassessed); 1973; 1975; 1979; 1984.

47 Andreae 1968-69; 1969; 1970; 1971; 1977; *ASR* I 2 (1980); 1981 in which he summarises works published on sarcophagi until that date); 1985; Andreae & Jung 1977. Fittschen (1972) took part in adjustments to the former chronological framework in a very important review article of Wegner's, *ASR* V 3 (1966). In this article he writes that Andreae's reassessment

the dating proposed by Rodenwaldt for the Mattei I sarcophagus from about 220 to 270-280 on the basis of stylistic analysis of the figures and the composition of the iconographic scheme.[48] As the Mattei I sarcophagus had been fundamental to the chronology established by Rodenwaldt, a new chronology had to be established. This was accomplished by Andreae in his contribution to *Die antike Sarkophagreliefs* (*ASR*) published in 1980.[49] However, this chronology is difficult to use, since the dating criteria used for establishing both the chronology and the stylistic development was never fully defined.[50]

Another significant feature that affects the understanding of sarcophagi is the several hundreds of years of admiration of their figural decoration. This fascination with sarcophagus reliefs has had its impact on their appearance as they are preserved today and many frontal reliefs have been separated from the coffin, with major implications for the study of their chronology. Since medieval times sarcophagi have been reused both for burials and as decorative elements, and during the late Renaissance and Baroque periods the coffins were used as fountains and planters, as well as decoration for the facades of Roman palaces.[51] A consequence of especially the decorative use on palazzo facades is an often extensive restoration of the reliefs, which alters the appearance of the figures to the extent that it becomes difficult to use them for stylistic evaluation and hence chronology, such a case being the Mattei I relief. The monumentality of many sarcophagi, together with previous periods' appreciation of the reliefs, has furthermore led scholars to perceive them as glamorous monuments and objects of art. This approach is expressed through frequently used terms such as *Prunksarkophage* and Gallienic Renaissance, terms that have led high quality sarcophagi to be grouped together in a relatively short period of time often with the consequence that probably too many sarcophagi are dated to the same period, around the middle of the third century.[52]

In spite of these difficulties, studies of style have provided the basis for understanding sarcophagus chronology to the extent that it is possible to go a step further and situate sarcophagi within the context of social values, self-display, and idealisation. In line with the general tendency in recent scholarship on sarcophagi, this book will be less concerned with tracing stylistic developments and the refinement of sarcophagus chronologies, given that most sarcophagi are datable within a relatively narrow time range. Even though the chronology of sarcophagi should be the subject of further reflection and discussion, I believe that the overall chronology that has been established for sarcophagi will not be changed dramatically by re-dating individual pieces. We must therefore accept a dating within a time span, and for the purpose of the statistics presented here, I have chosen an interval of 25 years based on the dates given in primarily the corpus *Die antike Sarkophagreliefs*, as well as other primary publications. Because of the difficulties involved in working with stylistic development in the third century and thus of giving precise dates, the iconography studied here

of the Mattei I sarcophagus is a precaution for understanding the stylistic development of the third century (first presented in Andreae 1968-69). Fittschen furthermore argues that the Mattei I sarcophagus cannot be dated to the 220s because the state commissioned art from this period did not show any evidence of a classicistic style, as found on the Mattei I sarcophagus (Fittschen 1972, 503, note 1). This argument is a classic example of how stylistic development as a method sometimes forces an inflexible linear development upon the material. Fittschen later confirmed this stylistic development again (1975, 12).

48 Andreae 1970, 88. The Mattei I relief is, however, a badly chosen building block for chronology, since the portrait is probably the only non-restored surface of the relief. The stylistic features of the relief are therefore problematic as illustrations of the style of the period. For more on this discussion, see Birk 2010/11.

49 The re-dating of the Mattei I sarcophagus was repeated in an article published in 1969 (Andreae 1968-69).

50 As A.M. McCann has observed, referring to both Andreae and Fittschen, "their arguments are based largely upon stylistic comparisons with other sarcophagi, which do not to appear to me to be fully convincing" (1978, 103, note 29). For Fittschen, see above n. 46.

51 Andreae & Settis 1983; Zanker & Ewald 2004, 9-24. For post-antique periods' interest in sarcophagi, see Guerrini 1982; Greenhalgh 1989, 183-201; Barkan 1999, 32, 60-1, 126; Danesi & Gambardella 2008.

52 For the concept of the so-called *Prunksarkophage*, see Andreae & Jung 1977. For the Gallienic Renaissance, see Rodenwaldt 1931, 319; Alföldi 1967, 263-81; Rössler 1997. Further discussion on the term and its impact on the handling of sarcophagi can be found in Birk 2010/11.

will not be based on the chronological developments of motifs. This seems reasonable since, despite general tendencies showing that some motifs were more popular in some periods than others, the possibility of choosing a motif according to the values implied in it was much more expansive than is often assumed. Therefore motifs that for some periods may seem 'old-fashioned' could still be produced in order to accommodate special needs. The Great Ludovisi battle sarcophagus (cat. no. 625) is an example of such conservatism, and it should make us aware that many other such cases are likely to be found among the corpus of sarcophagi.[53]

53 Most recently studied by Künzl (2010).

CHAPTER 1

Images for Contemplation

Soon you are made anew into various semblances: here shines Ceres in bronze,
here the Cnosian maid, in that clay is Maia, Venus (no wanton) in this stone.
The deities accept your beauteous features without complaint.
Servants stand around accustomed to obey.

Statius, *Silvae* V. I 231-35[1]

The Romans were well aware of the possibility of negotiating their identities through images and portraits, and this extended to *post-mortem* contexts.[55] This visual negotiation was a language that appealed to people from various social groups of Roman society, and besides being a strong communicative factor in public and private monuments, it is used metaphorically in written texts. Such a description is found in a poem by the first-century poet Publius Papinius Statius (see above). He describes a woman who has been represented in diverse forms on her tomb by her husband. These different representations are approved by the gods, and thus the woman is introduced into the divine sphere through her portraits. The text is fiction and the woman fictive, but what is of interest here is the description of a visual language used to construct an ideal memory. Self-representation through the shapes of goddesses can be interpreted in the context of *apotheosis*, but it is more likely to be read as a metaphorical construction of a person's virtues.[56] The diverse forms of the wife's portraiture all represent different aspects of her identity. By mentioning several deities, Statius implies that Priscilla's person was multi-faceted and possessed virtues that answered to those of the different goddesses. What we see is a tribute to the ideals of a first-century Roman wife: prosperity and motherly relationships (Ceres), the quality of the chaste maid Diana or the beautiful Ariadne (the maid of Knossos) combined with the virtues of piety and beauty (Maia), and finally love and the female virtue of modesty and chastity (the not immodest Venus).[57] In summa, by applying Priscilla's portrait to statues of the different goddesses and heroines, Statius transfers the virtues of these mythological figures to the personality of the deceased woman. Her identity was, by these means, negotiated *post-mortem*. It must be remembered, however, that we learn about Priscilla through the way her husband commemorated her, and that the statues were selected because they fitted the ideals of current society and thus also accommodated the husband's claim to status. For, as we will see, to show oneself as the patron of tombs and sarcophagi was just as important as commemorating the deceased.

The design of a sarcophagus and its often rich figurative decoration constitute a significant source for studying virtues and ideals within a relatively broad group of Roman upper-class society. Their figurative decoration conveys information about individuals in a time- and

54 *Mox in uarias mutate nouaris effigies: hoc aere Ceres, hoc lucida Cnosis, illo Maia tholo, Venus hoc non improba saxo. Accipiunt vulyus haud indignata decoros Numina: circumstant famuli consuetaque turba obesequii.* Trans. Shackleton Bailey 2003.

55 See, for example, Flower 1996; Stewart 2003, 79; Fejfer 2008, 105-37.

56 I am grateful to Zahra Newby for discussion about the meaning of the text. On *apotheosis*, see Cumont 1942; Engemann 1973; Wrede 1981.

57 For commentary on the text, see Gibson 2006, 162-65. There is some discussion as to whether the "Cnosian maid" is Diana or Ariadne; see Gibson 2006, 163. Shackleton Bailey suggests that she is Ariadne; see Shackleton Bailey, Statius, *Silvae* V, 1, note 23. Wrede (1981, 75-7) compares the description of Priscilla's portrayals with surviving examples of sculpture.

place-specific context, and is indicative of how people wanted to present themselves or their relatives for the future. Through the representations of women, men, and children as they appear on sarcophagi, it is possible to approach a wide variety of questions concerning social relations and gender roles.[58] In this study sarcophagi with portrait figures have been chosen as the primary source, because they possess great potential as building blocks in constructing a framework within which sarcophagus reliefs in general may be interpreted, i.e. those without portraits as well. Their potential lies in the fact that the portrait figure helps the viewer to focus on reading the scene, guiding the viewer to an interpretation that is as close as we may get to the patron's intended meaning.[59] The body type chosen for the portrait figure presents an allegory of different social categories and societal ideals, and together with portraits and inscriptions informing us of the sex and age of the deceased, we get an idea about what the person buried in the coffin was like.[60] Thus taking the portrait figure as the starting point of an interpretation provides us with some basic information about the commemorated person.

Sarcophagus reliefs can be compared with the description of Priscilla's tomb. On the oblong front the deceased is shown in one or more variations of ideal figures, acting through an iconographic language that emphasises his or her virtues. In this respect, the coffin is an honorary monument that, like the tomb, displayed the status of the family. It is a place of simultaneous commemoration and veneration of the dead; the coffin becomes a medium for reflection and contemplation, using mythological narratives and scenes of ideal life-situations to symbolise human situations and feelings. This "double identity" of the sarcophagus, and especially its portrait figures, means that both individuality and the social persona can be studied through its decoration.[61] In this chapter, I will explore sarcophagi as commemorative monuments set up as acts of bereavement and self-display. I will explain the key concepts of my approach to self-representation, which is situated in a well-established scholarly tradition of reading sarcophagi as expressions of social identity and symbolic meanings.[62] In order to do this, I will look at three external factors that impact the appearance of the decoration: the production, the funerary context of viewing, and the Roman concepts of the afterlife.

Patronage, Production, and the Funerary Context

Before we go into detail about how sarcophagus images can be interpreted in a funerary context, it will be helpful to consider some external circumstances, namely the questions of who were buried in sarcophagi, who bought them (and thereby approved of the decoration), and finally, for whom they were visible. The two first questions concern the identities we are talking about, whereas the last one approaches the meaning of sarcophagus images.

The Dead and the Patron

The portraits on sarcophagi are not exclusively of deceased people. Often the patron is portrayed along with the departed person. Patronage of funerary monuments was a way of positioning oneself in relation both to the dead and to surrounding society, i.e. the visitors to the tombs.

The patron is here defined as the person who commissioned the sarcophagus; he or she decided what motif was appropriate for commemorating the person who was to be buried in the sarcophagus. The patron

58 For role models and self-representation on Roman sarcophagi as expressions of values both in relation to society and the family, see, for example, Zanker & Ewald 2004, 179-201.

59 On theories of viewing, see Sharrock 2002; Clarke 2002, 2003; Elsner 1995. Clarke (2002) distinguishes between male and female viewers. I think that it can be difficult to differentiate the approach taken by the different viewers according to categories of sex, class, age, and status. More important is the notion of personal experiences and personhood, which of course in return depends upon the previously mentioned categories. Therefore I do not approve of the book's separation of viewers according to sex.

60 The idea of the individualising head and the symbolic body was first suggested by Brilliant 1974, 166-68 and is today generally accepted; see for example Hallett 2005a (who also sees the nude body as a "costume"), the approach taken by Zanker in Zanker & Ewald 2004, and Koortbojian 2008.

61 For the reflection of the social persona in funerary art, see Ewald 2004, 230. For "double identity" in the Roman tradition of self-representation, see Koortbojian 2008.

62 The latest volume on these issues, and the first written for an Anglophone audience, is Elsner & Huskinson 2011.

could therefore be either a near relative of the deceased or a person who chose a sarcophagus for him- or herself.[63] The presence of a still-living patron could be appreciated immediately through both inscriptions and portraits when entering a tomb. A well-preserved and rich example of how the patron was visually represented in a tomb is found in the mausoleum of Herma Valerius (Mausoleum H) in the necropolis beneath the Vatican.[64] The inscription of the tomb facade informs us that Gaius Valerius Herma founded the tomb for himself and his wife Flavia Olympia, his daughter Valeria Maxima, his son Gaius Valerius Olympianus, and for his freedmen, freedwomen, and their descendants.[65] Valerius Herma is recorded as a patron in inscriptions not only on the outside of the tomb, but also on several individual burials inside the tomb: he is identified as the father commemorating his two children on the tombs of his son and his daughter and as the patron of two additional burials belonging to foster sons, and he is also mentioned in the inscription on a freedman's burial of his wife, where Herma Valerius is designated as the good patron.[66] Patronage was a privileged way of securing one's memory that was only available to the few who had sufficient financial means. Patrons such as Valerius Herma took the opportunity to engage in their own self-representation while commemorating the dead. In a similar manner, the presence of patrons is felt strongly on sarcophagi, where portraits and names of the one who erected the monument are revelatory of his or her status and relationship to the deceased.[67]

Sarcophagi are, as a general rule, meant to hold one or at most two individuals. The interment of three or more persons in one sarcophagus is rare, but when it happened we are most likely dealing with a family consisting of parents and one or two children.[68] This use of sarcophagi as single burials, or in a very few cases for a family, is generally reflected in the number of portraits found on a single sarcophagus.[69] As we will see, the most frequent scenario involved one figure individualised through the application of portrait features, but as can be seen from Graph 1, sarcophagi with two portraits are not uncommon either. However, more than two portraits on one relief are rare.[70] In producing the statistic presented here, some sarcophagi with more than one portrait representation have been categorised in the group of single commemorations, if the portraits are considered to represent the same person. This means that sarcophagi such as the famous 'brother sarcophagus' from Naples (**Fig. 4 & 81**; cat. no. 641),

63 It was the responsibility of the family and the heir to arrange a Roman's funeral (Rawson 2003, 338).

64 Mausoleum H. For the publication of the necropolis, see Mielsch & Hesberg 1995; Liverani & Spinola 2010, 92-108.

65 The formulaic phrase *et suis libertis libertasque posterisque eorum* and similar formulations may have been written as part of the self-representation created to show the patron as a beneficial man and not primarily for securing the juridical rights of freedmen to be buried inside the tomb. For a discussion of this, see Bodel 2008, 212-14. For a full account of the inscription of Valerius Herma, see Toynbee & Ward-Perkins 1956, 101, note 59 or Wallace-Hadrill 2008, 68.

66 Wallace-Hadrill 2008, 66-76.

67 For a general introduction to inscriptions on sarcophagi, see Koch & Sichtermann 1982, 25-7.

68 An example mentioned by Dresken-Weiland (2003, 246) is a coffin bought by the wife for her family, both the wife (Aelia Euthenias), the husband (Acilius Primigenius), and a girl named Thuscolana (the daughter?) were supposed to be buried in the sarcophagus, and all three of them are represented together in a *clipeus* on the frontal relief. Another example is cat. no. 269, discussed below. The depiction of a family in a *clipeus* is unusual, and the sarcophagus, which is published in Giglioli 1942 with a drawing and a photo of the lid, may be equal to cat. no. 458. However, the drawing published by Giglioli shows a sarcophagus with columns at each end instead of lions. Another example of more than one interment in the same coffin is that of a woman named Aelia Sabina, who was buried together with her newborn daughter (Dresken-Weiland 2003, 247). A documented exception to the close familiar relation between the persons buried together is T. Manlius Prunicus, who bought a sarcophagus for his wife (Claudia Ianuaria) and later added the name of his brother, Manlius Cyriacus (Dresken-Weiland 2003, 257). In this case the family bond is between the patron and the deceased, and not directly between the two deceased.

69 I know of only one sarcophagus from Rome which bears the inscription "*sibi et suibus*". The sarcophagus was bought by Gladia Felicitas for herself and her family (Dresken-Weiland 2003, 265). This formula is normally added to the façade of a tomb built to house several inhumations, cremations, or sarcophagus burials.

70 The only exceptions are cat. nos. 100, 645, 114, 116, 249, and 458, and the sarcophagus mentioned in note 66. The Hylas relief (cat. no. 594) is here not considered to present more than two portraits, cf. Birk 2010/11.

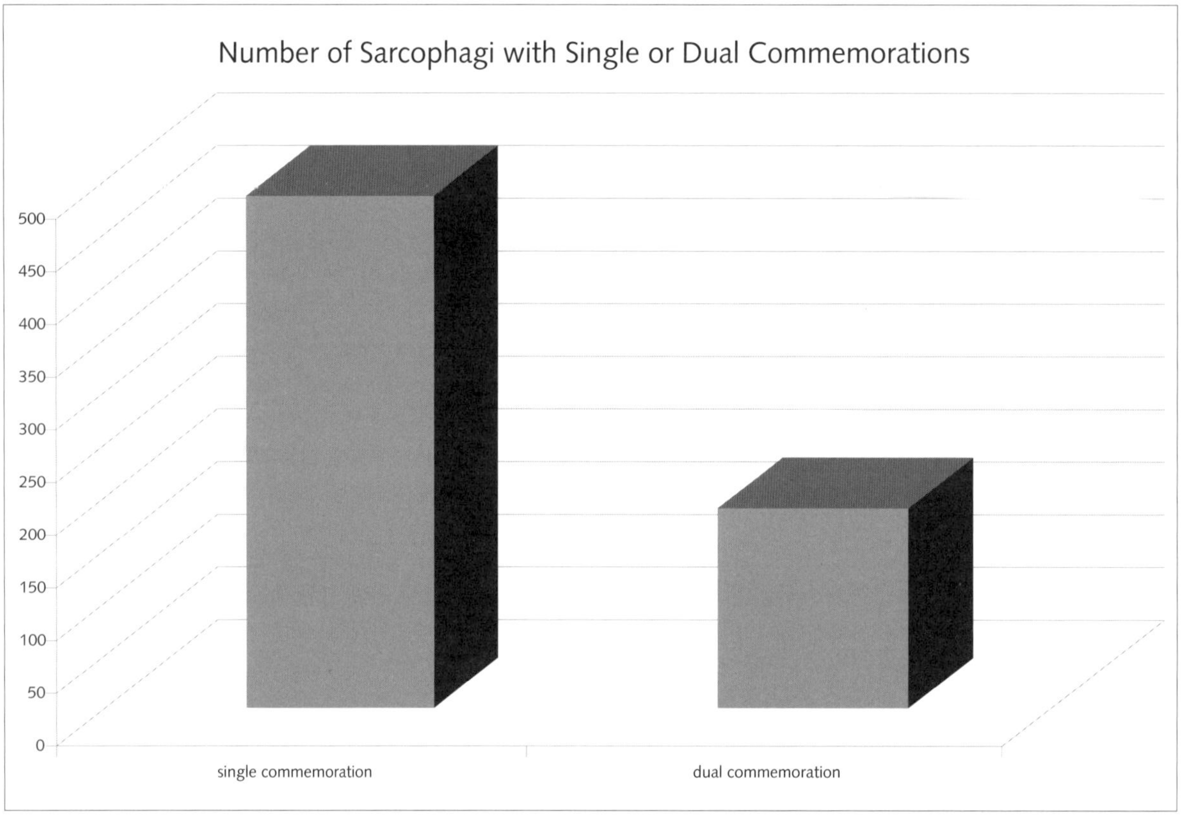

Graph 1 *Based on appendix A, showing the number of sarcophagi commemorating one person and two people.*

with four figures individualised through a portrait of the same man, is represented in the category of single commemorations.[71]

Judging from the rare instances in which bones have been found and registered during the discovery of a sarcophagus, this picture of the coffins as single burial places is confirmed. The relief on cat. no. 65 shows one portrait figure, that of a learned boy, and inside, the coffin housed a skeleton of a single individual. Another skeleton was found in a coffin from Ostia (**Fig. 43**; cat. no. 97). The decoration of this coffin represents the same woman as both a learned woman and a philosopher. A skeleton of a 12-year-old boy was found in a sarcophagus with the representation of the nine Muses (cat. no. 154), and on the frontal relief, the boy himself was represented as the ninth Muse.[72] The number of persons buried in one coffin therefore normally corresponds to the picture we get from the number of portraits carved on the relief and to the names given in sarcophagus inscriptions.[73] There are, however, some exceptions which can be explained by the re-use of older coffins or unexpected bereavement. A strigillated sarcophagus with a lion-deer group at each end of the coffin shows a bust with a scroll in a *clipeus* (cat. no. 142). A portrait of a young girl has been carved on the bust, but an inscription on the upper profile of the

71 For the four representations of the same man and the body types, see for example Hölscher 2008, 52.

72 Further sarcophagi with portraits that contained one skeleton are cat. nos. 215, 226 (of which we furthermore know that the sex of the portrait and the skeleton correspond), 265, 275 and 415.

73 For the complex relationship between text and art and their concordance on funerary monuments, see Koortbojian 2006. The examples he gives are from the first century BC, but the article illustrates well how inscriptions and iconography support each other.

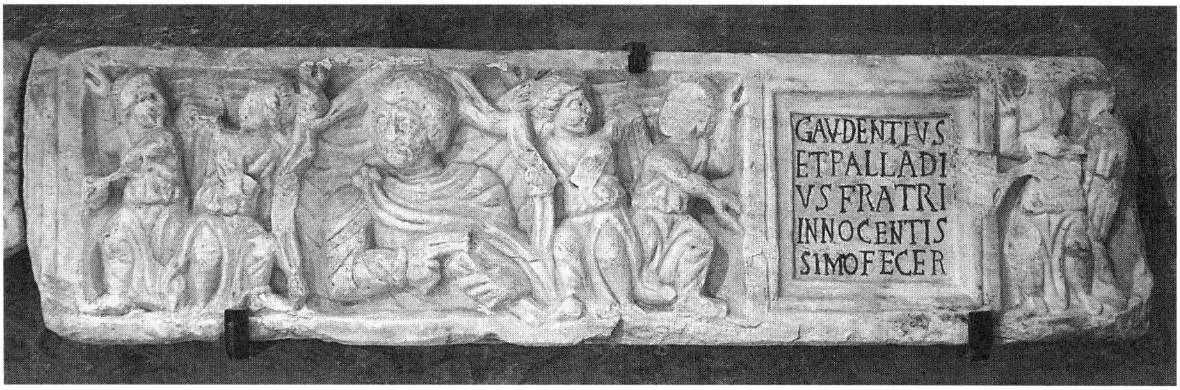

Sarcophagus lid (cat. no. 15). Avignon, Musée Calvet. Photo: Author, courtesy of Musée Calvet. **Fig. 6**

coffin mentions two names. It informs us that Valerius and Domitia, who were brother and sister, were commemorated by their father. Three things point to the fact that this coffin was reused and not bought from stock or designed especially for the siblings. First, the portrait features of a girl were carved on the bust, which means that the coffin at one point had been used for a girl. Second, the inscription is carved on the profile, which is only done in cases where there is either no inscription panel or the panel already has an inscription. Finally, the patron was a man, the father; the portrait subject cannot therefore be him.

When a single individual is represented by a portrait on a sarcophagus, we normally take it to be the image of the person who is buried in the coffin. What about sarcophagi with representations of two individuals? It can be difficult to determine whether such sarcophagi were used as the final resting place for one or two individuals, but again inscriptions can be helpful in solving this issue. When an inscription mentions two persons, the first person is designated as the deceased and the second as the patron who commissioned the sarcophagus. Frequently the patron was a spouse or a parent, and in the case of marital couples the coffin was most often destined for a woman.[74] The deceased and the patron (when they are not the same person) are almost always closely related, as is evident from the following examples:[75] cat. no. 3 is the coffin of a girl buried by her grandfather, on another lid the inscription mentions two brothers who had a sarcophagus made for a third brother (**Fig. 6**; cat. no. 15), a strigillated sarcophagus with cupids at each end is the final resting place of a boy buried by his parents (cat. no. 25), on the lid of a strigillated-lion coffin the inscription mentions a man who had been buried in a sarcophagus by his two sons (cat. no. 41), and another lid with harvesting cupids commemorates a wife buried by her husband (cat. no. 48). These are only a few examples from the much larger corpus. In conclusion, spouses, children, parents, grandparents, and siblings were all designated either as deceased or patron.[76] *Liberti* are practically absent from sarcophagus inscriptions.[77]

In the few cases where an inscription is preserved on a sarcophagus featuring two portraits of two different persons, the inscription furthermore informs us that one person is commemorated and the other is the patron, and this must be the case with the portraits as well. This use of double portraits enabled a dual memory construction, since the same sarcophagus commemorated the deceased and honoured the patron responsible for the commission. The visual decoration of such coffins therefore takes part in the negotiation of the identity

74 Dresken Weiland 2003, 200. A sarcophagus from the mausoleum of the Valerii is dedicated by a son to his mother (cat. no. 67).

75 Ewald comes to the same conclusion but also mentions a sarcophagus given to a patron by his freedmen (1999, 111, note 620).

76 Dresken-Weiland 2003, catalogue on pp. 239-80. Heirs are also mentioned, but in this context it is likely that they are to be found within the same category of family members.

77 Dresken-Weiland 2003, 211.

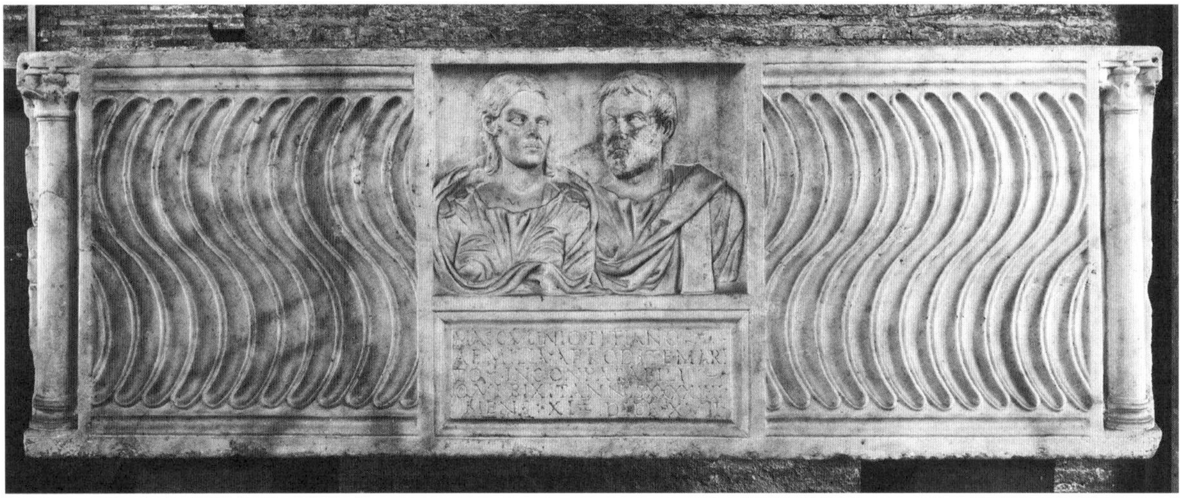

Fig. 7 *The strigillated sarcophagus of a married couple (cat. no. 304). Rome, Museo Nazionale Romano, inv. 115175. Photo: Soprintendenza Speciale per i Beni Archeologici di Roma.*

not only of the deceased, but also of the still-living patron. This can be seen from a strigillated sarcophagus in the Museo Nazionale Romano, which has a central panel showing two busts and an inscription (**Fig.** 7; cat. no. 304).[78] The inscription states the name of the deceased in the dative and adds to it the words *marito incomparabili.*[79] We therefore know that the wife bought the coffin for her husband and that only the man was buried there, despite the fact that both the man and the woman were represented on the front. It may be that the wife was later buried in the sarcophagus, but there was no room left for her name in the inscription. She therefore represents herself on the coffin as a patron and widow. As a consequence of this display of patronage, sarcophagi become media through which living persons could also negotiate their identities. Another example is a lid with *acroteria* of theatrical masks, Eros and Psyche, and two portrait busts (cat. no. 73). The busts represent the married couple mentioned in the inscription, but in this case the sarcophagus was meant to be the final resting place of them both. It was the husband, Marcius Hermes, who buried his wife but he added his name to the inscription followed by a *sibi*. He represented himself as a learned man, a husband, and as the counterpart of his wife, who holds a pomegranate, a symbol of prosperity. She is furthermore designated with the pronoun *dignissima*. Here it is not only the deceased wife who has been idealised, but the fact that the husband has placed himself in the context of his marriage with a pious woman and a symbol of knowledge (the scroll) connects his person with seminal Roman virtues, such as *dignitas*, *concordia*, and learnedness.

Marriage was an important relationship for visual emphasis on sarcophagus reliefs. A man who survived his wife and their two children dedicated a sarcophagus to his three deceased family members (**Fig.** 9; cat. no. 269); on the lid, a bust is present on each side of the inscription tablet, which identifies the man as P. Aelius Myron, his wife Aurelia Agrippina, his daughter Aelia Arria, and his son Crescens. The portrait subjects are in all probability the man and his wife, but whereas the wife is buried in the coffin, the man was still alive when the coffin was commissioned. The importance of representing oneself as the patron becomes explicit on this lid, since the father chose to put a portrait of himself on the sarcophagus instead of having the bust beside the mother re-carved to resemble one of the deceased children. It is P. Aelius Myron with his wife, and therefore their marriage, that is emphasised on this funerary relief. Unfortunately the coffin has not been preserved, but considering the standardised iconographic schemes of sarcophagi, it is unlikely that the children were represented in portraits on its reliefs. On sarcophagi that date from after the second century, children are rarely

78 Schauenburg 1963.

79 Cat. no. 445 is another example.

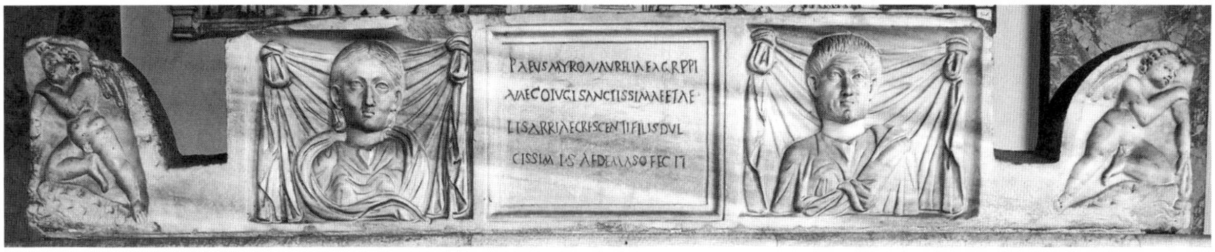

Sarcophagus lid of P. Aelius Myron and Aurelia Agrippina (cat. no. 269). Rome, Musei Vaticani, Cortile del Belvedere. Photo: Author, courtesy of Musei Vaticani. **Fig. 9**

represented together with their mother, father, and siblings. Instead they appear as individuals on an equal level to representations of adults or as a counterpart to a parent, yet another indication of the suggestion that sarcophagi were made for individual burials.[80]

A man and his wife are represented on a strigillated sarcophagus in the collection of Museo Nazionale Romano (cat. no. 434). The sarcophagus was given by the husband, Valerius Valentinianus, and his heirs to his wife, Marcia Iulia Baebia. The man and woman are represented in a *clipeus* through the standardised representation that shows him as a learned person and her as the supportive wife. The inscription honours her memory with words of praise and there is no indication that he was supposed to be buried in the coffin with his wife. The iconography emphasised the man as the most prominent figure on the relief; yet the sarcophagus was meant as the final resting place of his wife only. Another sarcophagus from the second century with a *clipeus* held by two flying *victoriae* shows two portraits, one of a man and one of a woman (cat. no. 436). The inscription informs us again that the sarcophagus was bought by the man for his wife, but that he was supposed to be buried in the coffin as well (*sibi*). Again we see how, while still alive, he used the opportunity to state explicitly that he was the patron of the sarcophagus and to represent himself as having had a harmonious marriage. One last example represents the patron (the mother) and the deceased (the son) side by side in an iconography that is meant to signalise equal status (cat. no. 43).

Another iconographic form that is used to insinuate patronage is found on the lid of a Lion hunt sarcophagus (**Fig. 63**; cat. no. 498). The father of the deceased boy is represented as a learned man while the son is shown as a lion hunter. It is a general characteristic that on sarcophagi with interacting figures, the patron is often represented in the form of a portrait bust on the lid, while the deceased is the figure that takes part in the scene. This placing of the two persons in different registers separates the spheres of the dead and the living in the particular context of mourning and commemoration. Whereas the interacting figure stands as a heroic figure in an idealised world, the bust on the lid is a more prosaic kind of self-representation with a lesser risk of crossing the line in displaying one's virtues while still living, a privilege that in the public sphere was only bestowed on those with public offices and members of the imperial house. The combination of these two realms is also seen on the Lion hunt sarcophagus (**Fig. 10**; cat. no. 512), which was found in the previously mentioned Mausoleum of the Valerii in the Vatican necropolis. A husband, represented as a lion hunter, is commemorated by his wife. On the lid she is represented as a learned woman, but her portrait was for some reason never finished.

The patron and the dead could act together in the theatrical representation of bereavement in a mythological landscape. Two sarcophagi, both of which will be treated in more depth later, illustrate how their relationship could be described by using a metaphorical language of loss and devotion. The first is the famous Alcestis and Admetus sarcophagus from Ostia, which shows a myth with a married couple represented as the two protagonists of the tale (**Fig. 11**; cat. no. 552).[81] The

80 For children's sarcophagi, see chapter 4.

81 Grassinger, *ASR* XII 1 (1999) cat. 76; Wood 1978; Fittschen 1984, 142, 160; Zanker & Ewald 2004, 2002-3; Newby 2011, 194-97, 200.

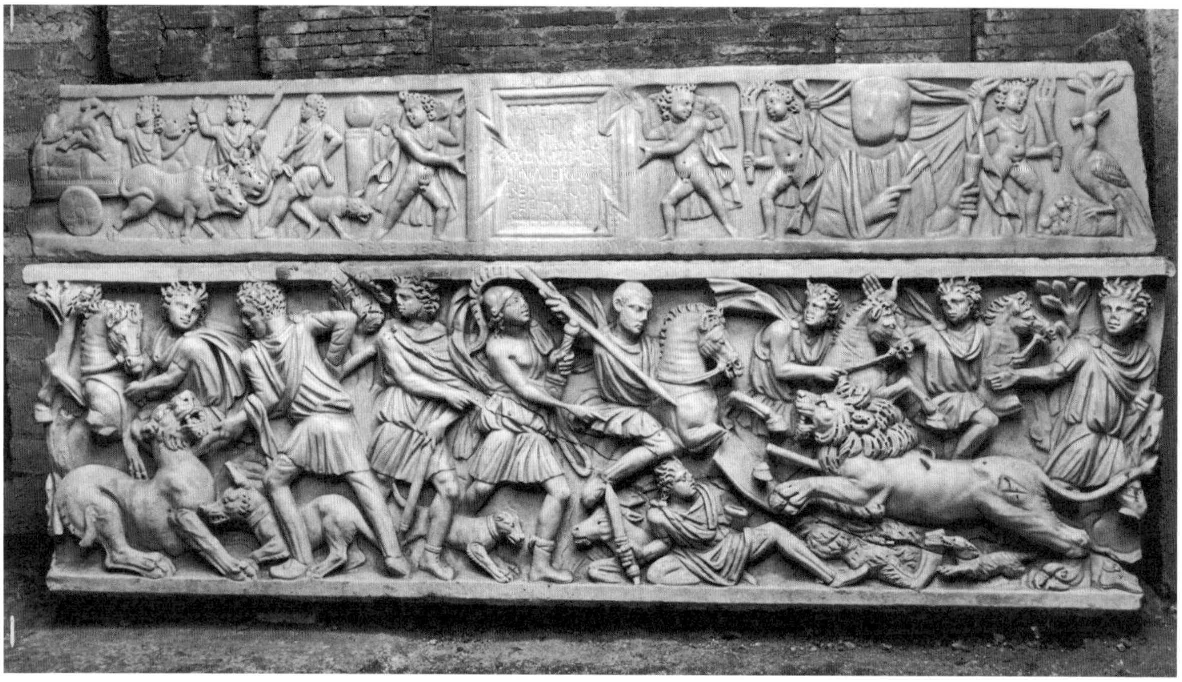

Fig. 10 *Lion hunt sarcophagus (cat. no. 512). Rome, Vatican necropolis beneath S. Pietro, Mausoleum H. Photo: D-DAI-ROM-78.83.*

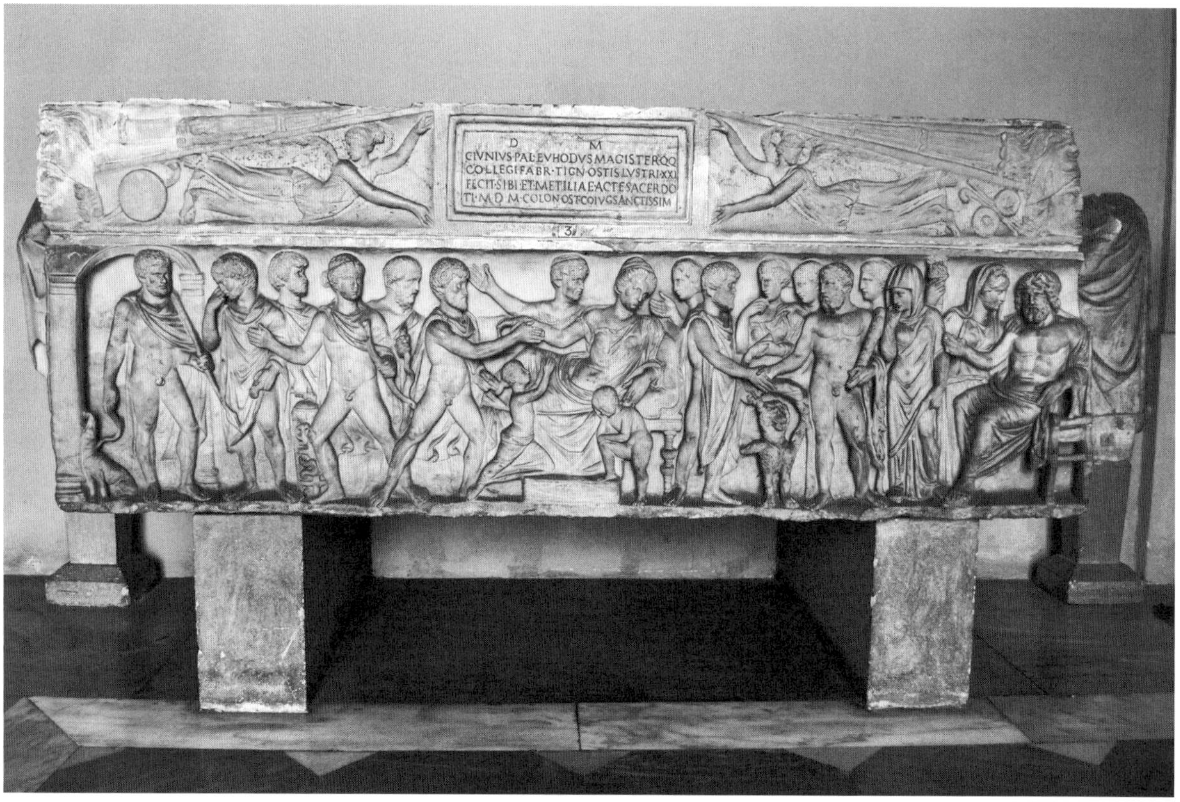

Fig. 11 *Alcestis and Admetus sarcophagus (cat. no. 552). Rome, Musei Vaticani, Museo Chiaramonti, inv. 1195. Photo: Author, courtesy of Musei Vaticani.*

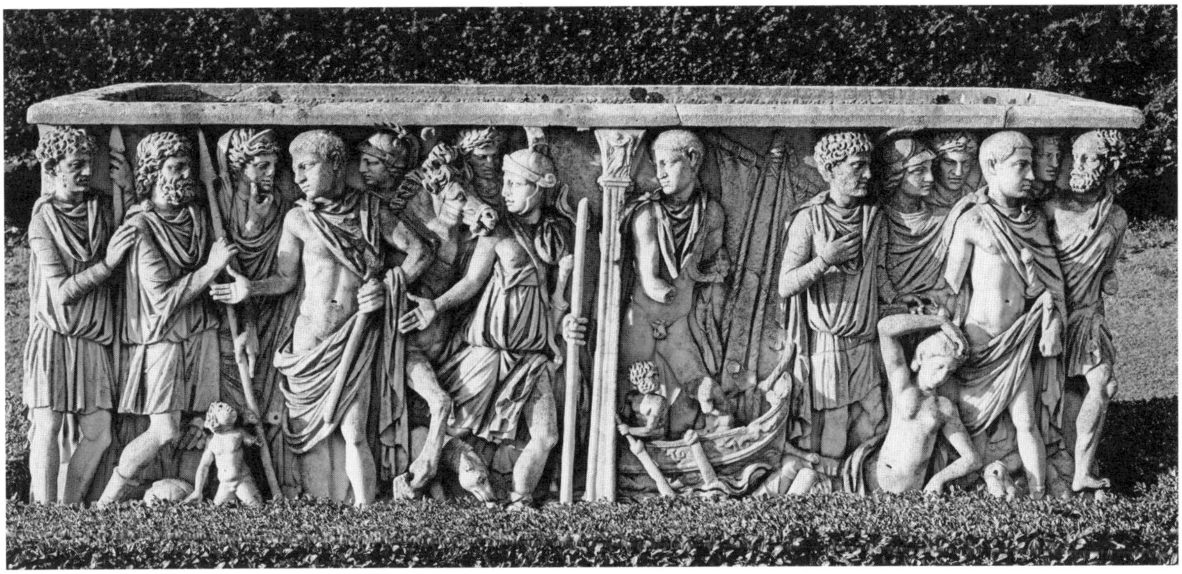

Theseus and Ariadne sarcophagus (cat. no. 612). Cliveden, Buckinghamshire. Photo: Copyright: ©NTPL/Derek Croucher. **Fig. 12**

husband, Euthodus, made the sarcophagus for his wife and himself while he (and maybe also she?) was still alive.[82] The other is the Cliveden sarcophagus with Theseus and the abandoned Ariadne (**Fig. 12**; cat. no. 612). The sarcophagus, on which both protagonists show portrait features, was given by a mother to her son. More simple compositions could also illustrate the relationship between the deceased and the patron. A female patron, Ofilia Marcella, had a strigillated sarcophagus with three figural panels made for herself and her late husband (**Fig. 13**; cat. no. 647). For the central scene, she chose a coffin with a *dextrarum iunctio* motif to symbolise their flawless marriage, and her emotions towards her husband are described in the inscription through the words *marito bene merenti*. But Ofilia Marcella wanted to express more than *concordia* about their relationship and she constructed an idea of both of them as persons with individual and complementary virtues. On the first and fifth panels, she and her husband are represented separately as learned figures, she with a scroll and he dressed like a Greek philosopher.[83]

Families could express themselves differently in the early production of sarcophagi than they did in the third century, when families are rarely represented together. On the sarcophagus of Marcus Cornelius Statius in the Louvre, the portrait of the deceased boy is carved on the relief together with his still-living parents (**Fig. 14**; cat. no. 615).[84] In the first scene, a woman breastfeeds a child while a man stands at her side. These two figures are both applied with a portrait of the boy's parents. In the next scene, the father, again identified through portrait features, holds the child, who is here shown as a little older. In the third scene, the boy drives a ram-drawn wagon: it is here that we can for the first time be certain that the boy himself is depicted with portrait features. The problem of recognising the portrait is due to the young age of the boy in the previous scenes. In the last scene, the father is represented as a seated philosopher tutoring the boy. According to the inscription and size of the coffin, only the child is buried there, but the decoration creates a memory of the whole family. The life course of the boy is the central theme of the relief, but the parents used the opportunity for self-display, and through their choice of motifs they represented themselves with virtues related to parenthood, *concordia,* and intellectuality.

82 For this sarcophagus, see also pp. 98-9, 146.

83 Ewald was the first to take note of this inscription (1999, cat. F 3). For further examples of the relationship between the deceased and the patron, see Birk 2012.

84 Amedick 1993, 143-45; Zanker 1995, 239-40; Huskinson 1996, 22, cat. 1.23; Dimas 1998, 67, cat. 386.

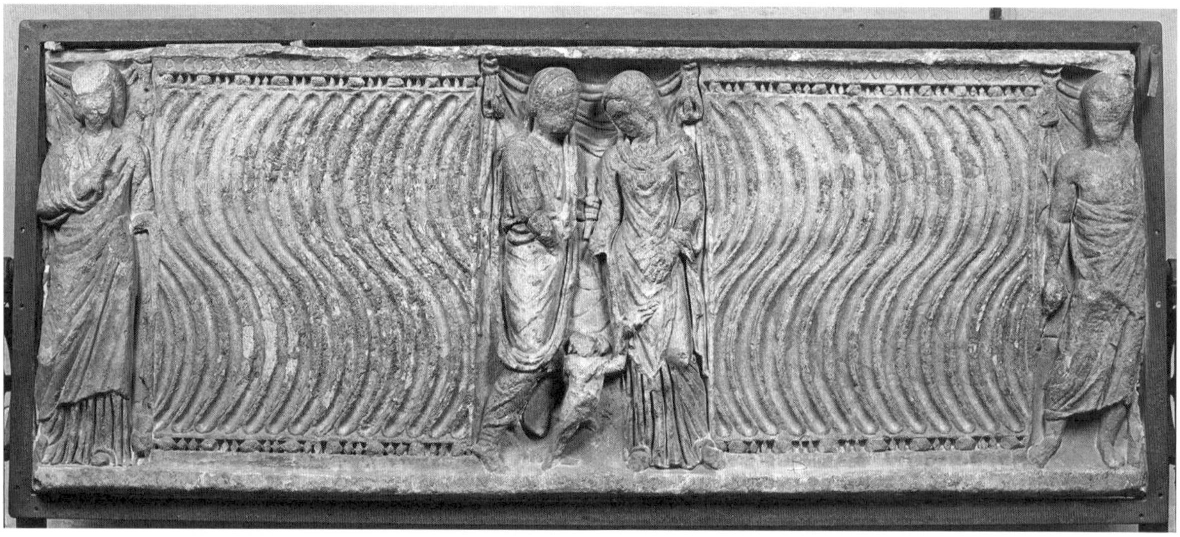

Fig. 13 *Strigillated sarcophagus with a learned woman, a* dextrarum iunctio *scene, and a philosopher (cat. no. 647). Rome, S. Sabina. Photo: D-DAI-ROM-96.1458.*

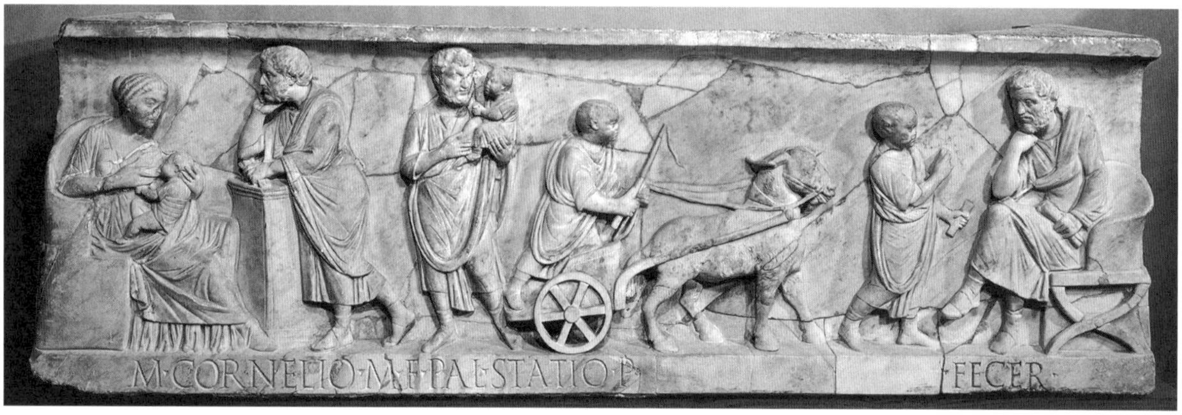

Fig. 14 *The sarcophagus of Marcus Cornelius Statius (cat. no. 615). Paris, Musée du Louvre, inv. MA 659. Photo: © RMN-Grand Palais (Musée du Louvre) / Les frères Chuzeville.*

However, sarcophagi were also put up without patrons exploiting the opportunity to promote themselves. On the sarcophagus of Lucius Pullius Peregrinus (cat. no. 120) only one portrait is carved of the two that were prepared.[85] Furthermore only one name is mentioned in the inscription, and therefore this coffin was probably not meant to house more than one person despite the blank portrait. The age of Pullius is given in the inscription in detail, which tells us that he was 29 years, three months, and half an hour old. According to Ewald the precise specification of his age means that he had a horoscope drawn up in order to know the exact time of his birth, which makes a connection with the philosopher iconography of the relief. The use of horoscopes flourished in "vulgär-philosophie" in Roman imperial times.[86] The specification of Pullius' age on his sarcophagus also means that he could not have had the inscription carved himself. We can therefore assume

85 Andreae 1969, 6; Fittschen 1972, 492-93; Ewald 1999, 152.

86 Ewald 1999, 115.

that another individual took care that the sarcophagus was put up after Pullius' death, but the patron remained both unnamed and faceless.

Two portraits carved on one coffin are therefore often not an indication of two burials. This is important for the purposes of studying identity as negotiated on sarcophagi. However, it is still possible to speak about identity without the secure knowledge of whether one or both of the portrayed persons were actually buried in the sarcophagus. Dead or alive, self-representation through portraits was used to show aspects of the identities of the persons represented. Both the deceased and the patron wanted to construct ideal memories, and both achieved this by combining metaphors of the right virtues with their portrait. Since this kind of self-representation was centred on the tomb, the role models of the portrayed persons, both the deceased and the patron, had to be appropriate for the sphere of the dead. There seems, however, to have been little variation in body types used for self-representation in tombs and houses. In *Historia Augusta* it is described how portraits of the emperor Tacitus were displayed in the house of the Quintilii representing him once in a toga, once in armour, once in a Greek mantle, and once as a hunter.[87] These are all body types that we know from portrait figures on sarcophagi. The only body type that is not frequently paralleled on sarcophagi is the heroic naked military man with a cloak. He is found on cat. no. 627, but apart from some appearances in mythological scenes, I know of no such examples. This homogeneity in the self-representational form probably explains why there is no variation in the body type used for the living patron and the deceased person, a situation that instead varied according to individual needs. The combination of figures in scenes does not necessarily reveal whether the people were dead or alive, apart from a tendency to place the portrait of the patron on the lid and the portrait of the deceased on the frontal relief in scenes with interacting figures.

87 For a discussion of this text in the context of self-representation and the values of body types from the Roman republic and into the imperial period, see Koortbojian 2008.

The Individual Choice

We have observed so far that sarcophagi as a general rule were commissioned for one person, and only rarely were meant to house more than two family members. It is also worth noting that portraits and inscriptions on sarcophagi put more emphasis on the relation between man and wife than on the family as a larger unit.[88] In cases where the coffin was purchased in advance of a person's death, he or she had an influence on the selection of motif. Otherwise it was the family who chose the coffin and found a suitable motif for the deceased. It remains, however, to be discussed how freely this choice of motif could be made. To answer this question some practical aspects of producing sarcophagi need to be touched upon. This will be done here through consideration of some of the working processes involved in carving a sarcophagus, since they are important for understanding the degree of flexibility involved in the production. Furthermore, the market mechanisms that sarcophagus workshops responded to potentially influenced the final product. Our first question, therefore, is whether sarcophagi were purchased from stock in a workshop that mass-produced them, or whether they were the outcome of a production system that responded to individual orders.

Previous studies of sarcophagi are often based on the idea that they were "on-stock products". It follows that they were "impersonal" and that the patron had only limited choice in the process of designing the relief.[89] It is easy to see why the idea of pre-fabrication and mass-production has almost completely overshadowed consideration of the influence of individual patrons in the analysis of sarcophagus images, since the standardisation of motifs makes such a system seem likely. The repetition of motifs is also evident from the categories

88 This picture might change when we look at the tomb as a whole. In the cases where sarcophagi were placed in family funerary complexes, one sarcophagus represents one individual or unit of the family, and the tomb symbolises the family in its entirety. It should, however, be kept in mind that sarcophagi were not always placed in a family tomb, see below.

89 Andreae 1984; Carroll 2006, 112-14; Cuomo 2007, 82, 94-5; Newby 2007, 233. For the most recent discussion of the meaning of the terms *industry* and *mass-production* in the context of sarcophagi, see Russell 2011 (121-23).

of the present catalogue. However, the repeated carving of the same motifs does not necessarily indicate a production-to-stock system. Standardisation can occur because of consumer demand generated by the specific function that the motif had in the narrowly defined context of commemoration.[90] Therefore, the notion of standardisation does not exclude individuality. Instead of seeing these products as impersonal, the repetition of motifs on sarcophagi could be equally explained by factors such as fashion, cultural codes, recognisability, and readability. I will in the following use evidence from the sarcophagi themselves to argue that the patron was able to choose the motif that he or she wanted, and that the notion of mass-production should not have such a dominating position in studies of sarcophagi. As a result, individuality becomes an important aspect in the choice of the decoration on the coffin.

It has been argued, using theories of stock-piling, long distance transport, and prefabrication, that the distribution of motifs was to a large degree dependent on social and economic factors.[91] This implies that many sarcophagi were shipped to Rome as half-finished products with roughly carved decoration, and that the sculpture workshops in Rome finished them as they were started. The decoration of the coffin was therefore decided upon a long time before the patron had the opportunity to influence its final appearance. This means that in any discussion of the choice of sarcophagus images, the significance of the quarry-based workshops that produced the coffins grows, and the influence of the individual patron on the motif diminishes.[92] The production-to-stock theory also implies that marble blocks for sarcophagi had to be imported by workshops without any security that they could dispose of the final product. This would be difficult for small workshops, but larger and well-organised workshops could probably afford to acquire raw material before the product was sold. In the last scenario, half-finished sarcophagi on stock could to be carved in haste, when necessary.[93] Following the line of enquiry of mass-production, images on sarcophagi tend to be explained as containing little information about the deceased and the patron since the choice of a sarcophagus in this scenario is a matter of 'what was available' in the workshop instead of 'what was wanted' (although the two must also have been interchangeable). There is, however, plenty of evidence for the involvement of patrons, and although the production to some degree was conservative in terms of motifs, sarcophagus reliefs were able to meet the wishes of individual patrons.

The first element to look at when studying the production of sarcophagi is the access to marble. Here it seems that Rome could provide marble for part of the production herself, and was therefore not wholly dependent on long distance trade.[94] Many sarcophagi were made from reused architectural elements, as has been revealed by a study of the reverse of sarcophagi.[95] A pattern of tool use often found on the reverse of the coffins shows that the block was reused and, in all probability, originally constituted architectural elements of larger buildings. The suggestion that they were made from reused blocks removes them from the discussion of stock-piling, since they did not arrive in Rome as half-finished products and did not have to be ordered a long time in advance. Additionally, the cost of the coffin can probably be lowered because the transport charges could be deducted. This is important in the discussion of the personal character of a sarcophagus because it suggests that often the relief was not pre-designed in a quarry workshop but designed in the workshop that the customer contacted. The group of sarcophagi that shows evidence of being made from a reused architectural element is relatively small in comparison to the majority of the production, but even in those cases where sarcophagi were pre-fabricated and half-finished,

90 Russell 2011, 136.

91 Ward-Perkins 1969; 1980; 1992 (see also Fant's review, 1995, 554-55).

92 Ward-Perkins 1992, 55-105 (especially the conclusion on p. 105).

93 For marble, quarries, and the transportation of marble into Rome, see Walker 1985, 18-36; Dolci 1989; Ward-Perkins 1992, 13-22; Maischberger 1997; Nuccio & Ungaro 2002. For an investigation of the interaction between quarry and workshop in Greece, see Nolte 2005.

94 The marble used for sarcophagi in Rome came from several quarries, see Ward-Perkins 1992, 31-7 with further references. For pre-fabricated sarcophagi and trade, see Ferrari 1966; Asgari 1977.

95 Bartman 1993, 58-9; P. Pensabene in Pensabene & Panella 1993; John J. Hermann in Van Keuren et al. 2011, 179; Birk forthcoming.

the decoration could still be adapted in line with the wishes of the customer.

When the design of half-finished sarcophagi was altered, it was in order to accommodate the wish of the patrons. In the following, I will give examples of sarcophagi that were intended to receive one kind of motif, but instead of finishing them as they were started, the workshop altered the design and carved it with a different motif, presumably to fulfil the desire of the patron. The first example is found on a lion sarcophagus (cat. no. 100).[96] It was changed from a standardised half-finished coffin to a specially commissioned piece with an individually chosen motif. What was first intended to be a frontal relief decorated with lion heads was turned back to front to make way for a new design with a representation of a learned family. On the reverse the two lion heads are still visible.[97] Another example is found on a strigillated sarcophagus where the bulks for the lion heads were carved as two half-length figures with portraits instead of lion heads (cat. no. 299).[98] This sarcophagus came to the workshop as a half-finished product, with two protruding bulks intended for two lion heads. Instead of finishing the heads, the workshop changed the layout, probably in order to accommodate a patron who wanted a different motif on his coffin.

In most cases the traces of such re-carving have disappeared, but, as described above, some sarcophagi bear evidence of the process. The impressive figural sarcophagus found at Acilia near Rome is decorated with close standing figures that occupy the entire length of the bathtub-shaped coffin (**Fig. 32**; cat. no. 645). The hands of the figures standing near the left end of the frontal relief project from the relief, whereas all the other figures are carved to the same depth.[99] At the right end of the relief, where the hands protrude, the marble block must have been thicker than elsewhere. This suggests that the relief was carved from a half-finished sarcophagus intended for lion heads.[100] One sarcophagus representing harvesting cupids shows a continuous scene of cupids and winemaking; the scene is interrupted at both ends by lion heads and the curving short ends are strigillated.[101] The layout probably originally corresponded to a canonical strigillated lion sarcophagus, but instead of furnishing the frontal side with further fluting, the workshop completed the relief with a scene of harvesting cupids.[102] Other sarcophagi had their layout changed after the coffin was finished because the patron wanted a different type of decoration than the one that was available. This was the case with a sarcophagus in the Capitoline Museum that shows the same man represented twice, once as a philosopher and once as a learned man with a scroll (cat. no. 113).[103] The learned man on the left panel was originally a female figure, which can be seen both from the outline of the rough block from which the portrait was carved and from the re-carving of the area around the feet, which originally was a long dress.[104] A comparable piece is found in the same room, but here the female figure has been preserved (cat. no. 112). One obvious example of such re-working is a sarcophagus from the Huntington Library and Art Gallery in San Marino, California (**Fig. 74**; cat. no. 246) where a female figure was re-carved as a male figure.[105] We will take a closer look at this sarcophagus later.

A final example of a design that has been altered after the figures have been carved is found on the so-called 'Plotinus sarcophagus' (**Fig. 46**; cat. no. 116).[106] The figure on the right of the central group has a female body and is dressed in a long garment. However, the head is of a bearded man, which indicates that what was originally intended to be a Muse was transformed into a sage. In this case it was not done to add an extra portrait since the figure is represented as a generic face, but to adapt the motif according to the wishes of a patron.

Both the transformed sarcophagi and those carved from reused blocks show that there were plenty of op-

96 See Reinsberg, *ASR* I 3 (2006) cat. 54 with further references.
97 Andreae 1984, 110-12.
98 I am grateful to J. Huskinson for making me aware of this example of re-designing the decoration.
99 For the dating of and the portraits on this sarcophagus, see Birk 2010/11.
100 Ward-Perkins & Throckmorton 1965, 207.

101 London, art market (Bielefeld, *ASR* V 2, 2 (1997) cat. 46, pl. 23, 1). For a definition of cupids, see Huskinson 1996, 41.
102 For the so-called lion sarcophagi, see Stroszeck, *ASR* VI 1 (1998). A nearly complete collection of sarcophagi with winemaking cupids is found in Bielefeld, *ASR* V 2, 2 (1997).
103 For a discussion of the re-working, see Ewald 1999, 192.
104 See Ewald 1999, cat. F 18; Birk 2011, 240-41.
105 Koch 1990.
106 For the re-working of the Plotinus sarcophagus and its research history, see Ewald 1999, 168-69, with further literature.

portunities for a patron to influence the decoration of the coffin. Though it can be difficult to detect such changes, the scenario was probably not uncommon. As I showed by discussing pieces such as the philosopher sarcophagus from Capitoline Museum (cat. no. 113), the fence-sarcophagus in San Marino, California (**Fig. 74**; cat. no. 246), and the so-called Plotinus sarcophagus (**Fig. 46**; cat. no. 116), figures were often altered in order to accommodate specific wishes. Both reused blocks and the re-carving of figures and designs play an important role in the discussion of whether a workshop responded to individual orders or worked on a production to stock system. The examples given here downplay the role of the quarry-workshop in designing the relief. Furthermore, it argues against the theory that sarcophagi were always on-stock products and that the choice of a sarcophagus was exclusively dictated by the products available in the workshop.[107] Besides suggesting a high degree of individuality in the choice of a motif, the phenomenon of reusing marble for sarcophagi also suggests that sculptural production was not entirely dependent upon the state of the imperial economy. The apparent boom in sarcophagus production during the third century, when the Roman Empire is generally considered to be in crisis, is therefore not such an anomaly as is sometimes suggested.[108]

The (In)Visiblity of Sarcophagi

To get the full picture of what a sarcophagus does in the context of commemoration, the most advantageous method would be to study the sarcophagus in relation to the tomb in which it was placed.[109] However, this is a field severely impaired by the lack of primary contexts since the coffins have for centuries been reused because of their aesthetic value. These missing archaeological contexts mean that many questions still remain unanswered, although recent studies have illuminated some of the ways in which sarcophagi were normally displayed.[110] In the following we will look at how different ways of displaying sarcophagi influenced their use as a means of self-representation.

There seems to be little evidence from Rome for the display of sarcophagi in open air contexts, but in the few cases that have been documented it seems that they were placed on a podium along the roads leading into the city.[111] This means that the coffin was put on public display. That such examples are rare can be due to several factors: from a practical perspective, the sarcophagus was vulnerable to weathering and human activities, such as plundering and desecration, when displayed outside of protective tomb buildings. Another explanation could be that these exposed sarcophagi for various reasons have been moved or destroyed, as when used for decorative purposes or new burials in post-antique periods. Furthermore, examples of limekilns have been found on Roman necropoleis, suggesting that the large amount of marble available in such places made them an attractive place to burn lime.[112] It is therefore very likely that more sarcophagi were displayed outside of the tomb than is suggested by the preserved evidence today. However, to judge from the shape of the coffin and the placement of the decoration (primarily on the frontal relief), sarcophagi were made to be seen from one side only and not to be gazed at from all angles. The low and often sketchy carving of the decoration on the short end reliefs and the high relief on the front make the latter the optimal angle for viewers.

A coffin located in a tomb would only have been ac-

107 Cf. note 86.

108 For the boom in sarcophagi production in the third century and the so-called *Prunksarkophage*, see Andreae & Jung 1977; Andreae 1981. On the third century 'crisis', see Fittschen 1975a; Schoenbeck 1936, 240; Dey 2009.

109 On Roman tombs and funerary architecture, see Hesberg & Zanker 1987; Hesberg 1992; Mielsch & Hesberg 1995; Liverani & Spinola 2006.

110 Dresken-Weiland 2003, 98. Meneicke 2010; 2012. A PhD dissertation on the original context of Roman sarcophagi was submitted to the Humboldt University, Berlin in 2009 by Katharina Meinecke. An overview article with preliminary results has been published on the internet:http://www.archaeologie-online.de/de/bibliothek/tagungsberichte/2008/cult_and_imagination/roman_sarcophagi_in_their_original_context_rome_and_vicinity (Accessed June 2010). For Christian sarcophagi burials and re-use of pagan sarcophagi, see Dresken-Weiland 2003, part III.

111 Dresken-Weiland (2003, 105) gives four examples where it can be assumed that the coffin was on display above ground, including cat. no. 358.

112 For examples of broken grave monuments and piles of marble pieces for the limekilns, see Gütschow 1938, 40-1, fig. 8; Herdejürgen 2000, 211. For a study of limekilns found in and around Ostia, see Lenzi 1998.

cessible to a limited number of people on normal days, probably mostly family and close friends.[113] Inside the tomb sarcophagi were ideally displayed in a way that encouraged their contemplation. Two sarcophagi found in 'Tomb VIII' at the Santa Rosa necropolis, today on the property of the Vatican, illustrate this kind of display.[114] It is one of the largest tombs in the area and can be dated to the first part of the third century. The floor is covered with a Dionysian mosaic and the walls had niches with painted floral figures and a peacock. The two sarcophagi (cat. no. 419 and a strigillated sarcophagus with learned figures belonging to a Publius Cesilius Victorinus) were placed on feet on the mosaic floor, in an optimum position for viewing. However, sarcophagi are not always displayed in such an optimal viewing position, and they are often found squeezed in between other structures that obstructed the views.

The previously mentioned tomb of the Valerii (Vatican cemetery, Mausoleum H) is embellished by figural decoration and sculptures.[115] The construction of the tomb can be dated to the second part of the second century, based on the wall decoration. It was built for both cremation and inhumation burials. The niches of the upper part of the wall were adorned with figures in stucco whereas the lower region had large *arcosolia*. We have already looked at some of the inscriptions from this tomb, but the extensive iconographic programme is just as informative as the epitaphs. The rich adornment of portrait figures in stucco reflects aspiration to public honorific statues, and sculptured portraits of marble and miniature pieces in stucco were displayed together with sarcophagi decorated with reliefs.[116] Both the marble portraits and those formed in stucco were images of deceased family members in different idealised forms. They were part of what can be called a kind of 'family gallery', constructed in the tomb with the purposes of both commemorating the individual and idealising the family.[117] The tomb also offers the largest assembly of death masks known, a feature that enhanced the private character of the tomb. It is in this context of private commemoration that the sarcophagi of the tomb should be read.

Placed against the northern wall was the abovementioned lion hunt sarcophagus (**Fig. 10**; cat. no. 512), and a strigillated sarcophagus was displayed in the northern *arcosolium* in the western wall (cat. no. 41). In front of the latter sarcophagus a third was placed that obstructed views of the first coffin. In the last of the two *arcosolia* placed on the western wall the sarcophagus of Titus Pompeius (cat. no. 67) was displayed, and centrally placed against the northern wall was an anonymous sarcophagus with an empty inscription panel and two blank portraits (cat. no. 444). Another twelve sarcophagi of terracotta and travertine were situated in the tomb, which all together may have housed up to 250 burials dating from a period of around 200 years.[118] Two of the sarcophagus burials in marble coffins are associated with hunting; one depicting hunters in a rural landscape and the other and merrier representation shows cupids performing the hunt (cat. no. 512; **Fig. 10** and cat. no. 41). On the first of these sarcophagi the deceased is represented as a lion hunter, whereas the other coffin is decorated with a portrait *clipeus*, hunting cupids, and a lion slaying a deer. The other two sarcophagi from the tomb are without figurative scenes, except for one lid that is decorated with sea-*thiasoi* (cat. nos. 67 and 444). The purpose of the decoration of the latter two sarcophagi is to elevate the image of the deceased by placing them on pedestals, and they thus commemorate the deceased in a manner that continues the tradition of public honorific monuments.

The imitation of the style of public honorary statues in tombs reaches as far back as the third century BC. The sarcophagus of Scipio Barbatus bears an inscription

113 Most often sarcophagi burial were found at large necropoleis, such as the Vatican cemeteries or Isola Sacra near Ostia, but they could also be us placed in tombs on private ground, as for example near a villa or in catacombs (Calza 1940; Baldassarre, Bragantini & Morselli 1996; Liverani & Spinola 2006). For an example of a sarcophagus close to a villa, see Kranz, *ASR* V 4 (1984) cat. 577. For examples of sarcophagi used for burials in catacombs, see cat. nos. 25, 369, (for a description of their context, see Gütschow 1938, 234-37), and 433.

114 Liverani & Spinola 2006, 91-4.

115 Toynbee & Ward-Perking 1956, 63-71, 82-8; Mielsch & Hesberg 1995, 143-208; Fejfer 2008, 120-23; Wallace-Hadrill 2008.

116 Fejfer 2008, 123. Four sarcophagi had a portrait figure: cat. nos. 41, 67, 444, and 512.

117 See also Wallace-Hadrill's (2008, 74-6) account of the portraits from the tomb.

118 Dresken-Weiland 2003, 340; Fejfer 2008, 120.

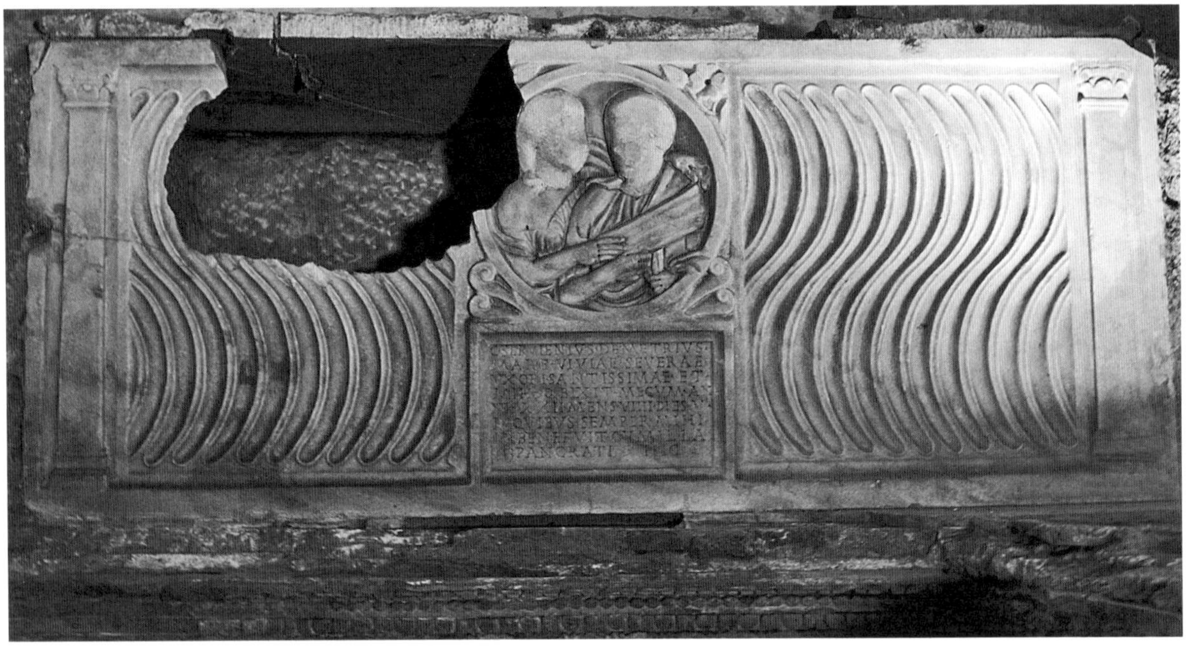

Fig. 15 *Strigillated sarcophagus of Servienius Demetrius and his wife. Rome, Via Latina, Tomb of the Pancrati (cat. no. 445).*

that represents him as a brave, wise, and attractive man and mentions his magistrate titles as well as the areas and tribes he had captured.[119] The wording of the inscription intended to make him a role model for contemporary readers to identify with: phrases such as *cursus honorum* make little sense if they were written for the darkness of the tomb, never to be read by living people. We must therefore conclude that the tomb was a livelier place and was more easily accessed than we tend to believe.

Another chamber tomb that housed several sarcophagi is the so-called tomb of the Pancrati.[120] It was originally built around the Hadrianic or Antonine period and the painted stucco ceiling of this period with mythological figure, cupids, and seasonal personifications is still preserved. Since the foundation of the tomb, several new burials had been added; this also changed the design of the room, which had to be altered in order to make room for inhumation burials. The tomb has two chambers, and sarcophagi were found in both of them. The motifs of all three sarcophagi found in the first chamber concentrates on a positive attitude towards death (cupids, seasonal personifications, and bucolic scenes), and they all have blank portraits (cat. nos. 30, 404, and 445; **Fig. 15**). Because of these blank portraits, it has been suggested that the tomb was furnished without knowing who was going to be buried there, so that a family or a burial association could make use of the tomb later.[121] In the main chamber with the painted ceiling, seven sarcophagi were found, three of which were richly decorated with mythological scenes and two of them had a portrait (**Fig. 55**; cat. no. 550).[122] The use of sarcophagi in the three chamber tombs mentioned here showed that the families or funerary associations sometimes picked related motifs, probably because they had a particular meaning to them. A large landscape painting on the wall behind one of the sarcophagi in the first chamber confirms the focus of the family on maintaining a positive attitude towards death. The sacro-idyllic character of the landscape places the deceased (mentioned in the inscription) in an ideal world of prosperity and divine presence.[123] A well in the floor of

119 Erasmo 2008, 166-68.

120 Herdejürgen 2000, 221-34.

121 Herdejürgen 2000, 79-80. For burial associations and columbaria, see Bodel 2008.

122 The other sarcophagus with a portrait is not preserved (Herdejürgen 2000, 229-30).

123 Tombs are often designated as *loci religiosi*. For this aspect, see Eck 1989, 58; Carroll 2006, 4.

the same chamber confirms that the living visited and used the tomb for feasts and other ritual activities.[124] They renewed their relationship with the dead by making offerings, contemplating the rich decoration of the sarcophagi, and sharing meals (funerary).[125]

The placement of sarcophagi in chamber tombs enabled the visitors to gaze at them and use them for contemplation, even though their visibility could be restricted, as in the case of cat. no. 41 (Mausoleum of the Valerii).[126] It is often the case that chamber tombs on Roman necropoleis were reused by several generations (though they did not always stay within the ownership of the same family).[127] A consequence thereof is that over time the chamber became filled with burials. This sometimes meant that sarcophagi had to be placed in front of each other, thus obstructing the viewing of those furthest back. That full visibility was not always the most crucial criterion for choosing a sarcophagus is, however, evidenced by other kinds of tombs housing sarcophagi. Sarcophagi could be put into buildings that scarcely left room for anything other than the coffin, and others were placed beneath the floor of a chamber tomb, a type of burial that made the coffin inaccessible after the funeral.[128]

Sarcophagi could also be buried in *fossa* tombs, meaning that they were placed directly in the ground. These ditches were sometimes lined with stone blocks and sealed with mortar.[129] In such cases the relief decoration was not meant to be seen after the burial. Some of these *fossa* tomb sarcophagi still seem to have been special commissions, since some had a unique motif or a portrait of the deceased applied to one of the figures of the relief.[130] When the sarcophagus was hidden beneath a grave monument or in a ditch, never to be seen again after the burial, the image had still, at some point between the workshop and the tomb, been an object for attentive consideration and contemplation.[131] When the sarcophagus was selected, someone had consciously thought about the motif and deemed it appropriate for the commemoration of one individual. This may have happened at the workshop where the motif was chosen, or outside the grave before it was sealed.[132]

The concealment of a sarcophagus in the ground or in a tomb does not contradict theories about the use of sarcophagi for commemoration and contemplation. The question is instead for whom the images were intended. Richly decorated graves, never visible for passers-by, are commonly known phenomena in human history, and their inaccessibility does not entail that these tombs were never part of a self-display that manifested the deceased's place in society.[133] The continuous visibility

124 Feasts were regularly held near the tombs. Lucian describes how funerary banquets were laid out and then burned in order to offer the food and drink to the dead (Lucian, *Charon*, Trans. Fowler & Fowler 1905, vol. 1, 181-82).

125 A description in a will of a tomb and of the activities that should take place there mentions the day the *cella* (tomb chamber) was opened. Furthermore, it is stated that the door of luna marble should be easy to open and put back into position; Toynbee 1971, 62-3. For the inscription, see *CIL* XIII 5708. The mention of "the day the *cella* was opened" and the importance of a door that could be easily opened and locked show that the patron of the tomb wanted the interior to be accessible. Wallace-Hadrill (2008) has also written about the internal and external features of the tomb and how both were used as a means of self-representation.

126 Other examples of sarcophagi that have been displayed in a similar way from this catalogue are cat. nos. 73, 97, 155, 226, 311, 374, 404, 460, 491, 511, 557, 604, and 631. Others were found in underground chambers such as, for example, cat. no. 595.

127 An assembly of 10 sarcophagi have been found in two connected underground rooms near the much debated Licinian Tomb (Bentz 1998; Kragelund, Moltesen & Østergaard 2003, 57-65). Whether or not the sarcophagi belonged to the same tomb as the altars found nearby is uncertain, but if they did we have an example of a burial complex used by the same family over several generations, from the early empire until some point in the third century (Kragelund, Moltesen & Østergaard 2003, 102-4).

128 For sarcophagus burials in narrow tomb buildings, see Dresken-Weiland 2003, 99-100. For sarcophagi below floors, see Dresken-Weiland 2003, 186-87.

129 Meinecke 2012. Dresken-Weiland enumerates the various examples found. It should however be noted that some of the sarcophagi mentioned by Dresken-Weiland are without relief decoration (2003, 186-88).

130 An example is cat. no. 154.

131 Zanker 2000, 8-9.

132 Because of the weight of sarcophagi, it is unlikely that they were a part of the funerary procession. Furthermore no sources, either literary or material, bear evidence of the presence of sarcophagi at this stage of the funeral.

133 Think about the Etruscan underground burial chambers with colourful wall-paintings and richly decorated Greek vases.

of the monument was not necessarily the main purpose of making it.[134] Its function was instead connected to funerary practices and varying beliefs, including those of existence in an afterlife and the destiny of the soul. In line with this, sarcophagi should be seen as closely connected to the tomb, the deceased, and the family, and not exclusively for public display of social status, despite the fact that it could work both ways.[135] An example of sculptures that were hidden, never to be seen after the burial, is found at the Vatican necropolis in a simple burial consisting of an amphora containing the ashes of one deceased person. Beneath the urn a statuette of a sleeping slave was found.[136] It is a likely possibility that the iconography of this little marble sculpture was closely related to the life of the deceased. Taking the primitive type of grave into consideration, he could himself have been a slave. The noteworthy thing is that the marble figure was put into the grave without any intention of making it visible for passers-by.[137] I would argue, therefore, that in order for a piece of sculpture to be an expression of the identity of the deceased, it did not have to be constantly visible. In discussing the visibility of the frieze of the column of Trajan, P. Stewart talks about "invisible" works of art, and argues that it would cause a loss of knowledge if modern scholars were to ignore what can be understood from such pieces just because restrictions were put upon the viewing of them in their original context.[138] Especially when working with sculptures made for what Zanker calls a new *Gefühlskult*, such as sarcophagi, discounting the value of those objects that were not visible to everyone would weaken the otherwise rich source material given to us in the archaeological material.[139] The act of concealing a relief-decorated sarcophagus in an earth-covered tomb only emphasises the fact that a burial was a personal matter, and often the size and decoration of the coffin related to the personality of the deceased (as exemplified by the statuette of the slave). Instead of claiming that the relief had no meaning because they could not be seen,[140] we should acknowledge that their lavish decoration and quantity is enough to prove their significance in Roman funerary culture. Sarcophagus images are therefore not only about aspiring to social status through self-display; they are also about private mourning and remembrance through ritualised acts, including the abovementioned concept of *Gefühlskult*.

In spite of their private character, it would be difficult to argue that sarcophagi were not made to emphasise status in the world of the living, in contexts both in and outside of the family. Those placed in chamber tombs, and those located in open air settings, were undoubtedly put on display. People outside of the deceased's close family may have had access to chamber tombs on special occasions, such as on the anniversary of the burial and during celebrations where people gathered at the necropoleis to commemorate the deceased.[141] Necropoleis were probably much more vivid places than we often imagine them to be. Physical arrangements

Another phenomenon from the world of sarcophagi is the few examples of sarcophagi with inscription and decoration placed inside the coffin. Here the message was not directed towards the living, but the dead (Dresken-Weiland 2003, 189-90).

134 See also Veyne's approach to "art without viewers" (1988).

135 Ewald states that sarcophagi were made for private viewing, but he also considers the imagery as part of a visual communication system, a standpoint in which it is implicit that more people are involved in the viewing (2004, 230).

136 Liverani & Spinola 2006, 79-80.

137 The concealment of grave goods and statues may have to be seen as an effort to prevent tomb raiders plundering the grave.

138 Stewart 2008, 125.

139 Zanker & Ewald 2004; Bielfeldt 2005, 1075.

140 For example Dresken-Weiland (2003, 193) "Ingesamt entsteht der Eindruck, dass die Menschen der mittleren Kaiserzeit und der Spätantike zu dem auf dem Sarg angebrachten Bild in vielen Fällen keine exklusive Beziehung entwickelt und diesem keine übergrosse Wichtigkeit beigemessen haben". Instead Dresken-Weiland thinks that it is the choice of a sarcophagus in itself, with or without relief, that conveyed a meaning (2003, 194).

141 Toynbee 1971; Zanker & Ewald 2004, 33-6; Koortbojian 1995, 15; Carroll 2006, 42; Jensen 2008; Hope 2009. A general overview of funerary rituals and traditions is given in Davies 1999, 125-86. The most frequently mentioned days of celebration are *Rosalia*, *dies Natalis*, the lightening of lamps at the grave at *Kalends Ides* and *Nones* of every month, and *dies Parentales* (13-21 February). The last day of the latter, *Feralia*, was reserved for public ceremonies whereas the others were for private celebration (Toynbee 1971, 63-4). See also Cumont (1922) 1959, 71-2 for *Parentalia* and *Lemuria*, where precautions are taken to keep the *lemures* (shades of the dead) away from the house.

were made to accommodate the living, including the installation of wells, cooking facilities, benches, and gardens with fruit trees, and it is clear that meals were an important part of the rituals undertaken in honour of the dead.[142] What these funerary banquets actually were and how the celebrations should be imagined are questions that are often debated, but the fact that they were a central part of the funerary culture and veneration of the dead is attested by the early Church fathers, who struggled to convince the converts, who had adopted the tradition for feasts of their martyrs and saints, that such banquets were a pagan custom that should be abandoned.[143] Secondly, both texts and iconography of funerary monuments were directed towards the living. Despite the fact that the buried person could have had an impact on the appearance of the monument, in cases when it was commissioned while he was still alive or when instructions were left in his will, it was the living that made the final arrangements and ensured that the burial took its proper form, meaning that it was understandable and acceptable in current society.

There are no indications that sarcophagi were part of the rituals that went on before the burial (i.e. the body's exposition or the *pompa*, funerary procession), but they were the objects for cultic veneration of the dead during and after the burial.[144] The celebrations of the dead had several purposes: they fulfilled the rituals that brought the necessary comfort to the immortal spirits, they ensured the survival of the dead in the memory of the living, and they enabled the living to contemplate the life of the deceased (and their own life) and honour them by keeping them alive through their memory.[145] The importance of the cultic practice that took place at the tomb is testified by a will left by Gaius Popilius Heracla. He asks for his tomb to be placed at the Vatican Hill near the Circus. What he probably requested was a chamber tomb similar to the one built by G. Herma Valerius (Mausoleum H), which we have already looked at. He asks that his freedmen and freedwomen were given the right, but also the obligation, to maintain the cult at the tomb, through which they could keep his memory alive; in other words he wanted his heirs to guarantee free admission to the tomb for all his and his wife's freedmen and their descendants.[146] Gaius Popilius thereby ensured that the tomb was open to those who could maintained his memory through sacrifices and cultic practices. We also learn from this document that those who could enter the tomb included not only heirs and blood-relations, but also the freedmen of the deceased's family.

To conclude, sometimes the memory of a person buried in a sarcophagus was constructed through remembrance during and after the funeral (i.e. invisible sarcophagi that had been buried and sealed). At other times it was constructed and re-negotiated through continuous visits to the tomb and by gazing at the sarcophagus, and the outcome was personal and depended on the relationship one had with the deceased or the purpose of the visit to the tomb. Therefore it can be argued that sarcophagi were made for contemplation, with all the possible uses that this entails.

Self-Representation and the Function of Sarcophagus Imagery

As we have seen, in its most frequently known context (the chamber tomb with room for several burials, as well as floor and wall decoration) the sarcophagus was a piece in a visual puzzle that aimed at satisfying the viewer.[147] The tomb as a whole represented the family, whereas the sarcophagus itself stood in for one individual or a family 'unit', such as a married couple, brothers and sisters, or a single child and a parent. The personal character of a sarcophagus has, however, often been questioned because of the repeated figural

142 For example, an oven was found inside tomb 87 at Isola Sacra (Balch 2008, 276), and a cooking niche is adjoining the main burial chamber of three tombs (E1, E3, and E4) on the Via Laurentina Necropolis at Ostia. The main burial chamber of these three tombs also functioned as a *triclinium*, as evidenced by the benches placed there (Heinzelmann 2000, 259-72).

143 Jensen 2008.

144 For representations on sarcophagi of the exposition of the body, see cat. nos. 537, 616, 620, 622, and 623.

145 Toynbee 1971, 51 and 61-2.

146 Toynbee & Ward-Perkins 1956, 10.

147 Bielefelt 2003. For a summary of the development of funerary architecture in Rome, and changes in the funerary customs that brought with it the popularity of sarcophagi, see Junker 2005/06, especially 163-67.

repertoire, the frequent lack of inscriptions, and the often unfinished portrait heads. However, seen in this original context, a sarcophagus was not an anonymous monument. The absence of written data can partly be explained by the fact that very often the inscriptions are not preserved. Names, ages, and family relations could be painted directly onto the individual burial places using perishable colours, such as carbon and red pigments.[148] These epigrams would have given the tomb a far more personal character than the often almost anonymous burial settings we face today. As exemplified by the tomb of the Valerii, such tombs had, besides the *titulus* on the entrance, several inscriptions inside the tomb that labelled the individual burials. The same phenomenon is known from a chamber tomb that has not been exposed to weather and human activities for centuries. The second century "columbarium 9" beneath S. Sebastiano is a fascinating example of a family tomb that has been used for several generations, and, besides its *titulus* inscription, it offers a variety of painted, incised, and carved inscriptions on marble and stucco that inform us of its inhabitants.[149] But despite the well-documented evidence for inscriptions in tombs, some sarcophagi were designed so that the figural decoration covered the entire surface and left no space free for an inscription panel.[150] In such cases, the images on the coffins could have helped the visitor to distinguish between the burials.[151] Self-representation is therefore a central issue when looking for the purpose of a sarcophagus burial. Such burials were usually the final resting places of one person, and its portraits, inscriptions, or figural decoration were the means by which the buried person could be identified. This means that each coffin is representative of one individual. In this analysis, sarcophagi will therefore generally be read in isolation from their original context (the tomb), since they are single monuments with a message about one individual or a family.

Self-representation in sarcophagus imagery was effected through portraits, which are applied to a standing figure, a bust, or a figure that interacts with the surrounding scene. Typically these portrait figures are shown in mythological surroundings or with attributes that symbolise certain qualities and virtues. The most popular types of figures belong to the learned sphere. The next most common are found in mythological narratives, on hunting scenes, and engaged in rituals. By combining the deceased's portrait with such a standardised scene the desired aspects of Roman *virtus* becomes directly transferred to the memory of the deceased. To illustrate how self-representation was used and negotiated on sarcophagus reliefs, we can turn briefly to an example of a sarcophagus that at first appears to be relatively standardised (**Fig. 16**; cat. no. 646). The sarcophagus in question is of the so-called strigillated type and decorated with two grooved and three figural panels. The scenes of these panels express virtues of the higher social classes that draw on concepts such as *concordia* and *paideia*. The central *dextrarum iunctio* scene is flanked by a panel with a learned woman and another with a philosopher. The *dextrarum iunctio* scene makes the sarcophagus an obvious choice for a marital couple, but the portrait tells another story. On this relief, the couple are not carved with portrait features; their heads are left roughly carved. Nor is the philosopher on the right panel carved with a portrait. His head is a generic representation of a philosopher. The person commemorated, a woman, is found on the left panel, and she is represented as a learned figure. She is the only figure applied with a portrait, and the qualities of the surrounding figures are therefore transferred to her. The marriage scene implied that she was married, but the woman did not choose the pious veiled woman on the marital scene for her portrait. She, or perhaps her family, had chosen not to emphasise her role as a married woman. Instead she is represented as an intellectual with all the qualities and connotations of learnedness that follows from this. This decision tells us that values other than the domestic were important to her, thus revealing aspects of personal preference and individuality. Through this process the sarcophagus was transformed from a standardised product into an individ-

148 Wallace-Hadrill (2008, 63) gives an example of *ollae* that have been labelled with carbon.

149 Taccalite 2009, 93-114.

150 Examples include cat. nos. 36, 12, 154, 219, 350, 395, and 592. It is likely that sarcophagi placed directly in the earth, or in a ditch with stone revetment similar to cat. no. 145, had a grave marker above ground, and that labels painted on walls may have identified the deceased.

151 Inscriptions could, however, also be added in places that were not designed for them, such as profiles; see, for example, cat. no. 221 and the aforementioned cat. no. 140.

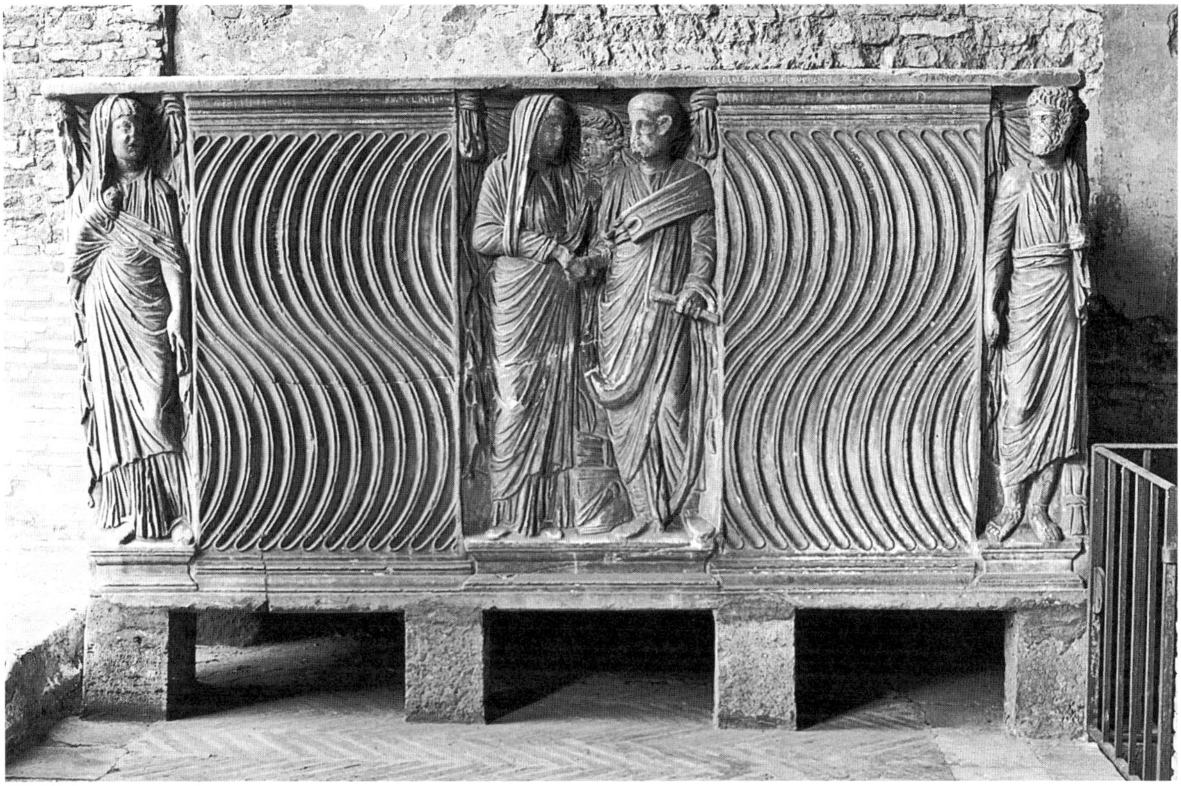

Strigillated sarcophagus with an individualised learned woman and a couple with blank portraits. Rome, S. Saba (cat. no. 646). Photo: D-DAI-ROM-65.262. **Fig. 16**

ualised commemorative monument. I will be arguing throughout this book that by putting together all of the glimpses of personhood offered by sarcophagus reliefs, we can gain information not only of the ideals valued by society, but also of the virtues valued by individual Romans in a funerary context. The sarcophagus represented in **Fig. 16**, cat. no. 646 offers one such glimpse.

Today's globalised world makes it important for many people in our society to define their identity, as a reaction to the extensive and constant incoming influence of other societies, cultures, and religions. The choices and possibilities that these debates open up encourage us to think about our own needs and place in the world, and this is reflected in the studies we make of other cultures.[152] In this context, the concept of identity is both popular and much discussed within archaeology, and as a consequence the discussion has been raised as to whether it is an empty term or a useful methodological tool.[153] Within archaeology the notion of identity has been used to explore objects from various angles; the approaches taken are multiple, since identity can be said to be implied in all aspects of human life.[154] Despite the fact that the term 'identity' did not exist in antiquity, it is a framework that ensures our recognition of the approach taken, and I find that the concept encourages us to reflect on issues connected to people, both as individuals and as members of a society.

Identity has been defined from various perspectives, but explicit definitions can be hard to find. In this book, R. Jenkins's definition of identity is used.[155] He defines all identities as social identities, and argues that identity

152 On the individual and its recent popularity in social science, see Meskell 1999, chapter 1.

153 Pitt 2007. See also Bell (2008, 20-4), who is of the opinion that the concept of identity does not fit for antiquity.

154 On identity within archaeology, see, for example, Laurence & Berry 1998; Miles 1999; Meskell 1999; Fowler 2004; Dias-Andreu et al. 2005; Casella & Fowler 2005; Revell 2009.

155 Jenkins 2006, 28.

is something that arises through all social interaction: one cannot talk about identity without social interaction, since identity is acquired by defining oneself in relation to other people. Therefore, it is about recognising, categorising, and defining yourself and the people with whom you interact. Through social interaction, identity is constantly negotiated and renegotiated, and as Jenkins states, there is also always the possibility of revising identity *post mortem*.[156]

To explain the mechanism of constructing memory and identity on Roman sarcophagi, the concept of "management impression", as defined by E. Goffman, can be useful.[157] The art of management impression is performed when a person acts in such a way that he controls the impression of him received by others, and thereby defines his own identity. To do so, a range of mechanisms needs to be controlled, such as a dramatic style and ability, idealisation, and so forth. According to Goffman these mechanisms refer to individual identification with collectively defined roles. This explains what occurs when a figure on a sarcophagus is individualised through a portrait. By representing oneself through a collectively defined figure (the body type), the patron sends a message with the purpose of controlling the impression the receiver gets of his identity. On sarcophagus reliefs, in contrast to Goffman's studies of contemporary societies, nobody had to perform; they merely chose an appropriate figure. Since an important purpose of creating a memory is to elevate the deceased in the eyes of the viewer, the roles must be socially accepted and generally recognisable in order for them to fulfil their aim, which, as argued by Zanker and Ewald, sarcophagus images are.[158] The advantage of this kind of self-representation is that the patron gains control of the memory constructed by viewers (family members, etc.) through their visits to the tomb, at least as long as the monument stayed within the sepulchral sphere. Still, the viewing positions can be difficult for the sender to control, since they depend on the viewer.[159] This is exactly why the notion of generally accepted cultural ideas is crucial. An example is the representation of the naked Ariadne. For us, Ariadne can seem like an odd choice of self-representation for a mother on the tomb of her son (**Fig. 12**; cat. no. 612), but the repeated use of this body type shows that it was perfectly acceptable to the Romans in the second and third century. They knew the image, and more importantly, they knew how to read it and which virtues it conveyed.

Besides issues such as sex, age, and gender, the concept of identity also encompasses ethnicity. On the question of ethnicity, I assume that all sarcophagi shared the same culturally defined language of Roman ideals, and we may therefore assume that both the deceased and the relatives saw themselves as Romans. Ethnicity is not reflected in the iconography of sarcophagi made in Rome, and therefore it seems to be a category of no or little importance here. One argument for taking this standpoint is that sarcophagi reflect such simplification.[160] In line with A. Wallace-Hadrill, I argue that the deceased were Romans in the way that they were a part of the cultural sphere in which this funerary culture was created, and they were familiar with the cultural codes on which the iconographic tradition relied, since it was them who created and negotiated it.[161]

The portrait figures were used to reflect the deceased's identity on two levels, both social and individual, meaning that the deceased chose a method of self-representation that not only idealised but also reflected on personal character. The perpetually repeated repertoire of figure types was readable for Roman viewers, since it was formed by the cultural system from which they had acquired their behavioural norms. This is in line with Zanker and Ewald's study *Mit Mythen Leben*, to which the approach followed here owes much. They examine the familiarity of myths to the average Roman observer and look in more detail at the use of portrait faces on sarcophagi.[162] Zanker sees this kind of self-representation in the tradition of Roman art as meaning bearing, and argues that the role models used

156 Jenkins 2006, 29.

157 Jenkins 2006, 96.

158 Zanker & Ewald 2004.

159 Elsner 1995 (for the approach to the concept of viewing, see especially 1-6), and more recently Elsner 2007, part 2. See also Berger 1972.

160 A comparative ethnographical study of Roman versus Attic sarcophagi is found in Ewald 2004.

161 Wallace-Hadrill 2008.

162 Zanker & Ewald 2004 (reviewed by Wood 2004; Bielfeld 2005).

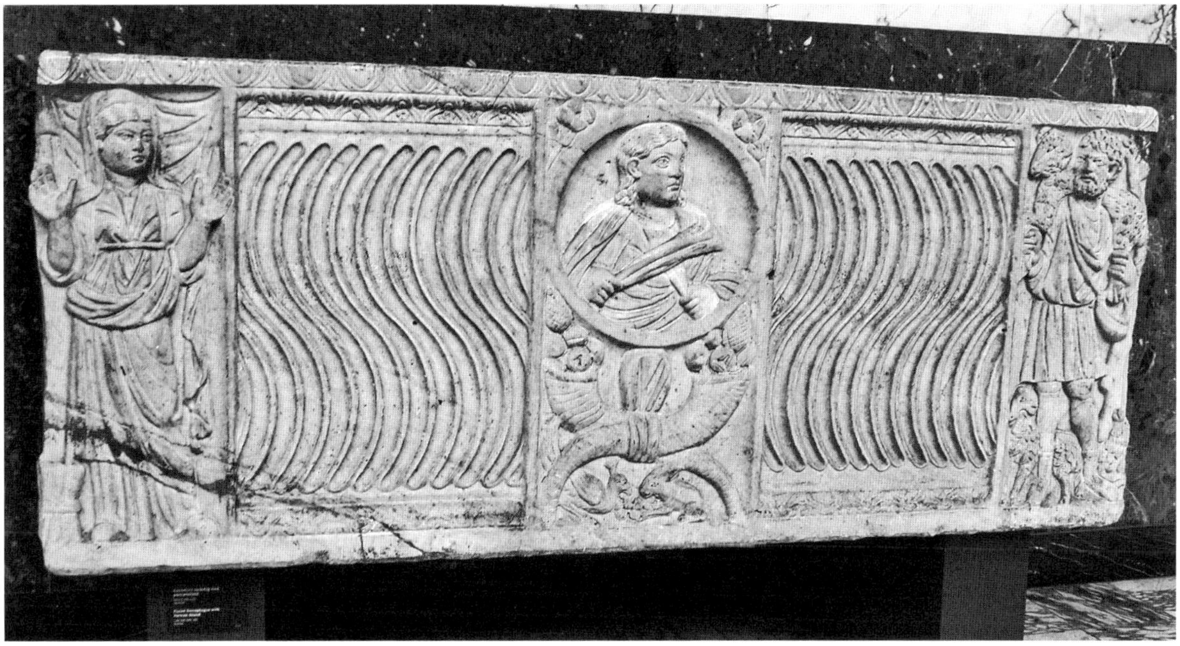

A strigillated sarcophagus with an Orans*, a bust of a learned woman, and a ram-bearer. The* Orans *and the learned woman are carved with portrait features (cat. no. 2). Copenhagen, Ny Carlsberg Glyptotek, inv. 2343. Photo: Author, courtesy of Ny Carlsberg Glyptotek.* **Fig. 17**

to construct identity had to be, and were, readily accessible to the ordinary viewer. The use of portrait figures on sarcophagi referred to a long standing tradition of self-representation in Roman sculpture. What we see on sarcophagi in some respects reflects the use of statue types, as they had been presented by the upper class since the Republican period in both public and private spaces.[163] By applying these traditional figures with a portrait on a sarcophagus, the deceased became a role model for the viewer.[164] The deceased therefore constructed his identity using a standardised iconographic language, and even though individuality is also reflected in the very choice of the figure, it could be further emphasised though minor manipulations of the scenes. In line with this, R. Bielfeldt's book on Orestes-sarcophagi argues that the previously assumed hermeneutic model, moving from a focus on mythological motifs to the popularity of images of everyday life, does not describe the material accurately.[165] She shows how mythological images were a rhetorical means that changed form over time in order to accommodate the changing society and to function expressively for its patrons.

A sarcophagus in the Ny Carlsberg Glyptotek, Copenhagen provides another good example of how standardised images could be manipulated in order to construct identity. It shows a woman or girl represented as a learned person with pious ideals and a view of life that alludes to philosophical ideals and bucolic peace (**Fig. 17**; cat. no. 2). The bust is represented in a *clipeus* that emphasises her status as a role model, and nothing but her hairstyle alludes to her femininity. She holds a scroll, an object frequently used in representations of both men and women on sarcophagi. Her dress is the normal tunic and *palla* worn by women, but in her case it is not used to enhance the feminine appearance of the body. In the right panel, she is represented again, as a figure in a praying gesture; this underscores her

163 For the repertoire of figure types, see Koortbojian 2008.

164 On the definition of role models, see Hölscher 2008, 45. Hölscher prefers the term 'role' instead of role models. Roles are performed by a person, but my understanding of his use of 'roles' is that when visually illustrated on, for example, sarcophagi, these roles become role models (see Hölscher 2008, for example, p. 52)

165 Bielfeldt 2005a.

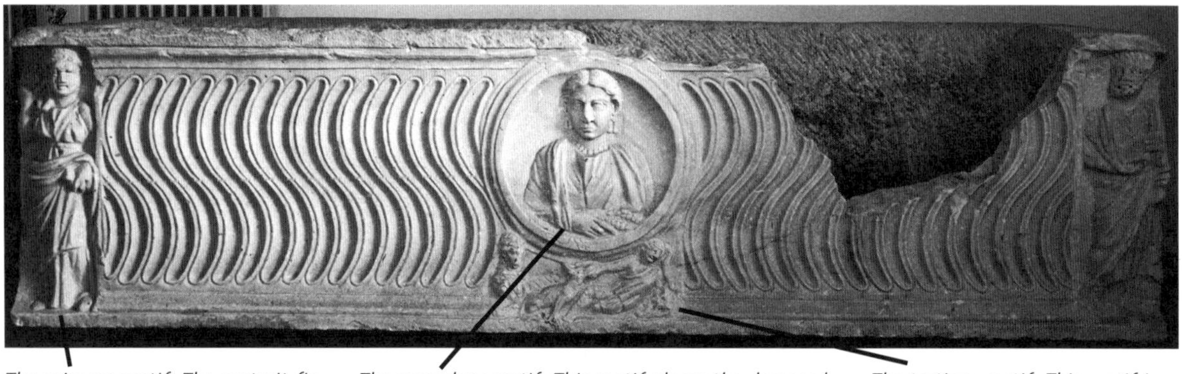

The primary motif: The portrait figure is the main focus of the decoration; in this case a portrait bust of a woman is placed in a clipeus.

The secondary motif: This motif places the deceased within a specific context, and usually the two panels allude to the same area of activity; on this sarcophagus the motifs refer to the intellectual sphere.

The tertiary motif: This motif is found beneath the clipeus. Often it looks as if the figures of this scene support the clipeus.

Fig. 18 *The figure illustrates the iconographic range and the possibilities for combining motifs on the frontal relief of a strigillated sarcophagus. It is according to this hierarchy of motifs that the catalogue has been divided. The example shown here is cat. no. 323. Ostia, Ufficio dell' Opera Nazionale Combattenti. Photo: D-DAI-ROM-69.773 (Hützel).*

pious nature. The qualities of the *Orans*, as this figure is called, are difficult to separate from those of the learned woman, a fact illustrated by the scrolls placed at her feet.[166] A ram-bearer represented in the right panel is the counterpart of the *Orans*. He is not shown with a portrait, and instead the virtues implied in this figure are transferred to the woman by the juxtaposition of the two motifs. The *cornucopiae* beneath the *clipeus* stand for prosperity and fertility, and the peacock and hare that eat grapes emphasise the notion of abundance in the iconography.[167] All these images reflect back on the woman. Through this self-representation, the woman becomes a role model to the public viewers, but to the people who knew her, it illustrates the ideal aspects of the woman that they wanted to remember.

Portrait Figures and Design

The decoration of the outside of the coffin was important to the memory that was constructed of the person inside, because the virtues represented through the figures were transferred to the identity of the deceased. The oblong shape of the coffin offered sufficient space onto which narrative scenes or figurative panels could be placed, and portraits indicated the connection between the scene and the deceased.

The prime mechanism for negotiating the identity of the deceased is the portrait figure. This figure will therefore be termed the 'primary motif'. On strigillated sarcophagi, similar to the one just described, the frontal relief is usually separated into five panels (see **Fig. 18**; cat. no 323). Panels number two and four are grooved, and the left, right, and central panels (panels number one, three, and five) are decorated with figures.[168] The portrait figure is most often found on the central panel, but is also seen in the other two, as on cat. no. 2 (**Fig. 17**). On the central panel, the portrait is often found on a bust in a *clipeus* or a shell, but it can also be placed in a rectangular panel, with one or more standing or seated figures. The deceased in the *clipeus* is generally dressed in a tunic and a *palla* or *pallium*. Normally the bust does not hold an attribute, but one of a limited number of objects – lyre, apple, or scroll – may sometimes be carefully selected to appear in the hands of busts.

166 For the meaning of the *Orans* and the learned figure, see chapter 2.

167 For the interpretation of the grape-eating hare on sarcophagi, see Bielefeld 1998.

168 Sometimes strigillation appears as straight vertical lines, for example cat. nos. 117, 336, 348, 446, and 403.

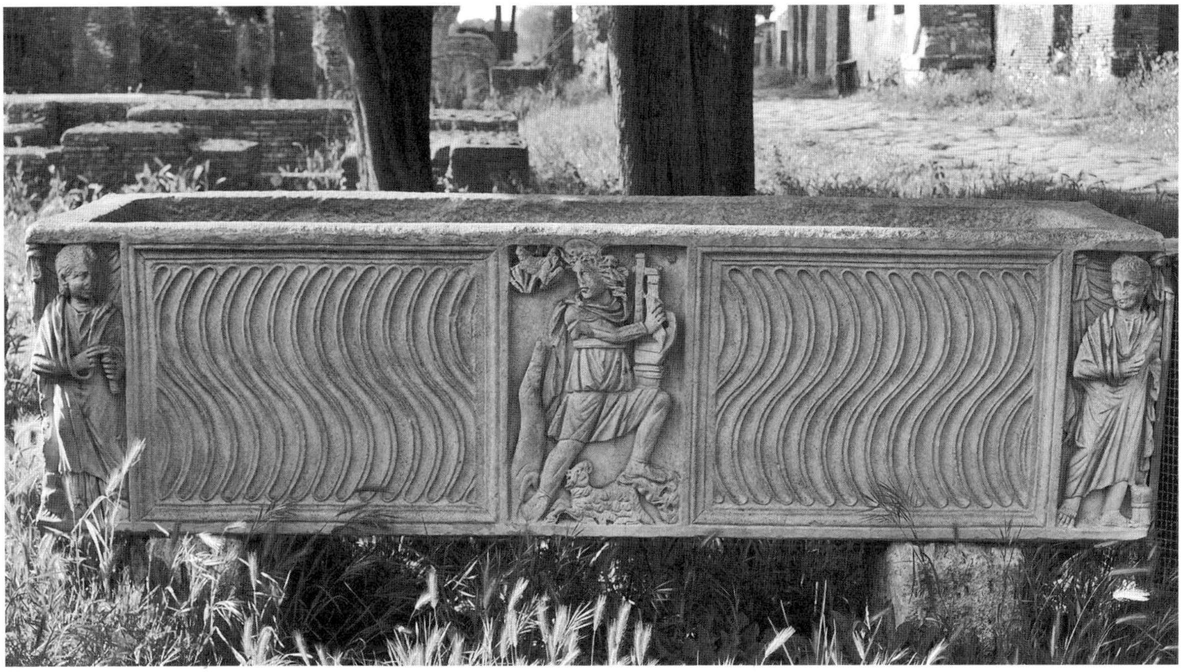

A strigillated sarcophagus with a learned woman and a learned man from Ostia. Orpheus is represented on the central panel (cat. no. 177). The piece shown on the photo is a copy. The original is in one of the office buildings on the site. Photo: Author. **Fig. 19**

If the portrait figure on a strigillated sarcophagus is placed in the first or fifth panels, any reading of the sarcophagus should take its point of departure there. In such cases, the central panel is most often decorated with motifs, such as a death door, a figural scene with, for example, a seated protagonist (see, for example, cat. no. 103 featuring a philosopher or cat. nos. 180 and 177 (**Fig. 19**), two practically identical sarcophagi with representations of Orpheus), or a small mandorla with varying figures.[169] Sometimes two portrait figures are juxtaposed, as, for example, cat. no. 2 (**Fig. 17**), where a portrait in the *clipeus* is combined with a portrait figure on the first panel, and the meaning of the design must then extrapolate to both of them.

The secondary motif is normally found on panels one and five, and these two figural panels often allude to the same area of activity, as in this case where both refer to the intellectual sphere (**Fig. 18**). The first panel shows a learned female figure or a semi-*Orans*, and the fifth panel shows a sage or a philosopher. Other themes typically found on these panels include sleeping cupids, lion-animal groups, seasonal personifications, and bucolic figures.[170] The subjects chosen for these reliefs either emphasised the virtues of the primary motif, by using motifs related to the same theme, or added new virtues to the identity established by the portrait figure. What I call the 'tertiary motif' is only found on sarcophagi with a *clipeus*, since it is placed beneath and often made to look as if it supports the *clipeus*. Frequently appearing motifs include theatrical masks, *cornucopiae*, acanthus leaves, pillars, and mythological or other narrative scenes. The latter type is found on our sarcophagus (**Fig. 18**). It shows a bucolic scene with an ibex, a sleeping shepherd, and his dog. The scene is a detail taken from a larger narrative and is related to representations of Endymion as well as to popular bucolic landscapes. With its three figural panels, strigillated sarcophagi offered a limited space for decoration,

169 For an overview of the form and type of sarcophagi, see Koch & Sichtermann 1982, 62-4. For the mandorla on sarcophagi and their motifs, see Batatta 2004.

170 For the interpretation of the different figures of the secondary motif, see chapter 3, *Gender Characteristics of the Secondary Motif*.

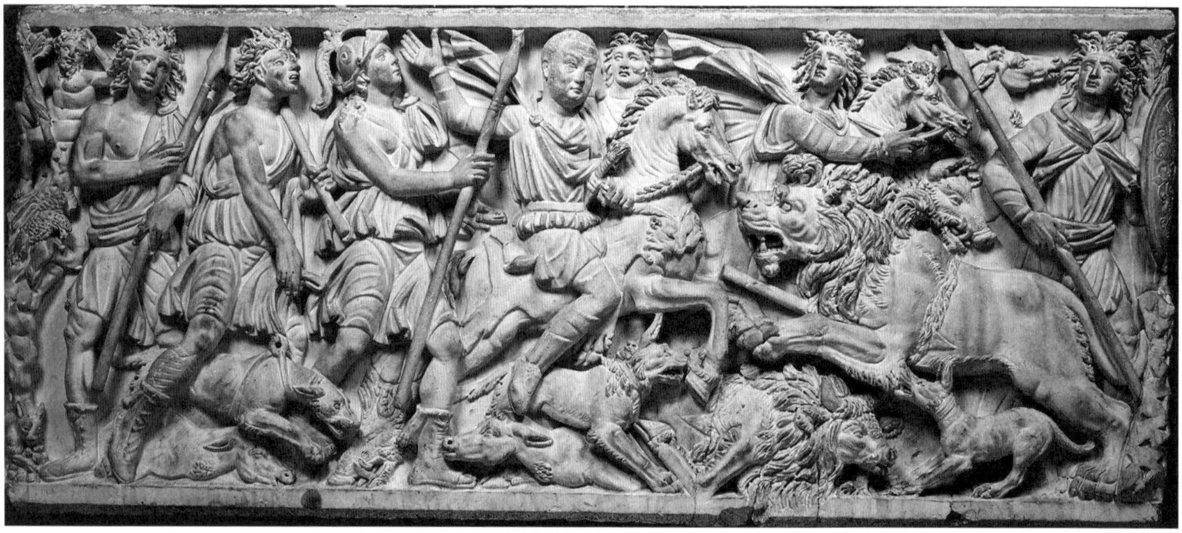

Fig. 20 *Lion hunt sarcophagus (cat. no. 482). Copenhagen, Ny Carlsberg Glyptotek, inv. 786. Photo: Ny Carlsberg Glyptotek.*

and only the essential parts of a motif are represented, in what is normally called an 'abbreviated' form.

A little less than one quarter of all sarcophagi with portrait figures are decorated with continuous narrative scenes, and they are therefore not as frequent as those with figural panels.[171] These elaborate sarcophagi show one continuous scene and present a detailed and vivid narrative style, but they do not offer the possibility of combining different areas of activity, as strigillated sarcophagi do. Again the portrait figure is the focal point of the representation, and in placing the deceased in a narrative setting, he or she is whirled into an imaginative world of heroes, gods, and other allegorical figures. In contrast to strigillated sarcophagi, the heroic and representative status of the portrait figure in a narrative scene is normally not emphasised by a *parapetasma*, columns, or any other kind of framework. Instead, the figure of the deceased interacts with the surrounding figures as the main protagonist. Through this action their function as a role model is stressed. This focus on the deceased as the main protagonist can be exemplified by the figures in a lion hunt scene on a sarcophagus in the Ny Carlsberg Glyptotek, Copenhagen (cat. no. 482; **Fig. 20**). All the figures are orientated towards the lion hunter, whose heroic gesture illustrates victory and power. His clothes, a cloak, and the elaborate harness of the horse aspire to high status, and the fact that he has just defeated the lion adds a heroic element to his personality. The question of how such iconography should be interpreted will be discussed in more detail in the following chapter. What I want to stress here is that in order to understand scenes on sarcophagi as commemorative images, the point of departure of any interpretation must be the portrait figure itself.

When reading sarcophagi, the lid plays a significant part, since its decoration adds yet another dimension to the negotiation of identity. However, lids have often been separated from coffins after, or even in, antiquity and are therefore frequently lost. Furthermore, lids and coffins that did not originally belong together are sometimes displayed together in museums to illustrate their function.[172] Another circumstance that complicates the matching of lid and coffin is that they do not necessarily

171 Sarcophagi with narrative scenes in the catalogue: cat. nos. 477-523 (hunt); 524-37 (reclining): 539-44 (carriage); 545-76, 569-81, 583-603, 605-12 (myths); 615-23 (children's life course); 625-26 (battle) 628, 29 (profession?); 639, 641, 645, 648, 656-61, 663-69, 671 (ritual).

172 Examples of lids placed on sarcophagi to which they did not originally belong are cat. no. 496 and 550. The lid (cat. no. 269) and the coffin (cat. no. 547) are today on display together in the Cortile del Belvedere (Musei Vaticani), but are not considered to have originally belonged to the same burial.

need to be carved from the same type of marble to have been made for the same burial. A workshop could use two different blocks of marble to make the lid and the coffin of the same sarcophagus. Therefore it is also the case that the length of the lid can vary from the length of the coffin, even though they may have originally belonged together.

Despite the previously mentioned shortcomings of the preserved material, the sarcophagus lids were always present for the Roman viewer visiting a tomb with sarcophagus burials. The motifs on the lid generally have a different theme from those on the coffin, and an inscription panel is typically the central motif.[173] On such lids, the bust is often placed on the right or left side of an inscription panel in front of a *parapetasma* held, for example, by cupids (as on **Fig. 87**; cat. no. 50). The name and sometimes the age of the deceased are mentioned in the inscription, and the deceased can be designated as *conjunx* or *filius*, with adjectives like *carissimo*, *inocentissimo*, etc. The inscription emphasised the personal character of the coffin in a similar way to the portrait, and it is therefore curious that the panel, like the portrait, is often left blank (see, for example, cat. no. 578).[174]

It has now been argued that both the form of the sarcophagus and the placement of the portrait figure in relation to the figural representations are important for how we read the relief. In addition, the Roman iconographic language offered a variety of attributes that emphasise the heroic aspect of the portraits. In the following, I will look at those most frequently used for heroisation on sarcophagi. The medallion or *clipeus* is on numerous occasions used to enhance the status of the deceased. As has already been stated, *clipeus* portraits are most frequently found on strigillated sarcophagi, where they are juxtaposed with allegorical figures such as seasonal personifications, learned figures, or a lion-animal group. The portrait enclosed by a *clipeus* served to reinforce the heroic image of the person.[175] This is suggested by the fact that the probable earliest representation of the scheme shows an image of a deity in the *clipeus*.[176]A mythological sarcophagus from the 160's represents Dionysus' Indian triumph, and the *clipeus* is used to attract attention to his cult image. Instead of using a *clipeus*, a portrait could also be framed by a wreath or a shell.

The *clipeus* or the wreath is also a means through which patronage can be symbolised. An example from the public sphere is found in Misenum on the Antonine *sacellum*, where the couple who had paid for the restoration of the building are represented in the gable in an oak wreath in a similar composition to those found on sarcophagi.[177] The wreath can thus enhance the status of the patrons, since it is a symbol used in cults, for triumphs, and for honorary awards in a military context.[178] It has therefore been suggested that the wreath symbolises immortality and the triumph over death.[179] This interpretation may be supported by a sarcophagus from Museo Nazionale Romano with triumphal iconography (cat. no. 624), dated to the middle of the second century.[180] It depicts a scene with Roman soldiers, captives, trophies, and a heroic naked young man with military cloak who shows mercy towards the barbarians. On the lid, a bearded man is represented on a cuirass-bust enclosed by a wreath. The wreath is carried by flying *victoriae* and yet more captive barbarians are flanking the scene. This triumphal iconography was popular in the second century, but not many of these sarcophagi show a portrait. In the context of sarcophagi it is not unlikely that the relief, beside showing one aspect of Roman *virtus*, was interpreted in terms of triumph over death. Another example, which should probably

173 Cat. no. 238 is just one example. Sometimes the panel is placed alongside a portrait bust, as on cat. nos. 5, 8, 15, 23, 43, 50-3, 197, 293-4, 322, 326, 397, and 562.

174 It is highly possible that the inscription could have been painted on the panel.

175 Krantz, *ASR* V 4 (1984) 38-9, especially note 176 for further literature; Jucker 1961, 142-50; Chiarlo 1976, 1338-40; Caronna 1983, 164. L'Orange (1953, 98) writes: "When the portrait of the dead is placed in the *clipeus*, the dead appears as elevated to the stars." In line with this, see Engemann 1973, 65-6 and Koch & Sichtermann 1982, 610, note 221 with further references to the argument of using a *clipeus* to symbolise *apotheosis*.

176 Zanker & Ewald 2004, 16, fig. 9.

177 Miniero & Zevi 2008, 174-251.

178 Bergmann 2010.

179 For this interpretation, see Baratta 2004, 201-2.

180 Other sarcophagi with a bust enclosed by a wreath are cat. nos. 310, 314, and 315.

be dated in the second half of the same century, shows another bearded man with a wreath on his head and a sword in a belt around his naked chest (cat. no. 627). He wears only a military cloak. The fragment is today used in the Trofeo Farnese in Palazzo Farnese in Rome. The *clipeus* in which the bust appears is carried on the back of two seated captives and is furthermore supported by Victoria on the left. Another heroic figure with a military cloak stands beside Victoria. Again the wreath is a symbol of the deceased's military triumph, but on the individual level the iconography, as a means of consolation, speaks in metaphorical terms about the possibility of him achieving a happy afterlife.

The portrait of the deceased in a wreath is not used differently from a portrait in a *clipeus*. When the *clipeus* is placed, as shown on **Fig. 18**, in a compositional scheme in which different themes and symbolical meanings are combined, the purpose was to glorify the deceased's memory; this is especially evident when the *clipeus* is carried in a procession of sea-*thiasoi,* flying *victoriae*, or seasonal personifications (for example, cat. nos. 186, 394, and 407).[181]

The heroic and commemorative aspect of sarcophagus imagery could, as a second possibility, be emphasised by depicting the figures on plinths or statue bases. This kind of figural representation is called 'statuesque' and is frequently found, not only on sarcophagi, but on funerary reliefs in general. The statuesque embodies the qualities of a real statue, and it has been suggested that they offer an alternative for those who could not afford a statue in the round.[182] However, sarcophagi were expensive commissions in themselves, and the purpose of the statuesque is to emphasise the ideal character of the individualised figure.[183] The same body type can be found with or without a plinth, and both generic figures and portrait figures could be carved as statuesque. This similarity of representation is an indication of the values implied in the individualised figure and shows that they, as well as the generic figures, had metaphoric significance. The two Muses flanking the deceased on cat. no. 13 are represented as statues on plinths, whereas the deceased is shown as a living person standing between them. On cat. no. 57, however, it is the two deceased individuals who have been placed on plinths, and they thus appear as statues. Whether the dead person is associated with ideal statuary figures or actually becomes a statuary figure him or herself, the intention of the scene was to place the deceased within the context of idealisation and commemoration.

The *parapetasma* is a third feature used to emphasise the status of the deceased. In contrast to the *clipeus*, it was not used exclusively for individualised figures; similarly to the statue base, the *parapetasma* was used to designate both individualised and ideal figures as role models.[184] The *parapetasma* could be carved either as hanging from the wall, tied in the corners with a knot, or it could be held by figures, such as seasonal personifications or cupids. The *clipeus* and the *parapetasma* are never used in the same scene, since both had a similar function and meaning, namely to idealise and heroise the person depicted.[185]

181 The *clipeus* is interpreted by L'Orange as *imago mundi* or the cosmos (1953, 90-102), and sometimes it is adorned with zodiacs (cat. nos. 425, 468, and 469). These are associated with seasonal personifications and the zodiacs are probably signs of cosmic significance that allude to the circle of the year and an abstract plan of life (for an iconographic study of the signs of the zodiac and their significance, see Hachlili 2009, especially p. 55).

182 Stewart 2003, 92-108. Stewart enumerates the various ways in which the statuesque has been analysed on funerary reliefs by different scholars, including imitation of tomb architecture and decoration (2003, 101-2).

183 Sarcophagi with statuesque representations: Cat. nos. 57, 100-2, 114, 124-25, 131, 133, 646, 649, 650, 655, 670, and 672. Statuesque is a typical feature of strigillated or other types of sarcophagi where the figure is not acting in a scene. Sometimes a *clipeus* portrait is placed on the plinth that characterises a statuesque (cat. nos. 351 and 356). For generic figures depicted as statuesque, see (examples are cat. nos. 330, 448, 637, and 651).

184 About one quarter of the sarcophagi in the catalogue show an individualised figure in front of a *parapetasma*. The *parapetasma* is frequently used behind learned figures and especially on reliefs with Muses. The fact that the *parapetasma* was not only suspended behind individualised figures speaks against the idea that it was used to symbolise apotheosis (Lameere 1939, 91, note 91).

185 Except for cat. no. 392, where the *parapetasma* is suspended in the *clipeus*. For an interpretation, see Brandenburg 1967, 227, 245, note 96. For further references see Krantz, *ASR* V 4 (1984) 55 with further references in note 305. See also Koch

Other attributes that could heroise the bust representing the deceased are acanthus leaves and *cornucopiae*. Acanthus leaves are often found on posthumous portraits in the round and have a specific symbolism in the context of death and burial.[186] *Cornucopiae* and acanthus leaves serve the same purpose in relation to function and meaning, since both are symbols of prosperity and fertility; they therefore offer an optimistic counterpoint to the portrait of the dead person that they carry.

As a final element in the design of a coffin, the short end reliefs should be mentioned. The coffin was supposed to be seen from the front, and the short ends were typically hidden in a niche, placed against a wall or close to another sarcophagus that therefore blocked the full view of the short end reliefs. Possibly for that reason, these reliefs are often more schematic and of secondary quality to the decoration of the frontal relief.[187] Like the reverse of a sarcophagus, the short end reliefs sometimes did not receive any decoration at all. In such cases they were normally roughly dressed. Despite the often anonymous character of these neglected parts of the coffin, both the short end reliefs and the reverse have value in that we can use them to understand the processes of production. Sometimes traces of the different stages in the production process can be seen on them, as figures are finished to different degrees or only sketched onto the marble.[188] It is likely that apprentices of the sculptural workshops were allowed to practice their carving on the short end reliefs.

When carved with figures, the motif of the short end reliefs often follows the theme of the frontal relief, in the sense that on, for example, a sarcophagus carved with a hunting scene, the short end is likely to show one figure from a hunt, such as a hunter with a spear and a dog. Another example is the hunt sarcophagus from Reims (cat. no. 494). The frontal relief shows one scene with Virtus and a commander and another with a lion hunter. On the short end reliefs, accompanying huntsmen are represented to illustrate the hunt party. Other popular motifs for the short end reliefs are shields and crossed spears or griffins. On *lenoi*, the bathtub-shaped coffins, the figural relief from the front typically continues onto the short ends.

Grief in Words and Images

Now that a framework for interpreting sarcophagi with an emphasis on self-representation has been established, the function of sarcophagus images as a means for consolation can be considered. Emotions were a major component in the choice and construction of a private funerary monument. With death follows grieving and sorrow, and the feelings experienced by the patrons of the monuments we are trying to understand are just as important as notions of social status and individuality.[189]

There are numerous ways in which people try to make sense of death, and some of these involve objects and images. An object can function as sort of token that symbolises the deceased person. Through the object the dead person can be felt to be present, and the simple action of looking at, touching, and holding the object can bring consolation. Images work the same way, and they can give connotations to actually experienced situations or feelings connected with the deceased. Images of myths, for example, work as allegories, and through this figurative mode of representation they say something about the order of the world. They furthermore make the bereaved think of experiences, situations, or right or wrong ways of acting or feeling. Myths were therefore chosen to decorate a coffin in order to allow the beholder to seek comfort and consolation (on the interpretations of myths, see chapter 2).

Emotions are implied in every human action, and in a funerary context it seems especially difficult to ignore their significance in the choice, erection, and use of a

& Sichtermann 1982, 610 with further references to *clipeus* and *parapetasma* (Koch & Sichtermann 1982, note 221).

186 Jucker 1961, especially 133-38; Turcan 1999, 131. Sarcophagi with acanthus leaves supporting the bust: cat. nos. 30, 46, 76, 79, 86, 281, 299, 424, 444, 447, 448, 450, and 470. All except for cat. nos. 281, 299, 444, and 470 are associated with learned figures.

187 See Koch & Sichtermann 1982, 64-6.

188 Birk forthcoming.

189 Tarlow 1999. Hölscher also suggests that such considerations should be taken into account (1992, 474), and Koortbojian has shown how funerary art can be both an expression of social status, conforming to formula in the iconographic and epigraphic language, and a revelation of individuality and real emotions and sentiments (2006).

monument.[190] That a sarcophagus was primarily made to commemorate one person means that the emotions and personal engagement put into the purchase of one coffin are directed towards one individual. However, emotions can be very difficult to concretise, whereas social status is more tangible. Paying more attention to this aspect of funerary culture can therefore lead us to further understanding of the functions of sarcophagus imagery.

Some sarcophagi are very explicit in expressing the desperate grief and sorrow of surviving relatives; one example of this is Valeria, the mother who in the middle of the third century purchased a sarcophagus for her son Artemidorus with the representation of the sleeping Ariadne and scenes from the myth of Theseus (**Fig. 12**; cat. no. 612).[191] Valeria suffered this loss when the son was just 17 years and 17 days old. Artemidorus had been a free man but engaged under imperial service (hence the inscription, *aug lib adlecto*). Valeria dedicated the sarcophagus to her son, to his spirit (*D M*) and in his memory (*a memoria*). Artemidorus was probably not married at the time of his death, and he was therefore commemorated by his mother, who called him the sweetest son (*filio dulcissimo*). The mother who chose this sarcophagus in the memory of her son grieved her loss, and she made a visual illustration of these feelings by letting herself be represented as the sleeping Ariadne, just after she had been abandoned by Theseus (he is shown with the portrait of the son Artemidorus). It is the very moment at which Theseus leaves Ariadne that is chosen for the sarcophagus, and it is a forceful metaphor for the situation at the tomb, as experienced by Valeria. Her son is gone and she is left behind. Comfort may have been found in knowing that like Theseus, who had defeated the Minotaur, so will the son defeat death, and be free to go on to his next adventure in the afterlife. On the left side of the sarcophagus Theseus/Artemidorus bids goodbye to his father, King Aigeus, and sails away. Again the separation of death and the journey to a new life is visually illustrated. The choice of the myth of Ariadne and Theseus therefore becomes a metaphor for loss and leaving the earthly world. Despite the formulaic character of the inscription and the images, the monument had a special meaning for Valeria, and its erection was a way for her to cope with her grief. As we will see, the recurrent focus on love themes in myths makes it clear that emotions played a significant role in the construction of memory.

On a child's sarcophagus from the third or fourth century the emotive words *in dolores patris* are inscribed to express what was felt at the loss of the child.[192] Despite of the formulaic connotations of phrases such as *carissima(us)* and *dulcissima(us)*, often used for children on epitaphs, they still have an emotional meaning.[193] Additionally more personal descriptions can be added: a girl who died at the age of three was addressed as having a sweet voice (cat. no. 631).[194] A Christian inscription mentions a wife who desired her husband beyond the limits of love, and spouses are often designated *benemerenti*, which describes well the feelings in a good marriage.[195] Some inscriptions can be heartbreaking to read; the inscription of a mother who lost two children, Laberia Alexandria aged 10 and Silvanus aged 6, must have evoked a great deal of pity in those who visited the tomb.[196] Her husband, the father of the children,

190 Tarlow 1999, 22-4. Tarlow 2000 is a review article of the study of emotions in archaeology. Within the study of sarcophagi, emotions have started to become an important issue. Examples of studies that involve such approaches are Zanker & Ewald 2004; Ewald 2005; Carroll 2006, especially 196-202. For a study of attic stelae that takes into consideration the emotional aspect of iconography, see Adams 2002.

191 Valeria's full name is not preserved. Blome 1992; Zanker & Ewald 2004, 47-8; Newby 2011, 201-5.

192 Dresken-Weiland 2003, 196-97.

193 For funerary inscriptions as indicators of emotions experienced by the dedicator at the death of the commemorated, see King (2000, 134-36), who explores how human feelings are transformed into formulaic phrases on epitaphs.

194 Carroll 2006, 196-201. 37 Roman inscriptions are found among the sarcophagi in the catalogue. Among these are the following examples of emotive adjectives: *Dulcissima/us*: cat. nos. 43, 50, 261, 263, 326, 612, and 639. *Carissima/us*: cat. nos.48, 182. To designate spouses: *Inconparabile*: cat. nos 41, 354, and 434. *Benemerenti*: cat. nos. 41, 67, 294, 512, and 647.

195 For the sarcophagus with the Christian inscription see *Rep.* I, cat. 778. The sarcophagus was given by a husband to his wife and both could have had their portraits carved, but the heads were left roughly carved.

196 *Dis Manibus Laberiae Alexandriae quae annos X menses V dies VII et Silvano qui annos VI menses V dies XIIII hoc in sarcophago genetrix duo corpora natoscondidit in felix semper-*

had died before them, and the woman states in the inscription that she will live a miserable life ever after.[197] Servienius Demetrius also makes a beautiful memorial for his wife on a sarcophagus from the tomb of the Pancrati (**Fig. 15**; cat. no. 445). Through two rough-carved or blank portraits, he shows himself and his wife together in a position that symbolises marital harmony. In the inscription he commemorates her as the most pious wife and mentioned in terms of years, months and days the time they had together in which she always did him good.[198]

Iconography, as well as inscriptions, shows that emotions play an important role when erecting a sarcophagus. Myths were used to illustrate the sorrow of the family and could show analogies to situations at the tomb, for example, by depicting scenes of parting. In a similar way, inscriptions help us understand the feelings between the departed and the patron of the coffin. Acts of grief were performed to seek consolation, and through texts, images and actions, the Romans had a whole variety of ways in which the afterlife could be imagined.

Contemplating the Afterlife

The large number of tomb markers and funerary monuments that have been preserved is evidence of the Roman preoccupation with death and the afterlife. We have looked at how the living approached the dead and how they visited the tomb, but to define what they thought or hoped for after death is a complicated matter, since the evidence for Roman ideas of an afterlife existence is extraordinarily varied.[199] Funerary inscriptions offer evidence for a total denial of a continuous existence, as, for example, an epitaph stating bluntly; *non fui, fui, non sum, non curo*,[200] while evidence of funerary cults on the Roman necropoleis shows that the spirit of the dead required attention and care.[201] The practice of making offerings at the tombs is confirmed in literature by Ovid, who describes how the *manes* or spirits of the dead only demanded modest offerings.[202] Festivals such as the *Lemuria*, *Rosalia*, and *Parentalia* were established practice, and both rites and festivals bear evidence of a repeated need to renew one's promises of devotion and affection towards the dead – actions that have no meaning if the existence of a person's *anima* after death was not presupposed.[203] Therefore we also find that the disbelief in the existence of the soul is combined with folkloristic ghost stories, which flourished among the Romans and though little has been written about this tradition, the stories are recorded by authors such as Pliny and Lucian.[204] These superstitious stories attest that the Romans did not believe that death was a total annihilation, and they testify to the fear of intervention by the deceased's spirit, which was felt as present in the world of the living. Therefore when interpreting funerary monuments, there are three main scenarios that should be considered: the possibility of extending one's life through the monument and the memory of the living; the hope for the survival of the soul in

que habitur adolorem quo superat vivet vita..que miserrimaducetCONIUge praerepto genitor quibusipse misellis. CIL VI, 20987 = *CIL* VI, 34135 = *CLE* 00504.

197 I am grateful to H. Sigismund Nielsen for making me aware of this inscription. It is difficult to date but according to Sigismund Nielsen, this type of inscription is usually given a date after 200.

198 See cat. no. 445 for the inscription.

199 Lattimore (1942, 342) believed that both Greek and Roman belief in immortality was neither widespread nor strong, and Dresken-Weiland assumes that the pagans had a negative or indifferent attitude towards an afterlife (2007, 285), but it has been shown by various scholars that the Romans believed in some kind of afterlife existence: Strong 1915; Cumont 1942; 1949; 1959 [1922]; Richmond (1950, 41) talked about afterlife beliefs as a world of opportunities for the Romans, from pure negation to an expectation of not only the survival of the soul but also of the individual; Toynbee 1971, 33-9; 1982; Andreae 1980 (for a short review mostly focusing on the lion hunt as a symbol of death, see Smith 1988); Koortbojian 1995, 78, 98-9; Turcan 1999; Davies 1999, 155-66; Felton 1999, xiii; Bremmer 2002; Zanker & Ewald 2004, 113-15, 117; Carroll 2006, 3-4; Erasmo 2008; Noy 2009; Hope 2009, 97-120.

200 "I was not, I was, I am not, I do not care", quoted from Toynbee 1971, 34. Lattimore 1962, 84-5; Hope 2007, 231.

201 One example of offerings and cultic activity by the grave is offered by the excavated necropolis along the Via Triumphalis (now in the Vatican), see the newest evidence in Liverani & Spinola 2010.

202 Ov. *Fast.* V 2.535-54; Zanker & Ewald 2004, 114.

203 For these festivals, see pp. 38-9; Gessert 2004, 224-26 considers the festival in relation to the use of sarcophagi; Hope 2009, 98-102.

204 Felton 1999.

the afterlife; and the belief that the tomb was the final resting place.[205]

The Romans' preoccupation with ensuring a persisting memory has been established by archaeological evidence and written testimony. Cicero wrote that "death is to be feared by those for whom everything is extinguished with their life, not by those whose renown cannot perish"; and Trimalchio wished to create a memory of himself through a tomb that was compared to a house decorated with statues.[206] Through the erection of a statue or a funerary monument the Romans aimed at ensuring remembrance that consequently could extend their lives on earth.[207] But while the monuments bear evidence of the importance of a non-perishable reputation on earth, images and words allude to hopes for an existence in the life beyond the grave.

> Bassa, wife of the poet Laberius, rests here in the deep lap of fruitful Earth, a wife of ancient morals. Her revered thoughts are with her husband, her soul has returned to heaven.[208]

The words are part of an epitaph composed by the poet Laberius for his wife and exemplify one way in which death could be approached. The husband's thoughts about where his wife has gone are equivocal: she rests below earth, her thoughts are kept with the husband through his commemoration of her, and her soul has returned to heaven. Laberius imagines that his wife is in the celestial realms, but the place of the Roman afterlife was not always located in the heavens; other accounts talk about the Underworld as the home of the dead.[209] Laberius furthermore alludes to a separation of the body and soul by giving the remains of his wife a location below ground and describing the soul as ascended to heaven, a thought that, as we will see, can also be illustrated on sarcophagi. It is with such equivocation in mind that funerary monuments and what they express about the afterlife and mourning should be interpreted. In the following, I will look at examples of how sarcophagus burials responded to the numerous and often ill-defined concepts of the afterlife by focusing on the example of the sleeping figures.

The sleeping figure could represent the deceased in the state that he or she was in after being put to rest in the tomb.[210] This does not necessarily imply a kind of afterlife, since sleep when it is equalised to death does not necessarily mean reawakening, but it does express a hope for the deceased to achieve an ideal state of eternal peace and rest.[211] The large number of altars and devices for offerings, such as tubes inserted into graves, found at Roman necropoleis testifies to a widespread belief in the continuous existence of the spirit of the dead in or around the tomb.[212] The belief that the tomb was the house of the dead is indicated by the fact that tombs could be furnished with doors, mosaic floors, wall paintings and beds.[213] Even sarcophagi often have an elevation in one end, which does not serve any real

205 Edwards (2007, 13-8) looks at the evidence for different approaches to afterlife existence in the introduction to her book on death in Rome.

206 Cic., *Parad. Stoic.*, II, 18. Patronius, *Satyricon*, 71.

207 Carroll 2011.

208 "*Bassa, vatis quae Laberi coniuga, hoc alto sinu / frugae martis quiescit, moribus priscis nurus. Animus sanctus cum maritost, anima caelo reddita est. Parato hospitium; cara iungant copora / haec rursum nostrae, sed perpetuae, nuptiae*" (*CIL* VI 13528). Translation from Erasmo 2008, 172. For the epitaph in its full length, see Erasmo 2008, 171-73.

209 Hope (2009, 107-12) gives a summary of beliefs in the survival of the soul in a heavenly sphere and in the Underworld (2009, 103-7).

210 Koortbojian (1995, 106) sees the sleeping Rhea Silvia as equated with death.

211 Richmond 1950, 40. On *somnus aeternus*, see Cumont 1942, 369.

212 Steinby 2001; Hope 2009, 98-102. It is worth noting that sarcophagi rarely had devices that made libation or other kind of offerings into the coffin possible. However, sacrifices probably took place anyhow, either on or near the coffin or on an altar, as is attested by Suetonius in his description of Nero's burial. He writes that Nero was buried in a porphyry sarcophagus and that the altar for sacrifices was placed above it; Suetonius, *Nero* 50.

213 See the discussion by Wallace-Hadrill (2008), who argues that the analogy between tomb and house is strong. He also sees the interior of the tomb as a place that provides a home for the dead among his or her family, whereas the exterior of the tomb, like the house, represents the household to the world. For the tomb as a house for the dead, see furthermore Zanker & Ewald 2004, 28-9; Hope 2009, 101, note 6. The idea is also described by Cumont 1959 [1922], 44-69 and Toynbee 1971, 38. For the restless spirit, see Hope 2009, 99-100, 116-17.

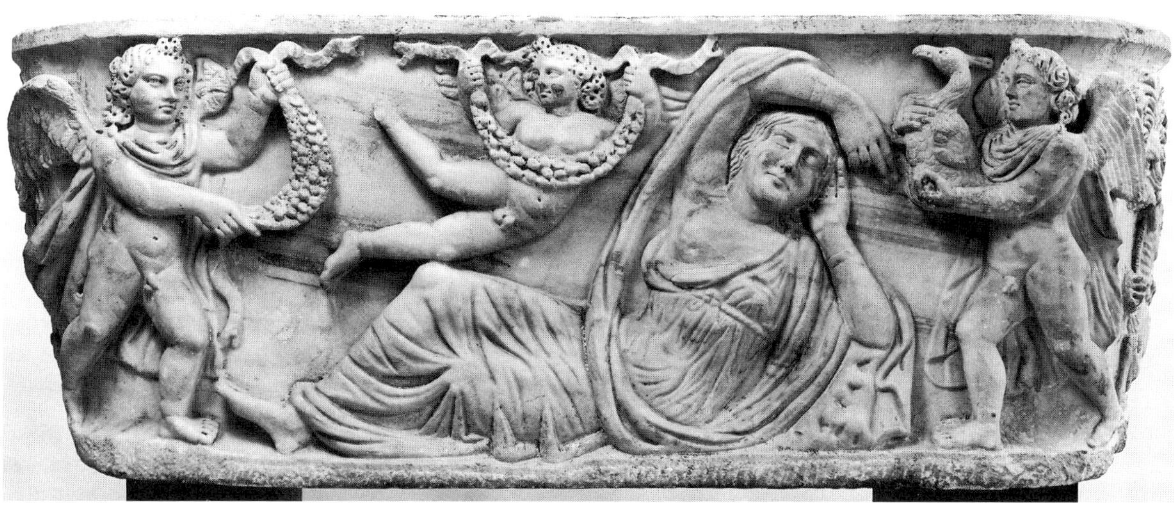

Sarcophagus with a woman in a similar posture to that of the sleeping Ariadne. Winged cupids bring her presents (cat. no. 556). Copenhagen, Ny Carlsberg Glyptotek, inv. Sc.784a. Photo: Ny Carlsberg Glyptotek. **Fig. 21**

function, but was meant as an illustration of a pillow on a bed. To find rest in the tomb was considered an optimal state of mind for a deceased person, whose spirit in the worst case could be deemed to wander restlessly. On cat. no. 556 (**Fig. 21**), the sleeping Ariadne is taken out of the mythological context, a scene that in itself emphasises the allegory of death.[214] Instead of the arrival of Dionysus, naked cupids with garlands surround her and underline the funerary meaning of the motif. Garlands are mentioned as presents to the dead by Ovid, and Lucian describes how glorious garlands rest upon the bier and flowers crown the dead during the funerary rituals.[215] Furthermore, garlands symbolise *pietas* as they are a traditional device used at sacrifices and in other religious contexts.[216] The sleeping figure is a symbol of death as a physical state similar to sleep, and Ariadne on this piece becomes a symbol of the peace that the patron hoped the deceased would find in the tomb.[217]

When Ariadne is represented in the broader mythological narrative, she is found sleeping by Dionysus after her abandonment by Theseus; this scene can be seen as an allegory of a hope for a happy existence after death. This representational form is the most frequent type of Ariadne scene on sarcophagi.[218] Before her sleep, Ariadne was unhappy because she had been abandoned by Theseus. But the life that awaits her after her sleep is a joyous life among gods, with Dionysus and his merry *thiasoi*.[219] Such poetic language about death could bring consolation to the bereaved, as it did for Cicero when he expressed his hope that his deceased daughter found a place among the gods, and it creates an illusion of death as a non-definitive state.[220]

Another way of approaching death was to use the various myths of the journey to the Underworld as metaphors.[221] Tales of the Underworld helped people

214 Another example is cat. no. 559. Here scenes with cupids, wine harvest, and (circus?) horses surround Ariadne.

215 Toynbee 1971, 64; Lucian, *On Morning* (*On Funerals*), trans. Fowler & Fowler 1905, vol. 3, 214-15.

216 For the garland sarcophagi as expression of *pietas*, see Herdejürgen 1996a.

217 Koortbojian 1995, 106-10; Zanker & Ewald 2004, 204.

218 Cat. nos. 555, 557-8, 560-66, and 612.

219 On Dionysian motifs as expressions of a happy *post mortem* experience, see Richmond 1950, 27-8; Zanker & Ewald 2004, 135-59.

220 See the letter from Servius Sulpicius to Cicero in which he tries to comfort him (Cic. *Epistulae ad familiares* IV 5-6). Cumont (1922) 1959, 32. According to Haskell (1964, 251), Cicero tried to convince himself that the soul had an external existence. On Cicero's concept of the afterlife, see Hill 2004, 52-4.

221 The journey is, however, more profound in Greek beliefs about afterlife, where the texts of the so-called Orphic gold tablets guide the deceased on the journey. They warn the

to make the sphere of the dead tangible, and though there was nothing like the Christian afterlife either in heaven or in hell, people were sometimes placed in different spheres according to their deeds in life or the way in which they died.[222] When Anchises describes to Aeneas the fate of the souls after death, purification of the soul or punishment for unjust deeds and other kinds of differential treatments of the souls are mentioned.[223] The pure souls are sent to Elysium, where according to Homer the heroes and good souls belonged, and some of them even received new bodies.[224] Whether the Romans believed in such concepts of the afterlife is difficult to tell, but they used the stories metaphorically to refer to the faith of the dead.[225] The decoration of cat. no. 597 has been interpreted as a scene that alludes to the Island of the Blessed and is thus part of a metaphorical language that uses myths to talk about death and the situation at the tomb. A number of sarcophagi (cat. nos. 697-11) use the myth of Proserpina and her abduction by Pluto to illustrate the dead having been torn away from the world of the living.[226] That this motif is meant to say something about death and afterlife is clear from one of the short sides of a sarcophagus (**Fig. 50**; cat. no. 608). The relief shows a veiled woman, the veil being a common way of representing the deceased or his or her soul, and Pluto. Between them are Hermes in his character of Psychopompos, who has led the deceased woman to the king of the Underworld.

Another way of illustrating afterlife hopes uses the myth of Endymion and Selene (cat. no. 574-86), which is rather popular on sarcophagi. In this myth, we see a positive attitude to the afterlife that alludes to a possible renewal of existence and a hope for a reunion after death.[227] Whereas in the case of the Ariadne myth, it was only Ariadne, and not Dionysus, who is seen with a portrait, both Endymion and Selene are represented with individualised features, thus emphasising the bond of love as transcending death.[228] The two figures can be understood as the deceased and the patron. It was sometimes believed that through sleep access was opened to the sphere of the gods, and the dead could contact living people, as Julia did in Lucian's *Bellum civile* when she addressed Pompey in a dream, though her appearance had more of the character of a pursuit than a happy encounter.[229] The dead would come to the person in his or her sleep, as is visually described by Selene approaching Endymion in her wagon. The encounter between Endymion and Selene expresses the hope that two people will meet again in another sphere, either after death or through sleep.[230]

The representation on sarcophagi of Endymion therefore seems apt for a funerary context, and like the previously discussed representation of Ariadne (**Fig. 21**; cat. no. 556), the sleeping Endymion can be shown as an 'abbreviated' form taken out of his mythological context. On cat. no. 576 Endymion is surrounded by flying cupids with garlands or grapes (**Fig. 80**). This representation, again closely connected to the funerary sphere through the cupids with garlands, puts emphasis on Endymion and the eternal sleep that Selene had

deceased about dangers and tell them what to do to obtain a blessed afterlife. Myths such as Aristophanes' *Frogs* and Plato's *Phaedo* also speak about the journey as a transition from life to the afterlife; see Edmonds 2004.

222 Hope 2009, 106.

223 Virgil, *Aeneid*, VI 559-627 (punishments of the gods); 739-44 (judgment of the soul); 745-47 (purification of the soul).

224 *Oxford Ancient Dictionary*, second edition, 1970, 23-4. On the renewal of the body, see Virgil, *Aeneid*, VI 713-23; 749-51; Edwards (2007, 16-7) who compares the account with the myth of Er in Plato's *Republic*.

225 An example is an epitaph from Rome lamenting a seven-year-old girl. It mentions both the inhabitants of the Underworld and the Elysian fields (Warrior 2006, 40 and *CIL* 6.21846).

226 Newby 2011, 219-24.

227 Koortbojian 1995, 107. On Endymion as an eschatological theme, see Zanker & Ewald 2004, 204-8; Newby 2001, 205-9.

228 Except for the one example in which Ariadne is not sleeping but shown with Dionysus seated on a rock, cat. no. 564.

229 Brilliant 1992, 1036-7. Lucian, *Bellum civile*, and for a translation, see Erasmo 2007, 195-96.

230 Koortbojian 1995, 108-9. For the eschatological meaning of Endymion in this context, see Balch 2008, 275. Inspired by Pythagorean and Stoic thought, some believed that the moon was the place where the boundary between the world of the living and the dead was found, and as the soul left the body and the deceased entered the sphere of the moon, he or she could reveal him- or herself through sleep to the living, Cumont 1942, 246-50; 1959 [1922], 24-5. Nock (1972 [1948], 630). However, Nock did not believe that dreaming of intercourse with a deity, as Endymion does, had anything to do with afterlife beliefs. He saw the images as expressions of feelings and cultural inheritance rather than of concepts specifically held (p. 641).

caused him to endure. The man is shown in a state that alludes to the idea of death as eternal sleep from which one never wakes.[231]

The third and last myth with a sleeping person is that of Mars and Rhea Silvia (cat. nos. 598-600).[232] On sarcophagus reliefs, the composition is similar to that of Endymion and Selene, but the characters have been changed and the narrative takes place in a mythological Roman past (**Fig. 22**; cat. no. 600). Rhea Silvia is sleeping, young and beautiful, and Mars is approaching her. Around them, gods and personifications represent the cosmos. We see Tellus as representative of the earth, a herdsman that illustrates the idyllic setting, and nymphs that personify springs and groves. The upper register is the sphere of the gods, and here divinities are represented. Just as Aeneas in the Underworld offered understanding of the nature of the cosmos, the representation of the myth of Mars and Rhea Silvia was used to reflect upon the meaning of death, life, and the order of the universe.[233]

Death can be difficult to deal with, and most people have probably been in a situation where they found themselves indulging in a hope that the spirit or soul of a deceased person still existed beyond the grave. Such a hope is not necessarily to be seen as an expression of a belief in the afterlife, but as an expression of a wish for maintaining a relationship with the deceased. Through the idea that the person is not gone forever, one can find consolation in times of bereavement. It is in this sense that I see sarcophagi with portraits as important factors in understanding how people in Rome felt about death and what they thought was the fate of the soul. As such, the portrait takes part not only in the process of individualising the monument by showing the facial features of the deceased, but also in extending the life of the deceased on earth through the memory created of them by the viewers. In contrast to earlier debates of the symbolic meaning of sarcophagus decoration, I think these hopes should be read not as a necessary consequence of religious or philosophical beliefs in an afterlife, but as a way for the bereaved to cope with

231 Cumont 1959 [1922], 10.

232 Newby 2011, 209-13.

233 Edwards 2007, 17.

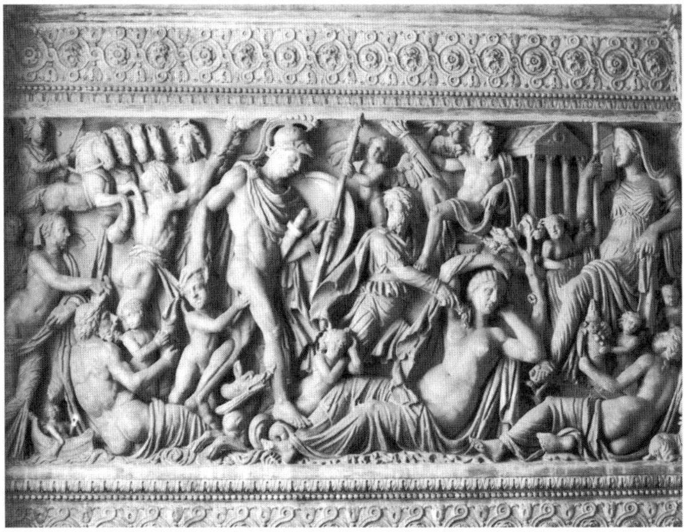

Mars and Rhea Silvia sarcophagus (cat. no. 600). Rome, Palazzo Mattei, built into the staircase. Photo: Author. **Fig. 22**

death.[234] In the end, the Roman afterlife was a personal matter.

Unfinished Portraits as Faces of the Dead

A final aspect worth discussing in the light of the previous discussion of ideas about the afterlife is the astonishingly high number of unfinished heads that are found on sarcophagi. On 201 out of 677 sarcophagi with portrait figures, one or more of the heads that were prepared to receive a portrait never had the facial features or had the hairstyle added.[235] This is a rather high percentage when one takes the entire production

234 I am here referring to the Cumont-Nock (Cumont 1942; Nock 1946) controversy, and though I want to see sarcophagus images as evidence that the Romans sometimes believed in an existence after death, I do not want to write the images into philosophical or religious narratives. Instead, I see the use of such metaphorical scenes as part of the process of consolation. For the newest comments on the discussion, see Newby 2011, 190 with further references in note 7.

235 Around 30% of the sarcophagi have a blank portrait. The distribution of these roughly carved heads is almost equally shared between men, women, and children. Only couples show a slightly higher percentage than the other groups (approximately 24% of the male, 26% of the female, 20% of the children's commemorations, and 42% of sarcophagi commemorating a couple have unfinished heads. See appendix B).

of sarcophagi with individualised figures into account. Unfinished or blank portraits, as I prefer to call them, can take many forms. Sometimes it is no more than a rough block (cat. no. 619); others have the facial features sketched on the block with very coarse strokes (cat. no. 314); and yet others are detailed, with features such as a faint suggestion of nose, mouth, and eyes or a polished surface. Occasionally the head was no more than a plain surface.

The interpretations that have been put forward of the blank portraits span from seeing them as a purely practical matter, embedded in the working process of making a sarcophagus, to meaningful symbols.[236] It has, for example, been suggested that the sarcophagus was purchased by a person in advance of his death, and that the patron did not want his portrait to be carved before he had died, for superstitious reasons.[237] However, there are sarcophagi such as the aforementioned cat. no. 612 that speak against this (**Fig. 12**). On this sarcophagus the mother, whom we have already met, is portrayed as Ariadne. She commissioned the sarcophagus for her deceased son, represented as Theseus. The mother was still alive, and only the son is buried in the sarcophagus, but they are both represented through portraits. On sarcophagi with two portrait figures, it is not unusual that only one of them had the portrait carved. It has thus been speculated that the portrayed person was the deceased, and the blank portrait was reserved for a husband or wife who was still alive at the time of the first burial. The blank portrait was then supposed to be carved when the other person died, but for some reason it happened that the person never came to be buried in the sarcophagus. This could be the case for the Muse and philosopher sarcophagus of Pullio Peregrino (cat. no. 120), but since the inscription leaves no room for another name to be added, I do not find this a likely suggestion. Another possible explanation is that the head was left roughly carved because it had been covered with plaster in which the facial features were modelled.[238] Remains of plaster have, to my knowledge, never been found on roughly carved heads. Others suggest that the portrait features were painted on the roughly carved surface, which seems an awkward explanation as no painted portrait features have yet been found on blank portraits.[239] Furthermore, we also know that portraits in the round were normally carved in detail before being painted, like sarcophagus portraits, which were coloured as the rest of the relief seems to have been.[240] A sarcophagus in the Ny Carlsberg Glyptotek, Copenhagen under current investigation shows that the hair and the head of a blank portrait were painted with red pigment but no portrait features were added. The only outline was a red line enhancing the portrait and the bust (cat. no. 3).[241] This suggests to me that the portrait and the hair were never intended to change appearance, neither by carving nor by painting, after the sarcophagus was taken into use and that, because of the covering slip, the blank portrait was intended to remain as such.

There are two final explanations of the phenomenon of the blank portrait to be mentioned. The first is that the unfinished head proves that a sarcophagus never left the workshop, which has been disproved archaeologically.[242] The other suggestion is that the patron of the sarcophagus did not want a portrait, but just took a sarcophagus on stock which happened to have

236 For the roughly carved head as an unsolved problem see Andreae 1984; Huskinson 1998; Newby 2011.

237 Koch & Sichtermann 1982, 611, with further references (note 233).

238 This was first suggested by Wilpert (1929-36, 100) and then by Gütschow (1938, 169-70). The use of plaster has been dismissed because no archaeological evidence for plaster has ever been found, and because the size of a *bosse* covered with plaster would have made the head too big for the body.

239 For the suggestion of painted portraits, see Sande 2010; Prusac 2011, 119-20.

240 Østergaard 2010 (http://www.glyptoteket.dk/tracking-colour2.pdf, accessed November 2011); Brinkmann 2004. Traces of paint can be seen on several sarcophagus portraits when they are examined carefully.

241 I am grateful to J. Stubbe Østergaard for sharing these results with me and for discussion on this topic. In a recent research report Østergaard suggests that the outline of an eye and the pupil is made with black colour. The evidence is, however, not convincing and, as Østergaard himself states, further investigation is needed, both of this piece and of other blank portraits (2011, 16-9).

242 Koch & Sichtermann 1982, 611-14 with further references (note 246). Huskinson also summarises the different proposals that have been put forward (1998, 143-4, note 25). Engemann (1973, 78) rejected this theory, that has been proposed by among others Bianchi Bandinelli 1970, 306.

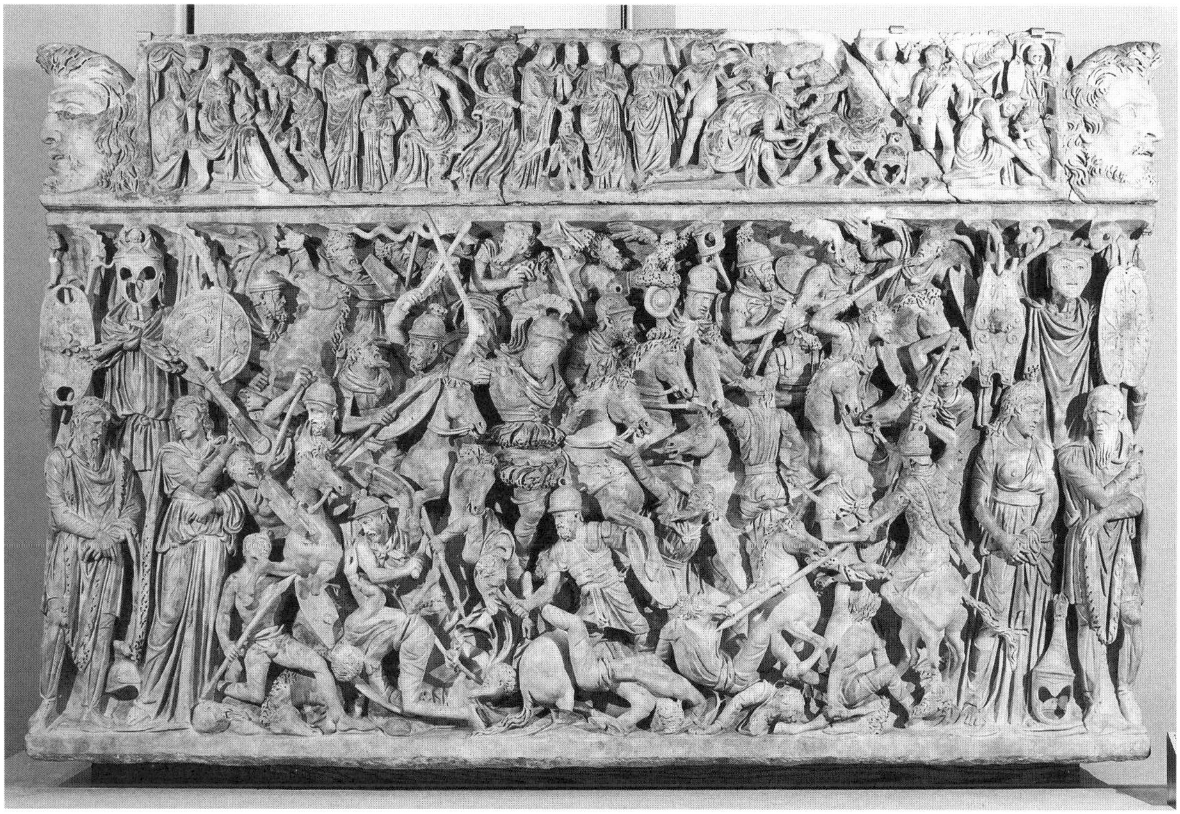

The Portonaccio sarcophagus depicting a battle on the frontal relief and life course scenes on the lid (cat. no. 626). Rome, Museo Nazionale Romano, Palazzo Massimo, inv. 112327. Photo: D-DAI-ROM-2006.1365 (K. Anger). **Fig. 23**

a head prepared for a portrait. This sounds unlikely to me for several reasons; first, purchasing a sarcophagus was expensive and must for many have been a matter of priority.[243] Therefore it seems surprising that the head was not at least finished as an ideal face without individualised features.[244] The carving of a generic face would not have taken a long time and could be carried out wherever necessary. Secondly, several sarcophagi with blank portraits seem to have been special commissions, which suggest that they were not made for a stock market. Examples include the battle sarcophagus from Portonaccio (cat. no. 626; **Fig. 23**), which because of its dimensions and elaborated carving must have been so costly that it is difficult to imagine it as a stock product. That the blank portrait was not carved into a new kind of figure is also curious in the light of the many re-carvings that took place on sarcophagi. Examples of sarcophagi that changed appearance during their carving are cat. nos. 100 and 299.[245] Therefore the blank portraits cannot alone be explained by the fact that they were pre-carved and purchased from stock, and since these blank portraits are preserved in such high numbers, they must have been a sight that frequently confronted the Roman viewer. Therefore, even though they may not have had a deliberate function in the early sarcophagus production, they must at some point have obtained a meaning for viewers over time. What they may have come to mean for the mourners will be explored in the following. It is, however, not my intention to decide whether or not they were left roughly

243 Fittschen 1975; Zanker & Ewald 2004, 30. On the costs of sarcophagi, see Russell 2011, 122.

244 Half-finished sculptures and sculptures with roughly carved reverses are, however, not an uncommon phenomenon in Roman art.

245 See the previous discussion, pp. 31-4.

carved deliberately, but to point to the fact that a blank portrait was frequently seen and reflected upon when a tomb was visited. As such, I argue that they obtained a social value.

As already stated, I take portraits on sarcophagi as representations of the deceased rather than as true likenesses. What a portrait offers is a glimpse of a person fixed at a certain moment in their life, and its appearance is therefore just as negotiable as all the other metaphorical images used to represent virtues on funerary monuments. This puts emphasis not on the likeness but on the portrait as a symbolic representation of the deceased; and the faceless head could symbolise the dead person in a similar manner. This means that the faceless figure maintained the same function as the figure with a portrait since both types of portraits symbolised the deceased individual. In the context of idealisation and self-representation they should therefore be treated equally with the figures on which the portrait features have been carved. Following this idea, the faceless figure is not only a symbol of the deceased, it is furthermore indicative of how death was perceived. Death meant annihilation of the person, and in this context the sarcophagus can be seen as an animated substitute for the body, whereas the soul, which was intangible, was not necessarily bound to the tomb. It is therefore possible that for some members of Roman society in the third century, the faceless figure symbolised a kind of separation of soul and body. The blank portrait was a visual way of illustrating the fact that the deceased has left his existence among the living, and the missing portrait features signalised to the viewer that his or her former self did not exist anymore.[246] Instead the soul has been liberated and the deceased was thereby not bound to the tomb. The empty shell that the blank portrait became an illustration of showed that the person's memory could be maintained, but not the person him- or herself.[247] This also explains why the head did not receive a generic head instead of a portrait. It would have required little effort for the craftsman to re-cut a roughly carved head into a generic face, if no meaning was given to it. As has already been said, the blank portrait was probably not deliberately given a symbolic meaning from the beginning, but their large numbers and their continuous production throughout more than a century proves, in my opinion, that they acquired a meaningful effect in a commemorative context.

Figures did not need to convey the same meaning for all viewers, but the fact that the separation of soul and body through death was an issue for some is illustrated by a sarcophagus with a reclining boy depicted among the Muses (cat. no. 620; **Fig. 96**).[248] The central motif of this sarcophagus is an illustration of such a belief. The reclining boy has portrait features, but his naked body that lay beneath the *kline* is faceless. The boy on the *kline* is an expression of the personhood of the boy, and the surrounding imagery shows that he possessed qualities that caused him to be accepted among the Muses. He, or his soul, has left the body, which now lies lifeless and, very importantly, faceless, as an empty shell on the ground. The blank portrait and the faceless head symbolise a conception of death in which the body and soul have different destinies. The figure with the roughly carved head thereby becomes a physical statement of the individual that once existed.

246 For reflections of this, see Huskinson 1998, 154-55.

247 Huskinson 1998, 134.

248 Wegner, *ASR* V 3 (1966) cat. 126; Fittschen 1972, 492; Wrede 1981, cat. 241; Amedick 1993, 147; Giuliano 1988, cat. 28; Amedick, *ASR* I 4 (1991) cat. 177.

CHAPTER 2

Exempla Virtutis: Portraits and Self-Representation on Sarcophagi

Contemplating the portraits of past generations was important in order to maintain their memory. Besides ensuring remembrance, funerary monuments and their images aimed at consolidating the family and inspiring new generations.[249] The body types and scenes used to commemorate the deceased and to console the mourners are here studied more closely. I will focus on a selection of figures that were individualised with a portrait, knowing that consequently many issues that are both interesting and germane will be left out. What is offered is therefore not an exhaustive interpretation of sarcophagus images but suggestions as to how the individualised figure can contribute to the study of commemoration and individuality through sarcophagi. The focus will be on how identity could have been constructed through iconographic choices, and on how virtues are expressed differently according to the social context in which the figure is represented. Four groups of individualised figures will constitute the framework for interpretation: figures on ritual scenes, learned figures, mythological figures, and figures on hunt scenes.

The group of so-called biographical sarcophagi or more precisely, those with scenes of military superiority, sacrifices, or the traditional joining of right hands to symbolise marriage – has been chosen as the material for this analysis because they started a fashion that lasted throughout the production.[250] In this group of sarcophagi, we find the earliest scene depicting a man and his wife; these figures convey traditional Roman virtues and bring the concept of *concordia* to the fore. As the production of sarcophagi grew and this form of burial became available to a larger group of people, scenes of rituals became popular on for example strigillated sarchophagi, replacing the military focus. In the same period, the learned figures emerged as, almost without competition, the most popular way of self-representation. It is not an overestimation to say that no other self-representative figure gained such popularity in the history of sarcophagi. They appear in combination with a broad variety of other motifs and are used to commemorate men, women, and children. This type of portrait figure is, together with busts (prevailingly of couples), the only one that continued in the Christian production of sarcophagi.[251]

Mythological characters with individualised facial features are probably the most widely discussed type within the study of sarcophagi. On these intriguing scenes, the deceased, and sometime the patron, interact with the mythological world in narratives of personal histories, bereavement, and social status, and they are a forceful way of engaging with metaphors of death and ideals. Finally, the hunt scenes are included here because of the iconographic ambiguity of their seemingly realistic situations. They use a language that combines representations of everyday life and mythological hunts. All of these scenes are significant in understanding self-representation as it is conveyed through sarcophagi.

249 Flower 1996; Højte 2002. For the latest contribution to the use of portraits and their different physical contexts and meanings, see Fejfer 2008.

250 On 'biographical' sarcophagi, see Rodenwaldt 1935; Andreae 1969; Fittschen 1971a; Kampen 1981; Whitehead 1984; Reinsberg 1995; *ASR* I 3 (2006); Ewald 1998; 2003; Wrede 2001. Specifically on battle sarcophagi, see Andreae 1956; Wrede 2001, 21-43.

251 On the learned female figure, see Huskinson 1999.

Figures in Ritual Scenes

Biographical Scenes, Pietas, *and Marital* Concordia

The group of sarcophagi with representations of rituals encompasses the early military commander sarcophagi as well as what has been called its 'abbreviated' form (cat. nos. 630-76).[252] It is generally believed that these sarcophagi mirror the ideal of self-representation within the senatorial class.[253] However, as Ewald has pointed out, such categorisation can limit the expressive value of the sarcophagi's decoration. Instead the abbreviated form should be studied in a broader socio-historical perspective, because they are products of new attitudes towards gender roles and a changed mentality that builds on new ideals.[254]

The so-called biographical sarcophagi are the earliest in this group, and they are characterised by a frieze of continuous scenes. Their representations of an ideal public life are characteristic of sarcophagi of the second and early third century, and the iconographic expression draws on the so-called historical reliefs of high imperial art.[255] In the figural scenes that allude allegorically to the Roman virtues of *virtus*, *clementia*, *pietas*, and marital *concordia*, the qualities of these private men (and women) echo those of the emperor.[256] However, a relatively limited number of these scenes have portrait figures. On all of the six such sarcophagi represented in the catalogue (cat. nos. 656-61), the conventional representations of the deceased as the protagonist appear on three scenes shown in the following order; the deceased as commander ready to receive a submissive barbarian family, the deceased sacrificing to the gods, probably a *Profectio*-sacrifice, and the joining of hands of a man and a woman in the gesture interpreted as a *dextrarum iunctio*.[257]

The first scene symbolises both the distinct aspect of Roman *virtus* that showed military power, and *clementia*.[258] The battle represented behind the commander positions the deceased in the context of male strength, whereas his gesture towards the submissive barbarian family shows his mercy. The presence of the female personification of *virtus* behind the man emphasises his courageous character. The second scene contains a flute-playing acolyte by a burning altar, and two *victimarii* with a bull as the sacrificial animal. The protagonist again shows portrait features but he is represented in a different social role, as he is sacrificing at an altar. In the background, a temple with columns and sculptural decoration is visible, which situates the event in a civic or political sphere. All the components of the scene are also found in Roman imperial art on scenes representing the emperor's *pietas*.[259] Therefore, besides emphasising the piety of the deceased, the choice of such a sacrificial scene shows the deceased as a man of high status, with a sense of societal duty.[260]

In the scene found at the right end of the relief, the deceased has moved from a context of public affairs into one of private relations. The scene shows the traditional joining of hands that symbolises concord, here of the family. In some of these scenes, both the man and the woman are given portrait features. The joining of hands as a sign of harmony within the family is again known from state reliefs, and because of the distribution and public display of these reliefs, the message of *concordia* in the representation of marriage was probably easily understood by the viewer.[261] It is in these marital scenes that we find the only type of female figure with portrait features on biographical sarcophagi, indicating the role of women in relation to their husband in this early period of self-representation on sarcophagi. Later in the third century, the female role on marital sarcophagi becomes more varied and was not limited to the role of the good wife in a male gendered environment.

More or less contemporary with the group of biographical sarcophagi are those with procession scenes

252 Ewald 2003, 562.

253 For this approach, see the important study by Wrede (2001).

254 Ewald 2003.

255 Stewart 2008, 121; Künzl 2010, 41-6.

256 The idea that the sarcophagus relief reflected the cardinal virtues originated in Rodenwaldt (1935) and is still brought into the discussion of the meaning of the reliefs: Kampen 1981; Wrede 2001; Stewart 2008, 72.

257 On the *dextrarum iunctio* motif, see Reekmans 1958; Rosssbach 1973, 11-37; Baratta, 2004, 197.

258 For a discussion of the representation of *clementia* on Roman sarcophagi, see Dowling 2006, 262-69.

259 Gordon 1990.

260 Reinsberg 1995; Stewart 2008, 72.

261 On the use of gesture on this type of sarcophagi, see Brilliant 1963, 157-61.

(also known as *Hochzeitssarkophage*, cat. nos. 663-69).[262] Their common structure shows a body of people arranged formally and partaking in a ceremony performed by a man and a woman. Furthermore, like the biographical sarcophagi these reliefs are characterised by a general homogeneity in the choice of figures represented in the scene, and by the fact that, in contrast to the biographical sarcophagi, the military aspect has been left out.[263] The different figure types, all taking part in the ceremony, typically consist of two or three women with chests and garlands, and juxtaposed with them on the other end of the relief are male chaplains and acolytes with sacrificial animals. The focus of the composition is either a matrimonial ceremony (cat. nos. 663 and 665) or a sacrifice (cat. nos. 664 and 668-69). Both types of scenes are inspired by similar scenes on biographical sarcophagi. The iconographic similarity between these two ritual scenes is close, both in meaning and appearance, and sometimes they are even combined on the same coffin (cat. nos. 665 and 668; **Fig. 24**). These conventional representations of an offering and a marital ceremony are generally seen as ideal representations of real situations, and they do not necessarily represent an actual scene from the life of the person buried in the sarcophagus. Instead the individualised figures should be viewed as symbols of social roles that illustrated the social status to which the deceased aspired.[264]

The procession relief from the Sala delle Muse in the Vatican (cat. nos. 665) represents the earliest *dextrarum iunctio* scene known from sarcophagi with portrait figures. The marital scene on the right end shows the husband with a portrait and the bride with her face covered by a veil.[265] An actual sacrifice is not represented, but the animal and chaplains in the procession behind the marital scene allude to the sacrifice that was traditionally part of the ceremony. The man's high public status is symbolised by the *cella curulis* on which he is seated, and the person behind him, who is honouring the deceased by putting a crown on his head. It is uncertain whether the ceremony is undertaken in connection with the marriage, his office as a magistrate, or a *post-mortem* commemoration of him.[266] All three interpretations are possible, but the cupid with a torch is a figure which connects the scene with death and the Underworld, requiring an interpretation within a funerary context.

Examples of later procession sarcophagi are the sarcophagus from S. Lorenzo fuori le Mura (cat. no. 668; **Fig. 24**), and a sarcophagus in St. Petersburg (cat. no. 669; **Fig. 25**). The two sarcophagi follow the same iconographic scheme and are both dated to the late second century. The central motif of the one in S. Lorenzo fuori le Mura is a sacrifice performed by a man and a woman standing on either side of an altar. On the right end of the relief, a marriage scene takes place: the man holds a scroll, and the woman is veiled. This female type came to be a popular form of self-representation for women in scenes of sacrifice and other *vita romana* representations in the following century.[267] The focus of the scene is the marriage vow; the two portrait figures join hands and a personification of *concordia* stands between them. A female attendant with a naked shoulder is seen behind the woman, and two male attendants stand behind the man.

In the centre of the relief the sacrifice is shown. An idealised representation of a woman with a naked shoulder and a veiled man with portrait features flank an altar, which has been laid out with fruit. Three personifications stand behind the woman. The first figure is female and holds a garland. The next person is a young man with a scroll; he has been interpreted as Honos, and because of the scroll he should probably be identified with an honour given in relation to a magisterial office. The last person is Fortuna with a crown and a *cornucopia*.[268] A *camillus* and a flute player attend the sacrifice, and a ram and a pig are the sacrificial animals, in contrast to the bull, which we find on the sarcophagus in St. Petersburg (cat. no. 669; **Fig. 25**). The bull makes us think of a sacrifice undertaken for the health of the empire, whereas the minor animals may be more

262 Wrede (2001) and Reinsberg, *ASR* I 3 (2006) also treat these sarcophagus reliefs as part of the same motif sphere.

263 The most recent discussion of these sarcophagi is found in Reinsberg, *ASR* I 3 (2006) 109-29.

264 Koortbojian 2008, 75.

265 For the evidence of the use of a veil for brides, see Freier 1963, 128-33.

266 Reinsberg (*ASR* I 3 (2006) 109-15) sees the procession as a magistrate procession, whereas Rossbach (1973 [1871], 94-105) connected it to the marital ritual.

267 Reinsberg 1996; *ASR* I 3 (2006) 152-54.

268 Reinsberg, *ASR* I 3 (2006) 127-29.

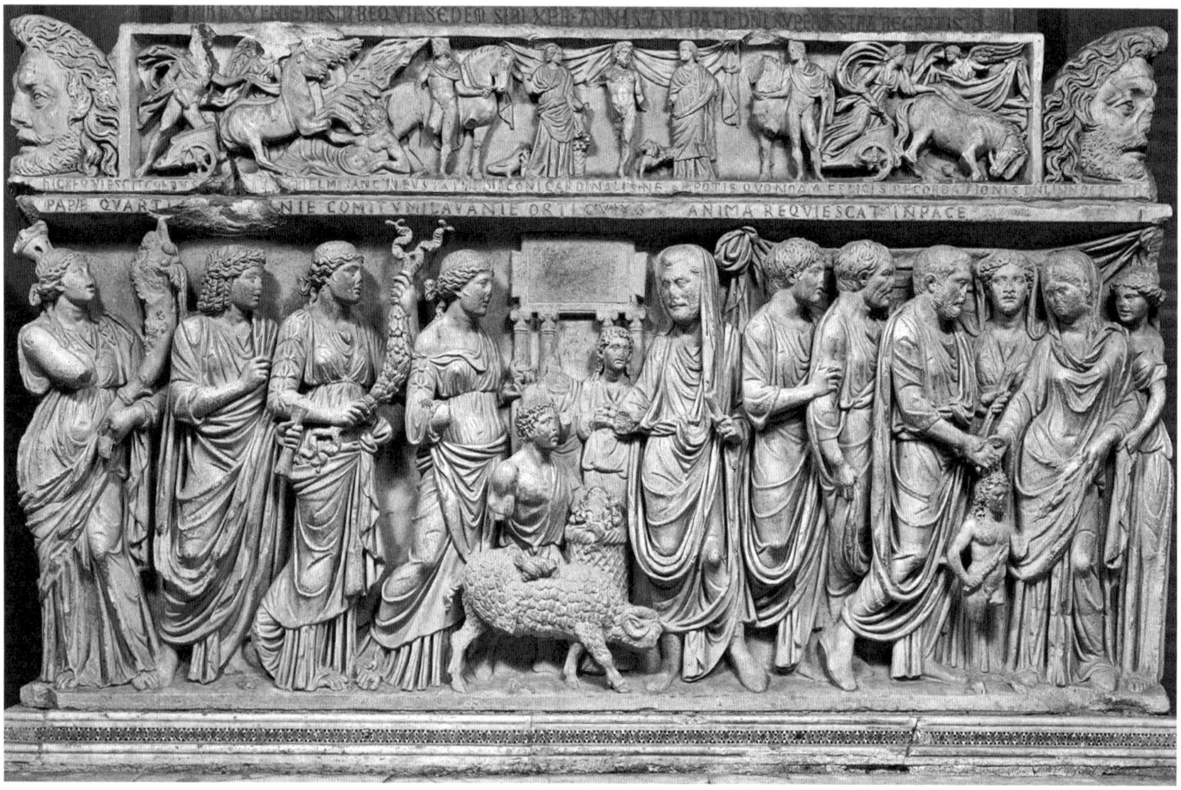

Fig. 24 *Sarcophagus depicting a ritual. Divinities related to death and the Underworld are represented on the lid (cat. no. 668). Rome, S. Lorenzo fuori le Mura. Photo: D-DAI-ROM-57.320*

appropriate, but still expensive, gifts to the gods on the occasion of a marriage or funeral. On the right short end relief, which is behind the woman, are three female priestesses; one carries a casket, one an incense box, and the last a mirror. The procession represents the female aspects of the ceremony, *pietas* and feminine beauty (the mirror and naked shoulder), and shows the woman as a Roman *matrona* of high status and with female values.[269] The male attendants, a young and an old man in toga, represent the public status of the husband and his career.[270] The Dioscuroi on the lid further emphasise the *concordia* of the patron and the wife. The Dioscuroi are frequently used on sarcophagi, and are suitable as a funerary motif since the twin brothers constitute a framework of harmony within which the main events take place.[271] Furthermore, they encourage reflection on the cycle of life at the tomb and their twin identity emphasises the image of a harmonious couple.

The sacrifice on the St. Petersburg sarcophagus is of the same character, but as we will see, its decoration is less explicitly about death, apart from the scene on the lid, which reminds us of the funerary context through its representation of the *Moirae* (Fates) flanked by the Sun and the Moon (cat. no. 669; **Fig. 25**).[272] The scene on the frontal relief focuses more on the virtues of the portrayed individuals. Venus and Eros are placed behind the woman and represent her virtues, whereas Victoria is placed behind the man to show his qualities. On the 'female' end of the coffin, the female attendants familiar from the S. Lorenzo coffin are again present but this time they are concentrating on a casket with

269 For the representation of feminine *pietas* through the four figures, see Reinsberg *ASR* I 3 (2006), 127.

270 Wrede (2001, 48-50) discusses this sarcophagus and the ritual taking place.

271 Sarcophagi with representations of rituals framed by the Dioscuroi are cat. nos. 649-50, 652-55, 658, and 668.

272 Reinsberg *ASR* I 3 (2006) 116-17, cat. 137.

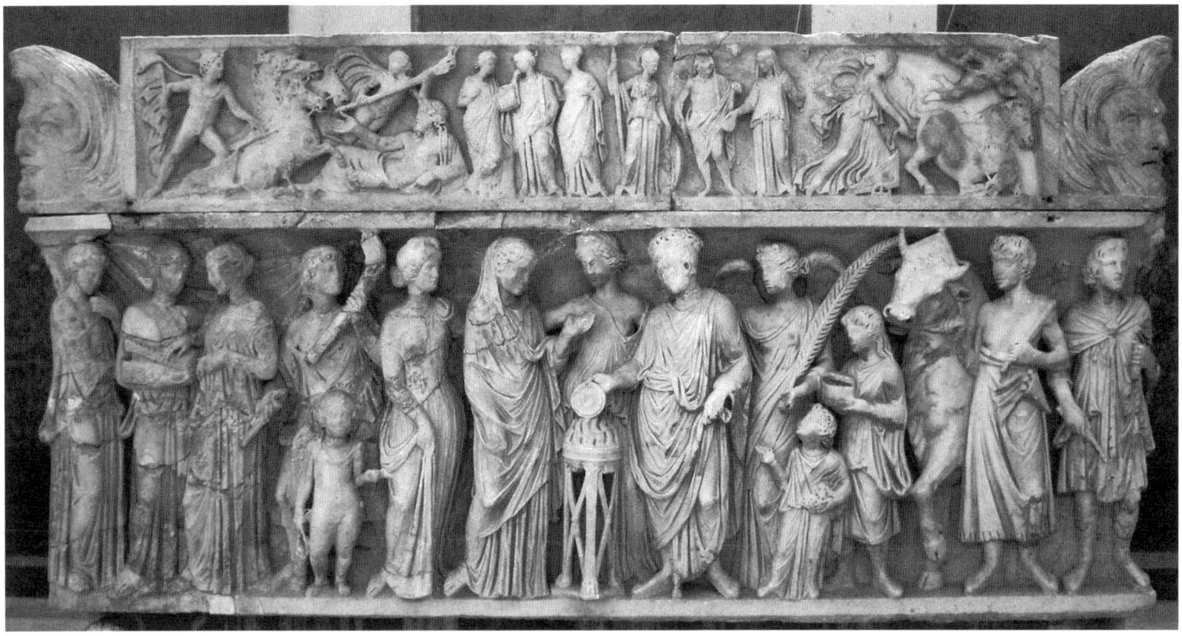

Sarcophagus depicting a sacrifice undertaken by a woman and a man (cat. no. 669). St. Petersburg, Hermitage, inv. A 433. Photo: Author, courtesy of The State Hermitage Museum, St. Petersburg. **Fig. 25**

a cloth, which may be either a votive or a bridal dress. On the 'male' side, there are two *victimarii*, the bull, and two boys with cultic objects who are represented as his helpers. This iconography is not unique and similar representations of the deceased person's virtues are found on other sarcophagi, for example, one that commemorates a couple in the Cortile del Belvedere in the Vatican (cat. no. 664). The frontal relief of this coffin shows a procession and a sacrifice at a burning altar, a *dextrarum iunctio* scene is represented on the left short end, and a scene with a hunter is carved on the right. Concordia stands behind the burning altar, Hymenaios, Venus, and Eros behind the woman, and behind the man are the sacrificial animal (a bull) and Victoria. The last figure on the right end is a priest.

Sacrifices are a recurring motif on sarcophagi, and the Roman sacrifice was undertaken in the honour of the gods on diverse occasions to secure public as well as private matters. The tomb constitutes a special case, since here not only the gods but also the dead received cult and sacrifices during festivals.[273] For example, a ram needed to be sacrificed on the spot in order to inaugurate the place as a tomb, giving it the special status of being sacred to the dead. Furthermore, the fact that processions were held in honour of the dead as well as during public sacrifices makes it difficult to separate the private funerary activities from the public religious. It is therefore hard to decide from the iconography which occasion the sacrifices on the two sarcophagi are celebrating and whether the ram of the S. Lorenzo relief is a reference to the animal that sanctified the tomb or a ordinary sacrifice animal.

On the S. Lorenzo sarcophagus, the altar is laid out with fruit, whereas a burning fire is shown on the altar of the St. Petersburg sarcophagus. It is likely that this difference indicates that the two reliefs do not represent the same ritual, a suggestion originally made by H. Wrede.[274] Furthermore, on the two lids, different figures are chosen to be the actors in the otherwise standardised iconography. The lids of other biographical and procession sarcophagi show the same composition of figures: the Sun and the Moon framing a central scene with the Dioscuroi or Tellus and Oceanus.[275] The

273 Beard, North & Priece 1998, vol I, 31.

274 Wrede 2001, 49.

275 The same kind of lid is found on cat. no. 658

Capitoline Triad is placed at the centre and sometimes the Fates are shown as well.[276] On the S. Lorenzo sarcophagus the Fates are missing and the Capitoline Triad has been exchanged for the triad of the underworld gods, Persephone, Dis Pater, and Ceres, to whom the sacrifice may be dedicated. It has also been suggested that the unidentified structure decorated with columns and an inscription panel (a *titulus* inscription?) behind the marital scene stands for the wife's tomb. On the other sarcophagi of the same type, the structure behind the couple can be recognised as a temple. In the latter case the sacrifice may have been undertaken to satisfy the gods of the temple, whereas the S. Lorenzo sacrifice is probably related to the funerary sphere.

Wrede suggests that since the woman in the S. Lorenzo sacrifice is not represented with a portrait, in contrast to the man, she was probably already dead at the time of the sacrifice. It is therefore plausible to see the man as a husband who sacrifices by the tomb of his deceased wife to honour her and the spirits of the dead. That she attends the sacrifice herself is an illustration of the brief social contact established between the living and the dead during offerings and other funerary rituals. Together with her *pietas*, the sarcophagus commemorated her female virtues, their marital relationship, and his public status as a magistrate. In this way the S. Lorenzo sarcophagus is explicit in its statement about death, and at the same time celebrates the social position of the man.

The 'Abbreviated' Form – Representations of Rituals

In the third century, the conventional scenes of so-called biographical and procession sarcophagi were transformed.[277] After this time, the frieze of continuous scenes is rarely seen, and instead scenes of marriage and sacrifices with few figures appear, isolated from each other by means of, for example, grooved panels or columns. This means that scenes from the 'real' and the mythological worlds, which earlier could not be easily combined, were easier to depict on the same relief because they appeared on different panels.[278] On these 'abbreviated' scenes, the portrait figures are often associated with figures from the mythological and learned sphere, the latter being more popular than the former.[279] It is suggested that this change in sarcophagus images is due to new types of self-image that emerged among the Roman senatorial class, which needed a different kind of representation.[280] Instead of representing ideal life courses, third century sarcophagi were made with abbreviated scenes to express personal ideals in a period when the focus on the individual was growing, as the popularity of portraits on sarcophagi testifies to.[281]

The S. Lorenzo sarcophagus (**Fig. 24**; cat. no. 668) initiated this new type of sarcophagi that downplayed public roles and deeds and instead upgraded the importance of private relations. The emphasis that is therefore put on personal qualities is symbolised through combinations of rituals and mythological figures and allegories. The abbreviated form was flexible, since the meaning was not fixed by an unnecessarily high

276 The similarity in the composition is well illustrated by Reinsberg (*ASR* I 3 (2006), pl. 51, 2-6.)

277 On the transformation of style in second- to third-century sarcophagi showing a ritual, or as Wrede calls them *Senatorische Sarkophage*, see Wrede 2001, 60-65; Ewald 2003.

278 A further element that can be used to separate the scenes is a so-called death door, as on cat. no. 634.

279 The sarcophagi here considered are those showing rituals and include secondary motifs of bucolic figures, cupids, a decorative scheme, death doors, mythological figures, learned figures, and seasonal and other personifications. Ewald sees the popularity of the philosopher on third-century sarcophagi as an aristocratic ideal of self-control. In the same article (a review article of Wrede 2001, *Senatorische Sarkophage*), he criticises Wrede for being too focused on status and class in his approach to sarcophagus imagery, and writes that other issues are involved, such as ways of coping with death and the need for new spiritual advice (2003, 567-68). Motifs of philosophers and the learned sphere in general will be discussed in the next section, pp. 73-93.

280 Wrede 2001, 20; Ewald 2003, 561.

281 In line with this, Ewald (2011, 362-63) suggests that the explanation for the decrease in cremation burials in relation to the increasing numbers of inhumation burials in the second century should be found in a new discourses about the body and the self. He furthermore suggests that the popularity of relief decorated sarcophagi from the second century and onwards was generated by the opportunity they offered for visually telling a story of the self. The third century is also the period when Neoplatonic philosophy was influential, and Plotinus' focus on inner knowledge as true happiness may have helped to impel such a new awareness of the self, cf. Ousager 2004, especially chapter 1.

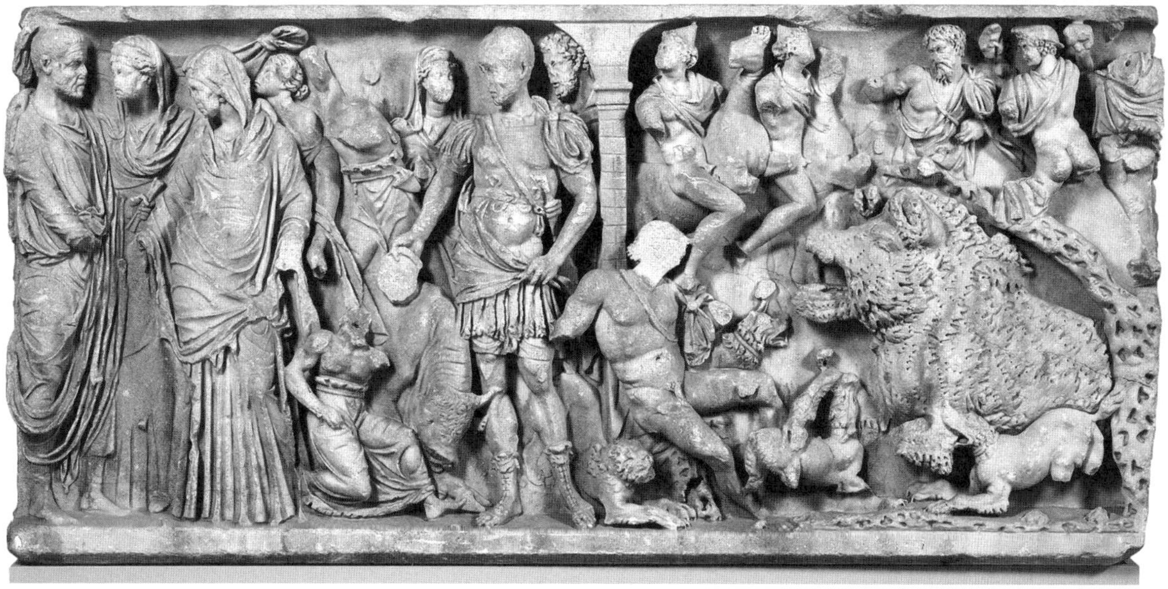

Fig. 26 *Sarcophagus showing a* dextrarum iunctio *scene, a sacrifice on the left end of the relief and on the right a scene shows Meleager wounded by the boar (cat. no. 648). Berlin, Staatliche Museen, Antikensammlung, inv. 1987, 2. Photo: Staatliche Museen zu Berlin, Preußischer Kulturbesitz.*

number of secondary figures. On these sarcophagi, it can therefore often not be decided if a sacrifice was a symbol of the veneration of the dead, of marital *concordia*, or of *pietas* towards the gods. Furthermore, women were liberated from the symbolism of the good wife, and she could be shown in a wider variety of roles than on biographical sarcophagi, on which the specified setting of the scenery had defined her social role.[282] Thus, instead of focusing primarily on ideal lives, the new compositional form is expressive of individual virtues and, most importantly, they could offer the same roles to women as to men.

The earliest example of this type, a Meleager sarcophagus in Berlin (**Fig. 26**; cat. no. 648), is not abbreviated in the real meaning of the term. The relief shows a fusion of a biographical scene with a mythological scene. Both the man and the woman in the marriage scene, as well as the man in the sacrificial scene, have portrait features. Two things help us to make the conclusion that this sarcophagus commemorates a man: firstly that the male figure is represented twice with portraits and the woman only once, and secondly that the protagonist of the mythological scene is a male hero. The veiled and pious woman with adverted eyes is probably a representation of the patron, who purchased this commemorative monument for her husband. Her female character is also shown in the depiction of her as the good wife, a role that not only shows her own feminine qualities but also emphasises the male virtues of a courageous military man and learned husband.[283]

On the left end of the relief, there is a marriage scene as well as a sacrifice. However, instead of the traditional *clementia* representation normally found on the left end of biographical sarcophagi, the wounded Meleager is represented during the hunt in a mythological landscape. The relief shows three steps in the man's life. First, his marriage is shown, as the event that marks his entrance into adult life. Then his pious life and his military status is illustrated by the representation of the deceased in a cuirass pouring a libation, while

282 The sarcophagus cat. no. 646 from S. Saba, which we have already looked at, is an example of these new ways in which women could construct their identity through the decorative scheme.

283 For the representations of patrons on sarcophagi, see Birk 2012.

a *victimarius* kills a bull. The adoption of these two conspicuous roles was important to advance in a public career. The mythological scene in which Meleager is confronted and defeated by the boar, symbolises the last event in his life: his death. The similarity of the representations of the wild boar to Cerberos watching the gate of Hades strengthens the symbolism of the deceased man's confrontation with death. It is one brief moment in the larger narrative of the myth that is carved, but in that scene both the allegory of death and the ideal virtues of a hero, namely Meleager' strength, courage, and ideal body told a Roman viewer everything he needed to know about the deceased person. While the Meleager scene illustrates death, the marriage scene emphasises the sense of harmony in the patrons' marital relationship. The marriage is probably not only a symbol of their earthly marriage, but also of their continuous devotion after death.

Turning to the female figure, one of the Fates is placed behind the woman. The presence of Fate emphasises the fact that the scene is to be read in a funerary context. Her presence encourages reflection on human fate and helps the bereaved to deal with the feelings involved in visiting a tomb. Furthermore, she binds the two scenes together by symbolising the destiny of the deceased as well as of Meleager, whose life was bound to a prophecy made by the Fates at his birth. Furthermore the failure of Meleager, who ultimately killed members of his own family, causes his death and the scene therefore encourages the viewer to reflect on life situations and morality. To show the death of Meleager together with the two representations of the deceased man presents an allegory of the separation that follows from bereavement, and is thus an expression of the emotions on behalf of the patron involved in the burial of a loved one.

The combination of single scenes from biographical and mythological sarcophagi became more popular throughout the third century, and enables the virtues of the individualised figures to be symbolised by a variety of allegorical figures. A column sarcophagus in Florence (**Fig. 27**; cat. no. 649) provides us with an example of how the traditional male and female roles are transformed into this new decorative form. The sarcophagus has a lid imitating a pitched roof with sculptural *acroteria*. The profiles and the niches on the frontal relief are also carved in the style of column sarcophagi from Asia Minor, but the coffin is believed to have been made in Rome with inspiration from Dokimeian craftsmen.[284] Two persons, probably the deceased and the patron, are displayed together in the central space, and separately in the two flanking niches. A Dioscuros is found between columns on each end of the relief.[285] The body types that have received portrait features are a commander, similar to the type known from *clementia* scenes (as, for example, cat. no. 657), and a veiled woman on either side of the central niche. On this sarcophagus the previously popular *clementia* scene is moved to the left short end; this is an indication of the decreasing significance of this virtue for men in constructing *post-mortem* identity. The sarcophagus thus illustrates two characteristic features of third century iconography: the narrative scene is taken out of the public sphere by removing the surrounding figures and architecture, and the victorious aspects of war are downplayed. On this sarcophagus the man still uses the power of military iconography for self-representation, but the woman undertakes the sacrifice herself. This would have been an odd choice had the husband and wife been represented on the same scene, but the abbreviated form enabled new roles of mutual respect and status to take a visual form on the same relief. A further characteristic of sarcophagi with the abbreviated marriage and sacrifice scenes is the use of a plinth on which the figures often stand. The Florence sarcophagus (**Fig. 27**; cat. no. 649) and a coffin from Via Flaminia in Rignano (cat. no. 670) are apparent examples of this since the bases on which the figures stand are carved with ornaments. Representations of statue bases emphasise the ideal status of the individualised figure in a way that is not found on sarcophagi with processions, placing the person within an idealised sphere of heroised individuals.[286]

---

284 Wrede 2001, 117. For a short introduction to sarcophagi from Dokimeion, see Koch 2010. Columns are a frequently seen architectural element on sarcophagus fronts (see, for example, cat. nos. 635-37 and 670).

285 A fairly large number of column sarcophagi shows the Dioscuroi flanking a sacrificing marital couple (cat. nos. 649-50, 652-55).

286 On biographical sarcophagi the military man stands on what appears to be a plinth but probably is a representation of the podium on which commanders often are seated when receiving a submissive barbarian.

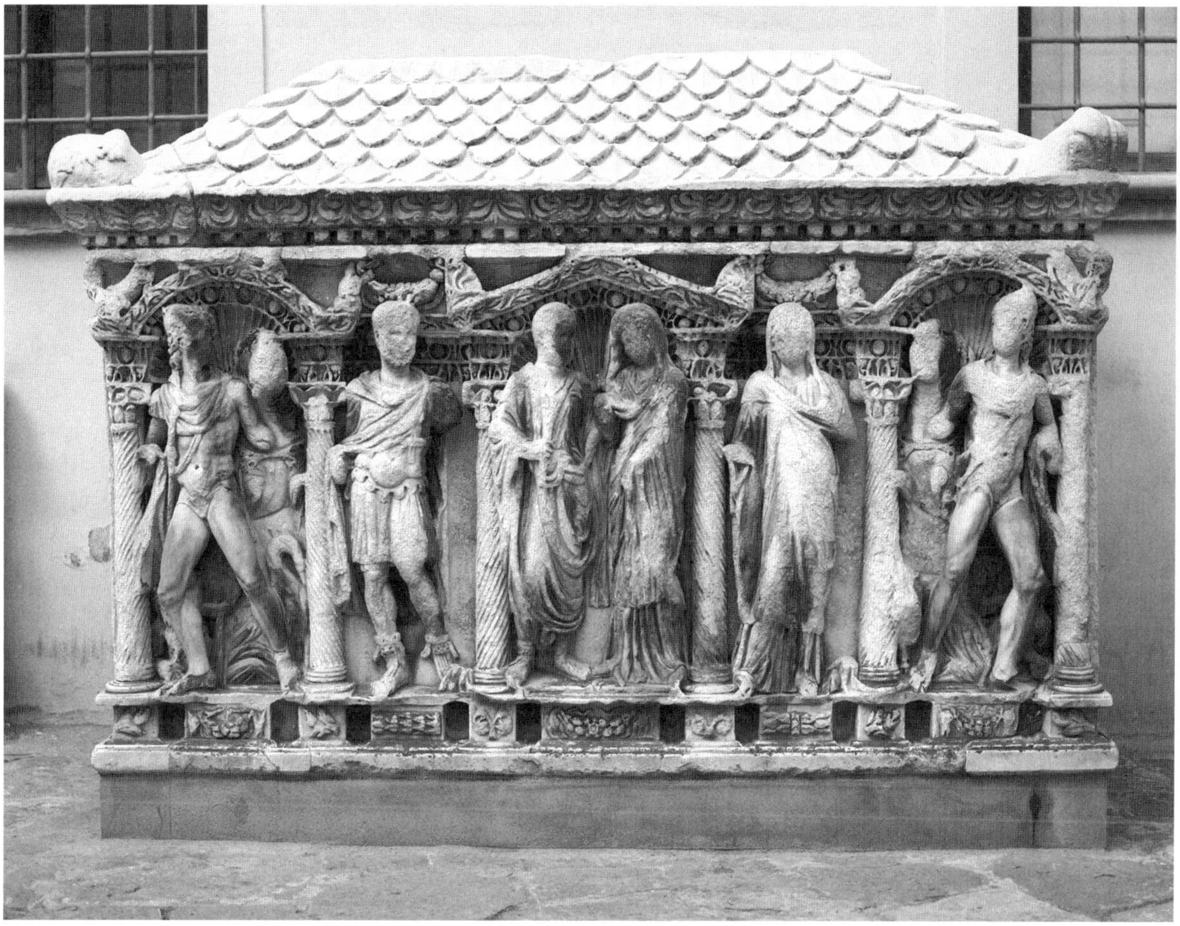

Column sarcophagus with a sacrificing woman, a commander, and a marriage scene (cat. 649). Florence, Museo dell' Opera del Duomo. Photo: D-DAI-ROM-75.230. **Fig. 27**

The military element that was present, if less central, on cat. no. 649 (**Fig. 27**) has vanished totally on a sarcophagus from Tipasa (cat. no. 655).[287] Instead in the two central niches, the man is dressed in toga and the short ends of the coffin each show a *victimarius*, who functions as an addendum to the sacrificial scene on the frontal relief. As on the sarcophagus in Florence (cat. no. 649) the frontal relief of the sarcophagus in Tipasa (cat. no. 655) is divided by columns, in this case into four niches: in the second niche from right a sacrifice is depicted, in the third niche is a *dextrarum iunctio* scene, and in the flanking niches the Dioscuroi are shown. In the marital scene both the man and the woman have roughly carved heads, and unfortunately none of the heads have been preserved in the sacrificial scene. With the removal of the military elements, the martial and the sacrifice scenes came to stand as an expression of the couple's shared pious virtues and harmonious relationship. The decreasing popularity of depictions of public and military deeds can be explained by their dwindling importance over time; it was, however, still possible to use such iconography when its traditional virtues were desired by the patron. Military iconography sporadically appeared on sarcophagi throughout the third century.

The new abbreviated design probably fulfils a desire to present the realistic and mythological spheres

287 Wrede 2001, 23, 38, 61 (where he places the sarcophagus in the discussion of the development of motifs, giving it a role in the transition from military to civil iconography). Other examples of the sacrifice are cat. nos. 650 and 652 (with columns) and 670 and 672 (with strigillated panels).

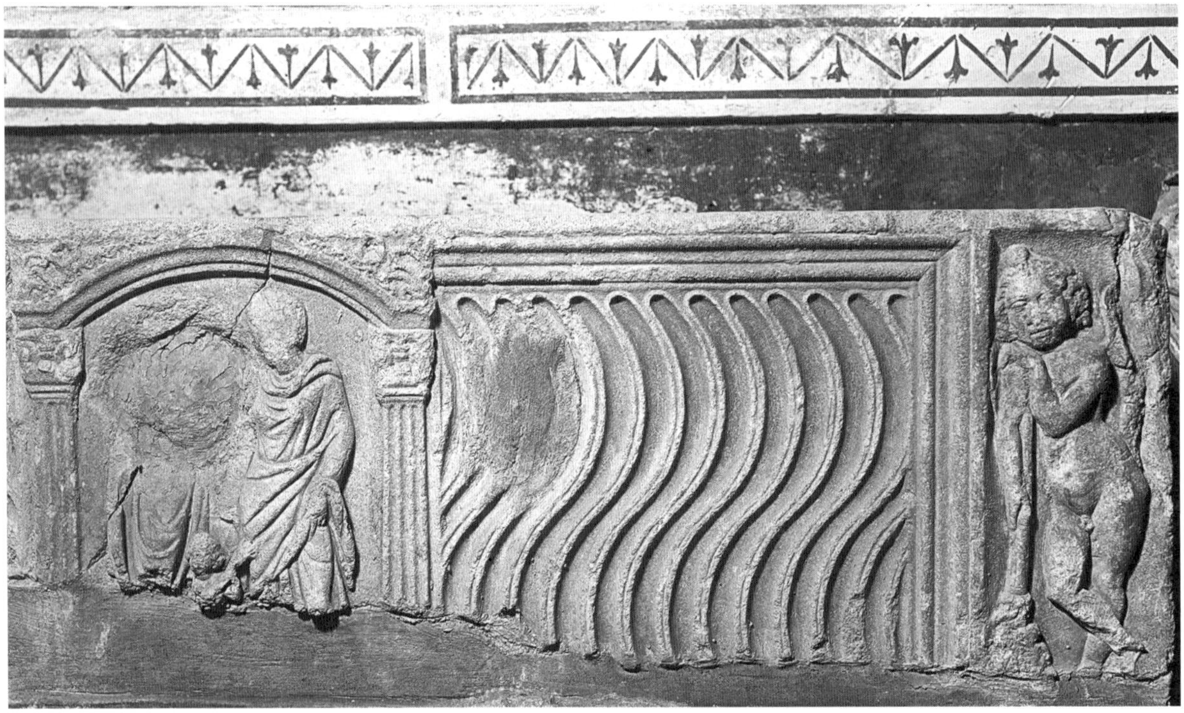

Fig. 28 *Strigillated sarcophagus showing a man and a woman in a marriage scene. A sleeping cupid is presented on the fifth panel (cat. no 633). Rome, S. Cecilia in Trastevere, Museo. Photo: D-DAI-ROM-32.168.*

as complementary to each other. The compositional separation of figural scenes allowed for a combination of figures that could not normally be found in the same scene making it possible for men and woman to appear with the same virtues. Instead of requiring a whole story like the continuous narrative scene, the singular mythological figure on column sarcophagi symbolised the virtues of the deceased and could express something about their view of death. For example, on one sarcophagus where both the man and the woman are sacrificing at a burning altar, Amor and Psyche symbolise the love of the sacrificing couple (cat. no. 637). Another coffin represents a statuesque of Narcissus and Amor (cat. no. 651). In the two identical scenes on the first and fifth panels on this strigillated piece, Amor presents Narcissus to love by showing him his own reflection, illustrated by a face depicted at Narcissus' feet. This love reflects back on the marriage couple on the central panel. Yet another piece shows sleeping cupids, which push the marital *concordia* beyond the limits of death (**Fig. 28**; cat. no. 633), while on another example of marital sarcophagi the three Graces are personifications of the wife's womanly virtues (**Fig. 29**; cat. no. 183).[288] On this sarcophagus the three Graces are shown on the central panel, while the man and the woman are placed separately on the first and fifth panels, both with blank portraits. The woman is accompanied by a female servant with a box containing either incense or cosmetics. Here two sides of the woman's identity are shown: the three Graces emphasise her womanly virtues, while the woman herself is shown with a scroll. She is thus at the same time an expression of both female beauty and learnedness. The husband, probably the patron, shows himself as the equally educated partner on the fifth panel.

This kind of relationship between man and wife on sarcophagi becomes even more pronounced during the turn of the fourth century, as can be exemplified by a much-restored sarcophagus today at Ince Blundell (**Fig. 30**; cat. no. 639).[289] Four figures may have had portrait features but only two are preserved, an *Orans*

288 Rossbach (1973 [1871], 179) saw *Hochzeitssarkophage* as expressions of marital harmony in both life and death.

289 For the restorations, see Reinsberg, *ASR* I 3 (2006) 199.

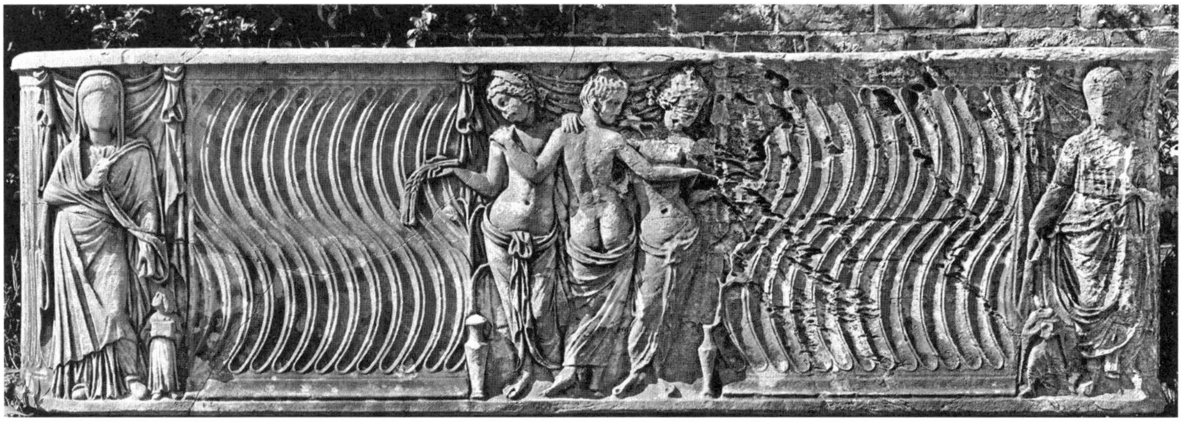

Fig. 29

Strigillated sarcophagus with a woman and a man on the first and fifth panels respectively and the three Graces on the third panel (cat. no. 183). Withington Hall (Chelford). Photo: Köln-FA1462-09_31563.

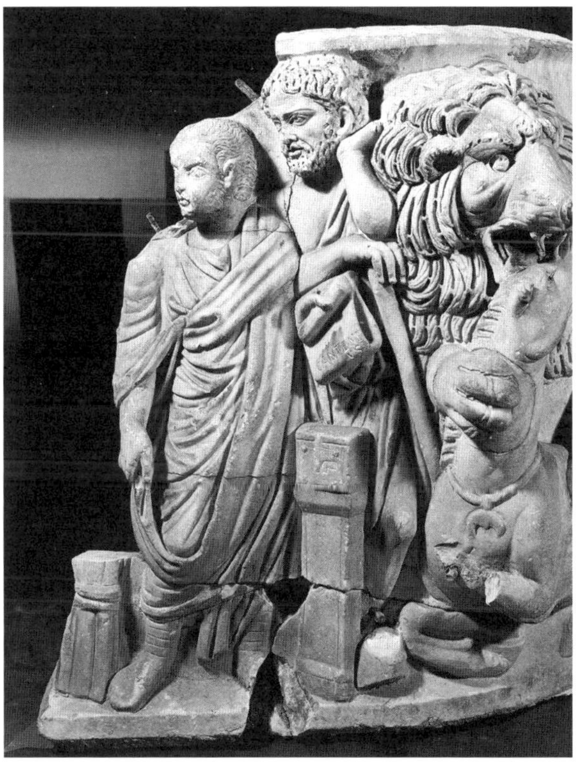

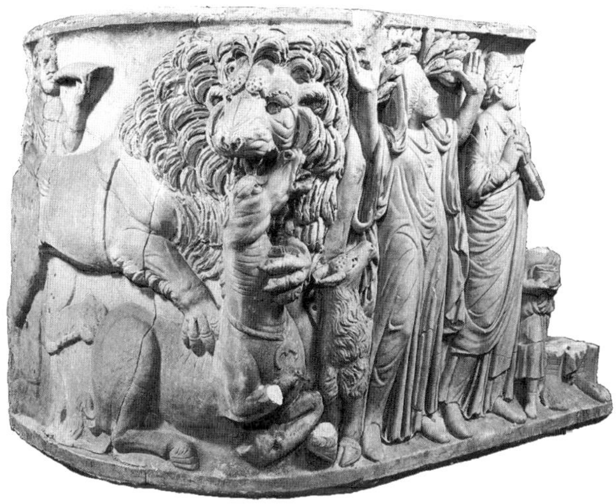

Fig. 30

Lenos-*shaped sarcophagus showing an* Orans, *a learned woman, a sacrificing man, and a boy (cat. no. 639). Liverpool, Merseyside Country Museum, inv. 1959.148.229. Once at Ince Blundell Hall. Photo: Liverpool Museum, photo number: N1990.1830.*

and a *togatus* on the left and right side of the central woman and man. A part of the woman's necklace is still preserved, a feature that is normally found on portrait figures from the late third and the fourth century, indicating that this was originally a portrait. The role models used to represent the couple are a learned man and a learned woman attended by a servant with a box. These role models are also known from the Withington Hall relief, but on this piece they are combined in one scene, which is unusual in the third century. The figures that emphasise their virtues, in this case with portrait features, are located behind them, and the separating elements are gone. Behind the man stands a learned boy and a philosopher, and behind the woman an *Orans*. The central woman and the boy are probably representations of the deceased, because the scrolls that they hold

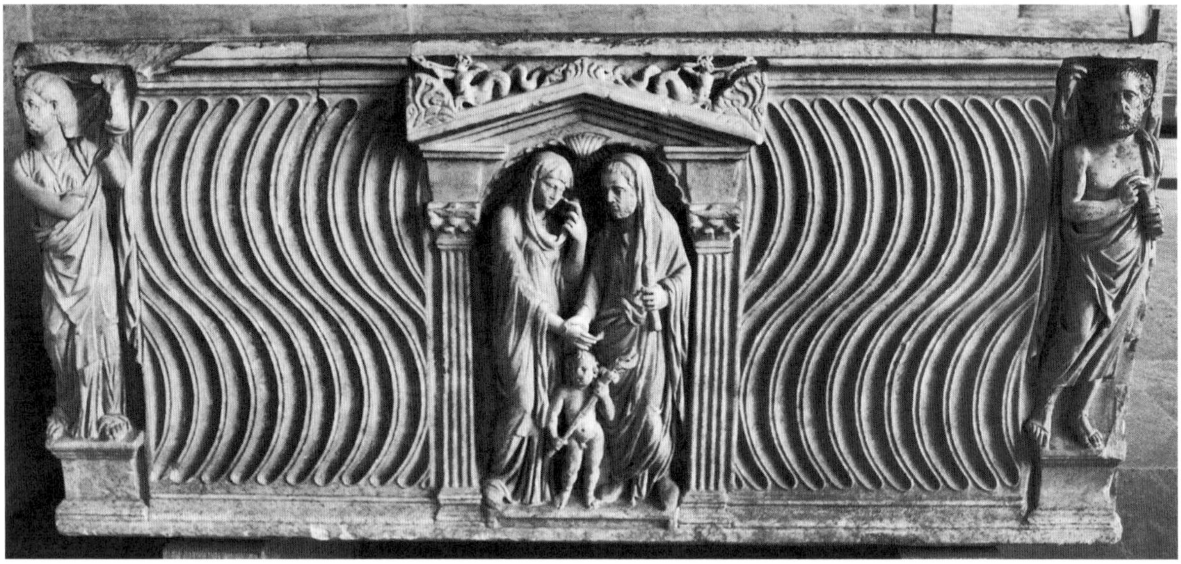

Fig. 31 *Strigillated sarcophagus with a couple. The woman is represented again as a Muse on the first panel (cat. no. 640). Munich, Glyptothek inv. Gl 533. Photo: Troels Myrup Kristensen, courtesy of Staatliche Antikensammlungen und Glyptothek München.*

bear their names; the man is the patron who has buried his wife and son, and the *Orans* may be a fourth family member.

The juxtaposition of a marital couple with other types of ideal figures thus shows how virtues can be ascribed to the deceased by simple means. On a strigillated *dextrarum iunctio* sarcophagus in Munich this is expressed by social roles and simple symbolism (**Fig. 31**; cat. no. 640). The two panels at the left and right end show a deceased couple as a Muse and philosopher on two square bases. On the central scene, the couple is depicted in a *dextrarum iunctio* gesture, and behind them is carved a shell. The shell here is an unusual feature since it is normally used for busts, but it is placed behind the figures as a mandorla and connotes the merry world of sea-monsters and nymphs, some of which decorate the gable of the niche. Between them is a cupid with a torch. The Muse and the philosopher are symbols of the virtues of the two persons in the niche, and elevate them to a level of mutual education. On top of the fact that it had become possible for women to be learned, the woman on this sarcophagus is represented as the Muse to her husband, the philosopher. The method of representing the virtues of the man and the woman as complementary to each other is a typical way of making gender distinctions, and it is these virtues – feminine education and male wisdom – that, as we will see, continue as ideals for couples on marital sarcophagi throughout the century.

The virtues of the man and woman in the context of marriage are gendered in a similar way on cat. nos. 643 (**Fig. 65**) and 644. Again the secondary motif (the allegorical figure) ascribes virtues to the woman that relate to female beauty and *pietas*, whereas the male qualities have to do with learnedness and mental guidance. These ideals continue even during the Christian period, and on two fragments from the same sarcophagus found at Ostia the marital couple is accompanied by a philosopher and a veiled female *Orans* (cat. no. 642).[290] However, this kind of gender differentiation is predominantly found in a marital context when the couple aspires to learnedness, as we will see in the next section on learned figures. Other secondary motifs on marital sarcophagi are more gender neutral. Examples of such popular secondary motifs are bucolic motifs, including ram bearers (cat. nos. 630 and 632), and sea-

290 Another example is cat. no. 639. Cat. no. 642 is made for a Christian patron, which can be seen from the fragment of a naked Eve with a fig leaf behind the *Orans*. This fragment of the sarcophagus came to my notice when the catalogue had been finished, but with the knowledge of the representation of Eve it should not have been included in this catalogue.

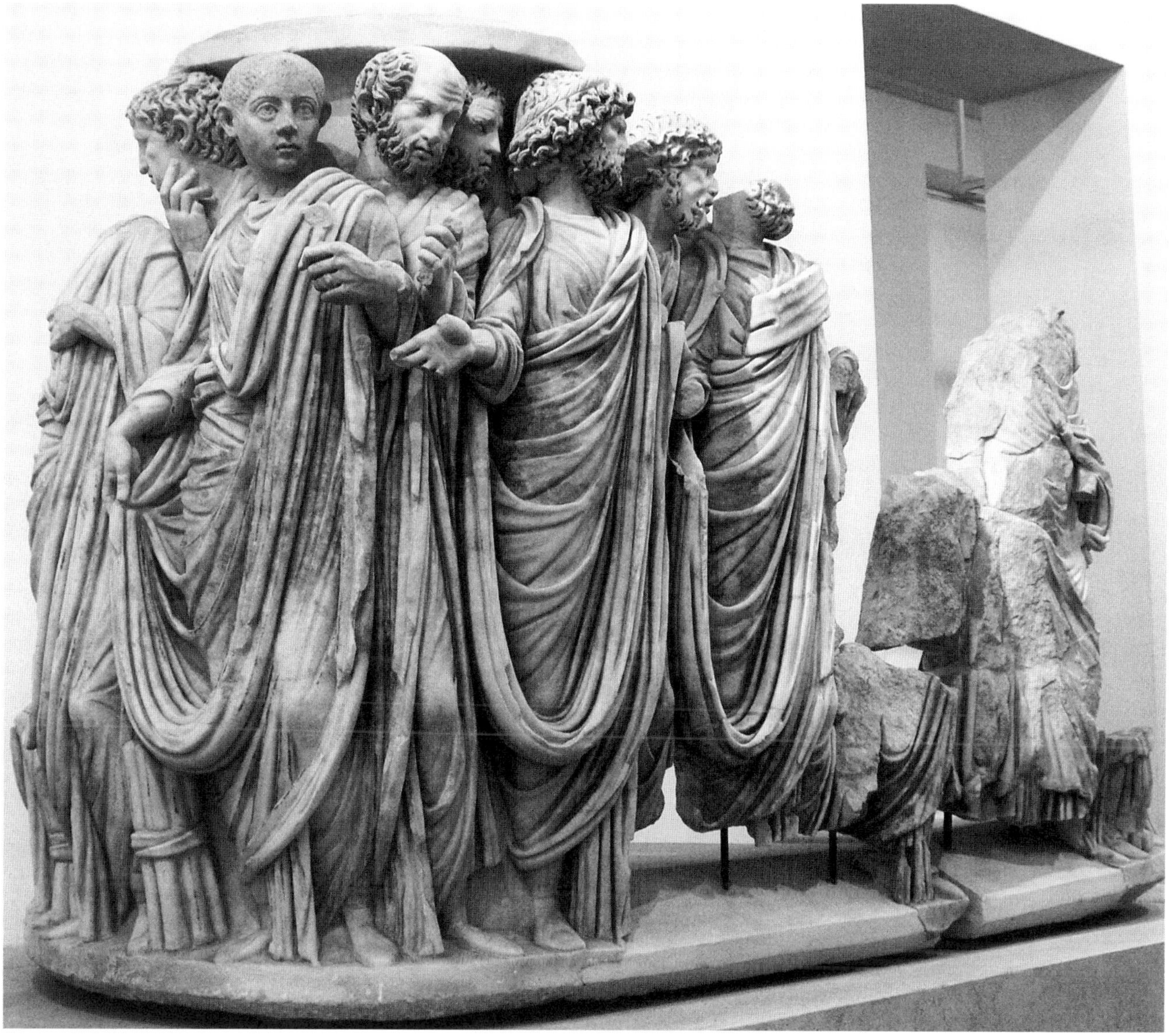

The Acilia sarcophagus (cat. no. 645). Rome, Museo Nazionale Romano, Palazzo Massimo, inv. 126372. Photo: Author. **Fig. 32**

sonal personifications symbolising prosperity and the cycle of life (cat. nos. 673 and 674).

A few sarcophagi continue the style of the procession scene long into the third century, but instead of illustrating specific events, they symbolise the deceased's virtues through a row of generic figures or personifications.[291] We have already looked at one from the early fourth century (**Fig.** 30; cat. no. 639), but another that should be mentioned is the so-called Annona sarcophagus (cat. no. 666).[292] The figures on the frontal relief are all represented in front of a *parapetasma* which makes them appear as a group. A couple is represented at the centre of the composition. The woman puts her left

291 The so-called brother sarcophagus from Naples (cat. no. 641) is one of them but its iconography will be discussed in chapter 3. Himmelmann-Wildschütz (1962) suggests that the deceased portrayed on this sarcophagus was a Roman magistrate.

292 Uggeri 1967/68; Andreae 1970, 85-6; Giuliano 1985, 46-51; Sapelli 1998, 37-9; Reinsberg *ASR* I 3 (2006) 124-25.

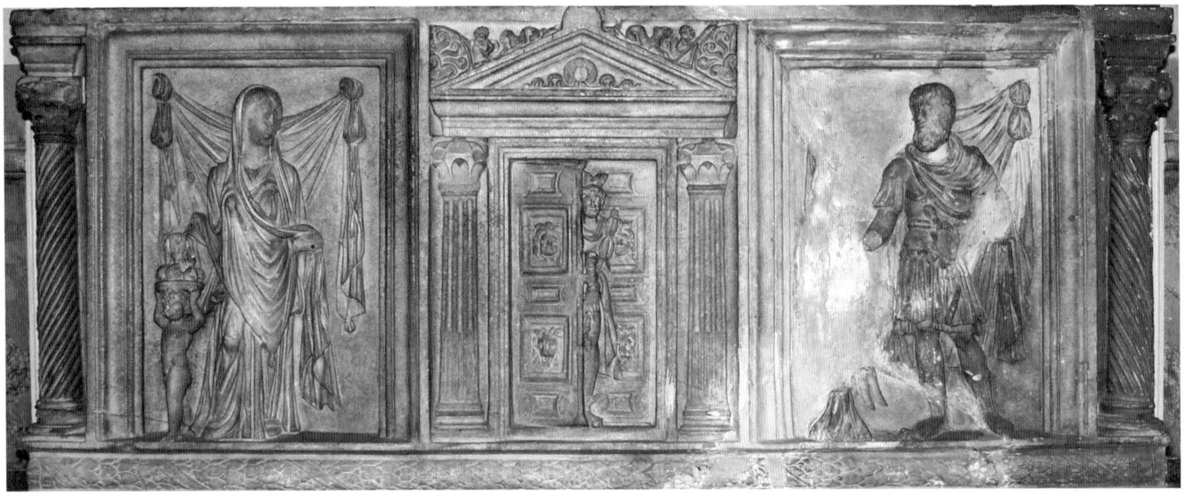

Fig. 33 *A sarcophagus showing a sacrificing woman and man placed on each side of a half open door representing the entrance to the tomb(?). Hermes stands in the door ready to lead the soul of the deceased to the Underworld (cat. no. 634). St. Petersburg, Hermitage, inv. A 889. Photo: Author, courtesy of The State Hermitage Museum, St. Petersburg.*

hand on the man's shoulder while her right hand grasps his hand. Concordia is represented behind them, and a burning altar stands between them. The altar symbolises their *pietas* and the ritual aspect of the scene. The four female personifications on both sides of them are all connected with grain. The woman with the elephant scalp has been interpreted as a personification of Africa, the source of most of Rome's grain; beside her stands Fortuna with a *cornucopia*, fruit, and sheaf; on the other end of the sarcophagus, a woman with a lighthouse and *rostrum* represents Portus; and next to her is a personification of Annona or Ostia with rudder and tablet. It is the magistracy of the man that is celebrated on this scene, which is further emphasised by the *togatus* behind him.[293]

Another example of this late processional type is the Acilia sarcophagus (**Fig. 32**; cat. no 645).[294] Its reliefs show an assembly of men and women. The figures stand close together and extend from the lower to the upper profile of the relief. The men are toga-clad and the women, of whom not much is preserved as the right end of the coffin is lost, wear long dresses. The central part of the frontal relief is also lost. Presumably, a marital scene was once placed here, but only the woman's feet, part of the man's body, and the lower part of his face are preserved. It seems likely that his head was once a portrait because of the traces of a chisel on the surface. The best preserved part of the Acilia sarcophagus is the left short end, whose decoration is a continuation of the frontal relief. Here, among the generic types, is a figure with a well-preserved portrait of a boy. This person is dressed in a *toga virilis* and – like the clothes – the hands evidently belong to an adult. This is a contrast to the portrait, which is clearly that of a boy, and suggests that the craftsman originally had a different intention for the figure.[295] The boy's portrait appears to have been carved in a secondary phase of production, probably immediately after the completion of the sarcophagus.[296] As the sarcophagus appears today, the focus is on the boy since he is the only portrait figure preserved, but the

293 Recently studied by Meinecke 2012.

294 First published by Bianchi-Bandinelli 1954; Lücken 1965; Andreae 1969; Himmelmann-Wildschütz 1973, 6-11; Guiliano 1979, 298-304 with bibliography upto the year 1979; Koch & Sichtermann 1982, 102-3; Fittschen 1984, note 38; Sapelli 1998, 30-3; La Regina 1998; Heinze 1959, 188; Wrede 2001, 72-3, 75, 78, 95; Reinsberg, *ASR* I 3 (2006) 145-47, cat. 88; Birk 2010/11.

295 It has been suggested that it was the sarcophagus of the emperor Gordian III, cf. Bianchi Bandinelli 1954, 200-217; Gullini 1960, 5; Guiliano 1979, 300. The suggestion is, however, not generally accepted.

296 For a discussion of the chronology of the portrait, see Birk 2010/11.

original focus of the composition was probably the man and woman on the marital scene. Here their marital harmony had been combined with learnedness, in the guise of both philosophers and generic magistrate representations, in a similar way to the brother sarcophagus in Naples that will be discussed later (**Fig. 78**; cat. no. 641). However, on the Acilia sarcophagus, the woman was commemorated together with the man and the lost female figures on her right side probably emphasised her qualities, whereas the magistrates and sages emphasised his.[297]

In the group of sarcophagi representing rituals, the virtues of *pietas* and of agreement, understanding and marital harmony, changed character, yet continued to be ideal virtues in the third century. What was different was that the strong emphasis on military aspects of biographical sarcophagi had vanished, as it had been known from scenes showing, for example, a commander and submissive barbarians.[298] Instead of finding a role model in the narration of a military man's life, new emblematic virtues were found in couples represented with individual virtues. The learned iconography, which we will look at in the next section, emphasises this new self-image in particular. Reminiscences of the traditional male virtue of military strength continued on some sarcophagi, for example, on the death door sarcophagus in St. Petersburg (**Fig. 33**; cat. no. 634). The traditional gender relationship between the man in cuirass and the veiled woman is therefore maintained; the difference is that the woman plays an active role, as she is performing the sacrifice.

The Learned Figure

The learned figure is one of the most popular figures on third century sarcophagi with portraits.[299] Muses and philosophers had been represented on sarcophagi since the earliest production in the second century, but during the third century, the learned figure took a new form.[300] In this period, motifs related to the learned sphere became increasingly popular (see graph 2). The representation of a man with a scroll, a figure type already known from biographical sarcophagi with *dextrarum iunctio* scenes, was frequently used for self-representation.[301] The female equivalent, the learned woman, was an innovative figure that emerged around the same time as the learned man on non biographical sarcophagi. Placed in a setting of the nine Muses, philosophers, sages, or holding a scroll, the deceased woman could now enter the intellectual sphere as a role model.

The different categories of learned figures have interested scholars for several decades. Rodenwaldt defined the term "philosopher sarcophagus" in 1936 and one year later, H. I. Marrou published his oft-cited work on scenes of intellectual life on Roman funerary monuments.[302] He was the first to divide the figures into categories on a major scale, and he interpreted the figure types as expressions of an iconography of *L'homme cultivé*. Max Wegner's book *Die Musensarkophage* is, as all *ASR* volumes are, a collection of all the then known sarcophagi with Muses.[303] A couple of years later L. Paduano Faedo made her contribution to the interpretation of sarcophagi with Muses,[304] and in the 90s Zanker used the vast material of learned iconography on various media from classical antiquity to argue that the image of the intellectual was an ideal in the late Roman Empire.[305] As acknowledge by Zanker, this material was, however, first collected and discussed as

297 One further sarcophagus could be mentioned in this context, the Museo Torlonia sarcophagus (cat. no. 667). It has, however, been restored to such an extent that its appearance has changed radically. It is thus a difficult piece on which to base an interpretation. Reinsberg, *ASR* I 3 (2006) cat. 94.

298 Köhler 1995; Kampen (1981, 58) sees the narrative as well as the "abbreviated" scenes as illustrating a continuous wish to associate oneself with the republican past and elevate one's social status by alluding to the *mores maiorum*.

299 The term 'learned figure' encompasses all individualised figure types from the learned sphere, i.e. Muses, philosophers, and men and women with scrolls or a musical instrument.

300 For the development of the Muse iconography, see Ewald 1999, 30-53. On Muse sarcophagi, see Wegner, *ASR* V 3 (1966); Panella 1967; 1968; Fittschen 1972 (review of *ASR* V 3); Paduano Faedo 1981; Rudolf 1981.

301 For reading scenes, see Klauser 1960; Zanker 1995, 186-89.

302 Rodenwaldt 1936; Marrou 1938. For a literature review with emphasis on the interpretation of the learned iconography in a funerary context, see Ewald 1999, chapter 2.

303 Wegner, *ASR* V 3 (1966).

304 Paduano Faedo 1970.

305 Zanker 1995.

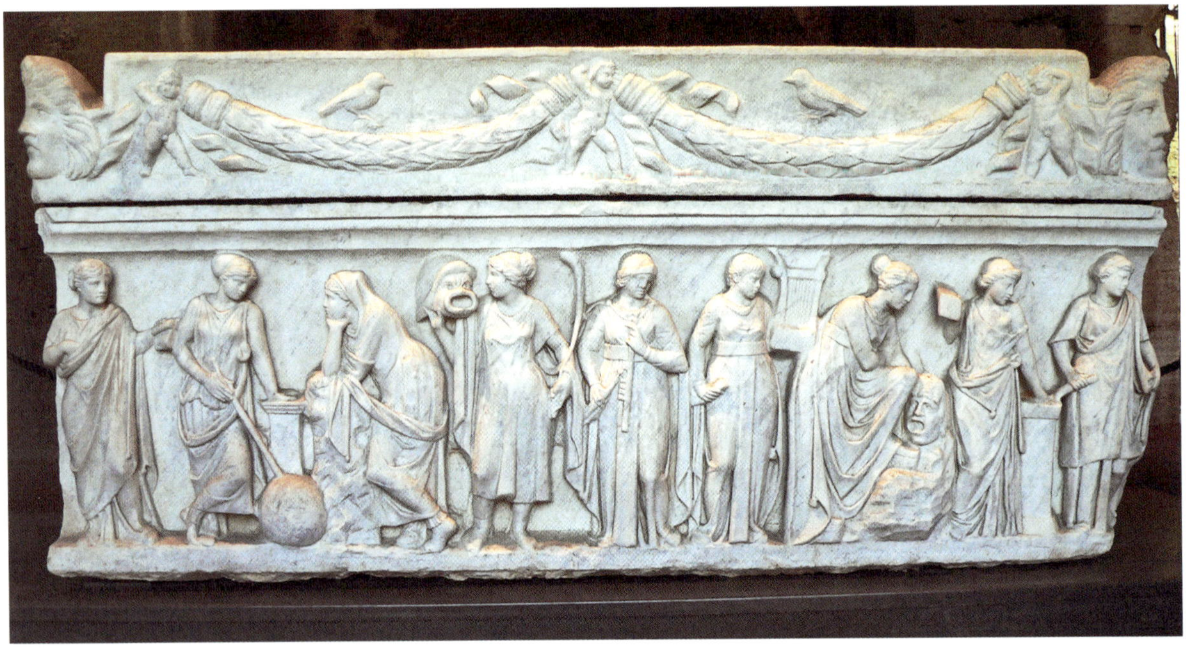

Fig. 34 *Muse sarcophagus. The deceased boy is represented with portrait features as the fourth Muse from right (cat. no. 154). Civita Castellana, Forte Sangallo, inv. 59646. Photo: Author, courtesy of the Soprintendenza per i Beni Archeologici dell'Etruria Meridionale.*

a group by Ewald, who later published a monograph on representations of the philosopher on sarcophagi.[306] The monograph offers a comprehensive literature review of the history of the learned figure and a study of its typological development on sarcophagi.[307] Zanker also included the female figure, in his previously mentioned monograph, and focused on the role that female self-representation played in scenes of intellectual life on sarcophagi.[308] The issue was followed up by Huskinson in two articles, where she analyses the female aspect of the learned iconography.[309] She uses the individualisation of a figure through a portrait as a way of looking for identity and to understand the social relationship between the deceased and other individuals. The latter articles suggested that there was more to be said about the use of learned iconography on sarcophagi. Continuing in this line of investigation, the present text offers a nearly complete collection of the individualised learned figures on sarcophagi with the intention of studying the significance of the figure in a social context.[310]

The History of 'Learned Men' and 'Learned Women' on Sarcophagi

From the beginning of the production of Roman relief-decorated sarcophagi in the second century, Muses and philosophers could be individualised with portraits of men, women, and children.[311] Among the first that show a learned figure individualised with a portrait is a sarcophagus used for the burial of a boy (**Fig. 34**; cat. no. 154). The sarcophagus can be dated to the early Antonine period based on a coin found in the coffin.[312] The frontal relief is a representation of the nine Muses, and the boy himself appears with a lyre in the guise of Erato or Terpsichore.[313] Another example that also

306 Zanker (1995a) refers to Ewald's MA thesis on the same topic from 1993.

307 Ewald 1999 with a full bibliography. Previously Piacentini had, among others, published an article on the philosopher on sarcophagi (Piacentini 1961).

308 Zanker 1995, especially the chapter "The Cult of Learning Transfigured".

309 Huskinson 1999; 2002.

310 The learned figure: Appendix C.

311 For philosophers on sarcophagi in the second and early third centuries, see Ewald 1999, 31-3.

312 Ewald 1999, 208, cat. H 2.

313 Ewald 1999, 31. For a discussion of the sex of the portrait

transcends the categories of learnedness and children's life course sarcophagi is an already mentioned sarcophagus with a family portrait (**Fig. 14**; cat. no. 615).[314] The coffin commemorated a boy, which is mentioned in the inscription, but the whole family is represented in portraits. The mother is shown breastfeeding the child while the father looks on, dressed as a philosopher. Various other scenes follow; the final one is a reading scene in which the father, again represented as a philosopher, teaches the son, who is standing with a scroll in his hand. This sarcophagus, together with the one with Muses that commemorated a boy (**Fig. 34**; cat. no. 154), are among the earliest known with portrait heads, and it is not much later, probably around 200, that the first example of a female portrait figure presented with the Muses appears.[315] It is on a sarcophagus from Camposanto in Pisa (cat. no. 162).[316] This particular example has a central *clipeus*, framed on the left side by a bucolic scene with a ram-bearer and sheep, and on the right side by the Muses.[317] Only eight of the nine Muses are depicted, which makes the woman in the *clipeus* a substitute for the missing ninth Muse; she could be said to be the ninth Muse.

Intellectual men with scrolls were recognisable figures when they started to appear as portrait figures during the first twenty years of the third century, but the learned woman with a scroll has no typological predecessor.[318] Still, she appears concurrently with the male individualised learned figure on sarcophagi and became increasingly popular thereafter (see graph 2). Concurrent with the introduction of both learned men and women, a new representation of the marital couple occurs. In the context of Muses and philosophers, a marital couple could be shown either seated at each end of the relief facing each other – the so-called Lycian motif – or as two busts enclosed by a *clipeus*.[319] On these reliefs, as on the previous marital sarcophagi, men and women were seldom represented as equals; instead they were ascribed with two different sets of virtues. The emergence of the different kinds of learned figures, the male and female, in the same period is an important factor for our interpretation of such figures.[320]

Before I explore the role of the learned person further, I will explain what is meant here by the terms 'learned woman' and 'learned man'. I have chosen to use the word *learned* to describe all individualised figures that are related to the intellectual world in some way. The reason for this is that my intention is to look at the construction of identity through virtues and qualities mediated by the appearance of an individualised figure. Here I found that the nuances between ideals conveyed through, for example, a woman represented as a Muse and a learned woman with a scroll, are so slight that it seemed inappropriate to divide the figures into different groups. I furthermore found that the nuances in meaning depended on the interpretation of each individual relief, its social context, and different viewing positions. I therefore consider the figures described here as 'learned women' to be based on the same ideals and to embody the same virtues. In all her representational forms, the learned woman symbolises status and qualities that relate to the intellectual sphere, in the spirit of the time of the Second Sophistic.[321] Therefore, the category *learned woman* encompasses Muses, women with lyres, women as philosophers, and, not least, women with scrolls.

figure and the meaning of the cross-gendered image, see Ewald 1999, 208; Fittschen 1992; Sande 2010; Birk 2011.

314 The sarcophagus is a so-called 'life-course' sarcophagus of Marcus Cornelius Statius (see p. 29). Amedick, *ASR* I 4 (1991), 64-5.

315 Both sarcophagi will be discussed later (pp. 170-71, 176).

316 The sarcophagus has been dated to the end of the second century based on the typology of the motif and the women's hairstyle; see Arias et al. 1977, 54.

317 Arias et al. 1977, 53-4, pl. 2.

318 For the representation of magistrates on sarcophagi, see Wrede 2001; Reinsberg 1995; Ewald 1999, 54-62. For the representation of magistrates on Roman reliefs in general, see Ronke 1987, and for statues representing a magistrate, see Fejfer 2008, 183-200.

319 Another motif is the already discussed *dextrarum iunctio* scene (cat. nos. 630, 632-33, 635-36, 638, 640-41, 643-53, 655-68, 670-74, and 675-76). For further thoughts on the Lycian motif and for *clipeus* busts of a marital couple, see pp. 151-55.

320 Ewald (1999, 29-53) offers a careful description of the typological development of the learned iconography and the appearance of the individualised learned figure on sarcophagi. His iconographic study is supported by the categorisation of the different motifs in his catalogue.

321 For the Second Sophistic, see Zanker 1995a; Borg 2004; Stirling 2005.

The category *learned men* is basically defined by the same criteria, with an emphasis on the virtues conveyed by the figure with a scroll. The learned man appears as the philosopher, a magistrate, a poet, the husband on a marriage scenes (when represented with a scroll), and a full-length figure or bust with a scroll. In the few cases where a man is represented as a philosopher with a naked chest and *pallium* but without the scroll, I have considered him to be learned as well.[322] When I specifically refer to a *learned woman/man with a scroll*, I am talking about the types that do not embody any formulaic figure type such as the Muse or philosopher. In conclusion, the learned woman/man with a scroll is a representation of the deceased standing or seated dressed in toga or *pallium/palla* and a tunic or *chiton* with a scroll in one hand or at his or her feet.[323]

The Symbolic Meaning of the Scroll

It has been suggested that by the middle of the third century the scroll had lost its proposed meaning as a marriage contract, a signifier of a magistrate profession, of practice in public oratory, or of private philosophy and instead simply showed that the person possessed some level of learnedness.[324] The argument continues that the woman was thus given the scroll by default, as a consequence of the generic production of unisex busts on sarcophagi, in contrast to the man, for whom the scroll was originally intended. It is, however, difficult in the context of its popularity to deprive the scroll of so much of its meaning, and say that it had already lost its significance by the middle of the third century, a period when it had actually just started to gain popularity. The scroll in the hand of a portrait figure may have changed its meaning in the third century, but it remained significant, and since the learned man and woman entered the stage of sarcophagus iconography at the exact same time it would be missing its real meaning to consider one of them as the *prototype*. What we instead observe is that in the third century there was an overall acceptance of women as learned, and as a consequence, that men's and women's virtues could be presented as one and the same. It is true that the motif of a scroll-carrying man had a longer history than the women with scrolls on sarcophagi, but its meaning was different and in second-century individualised sarcophagus iconography men with scrolls were predominantly found on marriage scenes on biographical sarcophagi.[325]

My interpretation of the use of the scroll in the third and early fourth centuries sees it as a sign of both status and power. The scroll had the obvious value of associating the deceased with knowledge and the intellectual virtues of the upper classes of Roman society.[326] The symbolic power divined into the scroll can be seen in a study of the relationship between the deceased on sarcophagi with two portrait figures. Women could hold a scroll, as could men, and they could even do so together on the same sarcophagus, but rarely in the same scene. When represented as a marital couple, only the man has a scroll, demonstrating his superior position in comparison with the woman. If, on the other hand, two women are represented together, the eldest of them has the privilege of holding the scroll. We will return to representations of couples later.

322 On the problem of defining the learned male figure see the discussion in Ewald 1999, 11-20, especially p. 13 where he discusses the different interpretations of the figure with a *pallium*, or Greek mantle, and its meaning when a tunic was worn beneath the mantle and when it was not. Ewald distinguishes between the learned types that I have here grouped together and he did not include *pallium* busts in his catalogue. In collecting all of them I learned that in terms of how they were combined with secondary themes they are not used differently. I therefore consider the figures, in their function as role models, to represent the same cultural ideal and the same virtues. Ewald also concludes that the sarcophagus workshops were flexible in their use of figure types and that the material actually did not invite such categorisation (cf. Ewald 1999, 13). Wallace-Hadrill (2008, 41-57) has discussed the differences in the appearance and use of the toga and the *pallium* in Roman sculpture and as a form of dress. He sees the two body types as merging into each other.

323 On the different ways in which a scroll can be represented, see Marrou 1938, 24-7. In the context of interpretation, I do not distinguish between the different scrolls. The scroll is here considered as a symbol belonging to the intellectual sphere.

324 Huskinson 1999, 199.

325 Except for cat. no. 668 where the man holds a scroll on both the sacrifice and the marriage scene.

326 For the learned culture of the high Roman Empire, see Swain 2006.

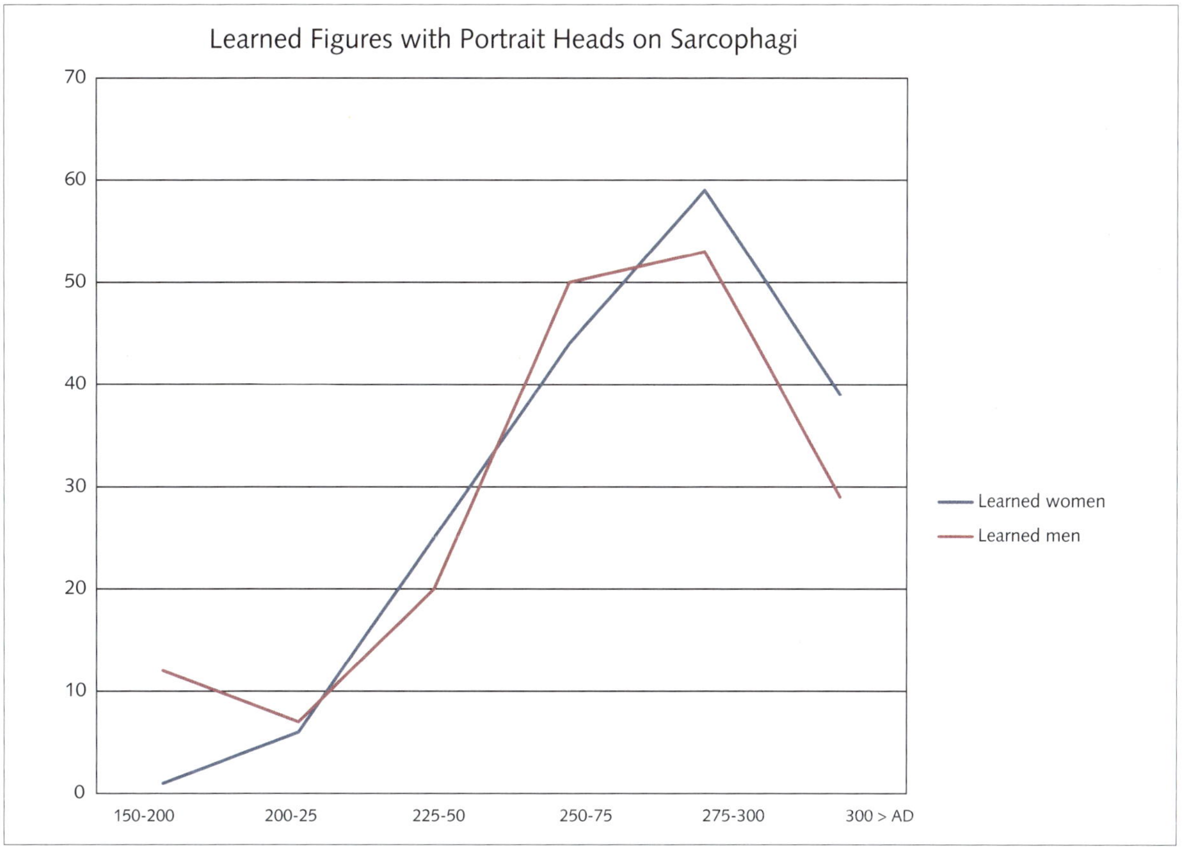

Graph 2

The graph shows the number of learned women in relation to learned men on sarcophagi. All kinds of learned figures have been included in the data (philosophers, men and women with scrolls, Muses, female philosophers, and lyre- and lute-playing women), independent of associated motif. The table is based on Appendices C1 and C2.[80]

The Learned Figures and Self-Representation

What follows is an account of the appearance of the learned figure on second- through early fourth-century pagan sarcophagi. The text is divided into two main parts. I shall first look at the representation of the female learned figure and afterwards consider how this corresponds to the representation of the male figures.

From the number of representations of the learned woman carved on sarcophagi, we learn that after her introduction she immediately became the most popular form of self-representation for women. Out of around 382 sarcophagi with women individualised through a portrait, including those commemorating a couple, about 160 sarcophagi commemorate women through a learned figure.[327] From the sarcophagi with learned women preserved with a dedicatory inscription, we furthermore learn that the majority of these portraits show the deceased woman and not the patron. Only on cat. no. 512, a hunt sarcophagus with an individualised hunter on the front relief and a learned woman on the lid is the patron represented as a learned woman. Cat. no. 43 is another example of a patron who has represented herself as a learned woman together with a learned man. An inscription tells us that the sarcophagus was given to a son, and the woman thus probably represents the patron and mother.

327 Based on appendices A & C1.

328 I have chosen to make chronological divisions of 25 years for graph 2, but I am aware of the difficulties of dating sarcophagi, which means that the dating of one sarcophagus sometimes spans several decades. For example, the dating of female portraits is often confused by the fact that the same hairstyle could last for decades. Furthermore, there

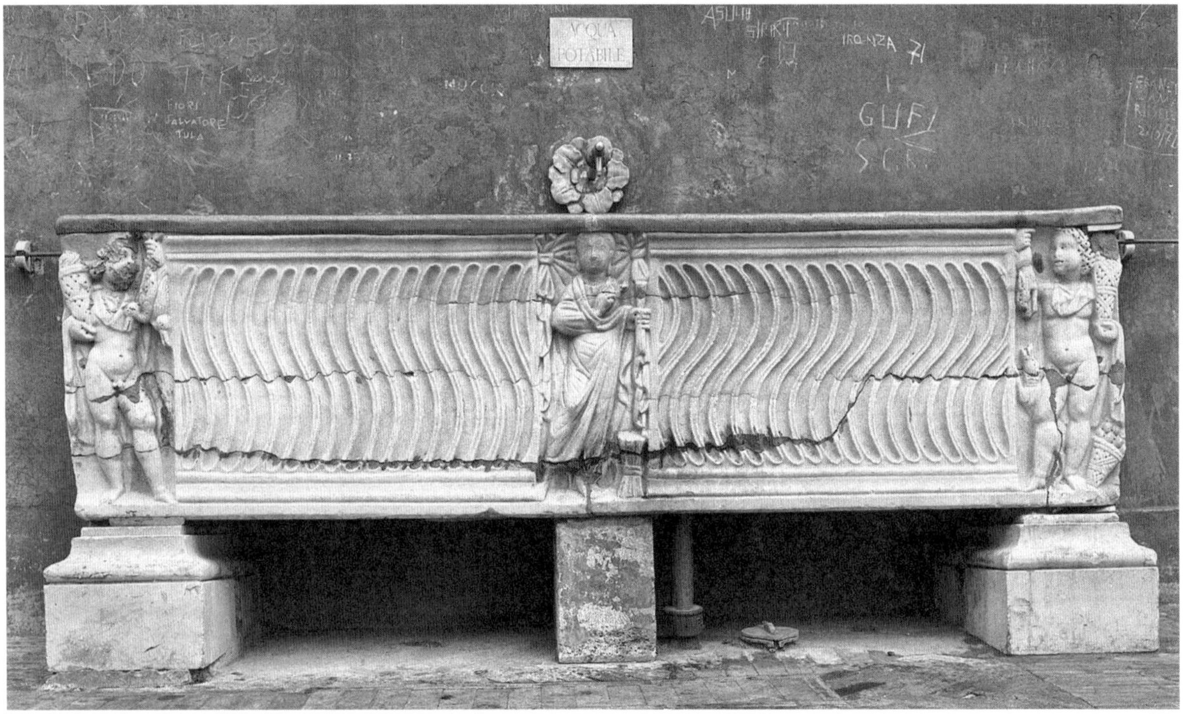

Fig. 35 *Strigillated sarcophagus. A learned woman with a blank portrait is shown on the central panel, and seasonal personifications are depicted on the first and fifth panels (cat. no. 236). Rome, Vatican, S. Pietro. Photo: D-DAI-ROM-71.996 (Hützel).*

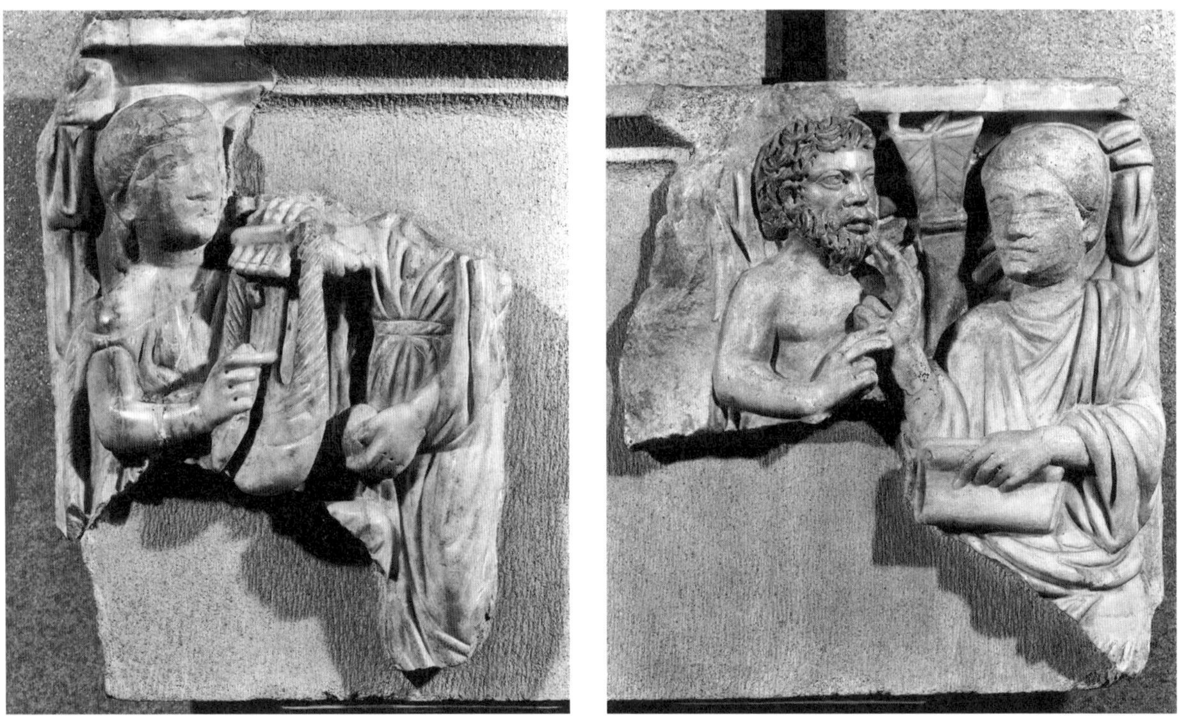

Fig. 36 *The left and right ends are preserved of what was probably a strigillated sarcophagus. On the first fragment a woman with a lyre is shown and on the second a man is seated reading a scroll. Both have blank portraits but their facial features are clearly indicated in the marble (cat. no. 93). Milan, Museo Castello Sforzesco. Photo: Raccolte d'Arte Antica, Museo d'Arte Antica e Pinacoteca del Castello Sforzesco, Milano. Copyright Commune di Milano, all rights reserved.*

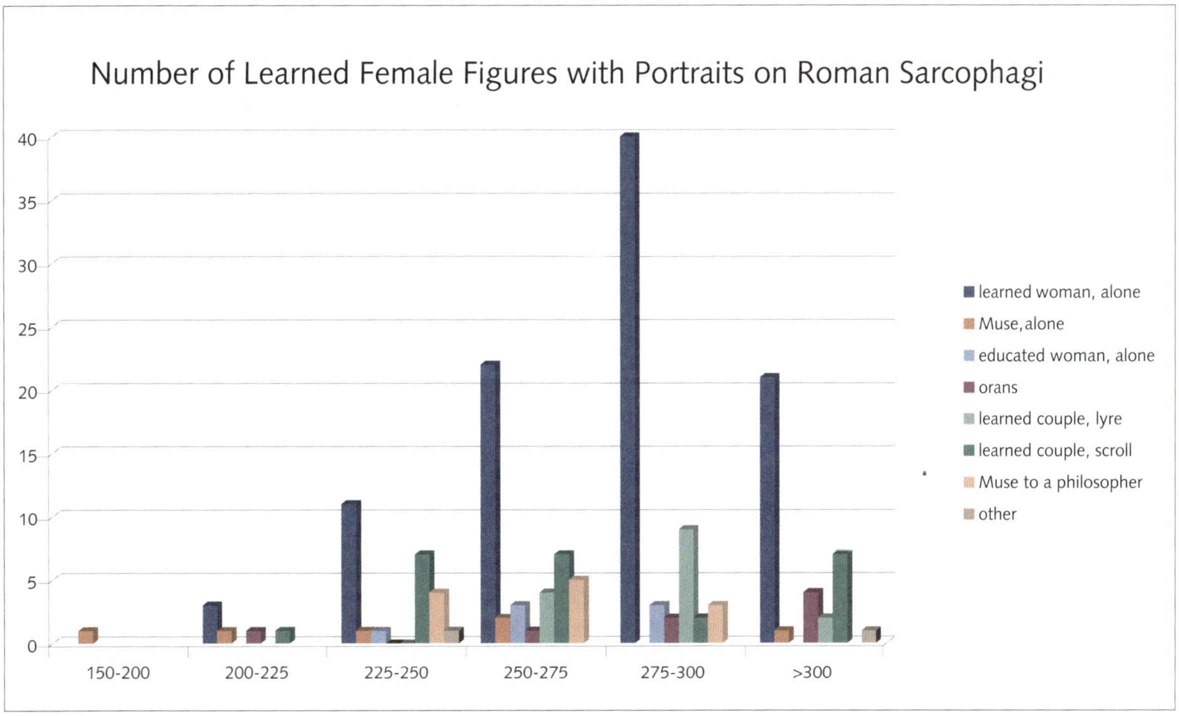

Graph 3

The graph shows the number of learned female figures with portrait heads from the catalogue. The category "learned couple, lyre" refers to sarcophagi with the so-called Lycian motif and sea-thiasoi sarcophagi with a bust framed by a shell. The category "learned couple, scroll" includes all other sarcophagi, on which a woman with a scroll is represented with a learned man. None of these sarcophagi show a learned woman represented with a non-learned man; this combination does not exist. The graph is based on Appendix C1.

The first representations of learned women with scrolls were seen within the first decade of the third century – except for the previously mentioned example with a Muse (cat. no. 162) – and afterwards her popularity increased rapidly to reach its peak around 260, which is illustrated by graph 2.[329] The decline in the use of the learned figures towards the end of the third century is mainly due to the general decline in production of sarcophagi and not to changes in the popularity of the motif. The graph should not be taken as more than a general visual illustration of the periods in which the learned figure occurs, and the point at which the figure reached its peak of popularity.

In graph 3 the different types of learned female figures are shown in relation to both their popularity and their chronological distribution. Examining the figure of the learned woman, the woman with a scroll was by far the most popular form of self-representation. The figure type can be exemplified by a strigillated sarcophagus depicting a learned woman on one panel and seasonal personifications on the other two panels (**Fig. 35**; cat. no. 236). Next comes the woman represented together with a man with either a musical instrument or a scroll, as exemplified by the fragments in Museo Castello Sforzesco, Milan showing a woman with a lyre opposed to a learned man (**Fig. 36**; cat. no. 93) and a strigillated sarcophagus in Musei Capitolini showing a woman and

is the danger of making a circular argument when dating sarcophagi on the basis of motif, since the dating of the particular sarcophagi then affects the dating of other sarcophagi. It can give a distorted picture of the distribution of different types of sarcophagi in relation to time. The graph therefore shows only a general picture of the chronological development of this motif.

329 Previous statistics for Roman sarcophagus themes, not only intellectual themes but in general, are offered by Ewald (2003; 2004) and Zanker (2005); the latter, as noted by Zanker, were produced by Ewald and G. Baratta. See also chapter 3 of this book.

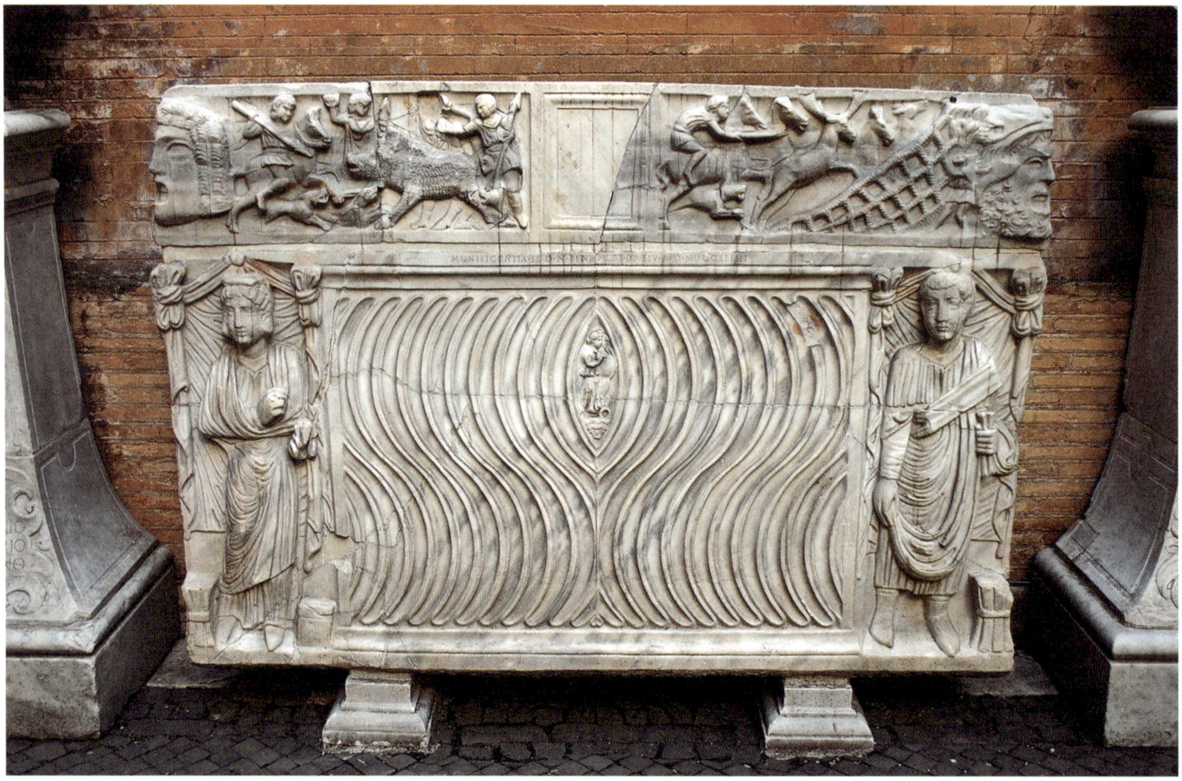

Fig. 37 *Strigillated sarcophagus with a learned woman on the first panel and a learned man on the third panel. The lid is decorated with a hunt scene. Though the figures have blank portraits the facial features are clearly indicated (cat. no. 82). Rome, Musei Capitolini, Palazzo Nuovo, inv. MCD 9/S (courtyard). Photo: Author, courtesy of Musei Capitolini.*

scrolls on one panel and a man on the other (**Fig. 37**; cat. no. 82).[330] The last type is the woman represented as one of the nine Muses, either alone or with a man, illustrated by **Fig. 38** (cat. no. 42) and **Fig. 46** (cat. no. 116).[331] In rare instances, I have defined a woman without a scroll as learned (an example is **Fig. 39**; cat. no. 102).[332] This type is included in the analysis because the figure type is similar to other learned women.[333] Furthermore, the woman on cat. no. 102 is so closely connected to the learned sphere, through the generic learned figures around her, that the purpose of the relief must have been to place her within an intellectual setting. A similar relief is found on cat. no. 131 (**Fig. 40**) but here the woman holds a scroll. The secondary motif is thus illustrative of the society in which the deceased wants to appear, and when individualised as a learned figure, they were placed in an intellectual milieu with a philosopher and/or Muses (other examples are cat. nos. 87, 92, and 97). The learned woman often appears juxtaposed with secondary motifs from outside the learned sphere, such as cupids, lions, or seasonal personifications (as for example on cat. no. 49; **Fig. 41** and cat. no. 140).

Depictions of female philosopher are rare, but they do exist. On cat. no. 97 (**Fig. 42**) two female philosophers are represented, and the use of a philosopher's virtues to commemorate a woman must have been a conscious choice. The two philosophers on the third and fifth panels have been carved with female portraits, whereas the learned female figure on the first panel has a roughly carved head. The sarcophagus belongs to a category of cross-gendered sarcophagi, which show that male figures could be used by women to represent

330 Other examples with a musical instrument are cat. nos. 45, 88, and 96; for examples with a scroll, see note 338.

331 Other examples are cat. nos. 91, 110, 120, 117, 128, 158, and 171.

332 This type is in graph 3 referred to as "Learned couple, scroll".

333 Cat. no. 103 is an example of a similar motif. On this sarcophagus the woman holds a scroll.

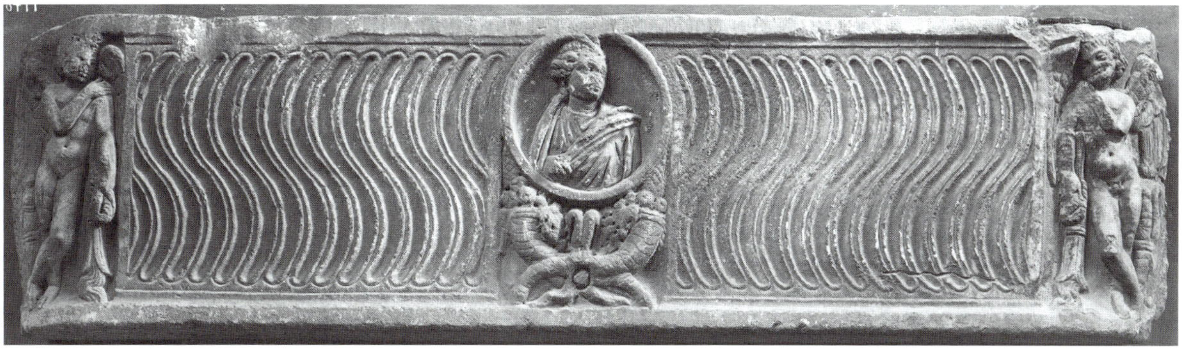

Strigillated sarcophagus with a portrait of a woman represented as a Muse (cat. no. 42). Rome, Villa Doria Pamphilj. Photo: D-DAI-ROM-8411 (Faraglia). **Fig. 38**

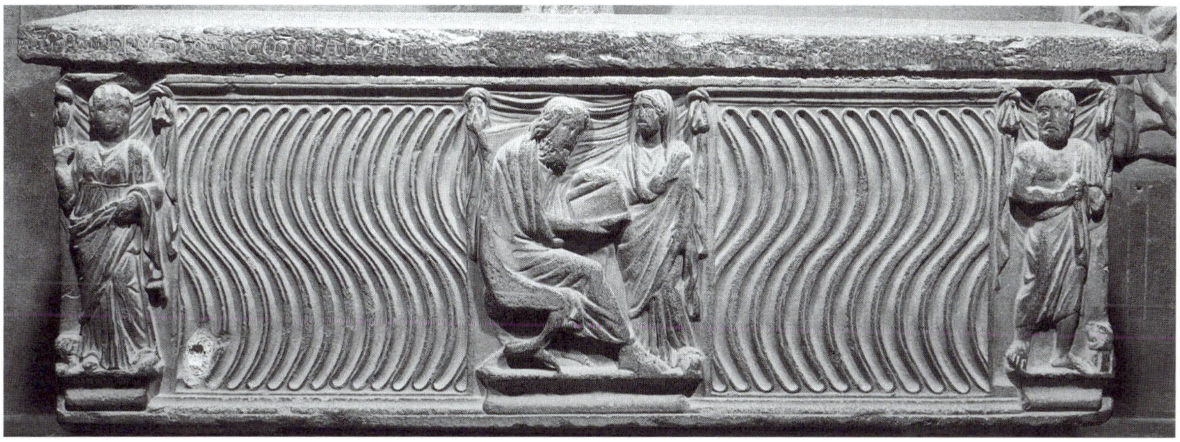

Strigillated sarcophagus showing a learned woman on the first panel. The third and fifth panels show scenes from the intellectual world (cat. no. 102). Pisa, Camposanto C 10 est. Photo: D-DAI-ROM-34.540. **Fig. 39**

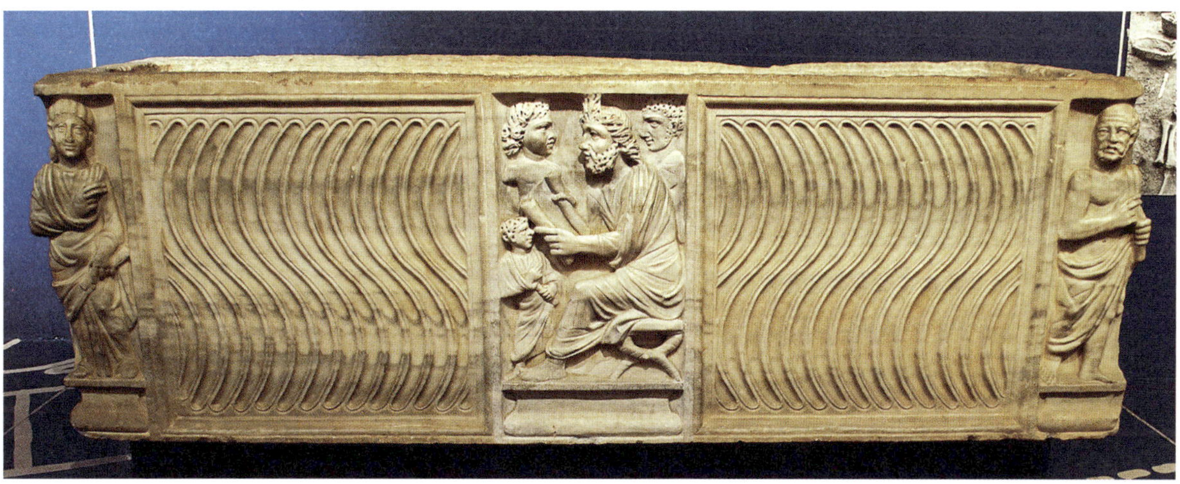

Strigillated sarcophagus with the deceased represented as a learned woman (cat. no. 131). Tarragona, Museu Nacional Arquelògic de Tarragona. Photo: Troels Myrup Kristensen. **Fig. 40**

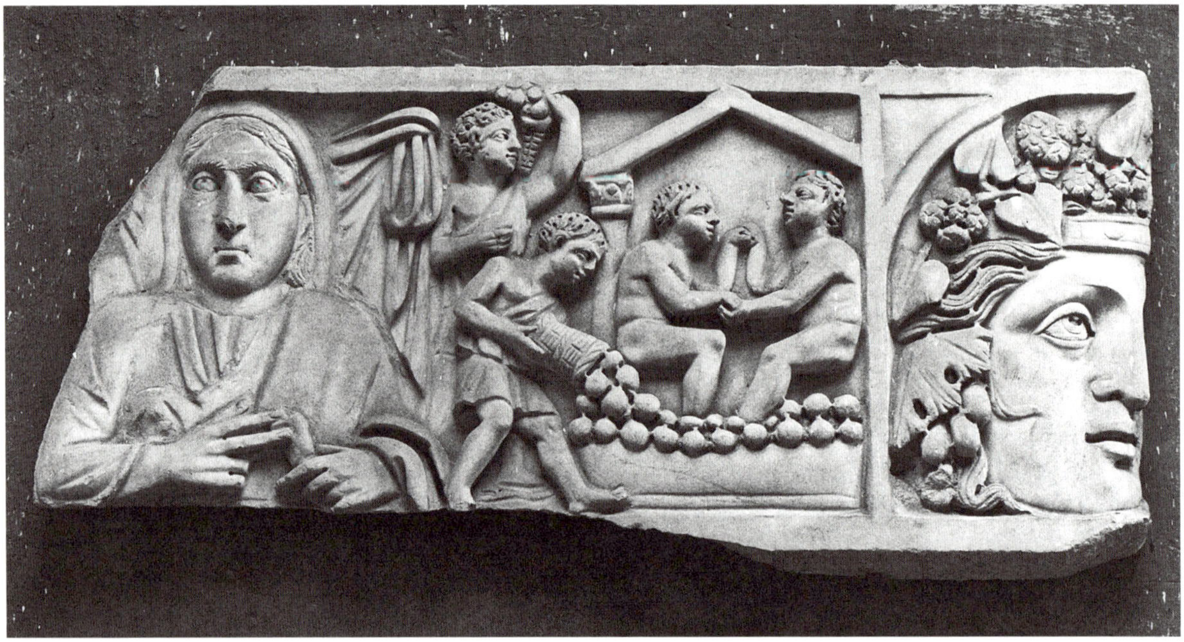

Fig. 41 *Fragment of a lid with a bust of a learned woman (cat. no. 49). Rome, Catacombe di Pretestato, Museo, inv. 21. Photo: D-DAI-ROM-68.976 (Hützel).*

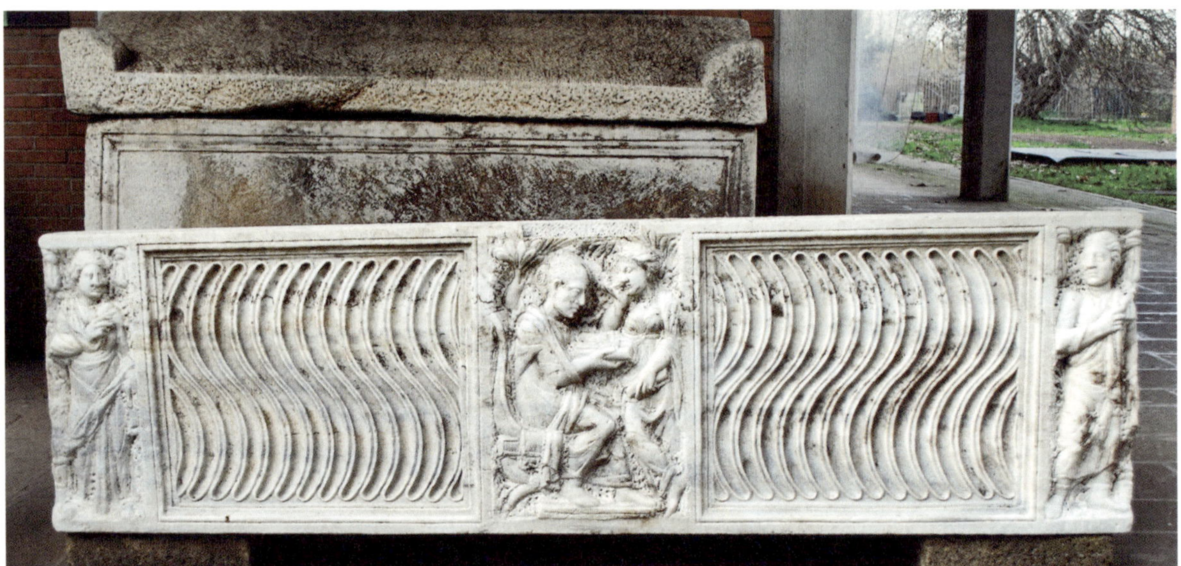

Fig. 42 *Strigillated sarcophagus with a learned woman and a female philosopher (cat. no. 97). Ostia, Museo, inv. 48277. Photo: Author.*

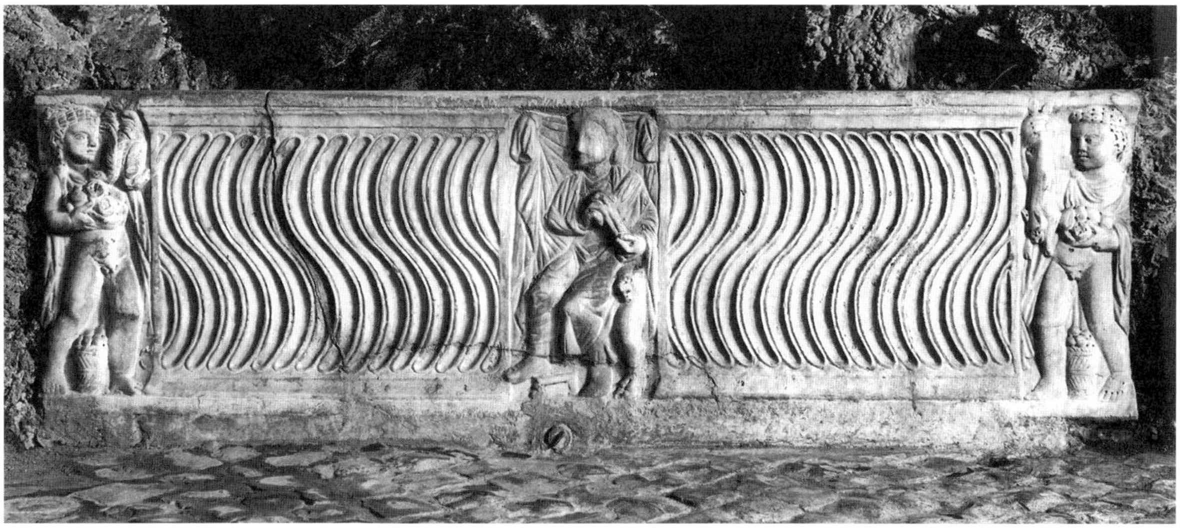

Strigillated sarcophagus with female philosopher and seasonal personifications (cat. no. 228). Rome, Palazzo Lazzaroni. Photo: D-DAI-ROM-70. 269. **Fig. 43**

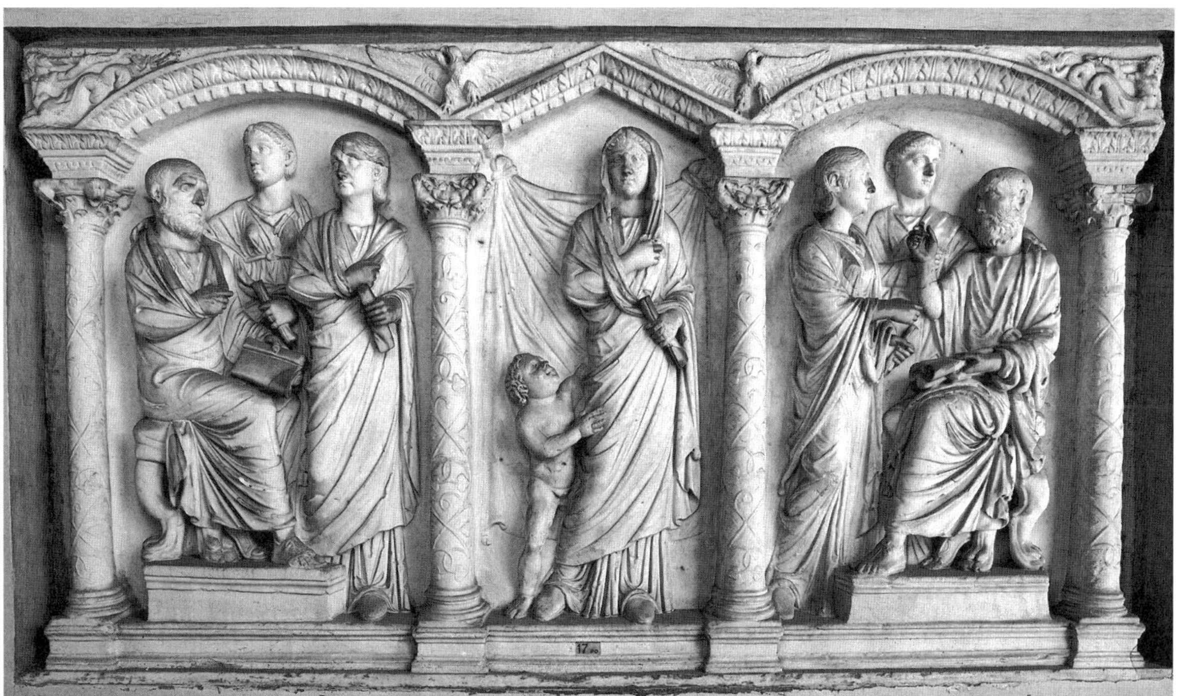

Column sarcophagus with a family represented as learned persons (cat. no. 114). Rome, Musei Vaticani, Cortile del Belvedere, inv. 871. Photo: D-DAI-ROM-93Vat 701. **Fig. 44**

personal virtues.[334] The seated female figure with a scroll is, however, not an entirely unknown image. Such a figure is found on a Prometheus sarcophagus, beside the lifeless body of the boy created by Prometheus.[335] She has no portrait features but is a generic representation of one of the four Fates. On our philosopher sarcophagus (**Fig. 42**; cat. no. 97), however, no reference is made to the Fates, and the other figures all belong to the learned sphere. A further argument for seeing this figure as a female philosopher is that cat. no. 97 is not the only sarcophagus with a seated female philosopher. A strigillated sarcophagus divided into five panels with a seasonal personification on the first and fifth panel shows a female seated philosopher on the central panel (cat. no. 228; **Fig. 43**). In her hands she holds a scroll, and a *parapetasma* is suspended behind her. Her head is roughly carved and the hair protrudes below the ears in a manner that shows that the *bosse* was prepared to receive a female hairstyle.[336]

Next in popularity to the woman represented alone with a scroll came the learned woman shown in combination with a learned man: a *learned couple*. A learned couple is defined as a woman with either a scroll or a musical instrument represented together with a man holding a scroll. On these sarcophagi, the secondary motifs often place the couple in an intellectual setting and thereby enhance their intellectual status.[337] Learned couples in which both the man and woman hold scrolls are prevailingly found on strigillated sarcophagi, meaning that the figures are separated from each other by the grooved panels and are thus not represented on the same scene.[338] The compositional scheme of such scenes is important, since two figures on the same scene often symbolise marriage, a relationship in which, it seems, both figures could not hold a scroll.[339]

The relationship between the learned couple separated by strigillated panels is, however, a difficult one. They could be married, but there do not seem to be any particular elements that symbolise marital bonds or *concordia*.[340] However, evidence from other sarcophagi with portrait figures and inscriptions, such as those with a scene showing a ritual, point to the fact that the relationship should be interpreted within the boundaries of the family. Ewald suggests that the internalisation of marriage changed through the second and third centuries, and women went from being "birth-machines" to becoming "life partners" or even friends.[341] In line with this, I see these representations as illustrations of a social relationship that builds on values of equality and mutual interests. Rather than focusing on marital aspects, the individuals who selected these representational schemes for their self-representation and burial are focusing on a partnership of equal qualities and equal status, issues that here are conveyed through the idealised iconography of learnedness. Only one sarcophagus that shows both the man and the woman holding a scroll seems to put family relations in the foreground (**Fig. 44**; cat. no. 114). Seven figures appear to have portrait features on the frontal relief and another six on the short end reliefs, which is unusual for Roman sarcophagi, where representations of families seldom consist of more than a couple.[342] The front is divided by columns into three niches. It is possible that the same woman is represented on all three panels. On the first and third panel she is seen together with a seated man represented as a philosopher. A younger woman stands behind them; this woman, interpreted as their daughter because of

334 For cross-gendered sarcophagi, see Birk 2011.

335 See Zanker & Ewald 2004, fig. 41.

336 For an almost identical sarcophagus with a seated male philosopher, see cat. no. 218.

337 *Clipeus* busts of a couple will be treated separately in chapter 3.

338 Cat. nos. 32, 43, 52, 54, 82, 92, 98, 111, 119, 114, 116, 163, 177, 180, 181, 241, 183, 639, and 646. Except from cat. nos. 32, 52, 114, 116, and 241 all are sarcophagi of the strigillated type or with another feature (door or inscription tablet) that separates the individualised figures. The three last mentioned examples (cat. nos. 114, 116, and 241) must be considered special commissions and will be discussed on pp. 33-4, 183.

339 Learned couples are also represented on sarcophagi with the so-called Lycian motif. On these reliefs the woman holds a lyre instead of a scroll. I will treat this group separately below (chapter 3).

340 Except for sarcophagi such as cat. no. 183, whose iconography is so close to the other sarcophagi with a sacrifice and a marriage scene that the figures must suggest the same virtues.

341 Ewald 2005, 55-6, 68-71.

342 The women on the short ends are said to have portrait features as well. The unusual decision to carve portrait figures on the short ends suggests that very specific wishes were involved in the purchase of this sarcophagus.

her young age, is situated in the place where Concordia traditionally stands on *dextrarum iunctio* sarcophagi.[343] There, the composition helps us to identify them as a marital couple negotiating their identity through family values.[344] Judging from the hairstyles, the three female figures on each end relief are represented with portrait features, which is highly unusual for figures on these surfaces. Four of the women wear a coiffeur similar to that of the daughter, and the other two women, standing in the middle in both compositions, have the same hairstyle as the older woman from the frontal relief. It is therefore likely that they should be identified as the mother and daughter from the frontal relief. The body types used for the six additional women are those of the Muses, and again we see how the secondary figures emphasise the motif of the frontal relief; we are most probably supposed to infer that the other three Muses are among the women on the front. By focusing on the central portrait figure and the iconographic support she is granted by the six Muses on the short ends, it seems that the sarcophagus commemorated a woman that through the presence of the other family members negotiated not only her own identity, but also that of her family.

A final type of learned figure that I have not mentioned yet is the *Orans*. As is clear from graph 3, the invidualised *Orans* is rare in the third century, but as the production gradually becomes dominated by motifs from Christian narratives, she becomes increasingly popular. We will return to the use of this figure in discussing the learned woman on Christian sarcophagi (p. 89).

In light of the current discussion of gender roles in Roman society, it is interesting to see how the number of learned men relates to that of learned women. This relationship is illustrated by graph 3, from which it can be seen that the number of female representations is almost equal to that of the male representations. More than one learned figure can be carved on one sarcophagus, and graph 4 shows the number of learned figures with portraits, rather than the number of sarcophagi that depict such figures. Huskinson has noted that a preliminary count of sarcophagi from the *ASR* V 4 reveals a slightly higher number of female portrait busts with scrolls, compared to male ones.[345] This picture is confirmed by my study, which encompasses all the learned women on sarcophagi, independently of associated motif.

Whereas graph 4 showed that representations of the female learned figure were almost equal in number to the male equivalent, on sarcophagi with only one portrait figure the number of representations of a learned woman with a scroll is higher than the number of single male figures with a scroll (compare graphs 3 and 5). The scholarly narrative of the learned male figure is, however, much more elaborate than that of the female. We have multiple interpretations of the male figure with a scroll: as a philosopher, magistrate, orator or poet, but women similarly represented are just characterised as "learned", or in a few cases as a Muse.[346] This unequal characterisation is caused by the fact that we can relate the representation of the learned man to professions that we know, from literary sources, that men could possess. The interpretation strategy changes when it comes to women; we see them as metaphors instead of roles because we have difficulties imagining Roman women in the same roles as men.[347] However, the male and female learned figures should be looked at from

343 For the description and discussion of the composition, see Ewald 1999, 171-72.

344 An example of a *dextrarum iunctio* scene with Concordia in this place is cat. no. 666.

345 Huskinson 1999, 197.

346 This problem of defining women's roles is well illustrated by Davies, who mentioned a number of male roles but could not find any parallel roles for women (Davies 2008, 208). On learned male figures, see Wrede 2001; Ewald 1998; 1999, 54-62. On male and female learned figures including Muses, see Marrou 1938. On Muses, see also Cumont 1942, chapter IV; Centanni 2006.

347 This way of thinking is expressed by Hansen (2008, 279), who writes that "The gendered image is therefore constructed not solely on the basis of a contrasting relationship of active masculinity to passive femininity but also on a relative relationship in which learned women interact with men, just as learned men interact with political authority." Reinsberg (1995) describes the different public roles of learned men on biographical sarcophagi. Still, she does not assume a direct identification between the deceased and the office represented but sees it as an ideal representation of the social range to which the deceased belonged (1995, 369).

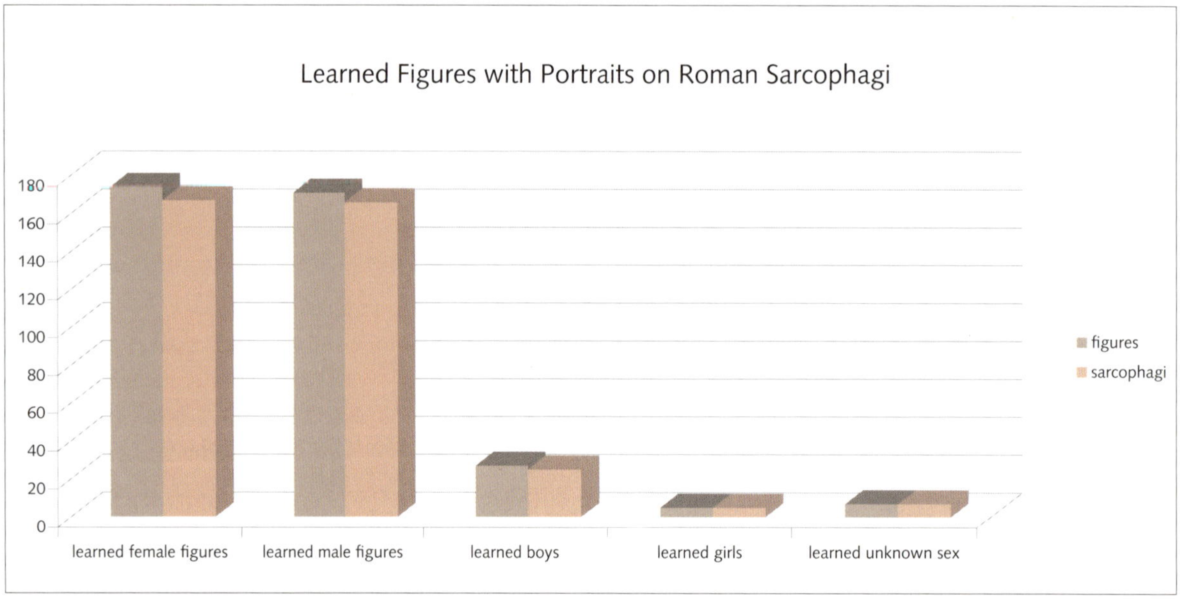

Graph 4 *The learned woman is found almost as frequently on sarcophagi as the learned man. This fact should make us reconsider the place of women in the intellectual milieu. The graph is based on Appendix C1-4.*

the same perspective. If we do this, then the learned figures, whether male or female, illustrate generally accepted cultural ideas about how to represent a person of the right moral standard and virtues, and not only of the 'right' sex.

Turning to the chronological development of the appearance of the learned figure on sarcophagi, men and women with a scroll could, to a higher degree in the beginning than later on, be distinguished by their clothing. But as time passed the representations somesometimes became so generic that it is sometimes impossible to distinguish one sex from the other, were it not for the portraits.[348] I will give an example to illustrate this point. The representations of the seated philosopher on cat. nos. 228 and 218 look identical (**Figs. 43 & 45**). The philosopher on the woman's sarcophagus (cat. no. 226) has a roughly carved head, but the *bosse* has been laid out to be carved with a female hairstyle. On the other sarcophagus (cat. no. 218) a male portrait has been applied to the philosopher. This confirms that the same figure, representing the same virtues and ideals, was prepared in the workshop to be used to commemorate both women and men.

My conclusion is therefore that men's and women's roles were limited and determined by sex *only* when the figures were set in relation to each other on one scene, and not when they were represented individually. The sarcophagi from the catalogue interestingly show that the learned sphere was not the only context in which men and women could be represented by the same figure type. In fact, most male figure types had an equivalent that could be used for representations of women and *vice versa* (see chapter 3).

The figure of the learned man also requires consideration. His appearance is less varied than his female counterpart, who acted in the learned sphere in a more varied repertoire of roles (*Orans*, Muse, learned woman with scroll, educated woman, and philosopher). He could be shown as a poet, a philosopher, or a learned man with a scroll, a mode of representation that is sometimes in literature referred to as a magistrate.[349]

348 Huskinson 2002, 25; Ewald 2005, 69.

349 For representations of magistrates on sarcophagi, see Ewald 1998; Wrede 2001, 66-76. I have chosen to designate all standing men with a scroll as learned and not to separate them into the different categories of poet, magistrate, teacher etc. because my interest here is in the virtues that the figure conveys. It is the intellectuality of the figure that is considered the main virtue here.

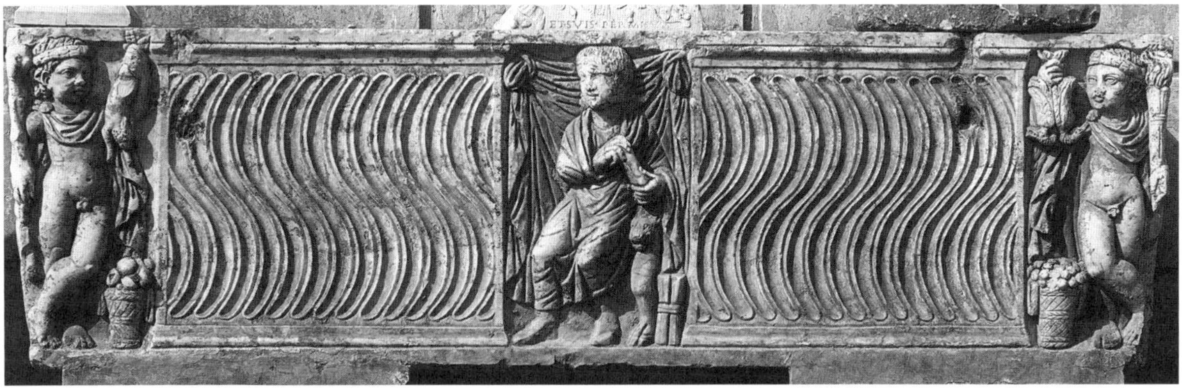

Strigillated sarcophagus with a philosopher and seasonal personifications (cat. no. 218). Rome, Museo Nazionale Romano, inv. 12265. Photo: D-DAI-ROM-1220. **Fig. 45**

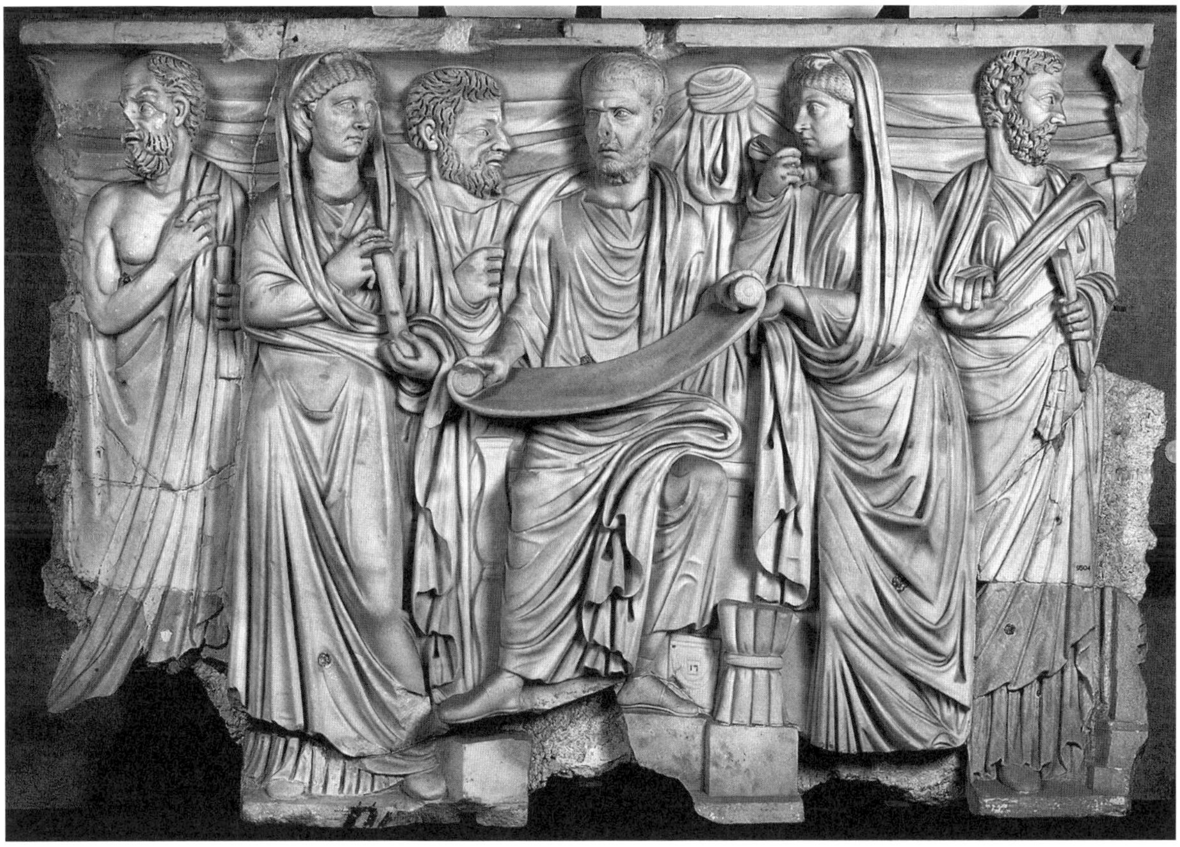

The so-called Plotinus sarcophagus (cat. no. 116). Rome, Musei Vaticani, Museo Gregoriano Profano, inv. 9504. Photo: FA-S_41102,02. **Fig. 46**

Applied with a portrait, he did not come into vogue until after 240, though there are a few earlier examples. The philosopher is represented as either a seated figure with a tunic or naked chest or a standing figure wearing a *himation*. Often the philosopher is accompanied by one or more representations of Muses (sometimes with a portrait) and sages. Examples of a philosopher and Muses with portraits can be found on (cat. no. 120) and **Fig. 46** (cat. no. 116). The learned man with a scroll, just like the learned woman, can be represented as a full

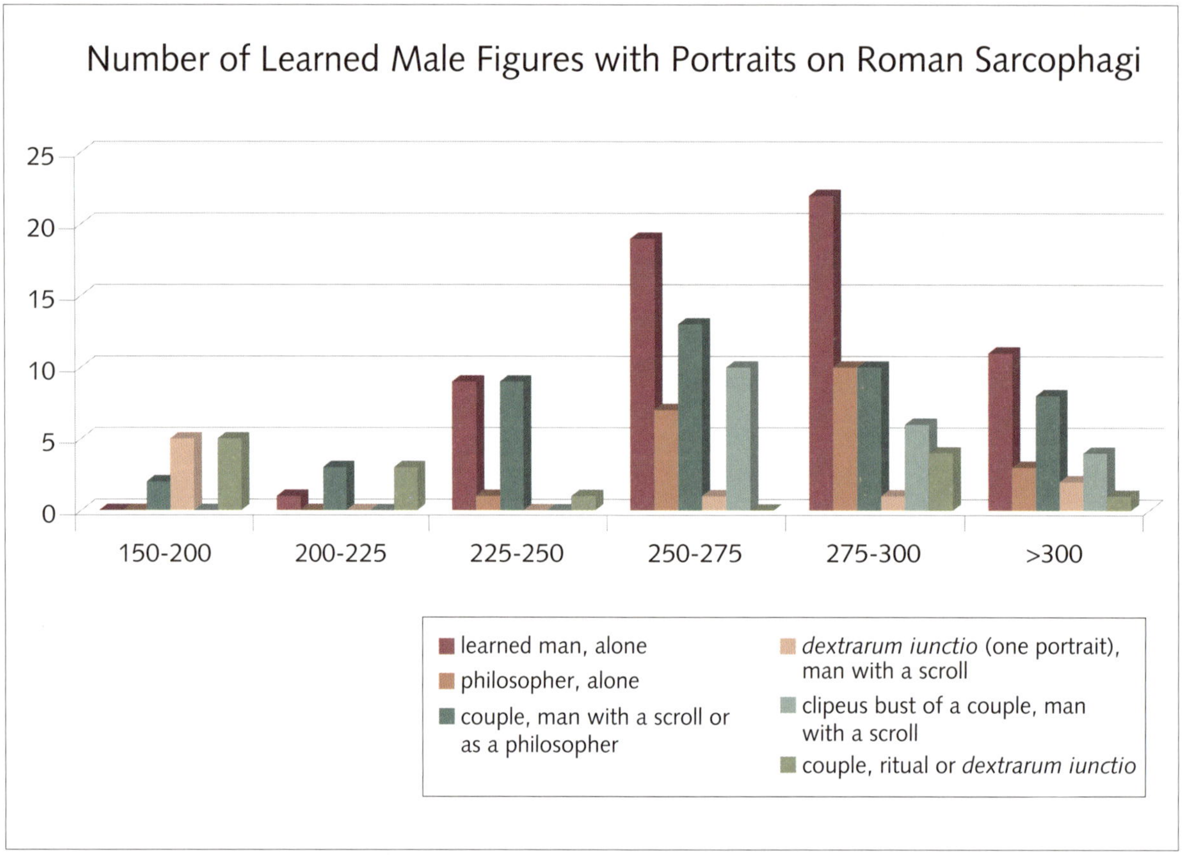

Graph 5 *The graph illustrates the popularity of the different types of learned men in a chronological perspective. The data used are the same as those used for graph 2. The graph is based on Appendix C2.*

figure or as a bust enclosed by a *clipeus*, and may be given a variety of associations through secondary and tertiary motifs. In contrast to the learned woman, who was most often represented alone (graph 3), the male equivalent is seen almost as frequently as one part of a couple as he is alone.

Graph 5 shows the chronological distribution of the different types of male learned figures, including the different social relations in which they are portrayed. Included are the learned men from the marital sarcophagi discussed above, which explains the group of men with scrolls belonging to the second and early third centuries, and sarcophagi with *clipeus* busts of a couple. Neither of these two types are included in the statistics on learned female figures, because in these motifs the woman is never represented as learned.[350] C. Reinsberg sees sarcophagi with learned figures (such as cat. nos. 641, 645, and 667) as direct iconographic continuations of the group of biographical sarcophagi.[351] According to her, both kinds of sarcophagi show representations of magistrate offices and social roles for men in the context of the career of a Roman man of senatorial class. I agree about this iconographic similarity and the influence of the learned men sarcophagi on those with representation of rituals, but think that a different meaning should be read into the new compositional scheme. The man in *dextrarum iunctio* scenes is repre-

350 Except for cat. no. 446, where both the portrayed persons are women.

351 Reinsberg 1995, especially p. 360-61.

sented with both learned and domestic qualities, the former by the presence of a scroll and the latter by the emphasis put on his relationship to his wife. As I have already argued, these scenes, like the abbreviated forms on other sarcophagi, make it possible to combine more virtues on one relief, and they therefore often concern themselves more with individual qualities and personal identity than with institutional norms. All suggestions of such norms through architectural elements and military iconography from life course representations have disappeared. It is therefore the new opportunity for men and women to represent themselves individually in new social roles of private values that should be read from these scenes.

As illustrated by graph 2, the images of the learned man began to appear concurrently with the female form and continued throughout the third and into the fourth century, but it is clear that the learned man with a scroll was most popular from around 260 until 300. An important conclusion to draw from this fact is that the learned man was not used as a prototype for the representation of the learned woman. The decrease in the use of the learned figure by the end of the third century was due, as has been mentioned, to the downscaled production of sarcophagi with traditional Roman motifs. Had the graph continued chronologically to encompass the Christian production as well, which is discussed briefly below, it would have shown that the popularity of the male learned portrait figure continued to fall while the use of the female figure remained constant for a couple of decades.[352]

The Learned Woman on Christian Sarcophagi

When Rome became Christian, the iconography on its sarcophagi changed and so did its role models of the ideal man and woman. The two popular female figures used for self-representation in this period were the *Orans* and the learned woman, two female role models whose numbers in the fourth century exceeded those of the male individualised figure on sarcophagi with biblical motifs.[353] Very few other types of role models were used for individualisation through a portrait in this period, with the exceptions of portrait busts most often without any attribute. The marital iconography that continued into to the fourth century comprised the *dextrarum iunctio* scenes and the couple enclosed by a *clipeus*. Though these scenes are not manifold, they showed the woman in her traditional wifely roles. Whether the patrons of such sarcophagi were Christian is in many cases impossible to decipher from the iconography.[354] An example would be the seasonal sarcophagus from Dumbarton Oaks (cat. no. 468), which has a relief showing the portraits of a man and a woman in a *clipeus* with zodiacs placed between four winged seasonal personifications, and additional bucolic scenes.[355] By the end of the third century, seasonal scenes had lost some of their original meaning of alluding to the natural cycle of life, and a sarcophagus like this may have used the motif to show a positive attitude towards death or a hope for a happy afterlife existence.[356] The woman with the wind-blown veil known from Venus and Nereid iconography and the man with a scroll continues the tradition of the previous century of showing marital *concordia* on sarcophagi.[357] The motif could therefore accommodate both pagan and Christian audiences.[358]

The iconographic language of the *Orans* originated from the learned woman, and the meaning suggested by the *Orans* illustrates this development.[359] The *Orans*,

352 For the decline of the pagan production, see Koch & Sichtermann 1982, 61-2; Koch 1993, 66.

353 This impression is achieved through a study of the sarcophagi published in *Rep.* I.

354 Two fragments show the two female types on the same sarcophagus relief (cat. no. 641). One exception is a canonical hunt sarcophagus from S. Elpido a Mare (cat. no. 520) that represents the commemorated persons as a hunter, a commander, and Virtus. The sarcophagus can be seen as a renewal of the early lion hunt sarcophagi (see below for the lion hunt motif).

355 Hanfmann 1951 (I & II).

356 Zanker & Ewald 2004, 257.

357 Cat. no. 241 is another example of "pagan" iconography in the period in which Christian iconography otherwise dominated the production of sarcophagi.

358 Numerous Christian sarcophagi use these kinds of *clipeus* busts, both for marital couples and for people with other social relations. For a new way of interpreting the so-called Brother sarcophagus in Museo Gregoriano Christiano, see Sande 2010.

359 Dresken-Weiland 2010, 38. Both Zanker and Huskinson note that the "old images of worldly learning are converted to depict study of inner peace and spiritual salvation" (Huskinson

too, is dressed in a *tunica* and a *palla*, but her arms are raised and her palms turned towards the viewer. The learned woman often stands in front of a *parapetasma* with a *palla* around her and a scroll in one hand. Additional scrolls can be placed at her feet, as is the case on a strigillated sarcophagus with a learned woman as the central motif and seasonal *genii* in the place of the secondary motif (**Fig. 35**; cat. no. 236). On a strigillated sarcophagus from Camposanto, Pisa, with a central representation of a philosopher and a Muse, the individualised female figure on the front left end panel is of the same figure type (**Fig. 39**; cat. no. 102). Her *palla* does, however, not cover the upper part of the dress. Instead it is tied around the chest with a belt, like the dress of the Muses. Scrolls are placed at her feet as well, which again confirms her connection to the learned sphere. However, instead of holding a scroll, her right arm is raised and the palm is turned towards the viewer. She is a hybrid of the learned woman and the *Orans*, and she is a good illustration of the connection between the two figures, both in iconography and meaning. The *Orans* starts to appear on sarcophagi in the late third century and the first examples are found on sarcophagi that again are not explicitly Christian (graph 3).[360] On another sarcophagus which does not invite categorisation as either pagan or Christian, the *Orans*, like the learned woman, is placed in front of a *parapetasma* (**Fig. 17**; cat. no. 2). She is dressed like a learned woman but she is also veiled; a veil covering the hair is not seen on a learned woman before the later part of the third century.[361] Scrolls are placed at the feet of the *Orans*, confirming the concurrence of the virtues implied by the *Orans* and the learned woman.

When placed in a Christian context on sarcophagi with images from the Old and New Testament, the *Orans* is often flanked by two men, probably representations of apostles, as seen on the Via Lungara sarcophagus in Palazzo Massimo.[362] Here she is veiled and her palms are turned towards the viewer. On either side of her, several scenes from the biblical narrative tradition have been set closely together. The scenes chosen (the wine miracle in Kanaa, the multiplication of bread, the resurrection of Lazarus etc.) to decorate the frieze are common on sarcophagi and in catacomb paintings.[363] More frequently, however, the *Orans* is represented alone, separated from the rest of the composition by a *parapetasma*, a *clipeus* or a column; she does not interact with any other figures. As well as the *Orans*, the learned woman with a scroll also continues to be represented on Christian sarcophagi, and in these representations she looks as if she is preaching or teaching the men on either side of her.[364] These similar methods of presenting the woman with a scroll and the *Orans* confirm the close connection between the symbolic meanings of the two female figures. The *Orans* is a personification of piety and faith.[365] At the same time she embodies intellectuality and literary knowledge, now related to Christian religious texts instead of the pagan philosophical ideology and traditional education that is illustrated by the learned woman on traditional sarcophagi.[366] One of the most interesting things about the *Orans* and the learned woman is that, besides being allegories of the virtuous woman, they are suggestive of some of the social roles that were open to women in early Christian society. She could apparently teach, preach, or act as a spiritual leader – even for men.[367] Such an interpretation does

1999, 202; Huskinson refers here to Zanker 1995, 286-87). For the figure of the *Orans*, see Otranto 1989, 74-5; Koch 2000, 21-2.

360 Cat. no. 20 is a *clipeus* bust sarcophagus with a portrait of a veiled woman, an *Orans*. The sarcophagus has been dated to the late Severan period based on stylistic data of the figures (Paroli 1999, 230). However, neither the hairstyle nor the carving of the eyes suggests that the portrait could not be dated to the later part of the third century.

361 Examples are cat. nos. 32 49, 92, 110-12, 119-20, 116, 181, and 646.

362 Koch 2000, 250.

363 For the latest interpretation of the iconography and meaning of these scenes, see Dresken-Weiland 2010.

364 Lange 1996, 28-9; Huskinson 1999, 205.

365 Klauser 1959; 1964; 1956-66, 127-28. Dresken-Weiland 2010, 38, who in Christian iconography also sees the *Orans* as a symbol of the soul of the deceased (for the iconography, see pp. 38-76).

366 On Paideia and status, see Brown 1992, 51-64.

367 On women with an intellectual status of their own, see Huskinson 1999, 205; on educated women in Late Antiquity, see Rousseau 1995. On teaching and preaching women, see King 2003. On the role of women in the spread of early Christianity and establishment of the Christian Church, see

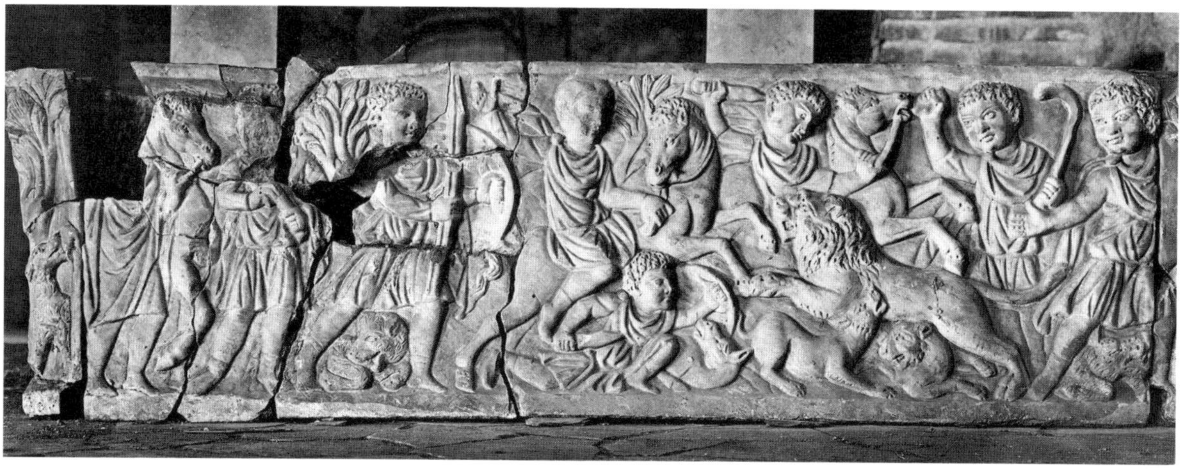

Lion hunt sarcophagus (cat. no. 495). Rome, Catacombe di S. Callisto. Photo: D-DAI-Z-NEG-9716_132125,01. **Fig. 47**

not, however, mean that the person who chose this iconography for her funerary monument was necessarily a religious female leader herself: by using the motif she placed herself in an ideal female role. This role contains ideals and norms that all reflect currents in society; the figure illustrates the intellectual status that could be held by women at the end of the third century.[368] The impression that we have of early Christian women from literary sources is one formed by a Christian tradition in which church fathers have literally written women out of the history.[369] However, in this formative period of Christianity in Rome it seems there were other possibilities for women to negotiate their social role than those represented in the Christian literary tradition. These possibilities are symbolised by the individualised female portrait figures: the traditional Roman way of showing social status and power was transferred to Christian ways of constructing identity.[370]

Learned Figures outside the Intellectual Sphere

As we have already seen, figures from the learned sphere were an extremely popular form for self-representation on sarcophagi. The popularity of the virtues they expressed sometimes caused them to be represented in unexpected contexts; examples of this can be found on two lion hunt sarcophagi (cat. no. 495; **Fig. 47** and cat. no. 511; **Fig. 59**). On these two reliefs the learned man has strayed into a scene which is normally described as the departure of the hunter. He is found on the left part of the frontal relief, beside the servant that holds his horse. He takes the place of a figure that is usually found holding a sword on similar sarcophagi; on many examples this figure is a military man with a cuirass.[371] These two male figure types, the military and the learned man, symbolise very different qualities: it is a long way from the military man, who is an embodiment of male *virtus*, to the learned man, who originates in the intellectual milieu. On the two coffins (cat. no. 495; **Fig. 47** and cat. no. 511; **Fig. 59**) heads of the learned men in question are lost, but it is likely that they were carved with a portrait, as is often the case with this figure on conventional hunt sarcophagi

Ide 1986. For influential women in the Christian community in Rome, see Denzey 2007 (reviewed by Burrus 2008).

368 On representations of learned men and women on Roman sarcophagi, see Zanker 1995, 256-80. On representation of the learned woman specifically, see Huskinson 1999, 207-8; Huskinson 2002. For women as leaders, apostles, and prophets, see Irvin 1980 (For a counterargument to Irvin's articles, see Irwin 1984); Jensen, 2001. For women as leaders and bishops, see Ide 1984.

369 Clark 1998, especially p. 170. Tulloch (2004, 302) writes "unlike the early Christian literary tradition, in which women are largely invisible, misrepresented, or omitted entirely, female figures in early Christian art play significant roles in the transmission of the faith."

370 For examples of social roles and intellectual influence in the early Christian period in Rome, see Denzey 2007.

371 The figure is found on cat. nos. 480, 493, 507, 509, and 520.

with two scenes.[372] Both sarcophagi can be dated to the end of the third century and belong to the period during which older conventions began to dissolve. The figure should not, however, be seen as a misinterpretation of outdated symbols. Lion hunt scenes were never intended to represent an actual hunt, nor were they designed to refer to the hunting prowess of an upper-class Roman man. Instead, the hunt was an allegory for the ideal virtues possessed by the deceased. When the protagonist is represented on the same scene as possessing both male *virtus* (the hunter) and intellectuality (the learned figure), he takes full advantage of the symbolic potential of sarcophagus iconography to display the multifaceted nature of his identity. Besides being an example of how scenes on sarcophagi should be understood as depicting the qualities of the deceased, the appearance of the learned figure on the hunting scenes shows the importance of intellectual virtues in third-century Rome.

Another sarcophagus shows the same combination of male *virtus* and intellectual abilities in one scene (cat. no. 238).[373] Dated to the early fourth century, it is nearly contemporary with the two lion hunt sarcophagi. The sarcophagus is adorned with seasonal *genii* and cupids. A boy stands in front of a *parapetasma*, wearing a cuirass and holding a scroll in his hand. An inscription tells us the name of the boy, Florentinus Domitius Marianus, and states that he was commemorated by his parents. The cuirass and the inscription – *equ(iti) r(omano)* – indicates that he was of equestrian rank, and the cuirass reveals that the boy had the courage it would take to fulfil this role. The scroll shows a further side of his identity, showing him to be well-educated and versed in classical literature. In short, the iconography symbolises both the boy's male *virtus* and his level of education.

Another unusual context – that is, one outside of the formulaic learned iconography – in which learned figures appear is a scene showing people driving a carriage through a city.[374] These sarcophagi have been categorised as depictions of *vita humana* by scholars working on *Sarkophagstudien*.[375] The patrons who chose these representations of the ideal human situation (we should not see them as historical records of real events) are speaking explicitly about social status in a manner that can be compared to that of the biographical sarcophagi of the second century. They use symbols that are related to official magistracies, the sceptre held by the figures on cat. no. 539 and the scroll on cat. nos. 540-44, and also suggest their high social standing through the image of the ride through the city in a carriage. One of the reliefs shows the carriage, surrounded by houses, being led by a driver through something that looks like a city gate (**Fig. 48**; cat. no. 543). The couple in the carriage are engaged in a scholarly discussion, the man with a scroll turning towards the woman, and their entrance into the city is prepared by a man walking in front of the carriage. Only the woman can with certainty be said to have a portrait head. The people of the city, who are shown greeting the couple, are smaller than them. The person commemorated by this sarcophagus is a woman, and will be discussed in the next chapter.

The relatively broad range of secondary and tertiary themes that could be associated with learned individualised figures shows that they were meant as a supplement to the virtues implied by the portrait figure. Since the secondary motif generally does not depend on the type of role model used, I will not go into too much detail here, but will limit my discussion to the most popular secondary theme: seasonal personifications (cat. nos. 191-247).[376] Seasonal personifications belong to the reflective or contemplative iconographic category, as the seasons are a common and neutral symbol of fertility and the cycle of life.[377] They symbolise both decay and renewal, and the *genii* are described in funerary epigrams as those who bring gifts to the grave. They may

372 Another combination of hunting scenes and a learned figure, here a woman called Valeria Florentia, is found on cat. no. 512. A bust of a learned woman is represented on the lid of a hunt sarcophagus while her husband, who died at the age of 21, is represented as the lion hunter on the coffin.

373 Huskinson 1996, cat. 8. 12.

374 Cat. nos. 539-44.

375 Amedick, *ASR* I 4 (1991).

376 The secondary motifs are reflected in the composition of the catalogue, in which sarcophagi with different types of role models have been categorised according to related motif. The other secondary motifs used in relation to learned figures are: Bucolic, cupids, Eros and Psyche, death door, garlands, and, lion attacking an animal.

377 Bielefeld, *ASR* V 2, 2 (1997), 89. On the interpretation of seasonal personifications, see also Hanfmann 1951 and Kranz, *ASR* V 4 (1984).

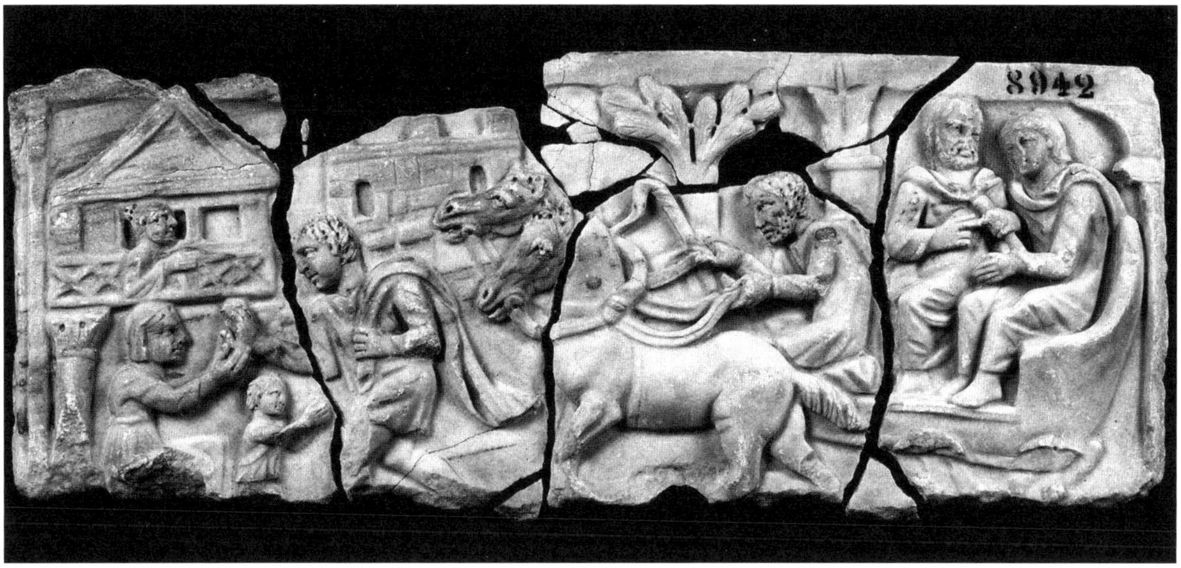

Sarcophagus showing a couple driving in a carriage (cat. no. 543). Rome, Museo Nazionale Romano, inv. 8942. Photo: Mal1629-07 (B. Malter). **Fig. 48**

additionally, as suggested by Ewald, reflect the situation of the family members, who regularly visited the tomb with gifts, such as garlands and other kind of seasonal fruit.[378] Using seasonal *genii* on sarcophagi is consequently not necessarily a way of suggesting the personal qualities of the deceased, but an encouragement to viewers to reflect on the cycle of life and the situation at the tomb. However, these symbols of rich and harmonious nature – together with bucolic landscapes, which were also juxtaposed with learned figures – are part of a narrative of the coveted *otium* and life of *luxuria*, and as such an appropriate motif to use in the context of philosophy and learnedness.

The Learned Figure as a Role Model, Conclusion

This discussion of learned figures has revealed aspects of the mental climate of the third century by showing how the female figure could enter the world of learnedness, and by proposing that there were more accepted ways of constructing social relations between men and women than has often been supposed. A hierarchy of gender has been revealed, but it has also been shown that the same role models were used for constructing both men's and women's identities. Thus, as will be discussed further in the next chapter, we can recognise an attitude towards gender roles through self-representation on sarcophagi that shows a high degree of flexibility in terms of which virtues and qualities were acceptable for ideal representations of the deceased and the sometimes still-living patron. Perhaps this attitude does not allow us to make a direct identification with the roles undertaken by the commemorated in society, but it shows a mentality that enables women especially to possess a larger variety of roles than has hitherto been ascribed to them, at least when we look outside marital relationships.

In the creation of a posthumous reputation, the intellectual sphere was a territory shared by both men and women: both genders could hold a scroll. The implications of such representations only became clear when they were represented as a marital couple, which can be explained by the allusion made to the iconography of the Muses. The use of the Muse as a role model not only showed the deceased woman's personal qualities, it was also an allegory of the devotion she felt to her husband: the woman was to her husband what a Muse was to a philosopher.

The concept of the ideal marriage, which changed from being mainly focused on the social roles of the man to become more equal in terms of ideals, was discussed in relation to scenes showing life course scenes and scenes with rituals. In scenes of marriage (such as

378 Ewald 1999a, 345.

cat. nos. 630 and 632-76), a man with a scroll is quite common, but it is also a fact that the woman rarely held one. The scroll might symbolise the marital contract, as suggested by some,[379] but in the end it should be read as a symbol of power. The person with a scroll signalises a higher level of knowledge that the person without a scroll. In chapter 3 we will look further into the relationship between men and women, and how it is expressed on portrait figures on sarcophagi.

Mythological Figures

The mythological figure, which may be either a divinity or a hero/heroine, is the third most popular form for self-representation through portraits on sarcophagi.[380] While the learned figure was usually frontally oriented and therefore had a rather stagnant appearance, the mythological figures interact with their surroundings.

The majority of sarcophagi which place real people into mythological contexts can be identified as belonging to the first half of the third century, but the first examples were seen around the middle of the second century.[381] The second part of the third century presents a decreasing number of this type of sarcophagi, and in the beginning of the fourth century their production continued to decline. Most recently Newby has looked at the mythological sarcophagi with portrait heads as a group, and she confirms that most examples can be found between 200-250.[382] Previous work on mythological portrait figures has been carried out by Wrede, who made an overview of the chronological division of mythological sarcophagi, and other sculptural forms, individualised through a portrait.[383] Though there are more mythological portrait sarcophagi in existence than are examined by Wrede, his selection reflects the chronological picture described above. The deceased in the guise of a mythological figure, or as Wrede expressed it, a 'deified figure', is known from early imperial times in sculpture in the round, and our individualised mythological figures should be seen as a part of that tradition since, as has been suggested, such examples portraying private persons belonged to sepulchral contexts as well.[384] In the early scholarship on the subject it was argued that this stylistic development affected the way mythological sarcophagi should be interpreted, and that the Greek classicising style of the second century had a different meaning from the third-century Roman allegorical style. This is no longer the case.[385]

On sarcophagi, individualised mythological figures seek to commemorate the deceased in a heroised form that brings out his or her lived experiences and beliefs as well as personal qualities on a symbolic level. In taking this approach, I follow a line of enquiry introduced in the late 1980s which is still influential (see below).[386] It interprets mythological images as allegories in which actual lived experiences are balanced with the myth's symbolic meaning.[387] It functions well, since the individualised figure in the mythological setting appears in a landscape of metaphors and allegories, so the scenery encourages the viewer to reflect upon questions of life and death. The approach taken by Zanker and Ewald in particular has gained ground in the last decade.[388] They combine self-representation and identity construction with bereavement and consolation, interpreting the coffins from the perspectives of the patron, the deceased, and the viewer.[389] This offers multiple reading possibilities, because similar images can be used for different purposes. This approach of multiple levels of reading was anticipated by Koortbojian when he suggested that mythological sarcophagi presented analogies and not identifications with the life histories of the deceased.[390]

379 Wrede 2001, 50 (on *dextrarum iunctio* scenes on Roman sarcophagi, see pp. 60-73). On the *dextrarum iunctio* motif as a symbol of status, see Brilliant 1963.

380 The learned figures and portrait bust representations are the two largest groups, see the index of the catalogue.

381 The earliest mythological sarcophagus known, but without a portrait figure, is the so-called Thetis and Peleus sarcophagus in the Villa Albani, Rome, see Müller 1994.

382 Newby 2011, 192. See also Zanker & Ewald 2004, 45-50.

383 Wrede 1981, 140.

384 Wrede 1981, 179.

385 For the second-century examples, see Blome 1977; 1978. For an evaluation of this approach, see Bielfeldt 2005a, 19-22.

386 First explored by L. Giuliani (1989 and latest 2003, especially pp. 281-92) and pursued by scholars such as Koortbojian (1995), Zanker (1999), and Bielfeldt (2005).

387 Lorenz 2011, 310.

388 Zanker & Ewald 2004.

389 See also Gessert 2004; Newby 2011.

390 Koortbojian 1995.

The symbolic value of mythological images on sarcophagi has been discussed intensively, and there is a long tradition of interpreting them as expressions of the hope for an afterlife.[391] Wrede's book on *apotheosis* or deification employs this line of argumentation. The weakness of his argument, however, is that he did not include all the different kinds of individualised mythological figures but tended only to study those that supported the argument of deification.[392] A parallel line of inquiry is that of interpreting the mythological portrait figure as a way of constructing identity, and to see the figures as expressions of virtues, qualities, and personality traits on an abstract level.[393] From this perspective, myths on sarcophagi are versions of a traditional tale whose components and events derive their meaning from society at large by reflecting moralities and accepted roles. As such, the patron of sarcophagi, by adapting and manipulating these myths into the funerary culture, exploited a communicative device that conveyed meanings to the Roman viewer. Through this adaption, the mythological figures work as *exempla*, since the exemplary behaviour of the legendary characters is transferred to the identity of the deceased and his or her life course.[394] This is a plausible approach to the relationship between the mythological figure and the identity of the deceased, but it does not unfold the full potential of mythological sarcophagi since it focuses mostly on representation and less on commemoration and bereavement, an approach argued for by Fittschen.[395]

There are 66 sarcophagi in this catalogue on which a mythological figure has been given portrait features.[396] However, 50 different myths are known to have been depicted on sarcophagi,[397] but not all myths were suitable for the insertion of a portrait figure. 19 different myths were used for this heroised kind of self-representation, which is a rather selective repertoire. In these myths, 31 different characters appear with a portrait head (see the

391 Cumont 1942 (for a negative response to this, see Nock 1946); Strong 1915; Lameere 1939; Turcan 1978; 1999; Engemann 1973; 1982; Andreae 1980, 135; 1985.

392 For example, while Ariadne is included, Endymion is not; Wrede 1981. For a review, see Mottahedeh 1984.

393 Among those who are discussing this method of interpretation of myths on sarcophagi are Sichtermann 1966; D'Ambra 1988; Blome 1992; Brilliant 1992; Müller 1994; Koortbojian 1995; Grassinger 1998; Zanker 2000; Junker 2005/06; Hansen 2007; and most recently Ewald 2011 and Newby 2011.

394 Gessert 2004, 218; Hansen 2007, 111.

395 As in his interpretation of Medea or Kreusa sarcophagi; see Fittschen 1992a, which was followed by Zanker & Ewald (2004, the chapter "*Klage, Trauer und Trost. Mythen als Trauerhilfe*" and especially pp. 65, 76, and 113-15).

396 Cat. nos. 545-68 and 573-614. To this may be added four sarcophagi with cupids as Dionysian *thiasoi* (cat. nos. 569-572). The focus here is on sarcophagi with mythological portrait figures. It should be noted that references to the mythological sphere are made on many sarcophagi with other themes; for example, one or more mythological figures may be inserted into an otherwise non-mythological scene (an example is cat. no. 651, where two representations of Narcissus flank a *dextrarum iunctio* scene). Since this chapter was written, a study by Zahra Newby has appeared (2011). Her study looks at mythological sarcophagi with an individualised mythological figure interacting in the scene. She numbers 70 known examples (p. 191), though she only enumerates 64 in her graph (graph 1, p. 192), and an additional two in note 11. The numbers of sarcophagi in each category differ from mine. For example, she has 9 sarcophagi with the representation of Achilles and Penthesilea whereas I only have 4, 14 with Ariadne where I have 12, and 17 examples of Endymion against my 14. These differences are caused by the difficulties involved in identifying a Roman portrait on a weathered or restored surface, as well as the boundaries between idealised and portrait features, and because she includes local workshops, whereas I am working only with those made in Rome. For example, a Campanian workshop that had been identified as having produced a number of Achilles and Penthesilea sarcophagi was included by Newby (*ASR* XII, 1, cat. 137, 138, 140, and 141); in contrast, I have considered them to be local imitations of the main production. I am grateful to Zahra Newby for sharing her data with me.

397 Koch & Sichtermann 1982. For an overview of the popularity of myths on Roman sarcophagi, see Zanker 2005. The article is based on statistical evidence and Zanker shows how the tendencies evinced by the choice of motifs show a transition from linking death and sorrow toward a more positive view of death. His statistical analysis is based not only on narrative mythological scenes, but also on scenes with seasonal personifications, bucolic settings, motifs of learnedness, and cupids. He makes a connection between the decreased popularity of myths in favour of more 'neutral' motifs (for example bucolic, learned, and seasonal figures) and the coming of Christianity.

catalogue).[398] Several of the myths represented on sarcophagi are only known in a small number of examples, whereas other myths, such as the sleeping Ariadne and Endymion, were much more popular. This differentiated mythological vocabulary is explained by Ewald by the fact that it allowed for distinction and exclusivity in a culture in which a sarcophagus burial was accorded to all social classes that could afford it.[399] In the following I will go deeper into the interpretation of some myths than others, but my overall purpose is to look at what the juxtaposition of individual actors and mythological narratives is able to express about the people they commemorated in terms of identity, social roles, and bereavement.

In general, mythological scenes on sarcophagi, both with and without a portrait figure, are formulaic. Often a myth is represented by the same single scene on several coffins, which includes the same selection of figures and the same composition. This repetition of scenes makes the myths recognisable for the viewer and ensures that they are not misinterpreted. Furthermore, standardisation gives us a hint as to which aspect of the myth the patron found most important, and it helps us to identify the emblematic virtues and moral standards the patron wanted to convey. The formulaic tendency is also repeated in the selection of figures that could be given portrait features. When a specific myth was chosen for commemoration, it is always the same character that is given a portrait. This is due to the fact that only some of the figures possessed the appropriate virtues to commemorate a deceased person or a patron. While some motifs were found suitable for commemoration and repeated again and again, others disappeared from the workshop's repertoire as the production of sarcophagi developed. Among these disappearances were the motifs of despair found on second century sarcophagi such as the representation of the rape of Niobe's children. Such motifs do not appear in the figural repertoire of the third century, when scenes implying an optimistic view of life and death became more popular; we seem to find a wide variety of ways of coping with death and afterlife expectations on the sarcophagi produced in this later period.

The level of knowledge required to read the myths, and the question of whether the mythological scenes were familiar to the viewer, have been much discussed.[400] Cumont supposed that both the patron and the intended viewer of mythological scenes possessed a high level of education in philosophy and astrology.[401] The need for such a high level of knowledge has, however, been questioned, and it is now generally accepted that the myth only needed to be recognisable in general terms.[402] When recognised as a particular representation, the myth could be interpreted individually according to both context and the personality of the viewer.[403]

One of the first examples of a mythological figure with portrait features portrays a middle-aged Roman woman as Ceres in her wagon.[404] The goddess is riding in a wagon in search of her lost daughter Proserpina (cat. no. 620). The myth is probably used as an allegory of the situation at the tomb as experienced by a mother who has lost a child.[405] In this scene Ceres is a figure of despair and grief, as Proserpina has been abducted by

398 I have chosen to include the small group with the deceased represented as drunken cupids together with mythological figures in the catalogue, because these cupids belong to the Dionysian sphere (cat. nos. 569-71). I have, however, studied them together with children's sarcophagi; see chapter 4.

399 Ewald 2004, 236

400 On myth and society and the familiarity of myths, see Cameron 2004, chapter 9.

401 Cumont 1942.

402 Zanker & Ewald 2004, especially 42-3.

403 Zanker & Ewald 2004. In an article Elsner (2000) uses Philostratus' *Imagines* to suggest how works of art should be read. He makes a comparison between the text and mosaics and sarcophagi with seasonal representations to illustrate the different ways in which the viewer could interpret the images. Koortbojian also concludes that the same mythological scene could be interpreted differently with regard to life, death, and any existence beyond them (Koortbojian 1996, 98-9).

404 The fragment is dated to 140-150 based on the similarity of the hairstyle to that of Faustina (Zanker and Ewald 2004, 94).

405 With reference to Burke (1992, 197), Smith (2008, 123) notes that "The modern concept of allegory sits a little uneasily with an ancient society that believed in classical goods and worshiped them." Despite this observation, I find that allegory is still a useful term when working with images from a funerary context, since it elucidates the capacity of mythological figures to make people reflect upon moral standards and lived situations related to both life and death.

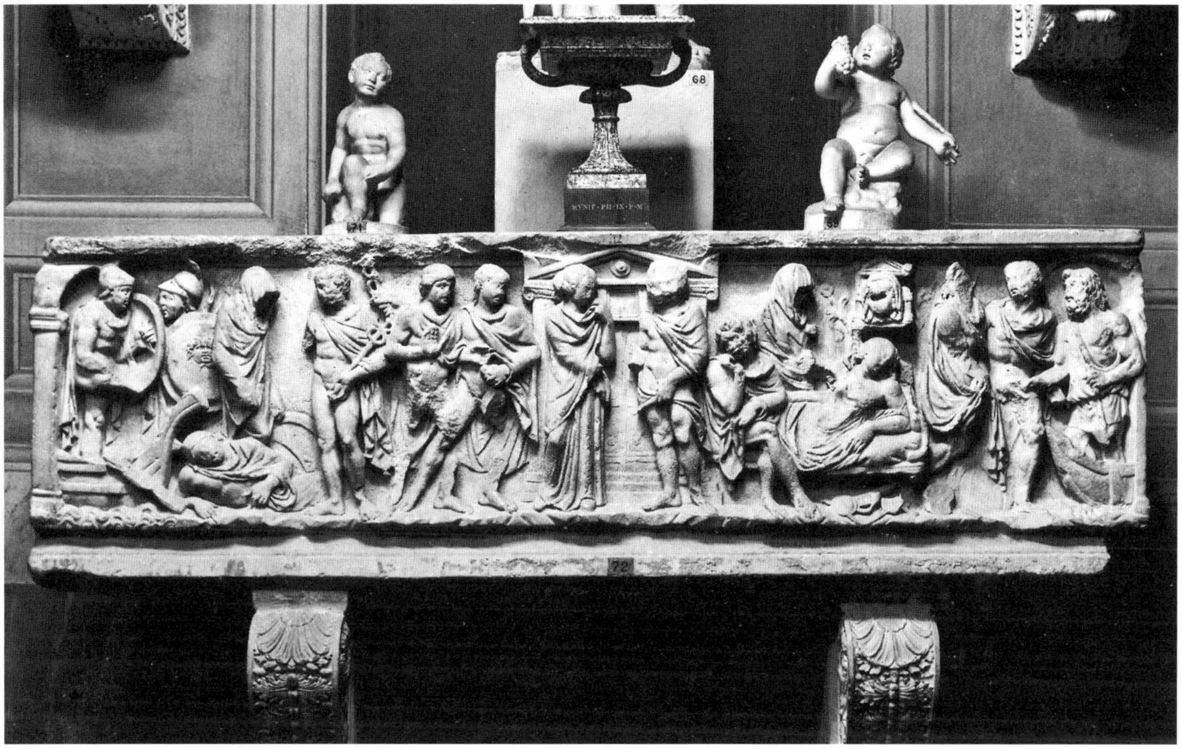

Laodamia and Protesilaus sarcophagus (cat. no. 595). Rome, Musei Vaticani, Galleria dei Candelabri, inv. 2465. Photo: D-DAI-ROM-72.612 (Singer). **Fig. 49**

the ruler of the Underworld, Pluto; the myth consequently constitutes a suitable parallel for experience of the loss of a child. Despite her desperate circumstances, the mother is represented as a beautiful goddess with a naked shoulder and a billowing veil. Ceres is an appropriate role model for a Roman *matrona*: she is associated with fertility and, in this myth, motherly love and concern.[406] In this early example of mythological self-representation the different levels of interpretation here suggested for sarcophagi were already defined and in use: that is, the scene is an expression of an individual's grief and search for consolation, as well as constituting an idealised self-representation through a role model.

Another early representation of portrait figures in a mythological narrative is found on a relief on which a man and a woman take the roles of a marital couple in the myth of Laodamia and Protesilaus (**Fig. 49**; cat. no. 595).[407] Here it is the composition that endows the patrons with the appropriate virtues. The relief shows af mythological narrative consisting of four scenes divided into two halves by the scene with the couple, who both have a blank portrait. The woman, closely draped with a himation, stands together with a naked man with a cloak, in a composition that is reminiscent Roman marriage scenes showing the joining of hands, thus connoting the highly valued family virtues. Behind them is a door framed by columns and a pediment that, judging from the *tabula* inserted above the door, is a representation of their own temple tomb.[408] The scenes on each side of the couple constitute the narrative setting for the protagonists, and the virtues of these scenes are transferred to them, an interpretation that is reinforced by the fact that the couple are dressed in

406 Zanker & Ewald 2004, 94.

407 Blome 1978; Zanker & Ewald 2004, 101-02; Newby 2011, 197-99, 375-77.

408 It can also be a visual illustration of the entrance to Hades, but since the tomb is a mediator between the Underworld and the living world the symbolic meaning stays the same; see Zanker & Ewald 2004, 376.

clothing similar to that of Laodamia and Protesilaus.[409] The left scene shows the death of Protesilaus as he first steps off a ship on the shore of Troy. His body lies on the ground and his soul is represented as a wrapped figure, led to Hades by Hermes. The next scene shows Hermes leading him back from Hades. On the right half of the relief, Laodamia is represented on her deathbed, which is the conclusion of the event represented on the central scene on the relief, namely the couple's three-hour long reunion that had been granted them by the gods. When Laodamia loses Protesilaus again her grief is so profound that she kills herself. At her feet sits a grieving Protesilaus and behind her bed her soul is represented as a wrapped figure. An *aedicula* or funerary monument that holds a female veiled portrait is placed on the wall in the background. It is therefore likely that we are dealing with the commemoration of a woman, whose soul we see leaving the body and whose portrait is placed in a niche, similar to the bust niches we know from the tomb of the Haterii.[410] Laodamia is, together with Alcestis, a perfect choice to symbolise the virtues of a faithful and pious Roman wife.[411] The separation caused by death and the despair that follows, so poetically expressed here, brings the interpretation of the relief to an individual level, while the choice of the myth itself alludes to the patron's level of education, and finally the message of the myth is one of despair and lost love. Even though the myth is used to express private feelings, the role models used are customised to suggest socially accepted, and even ideal, roles of both the man and the woman. The short end reliefs emphasise the funerary theme: the left short end shows a veiled female figure (deceased) taking leave, and the right end shows the sufferings endured in Hades by Sisyphus, Ixion, and Tantalus. The choice of the myth seems to be unique; it is not known from other examples.[412]

An oft-cited sarcophagus dated from around 160 uses a myth to illustrate both the situation of bereavement and the deceased's virtues.[413] The coffin in question is the elaborate Alcestis sarcophagus in the Vatican (**Fig. 11**; cat. no. 552).[414] The sarcophagus is fascinating for several reasons, firstly because the two deceased persons, Junius Euhodus and Metillia Acte, who both are mentioned in the inscription, have had their portraits carved on the figures of Admetus and Alcestis.[415] The focus of the relief is the narrative, and three scenes from the myth are depicted: the prophecy of Admetus' early death, Alcestis' death and the family's bereavement, and her return from Hades. The portrait of Metillia is only applied to the central scene, in which Alcestis lays on her deathbed. Euhodus, on the other hand, is represented as Admetus twice. He is depicted in the death scene, parting ways with Alcestis, and he also appears in the return scene, in which he is reunited with Alcestis. A woman, probably Metillia's mother, and a man, probably her father, are the portrait subjects of two figures behind the deathbed. Metillia and Euhodus's children may be represented by the grieving children at Alcestis' side, though they do not have portrait features. The reunion scene to the right of the dying Alcestis looks very much like a traditional *dextrarum iunctio* scene, though in this case it is Hercules who has brought back Alcestis that holds Admetus' hand. Euhodus and Metillia thereby compare their marriage to that of Admetus and Alcestis. Several aspects of their social identity are revealed through the myth. Metillia's virtues are identified through the willingness of Alcestis to sacrifice her own life for her husband. Emphasis is put on their marital bonds as well as on her *pietas*, faith, and devotion: important qualities for a good Roman wife. Euhodus appears on the two scenes as devoted to his wife, but is also commemorated by heroic virtue, as illustrated by his semi-nakedness and his role as a mythological figure and hunter.[416]

From the inscription we know that Metillia was a priestess of the Magna Mater cult in Ostia while her

409 Newby 2011, 197-200.

410 Sinn 1996; Leach 2006.

411 Something that is also recognised in funerary poems; see Zanker & Ewald 2004, 374-75.

412 Except for one without portrait figures in Santa Chiara, Naples (Zanker & Ewald 2004, 101-2, fig. 85).

413 Koch 1993, 50-1.

414 For the dating based on the inscription mentioning the magistrate position the man held, see Robert, *ASR* III 3 (1919) 32; Fittschen 1984, 142.

415 For the sarcophagus, see Wood 1978; Mucznik 1999, 36-8; 1999a; Gessert 2004, 119-22; Newby 2011, 194-96. For Alcestis representations in Roman art, see Mucznik 1999. The portrait of the woman is dated to around 140, the man to the reign of Antoninus Pius, and the inscription to 160.

416 Wood 1978.

husband, who commissioned the sarcophagus, served as magistrate of the guilds of carpenters in the 21st *lustrum*.[417] The information that he came from the tribe of Palatina gives us an idea of the social status of the deceased. The family was not part of the aristocracy, but they were well-to-do people with some significance in the public life of Rome's harbour city, Ostia. We know from the portraits, which show some signs of age, that they were middle-aged at the time of their death. We also know that they were married and, from the children placed by the deathbed, that they probably had children themselves. From the myth's focus on the return of Alcestis, we can deduce that they probably hoped for a reunion after death, which makes sense when we consider her role as priestess in the cult of Magna Mater.[418] Euhodus and Metillia appear to have been individuals with strong religious and moral faith, and the sarcophagus was probably ordered especially to accommodate their needs. This is is interesting because religious manifestations are rarely explicit on sarcophagi. In the Roman production of sarcophagi, iconography seldom shows which cult or religious belief the deceased aspired to, which contrasts with its emergence as a focal point for the early fourth-century production of Christian sarcophagi.[419]

There are not many sarcophagi telling the story of Alcestis, and all of them can be dated to the early part of the third century.[420] The individual choice of decoration for this sarcophagus is also confirmed by the fact that only one further example of portrait features given to the image of Alcestis is known (cat. no. 551). It is a rather small fragment of a frontal relief showing a deathbed scene, and its identification as a representation of Alcestis is uncertain.

Fittschen notes that the dating of the portrait of Metillia, whose hairstyle is similar to that of the early Antonine period, diverges by some 20 years from the dating of the relief based on the inscription, but the portrait does seem to have been carved on the sarcophagus at the same time as the rest of the relief.[421] It has therefore been proposed that Metillia was initially buried in another tomb and then later commemorated together with her husband through the images on the sarcophagus, even if her remains were not actually transferred to the new tomb. Another possibility is that she simply continued to wear an old-fashioned hairstyle until her death.[422] However, like the portrait figures on sarcophagi, the hairstyle may symbolise the person's qualities instead of providing a life-like representation of the deceased. As such, the choice of the Antonine hairstyle was perhaps meant to be suggestive of virtues connected with the female ideal of the period.

Between 220 and 260 a certain density of individualised mythological figures can be postulated; the mythological portrait figure reached the peak of production at this time. In this period, the popular representations of the sleeping figures begin to appear. Both in quantity and variety they outnumber all other narrative mythological reliefs. Endymion is the most popular motif in the group of sleeping figures (cat. nos. 573-86).[423] The total number of sarcophagi with depictions of Endymion is around 120, but only a small proportion of them shows a portrait figure.[424] The production of 14 examples with portraits can be ascribed with certainty to workshops in Rome. Generally Endymion is shown in the scene in which Selene comes to him while he is sleeping, but in two instances

417 On her role as a Magna Mater priestess, see Mucznik 1999a.

418 Wood 1978, 503; Mucznik 1999, 75-6.

419 There are, however, some rare examples of secondary incisions that could be religious manifestations. The commander on cat. no. 625 had a *sphragis* incised on his forehead. This cross might be a religious symbol, but when and why it was made are questions that have been much discussed. A bust of a man, evidently the same man, has a similar cross on his forehead, which points to the fact that the crosses were probably made around the period of production. The interpretation of the cross is much discussed. It has been thought of as a military sign, and connected to the cult of Mithras, as well as with other cults, including Christianity. Dölger suggested that both the +- and X-shaped crosses in early Christian times were connected with the name of Christ (Heintze 1957; Rodenwaldt 1936; Dölger 1930; Künzl 2010, 69-72). For cross-markings on bodies and heads in Roman sculpture, see Kristensen 2012.

420 Blome 1978, 435-45; Grassinger, *ASR* XII 1 (1999) cat. 76.

421 Fittschen 1984, 141-43.

422 Newby 2011, 195.

423 For the use of the figure of Endymion in Roman houses and his transformation into representations of Jonah, see Balch 2008.

424 Robert, *ASR* III 3 (1919).

he is shown alone (cat. nos. 576 and 582; on cat. nos. 573 and 575 only Selene has portrait features, and on cat. no. 585 the head of Endymion is not preserved). Ariadne is another sleeping figure. I have been able to identify 12 Ariadne sarcophagi on which she has been given portrait features (cat. nos. 555-66), but whilst Endymion sarcophagi were often used to commemorate a couple, the Ariadne motif was found most appropriate for single commemorations.[425] Only one sarcophagus depicts Ariadne with Dionysus, and it also differs from all the others in that it does not show the sleeping scene (cat. no. 564).

The last myth with a sleeping figure that should be mentioned is an indigenous Roman myth whose representative form has been customised by the traditional Roman language of representing myths. It is the tale of Mars and Rhea Silvia, the virgin's encounter with the warrior god. Only three individualised examples are known, and they can all be dated between 210 and 250 (cat. nos. 598-600).[426] The popularity of the sleeping figure seems to last until around 270,[427] but the precise dates are much debated.[428]

Most of the myths represented on sarcophagi are Greek in origin, but they have undergone what some have termed a process of "Romanisation".[429] In the adaption of Greek myths to a Roman funerary context, portrait heads help to reinforce the Roman values intended by the patron by putting emphasis on a specific motif; mythological figures on Attic sarcophagi were never given portrait features. This Romanisation is especially evident in the development of both the style of the representation and the choice of scenes.[430] According to Blome, the development takes place from the second-century classicistic style to the late third century, more typically Roman style. In this period iconography turns towards a "native" language, and the emphasis lies on ideal Roman virtues. However, I am not sympathetic to the idea that the early sarcophagi were less "Roman" in their expression than the later third-century sarcophagi. Roman sarcophagi should from the beginning be interpreted in relation to Roman culture and ideals, and it is more likely that the mentality and the funerary traditions changed during the third century in a way that facilitated new visual expressions, than such developments in expression were due to a process of Romanisation.[431]

Achilles and Penthesilea and hunters such as Meleager and Hippolytus are mythological figures that are individualised in some numbers, but in relation to the quantity of sarcophagi representing the same myths, the individualised examples are more the exception than the rule.[432] By the end of the third century, mythological figures have decreased in popularity, but they continue for as long as pagan sarcophagi were made with portraits of patrons. A Roman woman appears as Venus on a column sarcophagus from the end of the fourth century (cat. no. 614), and Meleager is found on a narrative sarcophagus from around 300 (cat. no. 601).

To examine one of the myths that were repeatedly individualised in the period in which mythological allegories first started to gain popularity, let us return to Ceres and the story of her lost daughter Proserpina. We shall look at the abduction and how the individualised image of Proserpina was used to take consolation in sorrow.[433] More than 90 representations of the abduction of Proserpina are known, but only five sarcophagi show the patron represented as Proserpina. On one sarcophagus, Pluto is given individual features as well (cat. no. 610). This may illustrate a case in which a male family member died first. Later a female portrait could be added to Proserpina, but in the meantime the

425 Mucznik 2000; Matz, *ASR* IV 3 (1969) 360-404.

426 Koch & Sichtermann 1982, 184-85.

427 See, for example, cat. nos. 557, 574-75, 578, and 584.

428 For interpretations of the sleeping figures, see chapter 1.

429 Blome 1992 (see also Blome 1977). The story of Mars and Rhea Silvia is the only original Roman myth, but it is represented in much the same manner as the 'adopted' myth of Endymion and Selene. For an interpretative approach to Greek myths on Roman sarcophagi, see Fittschen 1992a.

430 On the concept of visual narrative in mythological sarcophagi, see Brilliant 1984, 124-65.

431 For the uses of Greek myth in Roman society, see Goldfarb 1994, and on sarcophagi, see among others Sichtermann & Koch 1975; Koortbojian 1995; Zanker 2000; Zanker & Ewald 2004.

432 For Achilles and Amazons, see Sichtermann, *ASR* XII 2 (1992); for Meleager sarcophagi, see Koch, *ASR* XII 6 (1975); for Hippolytus, see Koch & Sichtermann 1982, 150-53.

433 For interpretations of the myth, see Blome 1978; Lindner 1984.

individualised Pluto and the faceless Proserpina were symbols of the situation at the tomb. When visiting the tomb, the patron, probably the wife, saw an image of her husband and his fate through an allegory of the Underworld. In the Underworld, the husband, personified as Pluto, was ready to be reunited with her, since he was a personification of the death that one day would come to her as well. A similar interpretation has been suggested for a Hylas sarcophagus (**Fig.** 79; cat. no. 594, see chapter 3).[434]

The other four individualised Proserpina sarcophagi are of a similar compositional type, and the period of production spans from the early years – that is, 150 – to around 240 (cat. nos. 607-11).[435] They show a lively composition packed with figures. On the left half of the reliefs, Proserpina is surprised by Pluto while picking flowers, and on the right half, Pluto takes her away in his wagon.[436] Interpretations of Proserpina's abduction are manifold. However, one way of reading Proserpina's abduction is as an allegory of an untimely death that took a daughter or wife away from her family. The endless search for Proserpina by her mother is, in such a reading, an analogy of the survivors' grief for a lost relative.[437] This interpretation is supported by the inscription *abreptio Vibies et discensio*, which appears with a wall painting showing the same motif from a mausoleum in the Catacombs of Praetextatus.[438] The inscription is from the Christian period, but it was not unusual at this time to use pagan allegories to show, for example, grief in Christian contexts. Such influence was possible because the pagan iconographic language was part of the early cultural background of the Christians.[439] The representation of Hermes leading the deceased soul to Hades on the right short end of the coffin in the Musei Capitolini furthermore shows that the abduction motif is about the descent to the Underworld (**Fig.** 50; cat. no. 608). The myth thereby analogises the situation of death and bereavement in both Christian and pagan funerary contexts.

The abduction motifs are also interpreted in terms of an allegory of *apotheosis*, but a *port-mortem* deification of individuals is only one way of reading the motif.[440] If we look beyond *apotheosis* as a possible explanation for the individualisation of gods and heroes on Roman sarcophagi, the value of the motifs is increased significantly. The scenes show allegories of human feelings, including the emotions that must have been part of the act of commemoration.[441] Some viewers could have seen Proserpina's annual return to earth as a symbol of rebirth or as an allegory of the happiness that comes with the release of death, whereas yet others might use the metaphoric narrative of death for contemplation at the tomb to cope with the feelings involved. Proserpina's abduction also showed that death was not to be feared and that it is the bereaved, and not the deceased, who experiences death as a terrible thing. This is especially prominent on the piece from Musei Capitolini, on which Proserpina received Pluto without fear and follows him willingly (**Fig.** 50; cat. no. 608).[442] In contrast to the relief showing a man represented as Pluto, on this coffin Proserpina is individualised as she is standing in the wagon. She is as beautiful as Venus in her nakedness, and makes no objection to Pluto's advance. Another earlier example does not use either of the two previously mentioned

434 For Hylas, see Zanker & Ewald 2004, 96-8.

435 This type is also the most frequently used. Koch & Sichtermann 1982, 175-80; Zanker & Ewald 2004, 91-4; Blome, 1978, 449-57.

436 Robert, *ASR* III 3 (1919) 450-95.

437 Another abduction myth is the tale of Hylas (cat. no. 594). For myths as expressions of grief and sorrow or as a reaction against a relentless fate, see Fittschen 1992a.

438 Wrede 1981, 151; Lindner 1984, nr. 31; Der Neue Pauly, Proserpina. Gessert (2004, 235) interprets Vibia as a worshipper of Sabazios, and uses the inscription to deduce the same meaning as is suggested here.

439 For an approach to the assimilation process that took place in the workshops when pagan motifs were used for Christians, see Elsner 1995.

440 For an historical introduction to apotheosis and "Privatdeifikationen" in the study of Roman art, see Wrede 1981, 1-5. For a Dionysian motif as an expression of *apotheosis*, see Matz 1958, 127, 130, 142. For images on sarcophagi as expressions of *apotheosis*, see Wrede 1981, 139-57; Andreae 1963 and especially 131-62 and note 14 with further literature; Dimas 1998, 48-52 (on children's sarcophagi).

441 For the scene as an image of consolation, see Zanker 1999, 27; Ewald 2005, 64, particularly p. 64. For the scene as an expression of the relationship between life and death and the emotions evoked by the loss of a person, see Zanker & Ewald 2004, 90-4, 370-73.

442 Newby 2011, 223.

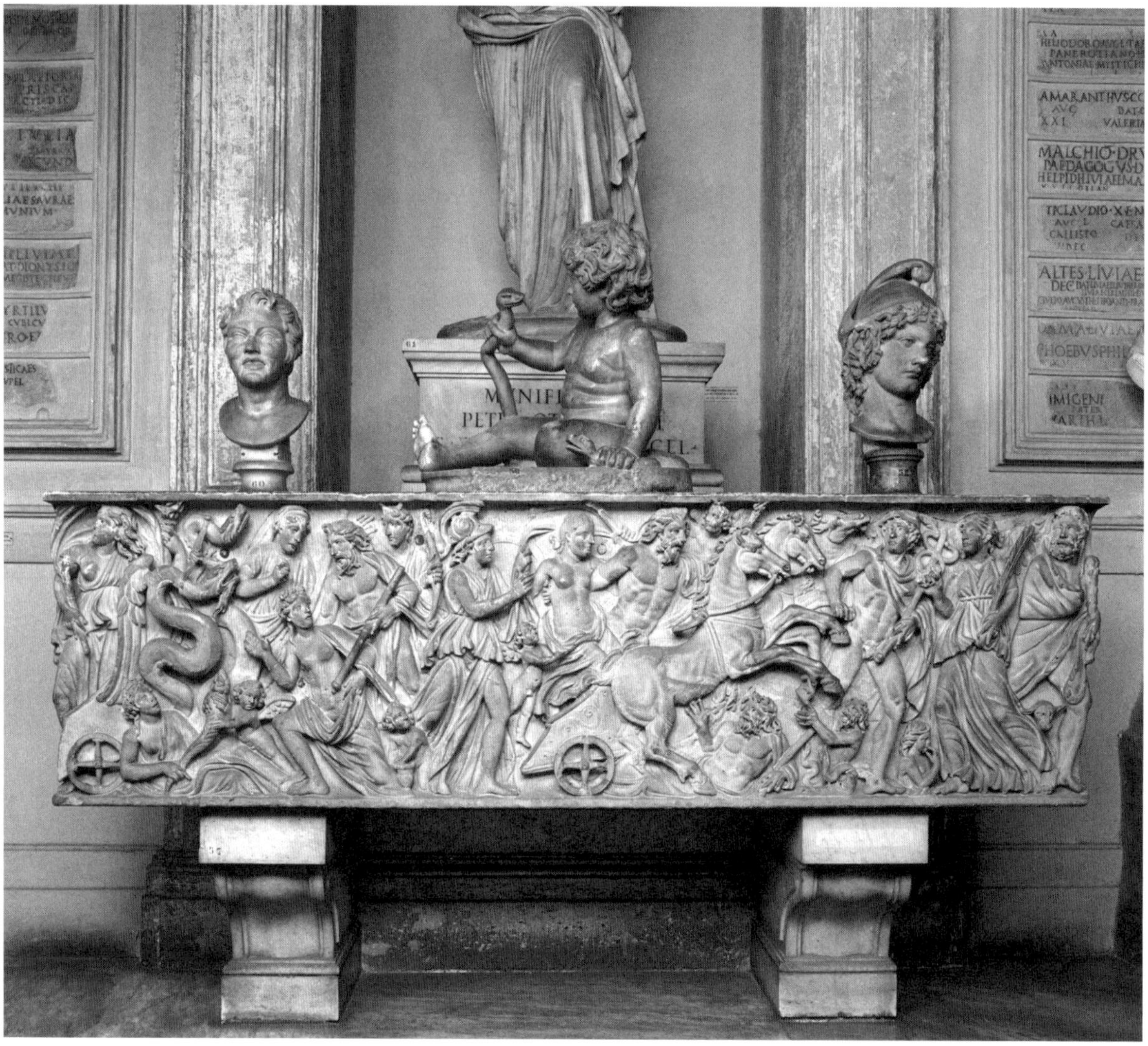

Fig. 50 *Proserpina sarcophagus. The deceased is represented as the young maid Proserpina, who was abducted by Pluto (cat. no. 608). Rome, Musei Capitolini, galleria 56, inv. 249. Photo: D-DAI-ROM-72.688 (Singer).*

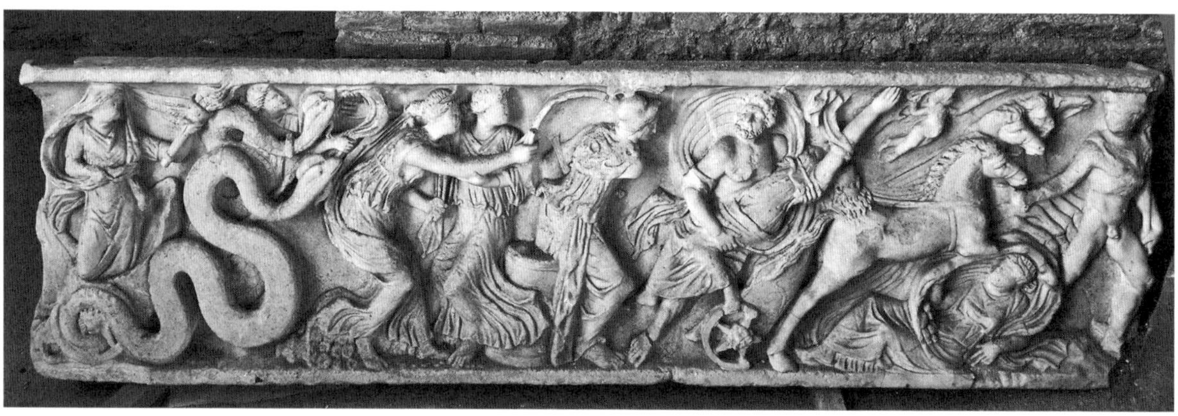

Fig. 51 *Proserpina sarcophagus. The deceased is represented as the queen of the Underworld in a snake-drawn wagon (cat. no. 609) Rome, Museo Nazionale Romano, inv. 255953. Photo: Soprintendenza Speciale per i Beni Archeologici di Roma.*

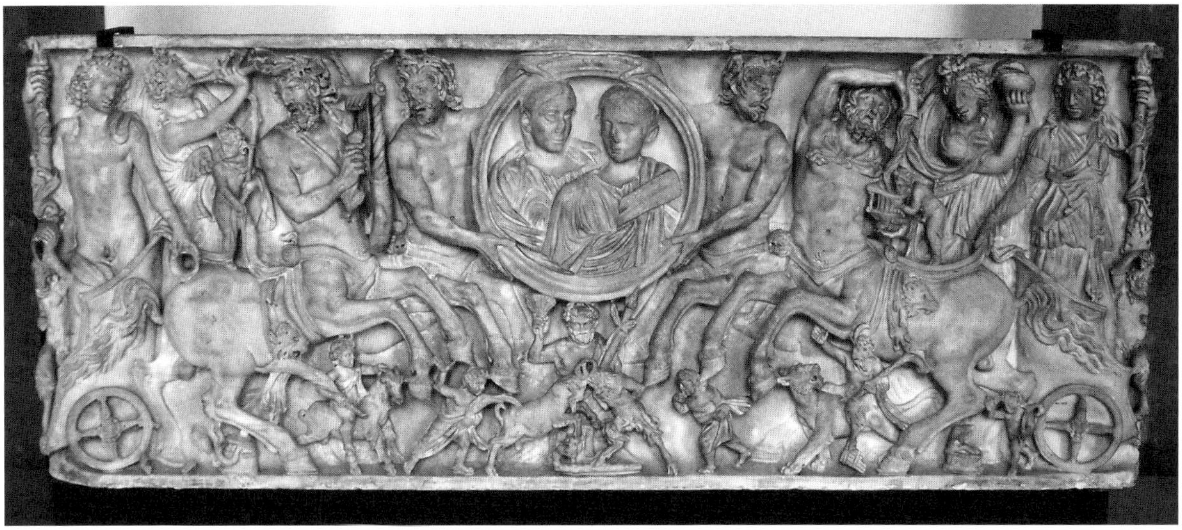

Sarcophagus showing a clipeus *carried along in a Dionysian procession (cat. no. 461). Paris, Musée du Louvre, inv. F 243. Photo: Author.* **Fig. 52**

scenes of flower picking or riding in Pluto's wagon to individualise Proserpina (**Fig. 51**; cat. no. 609). On this sarcophagus the individualised figure is represented in the snake-drawn wagon of Proserpina, in a triumphal gesture. The two scenes of abduction and Ceres' despair are shown to the right of her, but these figures have not been individualised. These ways in which the portraits are used to emphasise different interpretations of the same myth are examples of how myths could be used individually to reflect different situations. The portrait figure helps us to understand the intended meaning. It is impossible to say that one or another interpretation of a myth was effective in comforting the bereaved in their grief. As a result of the contemplative function of sarcophagus decoration, the viewer could use the myth in the way or ways that gave him/her the most consolation.[443] It was this flexibility that made myths so popular in the funerary context.

When the bereaved used sleep as an image of contemplation, depicting Mars as he comes to the mortal Rhea Silvia in her sleep, it could be done in an effort to establish an inner dialogue with the deceased (see, for example, the Palazzo Mattei relief, **Fig. 22**; cat. no. 600). In the case where the sleep of mortal mythological figures can symbolises death, the sleeping figure can be seen as placed in a joyous situation.[444] But, the scene of Mars and Rhea Silvia is also an image of the process of dealing with grief, instead of just a symbol of death. The image of an arriving divinity that took care of the deceased brought hope to the relatives since it suggested an idyllic setting where the dead were in good hands.[445] In the myth of Rhea Silvia we find both immortal and mortal characters, and as such the patron can use the mortals and their connection to the living world to speak about the universal order. Through personifications placed around the central couple of Mars and Rhea Silvia, the cosmos is represented: Tellus and Oceanus are the earth and the ocean, omnipresent divinity is shown by the placement of Vulcan and Venus in the right corner, Sol drives his wagon across the celestial concave, and Horus symbolises the seasons. In front of Horus, wrongly restored with a male head, a naked female figure with a torch personifies a wind god. Two goats in the upper right end establish the rural setting of the scene.

Despite the fact that myths are often used to express despair, they can also imply a positive attitude

443 Zanker 2000, 28.

444 See the section on afterlife, chapter 1. For the parallel between sleep and death, see Mucznik 2000, 134.

445 For the myth as a framework for human existence, see Fittschen 1992a.

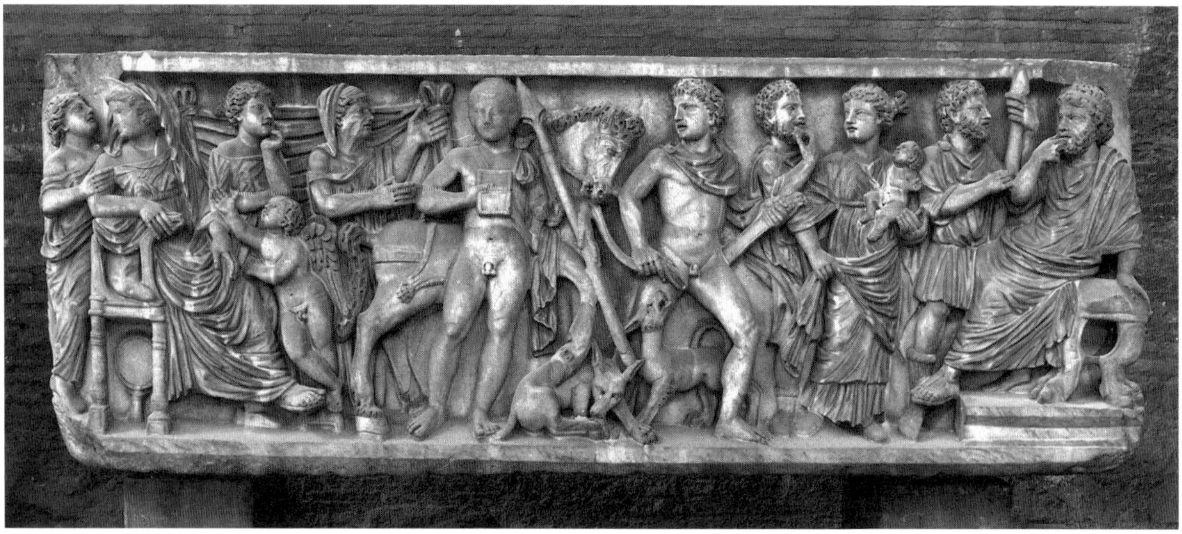

Fig. 53 *Hippolytus sarcophagus (cat. no. 592). Rome, Museo Nazionale Romano, inv. 112444. Photo: Mal 1614_04_17547.*

towards death. An optimistic view of death is illustrated on a range of sarcophagi, one being the Dionysian sarcophagus in the Louvre (**Fig. 52**; cat. no. 461). It shows a *clipeus* with a merry Dionysian procession and two centaurs holding a *clipeus* with a portrait bust of a woman and a boy.[446] The scenes have been interpreted as expressions of *Lebensfreud* and *Glücksvisionen*, because Dionysian motifs offer, together with scenes of sea monsters and bucolic motifs, an optimistic vision of the afterlife.[447] In their capacity to reflect on situations and states of mind, these motifs engage with human life.[448] Following that thought, it has been suggested that the use of myths in sepulchral contexts had more to do with life than death.[449] This is in some respects true since sarcophagi, as the focus of a family's commemoration of their deceased, were meant for the dead but had agency in the world of the living.

Accepting the allegorical method of reading myths in terms of lived situations and human feelings means that emotions such as hope, grief, love, and loss, become central to their interpretation. When we focus on emotions instead of on the details of the mythological narrative, it becomes easier to explain scenes such as those of Achilles and Penthesilea on sarcophagi (cat. nos. 545-49).[450] Patrons commissioning such imagery could hardly have wanted to pursue direct parallels to the actual deeds of Achilles.[451] If the individualised figures of Achilles and Penthesilea were meant to be read as a married couple, what ideal virtues can be deduced from an image of a husband who kills his own wife? The real issues here are the sudden death of a beloved wife, the survivors' grief, and a message of love.[452] In this kind of reading, it is not presupposed that the viewer was familiar with the myths in every detail. Actually, it only demands that the viewer could read the iconographic language and thereafter interpret it in the way that she or he found most consolatory. It is likely that sarcophagi with depictions of Achilles and Penthesilea

446 For the use of Dionysian motifs on late Roman mosaics as *exempla* of social and universal rules of morality, see Monteagudo 1999, 54.

447 "the Bacchic mysteries promised a blessed afterlife to those who were initiated," cf. Mucznik 2000, 135.

448 Zanker & Ewald 2004, 116-77.

449 Cameron 2004, 223.

450 As Turcan also says (1992, 1102), the dissociation of myths from their original context (the Greek society) has consequences for their meaning and interpretation. The myths must therefore be reinterpreted according to the Roman funerary context. For *interpretio romana* of Greek myths, see Bremmer & Horsfall 1987.

451 For a description of the scene showing Achilles and Penthesilea, see Grassinger, *ASR* XII 1 (1999) 153-54, and 181-82. For an interpretation, see Grassinger, *ASR* XII 1 (1999) 183-85.

452 Ewald 2003, 571; Zanker & Ewald 2004, 53-4, 286-87; Newby 2011, 213-14.

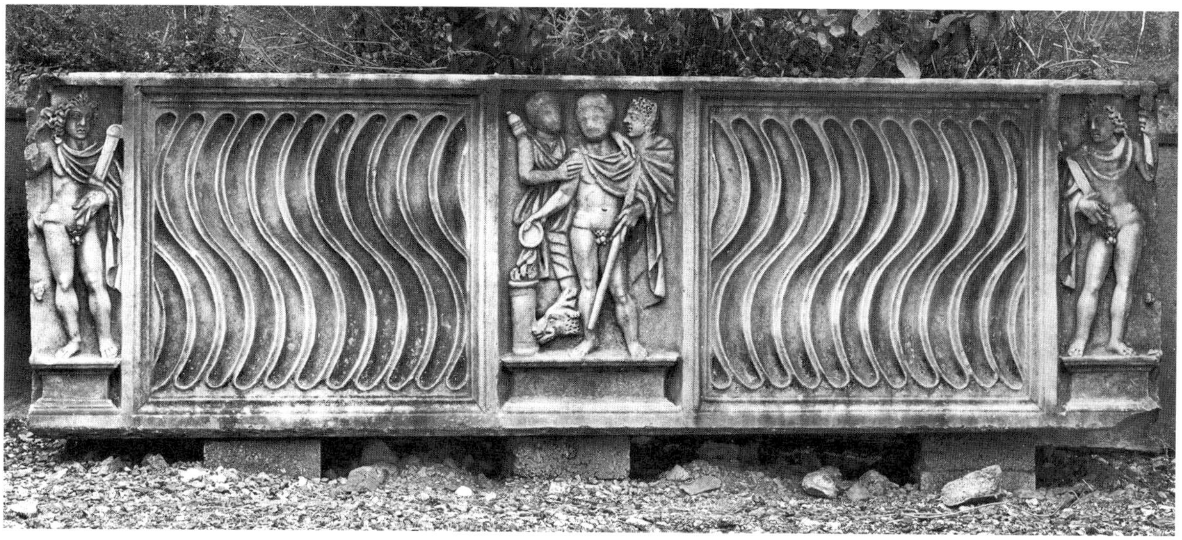

Strigillated sarcophagus with Meleager and Atalante sacrificing; both are carved with blank portraits (cat. no. 604). Wilton House, Wiltshire. Photo: FA 2542-07_23094.220 **Fig. 54**

commemorate the deceased woman only, since she is the one who dies in the scene. In such a scenario, the male portrait is an image of the patron who commissioned the coffin. By portraying both the deceased and the patron, a memory is created that unites both of them in eternal *concordia*, and at the same time gives status to the husband who was still alive.

This focus suggested by the myth of Achilles and Penthesilea required that the learned viewer, who would have been familiar with myths, put aside central aspects of the story. A further example is provided by a Hippolytus sarcophagus (**Fig. 53**; cat. no. 592).[453] In its left-hand scene, Phaidra mourns Hippolytus' rejection of her, and later his death.[454] The central scene shows the heroically naked Hippolytus with a blank portrait, and in the right-hand scene Theseus receives the tragic news of Hippolytus' death and Phaidra's suicide. Again the relief should be seen as suggesting the feelings evoked by a sudden separation caused by death and the subsequent grief of the survivors.[455] The fact that it was Phaidra's love of her stepson that brought about the hero's death cannot have been the primary message of the motif. The learned viewer might have been able to make that connection, but the symbolic value and the allegorical way of reading the motif must have been the main purpose behind the choice of such motifs. The sarcophagi reliefs showing Achilles, Penthesilea, and Hippolytus can thus be seen as examples of myths used to convey states of mind and help the mourners through their grief.[456]

Though it was not necessary for the viewer to have an exhaustive knowledge of myths, there must have been a shared cultural conception of the virtues that could be conveyed through them. This would have been necessary in order for myths to become *exempla* for people in situations in daily life.[457] Myths constitute a valid framework for approaching questions related to life and death; in this narrative the protagonist becomes a symbol of social and moral rules, through which the individualised figure acquires its legitimacy as a role model.[458] Meleager is one such

453 On this myth on sarcophagi, see Robert, *ASR* III 2 (1904); Lawrence 1976; Lewerentz 1995; Zanker 1999.

454 For representations of Phaidra on sarcophagi, see Mucznik 1999, 89-9.

455 Zanker 1999.

456 As Veyne states: "It matters little which myth is represented; the point is that the Romans fled death through myths." (1987, 233).

457 Griffin 1986, 17; Gessert 2004, 237.

458 For the concept of role models in Roman art, see the contributions in Bell & Hansen 2008. In Bell 2008 "role model" means *exempla* or the ideal way of being, which in art is

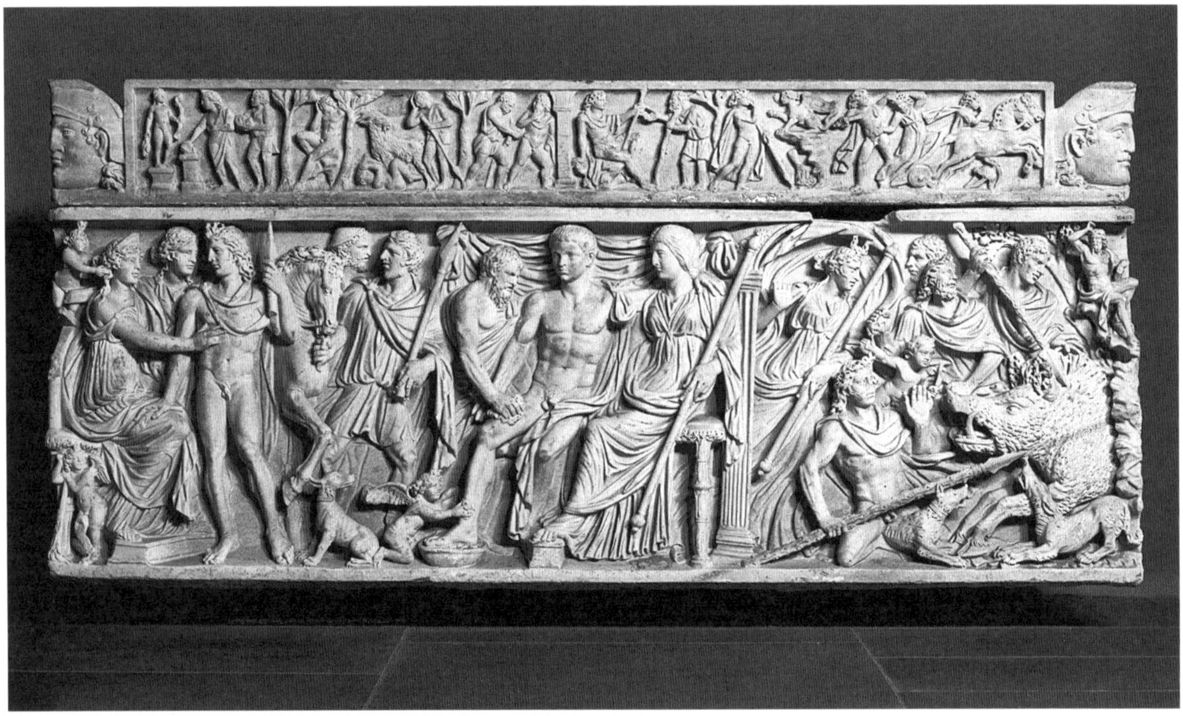

Fig. 55 *Adonis and Venus sarcophagus (cat. no. 550). Rome, Musei Vaticani, Museo Gregoriano Profano, inv. 10409. Photo: D-DAI-ROM-71.1762 (Singer).*

ideal figure.[459] He is depicted either heroically naked (cat. nos. 601-4; **Fig. 54**) or as a Roman hunter (cat. no. 605).[460] The tale of Meleager is about a hero who despite his emblematic qualities has a character flawed by human temper, pride, and fury; his story makes it clear that there were limits to both what he could do, and what morally he was allowed to do. For example, when he goes hunting, he takes Atalante with him. She wounds the boar and therefore makes it possible for Meleager to kill it. This means that his deed is not his own; an argument followed because Meleager wanted Atalante to have the hide, as a consequence of which he kills two of his relatives. This obviously exceeds the limits of what is morally acceptable, and he is killed when the branch that symbolises his life is deliberately burnt in order to bring a halt to his disgrace. Still, in the context of sarcophagi, he is an ideal figure that people wanted to identify themselves with, an *exemplum*. His character contains both good and bad elements. Male virtues have been read into his heroic figure, but at the same time he is not infallible: he is subject to cultural rules, and his story is therefore a good parallel for human situations.

Representations of myths and human life should not be considered separately, a point that is illustrated by a biographical sarcophagus today in Berlin (cat. no. 648; **Fig. 26**).[461] We saw that the iconographic language of this sarcophagus was equivocal, because it spoke in terms of both 'real' human life and mythology.[462] In its use of the myth of Adonis, Adonis becomes an allegory of the virtue possessed by the deceased man, and at the same time he illustrates the vulnerability of life.[463] On another Adonis sarcophagus there are no representations

imitated by people. For role models and self-representation on Roman sarcophagi as expressions of both social and familial values, see Zanker & Ewald 2004, 179-201.

459 For an interesting interpretation of the myth, see D'Ambra 1988.

460 Koch & Sichtermann 1982, 112-14; Sichtermann, *ASR* XII 6 (1992) 161-66.

461 For this line of interpretation, see note 12.

462 For an discussion of this sarcophagus, see p. 65.

463 Cumont 1959; Brilliant 1992, 1032.

of *vita humana* (**Fig. 55**; cat. no. 550);[464] instead the myth has itself become a representation of the deceased's situation through the portraits given to the protagonists, Adonis and Venus. They sit on a rock, and together they illustrate the mutual affection of the couple. The myth is used to parallel the circumstances of the couple they represent, by showing the untimely death that has torn them apart. The death is shown in the scene of Adonis' hunt behind them, while grief is illustrated by the farewell scene on the left end of the relief.[465]

In conclusion, myths illustrate human situations, and their ability to bridge the gaps between the terrestrial and celestial, sleep and waking, and not least, humanity and divinity, made them perfect vehicles for the idealisation of the deceased.[466] As the scenes are also allegories for emotions provoked by the loss of a relative or loved one, they are used in the search for a meaning in life and death. They tell of the cosmos and the order of the world; they elucidate moral and social rules; and the portrait figures help the viewer to focus on the important aspect of the myth.

Hunt Themes

Lion hunters individualised through the application of a portrait, interacting in non-mythological hunting scenes, were one of the popular role models for men.[467] Non-mythological hunt scenes were not used on sarcophagi before the Severan period, and the lion hunter was therefore a new and characteristic figure in the third century.[468] Hunt scenes are based on a formulaic iconographic scheme; as a general rule, the possibilities for variation were limited, but if one looks at them in detail, it becomes evident that no two scenes were carved identically.[469] Hunt sarcophagi have been extensively studied in connection to both chronology and their iconographic scheme.[470] When studied as a group within the *ASR* corpus, they are treated under the broad term *Vita privata* or *Vita romana*. Even though the hunting scenes were never representations of real hunts, their non-mythological character and the Roman style of the hunter's dress have caused the scenes to be considered as allegories of private experiences.[471]

Traditionally, hunt sarcophagi are split into four groups according to the kind of hunt they depict: a lion hunt scene, boar hunt scenes, and scenes of battue with a net are present on a number of sarcophagi, whilst a small group do not conform to any of these categories.[472] The earliest examples all show lion hunts, and this type continues throughout the third century, but it is characteristic of the later third-century hunt scenes that a lioness appears as one of the victims of the hunters. Scenes of boar hunts and battue with a net belong generally to the later part of the third century as well.[473] These hunt scenes are inspired by the representation of hunts on mythological sarcophagi, such as those showing scenes from the lives of Hippolytus, Meleager, and Adonis, and some of the characters from these scenes were transferred into the third-century hunt sarcophagi.[474] Examples are the heroic, naked men with a horse often seen at each end of the frontal relief, usually interpreted as the Dioscuroi.[475] The representation of Virtus,

464 For interpretations of this sarcophagus, see Brilliant 1992, 1034; Zanker & Ewald 2004, 210-11, 290-92.

465 For an approach to how the myth of Adonis and Aphrodite on Roman sarcophagi can be read, see Koortbojian 1995, 23-62.

466 Brilliant 1992, 1035.

467 Of around 251 sarcophagi with hunting as the main theme on either the frontal relief or the lid, 38 have one or more figures with a portrait head. The numbers derived from an account of hunt sarcophagi from Andreae, *ASR* I 2 (1980) and Blome 1998.

468 The main publications of hunt sarcophagi are: Andreae, *ASR* I 2 (1980); Andreae 1985; Vaccaro Melucco 1963/64.

469 For an account of the canonical lion hunt scheme, see Andreae 1971, 119-20.

470 Most importantly: Rodenwaldt 1936; Vaccaro Melucco 1963/64; Andreae 1971; *ASR* I 2 (1980); Koch & Sichtermann 1982, 92-7.

471 Andreae sees a lion hunt as a symbol of death or the victory over death by the deceased (Andreae 1985, 11-4). As has also been pointed out by Smith, there is no evidence for such an interpretation. He also dismissed Andreae's theory from the same article about a connection between state-reliefs and lion hunt sarcophagi (Smith 1988).

472 Koch & Sichtermann 1982, 93.

473 Andreae, *ASR* I 2 (1980) chapter 4-4.1.5; Rodenwaldt 1921/22.

474 Rodenwaldt 1936, 84; Andreae, *ASR* I 2 (1980) chapter I.1-3; Andreae 1985; 1995, 28; Wrede 1981, 150.

475 The most obvious example here is cat. no. 496. On the Dioscuroi, see Andreae 1977, 121; 1973, 396, Rodenwaldt 1936, 84. See also note 271.

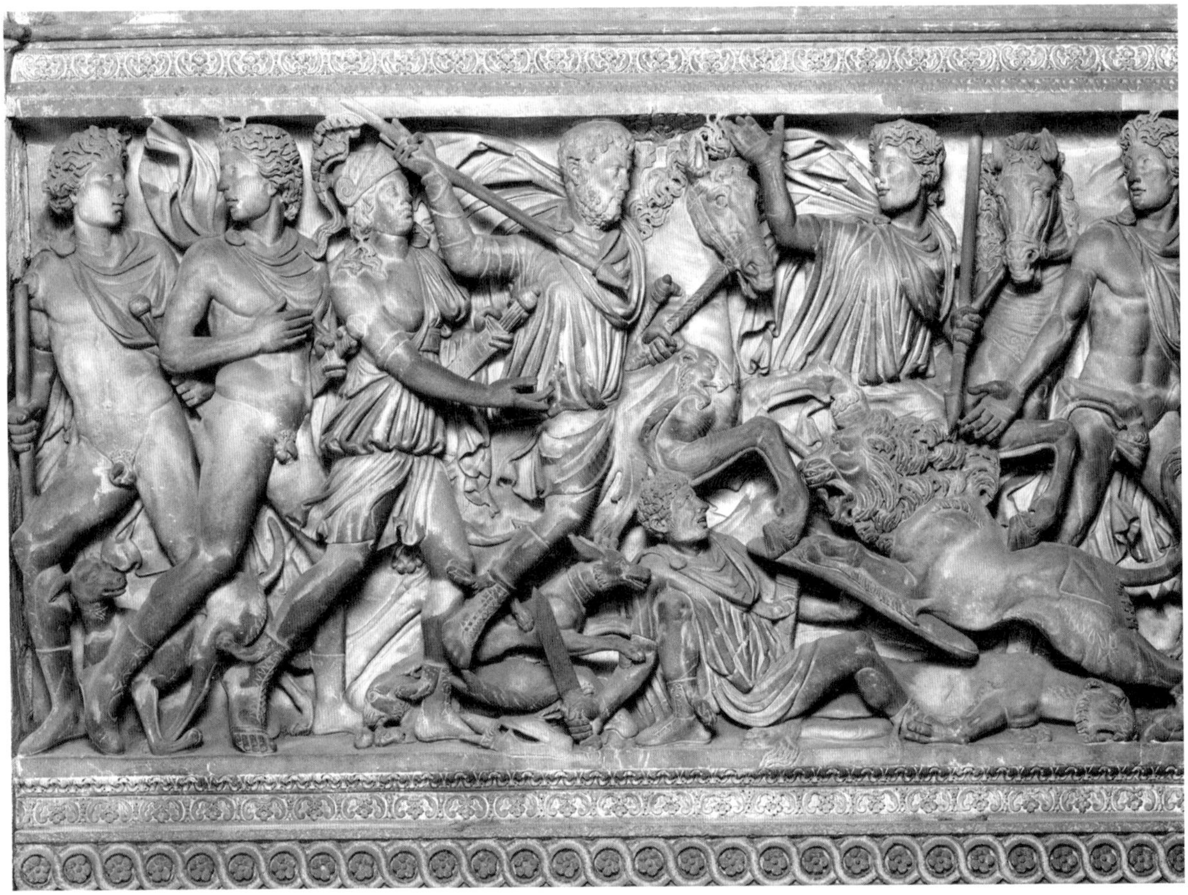

Fig. 56 *Lion hunt sarcophagus. The so-called Palazzo Mattei I (cat. no. 508). Rome, Palazzo Mattei. Photo: D-DAI-ROM-80.934 (Schwanke).*

who accompanies the central hunter, also derives from the mythological hunt scenes.[476]

The Lion Hunter, Virtus, and the Roman Ideal

On hunt sarcophagi with portrait figures the patron is generally represented as the central hunter on horseback, a scheme that can be exemplified by a much restored relief in Palazzo Mattei in Rome (**Fig. 56**; cat. no. 508).[477] He is about to spear a lion or a boar, and on some sarcophagi he anticipates his victory, raising his arm in a triumphal gesture before the animal has fallen.[478] On the earliest lion hunt sarcophagi with two scenes, the right-hand scene shows two figures that have been interpreted as Diana and the huntsman departing before the hunt (see for example **Fig. 57**; cat. no. 479).[479] As a variation of this scene, the

476 Andreae 1971, 121; *ASR* I 2 (1980) 18-22. Koch & Sichtermann 1982, 93. Most recently on the representation of Virtus on sarcophagus reliefs; Hansen 2007.

477 Exceptions are: cat. no. 81 is a lid with a bust, a *sigma-mahl* and a hunting scene; cat. no. 320 is an unusual combination of a *clipeus* with a bust held by two Victoria framed by hunting scenes; and cat. no. 496. On this sarcophagus, the hunter is naked and fights the lion on foot with a stone in his raised hand. He can be sure of his fortune because Virtus stands behind him and supports him. Virtus has a portrait of a woman. The hunter is probably the main protagonist of the scene, despite the fact that he is not the usual type of "hero" on a hunt sarcophagus.

478 Examples of hunters making the triumphal gesture are cat. nos. 495, 500-01, 511, and 520.

479 Cat. no. 479. For the connection between the so-called Venator sarcophagus (cat. no. 593) and cat. no. 479, see Andreae, *ASR* I 2 (1980) 18-24.

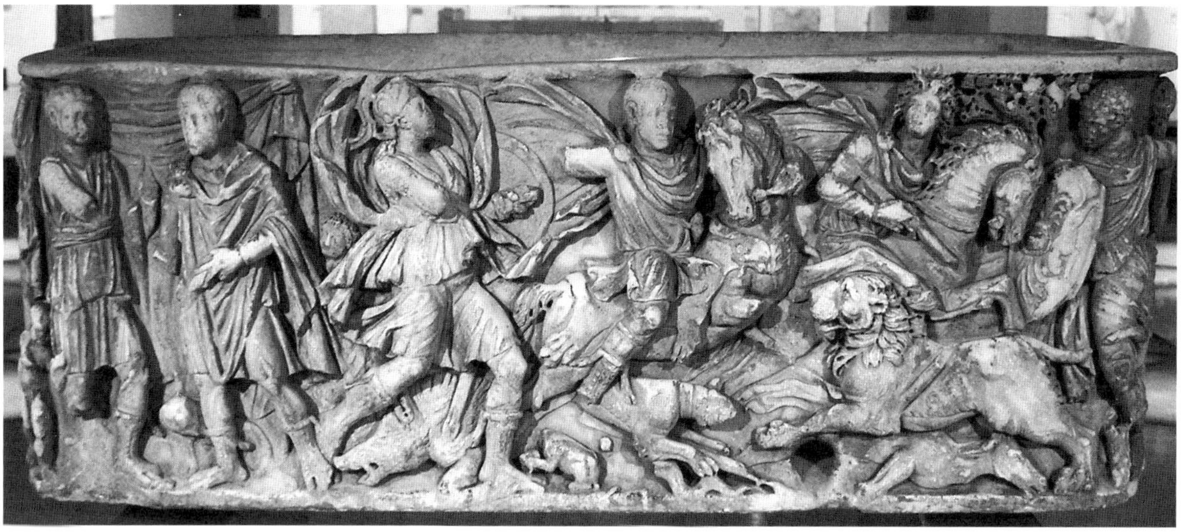

Lion hunt sarcophagus (cat. no. 479). Barcelona, Museo Archeológico, inv. 870. Photo: Author. **Fig. 57**

hunter is sometimes represented alone (cat. no. 492). The first examples are traditionally dated to the 230s, but lion hunt sarcophagi with two scenes continue well into the fourth century.[480] In the period between 230 and 330, the man on the farewell scene is often, but not always, dressed as a commander in a cuirass.[481] On hunt sarcophagi with two scenes, the deceased is often represented twice; once as a military man on Virtus's right side, and once as a hunter on her left side. This shows that there is a connection between the virtues divined into the military man and those of the triumphant hunter; they represent a male ideal based on strength, courage, and triumph. The military iconography known from biographical and battle sarcophagi is, as mentioned above, rarely seen in the third century.[482] The hunter may therefore be seen as a new allegory elaborating on the 'old' virtues that previously were symbolised through the military man. Occasionally the two figures even merge into one: in the lion hunt sarcophagus in Musei Capitolini (**Fig. 8**; cat. no. 499), the commander has taken the role of the central hunter.[483] The scene uses the canonical lion hunt figures, but in an abbreviated form.

The focus on male *virtus* is made explicit by the presence of the personification of *virtus*. She is shown with a helmet, boots, and a bound-up tunic, and she always accompanies the hunter. Her very presence heroises the central hunter and the military man on the farewell scene. She is an embodied expression of the virtues that the hunter possessed. These three main characters of the hunt scenes can be individualised with portraits; the male expression of *virtus* (the hunter) is regarded as the vital male quality, whereas the female figure is interpreted in terms of the male role, as his supporter.[484] The coupling of Virtus and the hunter through the application of portraits is an example of the emphasis put on the relationship between man and woman as a couple in the construction of identity on sarcophagus reliefs.[485] The ideals that are expressed are therefore not only strength and male *virtus*, but also *concordia* and the mutual loyality of the couple.

Formula and Individuality in Lion Hunt Sarcophagi

The formulaic language of hunt sarcophagi made the motif immediately recognisable to the Roman viewer. For the modern reader its formulaic nature is advantageous because it makes it possible for us to study deviation from the norm, when it occurs. These un-

480 Andreae, *ASR* I 2 (1980) cat. 29 and 65.

481 Cat nos. 480, 494, 498, 507, 509, and 520.

482 Also noted by Muth 1998, 233.

483 Another example is cat. no. 509.

484 Muth 1998, 232-33.

485 Hansen 2007, for example, p. 5.

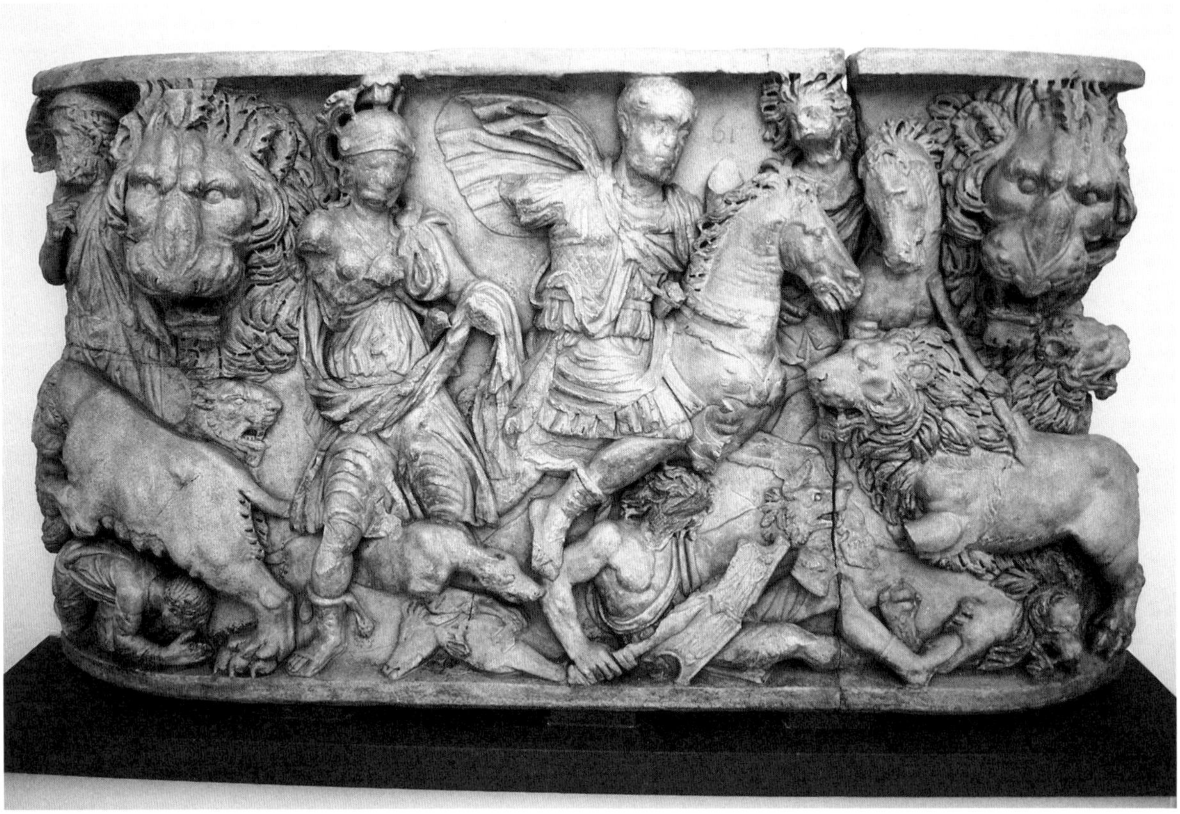

Fig. 58 *Hunt sarcophagus (cat. no. 499). Rome, Musei Capitolini, Palazzo Nuovo, Inv. S 221. Photo: Author, courtesy of Musei Capitolini.*

conventional features often reveal individuality. On two sarcophagi, already discussed in the context of the learned figure (cat. no. 495; **Fig.** 47 and cat. no. 511; **Fig.** 59), the men on the left scenes of the frontal relief show divergence from the norm. They are not wearing the military dress that, as I have stated, was the usual for this figure, but a short tunic, a mantle, and boots. What is more important is that instead of a spear or a sword, the two men hold scrolls in their hands. That these objects are scrolls, and not broken spears, is shown by the way they hold them: learned figures often hold the scroll with the left hand, and with the second and third finger of the right hand she or he touches the top end of the scroll, which is also the case with the figures on the two sarcophagi.[486]

The fact that the huntsmen hold scrolls instead of the usual swords or spears functions as part of the negotiation of identity that took place on sarcophagus reliefs. One conclusion that can be drawn from this example is that the hunt is an allegory not only of physical power, but also of psychic strength, here symbolised through learnedness. On a fragmented sarcophagus from the catacombs of S. Sebastiano (**Fig.** 59; cat. no. 511), this interpretation can be strengthened by the examination of another detail that deviates from the norm. Personal strength is probably the principal virtue that the patron of the sarcophagus wanted to project onto the identity of the deceased. The deceased is represented as the central hunter, and the slight alteration is only found when the portrait is studied in detail: the lion hunter is a woman. This relief is not unique; another female lion hunter is found on a sarcophagus now in Nieborow, Poland (**Fig.** 73; cat. no. 489). The two women deviate from the typical iconography of lion hunters only in the fact that they

486 See, for example, cat. nos. 4 and 7.

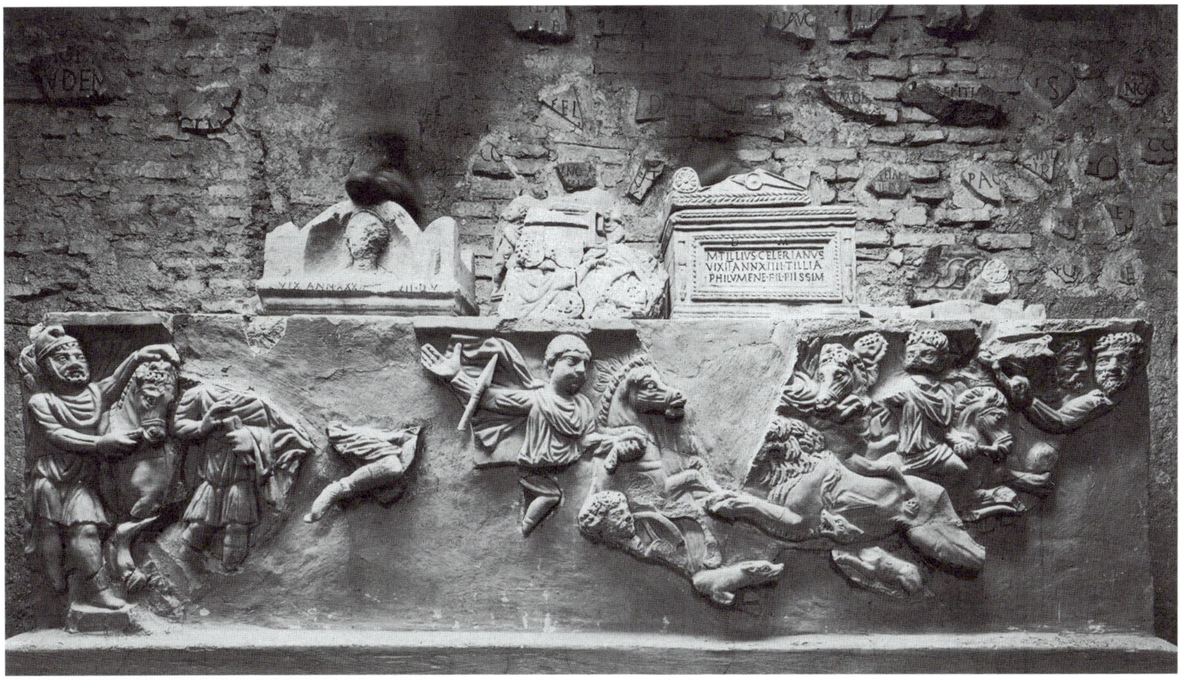

Lion hunt sarcophagus with a female huntress (cat. no. 511). Rome, S. Sebastiano, Museo II. Photo: D-DAI-ROM-37.1073 (Falber-Meyer). **Fig. 59**

are women and not men.[487] These reliefs are the last statements of two Roman women who used the permeability of genders to show their personal strength and thereby ensure their commemoration as successful Roman women, rather than selecting the more conventional representation of the learned women or the women in marriage scenes.

A Christian Lion Hunter

Another example of the capability of the lion hunt iconography to convey the deceased's identity is found if we revisit the sarcophagus from Cimitero Maggiore in Rome (**Fig. 60**; cat. no. 498, discussed in chapter 1 in relation to patronage of sarcophagi). It is a lion hunt sarcophagus with two scenes. The central hunter on the frontal relief has portrait features, and there is a portrait bust of a learned man on the lid. Beside the bust is an inscription. At some point, the first inscription on the lid was erased and a new inscription was added. Judging from the two male individualised figures, the sarcophagus must originally have been made for one man, or possibly two men. The bust on the lid is carved with a portrait of man with a beard; behind him is a *parapetasma* held by cupids. The scene on the opposite side of the inscription panel is a representation of a generic hunt. The portrait of the central hunter on the frontal relief is of a young man: his beard only grows on the lower part of his chin, and the face is smooth with large eyes. The second inscription mentions that a 24 year old son, Aurelius Tabula, was commemorated by his father. The son is in all probability represented as the lion hunter, and the father (the patron) is portrayed as the learned and older man on the lid.[488] The same scheme is also found on other sarcophagi, as for example the one from Mausoleum H in the Vatican necropolis. The inscription on this lion hunt sarcophagus (**Fig. 10**; cat. no. 512) tells us that the patron was a wife who purchased the coffin for her husband. The husband is represented as the hunter on the frontal relief, and there

487 The two sarcophagi are studied more closely in chapter 3.

488 The inscription furthermore dates this burial to after 313. As is recognised by Andreae, the phrase *servus dei* is unlikely to have been used before the Edict of Tolerance of Milan (Andreae, *ASR* I 2 (1980) 158, cat. 78).

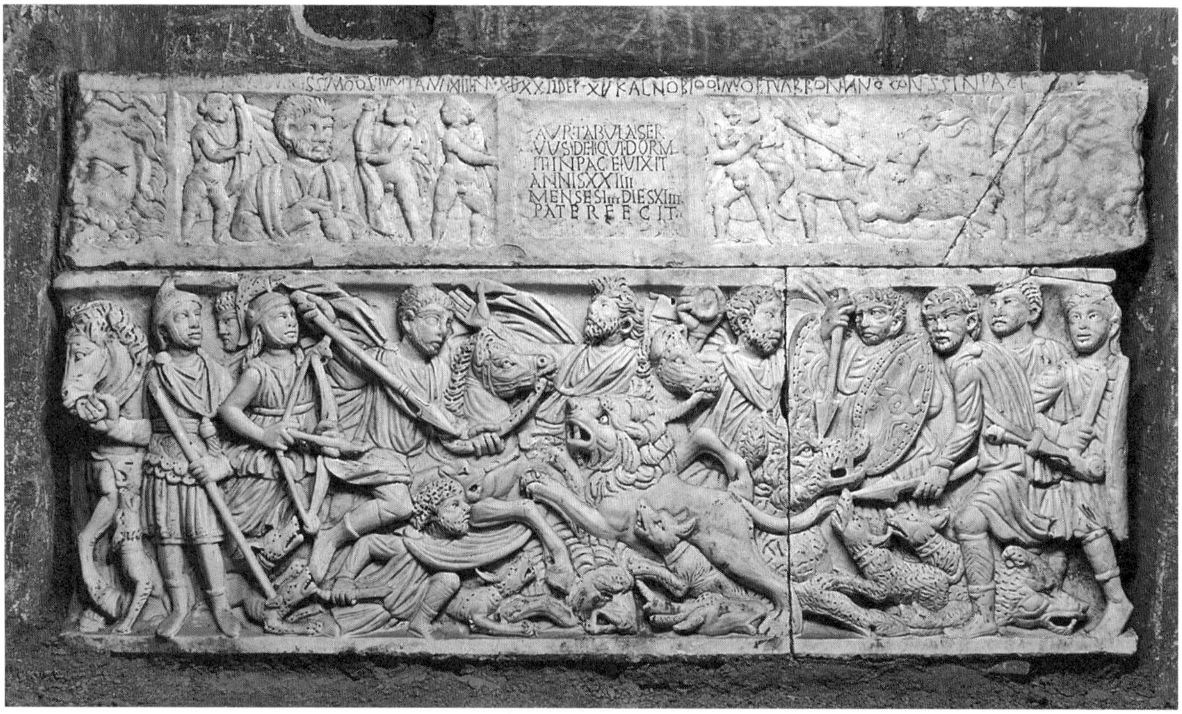

Fig. 60 *Lion hunt sarcophagus (cat. no. 498). Rome, Cimitero Maggiore, Regione delle Cattedre, Cubiculum K. Photo: D-DAI-ROM-78.106 (Rossa).*

was room for her portrait to be carved on a learned female bust on the lid.

Returning to the lion hunt sarcophagus with the two male portraits (**Fig. 60**; cat. no. 498), it is reasonable to assume that the inscription we see now may not be contemporary with the portraits, since the first inscription was erased. But the patron who reused the sarcophagus chose one with two portraits because the iconography fulfilled his needs: the time span between creation of the portraits and the inscription is therefore not important to the interpretation of the deceased's identity. For both the patron and the viewer, the portraits represented the two men mentioned in the inscription. In this case, history has repeated itself, and a third inscription was carved on the upper profile of the lid, giving the name of a 14-year-old boy, Valerius Sabbinus. He is referred to as *filio dulcissimo*, which tells us that he was also commemorated by a parent, and it may even be a father, who would then again be symbolised by the portrait on the lid. The inscription can be dated to 364 with reference to the names of the two consuls who are mentioned in the inscription. The last time the sarcophagus was thus reused was around a generation after it had been carved, which means that a relatively short time after the first burial the memory of this person was lost, and the sarcophagus was moved into a Christian burial place. Here it was used first to illustrate the virtuosity of a Christian man in the first half of the fourth century, and then once again for another patron shortly after.

The Christian identity of the second and third patrons are revealed by the inscription. Aurelius Tabula is called a *servus dei*, and on Valerius Sabbinus' inscription the phrase *in pace* is added. The fathers, however, used pagan iconographic language to express his son's *virtus* and his own social status.[489] The hunt motif was not uncommon in a Christian context, as can be illustrated by an example from Osimo (**Fig. 61**; cat. no. 490). The coffin is decorated with a canonical lion hunt, whilst the lid has depictions of biblical scenes. Christian identity in the early fourth century was not developed to a level at which the Christians saw themselves as inherently different from their pagan neighbours. They still

489 For sarcophagus burials in the early Christian period, see Dresken-Weiland 2003.

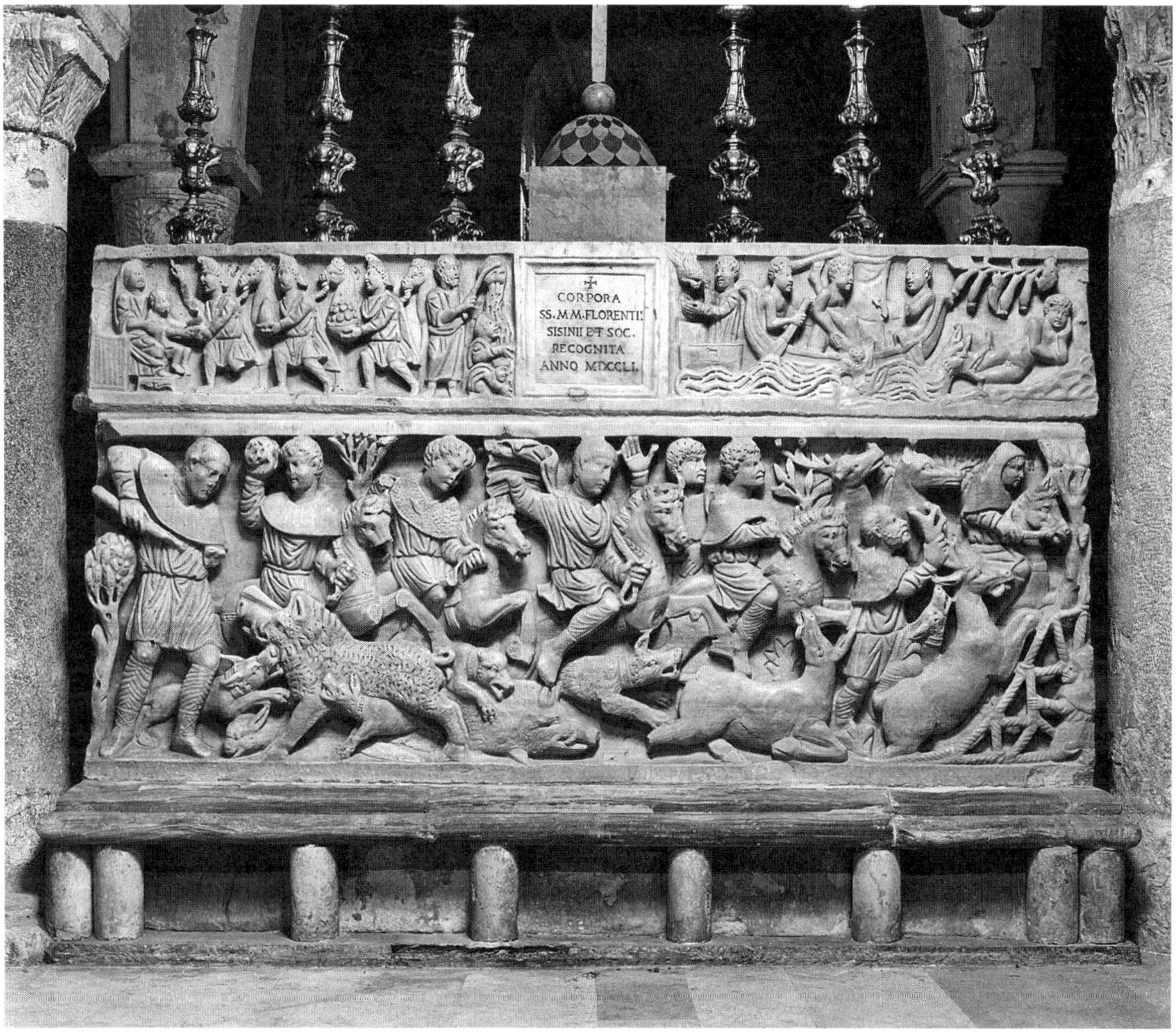

Hunt sarcophagus (cat. no. 490). Osimo, Cathedral, crypt. Photo: D-DAI-ROM-75.998 (Rossa). **Fig. 61**

aspired to the same upper-class ideals. To be Christian was therefore also to be Roman, and pagan and Christian graves were placed side by side.[490] Today religion is an important element in our funerary rituals, and cemeteries are divided according to religion. But before Christianity became the dominant religion, religious adherence and burials were not so strongly bound together, and specific religious beliefs were rarely expressed on Roman sarcophagi. The Christian family who reused the lion hunt sarcophagus (**Fig. 60**; cat. no. 498), chose to construct their *post-mortem* identity though a motif that traditionally symbolised status in society and not in heaven, in contrast to the iconography of more explicitly Christian sarcophagi that exclusively showed scenes of the miracles of the Christian religion. These expressions of Christian identity became stronger and more explicit as the fourth century progressed, and religious identity grew to be of the highest importance.[491]

Conclusion

Through the exploration of four categories of portrait figures (ritual, learned, mythological, and hunter/Virtus) used for self-representation, I have offered some

490 See Denzey's interpretation of Cubiculum N at the Via Latina catacombs, cf. Denzey 2007, chapter 2.

491 See the collection of Christian sarcophagi in *Rep.* I.

suggestions as to how to read sarcophagus imagery. I have pointed to the level of individuality that is found in the conventional decoration of sarcophargi by focusing on different ways of using the standardised scenes and by showing that iconographic deviation from the norm can signalise personal choice. Furthermore, in comparing some of the 'stories' told by the reliefs, the varied ways in which identity could be negotiated through the portrait figure have been illustrated. The conclusions of these analyses can be summed up briefly by saying that ritual scenes and those that included a learned figure revealed a hierarchy of gender that can be mapped within social relationships, but the learned figure also showed how this iconography developed to a level where the same role models were used for the construction of both men's and women's identities. Furthermore, we saw how analogies to human situations involving emotions and social relationships were used concurrently with a negotiation of the deceased's identity, as exemplified by the presence of mythological portrait figures on many sarcophagi. The main protagonists of hunt scenes, the hunter and Virtus, are, when they are displayed together, an expression of the traditional virtue of *concordia* between man and wife. However, the qualities suggested by these figures show the male and female as equally heroic and virtuous. Together with the learned figure, the hunt motif also showed how pagan expressions of virtues were assimilated into Christian iconography, when religion gradually became more important in the construction of identity. In the next chapter, gender roles and social relationships will be studied further through a comparative case study of the different portrait figures found on sarcophagus reliefs.

CHAPTER 3

Visualising Gender

...I have also written out for you the remainder of what I would have said on the topic that man's virtues and women's virtues are one and the same.

Plutarch, introduction to *On the Bravery of Women*[1]

In Plutarch's *On the Bravery of Women*, women are said to possess the same virtues as men, though they are differently expressed according to personality and individual qualities, rather than gender. Through his account of women's deeds, Plutarch does not present one ideal way of being female but instead he emphasises the women's individual ways of acting in different situations. In this chapter, I study the construction of role models for men and women through the use of the figure types that on sarcophagi were repeatedly individualised through the application of a portrait. My aim is to characterise male and female ways of self-representation in order to demonstrate the wide spectrum of roles that were available to people for use in constructing an ideal self-image. I furthermore want to establish how analogies were used to express both social identity and individuality; gender roles and the mutual relationship between the sexes will play an important part in this discussion. By examining the individualised figures, I will show that there is a difference in the choice of figure types that could be used for women and men when a person was represented alone, and when two persons were represented together.

The same pluralistic way of perceiving the qualities of gender that is present in Plutarch is apparent in the individualised figures of men and women on sarcophagi. Here, their various qualities and virtues are identified through the different kinds of self-representation, and the figures symbolising the deceased are subject to acts of both bereavement and commemoration. Therefore, as we will see, no single way of being either male or female is visually expressed on sarcophagi, and it is the individual qualities of the deceased that play the deciding role in selecting the motif that decorated the coffin. The body type of the portrait figure was a personal choice not limited by sex; only the social context of these figures restricted the range of virtues applicable to a person. This means, for example, that when a marital couple are represented, the man and woman generally conformed to ideal images of generic role models of matrimony. In a careful analysis of each individual's representation, a more nuanced picture of gender roles emerges. This is especially evident in examples of cross-gendered representations on Roman sarcophagi that will here be explored through the feminine and masculine ideals as they are expressed through these portrait figures.[493] The relationship between sex and gender, as it is expressed through visual imagery on sarcophagi, is revealing about social roles and suggests that the binary gender system, often assumed to be the basic gender relation in Roman society, was not the only, and maybe not even the prevailing, way of perceiving gender.[494] Texts written by elite male authors of the Roman era have played a seminal role in the modern perception of ancient gendering; as Clarke says about women in ancient literature, "The men put all the words in the women's mouths and attribute to them all the deeds they are supposed to have done".[495] The absence of women, who

492 Plutarch, *Moralia* III, *On the Bravery of Women* (introduction), trans. Babbitt.

493 See also Birk 2011.

494 Classical archaeology was first introduced to the criticism of male bias by Pomeroy's book *Goddesses, Whores, Wives, and Slaves: Women in Classical Antiquity*, published in 1975.

495 Clarke 2002, 149.

seldom have their own voice in literature, can to some extent be remedied by interpreting self-representation on funerary monuments as reflections of Roman ideas about gender ideals.

First, I will survey the categories of individualised figure types established in the catalogue by looking at the distribution of the sexes on sarcophagus reliefs. The intention is to enable a general understanding of which virtues and qualities were used in the construction of the posthumous reputations of men and women. The secondary motif, which adds new levels of meaning to the portrait figure, emphasised the commemoration of men and women in terms of virtues. They will be included in the discussion in terms of their symbolic meaning. Thereafter, the female, male, and marital ideals of self-representation will be approached separately. In doing this, I will focus on what kind of role the portrayed figures fulfil, as both active and passive agents, and how they take different forms according to the social relations displayed on the coffin, such as kinship. A key component of this is the symbolisation of ideals and personal qualities, which, however, is sometimes jeopardised in order to construct an individualised memory.

In my research on these issues, I found that children's sarcophagi did not always fit into a male/female categorisation. There seems to be a certain degree of fluidity in the formula of gender in representations of children before puberty. Children's sarcophagi and what they reveal about the Roman perception of childhood will therefore be studied separately in chapter 4.

Feminism, Gender, and the Body – An Introduction

In archaeology, the body has been studied in regard to the negotiation of identity, with particular focus on dress, nudity, and figure types, in order to understand the cultural norms established around the categories of sex and gender.[496] Gender itself has been an influential issue for decades, and feminist theory as well as queer theory has had a great impact on the way archaeological studies have dealt with what it means to be a man or a woman.[497] Today gender discourses are frequent within archaeology both in regard to the roles of men and women and in relation to their sex and sexuality.[498] During the formative periods of feminist studies, it was debated whether the body influences the construction of gender or if it was gender that influenced the appearance of the body. This is no longer one of the discourse's principal questions, since it has been shown that biology, as well as culture, plays a major part in the construction of gender. Today the main questions are how biological and/or cognitive difference is interpreted culturally in different societies, and what influence it has had on the evolution of the body and mind. Through discussions of these questions, emphasis on hierarchy has been replaced by highlighting differences and individuality.[499]

In writing that "one is not born, but rather becomes, a woman", Beauvoir claimed that gender is a process of interpreting the body, of giving it cultural form. This led her to the acknowledgment that being a *female* and being a *woman* are two different sorts of being.[500] *Female* relates to biology whereas a *woman* is a cultural construction. Throughout history, modern and early

496 On the naked and dressed body, see especially: Hallett 2005; Olson 2008. On the interpretation of the body in antiquity, see especially: Rousselle 1993; Monserrat 1998 (especially the Introduction and Meskell's contribution on "The Irresistible Body", pp. 139-61); Lee 2000, 114-15; Rautman 2000; Fabricius 2001; Hopkins & Wyke 2005; Sørensen 2006, 117-19.

497 Feminists here are exemplified by: Deckard 1975; Brooks 1997. For the history of feminism within classics, see Brown 1997 and Rabinowitz & Richlin 1993. For queer theory in archaeology: Herdt 1994; Moore 1999; Voss 2008 (with an extensive list of further references). Many both feminist and queer theoretical approaches to archaeology have built upon the work of the post-structuralist philosopher Judith Butler (1990, 1993).

498 Kampen 1996; Clark 1998; Meskell 1999; Gilchrist 1999; Leach 1999; McClanan & Encarnacion 2002; Meskell & Preucel 2004; Skinner 2005; Nelson 2006; Casella 2006; Varner 2008; Voss 2008. Many studies have focused on women: Pomeroy 1975; 1991 (a review article on the study of women until that date); Kampen 1981a; Cameron & Kuhrt 1983; Archer, Fischler & Wyke 1994; Kleiner & Matheson 1996; Lovén & Strömberg 1998; Hemelrijk 1999; Dixon 2001; Sørensen 2001; D'Ambra 2007; Davies 2008. On women's roles in archaeological research: Nelson, Nelson & Wylie 1994. For a review of the history of gender and feminism and the emergence of queer studies within archaeology, see Voss 2000.

499 Gilchrist, 1999, 1-16. For a short description of how *first*, *second*, and *third wave feminism* are defined, see Gilchrist 1999, 2 and Meskell 1999, 54-6.

500 Beauvoir 1949 (1973), 301; Butler 1986, 35-6, 47.

modern expectations about gender roles have too easily lead to narratives of woman as the performer of some roles and man as the performer of other roles. However, in our current society we do understand that male and female patterns of behaviours can be exhibited independently of the sex of the person, meaning that men and women use the same social roles to construct their identity, and it seems a likely possibility that the Romans also acknowledged this distinction.[501] When studying the way social roles are visually expressed on sarcophagi, the tendency to think about gender in terms of hierarchy in the classical archaeological tradition seems to be challenged by antiquity itself. The uniformity in terms of self-representation found in male and female portrait figures on sarcophagi, as, for example, illustrated through the learned figure type that was used to negotiate the identity of men and women equally, point in the direction of equality, and not hierarchy, of male and female visual ideals.

On sarcophagi there are numerous examples of how one could be female or male but still be placed in mythological or social contexts that are emblematic of the opposite sex. We also know of individualised figures of women represented with male physical characteristics, and *vice versa*. These cross-gendered images are explicit physical examples of how gender and identity could be constructed through representations of standardised social roles according to the wishes of an individual person. Still, the *feminine* in antiquity has often been regarded as secondary in comparison to the *masculine*, and it is supposed that feminine characteristics, such as a body with soft curvy lines, would never be accorded to a man.[502] However, as has already been suggested, several such representations can be found on sarcophagi.[503] As mostly middle-class Romans, the patrons of cross-gendered sarcophagi displayed their social identity in the most conventional way – by using traditional Roman iconography – and none of these sarcophagi indicate that the individuals commemorated diverge from societal norms. The explanation for such feminine or masculine characteristics worn by the opposite sex can be found in the need to display nothing but specific personal virtues, and as shown by Eric Varner, the feminine could be an ideal in itself, even for the emperors in official art.[504] Portrait figures on sarcophagi can therefore contribute positively to the discussion of gender roles in Roman society, and these figure types – and especially those with biologically different sexed body parts combined in one body – should be seen as a visual expression of ways of perceiving genders. As a consequence, sarcophagus images become an informative source for understanding the way that gender was lived and constructed in Roman society.

Spaces and activities are often associated with either one or the other sex, which often influences interpretations of scenes.[505] This can be exemplified by a relief on which two men are seen in a scene that includes a mirror. In the next panel, the portrait of one of the men is seen on a bust with Venus-associated iconography (**Fig. 62**; cat. no. 249). The men of this relief have been placed in a female environment by means of both physical characteristics and objects. We will return to this relief later. Another sarcophagus shows two men engaged in wool-making (**Fig. 63**; cat. no. 534). A third man is reclining on a coach attended by a woman and another scene, probably associated with a ritual of the cult of Attis/Cybele, is visible in the background.[506] The world of wool-making is traditionally associated with female *pudicitia*, but women engaged in wool work are seldom represented on sarcophagi. However, the man commemorated through this funerary relief seems to have had something to do with wool-making; he has portrait features similar to the wool-working man on

501 Bassler suggests that the Roman-Christian perception of gender in the first century was a spectrum, where the male was located at one end, the female at the other, and the individual person at any one point on the spectrum according to individuality; cf. Bassler 2008, 52. For an introduction to how gender has been perceived from the Hippocratic corpus, through Aristotle and Galen to Early Christianity, see Harlow 1998. On the way we think about gender today in the Roman world, see Montserrat 2000.

502 For example, Kampen (1996b, 18; cited in Huskinson 1999, 192) writes: "A man, taking on attributes of women, became suspect unless he was a youth or a god in whom androgyny was permissible". For the contrary attitude, see Varner 2008.

503 For example, cat. nos. 113, 216, 249, 533, and 538.

504 Varner 2008.

505 For gender analysis of space, see for example Wallace-Hadrill's article "Engendering the Roman House" (1996).

506 Koch 1988, 24-7.

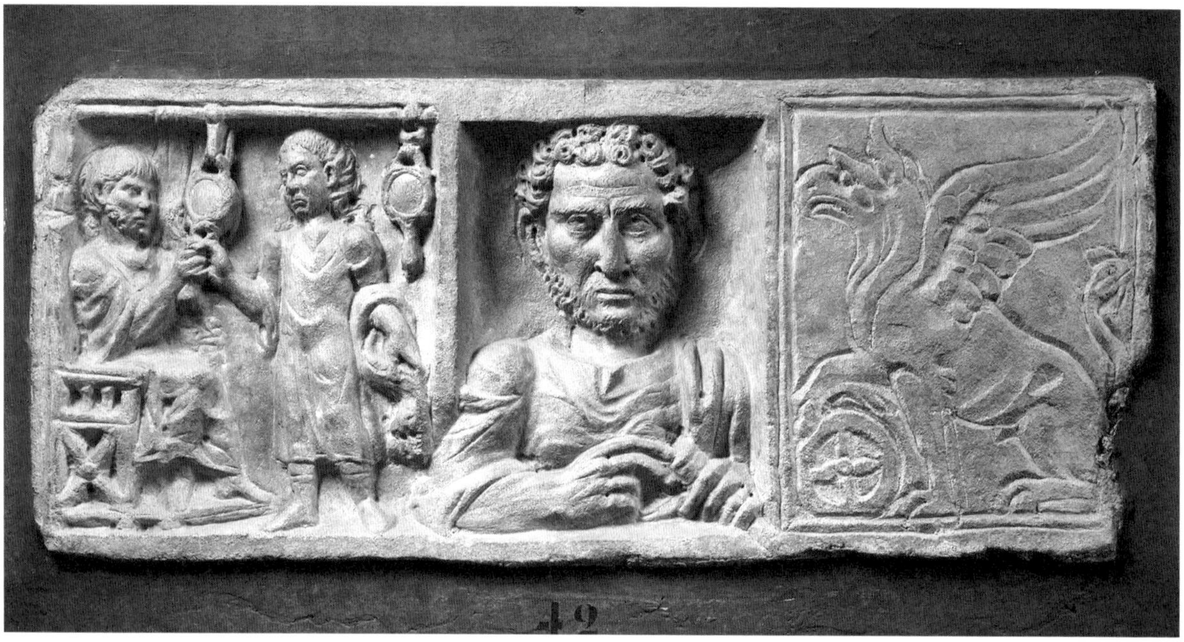

Fig. 62 *Sarcophagus lid or* loculus *plate with a scene with two men and a bust of a bearded man (cat. no. 249). Rome, Musei Vaticani, Museo Gregoriano Profano, inv. 9517. Photo: D-DAI-ROM-1963.0639.*

the left side of the relief. Occupation scenes are extremely rare on sarcophagi, but nonetheless the relief has been understood as commemorating a businessman engaged in the production of wool.[507] If the characters on the relief had been women, the interpretation would undoubtedly have located the scene in the household, representing female duties, since working with wool is traditionally considered to be a female virtue.[508] The obvious risk of making gender-stereotypical assumptions in such an approach has been discussed in relation to another group of material in an article on gender and space.[509] Here the presence of women in Roman fortresses was proved by the presence of spindle whorls, among other things. The problem is not that the researcher asserts the presence of women in fortresses, which I find very convincing, but the biased consensus of wool work as a female activity.[510] The argument could just as easily be turned around: the presence of spindles in a male-gendered space could be interpreted as evidence that men were engaged in wool-making for consumption purposes. The notion of wool work as typically female work is not wholly unambiguous either, but it illustrates well how modern ideas of gender roles control the interpretation of genders relations in antiquity.[511] The previously mentioned sarcophagus relief (**Fig. 63**; cat. no. 534) thus challenges our ideas about wool-working as an exclusively female occupation by showing that a man can express his virtues using a wool-working scene. Representations such as these incite us to take a more varied view of gender than the binary distinctions given by biological sexes.[512]

Gender Roles and Role Models: Men and Women on Sarcophagi (The Distribution of Sex)

Representations of men and women on Roman sarcophagi, and the reading of sarcophagus imagery as

507 For occupation scenes, see Zimmer 1982, and specifically on sarcophagi, see Whitehead 1984.

508 See Dixon 2001 (117-25) for a discussion of modern approaches to female involvement in commercial activities (especially cloth production) and the biased idea of women's activities as domestic versus the male commercial activities.

509 Allison 2006, and see particularly the response from M. L. S. Sørensen (2006a).

510 Allison 2006, 5, 7.

511 Cf. Casella 2006; Dixon 2001, especially 119-22.

512 Moore 1999a, 151-69; Monserrat 2000.

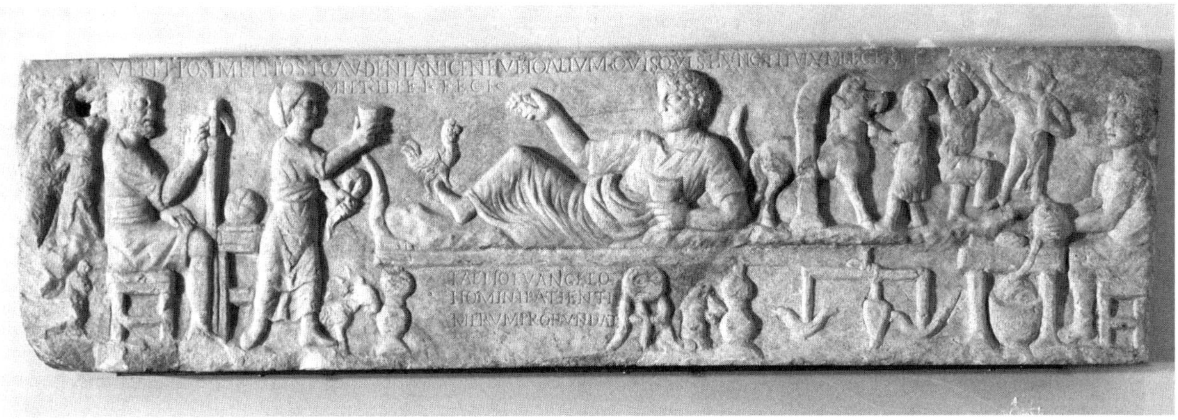

Frontal relief or loculus *plate showing a banquet scenes and people engaged in wool-working activities (cat. no. 534). Malibu, California, The Getty Villa, inv. 86.AA.701. Photo: With permission from The J. Paul Getty Museum, Villa Collection, Malibu, California.* **Fig. 63**

an expression of self-representation through gendered virtues, have been much debated lately.[513] In particular, representations of women have caught the interest of scholars, occasionally and unfortunately resulting in a hierarchic idea of women as inferior to men in Roman society.[514] As a general observation, most sarcophagi have no portrait, no inscription, and no skeletal material preserved. Determining the sex of the individuals who were buried in the coffins is therefore often a matter of interpretation based on sarcophagus imagery. The consequence is that gender determinations easily become subjective assessments of the personality of the deceased based on a biased idea of gender-specific motifs. In the following section, I hope to show that on sarcophagi the male role model was not superior to the female, and that a male-gendered iconography did not set the standards for sarcophagus imagery. The emerging picture is that the male and female spheres appear to be equally important in the construction of memory among well-to-do Roman society.[515] The group of biographical sarcophagi that dominates the second-century production gives the impression that in this period most sarcophagi were made for men.[516] However, looking at the portrait figures more broadly, it becomes clear that there is a slightly higher proportion of sarcophagi commemorating couples, due to the biographical sarcophagi, but otherwise men, women, and, in this case, also children were given portrait features equally often. When we enter the fourth century and the production of Christian sarcophagi dominates the

513 Among others: Huskinson 1999, 2002; Salathé 2000; Ewald 2004; 2005, 59-62; 2011; Zanker & Ewald 2004; Hansen 2007; 2008. Though not only concerned with sarcophagi, see also Denzey's excellent book on the lost women of early Christian society (2007).

514 Despite its excellent argument, such an attitude is expressed in Hansen 2008. She sees the learned woman as a Muse to a learned man, i.e. his inspiration instead of a philosophical figure herself. The same way of thinking about gender in term of hierarchy is implicit when Davis considers the high number of female statues in Roman society, which to her surprise is equal to that of men (Davies 2008).

515 See also Hansen 2007, who recognises a new female privilege to posses virtues equal to men, but who, however, continues to think about gender in terms of the passive female versus the active male. Mythological representations on mosaics have also been interpreted in terms of gender as a male/female dichotomy whose image sphere is dominated by an androcentric perception of the world (Muth 1998, Part III chapter A). This means that a naked body portrayed in the same posture can be interpreted differently accordingly to its sex. For example, a representation of a semi-naked Apollo (in a posture similar to the sleeping Endymion and Ariadne) is interpreted as an expression of the happiness of *Otium* (cf. Muth 1998, p. 236), whereas the female body is interpreted as suggesting ideals of beauty and erotic attractiveness (cf. Muth 1998, 238-43).

516 This was presupposed in, for example, Hannestad 1988, 290; Huskinson 2002, 12, note 2.

market it actually happens that the most popular portrait figures on sarcophagi were learned women. Only a few male portraits appear, and then they are mostly in the context of a couple.

With this assessment of sarcophagus imagery I attempt to open up new ways of reading gender into the funerary iconography, since the connection between sex and motif is not always straightforward. For example, the unusual find of a mummy from Grottarossa (Rome) showed that a girl could be buried in a sarcophagus decorated both on the lid and on the coffin with hunt scenes. When the girl was laid to rest, she was dressed in rich garments of silk and jewellery, and her personal toy, a doll, was placed beside her as a symbol of her immature death.[517] The iconography on the outside of the coffin does not make any reference to her sex, the feminine adornment suggested by her clothing, or her age. Instead, it prioritises other aspects of her identity by illustrating her virtues and social standing. It has been suggested that the purpose of the motif was to convey status among the members of an aristocratic or senatorial family, which is the social class she probably belonged to, taking the grave goods into consideration.[518] The iconography could, however, also be viewed in more personal terms, and the possible connection of the scene to Virgil's *Aeneid* then enrols her in a world of knowledge and education. As a result, both her virtuous character and her engagement with the intellectual sphere are illustrated. As this example shows, iconography, as the sole source of information about the deceased, can be difficult to address in terms of sex and gender without relying on another source, such as an inscription, a portrait image of the deceased, or skeletal remains. Since portrait figures are found on a representative segment of sarcophagus reliefs, the outcome of a study of this corpus and the relations between sex and iconography can provide us with guidelines of how to read gender into sarcophagus images in general, including sarcophagi without portrait figures. When a portrait or an inscription has helped us to identify the sex of the commemorated individual, the scenes can be studied in order to specify the individual character of the deceased and subsequently to see if the subject of most sarcophagus imagery really was men, as has been presumed.

The hunt motif of the Grottarossa sarcophagus did not commemorate a boy or a man, despite the male virtues that might easily be read into the iconography, and as we will see, military scenes do not necessarily commemorate the deeds of men either. My approach to sarcophagus imagery is therefore that the portrait shows the sex of the deceased individual and the iconography symbolises their gender. As a general rule, I do not consider the iconography itself to be gendered, and instead of referring primarily to the sex it might suggest, I interpret it as a pictorial narration of the virtues, qualities, and character of the deceased. To separate sex from gender in studying sarcophagus images opens up reinterpretations of male and female roles in relation to their reciprocal status and nature. I do not, however, intend to say that there are no gender distinctions to be found on sarcophagi. Nor is my intention to postulate that no motif is more appropriate for one sex than for the other. What I want to show is that looking at the way men and women were represented on sarcophagi can tell us that there is much more to be said about the gender roles of the upper classes in Roman society.

A look at the distribution of the sex and age of the commemorated individuals (graph 6) shows that men and women were commemorated on sarcophagi in equal numbers, and that the commemoration of couples was fairly popular. The purpose of the graph is to give an idea of the basic evidence on which the following study of gender and social roles relies.

An enumeration of the sarcophagi in the catalogue shows that 208 sarcophagi commemorate a single man and 199 commemorate a single woman; 186 sarcophagi show a couple and 80 sarcophagi were made for children. The number of sarcophagi with portraits that commemorate men and women are more or less equal. This gives us our point of departure for the following discussion, in which men and women are observed as sharing the production equally, and the decoration of their coffins shares similar iconographic components. As a consequence of this, I do not think that sarcophagi made for men constituted any iconographic basis upon which the decoration of sarcophagi made for women could rely. In all probability this picture can be applied to the production of sarcophagi in general, i.e. sarcoph-

517 La Regina 1998, 283-85 with further references.

518 Dresken-Weiland 2003, 343-44 with further references.

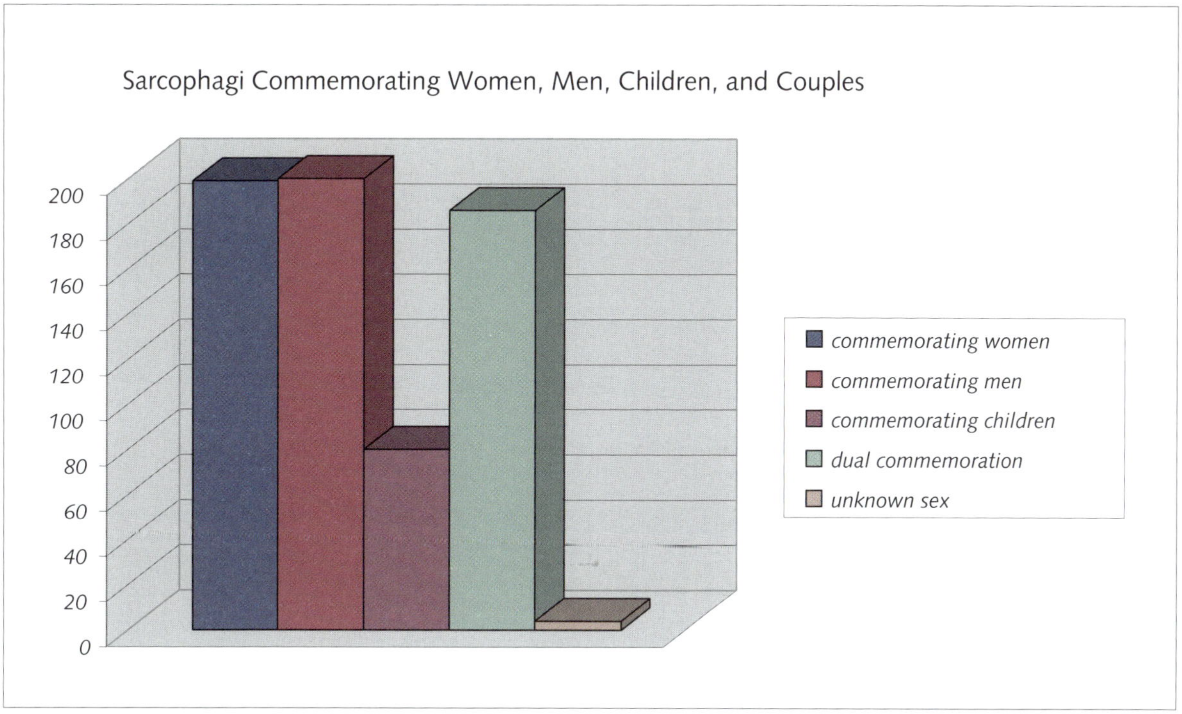

The statistics are based on sarcophagi from the catalogue. The graph shows the number of sarcophagi commemorating a single man, a single woman, a couple or a child. For details of which sarcophagi were assigned to each category, see appendix A. **Graph 6**

agi both with and without a portrait figure. Roman portrait statues also confirm this equality between men and women in visual commemoration: statues of gods or heroes were just as frequently carved with portraits of women and children as with portraits of men.[519]

A consideration of the types of self-representation and the figure types used for portrait representations suggests that there was a high degree of flexibility in terms of gender. This is illustrated by graph 7, which shows that men and women were represented through the same symbolic representations of virtues: the scroll appears in the hands of both sexes, and the iconographic scheme used for sleeping persons in tales of love affairs is the same for both, too. This concept of identity constructing roles applies to single commemorations, but changes when men and women are represented together. The graph therefore shows that more social roles can be used when the deceased is represented alone, and it is in this context that men and women may use the same figure types. Other ideals are expressed by the figure types used for marital couples; here it is their relationship that is central to their representation, rather than their individual characteristics.

The categories used to group the forms of self-representation in graph 7 are therefore not made according to the sex of the figure type but of the portrait. The figure types have been classified in line with the narrative contexts in which they take part, and emphasis is put on the ideals and qualities conveyed through the figure.[520] The graph also shows that, except for very few motifs – one being the hunting motif – that were predominantly used for male commemorations when

519 Fabricius 2007, 75.

520 For a statistical illustration of the distribution of themes on sarcophagi in general, see Ewald 2003, figs. 1 a-d. His figures 1 c-d make a good comparative basis for graph 7, and we learn that the popularity of a motif is not equal to the number of examples with individualised figures. To make a precise comparison between Ewald's figures and graph 7, it would, however, be necessary to know how Ewald's categorised, if indeed he did so, the many examples of learned women.

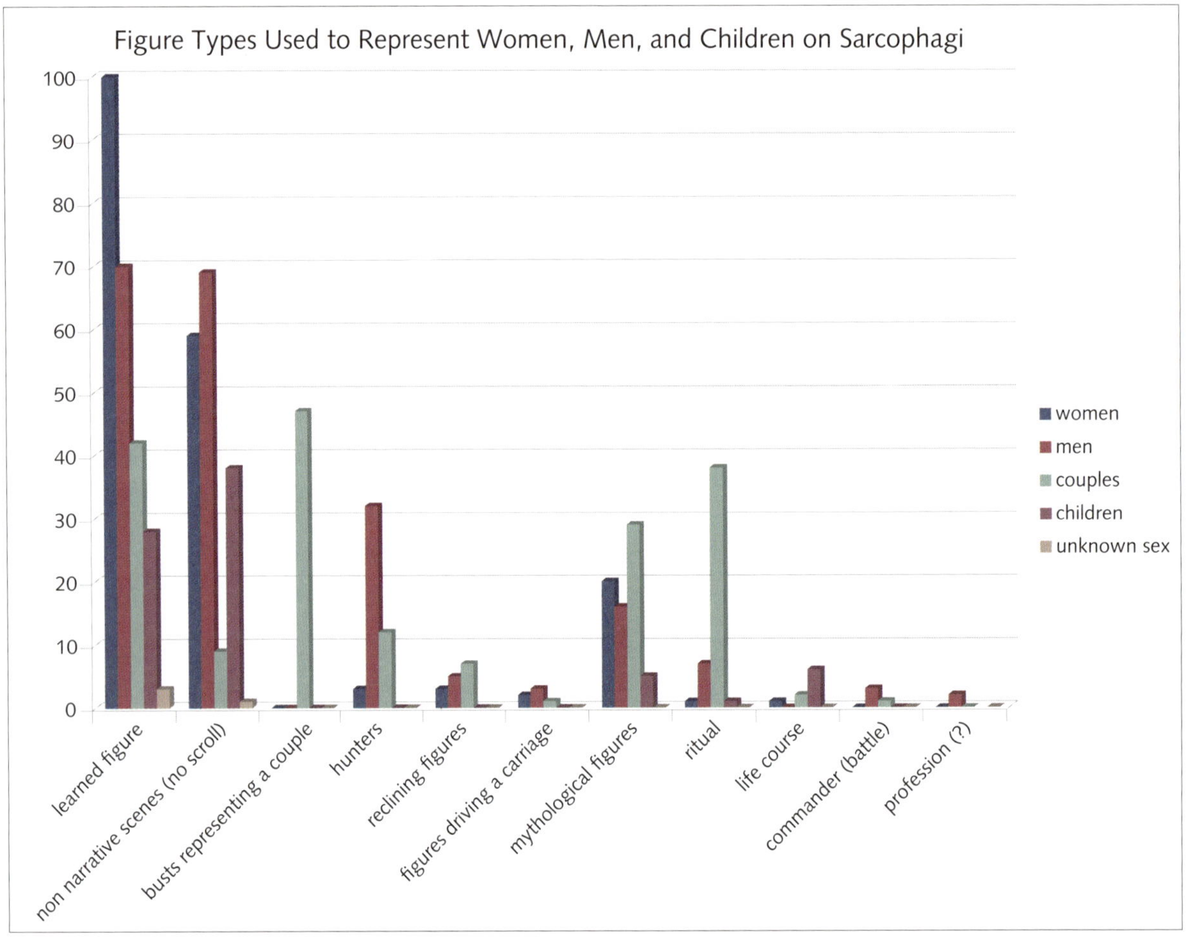

Graph 7 *The figure illustrates the number of sarcophagi showing the different figure types represented with a portrait of a man, a woman, a couple, or a child. It is clear from the graph that none of the categories of self-representation exclude either of the sexes from entering their iconographic sphere. The figure is based on the categories of self-representations that have been established in the catalogue; see also Appendix A.*

a portrait figure took part in the action, most forms of self-representation were accessible to both men and women. The fact that the categories of presumed profession and commanders only contain male commemorations is due to the small number of examples of these two categories (two in each case). As we will see, motifs from these categories are also found related to women. Therefore despite the fact that some portrait figures were preferred by women and others by men, the choice of a figure type seems not to have been limited by the deceased's sex but by personalities and ideals. As has already been said, the differences in the choice of roles for men and women are mostly found in the social contexts in which the figures are placed on the relief. This means that when men and women are represented together, their roles were defined differently from when they were represented as individuals. I look further into the values and meanings of both male and female figure types below ("The Female Ideal" and "The Male Ideal"), but first I discuss the use of secondary motifs (graph 8), with the intention of seeing if there is any pattern in the choice of the motifs decorating the coffin together with the portrait figure in relation to the gender and personal history of the deceased.

Gendered Characteristics of the Secondary Motifs

Secondary motifs, as I define them, are the scenes that add extra meaning to the primary motif (the portrait figure). Such scenes are for example found on fluted sarcophagi, which alternate sculptured panels with the

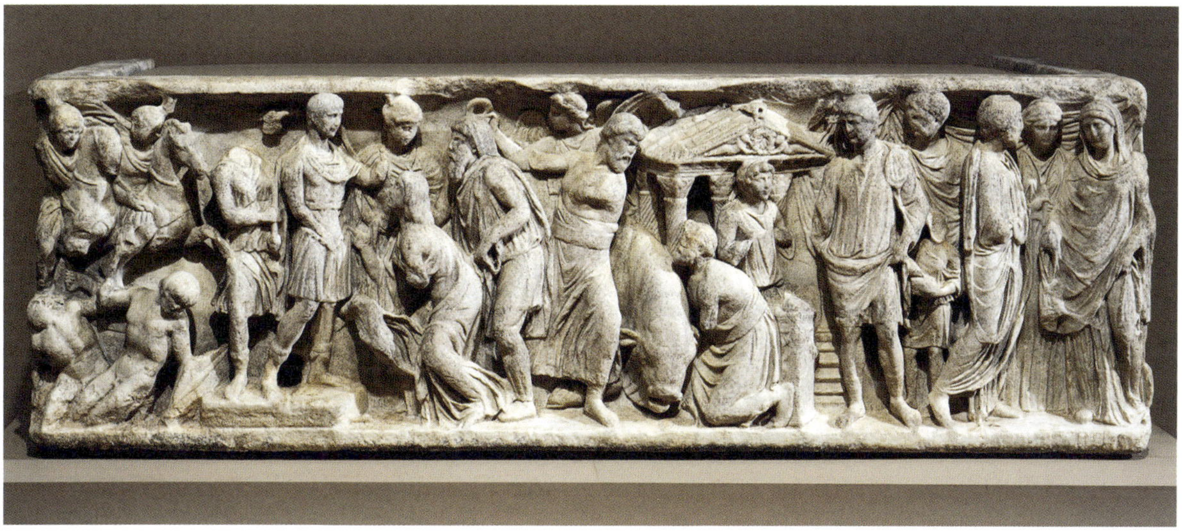

Fig. 64

The commander and the man making a sacrifice show portrait features. The dextrarum iunctio *couple has blank portraits. Los Angeles County Museum of Art, inv. 47.8.9. (cat. no. 659). Photo: © Photo SCALA, Florence.*

representations of the deceased or on sarcophagi with *clipeus* portraits.[521] Furthermore, the scenes on short end reliefs and lids are included in the discussion, since they also affect the meanings that can be read into the portrait figure. Sarcophagi are never identical and can be difficult to categorise, and in deciding what elements to classify as secondary motifs, I have tried to identify the second most important aspect of the decoration. This, of course, is not always easy and sometimes it becomes a matter of interpretation, but however difficult such categorisation seems, new methods of interpretation reveal themselves when the hierarchic relation between the primary and secondary motif is investigated. Viewing the narrative of scenes as a way of characterising the portrait figure can shed new light on sarcophagi that for decades have been considered suitable for male commemorations only. This is especially true for biographical sarcophagi that have traditionally been analysed from an explicitly male point of view. One example of such a life course sarcophagus is found in the William Randolph Hearst Collection in Los Angeles County Museum (**Fig. 64**; cat. no. 659).[522] From left to right, the viewer sees a battle, a *clementia*, a sacrifice, and a *dextrarum iunctio* scene. A man is given a portrait in both the *clementia* and the sacrifice scenes, and the heads of the man and the woman in the marriage scene have been prepared for portraits. The focus on military iconography has made scholars suggest that the sarcophagus commemorated a man.[523] However, the child's first bath scene on the right short end shows that the focus is not exclusively on military virtues, and the female portrait figure and the bath scene indicate that the sarcophagus does not only convey male qualities. With the portrait figures as the focal points, the scenes should be seen as having been made for a couple.[524] Some scholars have even reinterpreted it as the commemoration of a woman, but since the female head is left roughly carved and the man has been portrayed twice, I do not think this is a good example for an argument in favour of a female burial.[525] The inclusion of the first bath scene tells us that military iconography on sarcophagi was not only

521 The secondary motifs are reflected in the catalogue by the sub-categories into which each figure type has been divided.

522 Huskinson 2002, 15-7; Kleiner & Mattheson 1996, cat. 162, 207-8; Reinsberg 1993.

523 Contra Kampen & Matheson 1996, cat. 162, 207-8.

524 Reinsberg 1993, 141.

525 Kleiner & Matheson 1996, 207 followed by Huskinson 1999, 15. Another sarcophagus (cat. no. 595) that, because of its narrative scene, has usually been considered to have been made for a man has been re-evaluated on the basis of the portrait figure and is now supposed to commemorate a woman instead; see Newby 2011, 198.

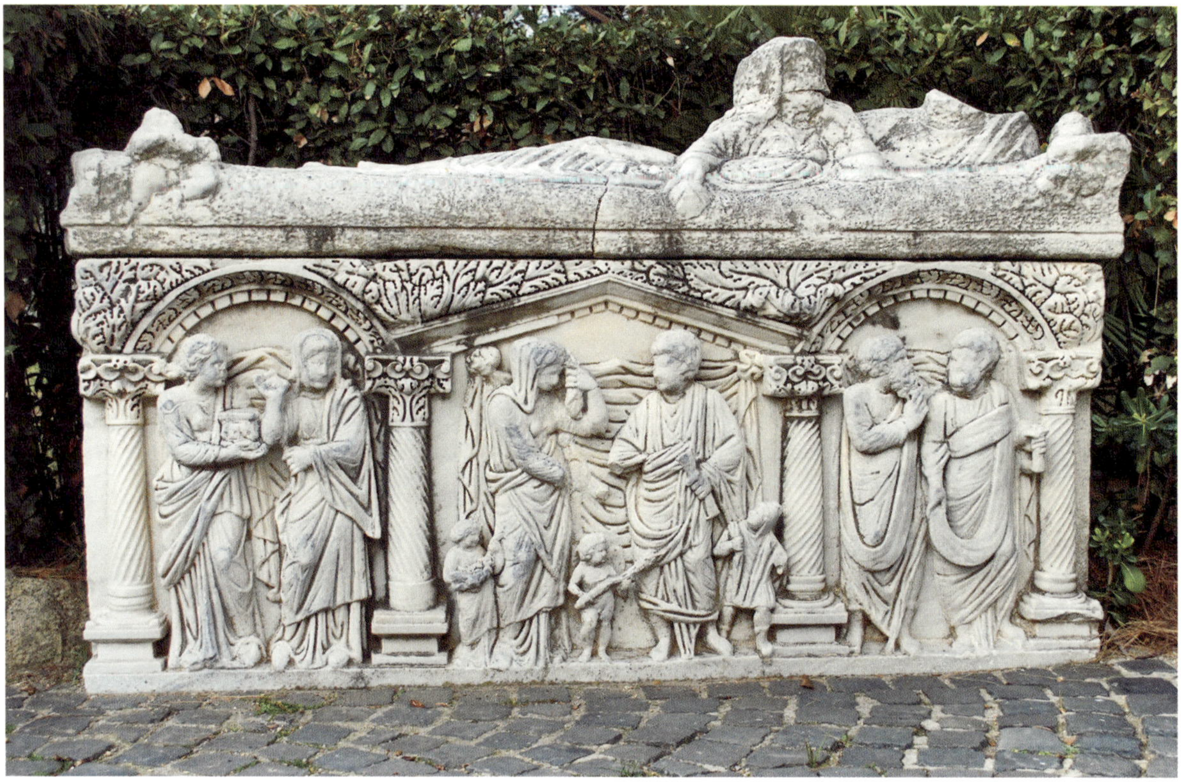

Fig. 65 *Column sarcophagus with a* dextrarum iunctio *couple. The woman on the left end has a blank portrait as well (cat. no. 643). Ostia, Museo. Photo: Author.*

about male virtues, but about characterising male and female roles in relation to each other, thus representing a marital couple with the right qualities. The idealised life course is an explicit statement of their social status, and the male *virtus* combined with the qualities of a mother and a wife emphasise the social norms of the couple. The military connection is probably at any rate an illusion and does not symbolise the man's profession as a military commander. Therefore the intended female commemoration on the sarcophagus is not an intrusion on the male sphere; instead, the mirroring of the male's virtues by female qualities emphasises his social position and thus his character. Judging from the portrait figures it seems likely that the patron was the wife, who bought the coffin for her deceased husband. That neither of the two figures in the marital scene have portrait features, but are carved with blank portraits, is probably due to the fact that at the time of completion of the coffin the wife had not yet died. The two blank portrait figures probably had to await her death, when the couple would have been reunited through the completion of the portraits. In the meantime the figures stand as a statement of the marital bonds of the couple that did not vanish because of one of them died, but which continued in an eternal agreement of *concordia*.

Another way in which a secondary motif can divine different virtues into the representation of a man and woman is illustrated by a *dextrarum iunctio* sarcophagus from Ostia (**Fig. 65**; cat. no. 643). The frontal panel is divided into three *aediculae*, each containing two figures. Because of the scroll in the hand of the male protagonist on the central scene and the two learned men in the right *aedicula*, the sarcophagus is here categorised as belonging to the learned sphere. In the central *aedicula* a woman and a man with blank portraits hold each other's hands in the *dextrarum iunctio* gesture. The woman is veiled, and the man holds a scroll. A little girl grasps the woman's dress, and a restless boy pulls at the clothing of the man. In the first and third *aediculae*, figures are displayed that emphasise the virtues of the woman and the man respectively in the marriage scene. The first of these figures shows the woman, again veiled

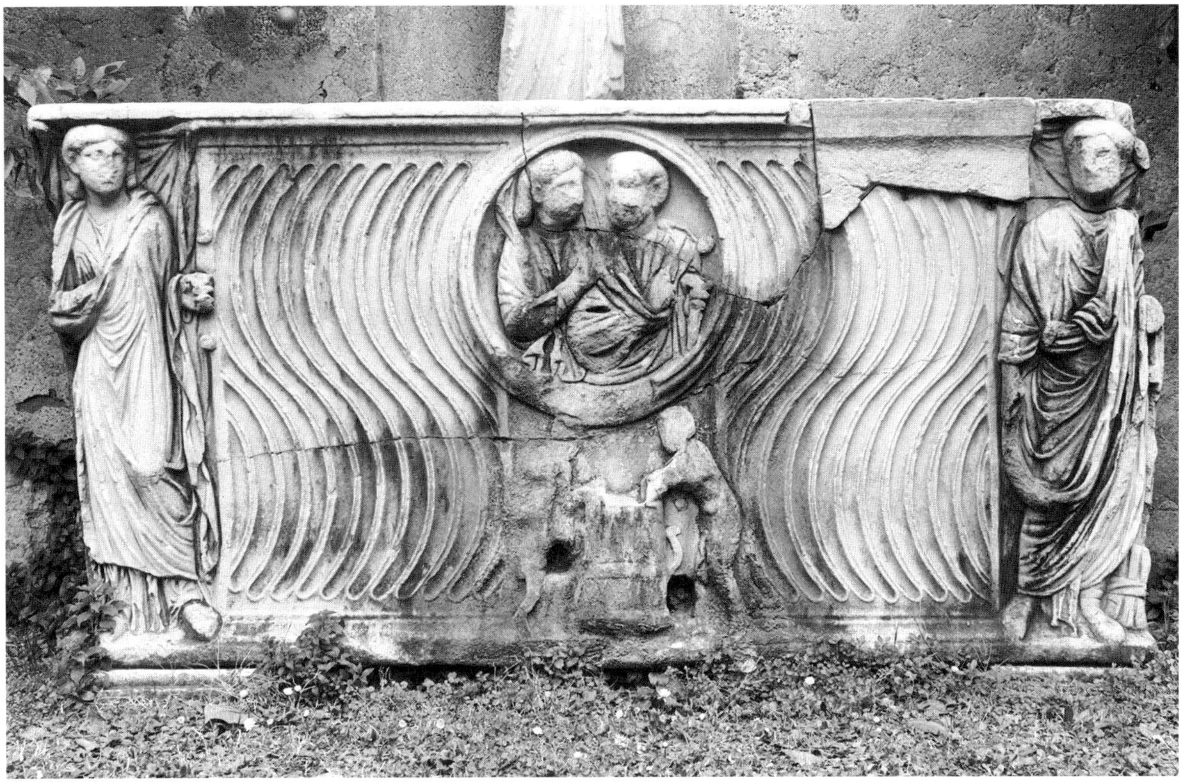

Strigillated sarcophagus with four portrait figures (cat. no. 454). Rome, Villa Medici, inv. 87. Photo: D-DAI-Rom-97.228. **Fig. 66**

and attended by a young woman holding an incense or beauty box. The third panel shows the man with a scroll in deep discussion with another man, a philosopher. The man takes care of the outward activities of political and philosophical discussion while the woman stands for the domestic virtues of beauty and child rearing. The panels represent the ideal roles of a man and wife within a traditional marriage.

The choice of a scene or even an object can signalise individual and personal histories, making the secondary and tertiary motifs important elements in the visual representation of an ideal identity. Short end reliefs are often adorned with more or less ornamental motifs, such as weapons or lion-griffins, symbolising watchful guardians over the dead, but they can also provide an opportunity to add personal information to an otherwise standardised decorative scheme.[526] A strigillated sarcophagus in Villa Medici in Rome shows four portrait figures with blank portraits on the frontal relief (**Fig. 66**; cat. no. 454):[527] enclosed by a *clipeus* is a woman dressed in a wind-blown veil who holds her arm around a man with a scroll, a learned woman is shown on the first panel, and on the fifth panel is a man with scrolls. The scheme is not unusual; it suggests the virtues of learnedness and mutual *concordia*. The tertiary motif below the *clipeus*, however, is of a personal character, since it is unique and probably provides information about the profession of the patrons. Two men wearing loincloths are shown together with a cask. One of the men pours an ingredient into the cask with a measuring cup. The scene is set in a bakery, which is confirmed by the end reliefs: the right represents a horse pulling a grinding mill, and the left shows a man with a spatula putting a bread into an oven.[528] The depictions of semi-naked men allude to the high temperature in

526 For griffins in funerary art, se Davies 2000, 33-4.

527 Ewald 1999, cat. F 32.

528 Zimmer 1982, 110, cat. 20.

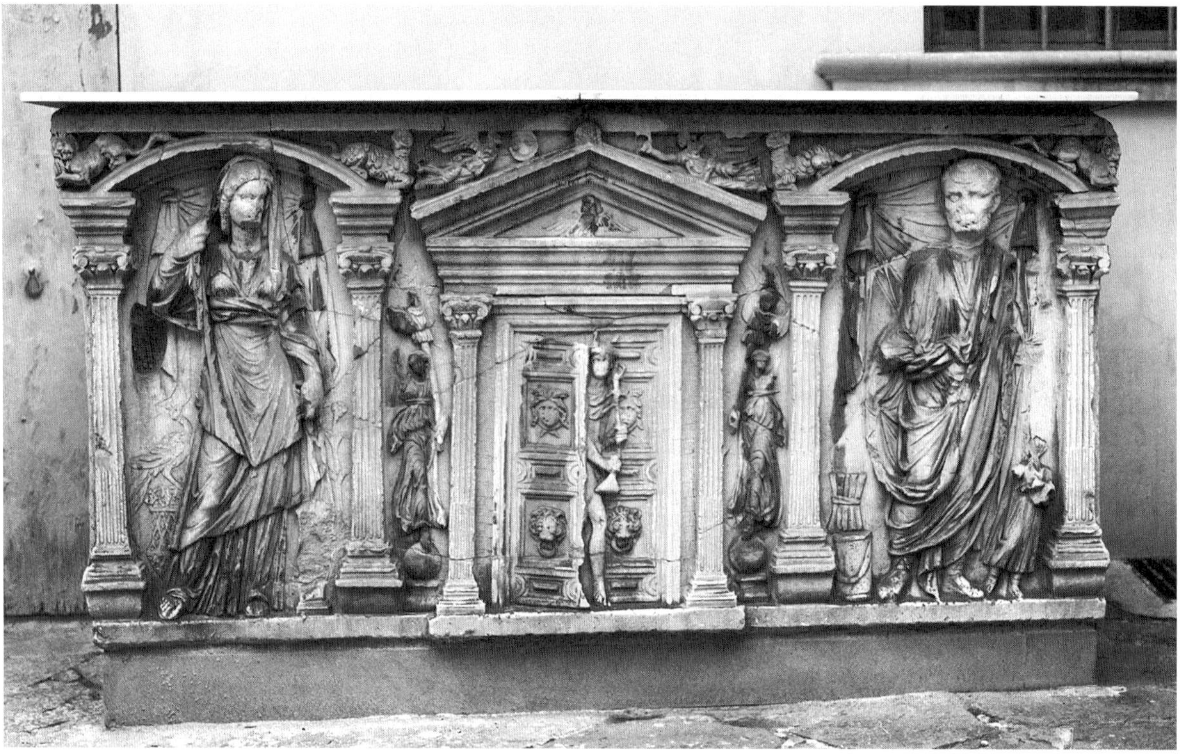

Fig. 67 *Sarcophagus showing a veiled woman and a learned man. Hermes looks out of the door that separates the two protagonists (cat. no. 55). Firenze, Museo dell' Opera del Duomo. Photo: D-DAI-ROM-75.236.*

bakeries, making the scenes appear more realistic. The relief, therefore, illustrates a situation as it could have occurred in daily life. Together with the ideal virtues of learnedness and *concordia*, the marital couple have here chosen to illustrate their profession and means of subsistence, which was the thing that gave them real status in society. This sarcophagus was therefore by all probability specially commissioned for a baker and his wife, who were so proud of their profession that they constructed their identity through scenes from their shop. The blank portraits on this sarcophagus, however, are curious. The production-to-stock theory cannot be used here, since the motif is so unique, and therefore the sarcophagus must have been commissioned while at least one of them was alive. The portraits could have been left roughly carved in preparation for their death, but, as argued previously, the frequency of blank portraits on sarcophagi combined with the evidence from sarcophagus inscriptions shows that this is not a satisfactory explanation. Blank portraits seem often to have gained a meaning as symbols of death and the immaterial nature of the soul (see chapter 1).

These three sarcophagi are individual examples of how secondary motifs and end reliefs can be used to attach additional meanings to the portrait figure. Next, the overall picture that emerges from an analysis of the categories of secondary motifs (graph 8) should be approached. While some themes construct identity, others seem merely to emphasise the funerary context through figural allusion to death or death cults. Despite their seemingly impersonal character, figural elements such as cultic objects can be understood in both active and passive terms. On one level, they symbolise the deceased's virtues, his adherence to cultic activity and his *pietas*; on another they are evidence of the sacred nature of tombs and allude to actual cultic activity at the grave without referring to a particular ritual.[529] However, in terms of gender the impression gained is again that most motifs were suitable for decorating the coffins of both sexes.

529 Herdejürgen looked at representations of cult objects, including garlands, *bucrania*, *patera*, and jugs, and evaluated their symbolic meaning; see Herdejürgen 1984.

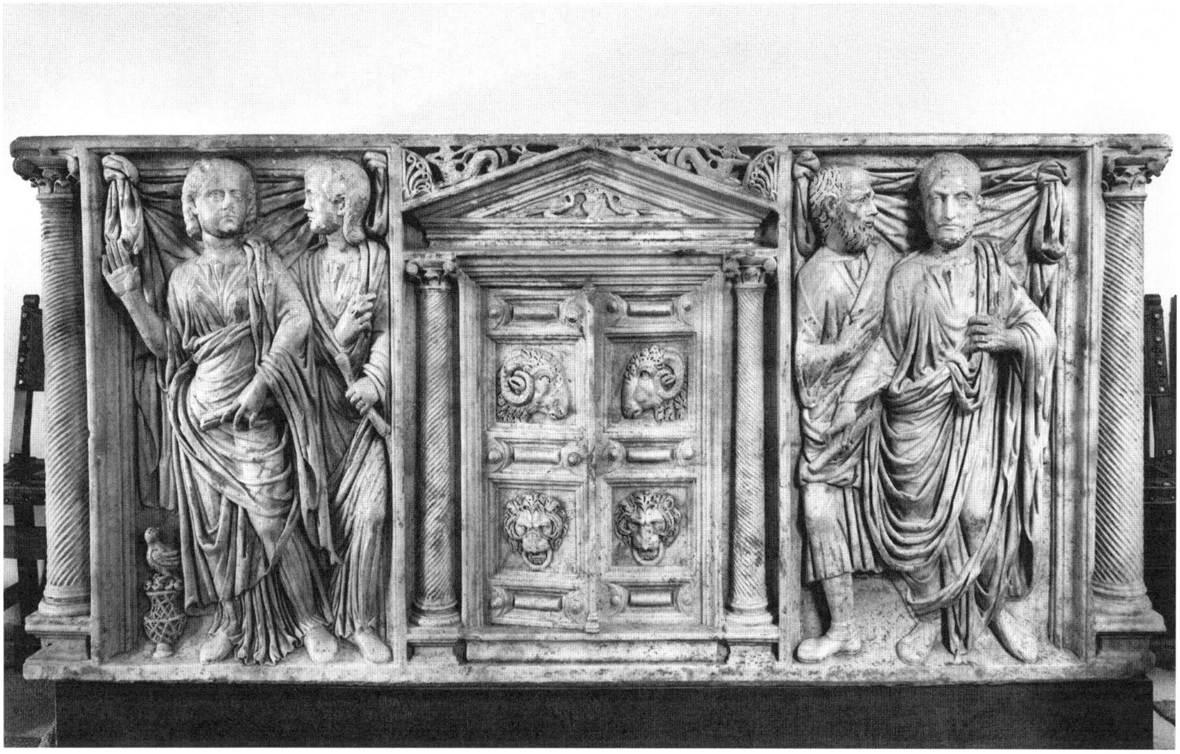

Córdoba, Alcázar de los Reyes Cristianos (cat. no. 54). Photo: D-DAI-MAD-FR-R-147-67-07. **Fig. 68**

This means that the choice of decoration is more likely to be based on the personality of the deceased than on their sex, a conclusion which can be drawn from graph 7 as well. Another convergence between graphs 7 and 8 is that children are represented in almost all categories, meaning that there is no very clear distinction between secondary motifs on the sarcophagi of children and adults. I will discuss children's sarcophagi below; here, my focus is on secondary motifs on sarcophagi made for adults.

As has been stated, the general impression given by graph 8 is that commemorations of men and women are represented in all categories; however, on closer examination of the graph, some motifs seem to have been designed mostly for couples. One example are 'death door' scenes, in which the couple stand on each side of a door.[530] In this category, the portrait figures are generally a learned man and a veiled woman either alone or with a female attendant and a girl with a cosmetic box (cat. no. 55; **Fig. 67**, cat. nos. 58 and 634; **Fig. 33**). Other death door sarcophagi are fluted and thus have less figural decoration than the two aforementioned examples (cat. nos. 56 and 57).[531] In such cases, the man holds scrolls, and the woman is represented without attributes. The conclusion must therefore be that this composition was seen as a perfect way of showing the ideal of marriage. The death door decoration of a sarcophagus in Córdoba is different, but it was therefore probably a special commission (**Fig. 68**; cat. no. 54). The design of the otherwise standardised death door sarcophagus has been slightly altered in order to accommodate individual needs. The woman is in many ways similar to the woman on cat. no. 55 (**Fig. 67**) – even the

530 Cat. nos. 54-8 and 634. For the door on sarcophagi as a symbol of the entry to Hades, see Haarløv 1977.

531 Though cat. no. 56 today only shows a portrait of a man, the female figure was probably intended to have portrait features as well (a close comparison might be made with cat. no. 57). In graph 4, cat. no. 56 is the only death door sarcophagus that is not registered in the category of couples.

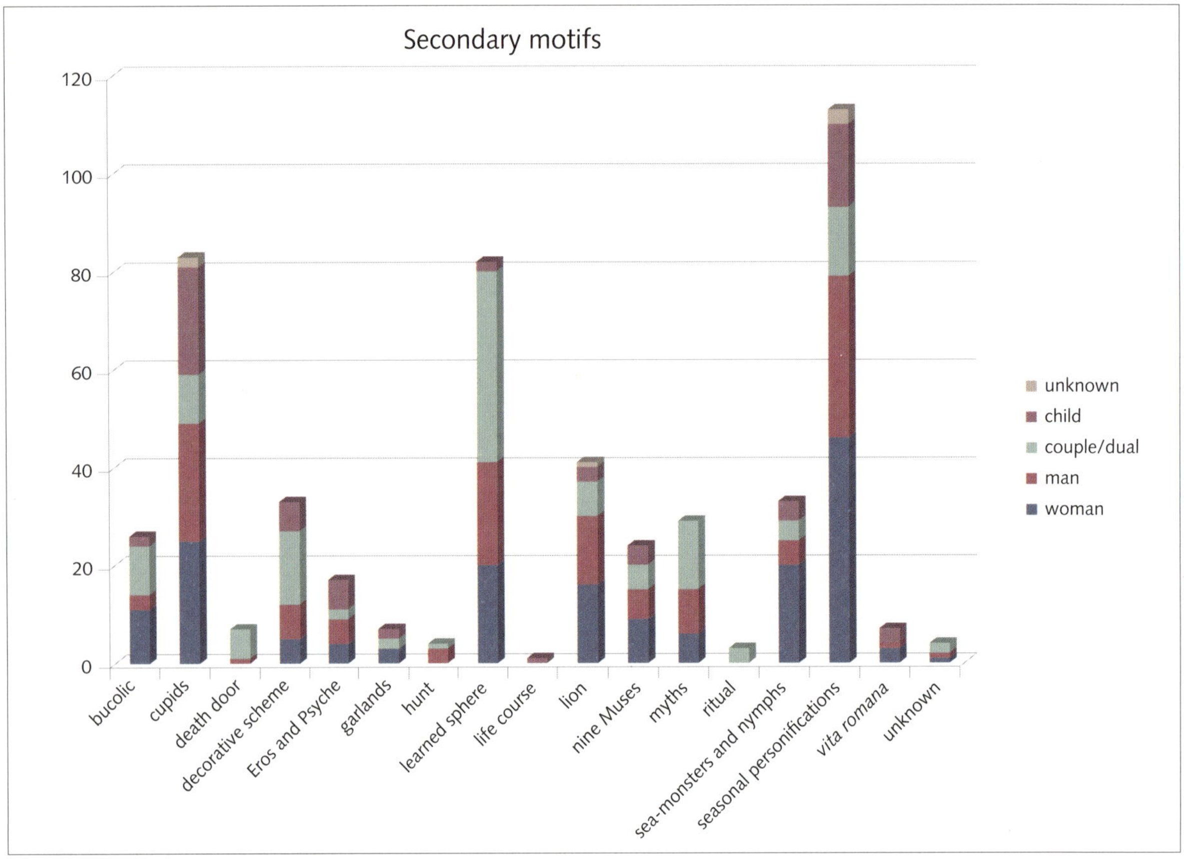

Graph 8 *The graph shows the secondary motifs that are associated with portrait figures. Sarcophagi with narrative scenes such as hunts and mythological scenes are not included, as they have only one type of scene. The graph is based on the catalogue.*

amphora with a basket-like ornamentation and a bird is found on both representations – but the woman on the Córdoba sarcophagus holds a scroll and so does her female attendant. This attendant shows portrait features as well, and instead of being the servant of a matron, she becomes the Muse of the learned woman.

Only two other categories seem to carry particular connotations of the gendered ideals. The first is sarcophagi with sea-monsters and nymphs. The portrait figures in this group are often represented with features that refer to Venus iconography, and the sea-creatures emphasis the virtues of the sea-born goddess. The group will be studied further below. The other theme that to some extent seems pre-gendered is hunting. However, only three sarcophagi show hunt scenes as the secondary motif (cat. nos. 81, 82, and 320), except for some lids and short end reliefs (see for example **Fig. 55**; cat. no. 550), and some of them include a woman as well as a man. The hunt motif is therefore, in the end, a motif that can be used to commemorate both men and women.

Though the secondary motifs can have different meanings depending on the portrait figure, there are some general remarks that should be made in terms of a common agreement about their interpretation. Seasonal personifications have been seen as symbols of the cycles of life and fertility.[532] They are often used as decorative figures in both sacral and sepulchral contexts as well as in private houses, and can therefore also be seen as neutral and always recognisable motifs that were also used for decorative purposes.[533] The seasonal personifications and their baskets of fruit may in a sepulchral context be paralleled to the offerings brought to the tombs,

532 Turcan 1966, 598; Batatta 2004, 197.

533 Hanfmann 1951; *LIMC* V1, 510-38; Gerke 1940, 30; Kranz, *ASR* V 4 (1984).

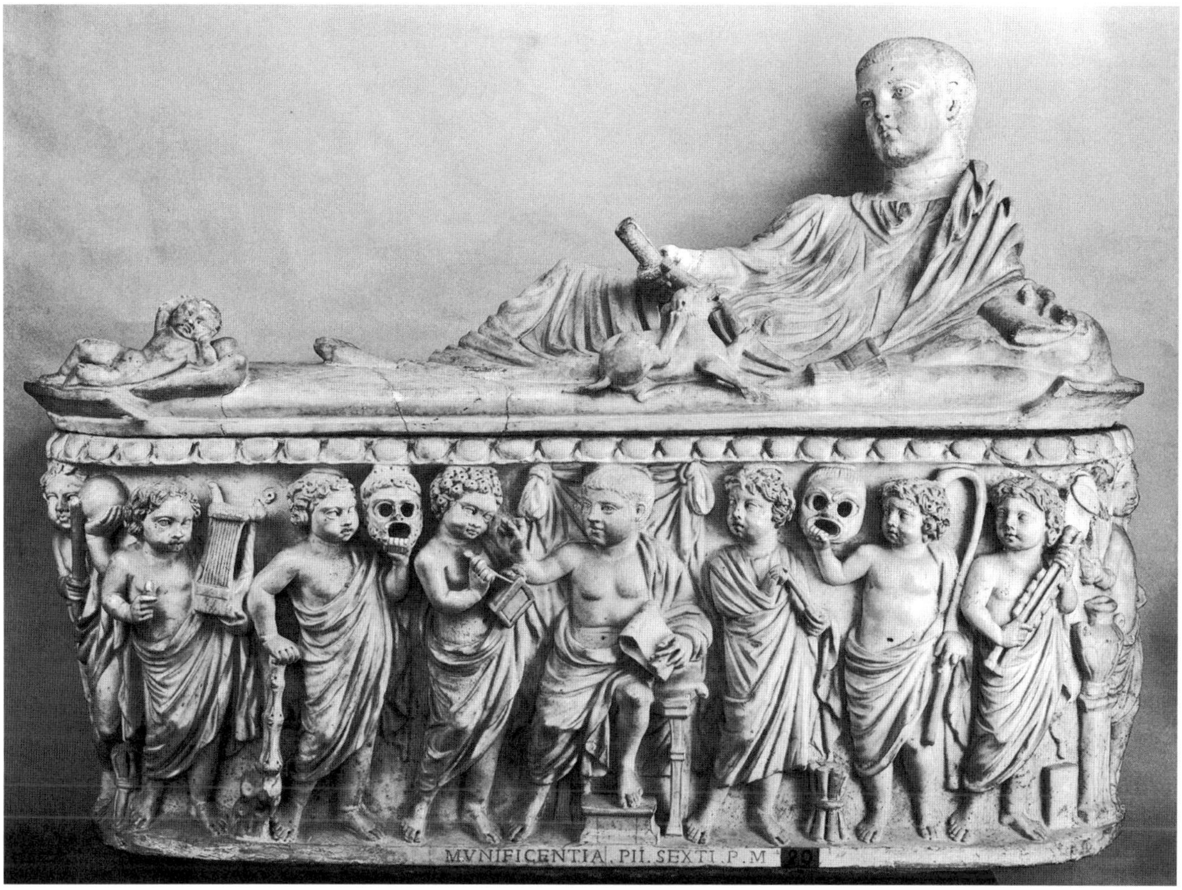

Fig. 69 *Sarcophagus showing a boy represented as a philosopher. The Muses on his left and right side are depicted a cupids or chubby* children. *The same boy is represented reclining on the lid (cat. no. 115). Rome, Musei Vaticani, Galleria dei Candelabri I 20, inv. 2422. Photo: D-DAI-ROM-41.935.*

as already mentioned.[534] Bucolic scenes belongs to the same sphere, but they are often seen with learned figures and thus allude to the philosopher-herdsman and the *vita felix*.[535] Bucolic figures increase in popularity on sarcophagi in the third century and, because they are often combined with other motifs, their juxtaposition with portrait figures is more frequent than the graph suggests. A five-panel fluted sarcophagus on the façade of Palazzo Sanseverino in Rome, for example, show a ram-bearer combined with an *Orans* with portrait features and a scene with a philosopher and a Muse (cat. no. 122). This combination of learned figures and a ram-bearer is frequently seen, especially towards the end of the third and in the beginning of the fourth centuries (for example cat. nos. 2, 4, and 14), and its popularity continued into the production of sarcophagi with Christian motifs.[536]

A lion attacking another animal, generally a horse, boar or deer, is typically used on *lenos*-shaped sarcoph-

534 Baratta 2004, 203.

535 For the meaning of bucolic scenes, see Himmelmann-Wildschütz, 1974; Himmelmann 1980; Dresken-Weiland 2010, 77-95.

536 For more on the relation of the bucolic and the learned spheres, and a discussion of the ram-bearer, see Ewald 1999, 62-76 with further references. Furthermore the ram-bearer is often connected with salvation and the Christian concept of humanitas; see Otranto 1989. Baratta (2004, 199-200) summarises the different interpretations of the ram-bearer.

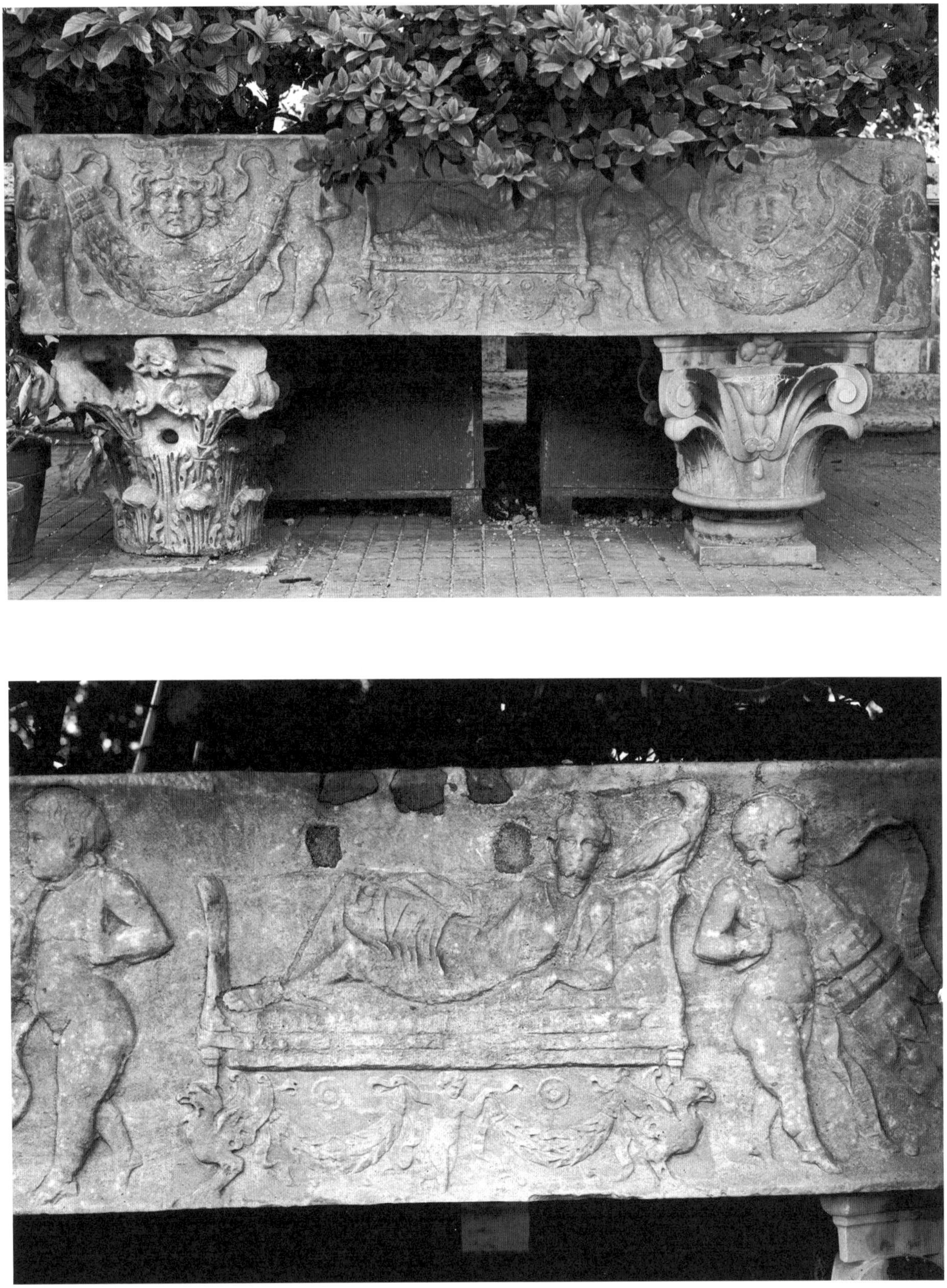

Fig. 70 *Sarcophagus with garlands and the deceased on a kline (cat. no. 537). Rome, Palazzo Pallavicini-Rospigliosi, Terrasse del Casino. Photo: D-DAI-ROM-81.4532 (Schwanke).*

agi.[537] This type of strigillated sarcophagus with a portrait figure, of which most are found in or near to Rome, often has a *clipeus* bust as the primary motif.[538] Another frequent and primarily decorative figure that appears on sarcophagi is the chubby, naked boy, sometimes represented with wings. The most frequent activities of these cupids on portrait sarcophagi are harvesting and resting or sleeping while leaning towards a torch.[539] As we will see, cupids also appear on children's sarcophagi, and in this context they help make the scenes fit the playful world of children (see for example **Fig. 69**; cat. no. 115). Another way of representing cupids is to show them as serving figures, in the sense that they can suspend a *parapetasma* behind the bust of the deceased (for example on cat. nos. 16 and 23) or support a *clipeus* or an inscription panel (for example cat. nos. 1 and 23). Torches often appear in the hands of cupids (for example cat. no. 20), and as the support for sleeping cupids who lean onto the torch (for example cat. nos. 17, 22, 25, 29, and 30). Such images are interpreted in the context of bereavement as an allegory of death.[540] Light has been connected, in various forms, to the cult of the dead; the use of torches and candelabras, and the importance of the custom of lighting a candle for the dead, have been long documented in the Roman funerary tradition.[541]

Another object used in funerary cults is the garland, and they appear frequently on funerary reliefs in general. Though only a few sarcophagi with portraits have garlands as their sole decoration, they are a popular decorative element on various kinds of scenes. Garlands, as well as torches and candelabras, are connected to funerary traditions and rituals.[542] The *atrium*, where people gathered to mourn the deceased on her *lectus funebris*, was decorated with garlands hanging from the walls; this scene of a dead woman lying in state in an *atrium* can be seen on the Haterii relief in the Vatican Museum, which is dated to the early second century.[543] Furthermore, funerary altars have been found that bear evidence of the place where the floral garlands were fastened.[544] A mid-second-century sarcophagus (**Fig. 70**; cat. no. 537) illustrates how garlands were often used. It represents a deceased woman on her deathbed with an eagle at her headrest. The eagle is rarely seen on sarcophagus reliefs, but is used in imperial iconography to symbolise the soul as it leaves this earth. Garlands carried by cupids are represented on each side of the woman, and even the bed is decorated with garlands. The garlands create an atmosphere of ritual and funerary feasts.

In conclusion, secondary motifs cannot be divided according to sex but should be grouped on the basis of the virtues they symbolise. It seems that in the funerary context, the Romans made distinctions between people based on their qualities and characters rather than their sex. This does not mean that an identity could not be constructed based on female or male virtues, nor that sex was not important to the Romans. But the fact is that they could construct their identities (as either men or women) by using the same images, and they could thus possess the same virtues.

What I have said here in terms of what kinds of motifs are found on sarcophagi is relevant to portrait sarcophagi only. A quantitative analysis of the distribution of the main themes of sarcophagi both with and without individualised figures has been made by Ewald, who enumerates 60 different themes.[545] From this study it is clear that sarcophagi in general represent a far wider variety of themes than are found on sarcophagi with portrait figures. However, sarcophagi with garlands, sea-creatures, cupids, seasonal personifications, and bucolic, Dionysian, military, and wedding scenes are the themes

537 The *lenos* shape as such has traditionally been associated with the Dionysian sphere, because of the shape of the tub used for pressing grapes; see Bianchi Bandinelli 1954, 200.

538 L'Orange 1976, 132; Chiarlo 1976; Caronna 1983, 163-64; Stroszeck, *ASR* VI 1 (1998).

539 For cupids on roman sarcophagi and their meaning, see Bielefeld 1995; *ASR* V 2, 2 (1997). Chariot racing and other kinds of activities involving cupids are also common on sarcophagi, though not frequently in connection with portraits. For the motif, see Schauenburg *ASR* V 2, 3 (1995).

540 Baratta 2004, 196; Backe-Dahmen 2008, 102.

541 Rushforth 1915; Cumont 1949, 49.

542 For sarcophagi with garlands, see Herdejürgen 1996; Isik 2000.

543 Sinn 1996, cat. 5.

544 Evidence has been found on altars for hooks that were used to hang flowers and garlands; see Liverani & Spinola 2010, 28. On the use of garlands in funerary rituals and celebrations, see Toynbee 1971, 64; Zanker & Ewald 2004, 34-5.

545 Ewald 2004, 233-37, ill.1.

that together with Muses, philosophers, and lion hunters constitute the largest groups of sarcophagi both with and without portraits.

Goddesses and Muses. The Female Ideal

Now that it has been shown that men and women could construct their identities by using the same iconography, the question is how can we characterise male and female role models? This section is concerned with identifying the female ideal by looking in more detail at the individualised female figure as she appears on sarcophagi commemorating one person, as opposed to sarcophagi commemorating a marital couple.[546]

The female portrait is most easily distinguished by its hairstyle, and less often by the portrait subject's characteristic facial features. Though we find some portraits in the Roman tradition of verism, for example old age is shown by deep lines on the forehead or similar features, the majority of the female portraits on sarcophagi have a strong tendency to show generic expressions. Therefore, the hairstyle is an important component in constructing an image of beauty and femininity for women.[547] Hairstyles were distinguished by and composed of plaits, windings, and artistic curls. These hairstyles were imitations of those of the empresses, who distinguished themselves by developing new hairstyles that turned them into icons of a specific female type. Following the fashions of these 'ideal' figures, women identified themselves with specific qualities and values. The hairstyle, therefore, was an identity marker in itself, which developed through time, and which women used in order to construct an ideal image of Roman femininity on their eternal resting place. The fact that women used hairstyles to construct identity sometimes resulted in portrait styles from different periods being combined on one relief, as, for example, the portraits of Mars, dated to the middle of the third century, and Rhea Silvia, whose hairstyle was compared to that of Julia Domna (cat. no. 598), on a relief in the Vatican.[548] Another example is the Mars and Rhea Silvia relief in the courtyard of Palazzo Mattei in Rome (**Fig. 22**; cat. no. 600), on which the woman wears a hairstyle similar to that of Julia Domna whilst, on stylistic grounds, the portrait of the man can be dated to about 30 years later, i.e. to the years between 240-50. Consequently, the sarcophagus has been dated to 250.[549] The choice of a female hairstyle that at the time of carving had gone out of fashion could be explained by a wish to be represented as a specific type of woman; however, it might have been the case that the woman continued to wear the hairstyle of her youth even when it became outdated, which has been suggested in the case of the Great Ludovisi battle sarcophagus (cat. nos. 625 and 248).[550] The portrait itself typically has as an oval face with round cheeks, a small chin, large eyes, and a straight mouth that shows no particular sign of emotion. The presence of a portrait conveys in itself a certain level of education, and was therefore indicative of the person's social standing. As such, individual characterisation of the portrait subject sometimes seems to have been less important than having a portrait that, despite its more or less generic facial features, symbolised the individual and represented the virtues and qualities of that person.[551] Some sarcophagi show a clear distinction between the male and female portrait tradition: some portraits aim to convey the seriousness of men and the beauty of women. On the so-called Plotinus sarcophagus (**Fig. 46**; cat. no. 116) the man, represented as a seated philosopher, is portrayed with signs of age whereas the female Muse at his side appears young and desirable. A second Muse on the right side of the philosopher wears the portrait of a woman that seems slightly younger that the first Muse. The three portrait figures probably should be read as a married couple and their daughter. The idealisation of the female portrait must have had an impact on the viewer, who evaluated the portrait in terms of personal qualities – and the aesthetic value of the portrait must have been important here for the ideals that the deceased aspired to.

546 For previous studies of a similar character, see especially Huskinson 1999, Salathé 2000; Hansen 2007.

547 Micheli & Santucci 2011.

548 Sichtermann, *ASR* XII 2 (1992) cat. 99.

549 Fittschen 1984, 149; Wrede 1981, cat. 202.

550 Fittschen 1984, 149.

551 The "not portrait" style of Greek portraits of women, as defined and studied by Sheila Dillon (2010), continued in the Roman period not only in public dedications, as she argues, but also in private funerary art. This idealised portrait style was a choice that could be made at the expense of naturalistic representation.

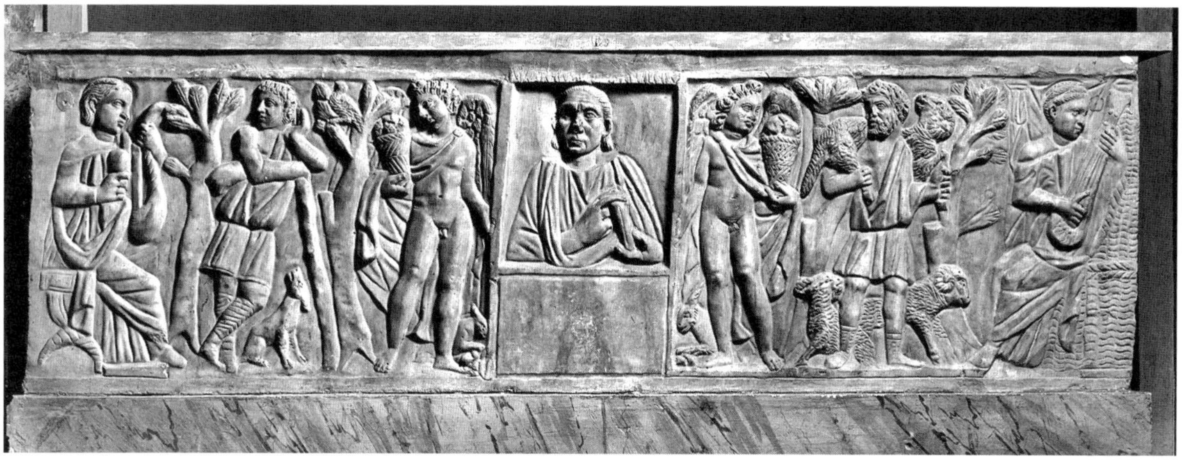

Sarcophagus commemorating three women (cat. no. 7). Rome, Musei Vaticani, Museo Pio Cristiano, inv. 128. Photo: D-DAI-ROM-3225. **Fig. 71**

The distinguishing of age between two women represented in the same scene is also seen on a previously visited piece showing a family portrait (**Fig. 44**; cat. no. 114). The frontal relief is composed of three niches. The left and right niches probably show the same family, whereas the central niche only contains the deceased woman, idealised as a learned figure. In the left and right niches, the father is represented with a long beard, wrinkles on his forehead, and deep lines around his nose and hollow cheeks. The portrait of the learned woman shows wrinkles between her eyes, and indications of age are modelled into the cheeks. Besides these conventional signs of age, the face of the learned woman has a fairly generic expression. The young woman standing behind the man and the learned woman has an idealised face in the form described above. She is probably the daughter. All these portraits are "standard" faces that conform to the role represented through the body type, in particular the bearded portrait of the philosopher. Therefore, I argue, the portrait in itself is an idealisation of the deceased, rather than a true likeness of the portrait subject that reflected personality.

Moving on from female portraits, I turn now to female figure types and the roles they convey. We have already looked at the learned woman and her qualities will only be touched upon briefly here. We saw how the category of learned female figures encompassed more than one social role; a learned woman could be educated and allude to the world of the Muses through an instrument in her hand, or she could show intellectual authority through a scroll. Sometimes she was even represented as a philosopher. The basic virtues suggested by this female type (learnedness, education, and authority) can be exemplified through the female figures on cat. no. 7 (**Fig. 71**). The sarcophagus shows a bust of a learned woman with a scroll, which symbolises the deceased woman's intellectual authority. She is framed on each side by a seasonal personification and a herdsman (a ram-bearer). Both bucolic scenes and seasonal personifications are, as argued, allegories of happiness (*Glucksvorstellungen*) and the prosperity and cycle of life. These secondary figures associate the woman with the concept of *vita felix*, and incite the viewer to reflect on questions connected to human life.[552] On each end of the relief, another two women are seated; both are individualised through the application of portrait features. One of the women plays a lyre and the other plays a lute. They represent the second of the learned woman's virtues, namely education. The lyre alludes to the Muses, and the instruments symbolise the educational ideals of the Roman upper class. On sarcophagi, the educated woman, with a lyre or shown as a Muse, is often juxtaposed with the learned man with a scroll, in order to differentiate the virtues of men and women. However, on this relief, the two educated women are presented as complementary figures to each other and

552 For the symbolic meaning of these figures when represented with learned figures, see Ewald 1999, 62-77.

their qualities reflect on the bust of the older woman with a scroll. The figures should probably be interpreted as two daughters and their mother, all equally educated, but the mother holds the highest symbol of wisdom or authority, the scroll. As we will see from reliefs with the so-called Lycian motif, the woman playing music is regarded as a figure complementary to her husband, embodying the virtues of a good wife. On cat. no. 7 (**Fig. 71**) the hierarchy that on many other sarcophagi is used to characterise the man and the women in a marital context is used to describe the relationship between a woman and her (presumed) daughters.[553]

In contrast to the scroll, which can be held by both male and female figures, instruments are attributes that on sarcophagi reliefs are used exclusively for women (see for example **Fig. 36**; cat. no. 93).[554] The allusion to the Muses effected by the instruments enhances the femininity of the portrayed woman, but it also shows her with a kind of female learnedness that is contrasted with male intellectuality. Such feminine virtues are normally significant only in a woman's relationship to a man, when they are represented together in the context of marriage. When the woman is represented alone she is rarely shown with an instrument; instead she often holds a scroll.[555] Cat. no. 7 (**Fig. 71**), however, illustrated that the opposition between the figure holding the lyre and the figure with the scroll is not necessarily to be found between the sexes, but in the figure's relationships with others.

The *Orans* is not a figure from the biblical narrative tradition, nor is she explicitly Christian, but she is the embodied personification of virtues that continued to be valued in a society that gradually became Christianised. Her form of dress, often with the head veiled, shows her to be a pious woman and the gesture of her arms signalised religious faith. She is often associated with the ram-bearer (for example, **Fig. 72**; cat. no. 14), or a bucolic setting, as on cat. no. 10. The female *Orans* is here placed in a rural landscape that suggests the idyllic character of the country life by showing a peasant with an ox-drawn wagon and a herd of sheep. At the same time, the philosophical ideal of the bucolic setting is presented: three herdsmen are watching their sheep while seeming to contemplate life. When the *Orans* is juxtaposed with a traditional learned Roman woman (**Fig. 17**, cat. no. 2) or with funerary cupids with torches (cat. no. 20), she symbolises the personal virtues of the deceased. These virtues belong to the religious sphere, but not necessarily the Christian faith, and they basically refer to the same pious female type that we know from second-century biographical sarcophagi. She is the sacrificing woman devoted and faithful to her duties, and possessing high moral standards. However, despite the fact that she is not necessarily Christian, the virtues she alludes to become increasingly popular towards the end of the third century and throughout the fourth, which is evident from the increasing number of sarcophagi with an *Orans* in this period. A last possible interpretation of the *Orans* sees her as a symbolic expression of a belief in the afterlife, making the *Orans* an illustration of the soul of the deceased.[556]

Mythological figures such as Ariadne, Penthesilea, Selene, Rhea Silvia, Proserpina, Laodamia, and Hippodamia were all known for their beauty and as victims of love in one way or another, and they were all used for self-representation by Roman woman.[557] On these scenes, the deceased is represented as imbued with feminine ideals, such as beauty and love, through which she becomes what has been called "a *prime exemplum* of a virtuous woman".[558]

The female mythological heroine is often used on sarcophagi made for dual commemorations, and the frequent juxtaposition of individualised mythological women with individualised men generally places their female virtues in the context of marriage. As such, the woman becomes a role model for wives, mothers, and daughters, and the perfect companion for a man who wants to be associated with traditional family virtues.[559]

553 Another example is cat. no. 252. See p. 154 and Birk 2011, 231.

554 The lyre is a female object (Ewald 2004, 238), with the exception being representations of Apollo, whose attribute is the lyre (for example cat. no. 553).

555 An exception is cat. no. 17, but it represents a child (a boy), and is therefore not relevant to the discussion of women's virtues.

556 Dresken-Weiland 2010, 38-76.

557 For the visual illustration of love as a new virtue on funerary reliefs, see Zanker & Ewald 2004, 182.

558 Newby 2011, 196. See also Grassinger 1994.

559 For examples of wives, see mythological couples, such as cat. nos. 545-48, 593, and 600. For an example of a daughter, see cat. no. 557. For an example of a mother, see cat. no. 655.

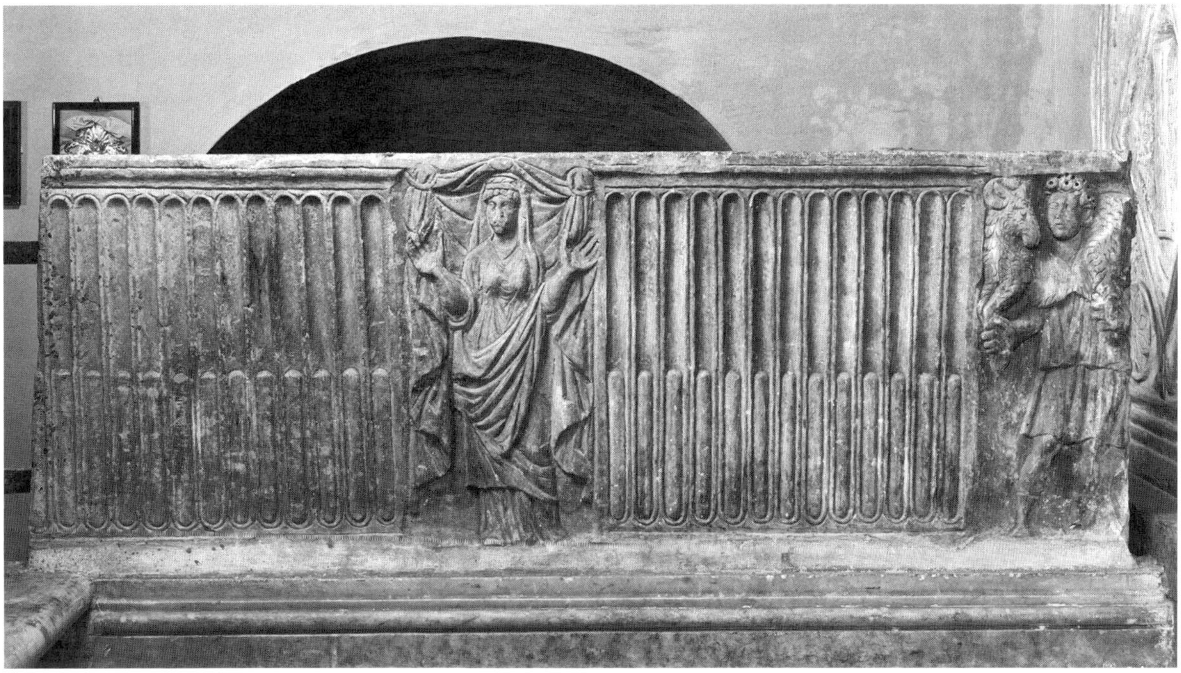

Strigillated sarcophagus with Orans *(cat. no. 14). Rome, S. Prassede. Photo: D-DAI-ROM-59.429.* **Fig. 72**

This information is important in interpreting the type of woman symbolised through heroines and goddesses, and as we will see, on these mythological scenes the gender roles are well-defined in terms of what the man and the woman respectively can do. Civic virtues such as marital *concordia*, are, for example, symbolised through couples represented as Achilles and Penthesilea, Mars and Rhea Silvia, or Dionysus and Ariadne. In these scenes the woman often has a passive part.[560] She is young, beautiful, and has surrendered herself to the situation, which is dominated by her male counterpart, who sometimes arrives on the scene to find the woman sleeping or who is a warrior watching the woman exhale, as in the case of Penthesilea.

Laodamia and Protesilaus are found on the previously mentioned sarcophagus showing scenes of Protesilaus' death and Laodamia's grief. The two scenes flank a couple represented in a third scene from the myth: the reunion of man and wife that lasted for the three hours the gods had granted them to relieve her of her immense grief (**Fig. 49**; cat. no. 595). The sarcophagus dates to the 170s, and presents the first individualised mythological couple on a sarcophagus relief. On the central scene (the reunion scene) the mythological figures have portrait heads and stand in a posture similar to that of *dextrarum iunctio* scenes. These facts, together with the doors of an *aedicula* or a tomb that are seen behind them, indicate that the scene should be interpreted in line with the *concordia* expressed on sarcophagi with death door scenes. In grave poetry Laodamia is mentioned as the loyal wife, and a portrait representation of her on a sarcophagus plays in a similar way on the marital virtues of her and the man with whom she is represented.[561] Such an iconic ideal wife is also conveyed through other mythological figures such as Alcestis (cat. nos. 551-52), whom we have already studied, and Hippodamia. A sarcophagus with scenes from the tale of the latter is today located in the garden of Villa Albani in Rome (cat. no. 606).[562] It has three scenes: in the first, King Oenomaus

560 For the representation of a Roman couple as Achilles and Penthesilea, see also Grassinger *ASR* XII 1 (1999) 153-54; Ewald 2004, 254.

561 Peek 1955, 189; Newby 1999, 2011.

562 For the sarcophagus and its iconography, see Bol 1998, 265-70. For the small group of sarcophagi with this motif, see Koch & Sichtermann 1982, 174-75.

receives Pelops at his court; the next scene shows the test of Pelops and the horse race against the king, who he must conquer in order to marry the daughter Hippodamia – King Oenomaus has fallen dead and Pelops is shown in a triumphal gesture; and the last scene shows the marriage of Pelops and Hippodamia. Her veiled head has a blank portrait and the composition of the two figures is similar to a traditional *dextrarum iunctio* motif. The civic virtues conveyed are *virtus*, *concordia*, *pietas*, and *pudicitia*, the last symbolised through the bride.[563] The four sarcophagi just discussed (cat. no. 595; **Fig. 49**, cat. nos. 551-52, and cat. no. 606) show unusual choices of decoration for a coffin, since portrait figures are only rarely placed into the narrative scenes of these three myths, and they should probably be considered as special commissions. However, the female body type and the virtues they convey in all four reliefs have clearly been chosen to represent the *concordia* of the marital couples, and to encourage the viewers to contemplate the harmonious marriages and high morality of these specific individuals.

Concordia expressed through mythological scenes is, however, not only present in the relationship between man and wife. On one piece (**Fig. 55**; cat. no. 550), Adonis and Venus are seated together with an arm around each other. The man (here a boy) is heroic and brave, which is symbolised by his naked body, and the woman (probably the mother of the young man) is chaste, shown by her fully dressed figure, seated with a sceptre.[564] The scene from the story of Adonis represented here is not related to his relationship with Proserpina, who desired Adonis and therefore would not return him to Venus after she had helped her to conceal him; this tale of Proserpina and the Underworld would not have been an appropriate setting for a sarcophagus commemorating a boy. Instead it is Adonis, the hunter, and the concord in his relationship with Venus that is the focal point of the decoration. It is this virtue, together with the bravery of Adonis and the affection of Venus, that the patron wanted to include in the memory of the deceased boy. The two representations of Venus on this coffin also show that the iconography aims at transforming the deceased persons into role models. The individualised Venus figure is a contrast to the generic representation of Venus on the left scene of the relief: the generic Venus figure is the sensual type with a naked shoulder, whereas the role of the woman is defined in relation to the boy (a son?), and her Venus figure is therefore dressed as a decent Roman mother.

Venus iconography becomes a popular method of self-representation for women in the third century and is, among other things, used to characterise the way women are represented on busts (for example on sea-*thiasoi* sarcophagi). Another full-length example of a woman presented using Venus iconography is found on the so-called Balbinus sarcophagus (cat. no. 671; another example is cat. no. 596, on which she is represented with Liber). The woman is represented with *peplos*, sceptre, and a necklace painted with gold onto her skin.[565] Amor is flying with a mirror behind her. She is paired with an individualised man in a cuirass and they are making a sacrifice together. The virtues of the two figures seem obvious (Venus the sensual exuding the desirability that comes from beauty, and the virtuous and powerful man) and they constitute the two poles of a gender line: the heroic, strong man and the beautiful woman. Mars is shown behind the man to emphasise his brave character and Victoria is crowning him. Virtus and Fortuna, together with Amor, are seen behind the woman, and the presence of Virtus shows another facet of the female repertoire of exemplary characters. She conveys the aspect of the female character that suggests strength, but she is also the figure that stands behind the man to emphasis his male virtues. The marital *concordia* of the couple is yet again indicated by the marital portrait group to the right of this composition and the reclining couple on the lid, all of which are given portrait features. Despite the unique character of this sarcophagus, it is a rather traditional piece. Though it uses a new composition of scenes, traditional figures and symbols are used to emphasise the well-known ideals of beauty, strength, *concordia*, *virtus*, and joint *pietas*.

563 For the virtue of *pudicitia* often implicit in the veiled woman on marital scenes, see Reinsberg, *ASR* I 3 (2006) 134, note 1156.

564 Koch & Sichtermann 1975, cat. 7; Wrede 1981, 139, cat. 2; Fittschen 1984, 138. For Adonis and Venus, see Der Neue Pauly 1, 119-22 Reallexikon für Antike und Christentum 1, 96. Pauly Wissowa 1, 391-92.

565 Reinsberg, *ASR* I 3 (2006) 214.

In the previously mentioned mythological scenes, the virtues of the woman can generally be said to be dominated by the male figure. There is, however, more to the female figure on mythological sarcophagi than soft virtues and marital *concordia*. In the scenes in which Selene appears before Endymion in his sleep, he (and not her) is the object of a love encouraged by his beauty, and the woman here takes the active part.[566] The role Selene embodies on these scenes can be compared with the male role models of Mars and Dionysus on scenes with sleeping female figures. The mythological woman, as well as being an object of male love, thus possesses both action and bravery. Penthesilea, for example, was a war heroine who, apart from being the object of male desire, also showed *virtus* herself.[567] Her warrior iconography and form of dress resemble that of Virtus on sarcophagi, and the bravery symbolised through the battle between Greeks and Amazons not only refers to the man, represented as Achilles, but also to the woman, represented as Penthesilea.[568] The dramatic battle scene and the tragic tale of Achilles and Penthesilea, a story of love and loss, pair the bravery of the patrons with the emotional setting of death and burial. Looking further into the visual manifestation of male *virtus* it materialises itself as a female personification, namely 'Virtus'. On hunt sarcophagi, she was, as we saw, a popular figure for the application of a portrait, and a similar role model is found in one representation of Diana (cat. no. 593) and one of Atalante (**Fig. 54**; cat. no. 604).[569] In these scenes, the woman is pictured behind the central hunter as his supporter. She is a feminine figure in a male-gendered environment, but she is not to be seen as inferior to the man. She is his actual strength and courage, and in her support of him she symbolises both *concordia* and mutual, equal personal strength.[570]

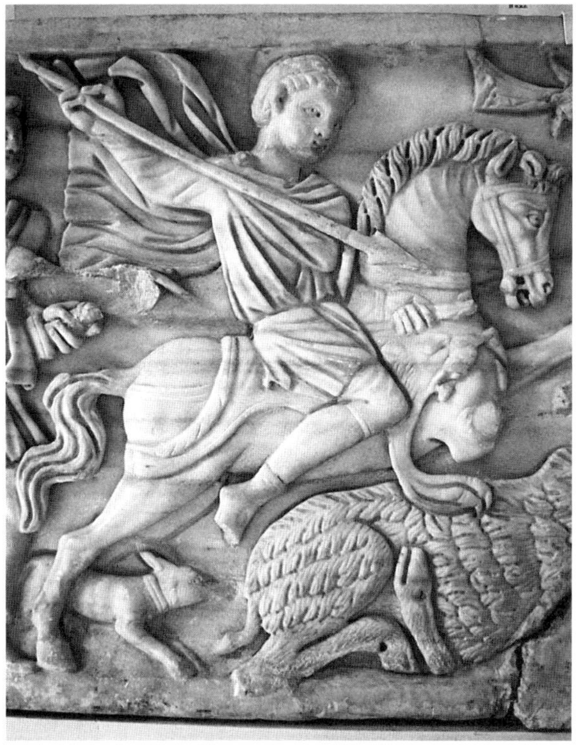

Lion hunt sarcophagus with female huntress (cat. no. 489). Nieborow Schloss (Poland), Arcadia, inv. Nb 2723 MNW. Photo: Author, courtesy of the Nieborow Schloss. **Fig. 73**

Women could also enter the male-gendered environment by representing themselves as lion hunters, accompanied by their own feminine personification of *virtus* (cat. no. 489; **Fig. 73** and cat. no. 511; **Fig. 59**). Two examples occur on lion hunt sarcophagi of the canonical type, one of which is now at Nieborow, Poland, and the other (fragmentary) at S. Sebastiano in Rome. On both sarcophagi, the central hunter has feminine features and a female hairstyle, rather than a male portrait (**Figs. 73** and **63**).[571] On the Nieborow sarcophagus the huntress is clearly accompanied by Virtus (and this was probably also the case on the other example as well, where traces of Virtus' spear may be seen across the huntress' gesticulating arm). The masculine qualities personified by Virtus are reinforced by the 'male' environment of the scene, with the attacking lion and the hunters with horses and

566 Cat. nos. 573-75, 577-81, and 583-86. On the interpretation of scenes with Selene and the sleeping Endymion in relation to reflections on life, death, and what lies beyond, see Koortbojian 1995, 63-99.

567 Hansen 2007, 113-16. For iconographic representations of Penthesilea and Achilles, see *LIMC* VII 1, 300-01.

568 Zanker & Ewald 2004, 52.

569 Hansen 2007, 108-13. For the meaning of Virtus, see Der Kleine Pauly, V, 1297.

570 Contra Hansen 2007.

571 Both sarcophagi are dated to the late third century. For a discussion of the huntress, see Sande 2010; Birk 2011.

dogs. Yet there is no doubt about the femininity of the huntresses. On the Nieborow sarcophagus, although her face is carved without much refinement, it is clear, for instance, that her mouth and chin are small, and her cheeks round. The arrangement of her hair is also unambiguous: combed from the forehead and backwards into locks, and woven into plaits from the neck, it is recognisable as a fashionable third-century fashion female hairstyle.[572] The two lion huntresses are obviously represented as one sex while they are acting as the other gender. What I mean by this is that the women are set into in a male-gendered environment, engaged in a presumably male activity. It seems that in choosing this motif for the sarcophagi, the personal qualities of the deceased were more important than the question of his or her gender.

The Nieborow sarcophagus does not show any signs of having been reused. The style of the portrait and the relief correspond to a method of rendering bodies, drapery, and hair that was common by the end of the third century and the beginning of the fourth. Andreae suggested that the S. Sebastiano sarcophagus was reused, meaning that the relief is of an earlier date than the portrait.[573] I do not, however, see any compelling evidence that the relief could not have been Constantinian as well, which gives the two sarcophagi a more or less similar dating. That these two sarcophagi were carved with images of a female 62 in the same period of time makes it likely that this was not just the outcome of some unintentional action by the craftsmen. Rather, the women who chose this image deliberately represented themselves in a male environment in order to illustrate specific elements of their identity. After all, if they had wanted a female role model, they could have chosen a mythological figure such as Diana or Artemis or the personification of Virtus herself, who would have proved a perfect vehicle to signal their strength as women. Instead these women chose to express themselves through the male bodies and through male iconography. The male *virtus* and the primary role of the huntsman were their ideals, and their own biological sex seems to have been no hindrance to their use of this iconography. These representations of women dressed in male clothing and involved in what are usually considered to be socially important male activities can help us to establish new ways of seeing gender. They make illuminating contrasts with the uniform imagery of female social identity that prevails on Roman sarcophagi, and offer glimpses of individuality at the micro-level of specific commemorations. The two sarcophagi are direct illustrations of my notion that, on sarcophagi, iconography expresses the gender of the deceased whilst the portrait expresses their sex.

There is compelling evidence that cross-gendered images, such as the two lion huntresses, were deliberately carved on sarcophagi. For a start, certain sarcophagi clearly show that the sculptor chose such a representation, even when there were other options. A graphic example occurs on a sarcophagus mentioned above that has three figural panels and two grooved ones (**Fig. 42**; cat. no. 97). The central panel shows a philosopher and a Muse, and a learned woman and a learned man are represented on the left and right panels respectively. None of the figural reliefs were finished and the back of the relief remains rough, with deep tool marks. The woman who was buried in the sarcophagus chose to be represented not as a Muse or a learned woman, but as a philosopher. By taking the male figure as a basis for her portrait, when two female figures were also available, the woman commemorated here deliberately displayed herself in a male role. It is, in the present discussion, of little importance whether the woman chose the image for herself or whether it was chosen for her. In either case, the female figure with the roughly carved head could have been used; and therefore either case prove to us that a woman's identity could be constructed by using metaphors that traditionally belonged to the masculine sphere. The deliberate choice of some cross-gendered images can also be proved in more practical terms. It is clear that even drastically re-cutting a figure to transform it from one sex into another did not pose a major problem to Roman craftsmen. This is seen from the aforementioned sarcophagus now in the Huntington Library and Art Gallery in San Marino, California (**Fig. 74**; cat. no. 246), on which a female figure was re-worked to represent a man.[574] The dress has been shortened, and cutting marks still visible around the

572 Bergmann 1977, 180-200 (cf. end of third century hairstyles).

573 Andreae, *ASR* I 2 (1980) 100.

574 Koch 1990; Birk 2011, 231.

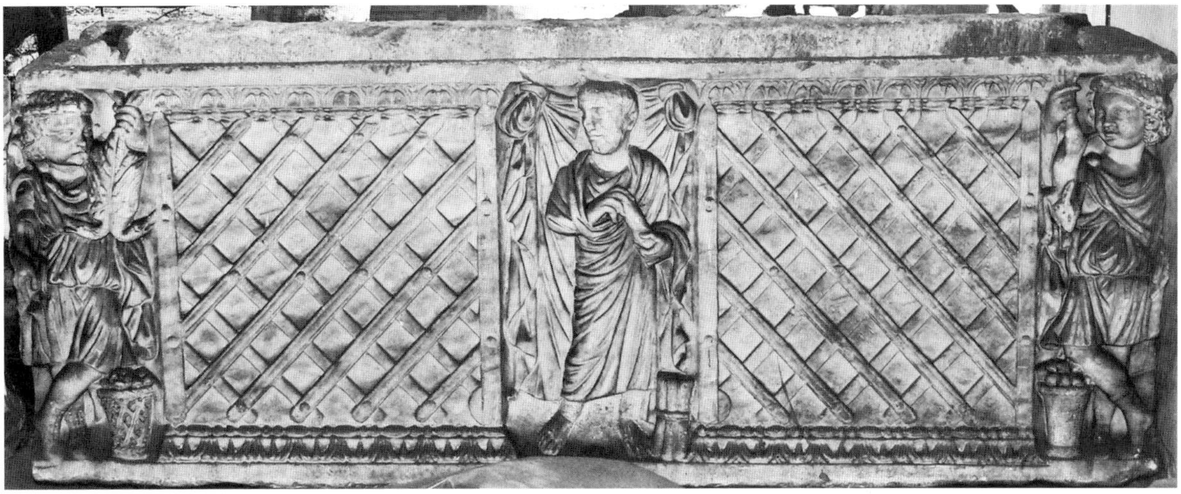

Sarcophagus with a learned man and seasonal personifications. The figure was originally female but was re-carved into a male figure; cutting marks are still visible around the feet and head (cat. no. 246). San Marino, California, Henry E. Huntington Library and Art Gallery, inv. 22.6. Photo: Author, courtesy of The Huntington Art Collections. **Fig. 74**

male portrait reveal that the original hairstyle was female (though it was probably never finished). The coffin may have been reused for a secondary burial of a man, with the figure being re-carved to suit the need of this man. It could also be that it was the only coffin of its kind available in the workshop, but the important point for this discussion is that the available figure did not suit the needs of the new patron and therefore it was altered.

Despite a general shared iconography, a group of sarcophagi exists that seems to have been predominantly used for female commemoration. This is the group of sarcophagi with depictions of marine creatures.[575] They never show full-length portrait figures but only *clipeus* busts or shells, with the exception of one which symbolises the birth of Venus by showing her kneeling in a seashell carried by sea-monsters (cat. no. 613).[576] There is a prevailing focus on feminine virtues in all the marine scenes.[577] For example, women are normally only represented with a musical instrument when accompanied by a man, but in this group, examples are found of *clipeus* busts of a woman playing a lute without the presence of a male companion. The emphasis here is not on the contrast between the man and the woman in a marital context, but on the feminine symbolism of the lute-playing women herself. The use of a shell instead of a *clipeus* similarly strengthens the connotations of female beauty. The shell is popular on sarcophagi with sea-*thiasos* but can also be used in other scenes; it typically shows a female bust, as the shell alludes to Venus iconography. It is probably its associations with the sea-born Venus that make the shell a suitable frame for female portraits.[578] It is likely that the connection to Venus conveyed so much femininity that the shape appealed mostly to women, but limiting the

575 For the group of sarcophagi with sea-monsters and nymphs, see cat. nos. 184-90, 362-83, and 463-65. Rumpf, *ASR* V 1 (1939); Brandenburg 1967; Sichtermann 1970; Engemann 1973, 66.

576 Rumpf, *ASR* V 1 (1939). For interpretation of the motif, see Brandenburg 1967. Brandenburg argues against the interpretation of the motif as a symbol of the journey of the souls to Elysium. He cautions scholars against seeing sarcophagi images as embedded in religious or eschatological contexts, and instead he interprets them as expressions of qualities of the dead person (Brandenburg 1967, 243).

577 For matrons represented on sarcophagi with characteristics of Venus and the female virtues she conveys, see Salathé 2000.

578 Cat. no. 613 shows a representation of Venus in a shell. The naked Venus wears the portrait features of a Roman woman. Venus iconography, especially *Venus-at-toilette* scenes, emerged with representations of sea-monsters and nymphs in the late second century (Taylor 2008, 41 with references to further iconographic studies of the sea-*thisaos* and Venus in note 80).

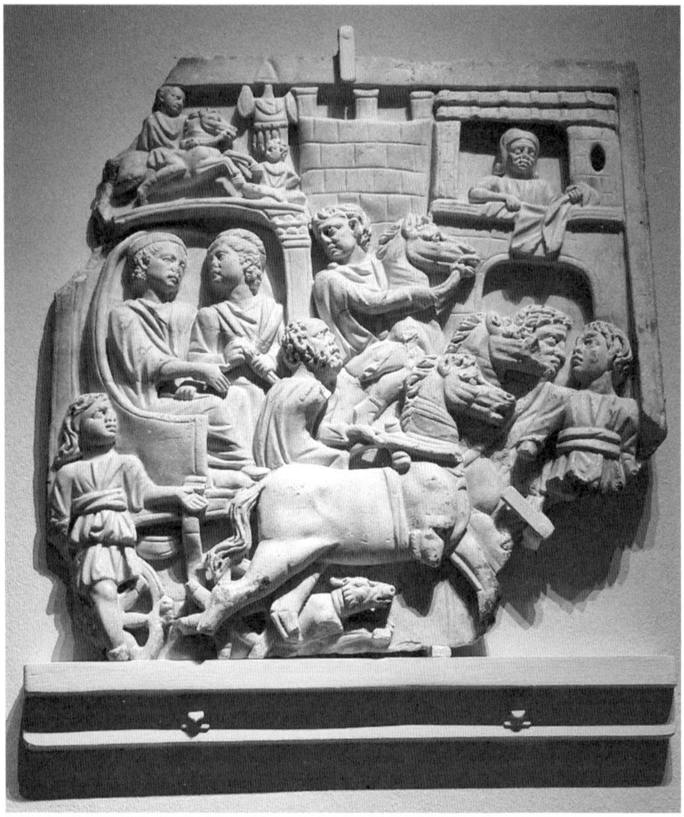

Fig. 75 *Fragment of a sarcophagus showing two women in a carriage (cat. no. 544). Stockholm, Medelhavsmuseet. Photo: Troels Myrup Kristensen.*

use of a motif to one sex is, as we have already seen, not a normal feature on Roman sarcophagi. In line with the general picture of the distribution of sex and gender on sarcophagi, and despite the fact that more than twice as many women than men are portrayed using this motif, men are also represented on sarcophagi with sea-monsters and nymphs.[579] They were also even sometimes framed by a shell.[580] Eros and Psyche, who were closely connected to Venus mythology, are also used as secondary motifs on sarcophagi for men and boys as well as for women. Psyche is an embodiment of the *anima* of human beings, whereas Eros is the personification of love and physical desire. As such, the two embracing figures have also been interpreted as the reunion of body and soul, rather than as a motif that bears female connotations.[581] The overall distribution of the scenes of secondary motifs and portrait figures in relation to sex can be illustrated by a scale composed of different degrees of gender dominated scenes: at one end we have the feminine sea-nymphs, and at the other end we find the male hunt scenes and battle scenes such those shown on the Great Ludovisi sarcophagus (cat. no. 625). In between, we find a variety of motifs that can be used according to personal preference, and we therefore see male commemorations that use motifs from the female end of the scale, just as female ones are represented by male imagery, such as in the case of the huntresses.

Men and women could use the same iconography for the images carved on their sarcophagi, even when entering the world of images representing public self-display. One particular group of sarcophagi provides a good illustrative example of this; the repeated motif on their reliefs is a carriage with two persons driving through or entering a city (cat. nos. 539-44). It is sometimes assumed that the composition was originally designed for two men, interpreted either in a funerary context as their 'last journey' or, in terms of public display, as a philosophical conversation.[582] However, a closer look at the portrait figures leads us to conclude that is was more probably designed for a couple. Generally, a man is shown holding a scroll, with another person seated at his side. The scroll gives him a position superior to the other person in the social construction of their

579 Men (6 examples): cat. nos. 187, 188, 367, 368, and 372 (carved from female bosses). A fragment from the Getty Museum was possibly also re-carved from a female head (cat. no. 378). Boys (2 examples): cat. nos. 366 and 381. Couples (3 examples): cat. nos. 463-65. Girl (1 example): cat. no. 371. Women (15 examples): cat. nos. 184-86, 189-90, 362-65, 370, 373-77, 379-80, 382-83, and 613. Unknown sex (1 example): cat. no. 369 (child).

580 Men or boys framed by a shell are found on cat. nos. 187, 366-68, 372, and 378. Two sarcophagi that do not belong to the sea-*thiasoi* group use a shell to frame a couple (cat. nos. 459 and 640). Women framed by a shell on sarcophagi outside the sea-*thiasoi* group are found on cat. nos. 144, 201, 233, and 252.

581 See Baratta 2004, 195. Eros and Psyche: Cat. nos. 68-75, 310-17, 637.

582 In favour of a male iconography: Sande 2010, 70. For the interpretation of the motif as a philosophical conversation, see Zanker 1995.

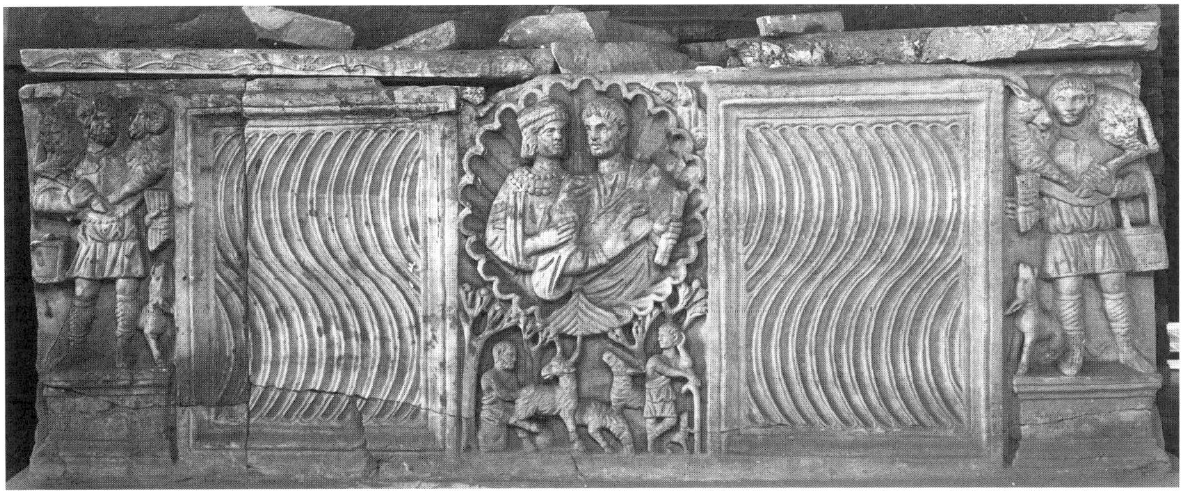

Strigillated sarcophagus with the deceased couple represented in a shell (cat. no. 432). Rome, Catacombe di S. Sebastiano. Photo: D DAI ROM 59.687 (Böhringer). **Fig. 76**

relationship.[583] On cat. no. 539, two men are seated in the carriage. This has been interpreted as a magistrate scene because one of the men holds a sceptre with a bust at the top; apart from the sceptre, the iconography is similar to the other carriage scenes.[584] On cat. nos. 540 and 541, the head of the second person is not preserved, but in the scene on the next two sarcophagi (cat. nos. 542 and 543) a woman is seated beside the man, and on cat. no. 543 they look as if they are engaged in a lively conversation. One last example, a relief on a sarcophagus now in Stockholm, there are two women in the carriage (**Fig. 75**; cat. no. 544), and one of them holds the scroll. The first five sarcophagi can be dated to the late third or early fourth century, and the sarcophagus from Stockholm with the two women should be dated in this period as well, which also corresponds well with the dating of the portraits. It is not clear from these examples that contain portraits that this iconography is particularly biased towards representations of men; instead, the sarcophagi in this group demonstrate that this image of public display of status, the carriage ride in a city, could be indicative of women's virtues as well of men's.[585]

It has been argued that the ideal ways for living women to signal power and status were through dress and jewellery.[586] However, the evidence for beautification objects, such as jewellery and clothing, is not common on sarcophagi. Jewellery is occasionally carved in marble (cat. nos. 280 and 323; **Fig. 18**) in the third century. However, during the fourth century it becomes more and more popular for female portrait busts to be adorned with, for example, necklaces. These adorned female portraits are often found together with a learned man in a martial composition, as on **Fig. 76** (cat. no. 432).[587] It is worth noting that earrings, bracelets, and necklaces could more often than the preserved evidence suggests have been either painted on or attached to the portrait figures. Similarly, dresses on portrait figures were almost certainly not as generic as they appear to

583 Cat. nos. 539-42. For the motif, see Weber 1978; Amedick *ASR* I 4 (1991) 46-55.

584 Ronke 1987, 186.

585 Prusac (2011, 199) discusses the portrait in terms of re-carving, and though she does not find traces of the "original" figure, she presumes that the portrait has been re-carved because the composition contains two women. She mentions that this head might not have been intended for sculptured portrait features after all, but for painted. This seems unlikely, firstly since it would be strange to have a painted and a sculptured portrait side by side, and secondly because as yet no painted portrait features have been clearly identified on roughly carved portraits. See pp. 55-8 for a discussion of roughly carved heads.

586 Olson 2008.

587 See also cat. nos. 11, 23, and 431-33.

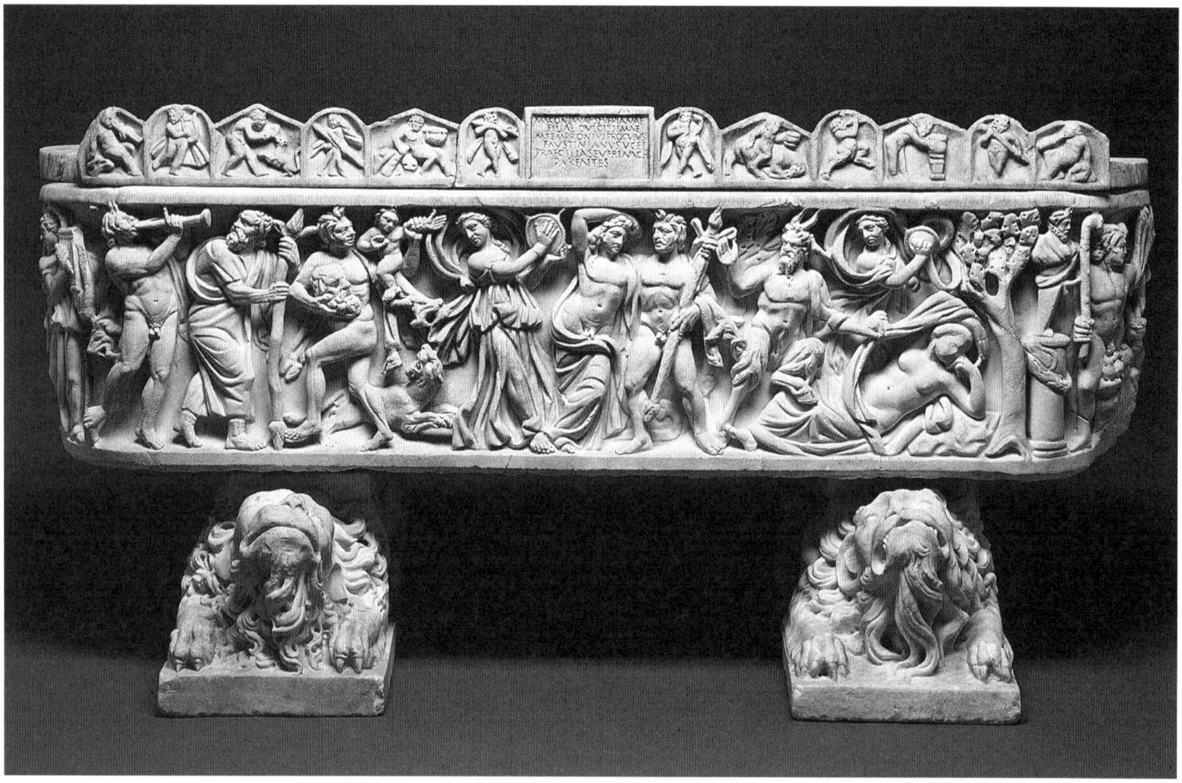

Fig. 77 *Ariadne sarcophagus (cat. no. 557). Malibu, California, The J. Paul Getty Museum, inv. 83. AA 275. Photo: With permission from The J. Paul Getty Museum, Villa Collection, Malibu, California.*

be today, since painted ornamentation has been found on close examination of the stone surface.[588] Clothing never seems to deviate from the traditional female fashion of tunic and *palla*. However, the evidence of paint on sarcophagi is just starting to have an impact on the analysis of the motifs. Visible to the naked eye are golden borders painted on the drapery to signalise the status of the patrons (for example cat. no. 666, on which the remains of gold paint are visible on both the portrait figures and the generic figures).[589] As the reliefs appear today in shiny, white marble, the bodies and clothes of some portrait figures seem so generic that they might just as well have been carved with the portrait of a man as of a woman, but it is possible that painted ornaments and jewellery were used to emphasise the status and gender of the deceased.

One type of 'beauty model' can, however, be recognised on sarcophagi today: the beautiful and desirable semi-naked woman disguised as a mythological heroine or a goddess. Though she became most popular in the first part of the third century, along with mythological sarcophagi in general, the first representations of a semi-nude woman belong to the years between 170 and 200 (e.g. cat. nos. 555 and 563). This semi-naked heroine is Ariadne, found by Dionysus while she is sleeping, and her pose emphasises her female curves and beauty (see for example **Fig.** 77; cat. no. 557).[590] The sleeping figure became very popular in the third century, and

588 Østergaard, 2011, 19-20.

589 For colours on Roman sculpture and sarcophagi, see also Østergaard (http://www.glyptoteket.dk/tracking-colour2.pdf). It shows that more details of the reliefs were emphasised through the use of colours, including details such as axe heads on the sketchy reliefs of the end short ends.

590 Another example alluding to the beautiful female body is a relief with Ceres in her wagon as she goes searching for Proserpina (cat. no. 567). She is not semi-naked but the naked shoulder suggests her feminine beauty. The sarcophagus is one of the earliest that shows a portrait head and is dated to around 150.

through representations of Ariadne and Rhea Silvia in their death-like sleep with naked torso and exposed breasts, the Roman woman was commemorated by means of allusion to her outer appearance. That the motif is about the power of beauty is underpinned by the myths themselves: when Achilles holds the mortally wounded Penthesilea in his arms, it is her feminine beauty and power that strikes him, symbolised by the heroic but still feminine representation of Penthesilea in his arms at the moment of her death. In a similar manner it is the youthfulness and beauty of Ariadne, as shown by her exposed body, that make Dionysus take her with him.

This display of the naked female body on sarcophagi is striking, because women who put their bodies on display in their lifetimes were considered unchaste.[591] This judgment obviously did not apply to a woman after her death: she could represent herself by a half-naked mythological figure type, and even when shown together with her husband on a *clipeus* bust, a woman chose a figure that suggestively exposed one shoulder. The graceful and half-naked figures reveal the femininity of a woman's body, and on sarcophagi her physical desirability was a positive quality, not a disgrace. From a male perspective these representations are about love and desire,[592] but for women they were most likely about creating an image of power and status. The men who fall in love with these mythological heroines are great heroes, such as Achilles and the god Mars, and identifying oneself with such a woman elevated one's own character to a divine level. Furthermore, the display of the naked body shows that women, as well as men, could use their natural attributes to define their place in a social context: through these images, they use their physical appearance to gain power over men.

As we have already seen, women's role models can take many forms. They may appear as independent and educated (the learned woman), as the beautiful objects of male desires (on mythological love scenes), as strong because of their feminine and sometimes male-gendered qualities (for example, the mythological figure and the lion huntress), and as supportive wives.[593] The latter type is especially found on *clipeus* sarcophagi with a couple, and on *dextrarum iunctio* scenes. On these scenes, the woman is represented as a chaste wife, sometimes with a veil and averted eyes, and occasionally in a gesture that symbolises *pudicitia*.[594] One role that is rarely emphasised on sarcophagi is that of the perfect mother and wife in a broader familial context. This role is only elaborated on some second century sarcophagi, such as the much-discussed coffin of the boy Statius (**Fig. 14**; cat. no. 615). On this relief, dated to around 150, the mother is seen seated while breastfeeding the boy. She is represented as a *nutrix*, a wet nurse; but since, as has been shown, sarcophagi are most often commemorations based on the relationships between parents and children or husbands and wives, the woman should be seen as an ideal representation of the mother. Another example is found on the lid of the Portonaccio sarcophagus (**Fig. 23**; cat. no. 626) from the late Antonine period, showing a woman watching her child having its first bath.[595] This motif is also found on some short end reliefs of biographical sarcophagi;[596] however, these feature no portrait heads. These examples are as close as we get to the female motherly role.[597] Another role that

591 Olson 2008, 95

592 A prevailing interpretation of beauty culture is that women's engagement with their looks was imposed on them for the gratification of men, cf. Olson 2008, 111.

593 Reinsberg (*ASR* I 3 (2006) 152-54) puts emphasis on the representation of *pietas* towards the gods, one's parents, and one's husband as an important virtue conveyed through the female figure represented with a man. On female virtues interpreted on the basis of mythological scenes on mosaics, see Muth 1998, 238-43.

594 This is typically seen on *dextrarum iunctio* and sacrifice scenes, as for example cat. no. 664. See Reinsberg, *ASR* I 3 (2006) 135, note 968, 1156, 1160.

595 Huskinson 1999, 15-7.

596 Cat. nos. 656, 659, 660, and on a life course sarcophagus from the same period, cat. no. 622.

597 There are two fragments that are exceptions to this rule. One shows a mother or a wet nurse with a short veil breastfeeding a child; it is dated to the end of the third century (cat. nos. 617). The other is a child's life course sarcophagus in the Vatican showing a woman with an infant watching another small child being bathed, but on this scene the woman has no portrait features and she is probably an old wet nurse. The sarcophagus is dated to the late third century (cat. no. 619). A child being bathed is also found on the short end of another child's life course sarcophagus from the third century; again this scene shows no portrait heads (cat. no. 623).

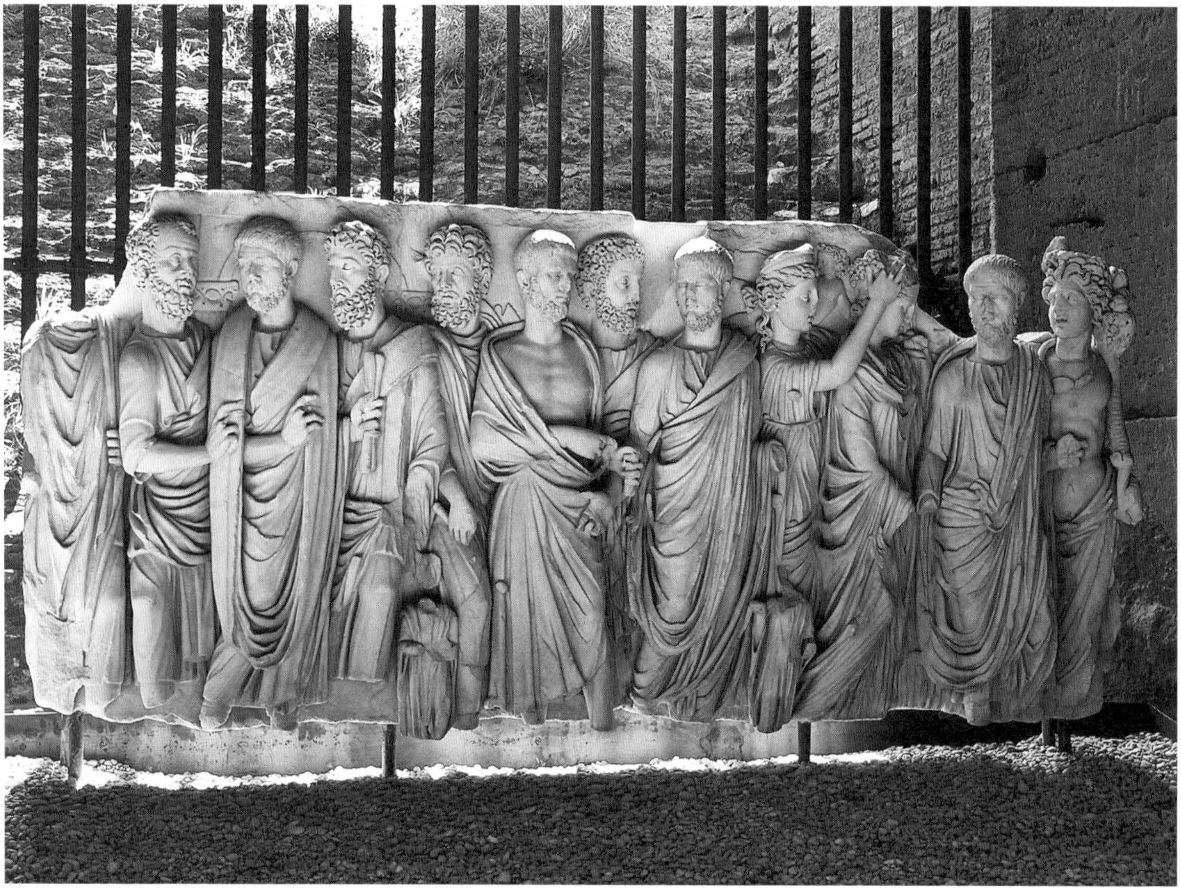

Fig. 78 *The so-called Brother sarcophagus from Naples (cat. No. 641). Naples. Museo Nazionale, inv. 6603. Photo: Author, courtesy of the Soprintendenza Speciale per i Beni Archeologici di Napoli e Pompei.*

is often used to characterise the ideal Roman woman is the woman who works with wool, the *univira*. She is never represented on sarcophagi, which is strange, since the wool-working woman and wife is often referred to in modern literature on Roman women.[598] We therefore have to accept that in the construction of funerary commemorations between the second and fourth centuries, other norms and ideals were in play than those emphasised in the literary sources, which were written by men.

Heroes, Hunters and Philosophers. The Male Ideal

On the so-called brother sarcophagus from Naples (**Fig. 78**; cat. no. 641), the learned male figure appears in its various forms, as if the aim were to provide a catalogue of the virtues divined into this figure.[599] The same man is represented four times with a portrait in different postures, clothing, and social contexts. He is illustrates the range of male role models that are popular on sarcophagi: he is shown as a Roman citizen dressed in toga, a magistrate, a philosopher in *himation*, and a husband

598 *I, Claudia* I (Kleiner and Matheson 1996, reviewed by Bartman 1998) and *I, Claudia* II (Kleiner and Matheson 2000) are examples of studies that paint this rather stereotypical picture of the Roman woman. The *univira* is a Christian type of ideal woman and she barely existed in the Roman period, except as an idealisation of women in Augustan literature. In funerary inscriptions the term is rarely used. I am grateful to Hanne Sigismund Nielsen for sharing her research with me.

599 Geyer 1978; Hölscher 2008, 52. See also Reinsberg, *ASR* I 3 (2006) 154-63 for the official role and status of this figure, as well as the man on marriage scenes.

clasping hands in *dextrarum iunctio*.[600] The sarcophagus demonstrates the different identities a man in his position could employ to present himself as a person of many virtues. This way of defining one aspect of an idealised personal character by setting it in opposition to another aspect is also found on sarcophagi showing two different persons. A piece in the Galleria Lapidaria in the Vatican depicts two men, one in a *sagum* without a beard and one clad in toga with a beard (cat. no. 62). Both men hold scrolls as a symbol of power, but whilst the man in the *sagum* conveys military status, the other man shows his engagement in a public career. The sarcophagus plays on the opposition of military versus public status, and through the juxtaposition of the two body types the virtues of military competences and magisterial power are given extra emphasis.[601] These two sarcophagi do not, however, show the full repertoire of male roles; there is a much greater variety of types that encompass different aspects of the male ideal. In a few cases, mostly from the second century, the commemorated man is represented as a father; sometimes on mythological sarcophagi he is seen as an object of love; and often the male role model continues the tradition of the heroic nature of male virtues: there are the military men in cuirass, the hunters on horseback, mythological heroes and gods.[602] Though the same figures were continuously repeated, some figures went out of fashion and others gained popularity as the repertoire of motifs was expanded. For example, the military role model of the second-century biographical sarcophagi with battle scenes was toned down on third-century sarcophagi; in fact only rarely is reference made to military ideals at this time. The Great Ludovisi battle sarcophagus (cat. no. 625) is a rare case, but it shows that motifs could be brought back into the iconographic repertoire to allude to traditional virtues. Except for a few other examples, the military man on third-century sarcophagi is only seen on lion hunt sarcophagi, and in the fourth century he is practically non-existent.[603]

600 Zanker & Ewald 2004, 186.

601 Amelung 1903, 286.

602 For the history of these body types in the tradition of Roman self-representation, see Koortbojian 2008.

603 Other examples, apart from the Great Ludovisi battle sarcophagus, are cat. nos. 100 and 248 (the latter probably the lid of the Great Ludovisi sarcophagus).

The male portraits on sarcophagi have generally strong physiognomy. The face thereby expresses the potent character of the portrait subject, a tradition that is known from the early republican period. Male portraits follow the 'period faces' established by representations of the emperors, in terms of both facial features and hairstyle, in order to construct an image of the deceased whose ideals were both easily acceptable and recognisable in current society.[604] However, individual features and especially old age (see, for example, cat. nos. 56 and 68; **Fig. 3**) can be recognised in sarcophagus portraiture. In private art forms, including on sarcophagi, there is indication that several portraits styles existed concurrently, in contrast to the imperial image that for ideological reasons represented only one style at any one time.[605] This means that a portrait could be chosen individually according to the male type with which one wished to be associated. As we have seen, some sarcophagi show two portraits that can be dated to different periods. The availability of different stylistic options to patrons makes the chronology of sarcophagi complicated, as has already been discussed in connection to the female portrait ideal.[606]

We have already seen that the learned figure was a popular method of self-representation for both men and women, but there are other parallels of male figures in the commemoration of women (see graph 7). In the mythological world, the abduction of a beautiful mortal is a theme that is shared by men and women.[607] As Persephone is taken by Hades, so Hylas is taken to the Underworld by spring nymphs, who could not resist his beauty and dragged him into the water (**Fig. 79**; cat. no. 594).[608] This relief is interesting since it is the only example known from the corpus of sarcophagi with a deceased person represented as

604 On the Roman male portrait, see Fejfer 2008, 262-85.

605 Fejfer 2008, 280.

606 For a summary of the problem of dating sarcophagus reliefs, see Birk 2010/11.

607 For an interpretation of male virtues communicated through mythological figures in mosaics, see Muth 1998, 228-38. Muth's theory is that through mythological protagonists, pictures of values and virtues in the relationship between men and women are formulated, cf. Muth 1998, 244.

608 For Hylas as the sexually attractive man, see Muth 1999, especially p. 129.

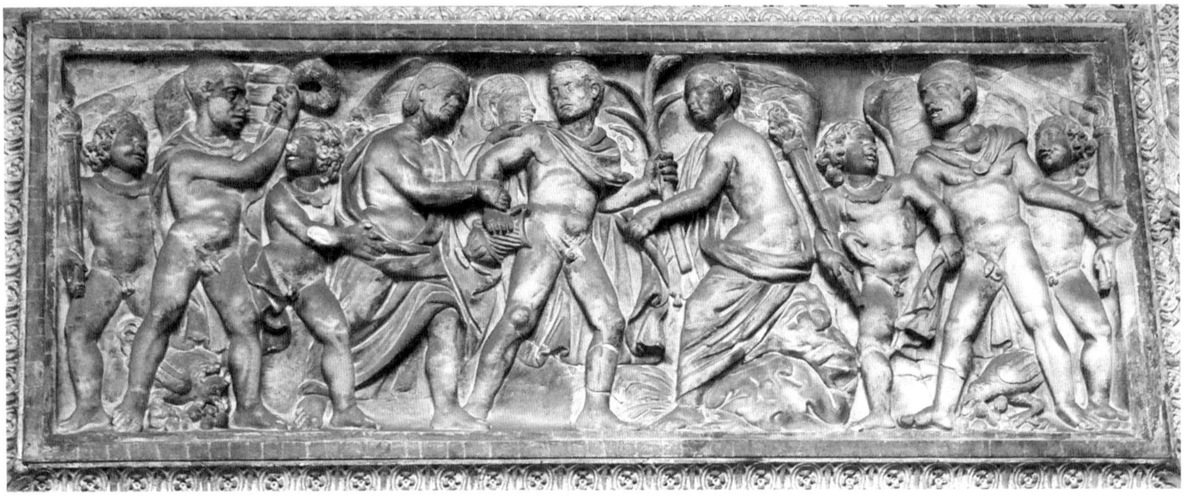

Fig. 79 *Sarcophagus relief showing the abduction of Hylas (cat. no. 594). Rome, Palazzo Mattei. Photo: Author.*

Hylas. It has undergone extensive restorations, and only two of the relief's four portraits can definitively be said to be Roman portraits, namely those of Hylas and the boy-nymph.[609] The scene is about death, symbolised by the cupids with torches who move between the protagonists, and loss, symbolised by Hercules and Polyphemos the Argonaut searching for their lost friend.[610] That the message of this relief is not about sexual desire is made clear by the fact that one of the nymphs is represented with the portrait features of a boy. He is probably an already deceased son, whose reunion with his father is suggested by the scene showing the boy-nymph dragging the man (Hylas) into the Underworld. It is known from other cases that funerary monuments could commemorate family members who had already died; for example, G. Valerius Herma built a tomb (Mausoleum H in the Vatican necropolis) for his family and two already deceased children, whose remains were probably transferred to the new tomb. The same has been suggested for the Alcestis sarcophargus (cat. no. 552). The Hylas sarcophagus may therefore have been chosen for the burial of a man, with the portrait of the already deceased boy being added to symbolise their reunion in death.

Another example of a male role that emphasises beauty is the sleeping Endymion, who, as he is represented on sarcophagi, constitutes a parallel to the sleeping Ariadne.[611] His beauty is expressed by the same means that were used for Ariadne and Rhea Silvia:[612] he is naked or semi-naked, has a slender waist, and his arm is elegantly raised above his head. Rhea Silvia, Ariadne, and Endymion all express physical beauty, and they are all the objects of a divinity's love (cat. nos. 573-86).[613] As Koortbojian says, the myth of Endymion, as it is represented on sarcophagi, reflects an idealistic beauty (Endymion), desire (Selene), eroticism (the encounter), and death (Endymion's sleep), and similar themes could be identified in the myths of Rhea Silvia and Ariadne.[614] The appearance of the three sleeping role models is so close that one could be carved into another with only minor alterations. A re-carving of an image of Ariadne

609 See Birk, 2010/11.

610 Zanker & Ewald 2004, 96-8.

611 According to Koch & Sichtermann, 23 representations of the sleeping Ariadne are known from sarcophagi (1982, 193). 11 of them have been individualised through a portrait (cat. nos. 555-58, 560-63, and 565-66).

612 On the unveiling of Ariadne, see Mucznik 2000. For Rhea Silvia, see *LIMC* VII 1, 615-20.

613 For a description of scenes on sarcophagi with Endymion, see Sichtermann, *ASR* XII 6 (1992) 35-9. Sichtermann says (*ASR* XII 6 (1992) 44) that portrait figures of Endymion start to appear on sarcophagi in the last quarter of the second century. This does not concur with the portraits analysed in my catalogue; here it seems that Endymion starts to appear with a portrait around 220.

614 Koortbojian 1995, 66.

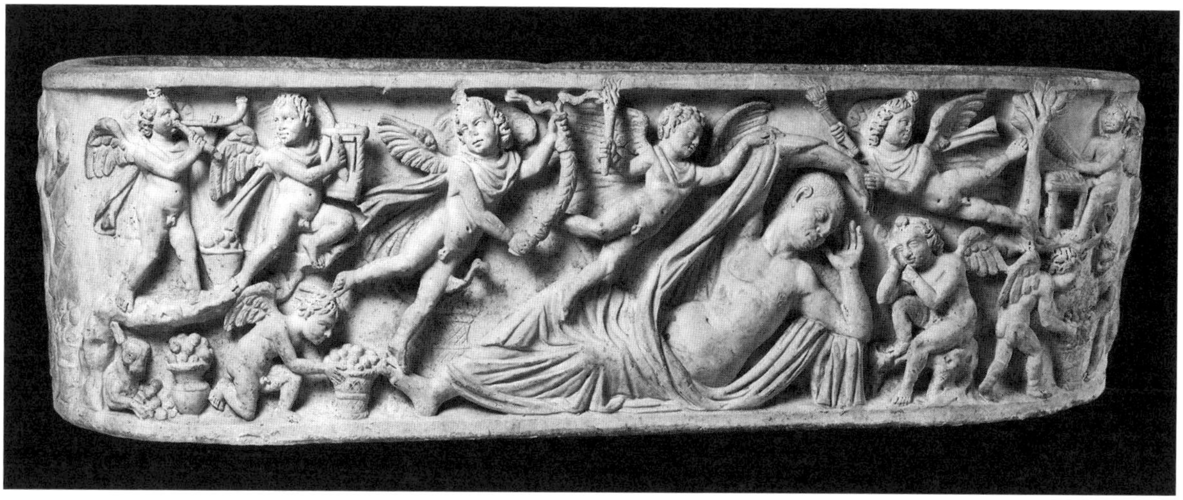

Sarcophagus showing the deceased in a position similar to the sleeping mythological figures (cat. no. 576). London, British Museum, inv. GR 1947.7-14.8. Photo: © The Trustees of the British Museum. **Fig. 80**

into Endymion is found on a sarcophagus in the British Museum (**Fig. 80**; cat. no. 576).[615] The graceful femininity of the body is still apparent, especially in the round belly and slender waist. The man has a portrait that enables us to date the sarcophagus to around the first part of the third century.[616]

What could be called feminine beauty is seen on yet another male figure on a sarcophagus mentioned previously (cat. no. 564). On this sarcophagus, Ariadne and Dionysus are seated on a rock in deep admiration of each other.[617] The young Dionysus has his genitals and slender waist exposed, whilst Ariadne is decently dressed and veiled. Both of them have a blank portrait. This relief demonstrates that there is no pattern in the symbolic meaning of naked or clothed figures in the sense of a gendered hierarchy: Dionysus is the one who uses his body to symbolise the virtues that he stands for, while Ariadne is dressed and veiled and thus recalls the traditional representation of the decent wife. There is, however, a cultural rule that specifies that when a couple is represented together, both of the figures cannot be naked.[618] The Roman craftsman took care to imply this kind of opposition between men and women when they were represented together, but it is not relevant when they are represented individually. This oppositional relationship, however, seems not to have been based on the sex of the persons, but on the fact that they were part of a social relationship, and marriage especially seems to have been governed by particular social rules.

The deceased man, like the deceased woman, could appear as a divinity that, encouraged by love, reveals himself to a sleeping mortal. In the female version this divinity was Selene; her male equivalent on sarcophagi is the god Mars (cat. nos. 598-600).[619] Mars, of course, stands for very different virtues, but in these scenes his actions and feelings towards the deceased (represented as the sleeping mortal) are the same as Selene's. These

615 The breasts were cut down and a penis was added to the figure. For discussion, see Sichtermann, *ASR* XII 2 (1992) 54-5.

616 Walker 1990, cat. 43.

617 Turcan 1966, 91, 95, 219-21; Matz, *ASR* IV 2 (1968a) cat. 76; Giuliani 1985, 188-90, cat. IV 5. For Ariadne, see *LIMC* III addenda, 1050-51.

618 For the naked body as an ideal in antiquity, see Himmelmann 1990, 1-28. For a cultural study of the limits of nakedness in Greek society in the fifth and fourth centuries BC, see Daehner 2006. For attitudes towards nudity in Roman art, see Hallett 2005a, 87-101.

619 For an interpretation of the mythological scene and the inversion of the roles of the protagonists on these "sleeping scenes", see Koortbojian 1995, 102-6. Koortbojian, furthermore, sees these sleeping figures as equated with death, but also as dreamers. He writes that they offer a positive image of the afterlife and therefore create a comforting image for the relatives (Koortbojian 1995, especially 100-13).

scenes show that the same meaning could be conveyed by a scenario in which the male and female roles were exchanged; the choice of motif was determined by the personality of the deceased person, rather than their sex. The composition of these Sleeping Beauty scenes are all alike: the mortal figure is situated in the lower right corner of the relief, and the god or goddess approaches from the left. It is, however, curious that on Ariadne scenes, Dionysus is never individualised. It seems as if something in the character of this somewhat unrestrained god was found inappropriate for the purpose of self-representation in this context. This cannot be explained by the character of the god, because he is individualised on other reliefs (cat. nos. 564 and 568); rather, it is likely that Dionysus's behaviour in the procession, drunk and lustful, was not appropriate for a Roman husband. Such behaviour seems only to have been appropriate when the man was represented alone (**Fig. 93**; cat. no. 568).

The mythological scenes and their male protagonists that have been discussed so far all had counterparts in female figures, but this does not mean that there are not some ideals that were more often preferred by men than by women, such as the lion hunter and war-related heroes like Mars or Achilles.[620] It is also worth mentioning here that patrons of sarcophagi always choose a god or a hero of the deceased's own sex for their representation.[621] This may be explained by the reciprocal virtues implied in the male and female mythological representations that make no such gross-gendered choice necessary. Though cross-gendering is known from mythology, such as when Hercules and Omphale changed clothes in order to participate in a bacchic ritual, patrons of mythological sarcophagi never exploited this possibility.[622]

In sarcophagus iconography, men could take on feminine physical characteristics, as well as being shown with feminine attributes. Although various kinds of cross-gendered images appear, the most common type consists of a male portrait applied to a female body. Sometimes the body was unambiguously presented as a female, with curvy lines and breasts visible beneath a long female dress. One shoulder might even be exposed in an allusion to the iconography of Venus (cat. no. 8). At other times it may simply be that a male body is represented in such a feminine fashion that it has become almost womanly (cat. no. 576).[623] The womanly male body is a not wholly unfamiliar phenomenon within Roman visual culture. For example, male gods like Dionysus or Priapus and young men like Narcissus and Hermaphroditus all show a great deal of femininity both in their behaviour and physical appearance.[624] As mentioned above the masculine hero Hercules also had an experience of being 'womanly', when he changes clothes with Omphale. Another way of illustrating gender qualities is by the addition of an object held by the person, such as mirror. On a sarcophagus in the Museo Gregoriano, in the Vatican, a man is depicted with a female body together with "soft domestic qualities",[625] symbolised by the children playing beneath the couch (**Fig. 81**; cat. no. 536).[626] The lid of this sarcophagus bears an inscription saying that it belonged to P. Caecilius Vallianus, a 63-year-old military man.[627] From a modern perspective it is almost impossible not to be intrigued by the way this military man chose to depict himself on his funerary monument. The reverse of the coffin is decorated with a hunt scene, and the face of the hunter may be a portrait as indicated, despite the sketchy character, by the facial features and especially

620 For the mythological hunter and the nude hero type as male ideals, see Ewald 2005, particularly p. 65.

621 Exceptions are Muses and nymphs. Varner (2008) shows that in imperial art this dichotomy of male and female mythological and divine figures was not adhered to, and emperors could be represented as goddesses (Varner 2008, 185-89).

622 Ovid, *Fasti* II 283-358. Kampen 1996a, 242. A portrait statue, probably from a funerary context, shows Omphale cross-dressed with the clothes and attributes of Hercules. On sarcophagi, however, Omphale is never shown with portrait features.

623 British Museum, inv. GR 1947.7-14.8; Walker 1990, cat. 43.

624 Cain 1997; Oehmke 2004; 2007.

625 Huskinson 1996, 26.

626 Huskinson 2002, 26. See also, Koch & Sichtermann 1982, 111.

627 Himmelmann-Wildschütz 1974, 47-8; Amedick, *ASR* I 4 (1991) 167-68. Whether the lid belongs to the sarcophagus or not has been discussed, but the argument that the discrepancy in the size of the lid compared to the chest is not enough to reject the possibility that the two pieces belong together (since this is relatively common for Roman sarcophagi).

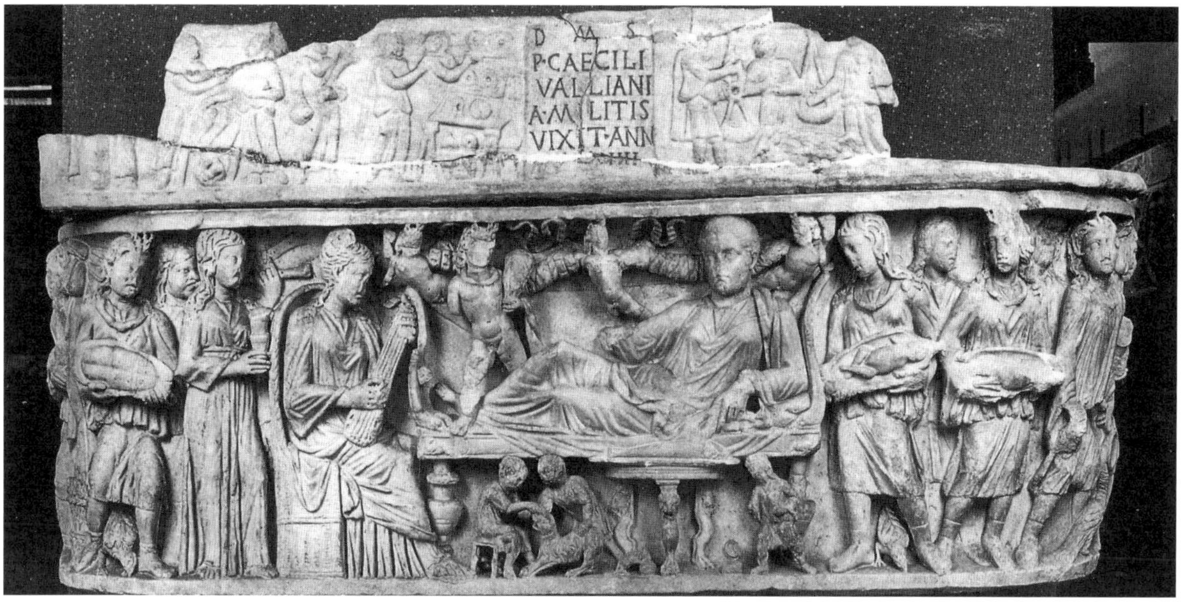

The sarcophagus of P. Caecilius Vallianus (cat. no. 536). Rome, Musei Vaticani, Museo Gregoriano profano, inv. 9538/9539. Photo: FA-S5718-01. **Fig. 81**

the beard. It is therefore likely that the coffin was designed to commemorate a man. S. Sande has recently suggested that the female body was made to make the reclining figure symbolise the deceased man's *anima* and his idea of an afterlife.[628]

Another example of the feminine ideal of men is found on a *loculus* relief in the Vatican (**Fig. 62**; cat. no. 249). The left panel of the relief depicts a seated man with what appears to be a scroll in his left hand. He stretches his right hand forward and grasps the hand of another man standing in front of him who, like the seated man, is dressed in a tunic with sleeves and has a *stola* around his left arm. Two mirrors and a curtain hang from a rod in the background. It seems as if the seated man is holding one of the mirrors, maybe ready to put it into the hand of the other man. As we have seen, the mirror was an object associated with Venus iconography and the female world: men who used mirrors were considered effeminate.[629] The heads of the two figures have been carved with portrait features, but it seems as if the portrait of the standing man with short hair has been re-carved from the face of a woman with long loose hair. The locks of the woman are still visible on the back of his head. The scene has been interpreted as a sales scene, a *dextrarum iunctio*, and a cultic scene,[630] but several questions still remain to be answered. If we accept that the long locks falling onto the shoulder of the standing man are reminiscent of an original female figure, the loose hair remains an unanswered question: Roman women always wore their hair up, and I know of no other example where portrait figures wear such hairstyle. Servants, captive, and grieving women wear long loose hair, and with the coming of Christianity Eve also appears with unbound hair.[631] In Eve's case, her appearance can be explained by her status as a sinner, in opposition to the modest and pious Mary, who is represented on sarcophagi with her hair pinned up under a veil, like a Roman *matrona*.

628 Sande 2010.

629 Sinn 1991, 48.

630 Sinn 1991, cat. 21; Amedick, *ASR* I 4 (1991) cat. 285.

631 An example of the first is the servant with a cup behind the *pandurium*-playing woman on the sarcophagus of Caecilius Vallianus, now in the Museo Gregoriano Profano in Rome (cat. no. 536). An example of a grieving woman on a deathbed is found on a sarcophagus from Louvre. Inv. Ma 319. Amedick, *ASR* I 4 (1991) cat. 115. Young women can let their hair fall loose to the shoulders. For an example from Ara Pacis, see Polaschek 1972, 147.

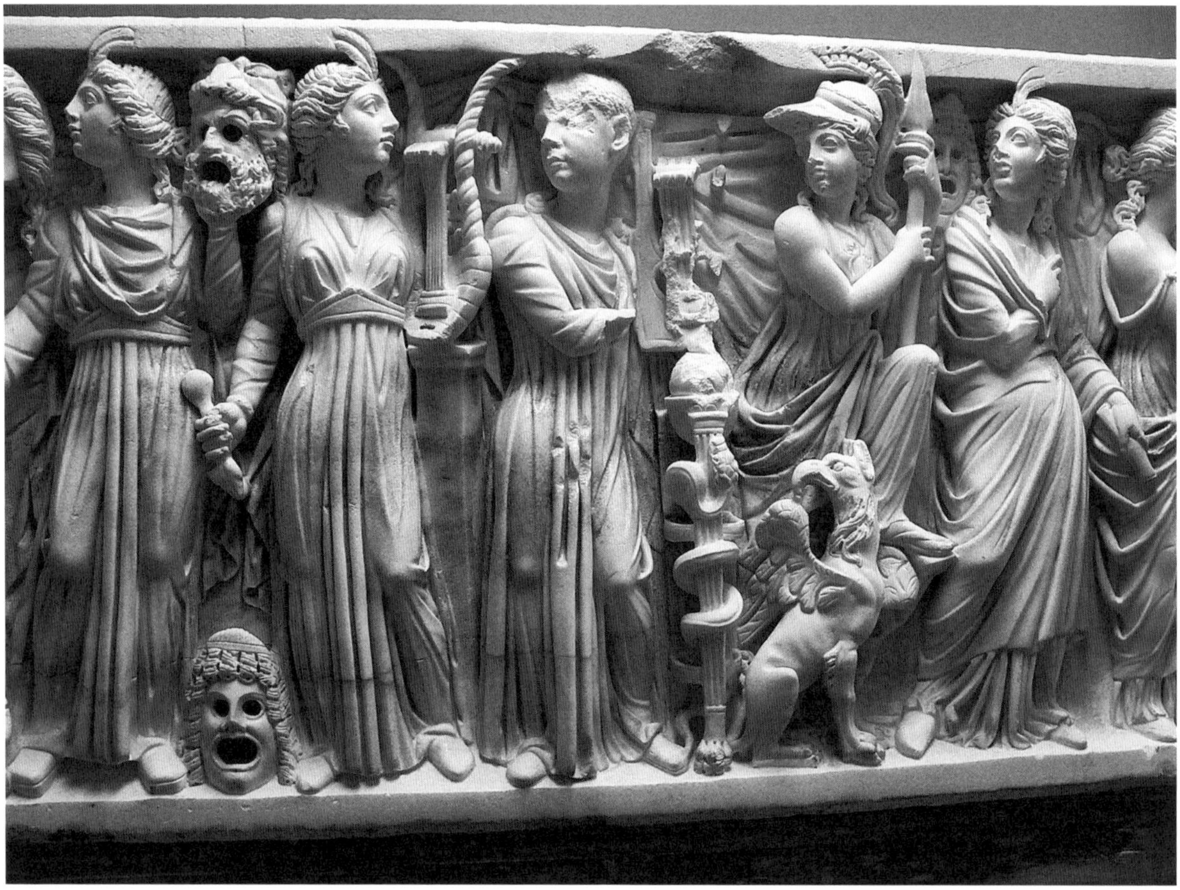

Fig. 82 *The deceased is represented as Apollo and the nine Muses (cat. no. 553). San Simeon, California, Hearst Castle, inv. P.C 6256. Photo: Author, courtesy of Hearst Castle.*

The question of how we should explain the long hair on this male figure is puzzling, but the *stola* and mirror might indicate that he is a representation of an actor. It was men who acted on the stage, and cross-gendering of actors is known from other sculpture. A statuette from Rome has been interpreted as a representation of an actor:[632] its generic face is round and soft like the face of a woman (or young man), and the hair is piled up; the face is veiled and the dress covers the feet; and a *palla* is draped around the figure. The outline of the body can be seen through the dress, which reverses our first impressions about its sex: the breast is flat and the waist is not narrow; the torso appears to be somewhat quadrilateral and no effort has been made to conceal the male genitals, which instead are emphasised by the tight-fitting garment. The sculpture shows a female character performed by a male actor. This could help us to understand why the man on the sarcophagus relief wears a *stola*. However, this explanation is not entirely satisfactory because most actors were men, and this figure seems originally to have been a woman. Furthermore, the figure has portrait features, which is not common for representations of actors.

The bust on the central panel supports the argument that this relief may be about cross-gendering, with the purpose of showing special virtues. The portrait bust is of a middle-aged man with a beard. He holds a scroll in his hands, which are large and masculine. In comparison to his hands the shoulders seem slightly too small, and though his drapery has slipped from his shoulder he seems to be wearing a tunic beneath the clothes. However, the outline of breasts, visible beneath the dress, locate the male figure in a Venus-like iconography. All

632 Savarese 2007, 79.

in all, it seems very likely that this figure was originally carved as a cross-gendered image.

Many pragmatic explanations can be found to account for such representations, especially where they involve some re-carving (a process that is often fraught with complicated questions); yet even so they do not change the fact that the resulting cross-gendered images were socially acceptable, and tolerated even on commemorative monuments.[633] As I have shown, male portrait figures on sarcophagi can be passive, epitomised by Endymion, and the femininity of men is conveyed through the beauty of Endymion and the effeminate Dionysus and Apollo (**Fig. 93**; cat. no. 568 and **Fig. 82**; cat. no. 553). Furthermore, there are examples of active women, such as the descending Selene, and women with masculine virtues, such as the warrior queen Penthesilea or the individualised Virtus. Common to all these mythological figures is that they were deemed to be appropriate for conveying a moral ideal; as such, they are role models for the living and the dead. It can therefore be difficult to try to explain the Roman way of dealing with the virtues of men and women using the modern model of a binary gender system.[634] There seems to have been no clear dichotomy between active men and passive women, or feminine and masculine, in the construction of role models.

The Marital Ideal: The 'Lycian' Motif and Busts of Couples in Clipei

Now that we are familiar with the character of the male and female role models, I want to open up for further interpretation by looking at the interaction of men and women in scenes where they are represented together. I use the example of learned couples to illustrate my point, by looking first at the motif sometimes termed "Lycian" and then at couples represented in *clipei*.[635]

633 Cross-gendering is also known from sculpture in the round: A statue in Athens represents Artemidorus, a mature youth, as Artemis with a female body, and a portrait head of Marcus Aurelius in the British Museum was added to a female statue (Varner 2008, 196, note 78, 201, note 129).

634 For other ways of perceiving sex, see Gilchrist 1999, 54-64; Meskell 1999, 73-7.

635 For an iconographic overview of the representation of marital couples on funerary monuments, see Lovén 2010.

The "Lycian" motif is seen on several sarcophagi and is mostly used in the late part of the third century, though a few examples are known from the fourth century.[636] It always shows a seated woman with a lyre on the left end of the frontal relief, and a seated man with a scroll on the right end.[637] The man and the woman both have portrait features and they face each other in the company of the nine Muses.[638] One sarcophagus (cat. no. 45) paraphrases this motif: the Muses, who are normally placed between the two seated figures, have been replaced by merry cupids with musical instruments. This substitution could indicate that the sarcophagus was intended for a child's burial, though the role models used for the portrait figures derive from adult iconography. Some strigillated sarcophagi also adopted the motif in an abbreviated form; they show the man and woman seated opposite each other on the left and right panels respectively, and the Muses are either left out or a single one is placed beside the portrait figure to symbolise the learned sphere into which the deceased has been accepted.[639]

The Lycian motif shows the man with a scroll and the woman with a lyre. Apart from this difference, they are depicted as equals, both attended by the Muses and both part of the learned milieu. The attributes that they hold, however, attach different meanings to the figures. Such conventions in the figural representation were not meant to make gender roles inflexible, but to symbolise the roles men and women embodied within the boundaries of a close relationship, such as marriage. As noted by Ewald, the combinations of a marital couple and intellectual figures are symptoms of an emotional re-

636 Huskinson 1999, 193. On the so-called Lycian motif, see Ewald 1999, 48-53.

637 For the Lycian motif, see Gabelmann, who sees the Lycian motif with Muses as prerequisite for the strigillated Lycian sarcophagi (Gabelmann 1968, 538); Kranz, *ASR* V4 (1984), 130-31; Ewald 1999, 48-53.

638 Cat. nos. 45, 157, 160, 164, 165, 173, and probably the fragments cat. nos. 161 and 176. Another sarcophagus with a similar motif is located in Rome, San Paolo fuori le Mura (Wegner, *ASR* V 3 (1966) cat. 184). The frontal relief is, however, so badly weathered that it is impossible to discern details. The sarcophagus is thus not included in the catalogue.

639 Cat. nos. 88, 93, 94, 96, 105, 107, 111, 121, 127, 167, and probably the fragments cat. nos. 99 and 129.

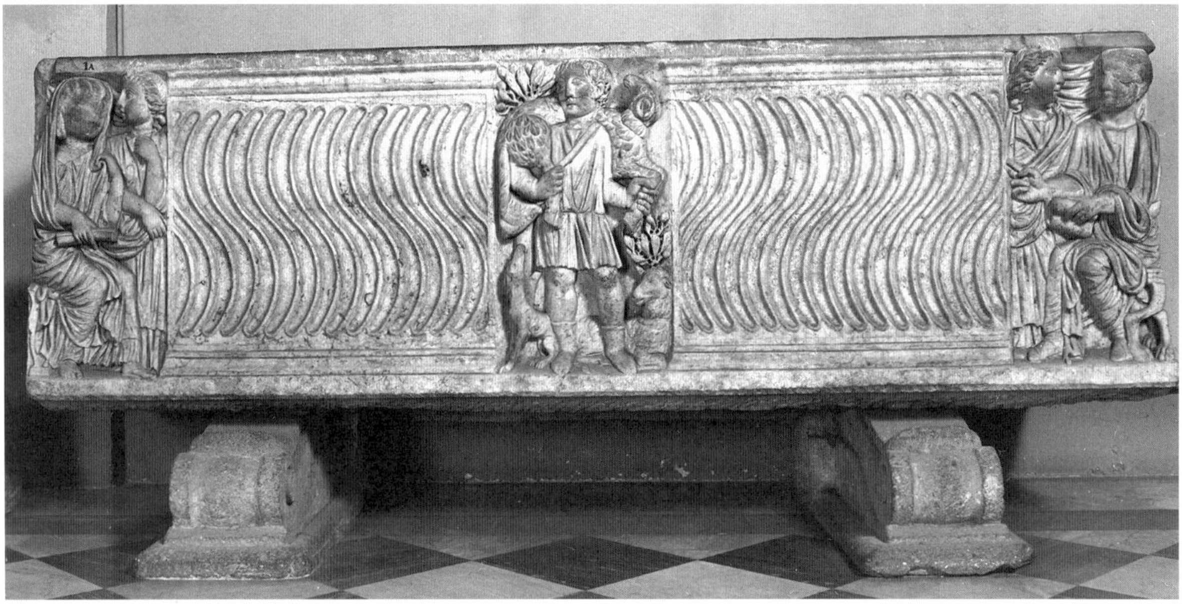

Fig. 83 *Strigillated sarcophagus showing a couple represented as a learned woman and a learned man (cat. no. 111). Rome, Musei Capitolini, Museo Centrale Montemartini, inv. MC1329/S. Photo: Archivio Fotografico dei Museo Capitolini, MC1329.*

evaluation of the marital relationship in the period.[640] In other contexts these gender roles were dissolved, as has been described above.

The 'educated woman' is the term I used to characterise the learned woman with a lyre or any other musical instrument. The instrument refers to her good education and musical abilities and thus only indirectly to her intellectual knowledge, and she therefore represents qualities different from those symbolised by the scroll. The lyre is an attribute of the Muses, and when the woman holds a lyre she signalises that she has been assimilated into their sphere. It shows her to be a well-educated woman commanding skills in areas such as poetry or music, and at the same time it creates a distance from the intellectual (and in some cases philosophical) abilities symbolised by the scroll held by the man. This relationship between the sexes is also expressed on sarcophagi which depict the man as a seated philosopher and the woman as a Muse (cat. nos. 92, 120, cat. no. 116; **Fig. 46**, and cat. no. 117). The philosopher is always the authoritative figure and the Muse his assistant or inspiration, and though the woman possessed virtues in herself, the female role is never emphasised at the expense of the male figure. This means that, as on *clipeus* busts of a couple, there is a tendency to portray women as the supportive figure to their husbands. I suggest that these scenes of Muses and philosophers, and Lycian compositions, stand for the institution of marriage and a relatively asexual relationship. In marriage, men and women have complementary roles, and the different attributes, scroll and lyre, reflect diverse qualities which help to fulfil the picture of the 'ideal' marriage.[641] In the Lycian motif, the presence of the Muses between the couple evoked a sense of that they belonged together and intensified the feeling of the marital context.[642]

As stated above, in the formulaic Lycian motif, the woman never holds a scroll – but no rules exist without exceptions. Cat. no. 111 is a strigillated sarcophagus with a couple seated opposite each other (**Fig. 83**). A Muse stands behind both of them. Strigillated panels separate the scenes showing the woman and the man, but unlike other sarcophagi with the Lycian motif, this woman

640 Ewald 2003, 569.

641 Huskinson 1999, 193. On Roman marriage, see Treggiari 1991a. On the Roman family, see Dixon 1992, and on the family as represented on Roman biographical sarcophagi, see George 2000. For marital relationships in the third century as expressed on sarcophagi, see also Ewald 2004, 250-53; 2005.

642 Zanker 1995, 275.

holds a scroll, too. This departure from the norm may be an expressions of individuality on sarcophagi; it may be argued that the scroll was chosen on the basis of the virtues and skills possessed by the woman during her lifetime. Alternatively, or perhaps concurrently, the presence of the scroll may be explained by the fact that women's roles in the intellectual sphere became more and more pronounced on sarcophagi as we approach the fourth century. As a result of this, the decision to include the scroll does not appear to be forced. Uses of attributes and modes of representation have shown to be effective tools in defining relations between the deceased. The group of sarcophagi showing a man and woman enclosed by a *clipeus* further supports this idea. In the following I look at how the framing *clipeus* could be used to emphasise marital bonds.

The composition of couples in a *clipeus* represents more traditional marriage ideals than compositions that show the man and woman individually, for example, on strigillated sarcophagi where they are depicted on separate panels.[643] The traditional, and rather stereotypical, idea of marriage is defined practically: the woman stands for domestic cares and the man for exertions out of doors, a relationship which is most explicit on second-century biographical sarcophagi.[644] These traditional roles, still alluded to on second-century sarcophagi, changed during the third century when new social relations developed within representations of marriage on sarcophagi; now men and women could be represented as equal partners, as expressed by the reliefs showing both the man and the woman holding scrolls.[645] The *clipeus* with a couple, however, represents a traditional attitude towards the marital institution that finds its place in sarcophagus iconography together with the aforementioned new form of self-representation that focuses more on the individual than on the family. The *clipeus* group includes sarcophagi with two busts represented shoulder to shoulder in the *clipeus* (cat. nos. 430-76). The iconographic formula of the *clipeus* busts is clear. The woman is always depicted behind the man, resting her hand on his chest as if she wanted to illustrate her support of him. On the majority of these sarcophagi, the man holds a scroll, but the woman never does. Instead she emphasises her femininity by exposing one shoulder (for example cat. no. 455), holding a billowing veil like a Nereid (for example cat. no. 449), or by wearing jewellery, a feature that on sarcophagi is mostly limited to the fourth century (**Fig. 76**; cat. no. 432).

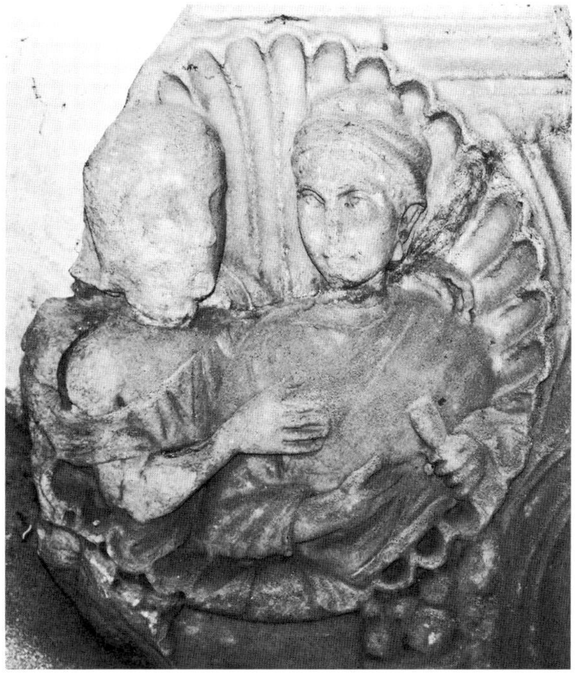

Fragment of the frontal relief of a strigillated sarcophagus (cat. no. 252). Rome, Museo Nazionale Romano, inv. 196637. Photo: Author, courtesy of Museo Nazionale Romano. **Fig. 84**

643 Here I refer not to sarcophagi with Lycian motifs, but to the strigillated sarcophagi on which both the man and the woman were represented with scrolls. Two busts represented together in a square panel, a *parapetasma*, or a similar frame are rarer (cat. nos. 241, 258, 304, and 395). The binding together of the figures by any type of frame conveys the same sense of belonging, and these examples should be interpreted in a similar manner to the *clipeus* sarcophagi with a marital couple.

644 Similar ideals were also described by the mid-first-century writer Columella: "it is only right, as I have said, that the female sex has been provided for the care of the home, the male for the out-of-door and open-air activities." ("*iure, ut dixi, natura comparata est mulieris ad domesticam diligentiam, viri autem ed exercitationem forensem et extraneam.*") *Rust.* 12. preface 4-5 (trans. Heffner Forster 1979). At the time of writing, Columella is, however, already describing a distant past.

645 Cat. nos. 43, 52, 54, 66, 94, 98, 114, 116, 119-20, 163, 177, 180, and 181.

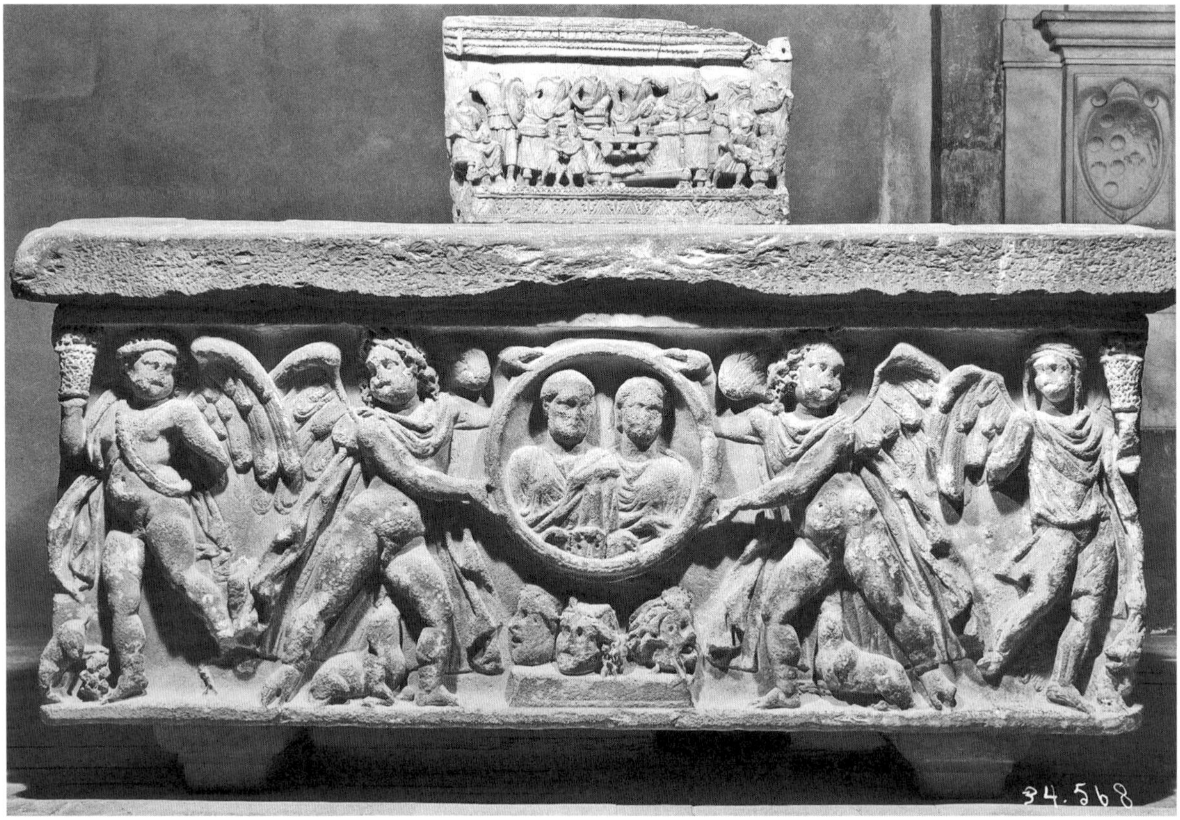

Fig. 85 *Seasonal sarcophagus. The male bust in the* clipeus *has been carved with a female portrait and the female bust with a male (cat. no. 470). Pisa, Camposanto, inv. 12. Photo: D-DAI-ROM 34.568 (Falbermeyer).*

These different ways of illustrating the virtues divined into the men and women represented together in a *clipeus* can be exemplified by the fragment cat. no. 252 (**Fig. 84**). The bust to the left is female and has an exposed shoulder; alluding to the iconography of Venus, and her head has been left roughly carved. The bust on the right is male and holds a scroll. The head has, however, been carved with a female portrait. The woman commemorated on this sarcophagus has specifically chosen to be carved onto the figure of a learned person, despite the fact that this figure was male. In doing so, she has chosen a social role that refers to her intellectuality instead of her physical beauty and femininity. Another example is cat. no. 470 (**Fig. 85**), on which both the male and the female busts show portrait features. The surface is badly damaged, but enough detail is preserved of their hairstyles to determine their sex. The male bust has been carved with a female portrait, recognisable by the hairstyle, and the female bust has been carved with a male portrait with a short hairstyle. It would be interesting to know what provoked this reversal of gender roles. I think, in this case, that the negotiation of gender roles is deliberate, and not a coincidence. This is demonstrated by the fact that the female bust was not carved, as is usually the case, with a naked shoulder, making the figure more suitable for a male representation. The focus was therefore not explicitly on the femininity of the figure but on their relationship, which seems to have been dominated by the female figure. The sarcophagus may therefore commemorate the woman. Other examples of the female figure represented in front of the male are found on cat. nos. 447, 448, and 450.[646]

646 Another fragment of a frontal sarcophagus relief with a similar iconography is in the National Gallery, Oslo (inv. NSG 29.01529). Only the *clipeus* with the busts of a couple and a hand of the *genius* holding it is preserved. The female portrait bust is placed in front of the male.

One sarcophagus with *clipeus b*usts representing a couple has a preserved inscription and it confirms that the social relation between the two persons was bound by marriage (cat. no. 434). The front shows a *clipeus* with two blank portraits and a bucolic scene, and the lid shows Jonah and the whale and a *Sigma-mahl.* The inscription informs us that the coffin was given by a husband to his highly praised wife. Another sarcophagus, however, raises the question of whether the two individuals in the *clipeus* necessarily had to be a marital couple.The iconography shows two women together in a *clipeus* (**Fig. 86**; cat. no. 446), and the relations between the two are interesting. The woman to the right looks older than the woman to the left. Judging by the other sarcophagi with two busts, it seems likely that this sarcophagus represents some kind of family relation, too. The two portrayed figures are probably mother and daughter. In this context it is worth noting that it is the elderly woman (the mother), who holds the scroll. This priority makes it evident that power relations were implied in the symbolic meaning of the composition. Another example of *clipeus bu*sts that do not represent a married couple is provided by a sarcophagus now in Paris: it seems to show siblings, a sister and a brother, represented in this context of family concord (**Fig. 52**; cat. no. 461). The motif is a Dionysian procession in which the *clipeus* of the deceased persons is carried, and this optimistic way of dealing with bereavement was combined with an iconography of social relations that was recognisable and therefore easily interpreted.

In conclusion, conventions in the figurative scheme of sarcophagi can be an informative source for studying individuals. For example, the formulaic use of the learned figures is informative about the relationship between the sexes. It may be a fictive and idealised picture, but it still contains some essential guidelines for how men and women could act. In general terms, the formulaic scheme of how men and women relate to each other, can be described as such: when represented as individuals, e.g. either separated from each other by relief panels or as the only individualised figure on a sarcophagus, men and women could possess the same virtues and qualities, independently of their sex. When represented together, as on sarcophagi with Muses and philosophers or with busts of a couple, men and women took different social roles and thus embodied different qualities.

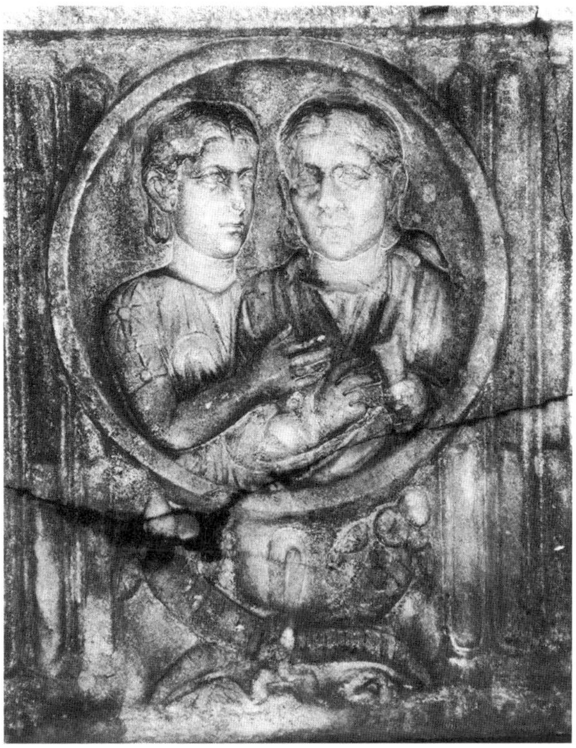

Fig. 86 *Strigillated sarcophagus with* clipeus busts. *This composition is normally used for a marriage couple but in this case both the portraits are female (cat. no. 446). Rome, Via Veneto 56, Palazzo Balestra, courtyard. Photo: Björn Christian Ewald.*

Conclusion

In this chapter I examined what visual imagery on sarcophagi reveals about the relationship between sex and gender. I will once more stress that the binary gender system, often assumed to be the basic gender relation in Roman society, was not the only, and maybe not even the prevailing, way of understanding gender. Rather, the representation of individuals on sarcophagi helps us to recognise a nuanced picture of how people could construct identity through sarcophagus imagery.

It was shown that role models were multiple and diverse, and that neither sarcophagi nor sculpture applied with a portrait supported the idea of a male-dominated iconographic language in funerary contexts. The same conclusion was reached through a study of the secondary motifs. For the Roman viewer, images may not immediately have signalised qualities categorised as either male or female. I therefore suggest that categorisation of sex was not the most important element of the construction of identity on sarcophagi. Other aspects seem to have been valued more highly, including status, virtues, and personal qualities, and the virtues suggested by these male and female role models were often complementary. Oppositions between men and women should therefore not be found in the figures' sex but in their relationship.

When men and women were represented together, there were some cultural rules that had to be followed, for example in scenes involving nudity. Nudity was not a taboo in funerary representations, and men and women were depicted in all their natural beauty, but they could not be naked together in the same scene.[647] Another example of a cultural rule is found in busts of couples. Here we saw that when a man and a woman were represented together, it was always the man who held the scroll. When two women were represented together the scroll was given to the elder, who would also be the one with the highest authority within the household.[648] The composition of the bust representations (and the scroll) is therefore a symbol of status and power, and it helps the viewer to define the male role in relation to the female. I chose the couple enclosed by the *clipeus* and the Lycian motif as an illustration of what may be termed traditional marital virtues, but other role models conveyed the same ideals, such as biographical sarcophagi, as well as those showing the ritual of *dextrarum iunctio*.

In modern scholarship, the Roman woman is often defined in relation to male society. This means that the *matrona* is considered to have been the ideal Roman woman. In this chapter, I offered a different picture of the ideal woman, one that includes intellectual virtues. Aside from sea-monsters, nymphs, and hunts, there are no obvious secondary motifs preferred by either women or men (see graph 4). Imagery on sarcophagi appears to be un-gendered in the sense that most imagery on secondary scenes could be used for both men and women as expressions of virtues, ideals, hopes, and desires.[649] It has not been my intention to downplay the role of the woman within the family, or ignore the fact that ancient authors often attribute domestic virtues to women and praise their abilities to be good wives.[650] I wished merely to note that other aspects of women were also highly valued, both by the women themselves and by men. In this alternative picture, the notion of a male-constructed or male-enforced intellectual world (which is particularly evident for the Christian period) is not dismissed, but merely nuanced.

Some of the stereotypical ideas of the wool-working woman as the ideal Roman woman are rooted in the concept of a universal woman. The female domestic ideal is probably traceable in other geographic, chronological, or social contexts, but in defining ideals, it is important to be explicit about, when, where, and what kind of context we are talking about.[651] The ideals of the wool-working woman, motherhood, and the 'one man woman' were not used to commemorate women on sarcophagi in third-century Rome. The popularity of the learned woman and the female lion huntresses showed that the ideals that mattered to them and their families were quite different. My conclusion is thus that sarcophagus imagery is not pre-gendered, and that it reflected not the sex, but the virtues and qualities of the deceased. My intention is not to imply that some methods of self-representations were not more popular, and thus more frequently used, for one sex than for the other: my point is that new interpretations can be generated by looking beyond the male-biased conception of sarcophagus imagery. I believe that this flexibility in the representation of men's and women's virtues on sarcophagi finds resonance in the Roman perception of gender roles in this specific context of self-display in third- and fourth-century Rome.

647 On nudity, see Wallace-Hadrill 2008, 51. As D'Ambra says, in the absence of the mythological conceit and its conventions, nakedness was not permitted (1996, 219).

648 Veyne 1987, 71-5. On the hierarchy of gender within the family in Roman law, see Treggiari 1991, 31-3.

649 Zanker & Ewald 2004, 183.

650 See for example the study by Hänninen (2007) of anecdotal Cornelia, especially p. 85.

651 Something that is often ignored, for example in Lena Larsson Lovén's article "Wool working and female virtues" (Lovén 1998). Another example of the stereotypical ideal of the wool-working woman is found in Taylor 2008, 34.

CHAPTER 4

Filiae Innocentissimae, Filio Dulcissimo: Commemorating Children

Like adults, children were commemorated on sarcophagi by figures individualised through the application of a portrait.[652] Unlike adult burials, however, the decoration of children's sarcophagi was chosen by a different social group from the one that it commemorated. Modern studies of life histories (based on personal events) and life scripts (describing commonly expected events) show that what children today define as important episodes in their lives differ significantly from those valued by adults:[653] children choose life scripts events from a life-fantasy or a current event, whereas adults follow a culturally defined set of important events, such as marriage, the birth of children, and a first job. In terms of Roman sarcophagi, what we learn about children from portrait representations of them is seen from the perspective of adults and their culturally defined set of norms. The standardised selection of motifs used for children shows an image of the child that was chosen in order to fulfil the expectations of the adults, which explains why children often appear as small adults in sarcophagus imagery.

The individual and the Roman life course have recently received much scholarly attention, as have Roman childhood and the representation of children, especially within research on sarcophagi and funerary monuments in general.[654] In approaching children's sarcophagi as a group, the idea of the culturally shared life script and its relevance for individual life stories will be taken into consideration. Roman society's attitude towards children will be explored through an analysis of the figure types to which the portrait of a child could be added.[655] The tendency to represent children in adult terms, as small grown-ups, instead of locating them in a childish world of fantasy and fairy tales is different from the way children's objects are often decorated today. Instead, on Roman sarcophagi we see the iconography of adult commemorations reflected in representations of children. On adults' sarcophagi, we saw how commemorators chose the same kinds of scenes to represent the personal identities of different individuals, despite the fact that peoples' lives were highly individual. This probably happened because people defined themselves in relation to others. The ideal life was therefore defined by a set of collective norms, which in the Roman world seems to have applied to the ideal life of a child as well.[656]

In separating children's sarcophagi from those of adults, I have taken a life course perspective in which childhood is defined as different from adulthood. This is, however, only rarely confirmed directly by the sarcophagus iconography itself. The ideal child life was generally not represented that differently from the ideal adult life. It is, however, possible to identify some special scenes of situations that were used to construct

652 80 sarcophagi in the catalogue commemorate children before adulthood; see appendix A. Apart from the examples mentioned in appendix A, which include sarcophagi with an indication of age in a portrait or an inscription, there may be more sarcophagi that commemorate children, the most obvious being cat. nos. 212, 220, 388, 423, and 557. They are, because of the uncertainty of the deceased's age group, included in appendix A among either men or women.

653 Bohn & Berntzen 2008; Berntsen & Bohn 2009.

654 Amedick, *ASR* I 4 (1991) 60-104; Huskinson 1996, 1999, 2005, 2007; Dimas 1998, 1998a; King 2000; Harlow & Laurence 2002; 2007; Rawson 2003; Gilchrist 2004; Zanker & Ewald 2004, 239-45; Revell 2005; Backe-Dahmen 2006; 2008; Sigismund-Nielsen 2007; Cohen & Rutter 2007; Baxter 2008 (with a literature review).

655 For portrait figures and children on sarcophagi, see also Huskinson 1996, section 13.

656 For cultural life script theory, see Berntsen & Rubin 2004; Berntsen & Bohn 2009.

the visual life script of children on sarcophagi. We will return to these scenes below. Taking the special representations of children's lives together with the scenes depicting adult activities, the discussion of children's iconography may contribute to the debate as to whether childhood was a socially differentiated stage in life with its own values, or if it was a stage whose particularities had little value in Roman society.[657] Furthermore, the choice of scenes on children's sarcophagi will be considered in order to understand which aspects of the child's identity were important to the family. An obvious function of children's sarcophagi was that they were put up to construct the identity of the family as much as to commemorate the child. However, since there is a curious lack of interest in depicting a family that consists of more than two persons, the focus of any interpretation must be on the virtues of the individual child and not on the child's role in the family.[658] We therefore face a self-representational tradition in which it was the individual who, through his or her personal virtues, contributed to the identity of the family.

In approaching the individual child through the decoration of a single coffin, some fundamental definitions must be made. First, it is important to define the age of the individual, and whether or not they are at a stage of life that can be called childhood. Second, we will have to consider how we can distinguish boys and girls when, as is the case for most of these sarcophagi, a portrait is the only indicator. Age can be difficult to determine using the small and sometimes scarcely detailed sarcophagus portrait, and many sarcophagi are difficult to categorise as belonging to either a child or an adult. Though perspectives will be given on older children when they are commemorated in a child-like way, the primary focus here is on young children's sarcophagi on which either an inscription or a portrait informs us that it is a commemoration of a child. This limiting of the material in question seemed reasonable, since age is difficult to determine in a society for which we do not know how to separate childhood from adulthood. As has been mentioned, inscriptions sometimes give an indication of the age group to which the deceased belonged by referring to the number of years they lived, but stages in life and particular events such as having one's own household were probably more important in the Roman categorisation of age than the actual number of lived years. Therefore, the end of childhood should be defined by various social factors, such as marriage, work engagements, or stages of education, instead of age.[659] However, age is often mentioned on epitaphs on sarcophagi, and must therefore have been important to the Roman viewers in defining the identity of the deceased in relation to his or her stage in life. Therefore, to be sure that the sarcophagi I am analysing belonged to children, I have chosen to focus on children younger than 9 years old, who we can assume had not reached further than the first stage in their 'life cycle'.[660] The decision has been made to separate young children from children who had already taken an adult role in life since it is likely that there were great differences in the way the two groups were looked upon, both by their families and by society. At 14, Roman boys had reached puberty and at 17 they could begin military training, which is the reason that one sarcophagus (cat. no. 326), commemorating a boy that lived for 17 years, is not included in this discussion despite the fact that his status as a son is referred to in the inscription (*filio dulcissimo*).[661] At that age, boys had already crossed the border into the adult world, and I therefore consider it an adult's sarcophagus. The words *filius* or *filia*, often found in epitaphs, are taken as an indication that the deceased was a child. Another example which shows that the use of this term did not necessarily refer to a child is found on a lid which has an inscription that mentions a mother who commemorated her son using the term

657 Ariès 1962; Rawson 1986; 2003; Dixon 1992; Backe-Dahmen 2006.

658 Kampen 2007, 127-29. On family and other social relationships expressed through epitaphs from Rome, see Sigismund Nielsen 2006.

659 Huskinson 1996, 2.

660 Here I use the notion of a life cycle system not firmly established before late antiquity. This life cycle system defines the end of infancy at the age of 7. However, the absolute value of a classification of age is debatable and depends on both social and cultural matters (Rawson 2003, 136, 139-41). My aim is not to go into the debate about age and children, but to study the sarcophagi of obviously young children. This means that they had not entered the adult world in a biological sense or through social relationships.

661 Rawson 2003, 136, and 138.

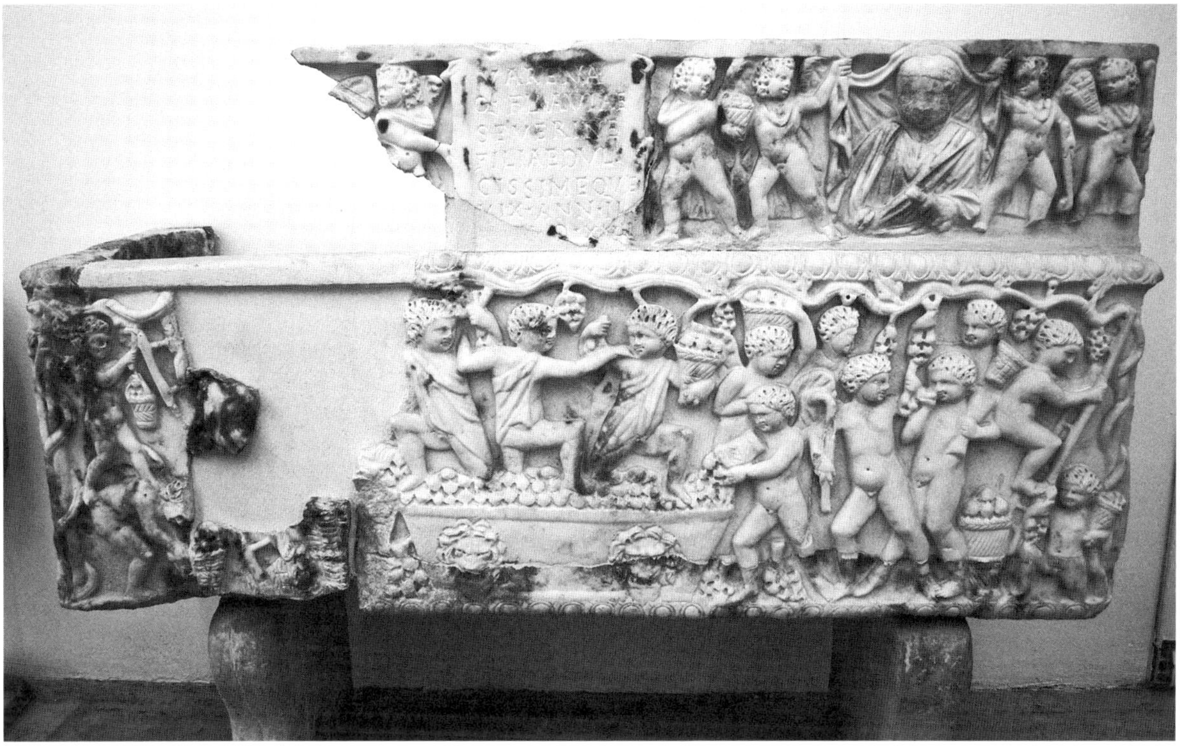

The sarcophagus of a two-years-old girl (cat. no. 50). Rome, Musei Capitolini, Palazzo Conservatori. Photo: Author, courtesy of Musei Capitolini. **Fig. 87**

filio dulcissimo, even though the son had reached the age of 39 years (cat. no. 43).[662] For similar reasons, the Ariadne sarcophagus in the Getty Museum (**Fig.** 77; cat. no. 557) commemorating Maconiana Serveriana with the words *filia dulcissima* has not been counted among children's sarcophagi, despite its length of 1.17 m, because there is no indication of age in the inscription, nor is there a finished portrait to inform any inference about the girl's age. It is likely that the sarcophagus was made for a child, but it could also have been used for a young woman, and I have chosen to make these sharp categorisations in order not to blur the general picture.

Apart from portraits, inscriptions, and iconography, the length of the coffin can indicate whether a sarcophagus was made for a child or an adult. Scholars have estimated that sarcophagi with a length of more than 1.70 m are not likely to have been produced for children.[663] This is, of course, only to be taken as a guideline.[664] The length of a coffin is a very insecure indicator, and therefore I do not used it as a primary factor in deciding if the sarcophagus was made for a child. An example of a small coffin used for an adult burial is the reused child sarcophagus with the remains of a *Horus* lock still visible behind the portrait (cat. no. 407): it is 1 m long but was used for the commemoration of a man. The length indicates that it may have been reused for the cremated remains of a man. At other times adult-size sarcophagi were used for the burial of a child, as, for example, a piece in Musei Capitolini decorated with cupids engage in harvesting and making wine (**Fig.** 87; cat. no. 50), which has an inscription commemorating a two-year-old girl.

The portraits of young women and youths can be almost impossible to distinguish from those of adults.

662 Dimas uses dedications from parents to define a child sarcophagus (Dimas 1998a, 28). I think, however, that this gives a less clear picture of what a child sarcophagus is, because the age span becomes too broad.

663 Huskinson 1996, 2; Koch 1997, 455; Dimas 1998a, 28.

664 Backe-Dahmen 2008, 110.

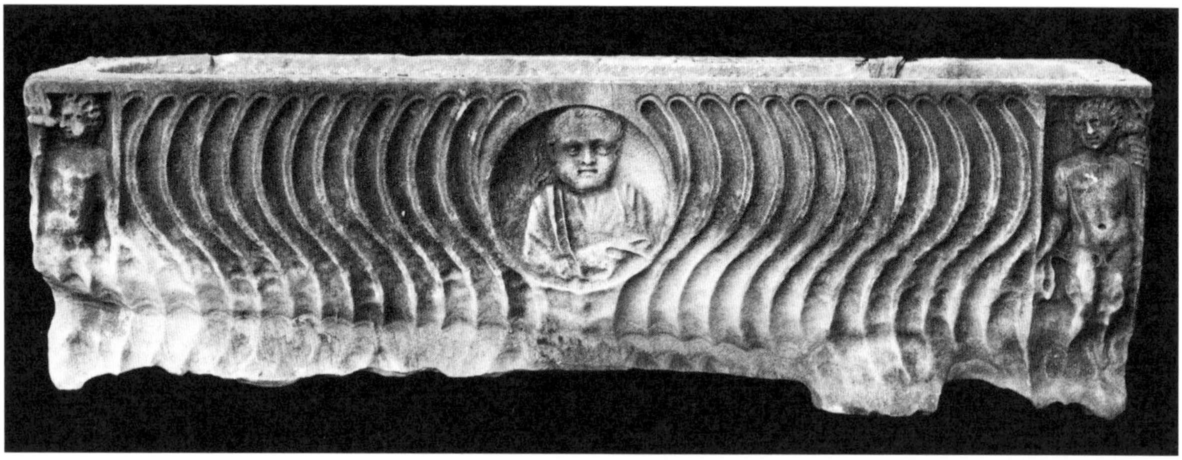

Fig. 88 *Strigillated child sarcophagus (cat. no. 279). Rome, Museo Nazionale Romano, inv. 135741. Photo: Soprintendenza Speciale per i Beni Archeologici di Roma.*

Portraits of small children are easier to recognise. They have a round face with voluminous cheeks, a protruding mouth, and a rather generic expression.[665] The chubby cheeks make the facial features appear smooth and soft, the hair is often short, and sometimes a *Horus* lock is added.[666] One example of such a portrait of a young child is found on a strigillated sarcophagus in the Museo Nazionale in Rome (**Fig. 88**; cat. no. 279).[667] The boy has a round face, large eyes, short hair, and a *Horus* lock. Another figure type that I take as an indication of the representation of a young child is the figure that imitates a child's chubby body, such as the boy on a piece showing the Muses (**Fig. 89**; cat. no. 159). The boy is the central figure among eight of the Muses and despite the chubby appearance of his half-naked body, he is represented as the ninth Muse. Another example is a boy-philosopher sarcophagus in the Vatican (**Fig. 69**; cat. no. 115) on which the Muses are again represented as chubby children.[668]

The second key question is how we can distinguish a boy's portraits from that of a girl when the portrayed person is a young child. This question may seem straightforward, but there are some complications in determining the sex of a portrait of a young child.[669] Young children tend to be carved with a short hairstyle regardless of sex, shown by a sarcophagus with an *Orans* that commemorates a girl named Optata who died at the age of three (cat. no. 631). She wears female clothing but has the short hairstyle of a boy. Another sarcophagus (cat. no. 312) commemorates Volusia Longina, who lived for four years, four months, and 18 days, and the portrait shows a child with a short hairstyle that may have led us to conclude that the sarcophagus belonged to a boy, had it not been for the inscription and the female bust. We tend to take it for granted that boys in Roman portraiture have short hair and girls do not, but this is a feature that depends on age rather than sex, and some portraits that seem to be of boys could just as well be depictions of girls, as has been demonstrated by Fittschen.[670] The general assumption that boys are more frequently commemorated on sarcophagi than girls may therefore be explained by the occasional difficulties in distinguishing portraits of young boys from those of young girls. In this study I have chosen to consider sarcophagi to be boys' commemorations when it would be prohibitively difficult to try to identify the sex of the child (such as on cat. nos. 406, 417, and 418), not because I am convinced that the portrait subjects are

665 Guiliano 1985, 384; Huskinson 1996, 87-8.

666 On *Horus* locks, see Backe-Dahmen 2006, 93-4; Backe-Dahmen 2008, 112-16.

667 Huskinson 1996, cat. 9. 45.

668 Huskinson 1996, 38-9; Ewald 1999, cat. D 5.

669 On this difficulty, see Sande 2010, 58 with further references in note 10.

670 Fittschen 1992.

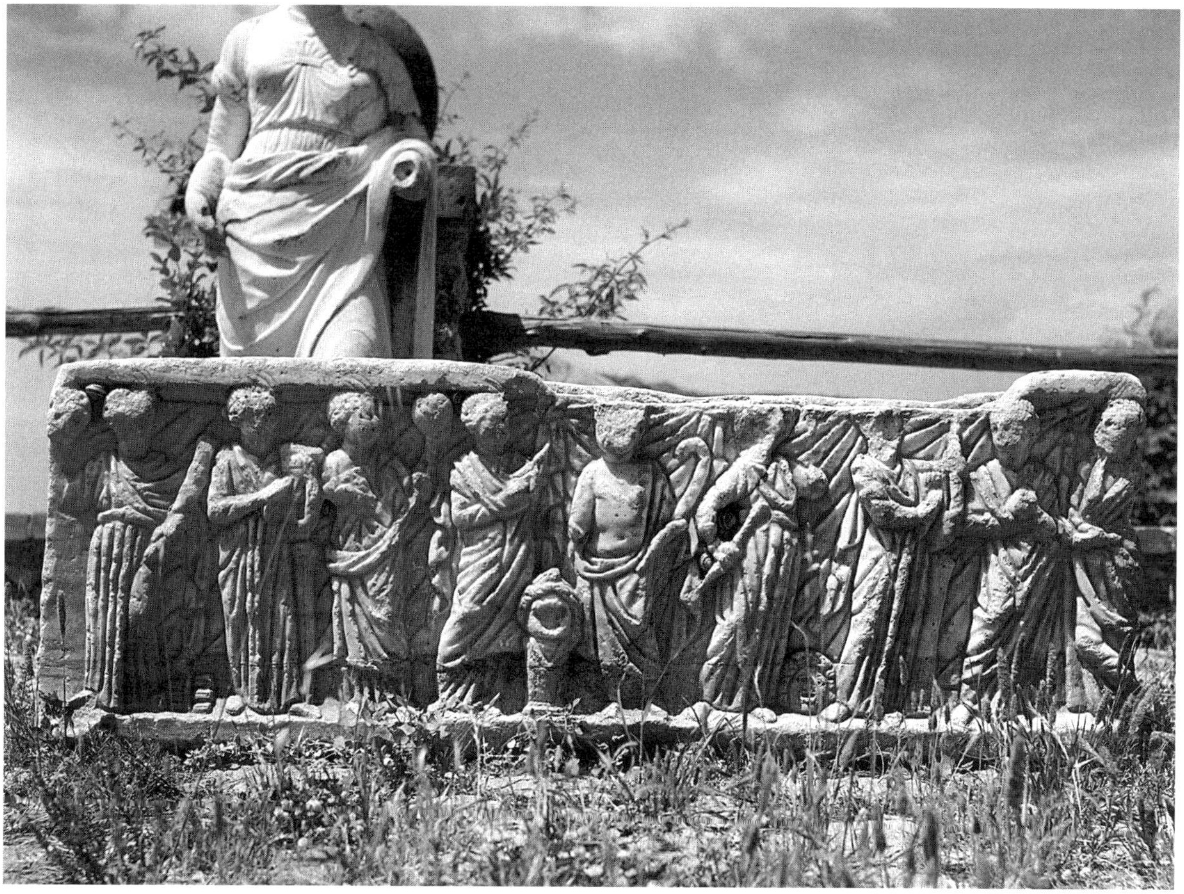

Child sarcophagus showing the deceased by among the Muses (cat. no. 159). Naples, Museo Archeologico Nazionale, inv. 205250. Once in Villa Mario Astarita. Photo: D-DAI-ROM-63.1251. **Fig. 89**

boys, but since, as I will argue, the sex of young children did not seem to be the most important factor in constructing their identities.

Some matters concerning the production should also be taken into consideration in identifying the themes that could be chosen for a child's sarcophagus.[671] Despite the high infant mortality rate, the death of a child was rarely expected in a way that would make the parents pre-order a child's sarcophagus. Therefore children's sarcophagi were probably made on stock, incidentally as a large proportion of adults' sarcophagi were.[672] In theory, this means that when the terrible loss of a child occurred, the parents could go to the workshop and choose a pre-decorated coffin. There may not have been hundreds of sarcophagi to choose from in one workshop, but the proportion of the production of sarcophagi that has been traced to Rome indicates that there were several workshops active at the same time.[673] Even though the coffin was pre-decorated, an appropriate piece that accommodated the parents' need to express their bereavement was chosen from a selection of motifs, and on some coffins details, such as a portrait, may have needed finishing before it was finally transported to the tomb. The presumed pre-fabrication of some children's sarcophagi does not mean, therefore, that the coffin tells us nothing about the people who chose it, but it suggests that there was a cultural code

671 For children's sarcophagi both with and without portrait figures, see especially Huskinson 1996; Dimas 1998; 1998a.

672 Backe-Dahmen 2008, 111.

673 For the discussion on workshops and production, see chapter 1.

for motifs that were acceptable for the commemoration of a child. If we can identify this code and point to specific methods of representation for children, then their iconography can be used as a guideline for understanding how children from the higher social classes in the Roman period were viewed culturally, especially when it comes to constructing status within the family and ultimately in society.

Children's *Iconography*

It is difficult to identify any iconography that was specifically designed for children, since the stereotypical repertoire of adults' sarcophagi seems to repeat itself in the commemorations of children. We can, however, make some suggestions as to how these standardised representations can be read as symbols of childhood. This is permissible since sarcophagus images offered the viewer the opportunity to interpret scenes differently according to context. Furthermore, sometimes it happened that some of these stereotyped motifs were slightly altered in order to fit the memory of a child.

In graph 7 it becomes clear that even though the general picture is that children's sarcophagi are found in all of the categories, one group, that of life course sarcophagi, was predominantly made for children, whilst the groups that contain sarcophagi with busts of a couple, professional and military scenes, representations of a couple riding in a carriage through a city, and reclining figures in a dining context were not used for children. Examining these categories, it becomes clear that the figure types that were unsuitable for children are those which refer to situations associated with marital relationships, such as the man and woman on *dextrarum iunctio* scenes, and the couple at a sacrifice or enclosed by a *clipeus*.[674] The obvious absence of marriage iconography on children's sarcophagi and the fact that children are generally never seen with their parents means that some of the standardised compositional types, such as death door scenes, are totally absent from the group of children's sarcophagi. Another rather large group that requires some commentary comprises the sarcophagi with hunt scenes. Hunting is an activity popular on sarcophagi made for adults, but it does not find use in children's sarcophagi, except for one showing Meleager and Atalante (**Fig. 54**; cat. no. 604). This situation is probably a consequence of the fact that the hunt did not symbolise an event in a life script that elevated the social status of the child. The male qualities of bodily strength, courage, and *virtus* expressed through hunt scenes were from the third century not qualities that a child needed to possess in order to advance in public life. Instead, education and intellectual skills were the key to a public career.[675] Generally, the ideal of male *virtus* is not often represented on sarcophagi with a child portrait figure. This is in contrast to scenes without the child portrait figure, where a range of images symbolising *virtus* can be found.[676] The difference between the two categories of sarcophagi can probably be explained by the fact that the portrait makes a direct link between the virtues of the figure type and the child, and from the Antonine period, during which portrait figures of children begin to appear, the qualities of education and potential to become a magistrate had already started to be more desirable for representations of a upper-class boys. We will return to the Meleager sarcophagus later.

There are some general rules for how freely the secondary motifs could be chosen. For example, children are not present in the group of sarcophagi symbolising the stoic life of herdsmen and philosophers in bucolic settings, apart for a few exceptions, such as the sarcophagus of a girl commemorated by her grandfather (cat. no. 3). On the lid of her sarcophagus bucolic scenes are represented alongside the inscription and her blank portrait. Common secondary motifs are instead sleeping cupids, garlands, lions, and especially seasonal personifications and acting cupids. Sarcophagi with cupids as well as seasonal personifications dominate the entire group of both children's and adult's sarcophagi in both variety and number.[677] It is also the case, however, that no compositional scheme with either of these two mo-

674 Except for one piece (cat. no. 616), where a boy on a life course sarcophagus is reclining while attended with food. A reclining child is normally found in *conclamatio* scenes, but here the iconography has been mixed with the adult meal scene; see for example cat. no. 536 (**Fig. 81**), which depicts children playing beneath the *kline*.

675 Wiedemann 1989, 162; Backe-Dahmen 2006, 116.

676 Backe-Dahmen 2006, 116-18.

677 Hanfmann 1951; Kranz, *ASR* V 2, 1 (1999); for an interpretation of motifs with cupids and a review of the different modes of interpretation that have been suggested, see Bielefeld, *ASR* V 2, 2 (1997, 89-93); Schauenburg, *ASR* V, 2, 3

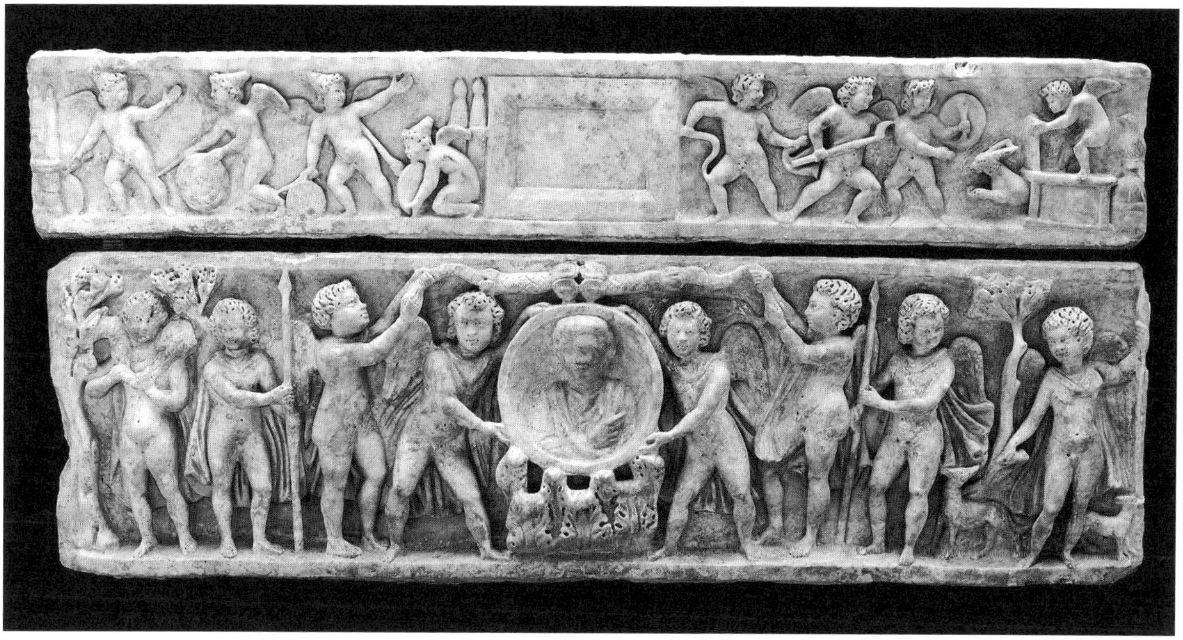

Child sarcophagus (cat. no. 281). Rome, Museo Nazionale Romano, inv. 229694. Photo: Soprintendenza Speciale per i Beni Archeologici di Roma. **Fig. 90**

tifs was made exclusively for adults or for children.[678] For example, scenes with cupids harvesting grapes are most commonly found on adults' sarcophagi, but they are also found on sarcophagi commemorating children (for example cat. no. 53). This ambiguity in the use of motifs is characteristic of Roman sarcophagi, and one piece, which transcends children's and adults' iconography, illustrates well how the harvesting cupids motif can accommodate the two groups and still carry meaning for both of them.[679] The front of the sarcophagus is decorated with a scene of cupids pressing and harvesting grapes (**Fig. 87**; cat. no. 50). The cupids picking the ripe grapes at several different levels are naked, though the three cupids pressing grapes in a tub are clothed. The scene seems playful and cheerful. The sarcophagus was, in all likelihood, carved for an adult, because of its length of approximately 2.10 m. However, the inscription tells us that it commemorated a two-year old girl. In an adult context the scenes would allude to the happy life of the Dionysian world and the prosperity it brings, but the playful cupids and their child-like bodies suit a child's world as well.[680] The piece shows how flexible the interpretation of such a scene can be, and how scenes can be read individually depending on the context in which they were used.

The general observation that the acting secondary figures on children's sarcophagi are cupids presented in different contexts is most obvious on scenes in which the cupids, dressed in adult clothing, take on the roles of different characters such as Muses (**Fig. 69**; cat. no. 115), hunters (cat. no. 281; **Fig. 90** and cat. no. 605), and Dionysian *thiasoi* feasting with the deceased boy (cat. nos. 569-72). It should, however, be noted that there are some motifs in which the secondary figures are only rarely depicted as cupids, as, for example, on life course sarcophagi (cat. nos. 620-23), those showing the learned sphere (cat. nos. 133, 154, and 160, with the exception of cat. no. 115), and those with sea-monsters

(1995); Matz 1958; Huskinson 1996, chapter 6; Dimas 1998a, 29-33.

678 For cupids on children's sarcophagi, see also Huskinson 1996, chapter 6; Backe-Dahmen 2006, 113-15.

679 On the problem of defining cupids and on cupids on children's sarcophagi in general, see Huskinson 1996, chapter 6.

680 Backe-Dahmen (2006, 113) suggests that the use of cupids transforms the potentially realistic scene into an unrealistic and ideal world.

and nymphs (cat. nos. 366, 369, and 371). The child-like behaviour and the fact that they resemble children physically probably explain the popularity of cupids on children's sarcophagi.[681] For example, on a relief showing a scene with the sea and a harbour, the figures of an otherwise realistic setting are carved as cupids (cat. no. 287). They are sailing, fishing, and playing instruments. In one boat Eros rows while Psyche relaxes with a glass of wine and in another she plays a double flute. One cupid has jumped into the water and the scene generally exhibits an unconcerned and happy attitude to life. On this sarcophagus the portrait of the deceased boy is shown in a *clipeus* in the right corner, and he is not interacting with the scene. It is a general characteristic of sarcophagi that, while the cupids are playful, the deceased child is not engaged in child's play; in fact, individualised children are never represented as doing specifically children's activities. Only the cupids' play and games refer to this aspect of childhood.[682]

Some seemingly standardised sarcophagi show a strong association with childhood, such as the aforementioned examples on which cupids imitate the adult world. On another two pieces the context of childhood is established by depictions of cupids playing with wheels (on the lid of cat. no. 281; **Fig. 90** and cat. no. 384). One of the coffins is decorated with cupids represented as hunters both on the frontal relief and on the right end of the lid (**Fig. 90**; cat. no. 281). The deceased child is shown in a *clipeus* on a pedestal of acanthus leaves and his or her image is adorned with garlands; the sex of the child is difficult to establish because of the blank portrait and the empty inscription panel, but the allusion to childhood is made by the iconographic choice of cupids playing and hunting. The other sarcophagus that similarly represents the adult world in a childish way is typical of the group of seasonal personifications (cat. no. 384): the child is no more than a couple of years old to judge from the round and chubby face, and the playing cupids on the lid connect this otherwise typical example of a seasonal sarcophagus with the child's young age. A tertiary motif that makes an otherwise standardized sarcophagus suitable for a child commemoration is the example of a woman breastfeeding a child as depicted beneath the *clipeus* of cat.no.313.

Pet birds are a motif that seems to have been used prevailingly for children, and a scene showing a child holding a bird in her hand is exclusively used for children (cat. nos. 292, 393, and 403). When birds are used on adult sarcophagi, peacocks in particular are popular. The first example of scene with a pet bird (cat. no. 292) shows a girl with a bird surrounded by playful cupids; judging from her portrait she was perhaps two years old when she died. The way the cupids are behaving, crawling on top of each other and falling on their backs, analogises the life stage the girl had reached before she died. The other two sarcophagi (cat. nos. 393 and 403) are strigillated and decorated with seasonal personifications on the first and fifth panels. On cat. no. 393 the central panel depicts a *clipeus* bust of a child holding a bird, to which he is offering grapes, and on cat. no. 403 the central panel depicts a standing boy with a bird. They can be dated to the 280s. Birds are furthermore used as mere decorative elements, such as the grape-eating birds on cat. no. 79; but they can be pictured engaging in the play of cupids, as exemplified by the two cupids riding a peacock (cat. no. 417), and thereby symbolise the playful world of children.[683] Furthermore, birds can be a symbol of a gift given to the dead, just as the Greeks used the cock as a gift of love from an older to a younger man: on one child's sarcophagus Eros is bringing Psyche a peacock to symbolise his love (cat. no. 313). When rare and expensive birds, such as peacocks, are seen on both adults' and children's sarcophagi one explanation is that they symbolise *luxuria*, and thereby elevate the status of the deceased.[684]

Another common motif on children's sarcophagi is the cockfight.[685] Scenes with cocks and two half-naked cupids encouraging the birds to fight are normally

681 See also Backe-Dahmen 2008, 94-102.

682 On children and play on sarcophagi, see Amedick, *ASR* I 4 (1991) chapter 6; Huskinson 1996, 16-7; Dimas 1998a, 30-1. On children's games in antiquity, see Backe-Dahmen 2008, 48-56.

683 For the grape-eating hare as a funerary symbol of prosperity and renewal of life, see Bielefeld 1998.

684 For birds as symbols of wealth, see Amedick, *ASR* I 4 (1991) 23. On the meaning of peacocks in funerary symbolism often, and especially in the early Christian period, interpreted as a symbol of immortality, see Murray 2004, 61-2. Animals are often used decoratively on sarcophagus reliefs.

685 For example, cat. nos. 36, 63, 77, 151, 271, 289, 312, and 313.

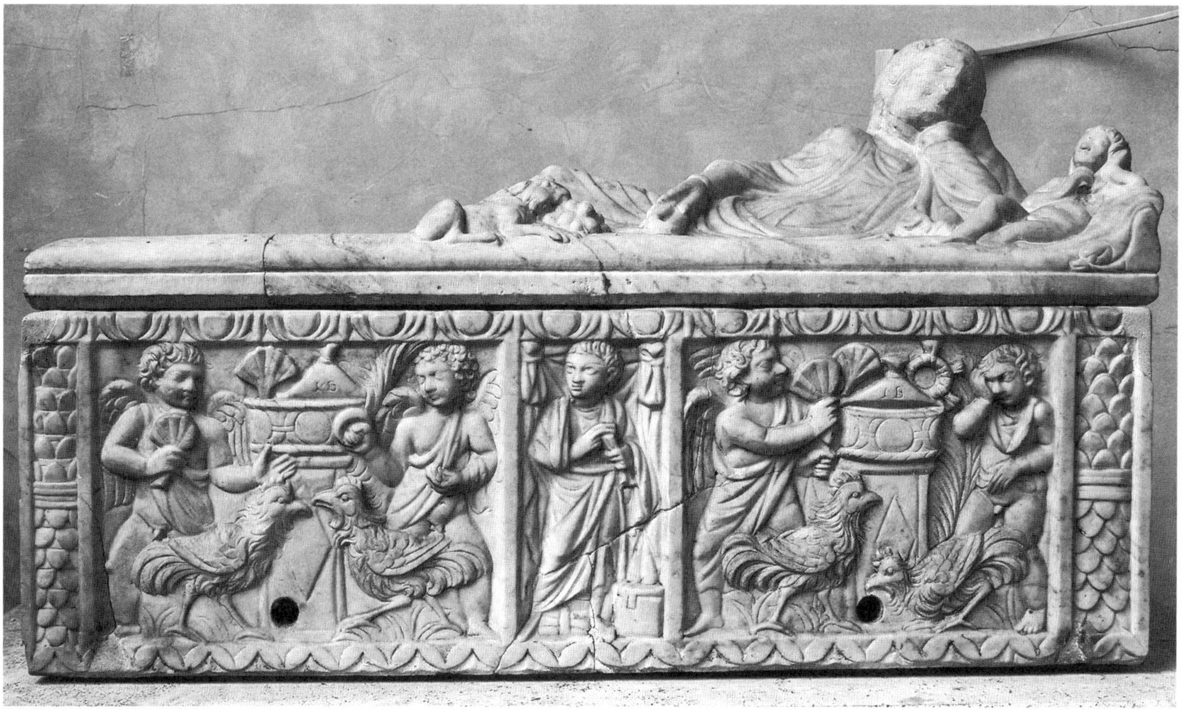

Child sarcophagus (cat. no. 36). Rome, Museo Nazionale Romano, inv. 65200. Photo: Author. **Fig. 91**

placed below the *clipeus*, but sometimes the fighting cocks are used as a decorative element without the cupids.[686] The cockfight can be seen as a symbol of children's play and a world of childish *virtus*; there is a strong emphasis on winning, as the prize is sometimes displayed near the fight (as on **Fig. 91**; cat. no. 36). Cockfights are not only seen on children's sarcophagi, however, and neither are they gender specific. In the catalogue there are at least six adult sarcophagi showing cockfights.[687] One of them is the aforementioned piece with a male *clipeus* portrait re-carved from a portrait that was originally of a boy (cat. no. 407). The *Horus* lock is still visible.

Children's *Role Models*

When playful and chubby cupids are represented on a child's sarcophagus, they refer to children's games.[688] Children represented in the guise of a cupid are typical examples of how adult motifs could be made childish by converting the figures into cupids. On a small group of sarcophagi (cat. nos. 569-72), cupids perform in a Dionysian procession with instruments and drinking cups, surrounding the deceased boy, who himself is represented as one of the followers of Dionysus (**Fig. 92**; cat. no. 570).[689] In these scenes, the deceased boy is supported by attendants as the most intoxicated of them all, the role that was usually taken by Dionysus. The image of an intoxicated person is used once on an adult burial, where the deceased man is represented on one of the figural panels of a strigillated sarcophagus (**Fig. 93**; cat. no. 568). He is naked and leaning against a satyr, who is trying to make him stay on his feet. The choice of a figure type that imitates the intoxicated Dionysus may find resonance in an adult life but as a child's role model the motif seems curious to us, especially in the context of the loss of a child. Such social

686 On cockfights, see Huskinson 1996, 19-20.

687 Cat. nos. 74, 227, 231, 234, 317, and 407.

688 Exemplified by the playful cupids on the lid of cat. no. 281. In spite of the motif, the sarcophagus is not treated as a child sarcophagus here, because of my decision to focus on the commemorations of young children.

689 On children's sarcophagi and Dionysian themes, see Huskinson 1996, chapter 3. On Dionysian themes in general, see Matz, *ASR* IV 1-4 (1968, 1968a, 1969, 1975); Turcan 1966.

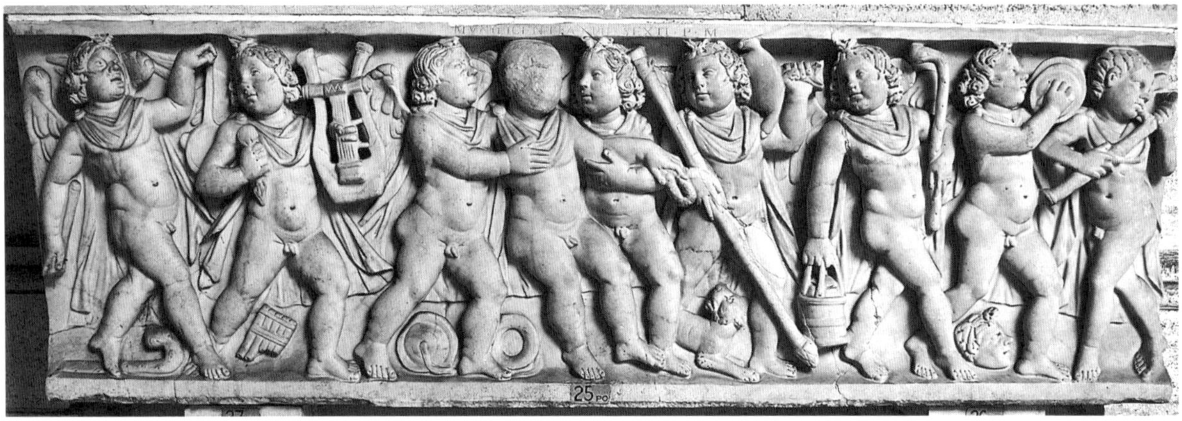

Fig. 92 *Child sarcophagus showing a boy in a Dionysian procession (cat. no. 570). Rome, Museo Nazionale Romano, inv. 65200. Photo: Author.*

behaviour seems to belong to an adult world, and these joyful scenes contrast with our expectations about the response to the loss of a child. The choice may, however, be explained by the fact that the purpose of the tomb and its iconography was to deal with the loss, and in this context the scenes of intoxicated figures and merry cupids show a positive attitude towards death, an attitude that implies a great deal of hope for an afterlife existence.[690] Seen in the light of a life course perspective, the scenes could also represent the deceased boy's initiation into the Dionysian mysteries, as an illustration of a kind of rite of passage.[691] Others have suggested that the feasting scenes represented events that could have taken place at the grave.[692] It was most likely the joyful approach to death that these scenes offered explains their appearance on funerary monuments. When equated with the carefree Dionysian *thiasoi*, the child becomes an allegory of the sorrow-less state of childhood, a state that is transferred to the hope for the child's afterlife. When the child's family came to the tomb for a ceremony, they may also have felt that they celebrated with the deceased, and Dionysian scenes may in general have been seen as a mirror of these funerary feasts. Dionysian motifs are otherwise uncommon on children's sarcophagi. They are, however, present as the secondary motif on the lid of one final piece (cat. no. 264), which has scenery imitating that of a garden, with sculptures and a depiction of Hermes. The deceased girl is not acting as one of the protagonists on this lid, unlike the scene with the drunken boy, but her bust is represented in a frame of garlands. The garlands point to a context of celebration and rituals, and emphasise the funerary implications of the motif.

There are more scenes inhabited by cupids imitating the world of adults than have so far been mentioned. One such scene is found on a sarcophagus in the Vatican Museum that represents the deceased boy as a philosopher with the body of a child (**Fig. 69**; cat. no. 115). The attendants of the philosopher boy are cupids dressed up as the nine Muses, and the scene gives the impression of children playing or acting in a play. On another example of a similar scene, the boy has a blank portrait and he is accompanied by cupids playing music rather than the Muses (cat. no. 33).

In contrast to adults, children are seldom represented as gods or heroes, with the exception of representations of the Muses. There is, however, one other exception that is worth mentioning: on cat. no. 605 cupids act out the myth of Meleager and Atalante.[693] Meleager, hunting

690 For scenes with wine related motifs that allude to the hope for a happy afterlife, see Zanker & Ewald 2004, 139-46.

691 For the suggestion that cupids on sarcophagi symbolised the deceased's inauguration in a Dionysian cult as proposed by Cumont, see the summary by Bielefeld, *ASR* V 2, 2 (1997) 89-90, as well as Huskinson 1996, 31; Turcan 1966, 425, 578-80.

692 Zanker & Ewald 2004, 36.

693 Backe-Dahmen 2006, 117, cat. S 17. Another sarcophagus shows a deceased child as a hero or god (cat. no. 554). The

the boar on horseback, has a portrait of a boy, whilst Atalante has a blank portrait. The other hunters are cupids. The interesting thing about the sarcophagus is that the composition is similar to that of the canonical hunt sarcophagi, otherwise not used for children, and again it gives the impression of a play staged by children.[694] This impression is reinforced by the fact that Atalante is shown with wings like Psyche's, a detail that indicates that the two figures are not only the deceased children playing together but that they have been transformed into Eros and Psyche. The transformation of the common iconographic repertoire of adults into scenarios appropriate for children is an expression of an ambiguous attitude towards children in Roman society. On one hand, childhood is recognised as a stage with its own characteristics, but on the other hand it is seen as a mere reflection of the adult world. The transformation of adult figures into cupids identifies the deceased as a child, but at the same time the patron uses this association to show the deceased as a person with adult virtues. Using adult virtues to heroise a child indicates that children were not seen to possess virtues that were socially valued in themselves in the context of funerary representation. Therefore, to idealise the deceased child and place him or her in the context of high social status, the virtues suitable for adults were imitated on children's sarcophagi. That children needed to be small adults in order to achieve social status is not an indication of a lack of empathy with children's lives on behalf of the adults (toys were sometimes used as grave goods for children, as in the case of the Grottarossa mummy), nor

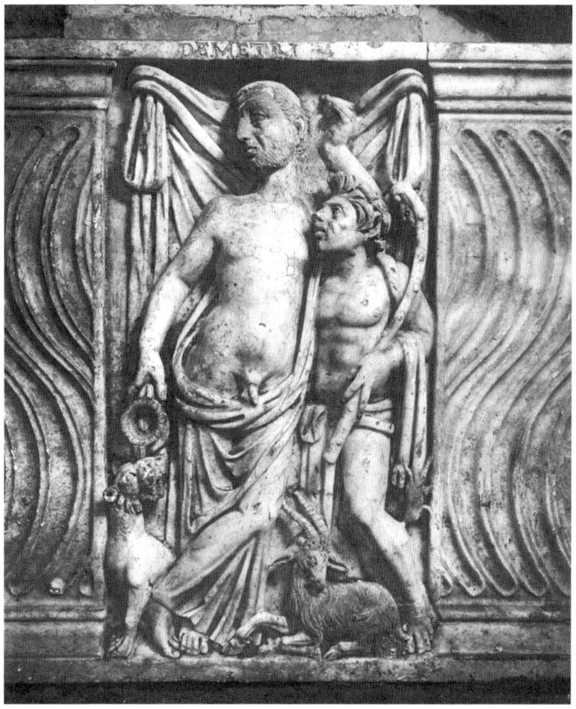

Strigillated sarcophagus with the deceased represented as Dionysus (cat. no. 568). Rome, Catacombe di Pretestato. Photo: D-DAI-ROM 29.434 (Sansaini). **Fig. 93**

can we conclude that Roman children did not experience a period of interest in playing and imagining. It is an outcome of the collectively agreed upon idea of what a life course should contain – a formula that develops in the minds of those who see status as the most important goal, namely the adults. In this ideal life course, the plays and games of childhood found no place.

Returning to the role models chosen for portrait representations of children, the learned sphere was another very popular theme, and here it is not unusual, as we will see, for boys to be presented as Muses or as learned, as in the case of the child-philosophers mentioned above. However, it is worth noting that girls were seldom represented as Muses.[695] The image of the Muses initially seems to be more appropriate for girls than for boys, but such distinctions are misconceived

frontal relief of one piece has been lost, but on the two short reliefs a boy is represented as Apollo together with Hermes and Dionysus with a maenad. Mythological sarcophagi without a portrait designed for children are, however, not that unusual; see Huskinson 1996, chapter 2. Most of the sarcophagi that she has categorised belong, however, to a period before the third century.

694 Cat. no. 495 may also show cupids who are acting in a lion hunt scene. The portrait is roughly carved and the size is above the average length of a child sarcophagus. I have therefore not categorised cat. no. 495 as a child sarcophagus. For lion hunt sarcophagi and their mythological predecessor, see Andreae, *ASR* I 2 (1980). On children's lion hunt sarcophagi in general, see Huskinson 1996, 9-10. Hunt scenes were more often used for children's sarcophagi when no portrait figure was displayed on the relief; see Backe-Dahmen 2006, 112-13.

695 For the identification of boys with Muses, see Amedick, *ASR* I 4 (1991) 74-5. Sarcophagi with boys placed in a learned sphere are cat. nos. 5, 17, 25, 33, 53, 72, 77, 115, 133, 154, 159, 160, 192, 194, 206, 216, 221, 229, 615, 616, 620, 622, and 623.

in the context of young children. The Muses symbolise virtues or skills that locate the deceased boys in a socially acceptable place in society, and they could, as suggested by Huskinson, refer to the educational stage the deceased had reached at the time of death.[696] When a boy was represented as a learned figure, it was not primarily to show him acting or playing a role as a living child, but to show his potential virtues, as conceived by his parents.[697] The learned boy or child-philosopher can, therefore, be read as an allegory of the parents' hopes for their son's future. These hopes should be interpreted more in terms of status than a future profession. Through this visual construction of memory, the parents present an ideal child, and take the opportunity to promote themselves. As mentioned above, in the third century a public career was acquired through learnedness rather than through military experience and physical strength. Consequently, status was expressed visually through images of education and knowledge, and not through military iconography. This situation is reflected in the corpus of children's sarcophagi. Even when military iconography is found on these sarcophagi, the learned element is still present. One boy, whose sarcophagus has not been included among child sarcophagi in my catalogue because the inscription says that he had reached the age of 9 years and the status *equites*, is represented in a cuirass and boots (cat. no. 238). The coffin was found together with a sarcophagus with Christian motifs, and the inscriptions on the two sarcophagi identify the deceased boys as brothers. The sarcophagus therefore was used in the period in which Christian and pagan motifs could be complementary to each other, a rather common feature of sarcophagi produced in the first quarter of the fourth century.[698] This cuirass-clad figure shows that, in pastiche, the military role model could still be used for boys towards the end of the sarcophagus production, but despite his military outfit the boy holds a scroll, and seasonal cupids and representations of Tellus and Oceanus are found on either side of him – iconography that is in line with the kind known from other sarcophagi with learned figures. We can consequently conclude that, for both adults and children, the learned figure was in this period definitely a more popular role model than any figure symbolising male *virtus* through physical strength.

The learned role model is not used as frequently for girls as it is for boys, but despite their less frequent occurrence, girls are not totally absent from the intellectual world in sarcophagus imagery. When they are represented as learned figures, they often appear with a scroll but seldom as a Muse. Four sarcophagi show learned girls, but whereas the girls of cat. nos. 36 and 70 are represented with portrait features, the girls of cat. nos. 3 and 50 (**Fig. 88**) are commemorated through blank portraits and inscriptions. These inscriptions mention the two-year-old Varena Quinta Flavia and an Aurelia Cyrilla.[699] That girls are rarely shown as Muses may have something to do with the combination of their female sex and young age. However, one strigillated piece (cat. no. 220), which was probably made for a girl and not a woman because of its size, shows a bust with a lyre and a plectrum. The portrait is blank but the head was prepared to receive a female hairstyle and one shoulder is exposed. In holding the musical instrument, she alludes to the skill of the Muses; she also recalls the way in which this iconography was used for married women, to show the two important female virtues of femininity and education. It has, however, not been listed among children's sarcophagi in the graphs because of the lack of evidence for the age of the deceased.

Another piece is decorated with garlands and two busts: one female bust with a portrait of a woman and one male bust holding a scroll with the portrait features of a girl (**Fig. 94**; cat. no. 78). The coffin was not carved as a child sarcophagus, but it was used or reused as the final resting place of a girl and possibly her mother as well. The use of the male bust for the girl's portrait confirms that the transition between the two genders were fluid in the context of the representation of young children.[700] The female bust wears a

696 Huskinson 1999, 125.

697 For an interpretation of the child-philosopher, see Huskinson 1993, 116. On children as philosophers on sarcophagi, see Backe-Dahmen 2006, 118; Amedick 1993, 147.

698 For Christian sarcophagi made for children, see Huskinson 1993.

699 There is no indication of age on cat. no. 3. The sarcophagus does therefore not necessarily commemorate a child before adulthood, but it is included here because she is commemorated by her grandfather, which indicates young age.

700 The sarcophagus has not been counted among children's

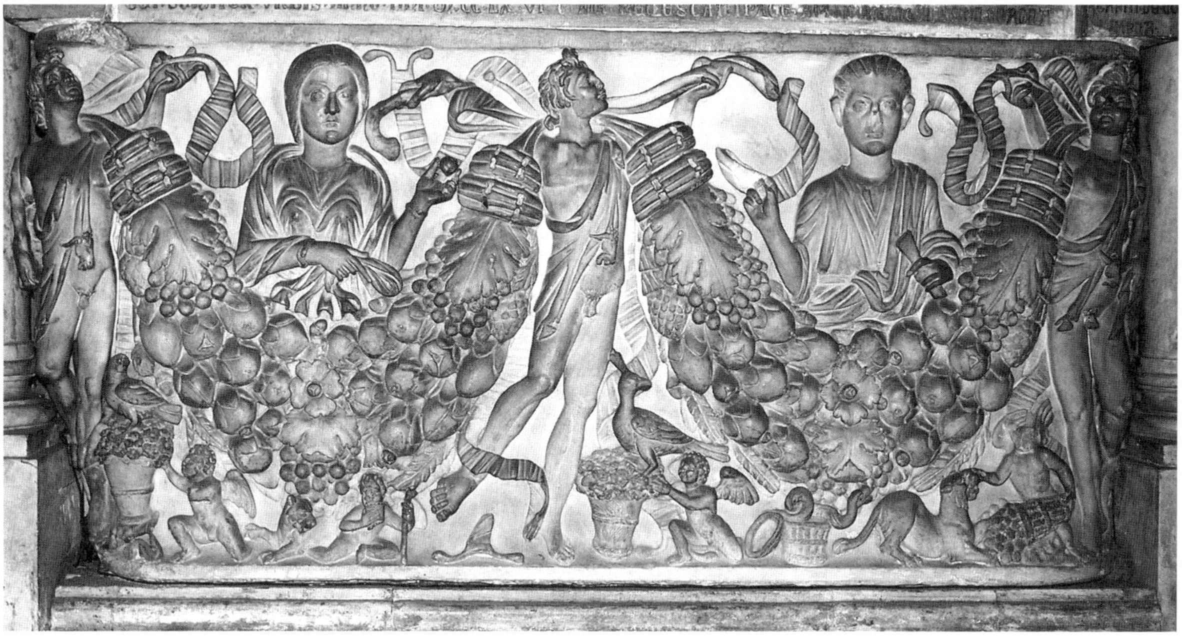

Garland sarcophagus commemorating a girl and a woman (cat. no. 78). Rome, S. Maria in Aracoeli. Photo: Author. **Fig. 94**

hairstyle that covers the ears and is tied into a bun, characteristic of the Severan period. The garlands held by satyrs and the small children playing with baskets of fruit or animals that also adorn the sarcophagus do not help us to understand the relationship between the deceased. The portrait of the girl, however, gives us some clues. The hairstyle is often used for young girls and is found on generic representations of playing children.[701] The young age of the girl is confirmed by two other sarcophagi that show a girl's portrait with a similar hairstyle (cat. nos. 289 and 315): on these coffins the busts are carved without indications of breasts. These apparently male busts probably symbolise that the deceased were of were pre-pubescent girls. Furthermore, the iconography of these two sarcophagi relates to the world of Eros and Psyche, as one shows the divinities themselves and the other cupids and a cockfight.[702] The early physical state of development in which the girl on the garland sarcophagus (cat. no. 77) is represented, combined with the fact that Eros and Psyche and cockfights are popular on children's sarcophagi, indicate that this girl was not yet married.[703] It is therefore likely that the portraits on this sarcophagus depict a girl and her mother, and following the tradition of depicting the patron alongside the deceased, it is likely that the older woman was the commemorator and the girl the deceased. One thing that speaks against a mother-daughter relationship is the fact that the girl holds a scroll, and the woman does not. The scroll can be a symbol of power, and therefore should be held by the person with the highest social rank (see p. 76). Nevertheless, the decision to let the girl carry the scroll may be an indication of the stage she had reached in her life when she died.[704]

sarcophagi because it represents both a young woman and a girl.

701 See, for example, the sarcophagus in the Vatican, Museo Chiaramonti inv. 1304, with playing children (Backe-Dahmen 2006, cat. S 13); and the statue of a girl playing with bones in Berlin Antikensammlung, Staatliche Museen zu Berlin (Backe-Dahmen 2008, fig. 22).

702 For the connection between the cockfight and scenes with Eros and Psyche, see cat. no. 313, where a cock is presented to Psyche as a gift of love. On other pieces, cockfights and Eros and Psyche are also combined on the same relief (see, for example, cat. nos. 74 and 312).

703 For Eros and Psyche as decoration on children's sarcophagi, see Backe-Dahmen 2006, 112.

704 For representations of girls being taught, see Dimas 1998, 104.

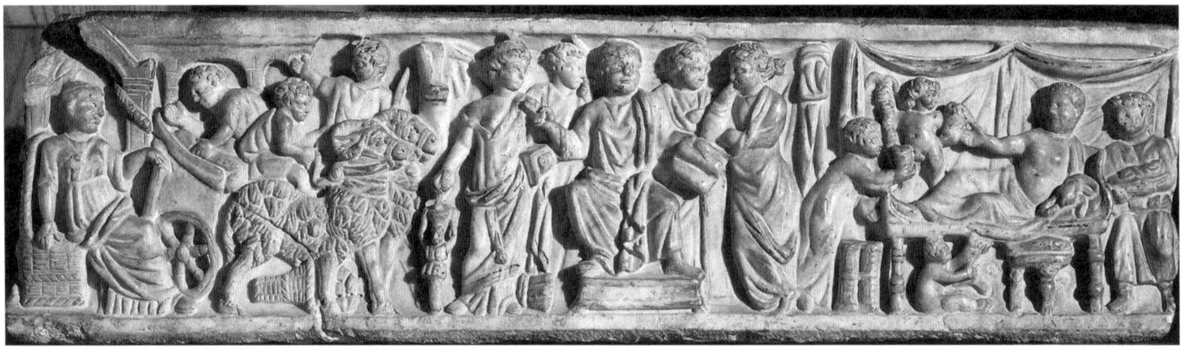

Fig. 95 *Life course sarcophagus commemorating a boy (cat. no. 616). Paris, Musée du Louvre, inv. Ma 1520. Photo: © RMN-Grand Palais (Musée du Louvre) / Gérard Blot.*

A last example of a learned girl that should be mentioned is a rare case of a child-sized sarcophagus decorated with iconography that was normally used for a marital couple. It is a strigillated sarcophagus with a central panel showing a seated philosopher with his Muse (cat. no. 117). The portraits are blank, and it is therefore only the size of less than 1 m. that indicates that it may have been made for a child. As has already been discussed, size is an ambiguous parameter to use in identifying for whom a coffin was intended, and this one may have been made for a cremation burial. Yet, considering the coffin as a commemoration of a child, the iconography can be compared with the playful cupids that imitated the world of adults, and the scene with a philosopher and his Muse alludes to the deceased's social status by endowing the child with the adult virtues of learnedness.

Except for the learned motifs, the ways in which girls were commemorated are not so easy to characterise as those used for boys, since the number of sarcophagi commemorating girls is smaller. However, the general picture is that the iconographic scheme and layout of children's sarcophagi not gender specific. This can be illustrated by the fact that the sarcophagus of Florentius (cat. no. 238) shows the same compositional scheme as two sarcophagi commemorating girls (cat. nos. 312 and 631). On all three sarcophagi two flying *victoriae* hold a *parapetasma* or a *clipeus*, and all three have lids with a square inscription panel and decorative figures on each side. Whilst on the boy's sarcophagus (cat. no. 238) the figures on each side of the flying *victoriae* are seasonal personifications, the girl's sarcophagi have a ram-bearer (cat. no. 631), and Eros and Psyche (cat. no. 312). Seasonal personifications, ram-bearers, and Eros and Psyche do not carry gender specific connotations. Furthermore, none of these figures were designed exclusively for children, which again illustrates a high degree of flexibility in sarcophagus imagery.[705]

Life course iconography was especially designed for children; sarcophagi in this group depict scenes that normally represent four steps in the life script of a child. The scenes often include the first bath and a *conclamatio*, thus representing the beginning and end of the child's life (for example, cat. no. 622).[706] They are known in their canonical form from the second century and their scenery is used and manipulated in the later production. However, the third-century life course scenes are few in number and appear as occasional reflections of the former scenes.[707] I will therefore revisit the sarcophagus of Marcus Cornelius Statius in order to give an example of this type of relief (**Fig. 14**; cat. no. 615).[708] The relief shows a number of events from the life script of the child. Judging from the portrait of the boy on the last scene and its still chubby facial features, M. Cornelius

705 For Eros and Psyche, see cat. nos. 68-75, 310-17, and 637 among which we find examples commemorating men, women, and children. On Eros and Psyche, see Huskinson 1996, chapter 7. See also Backe-Dahmen 2006, 112.

706 Dimas 1998, 16-22; Backe-Dahmen 2006, 114.

707 On life course sarcophagi see Amedick, *ASR* I 4 (1991) chapter 4; Huskinson 1996, 10-2; Kampen 1981a.

708 For cat. no. 615, see also Huskinson 1996, 11.

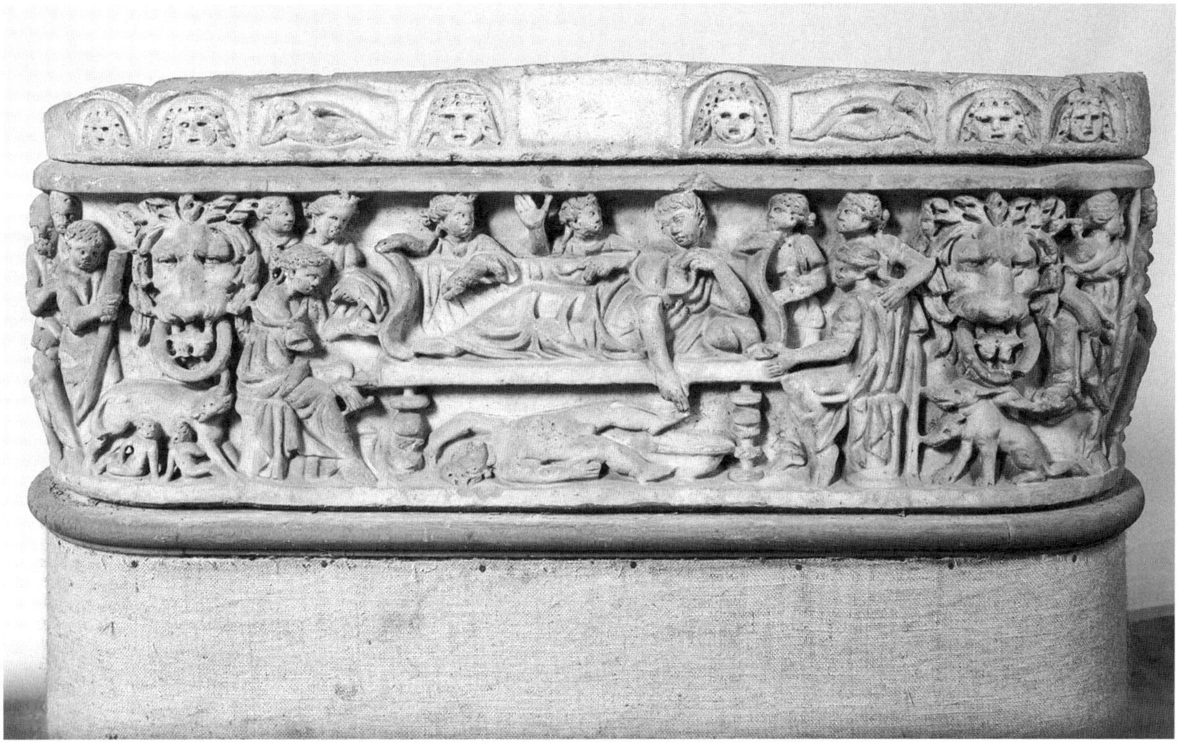

Sarcophagus with the deceased boy among the Muses (cat. no. 620). Rome, Museo Nazionale Romano, inv. 535. Photo: D-DAI-Rom-1965.1122 (Koppermann). **Fig. 96**

Statius seems to have died before he turned five. The scenes have clearly been chosen from the perspective of the parents, since the relief shows key events in their lives: motherhood is emphasised in the portrait of the woman, and the father is represented as a learned man at the point at which he, as the *pater familias*, had the responsibility for teaching the child.[709] The playful life of childhood itself is represented by the boy driving a toy chariot. Life course scenes with a portrait figure such as these are not frequently found, but the iconography is known from sarcophagi without portrait representations of the deceased. Apart from a unique example of a child scene, which will be described below (cat. no. 621), there are three more pieces showing life course scenes. One relief is from the third century and shows two scenes. The first depicts a mother with an infant and a child's first bath (cat. no. 619). The three Fates are represented in the background to symbolise the thread of the child's life being spun out in this period of the child's life. The other scene shows a child with a blank portrait driving a ram wagon probably illustrating a playful scene. Blank portraits of infants are found on another two third-century sarcophagi and the secondary scenes illustrate a first bath and a nurse or mother with a child (cat. nos. 334 and 618).

Another variant of the life course reliefs are those showing scenes of reclining boys (cat. no. 616; **Fig. 95**, cat. no. 620; **Fig. 96**, and cat. nos. 622, and 623). These scenes represent the boy in the final stage of his life, on his deathbed. Other themes that appear consistently on these four sarcophagi, though combined in different ways, are the bath, education, and the toy chariot. On two of them focus has been put on the *kline* scene which therefore occupies the entire frontal relief (cat. no. 616; **Fig. 95** and cat. no. 622), while other scenes from the life course repertoire occupy the short end reliefs. On these sarcophagi the focus is on death, in contrast to the above mentioned examples from the

709 For the educational responsibility of the *pater familias*, see Wiedemann 1989, 143.

second century that show imitations of everyday life.[710] Furthermore, the focus changes from the family to the individual child when the portrait representations of the parents disappear. The life course scenes follow the general trend of third-century sarcophagus production, which, in an effort to emphasise the individual person's memory, demonstrate an increasing focus on one (or two) central figure rather than on a broad narrative. On cat. nos. 620 (**Fig. 96**) and 623 the Muses and additional figures with raised hands in a gesture of mourning are shown behind the reclining boys. The boys wear robes that expose their shoulders, a sign of feminine beauty. The allusions to literary and musical abilities made by the Muses and the boy's assimilation among the Muses connect these two sarcophagi with others that depict boys as Muses (we will look at them below). Beneath the *kline* on cat. no. 623 we see a bird looking wishfully at the grapes in the boy's hand. The bird and the grapes can be a symbol of the transience of life. These two sarcophagi are here put forward as examples of scenes that were used exclusively for children, since figures in *Sigma-mahl*, or any other reclining figures, were not attended by or represented as Muses. One thing that needs to be recalled about cat. no. 620 (**Fig. 96**) is the soulless body of the deceased boy that is lying beneath the *kline* on which he is displayed. His body is naked and we can therefore see that despite the naked shoulder the boy on the *kline* is male; the naked shoulder is more likely a reference to his *post-mortem* acceptance into the sphere of the Muses. He has literally become one of the Muses, a statement made explicit by representing him with the body and dress of a Muse.[711]

Except for these few life course scenes, the adult role model is by far the most popular body type used for children's commemoration in the third century. Generally, the bust in a *clipeus* used for children cannot be distinguished from those used for adults and sometime breasts are even visible on the bust, evidence of the tradition of using the same figure types for all age groups.[712] The world of sea-monsters and nymphs, which carried particular connotations of female ideals, is also used to commemorate both boys and girls.[713] The sea-monsters have been interpreted as symbols of fertility and the cycle of nature and can be interpreted in the context of hopes for a happy afterlife.[714] Seen in this light, sea-monsters seem an appropriate choice for a child's sarcophagus. Though some motifs can be interpreted in the context of childhood, there is actually a quite large group of children's sarcophagi whose iconographic repertoire cannot be differentiated at all from that of adults, simply because these two age groups were commemorated by the same iconography. For example, the boy shown as a philosopher reflects an ideal commonly used for men (cat. no. 133), and the girl who is represented as an *Orans* takes a form that is by the end of the third century a fairly popular role model for women especially (cat. no. 631). The *Orans* sarcophagus was made for a Christian girl, and the same conclusions apply to Christian and pagan sarcophagi: the choice of subject matter on children's sarcophagi generally differs only a little from that on sarcophagi made for adults.[715]

Parents and Children

Sons and daughters were commemorated on sarcophagi by their parents relatively often, and as we have already seen, sometimes the parents are present on the relief together with the child or mentioned in the inscription.[716] The previously discussed Theseus-Ariadne sar-

710 Another sarcophagus from the third century that shows an increased focus on the child is cat. no. 618 (Amedick, *ASR* I 4 (1991) 63). It is a fragment of a sarcophagus that has been dated to the Tetrarchic period, showing a mother or a nurse breastfeeding a child. In contrast to the sarcophagus of M. Cornelius Statius, who as a baby was not depicted with a portrait, the child has a blank portrait.

711 This is not intended to be understood in terms of *apotheosis*. *Apotheosis* is a motif which is rarely found on sarcophagi: to my knowledge it only occurs on sarcophagi with life course themes that commemorate children. In the catalogue there is one example of an *apotheosis* scene (cat. no. 622). On this sarcophagus, the child is taken to heaven in a wagon driven by two horses. The protagonist himself wears a wind-blown veil and an eagle accompanies him. It actually looks as if he is seated on the eagle and standing in the wagon at the same time.

712 For example, cat. no. 371. It is 1.27 m long but the bust has breasts and a naked shoulder.

713 Cat. nos. 366, 369, 371, and 381.

714 Backe-Dahmen 2006, 115, note 1050.

715 Huskinson 1993; 1996, 69; Backe-Dahmen 2006, 121-26.

716 It is said of the Roman woman that "her role in society is that of wife and mother" (Treggiari 1996, 116). This is, however, not the picture found on third-century sarcophagi of

cophagus (**Fig. 12**; cat. no. 612) is an example of this. The inscription tells us that a mother commemorated her son, and on the relief both mother and son have been represented as mythological figures. On another sarcophagus, an adult son, Marcus Aurelius Secundus, is commemorated as "the sweetest son" (cat. no. 326). The portrait of the mother, who is the commemorator, is represented on one side of the inscription and the bust of the son is shown on the other side. Normally such pairs of busts are interpreted as a marital couple, but the signs of age on woman's portrait and the dedication to a son makes it clear that these are representations of a mother and her son.

Returning to the popularity of life course iconography in the second century, representations of parents and children are of a different character from those produced in the third century. On the lid of the famous battle sarcophagus from Portonaccio, scenes commemorating the different stages in an idealised life course are represented (**Fig. 24**; cat. no. 626).[717] These scenes are interesting with regard to the identity of the deceased person. In the first scene, a mother watching a child's first bath has a roughly carved head.[718] The second is a reading scene, a motif that, as on the sarcophagus of M. Cornelius Statius, was most often used for boys; it is interesting here that a girl is shown being taught. Her portrait features, however, appear somewhat generic. The teacher is not a male philosopher but a seated female figure. She could be a Muse: she is similar to one of the Muses pictured in the background. Beside them stands a veiled woman who may be the mother. The central scene is a *dextrarum iunctio*, and the fourth is a *clementia* scene. In the *dextrarum iunctio* scene both man and woman have roughly carved heads, and in the *clementia* scene, the seated man in a cuirass has a roughly carved head. Normally the sequence of life events found on the right half of this relief was used on children's sarcophagi only, but it is questionable whether the Portonaccio sarcophagus was made to commemorate a child. As on the Marcus Cornelius sarcophagus, the emphasis is on the family and especially on the virtues of the mother and the father, as suggested by the figures that were prepared for portraits. The relief constructs ideal identities for the two adults that draw on family virtues, but a special emphasis is put on the man: the male *virtus* represented through the central horseman with the roughly carved head on the frontal relief complements the virtue of the *pater familias*. It is likely that this family had a girl, since the presence of a girl in the reading scene is somewhat unusual, and she may have been buried in the sarcophagus together with her parents; however, the scenes chosen to commemorate her life were here assimilated into the context of an adult life course. This sarcophagus is a good example of how the iconography of children's sarcophagi reflected the virtues that were valuable in an adult world, because in this case they were used to construct the ideal identity of a man.[719]

A previously discussed sarcophagus from the second century also shows life course scenes with a special emphasis on the parents; they, as well as the child, have been provided with portraits (**Fig. 1**; cat. no. 621). The relief does not, however, show the canonical set of life course scenes. Instead the same scene showing the

---

women, who are rarely depicted as mothers. The image of the family, as it is seen on the second-century sarcophagus of the boy M. Cornelius Statius, was not a popular way of showing status in this later period. The four following examples could, however, represent a family:

Cat. no. 100: The so-called *brother sarcophagus* from Pisa. Two young boys are carved with portrait features, and a man and a woman have roughly carved heads. The scene probably represents a family and their two deceased sons (Fittschen 1984, note 38a).

Cat. no. 114: A woman is represented in an *aediculae*. She is flanked by two men and a young woman. It is probably a representation of herself and her family (her husband and her daughter).

Cat. no. 116 (so-called Plotinus sarcophagus): Two mature women flank a seated philosopher with the portrait of a middle-aged man. The right woman seems younger than the left which makes a mother-daughter relationship plausible.

Cat. no. 458: On this sarcophagus the traditional composition of a man and a wife enclosed by a *clipeus* has been altered to include a child as well.

717 Amedick, *ASR* I 4 (1991) 60, 62, 66, 80, cat. 179. Kampen 1981; Huskinson 2002, 15-7.

718 A child's first bath and a mother nursing a newborn are also represented on cat. nos. 334 and 618 respectively. For the iconography of the child's first bath, see Amedick, *ASR* I 4 (1991) 60-3; Dimas 1998, 64-71.

719 For the use of children's life course scenes on adult sarcophagi and an interpretation thereof, see Dimas 1998, 67.

parents in a wagon is repeated twice. This is probably an allusion to two different periods in the life of the child, since the child on the right scene is newborn and swaddled, whereas on the left scene he is seated at his parents' side. Between the wagon scenes two small boys are playing, the oldest with a bird and the other with a toy wagon, learning how to walk. Though it is not wholly clear whether the boys have portrait features, they are probably depictions of the same child at different stages of his life, as is the case in the two wagon scenes. Despite the fact that the boy is shown playing in these scenes, it is the wagon scenes that dominate the relief, reminding us of the scenes of public display made for adults' sarcophagi with a couple driving through a city (cat. nos. 539-44). The emphasis on the parents in the context of a child's life course shows that the representations on the sarcophagi are concentrated around the family and therefore it is as much an idealisation of the parents as of the child itself. The interpretation of this iconography should therefore be situated within an adult world, in the desire to construct an identity of the entire family. A small fragment from the third century shows a woman with portrait features holding a baby (cat. no. 617). The scene was probably similar to the nursing scenes in which the child had a blank portrait (cat. nos. 334 and 618), but not much of the composition is preserved. Further analysis of this piece is therefore difficult, but it is possible that we here have an illustration of what some modern scholars define as the 'good Roman wife'. It may be an illustration of a *nutrix*, but the figures that normally wear portrait features are parents, children, grandparents, and husbands and wives. Other social roles are seldom represented. The relief is therefore probably a fragment of an unusual life course scene, with a mother represented by a portrait. The only other examples which show the mother figure with a portrait are the lid of the Portonaccio sarcophagus (**Fig. 23**; cat. no. 626) and M. Cornelius Statius' sarcophagus (**Fig. 14**; cat. no. 615).[720]

In chapter 3, it was argued that two busts framed by a *clipeus* emphasised marital bonds, whereas sarcophagi with figures on separate panels, for example, on the first and fifth panel of a strigillated coffin, signal that the persons were socially connected but do not focus on marital virtues as the primary ideals. But the Roman formulaic iconographic language was not so uncompromising that it could not be bent. One example of busts in a *clipeus* that almost certainly do not illustrate a marital couple contains the portraits of a man and a child (cat. no. 456). The man stands behind the child as a protective figure, in contrast to the other *clipeus* bust sarcophagi on which the man is shown in the foreground and the woman stands behind with her arm around him, as a supportive figure. The difference in the size of the busts confirms that we are looking at an adult and a child. The portrait of the child is carved on a female bust, and the drapery has slipped from her right shoulder. The figure is smaller than the man, and the portrait is carved with round cheeks and short hair, both typical features of young children. The exposed shoulder and the visible breast beneath the dress recall the stereotypical female busts on *clipeus* bust sarcophagi, and despite the short hair the child is probably a girl. It is interesting that marital iconographic language is used to signal femininity on a bust that commemorates a child. A marital relationship is in this case unlikely because of the obvious difference in age between the girl and the man. Roman girls could be legally married at twelve and were considered to become women at fourteen.[721] Usually a girl was married in her late teens, though sometimes in her early teens. Upper-class girls could, however, be married very early. The girl cannot be more than five years old, because of the facial features and hairstyle, and therefore she seems too young to be interpreted even as a child bride.[722] The coffin must have been a special commission, since more details seem to have been re-carved to fulfil individual demands: the prominent position of the girl in front of the man, the fact that one bust is smaller than the other, and finally, the gesture in which he puts his arm around the girl to show himself as the protecting figure. These important iconographic alterations have been made in order to express the rarely depicted relationship between a father and a daughter.

720 Dimas 1998, 67-8.

721 Denzey 2007, 9-10 and note 19. For a study of the age of Roman girls at marriage, see Hopkins 1965.

722 Shelton 1988, 37. Her study is based on a statistical material based on inscriptions which show either the parents or a husband commemorating a girl. Shaw (1987) argues that Roman girls were generally married in their late teens.

The size of the sarcophagus is just above the average length for a child sarcophagus and therefore a little short for an adult; as such, it is likely that the man was never buried in it. Consequently we must see the father as the commemorator who bought the coffin for his daughter, and in doing so, he chose the motif with the explicit purpose of expressing his grief, emphasising his affection for his daughter and his urge to protect her, even in death.[723] The iconography can therefore be interpreted as a visual illustration of the rather common phrase *filia dulcissima* or *carissima* used to designate the deceased child in funerary inscriptions, a relationship that was otherwise rarely expressed through the relationship between the individualised figures.[724] The sarcophagus thus exemplifies how the social role of a daughter could be shown visually. The iconography tells us that the girl died so young that she was still under the protection of her father at the time.

Another sarcophagus that we have looked at before illustrates a similar affectionate child-parent relationship, between a mother and her grown-up daughter (**Fig. 86**; cat. no. 446). The portrait of the mother is carved as a learned figure. Signs of age are visible on her face, and she looks older than the woman behind her. The young woman has the same hairstyle but her cheeks are round and her mouth protrudes more; she puts her arm around the other woman in a protecting gesture. The differences in age illustrated through their facial features indicate that they belonged to two different generations, and were most likely mother and daughter.

Despite these examples, the emphasis on child-parent relationships cannot be said to have been a common phenomenon, and visual expressions of such relationships were not found among the standardised iconographic repertoire of portrait sarcophagi. Instead they found expression through the manipulation of standardised motifs, and sometimes it seems that the portrait of a child was added to an already completed coffin, as is the case with the boy on the Acilia sarcophagus, which was made for an adult couple (**Fig. 32**; cat. no. 645). This piece was probably made as a *dextrarum iunctio* sarcophagus, but the female portrait, which was presumably carved on the central woman, has been lost; the male portrait still can be recognised in spite of the fragmentary state of the relief. Perhaps as a later addition, a boy's portrait has been carved on an adult learned figure on one of the short ends. The inclusion of a child in a family commemoration is not a frequent scenario in the third century and may be due to an unexpected situation in which the boy died before the parents and was therefore buried in the coffin ordered by the parents for themselves in advance of their deaths.[725] Considering the rare expression of the parent role on sarcophagi, the modern focus on the motherhood role as one of the most important virtues of Roman women may have to be reconsidered.

Age and the Instability of Gender

We have seen that the social roles through which children were commemorated were, in most cases, comparable to those of adults, but how then can images of children be interpreted in terms of gender roles? As with adults, sex seems generally not to have dominated the choice of the decoration for a child's coffin, which was weighted with allegories of virtues symbolising the potential of the child and his or her personal qualities instead. Nevertheless, images of gender can be descriptive of the child's life course. In the following, I will look at children's sarcophagi from a gender perspective, taking a group of cross-gendered sarcophagi as my starting point. The majority of these examples commemorate boys, judging from the portrait; learned iconography, especially the nine Muses, will be central to their interpretation.

Deceased boys have in several cases been represented as one of the nine Muses, wearing her dress and attributes, and often they are flanked by the other eight in the frieze composition typical of Muse sarcophagi that was so popular in the third century.[726] Representations

723 In some scholars' views, Roman parents avoided physical and emotional involvement with infant children (Bradley 1991). S. Dimas, however, demonstrates how images of sorrow and loss were popular on children's sarcophagi (1998, part 2 A, especially pp. 15-6), and King has used the evidence of epitaphs to argue for Roman reactions to the death of an infant child, cf. King 2000.

724 Kleiner & Matteson 1996, 9, 12; Denzey 2007, 54.

725 For a discussion of the portrait and the date of the sarcophagus, see Birk 2010/11.

726 Wegner, *ASR* V 3 (1966); Huskinson 1996, 38-40; 2007, 336.

of boys as Muses or 'learned women' appear both on narrative reliefs and on sarcophagi with a *clipeus* or a *parapetasma*, but all the compositions evoke the intellectual sphere.[727] The scenes of men and women represented on body types of the opposite sex are discussed above, but a high percentage of such cross-gendered images depict a boy or youth as a Muse or some other intellectual female figure. This situation suggests that greater gender flexibility was allowed in the representation of children than of adults, and it is likely that the imagery of these sarcophagi should be seen as an illustration of the relationship between age and gender as it is formulated in the ideal life script of a child. It is known from other societies that the sex of a child can be perceived as neither male nor female, but undefined until fixed by a rite of passage or a socially significant relationship such as marriage or childbirth.[728] Thus, these cross-gendered images of boy-Muses may be seen as representing the relationship between gender and a particular stage in an individual's life course – which in the following cases is shown by the presence of the Muses to be a formative stage connected with education and learning.[729]

A Muse sarcophagus from the second century found near Cività Castellana (**Fig. 34**; cat. no. 154), is one of the first examples of a sarcophagus with a portrait figure. It shows the nine Muses, one of which is a cross-gendered image of a boy dressed like a Muse; we also know from the skeleton found in it that the deceased was a boy.[730] The boy holds a lyre – normally the attribute of Terpsichore or Erato – and is placed among the other eight Muses, so that visually he becomes one of them. His body is quite feminine, with clearly visible breasts. This image is a very direct projection of the virtues of the Muses on to the deceased boy.[731]

If we recall the aforementioned cross-gendered examples (in chapter 3) on adult sarcophagi, the justification of this combination of portrait and body was found in the very expressive way in which cross-gendered images could symbolise the personal qualities of the deceased. In the context of children's sarcophagi, the interpretation may be less complex since it was neither the effeminate body nor the traditional virtues of the opposite sex that the patrons wanted to allude to. The cross-gendering of boys as Muses should instead be seen in the context of their idealised life script, as an embodiment of the special virtues and characteristics of the intellectual sphere which transcend human gender. The boy who has been accepted into the company of the Muses on another piece in Naples (**Fig. 89**; cat. no. 159) is shown as the central figure, with four Muses on each side, and a mask is placed on a pedestal at his feet.[732] He is not dressed like a Muse but as a male philosopher, and his chubby and childish body appears with the attributes of an adult learned man. However, he is still meant to be regarded as a substitute for the ninth Muse, since he is the ninth person in the group.

The next example that further demonstrates the instability of gender in the sphere of the Muses is a sarcophagus that is now lost, but known through a drawing in the Dal Pozzo-Albani volumes.[733] Nine figures are displayed under five arches. Accommodating this number (recalling the nine Muses) appears to have been important for the craftsman, as he had to compromise the symmetry of the composition to do so: the second arcade contains only one figure whilst the others have two. All of the figures represent Muses except one in the central arcade, which is dominated by a male poet with portrait features. Although it is difficult to determine from the drawing whether he is a boy or a man, he has been described on the sarcophagus as a *young* poet.[734] Another boy-poet among eight Muses is seen on a sarcophagus in Verona (cat. no. 175). The portrait, though badly damaged, is of a boy. His hair has an unusual appearance, rendered by horizontal lines, and he wears the characteristics of the Muse Calliope, with his hips twisted in a sinuous pose. He takes the place of the ninth Muse, though the other Muses have the identifying feathers on their head and he does not.

727 Examples of both types will be provided below.

728 Strathern 1992, 66; Sørensen 2006, 119.

729 Gilchrist 2004, 142-60; Huskinson 2005, 102; Dimas 1998, 105.

730 Moretti 1975, 261; Huskinson 1996, cat. 5.1; Wrede 1981, 140, cat. 239; Ewald 1999, cat. H 2. Fittschen (1992) argues that the portrait is of a girl.

731 Huskinson 2007, 336; Wrede 1981, 140-41.

732 Museo Archeologico Nazionale, Naples, inv. 205250. See Wegner, *ASR* V 3 (1966) cat. 23.

733 Vermeule 1960, cat. 14, fig. 14.

734 Wegner, *ASR* V 3 (1966) 91. The sarcophagus is not in the catalogue since our only evidence is the drawing.

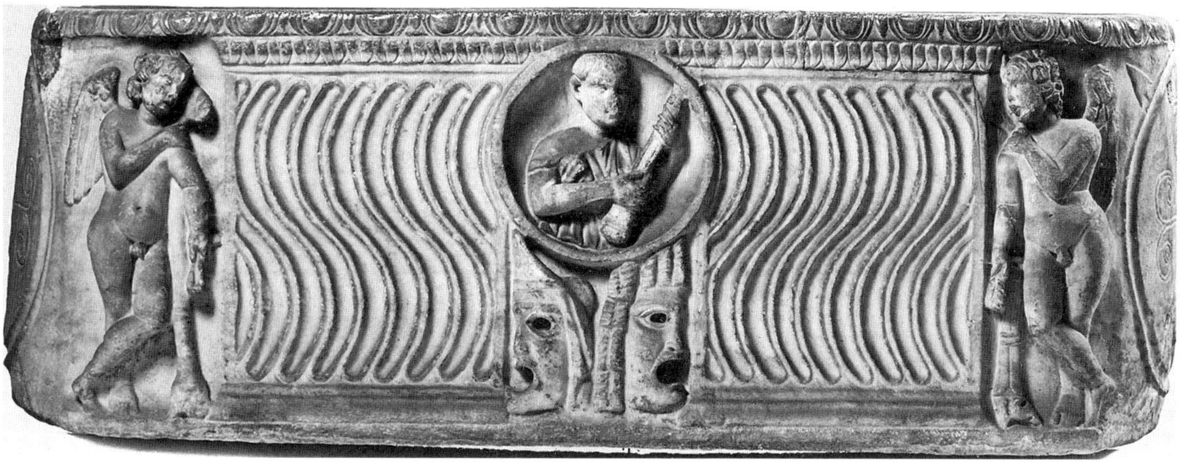

Strigillated sarcophagus commemorating a boy (cat. no. 17). Copenhagen, Ny Carlsberg Glyptotek, inv. 854. Photo: Ny Carlsberg Glyptotek **Fig. 97**

The absence of the feather sets the boy apart from the divinities, and though he embodies Calliope's virtues he is represented as a human. It is thus easier to illustrate his transformation from a human to an embodiment of ideal virtues, and for the commemorators to identify the Muse with the deceased boy.

A more feminine version of the boy-Muse is found on a strigillated piece in Copenhagen showing a boy in a *clipeus* with an exposed shoulder playing an instrument similar to a lute (**Fig. 97**; cat. no. 17). This piece, like the other boy-Muse sarcophagi, indicates that there was a degree of gender flexibility connected to the childhood years. Another example of a feminised male figure appears on a sarcophagus now in Palermo Cathedral (cat. no. 160).[735] The relief shows the nine Muses and two boys, who are each represented in different ways. They may be brothers, or it may be the same person represented twice, each figure embodying a specific gender role. Such dual representations of individualised figures are not uncommon in Roman art, and we have already looked at an example of a man represented in four different guises (**Fig. 78**; cat. no. 641). Two portrait figures representing the same person in diverse ways can emphasise different aspects of the person's life and virtues.[736] The young man on the right end of the Palermo sarcophagus is represented as a male seated philosopher: the scroll in his hand links him to the world of learning, and the Muses are his inspiration. The young man on the left side of the relief is represented by the figure of a Muse: the long dress, exposed shoulder, shapely breasts, and lyre firmly associate him with feminine qualities. There has been debate as to whether the portrait is of a girl or a boy. In an early contribution to this debate, Wegner pointed out that the portrait was originally female and was re-cut to represent a male.[737] Fittschen initially thought that the portrait was of a boy, but changed his mind and argued that it was a portrait of a very young girl.[738] In his discussion, Fittschen puts emphasis on the sex of the child instead of acknowledging the ambiguity implied in gender categories of very small children, which leads to discussing whether the motif was appropriate for a boy or a girl rather than attempting to understand what is meant by the motif in the context of childhood. The figures on the Palermo relief do not invite any categorisation according to sex and we cannot, as on other cross-gendered sarcophagi such as cat. no. 252; **Fig. 84**, explain this choice of mixed male and female iconography by their relationship with the other portrait figures on the reliefs. Instead, it seems that age played a significant role in the decision to use cross-gendered figures, and that androgyny seems to

735 Palermo Cathedral, Palermo. Wegner, *ASR* V 3 (1966) cat. 68; Ewald 1999, cat. A 13.

736 Hallett 2005a, 212-15.

737 Wegner, *ASR* V 3 (1966) cat. 68.

738 Fittschen 1972, 490; 1992.

have been more easily permissible for boys than for adults.[739]

Other sarcophagi use cross-gendered images of children to make more general points about age. A *clipeus* sarcophagus of a boy aged one year and 30 days, dedicated by his parents to their 'most sweet' son, is an example of how the same iconography could be used for both sexes to show that the child had not yet reached puberty (cat. no. 261).[740] The boy's portrait has been applied to a female bust with breasts. The sarcophagus can be dated to the end of the third century because of the hair, which is carved straight across the top of the forehead.[741] Another two sarcophagi with Christian motifs show how the use of female bodies did not intrude on the idealised aspect of a boy's commemoration. One has a boy's portrait carved onto a female bust in a *clipeus*; in the other case, the portrait is applied to a female *Orans* figure.[742] Neither of these examples have been interpreted as representing girls. The fact that girls could be represented by male figure types is illustrated by a sarcophagus without an individualised figure.[743] Octavia Paulina was six years, four months, and five days old when she died, and on her sarcophagus, she has been represented as a victorious girl athlete using imagery from representations of male athletic contests usually reserved for boys' sarcophagi.[744] On the centre of the relief she is depicted in her victory: she is putting a wreath on her own head with one hand and holding a palm branch in the other, a figure type usually used for boys. On the left end of the relief she is seen with two boys pouring oil on her body, and on the right end of the relief she is wrestling another girl. All the other fighting figures are boys, but since girls did not fight boys, her rival has been shown as female. The otherwise standardised motif has, in this way, been adapted to suit the commemoration of a girl.[745] The imagery of a girl fighting and competing is unusual, and must be read as a conscious decision to illustrate certain aspects of her life and personality, such as a sense of triumph, which her father Octavius wanted to commemorate.

Further testimony that changing gender was not particularly problematic as long as it took place before adulthood can be found if we revisit the Hylas sarcophagus (**Fig. 79**; cat. no. 594). As we saw, the scene depicts the abduction of Hylas by the nymphs, as well as Hercules and Polyphemos the Argonaut searching for him. The portraits on the figures of Hylas and the nymph on his right have been preserved (the rest are modern restorations).[746] Hylas has the portrait of a middle-aged man, resembling the portraiture style of Gallienus. The nymph has portrait features, but they are not those of a girl as would have been appropriate to the figure type; they depict a boy with short hair and a soft, round face.[747] The near-naked female body was obviously no deterrent to the addition of a boy's portrait, and the cross-gendered appearance of this figure is likely to be connected with the young age of the boy. He probably never reached the age at which he was allowed to wear the toga of manhood, the *toga virilis*, which could mean that his gender, in terms of social roles, was still in a formative stage.[748] The idea that small children were represented in Roman funerary art without a clear distinction of their sex illustrates an ambivalence that was probably intentional. Just as the representation of boys as Muses could be explained by their stage of personal and cultural development, so too could the other cross-gendered images be concerned with a child's young age or the progress they had made

739 For cross-gendering on funerary reliefs as expressions of sexual relationships, see Clarke 2003, 215-19; Varner 2008, 194. On sexual ambivalence in antiquity, see also Brisson 2002.

740 Huskinson 1996, cat. 9.36.

741 Walker 1990, cat. 36.

742 Rome, Capitoline Museum, Sala II, inv. 70. See Rep I, cat. 811. The sarcophagus with a boy's portrait carved on the bust of a female *Orans* is in Liebieghaus, inv. 1505, see Bol 1983, cat. 96.

743 Amedick, *ASR* I 4 (1991) cat. 67; Huskinson 2007, 338. A sarcophagus with a dedication to Publia Ailia Proba depicts a girl with a very "boyish" look. That she is in fact a girl is shown by the plait piled up from her forehead and pulled backwards (Stuart Jones 1968, 78-9).

744 Amedick, *ASR* I 4 (1991) 82-4; Dimas 1998, 156-58.

745 For Palestra scenes on children's sarcophagi, see Dimas 1998, 152-62.

746 The relief was once thought to represent a family, but close examination shows that the faces of Hercules, Polephemos, and the woman are modern. They can be connected with the extensive restoration of the reliefs from Palazzo Mattei in the 16th century. See Birk 2010/11.

747 Zanker and Ewald 2004, 97.

748 On the *toga virilis*, see Harlow & Laurence 2002, 67-9.

in their life course.[749] If so, we might argue from such images that children could be thought of as crossing from one gender to another at certain points in their lives.[750]

Conclusion: Death and the Child

It is clear that it was the adult world that set the frame of reference for children's representations, as shown by this survey, in which individualised children were shown to be typically represented by adult iconography.[751] These images were chosen by the parents to reflect the child's most important task, namely preparing for adult life. For example, the representations of a deceased boy and girl as Meleager and Atalante (cat. no. 605) showed the two children as actors in an idealised adult world symbolising the ideal of *virtus*. The scene is associated with childhood and its world of fantasies and playing through two distinct features. Firstly, the scene is set as if it were in a play, with Eros and Psyche acting in the mythological hunt scenes like playing children. Secondly, all the hunters are cupids that take the roles of adult huntsmen and transform the hunt into a game of children.

In this way adult iconography on children's sarcophagi could be linked to the world of childhood by transforming the figures in the scenes into cupids (another example of this is **Fig. 69**; cat. no. 115), and by decorating a secondary or tertiary scene with, for example, playing children, seasonal personifications, or cupids. Nevertheless, the use of cupids is frequent on adults' sarcophagi, too, and this particular choice is not direct evidence of the commemoration of a child. There were, however, some motifs that were rarely used for children's sarcophagi, such as hunters and military men. The apparent lack of these role models is probably a consequence of the fact that in the third century, being recognised as an adult was no longer associated with the state's need for citizens who could fight.[752] The route to obtaining a position in public life was instead by way of a knowledge of literature, and children's futures lay in their ability to acquire such skills. This is reflected in the many representations of learned children and boy-Muses, and it shows the parents' prioritisation of this life situation as one of the most important stages in the life script of their child. The seated philosopher with a boy's portrait (**Fig. 69**; cat. no. 115), the so-called brother sarcophagus from Palermo (cat. no. 160), and the philosopher with a naked chest (cat. no. 133) were examples of this. The large size of the Palermo sarcophagus and the motif otherwise only used for couples tell us that the sarcophagus was originally intended for adults. The fact that it was used for children is, however, just as telling as had it been designed for them from the beginning. It confirms that children were valued for the adult virtues that they potentially would possess in the future. This conclusion is only valuable in a funerary context, where the effort was put into displaying socially accepted ideals and values in order to construct an ideal identity for the family.

Other sarcophagi with a similar message showed a boy represented as a learned man enclosed by a *clipeus*. He does not interact with the other figures on the scene but is represented with iconography that does not differ from the popular representation of learned figures (cat. no. 221). The apparent dearth of sarcophagi commemorating girls is, I think, due to the fact that portraits of young girls and boys cannot always be distinguished. Since gender distinctions were not the most important part of the deceased child's identity, there may be more sarcophagi that commemorate girls which we have wrongly identified, on the basis of portraits, as commemorations of boys.[753] This lack of interest in demarcating the gender identity of boys and girls is also suggested by the use of a shared iconography in the secondary and tertiary scenes on children's sarcophagi.

It is in fact difficult to argue for a specific iconography of children, and the commemoration of a child seems to have been carried out with the same notions of representation that were used when adults were commemorated. Taking a chronological view of

749 Huskinson 1999, 195.

750 Fowler 2004, 44.

751 Huskinson 2007, 332-37.

752 Wiedemann 1989, 162.

753 The instability of gender among children has been cited by other scholars, for example by Huskinson in the description she gives of children's sarcophagi in general (see Huskinson 1996, 115). Varner also suggests that such ambivalence with regard to gender is present among representations of children in sculpture in the round (Varner 2008, 195).

children's sarcophagi in general, as Huskinson did, and not only those with portrait figures outlines the development of the children's iconography.[754] The long-term perspectives on motifs that were considered appropriate for the commemoration of children show a change in focus from life course representations to learned figures and cupids. Children's sarcophagi had their own iconographic development, despite the fact that this iconography mostly originated in the repertoire used for adults' sarcophagi. The individualised figure showed that the social roles through which children could be idealised changed during the period of sarcophagus production, but it also demonstrated that the majority of parents represented their children as they would have represented themselves. In the early period of the production there was a stronger focus on depicting children in a childlike world, for example, by events from their life script (such as on **Fig. 14**; cat. no. 615 and **Fig. 1**; cat. no. 621) or scenes such as that of a girl playing with a pet (cat. no. 292), a popular activity also attested by written sources.[755] These two motifs appeared exclusively on children's coffins. Other themes such as *conclamatio* (cat. no. 616; **Fig. 95**, cat. nos. 619, and 622-23) and intoxicated boys (cat. nos. 569-70, 571; **Fig. 92**, and cat. no. 572), though similarly infrequent, were also specially made for children. However, these two themes were not exclusively used for this age group; lament is symbolised on adult sarcophagi through mythological scenes and reclining figures, and the Dionysian sphere and scenes with Ariadne and Dionysus himself were just as popular. Aside from the abovementioned roles, all other individualised figures showed children as small adults, though the young age of the deceased was sometimes marked by transforming some of the figures into cupids, as well as by using secondary motifs that alluded to childhood in a similar way. It can be concluded that the adult dominance over the decoration of children's coffins was present in all periods, first in scenes of the ideal child life from an adult perspective and later in children's imitations of adult roles. The representations of the child as a small adult were a way for the bereaved relatives to show the world the potential virtues which had been lost when death took a child.[756] This practice also proved that the social significance of children was rooted in their futures, since children could only become a status symbol for their families when they were represented with adult virtues.[757]

754 Huskinson 1996; 2007a.

755 Wiedemann 1989, 146.

756 Huskinson 1996, 93. For a similar approach based on epitaphs, see Sigismund-Nielsen 1997, 193. She sees the language of the epithets used for young children as expressions of the unfulfilled expectations of parents.

757 Despite the fact that scenes of children's games are found on children's sarcophagi featuring no portrait figure, Backe-Dahmen reaches the same conclusion (2006, 121).

Retrospect

Sarcophagi with portraits have until now never been studied as a complete group. This book includes a catalogue of 679 Roman relief-decorated marble sarcophagi. The collection of such a vast quantity of material has the advantage of giving an overall picture of funerary self-representation over an extended period. It makes it possible to follow the general developments that occurred over the period of production of sarcophagi, and offers a quantitative expression of what can be determined about the virtues and moral rules of a society using such material. The ways in which people chose to represent themselves are here shown to be a rich source for studying both individuality and the social persona in the higher social classes in Rome over almost two centuries. We can use this source to help us understand the mentality of a stratum of society that is not well reprecented in literary sources and how they defined themselves in relation to previous periods. Furthermore we gain knowledge about the importance of the individual as it was evidenced through the many manipulations of scenes and figures.

The rich repertoire of portrait figures revealed in the catalogue suggests that the social roles as they were played out through these figures in many aspects did not conform to roles widely known from public art and literary sources. Instead it was shown how individual Romans negotiated issues of identity, gender, and status according to societal norms. These role models, while firmly rooted in the worlds of mythology and idealisation, reflected on and engaged with the world of the living. Therefore, in both mythological scenes and scenes imitating everyday life, the deceased (and his or her spouse) acted in accordance with the social ideals that were valid during their lifetimes. In this analysis, social class is difficult to determine since the fictive nature of funerary images means that people from different classes exploited the iconographic language to elevate their status and therefore idealise their memory. As a consequence, reflections of social structures should not be sought in sarcophagus images; this study has been more concerned with studying norms and the relationships between people than with defining the nature of the Roman family or any other kind of social group.

Self-representation through iconography can be said always to convey collectively defined ideals, and it would be obvious to explain these ideals as an imitation of the elite culture of the Roman aristocracy. Nevertheless, the popularity of sarcophagus burials in relief-decorated coffins in the third century should not be seen as an imitation of the iconographic forms of the elite.[758] Instead, the sarcophagus boom experienced in this period, and not least the popularity of portrait figures, is an outcome of a process through which a transformed middle class redefined Roman funerary culture in order to construct a new elite culture that echoed their need for self-representation.[759] In the formation of this funerary culture old traditions were combined with new ideals, as is evident from the expanded repertoire of individualised figures.The use of a coffin as a physical commemoration of a particular person indicates that great importance was put on the individual, though individuality itself can be difficult to find in a funerary tradition where it was important to conform to society. The tradition of sarcophagus burials evolved in a mental climate in which the concept of the self was being renegotiated, and the many individualised figures that appeared on these coffins should be seen as reflecting this interest.[760]

As a consequence of this changed mental climate, needs emerged for representations of new social roles. As has been argued, these roles expressed personal

758 Ewald 2004, 234.

759 In line with the way Wallace-Hadrill sees the formation of elite cultures (2008, especially p. 3).

760 Ewald 2003, 568-69.

virtues and qualities, rather than merely exploiting old and well-established family roles, such as the mother and the *pater familias*. These new roles only rarely reflected social roles directly, and profession, for example, is not symbolised through these figures. The repertoire of individualised figures showed that people were most often represented through fictive identities, which means that the genuine facts of the deceased's life were put aside in favour of an idealised representation of the deceased.

Even though individualised figures do not reflect the 'real' social roles of the deceased person, they mirror reality in the sense that prominent Romans would not have been portrayed in these diverse forms if they were regarded as inappropriate. Individualised figures are revealing of current mentalities and of how social roles were perceived and negotiated in society, especially in terms of what was allowed and possible, but also in terms of what was unacceptable. Even if the deceased never fulfilled the role embodied by his or her ideal portrait figure in life, the function of the portrait figure as a role model shows that this way of being a man or a woman was an integral part of cultural self-understanding. In this light, forms of self-representation on sarcophagi can tell us about the lives of Roman men and women in their social and cultural contexts.

The Roman perception of memory seems to a large degree to depend on visual means. It was through iconography and monuments that people from different social groups constructed a visual idea of what they thought was worth remembering. The way people expressed these ideas changed over time. By studying relief-decorated sarcophagi iconographic changes and ideals can be examined through a homogeneous material group that because of its constant form and presence over a long time span offers a solid ground for such analyses. The general picture is that after the first half of the third century, mythological portrait figures ceased to be used as role models.[761] At that time the learned figure had already entered the stage as another kind of role model that was capable of establishing an ideal *post-mortem* identity. This new role model quickly became very popular in the third century must have appealed to a wide audience of both patrons and viewers. The popularity of the learned woman in particular shows that new identities and roles were opening up for women.[762] I do not mean by this that the figure represented a role that could have been adopted by many ordinary Roman women. Nor do I think that society was made up of people enacting the roles suggested by the individualised figures on sarcophagi, but we can see that these roles appealed to people, probably because they suggested realistic types of role models.

The changes in the types of individualised figures that were used as *exempla* for the bereaved can help to evaluate the mentality of a period, since they are revelatory of socially accepted virtues and individual qualities in the act of constructing social status. When images were able to offer consolation in times of mourning, it is because through the images the bereaved relatives were encouraged to contemplate essential questions of life and death.

To us, sarcophagus relief decoration offers an opportunity to reflect on the roles of men and women in society. Throughout this study, it was shown that a hierarchy of gender was only significant when individuals were depicted in the context of a social relationship, particularly marriage. When a couple were represented together, it was important to make distinctions between male and female virtues, whereas in most other contexts, this was not the case. This may explain why the most popular form of self-representation was as a single figure that suggested a rich assortment of identities, independent of the sex of the individual. For example, the high number of women commemorated by figures holding scrolls, which exceeds the number of individual representations of learned men, shows that not only could the same role models be used for constructing identities for both sexes, but also that women could be seen in roles that are usually considered to be exclusively

761 For a summary of the iconographic development of what Wrede (2001) calls "senatorial sarcophagi", see Ewald 2003, 565-67.

762 As noted by Huskinson (1999, 208, 210). As was discussed in chapter 2, the learned woman as a role model continued to be influential in the Christian period, not only on the intellectual scene, but also in religious life. Arjava (1998, 257-66) noted that early Christianity did not change female roles or ideals, and that women's roles, including those related to the Church, first changed significantly after the sixth century (Arjava, 1998, 262; Ide 1986, 63).

male. The learned woman was not merely an imitation of male iconography. From the beginning, she conveyed virtues and values that are informative of a kind of ideal womanhood.

The general picture gathered from the variety of imagery on sarcophagus reliefs shows that there was a high degree of freedom for both women and men to influence their mode of self-representation. This also means that individuality could be expressed through both the choice of motif and, especially, deviation from the standardised compositions. The close study of the virtues and qualities expressed by individualised figures revealed some previously not widely accepted roles for both women and men. The continuation of the representations of learned woman in Christian sarcophagus reliefs suggests that late antique women played a greater role in the formation of Christianity in Rome than has previously been supposed. Furthermore it is notable that men were idealised with the same virtues as women in relation to both love and death (for example, in the figures of the mythological male sleepers). The same is the case with representations that allude to the domestic sphere, where women did not play a more pronounced role than men, who when shown in the context of domestic life could associate themselves with, for example, wool-working, children, or marriage. On the basis of this evidence, I suggest that we should assume a model of gender that encompasses a whole range of degrees of maleness and femaleness, variable in relation to individuals. This understanding of the concept of gender in Roman society leaves space for cross-gendered identities, such as those presented by male portraits on female figures and *vice versa*, which should be taken into account in studies of how the Romans perceived and experienced gender roles.

The patron's personal choice of motif in choosing a sarcophagus is important when dealing with emotions such as grief and the search for consolation, and the mechanisms of making sarcophagi seem to have allowed for a high degree of individuality in the choice of motifs. This personal choice is a prerequisite for understanding relief-decorated sarcophagi as media for constructing identity. It was suggested that sarcophagi were made as permanent statements of the deceased, substitutes for the decaying body, and that messages of ideals and virtue therefore could be conveyed through their iconography.[763] Sarcophagi were not just self-promoting monuments of a family; they took part in commemorative acts and exhibited religious awareness within a funerary context. Elaborately decorated sarcophagi were used for burials that were never opened after the funeral, a fact that shows us that the choice of a sarcophagus was made for private and personal use.

I hope that this book has opened up a discussion of the role of private commemoration and bereavement in the choice of sarcophagus motifs, and that the many indicators of private feelings in these choices will be explored further in future studies. I am convinced that sarcophagus imagery is capable of expressing a large degree of individuality in this otherwise standardised iconography, which is reflected in several unique representations of patrons and deceased persons on sarcophagi. I have looked at many pieces that are not particularly striking in their choice of motif but which nonetheless exhibit an individual choice of motif, such as the sarcophagus at Villa Doria Pamphili in Rome showing a couple represented on busts on a plinth (cat. no. 241). The plinth tells us that they could be seen as statuesque representations. The man is learned and the woman's figure alludes to Venus iconography with her naked shoulder and billowing veil; together they demonstrate a conventional representation of a marital couple. However, the woman also holds a scroll. This sarcophagus represents more aspects of the woman's identity than the male's, since she is represented as a wife and as learned at the same time. The sarcophagus combines gender roles that are not normally seen together despite its highly standardised iconography. Despite the shared morality of sarcophagus representations and the common iconographic framework of figures of self-representation, the possibilities for adapting and manipulating the conventional scenes are endless. Therefore, each sarcophagus has its own story to tell and ideally each should be approached individually.

It was not only the gender roles of men and women that were negotiated on sarcophagi reliefs; these reliefs were also involved in the construction of the social identity of children. However, it is difficult to explore the life course of individual children, since their lives were measured in relation to adult virtues. The repre-

763 Ewald 2011, 261-64.

sentations of children as small adults instead revealed social attitudes towards childhood. It is clear that a child's qualities were primarily represented through its parents' hopes for the child's future, and in the context of constructing social status, childhood seemed to play an inferior role. There were no representations of childhood associated with a portrait figure which indicated that it was considered to be a distinctive period in the life course of an individual. Instead ideals from the adult world were transferred directly into the world of children for their commemorative monuments.

The ways in which identity and gender roles were negotiated through the creative use of images on sarcophagi showed a high degree of flexibility in how individuals in the third century manipulated myths and stock motifs to express personal virtues and social ideals. The period is in many ways a turning point between traditional Roman culture and Christianity. The Augustan laws on family and marriage belonged to a distant past, and Christianity had not yet influenced the social rules of the family and women's authority. What it meant to be a woman or a man in this period of change could be explored even further by investigating the tension between the attitudes towards women in written texts and the ways in which they were visually represented in tombs, houses, and public spaces. The broader perspective of such a study would allow a fuller exploration and comparison of gender roles as they are negotiated through self-representation in both life and death. The results would contribute to a more exhaustive understanding of roles and to a more general study of the social lives of men, women, and children in the later Roman Empire. I have here made a start by attempting to answer some of the basic questions about gender roles and identity through theories of viewing and response, and it is my conviction that by paying closer attention to this extensive corpus of material, visual images can offer us vivid and realistic snapshots of life in this transitional period in Roman society.

Bibliography

ASR: Die antiken Sarkophargreliefs. Berlin.

MNR: *Museo Nazionale Romano, Le Sculture I-XII.* A. Giuliano, ed. 1979-1988. Rome.

Rep I: Bovini, G. & H. Brandenburg. 1967. *Repertorium der christlich-antiken Sarkophage I. Rom und Ostia* (*Rep* I.), F. Deichmann, ed. Wiesbaden.

Rep II: Dresken-Weiland, J. 1998. *Repertorium der christlich-antiken Sarkophage II. Italien mit einem Nachtrag Rom und Ostia, Dalmatien, Museen der Welt.* Wiesbaden.

Adams, G. 2002. "Familial Relationships, Hierarchy and their Representation on Athenian Grave Stelai." *Eras Journal* 4. http://arts.monash.edu.au/publications/eras/edition-4/adams.php.

Alföldi, A. 1967. *Studien zur Geschichte der Weltkrise des 3. Jahrhunderts nach Christus.* Darmstadt.

Allison, P.M. 2006. "Mapping for Gender. Interpreting Artefact Distribution inside 1st- and 2nd-Century A.D. Forts in Roman Germany." *Archaeological Dialogues* 13, 1-20.

Ambrogi, A. et al. 2008. *Sculture antiche nell'Abbazia di Grottaferrata.* Rome.

Amedick, R. 1991. *Die Sarkophage mit Darstellungen aus dem Menschenleben, Vita Privata. ASR* I 4. Berlin.

Amedick, R. 1993. "Zur Ikonographie der Sarkophag mit Darstellungen aus Vita Privata und dem Curriculum Vitae eines Kindes." In G. Koch, ed. *Grabeskunst der römischen Kaiserzeit.* Mainz, 143-53.

Amedick, R. & G. Koch, eds. 1998. *Akten des Symposiums "125 Jahre Sarkophag-Corpus". Marburg, 4.-7. Oktober 1995.* Mainz.

Amelung, W. 1903. *Die Skulpturen des Vaticanischen Museums* I. Berlin.

Amelung, W. 1908. *Die Skulpturen des Vaticanischen Museums* II. Berlin.

Andreae, B. 1956. *Motivgeschichtliche Untersuchungen zu den römischen Schlachtsarkophagen.* Berlin.

Andreae, B. 1963. *Studien zur römischen Grabkunst.* Heidelberg.

Andreae, B. 1968. "Zur Komposition des Grossen Ludovisischen Schlachtsarkophages." In *Festschrift Gottfried von Lücken, Wissenschaftliche Zeitschrift der Universität Rostock* 17, 633-40.

Andreae, B. 1968/69. "Imitazione ed originalitá nei sarcofagi romani." *RendPontAcc* 41, 145-166.

Andreae, B. 1969. P. Zazoff, ed. "Processus Consularis – Zur Deutung des Sarkophags von Acilia." In P Zazoff, ed. *Opus Nobilis, Festschrift zum Ulf Jantzen.* Wiesbaden, 3-13.

Andreae, B. 1970. "Zur Sarkophagchronologie im 3. Jahrhundert n. Chr." *JbAChr* 13, 83-8.

Andreae, B. 1971. "Die Entwicklung der römischen Löwenjagdsarkophage." *AA*, 119-22.

Andreae, B. 1973. *Römische Kunst.* Freiburg.

Andreae, B. 1977. "Zur Weiterführung des Gesamtplans des Corpus der antiken Sarkophagreliefs." *AA*, 475-78.

Andreae, B. 1980. *Die Sarkophage mit Darstellungen aus dem Menschenleben 2, Die römischen Jagdsarkophage. ASR* I 2. Berlin.

Andreae, B. 1981. "Bibliographie zur Sarkophagforschung nach Rodenwaldt, 1945-1980." *ANRW,* 2.12.2, 3-64.

Andreae, B. 1984. "Bossierte Porträts auf römischen Sarkophagen – ein ungelöstes Problem." *MarbWPr*, 109-28.

Andreae, B. 1985. *Die Symbolik der Löwenjagd.* Opladen.

Andreae, B. 1995. "Il sarcofago di Vitterbo nell'arte romana." In A. Emiliozzi, ed. *Il sarcofago romano dal monumento rinascimentale della Bella Galiana a Viterbo.* Viterbo, 23-53.

Andreae, B. & H. Jung 1977. "Vorläufige tabellarische Übersicht über die Zeitstellung und Werkstattzugehörigkeit von 250 römischen Prunksarkophagen des 3. Jhs. Chr." *AA*, 432-36.

Andreae, B. & S. Settis, eds. 1983. *Colloquio sul Reimpiego dei Sarcofagi Romani nel Medioevo.* Marburg.

Andreae, B., G. Oehlschlegel, & K. Weber. 1972. "Zusammenfügung der Fragmente eines Meleagersarkophages in Frankfurt und Kassel." *JdI* 87, 388-432.

Andreae, B. et al. 1995. *Bildkatalog der Skulpturen des Vatikanischen Museums.* Berlin.

Andrén, A. 1965. *Classical Antiquities of the Villa San Michele.* Opuscula Romana V. Lund.

Antonsson, O.A. 1958. *Antik konst. En konstbok från Nationalmuseum.* Stockholm.

Apollonj Ghetti, B., A. Ferrua, & C. Serafini. 1951. *Esplorazioni sotto la confessione di San Pietro in Vaticano, eseguite negli anni 1940-1949.* Vatican City.

Archer, L.J., S. Fischler, & M. Wyke. 1994. *Women in Ancient Societies. An Illusion of the Night.* Basingstoke.

Arias, P. E., E. Cristiani Gabba, & S. Settis. 1977. *Camposanto monumentale di Pisa. Le antichità.* Pisa.

Ariès, P. 1962. *Centuries of Childhood. A Social History of Family Life.* New York.

Arjava, A. 1998. *Women and Law in Late Antiquity.* Oxford.

Asgari, N. 1977. "Die halbfabrikate kleinasiatischer Girlandensarkophage und ihre Herkunft." *AA*, 329-80.

Babbitt, F. C. 1949. *Plutarch's Moralia* III. Cambridge, Mass.

Backe-Dahmen, A. 2006. *Innocentissima aetas. Römische Kindheit im Spiegel literarischer, rechtlicher und archäologischer Quellen des 1. bis 4. Jahrhunderts n. Chr.* Mainz.

Backe-Dahmen, A. 2008. *Die Welt der Kinder in der Antike.* Mainz.

Balch, D. 2008. "From Endymion in Roman 'Domus' to Jonah in Christian Catacombs: From Houses of the Living to Houses of the Dead. Iconography and Religion in Transition." In L. Brink & D. Green, eds. *Commemorating the Dead. Texts and Artifacts in Context.* Berlin, 273-303.

Baldassarre, I. 1991/92. "Tre sarcofagi figurati della tomba 34 dell'Isola Sacra." *Studi Miscellanei* 30, 305-22.

Baldassarre, I., I. Bragantini, & C. Morselli. 1996. *Necropoli di Porto*. Rome.

Balty, J.C. 2005. Review of Ewald 1999. *AntCl* 74, 635-36.

Baratta, G. 2007. "La mandorla centrale dei sarcophagi strigillati. Un campo iconografico ed i suoi simboli." In F. & T. Hölscher, eds. *Römische Bilderwelten. Von der Wirklichkeit zum Bild und zurück. Kolloquium der Gerda Henkel Stiftung am Deutschen Archäologischen Institut Rom, 15.-17. März 2004*. Heidelberg, 191-215.

Baratte, F. & C. Metzger. 1985. *Catalogue des sarcophages en pierre d'époques romaine et paléochrétienne*. Paris.

Barkan, L. 1999. *Unearthing the Past. Archaeology and Aesthetics in the Making of Renaissance Sculpture*. New Haven.

Bartman, E. 1993. "Carving the Badminton Sarcophagus." *MMAJ* 28, 57-75.

Bartman, E. 1998. Review of Kleiner & Matheson 1996. *BMCR*. http://bmcr.brynmawr.edu/1998/98.6.03.html

Bartman, E. 1999. Review of Huskinson 1996. *CW* 92, 4, 386-87.

Bassler, J. 2008. "The Problem of Self-Definition. What Self and Whose Definition?" In F.E. Udoh, ed. *Redefining First-Century Jewish and Christian Identities. Essays in Honor of Ed Parish Sanders*. Notre Dame, Indiana, 42-66.

Baxter, J.E. 2008. "The Archaeology of Childhood." *Annual Review of Anthropology* 37, 159-75.

Beard, M., J.A. North, & S. Price. 1998. *Religions of Rome* I-II. Cambridge.

Beauvoir, S. de. 1949 (1973). *The Second Sex*. Translated by H. M. Parshley. New York.

Bell, S. 2008. "Role Models in the Roman World". In S. Bell & I.L. Hansen, eds. *Role Models in the Roman World, Identity and Assimilation*. Ann Arbor, 1-40.

Bell, S. & I.L. Hansen, eds. 2008. *Role Models in the Roman World, Identity and Assimilation*. Memoirs of the American Academy in Rome 7. Ann Arbor.

Benndorf, O. & R. Schöne. 1867. *Die antiken Bildwerke des Lateranensischen Museums*. Leipzig.

Bentz, K. 1998. "Rediscovering the Licinian Tomb." *JWalt* 55/56, 63-88.

Berger, J. 1972. *Ways of Seeing*. London.

Bergmann, M. 1977. *Studien zum römischen Porträt des 3. Jahrhunderts n. Chr*. Bonn.

Bergmann, B. 2010. *Der Kranz des Kaisers. Genese und Bedeutung einer römischen Insignie*. Berlin.

Berntsen, D. & A. Bohn 2009. "Cultural Life Scripts and Individual Life Stories." In P. Boyer & J. Wertsch, eds. *Memory in Mind and Culture*. Cambridge, 62-82.

Berntsen, D & D.C. Rubin. 2004. "Cultural life scripts structure recall from autobiographical memory." *Memory & Cognition* 32.3, 427-42.

Beschreibung der antiken Skulpturen mit Ausschluss der pergamenischen Fundstücke 1891. *Hrsg. von der Generalverwaltung*. Berlin.

Bianchi Bandinelli, R. 1954. "Sarcofago da Acilia con la designazione di Gordiano III." *Bd'A* 39, 200-20.

Bianchi Bandinelli, R. 1970. *Rom, das Zentrum der Macht. Die römische Kunst von den Anfängen bis zur Zeit Marc Aurels*. Munich.

Bielefeld, D. 1995. "Zur Ikonographie attischer Sarkophage mit Eroten-Darstellungen." *RM* 102, 397-404.

Bielefeld, D. 1997. *Weinlese- und Ernteszenen. Die stadtrömische Eroten-Sarkophage. ASR* V 2. 2, Berlin.

Bielefeld, D. 1998. "Ikonographie und Bedeutung des 'Trauben naschenden Hasen'." In G. Koch, ed. *Sarkophag-Studien 1. Akten des Symposium "125 Jahre Sarkophag-corpus." Marburg 4.-7. Oktober 1995*. Mainz, 7-19.

Bielfeldt, R. 2003. "Orest im Medusengrab, Ein Versuch zum Betrachter." *RM* 110, 117-50.

Bielfeldt, R. 2005. Review of Zanker & Ewald 2004. *Göttinger Forum für Altertumswissenschaft* 8, 1067-79.

Bielfeldt, R. 2005a. *Orestes auf römischen Sarkophagen*. Berlin.

Birk, S. 2010/11. "Third-Century Sarcophagi from the City of Rome: A Chronological Reappraisal." *AnalRom* 35-36, 7-30.

Birk, S. 2011. "Man or Woman? Cross-gendering and Individuality on Third Century Sarcophagi." In J. Elsner & J. Huskinson, eds. *Life, Death and Representation. Some New Work on Roman Sarcophagi*. Berlin, 229-60

Birk, S. 2012. "Sarcophagi, Self-Representation and Patronage in Rome and Tyre." In S. Birk & B. Poulsen, eds. *Patrons and Viewers in Late Antiquity*. Aarhus, 107-34.

Birk, S. forthcoming. "Carving Sarcophagi: Roman Sculptural Workshops and Their Organisation." In T.M. Kristensen & B. Poulsen, eds. *Ateliers and Artisans in Roman Art and Archaeology*. JRA Supplementary Series. Portsmouth, RI.

Bisconti, F. 2004. & H Brandenburg, eds. *Sarcofagi tardoantichi, paleocristiani e altomedievali. Atti della giornata tematica dei Seminari di Archeologia Cristiana. Ecole française de Rome, 8 maggio 2002*. Vatican City.

Blome, P. 1977. "Begram und Rom. Zu den Vorbildern des Aktaion-Sarkophages im Louvre." *AntK* 20, 43-53.

Blome, P. 1978. "Zur Umgestaltung griechischer Mythen in der römischen Sepulkralkunst. Alkestis-, Protesilaos- und Proserpinasarkophage." *RM* 85, 435-57.

Blome, P. 1992. "Funerärsymbolische Collagen auf mythologischen Sarkophagreliefs." In *Giornate Pisane. Atti del IX Congresso delle F.I.E.C. 24-30 Augosto 1989* (=StIt 85), 1061-73.

Blome, P. 1998. "Der Löwenjagdsarkophag Ludwig im Antikenmuseum Basel." In G. Koch, ed. *Sarkophag-Studien 1. Akten des Symposium "125 Jahre Sarkophag-corpus." Marburg 4.-7. Oktober 1995*. Mainz, 1-6.

Bodel, J. 2008. "From '*columbaria*' to catacombs: Collective Burial in Pagan and Christian Rome." In L. Brink & D. Green, eds. *Commemorating the Dead. Texts and Artifacts in Context*. Berlin, 177-242.

Bohn, A. & D. Berentsen 2008. "Life Story Development in Childhood: The Development of Life Story. Abilities and the Acquisition of Cultural Life Scripts From Late Middle Childhood to Adolescence." *Developmental Psychology* 44.4, 1135-47.

Bol, P. 1983. *Bildwerke aus Stein und aus Stuck: von archaischer Zeit bis zur Spätantike*. Melsungen.

Bol, P. 1992. *Forschungen zur Villa Albani. Katalog der antiken Bildwerke* III. *Bildwerke in der Galleria della Leda, im ehemaligen Tempel der ephesischen Artemis und im Bigliardo*. Berlin.

Bol, P. 1998. *Forschung zur Villa Albani. Katalog der antiken Bildwerke* V. *In den Gärten oder auf Gebäuden aufgestellte Skulpturen sowie die Masken*. Berlin.

Borg, B., ed. 2004. *Paideia. The World of the Second Sophistic*. Berlin.

Boschung, D. 1987. *Antike Grabaltäre aus den Nekropolen Roms*. Bern.

Bovini, G. 1949. *I sarcofagi paleocristiani. Determinazione della loro cronologia mediante l'analisi dei ritratti*. Vatican City.

Bradley, K. 1991. *Discovering the Roman Family. Studies in Roman Social History*. New York.

Brandenburg, H. 1967. "Meerwesensarkophage und Clipeusmotiv. Beiträge zur Interpretation römischer Sarkophagreliefs." *JdI* 82, 195-245.

Brandenburg, H. 1978. "Der Beginn der stadtrömischen Sarkophagproduktion der Kaiserzeit." *JdI* 93, 277-327.

Brandenburg, H. 2004. "Osservazioni sulla fine della produzione e dell' uso dei sarcophagi a rilievo nella tarda antichità nonché sulla loro decorazione." In F. Bisconti & H. Brandenburg, eds. *Sarcophagi tardoantichi, paleocristiani e altomedievali. Atti della giornata tematica dei Seminari de Archeologia Cristiana. École Francaise de Rome – 8 maggio 2002*. Vatican City.

Bremmer, J. 2002. *The Rise and Fall of the Afterlife*. London.

Bremmer, J. & N. Horsfall. 1987. *Roman Myth and Mythography*. London.

Brilliant, R. 1963. *Gesture and Rank in Roman Art. The Use of Gestures to Denote Status in Roman Sculpture and Coinage.* New Haven.

Brilliant, R. 1974. *Roman Art from the Republic to Constantine*. London.

Brilliant, R. 1984. *Visual Narratives. Storytelling in Etruscan and Roman Art*. Ithaca, NY.

Brilliant, R. 1992. "Roman Myth/Greek Myth: Reciprocity and Appropriation on a Roman Sarcophagus in Berlin." In *Giornate Pisane. Atti del IX Congresso delle F.I.E.C. 24-30 Augosto 1998* (=StIt 85), 1030-45.

Brinkmann, V. 2004. *Bunte Götter. Die Farbigkeit antiker Skulptur*. Munich.

Brisson, L. 2002. *Sexual Ambivalence. Androgyny and Hermaphroditism in Graeco-Roman Antiquity*. Berkeley.

Brooks, A. 1997. *Postfeminisms: Feminism, Cultural Theory and Cultural Forms*. London.

Brown, P. 1992. *Power and Persuasion in Late Antiquity. Towards a Christian Empire*. Madison, Wis.

Brown, S. 1997. "'Ways of Seeing' Women in Antiquity." In A.O. Koloski-Ostrow & C. Lyons, eds. *Naked Thuths. Women, Sexuality, and Gender in Classical Art and Archaeology.* London, 12-42.

Buranelli, F. 2010. *Palais Farnèse*. Milan.

Burke, P. 1992. *The Fabrication of Louis XIV*. New Haven.

Burrus, W. 2008. Review of Denzey 2007. *Journal of Early Christian Studies* 16, 261-62.

Butler, J. 1986. "Sex and Gender in Simone de Beauvoir's *Second Sex*." *Yale French Studies* 72, 35-49

Butler, J. 1990. *Gender Trouble. Feminism and the Subversion of Identity*. New York.

Butler, J. 1993. *Bodies that Matter. On the Discursive Limits of "Sex"*. London.

Cain, H. 1997. *Dionysos. "Die Locken lang, ein halbes Weib? ..." Sonderausstellung Museum für Abgüsse Klassischer Bildwerke.* Munich.

Calza, G. 1940. *La necropoli del Porto di Roma nell' Isola Sacra*. Rome.

Calza, R. 1964/65. "Le sculture e la probabile zona cristiana di Ostia e di Porto." *RendPontAcc* 37, 155-257.

Calza, R. 1977. *Antichità di Villa Doria Pamphilj*. Rome.

Cambi, N. 1998. "Sarkophage aus salonitanischen Werkstätten." In G. Koch, ed. *Sarkophag-Studien I, Akten des Symposiums "125 Jahre Sarkophag-Corpus". Marburg 4.-7. Oktober 1995*. Mainz, 169-81.

Cameron, A. 2004. *Greek Mythography in the Roman World*. Oxford.

Cameron, A. & A. Kuhrt. 1983. *Images of Women in Antiquity*. Detroit.

Caronna, E.L. 1983. "Quattro sarcopfagi della Chiesa di S. Stefano Rotondo." *MemLinc* ser. 8, 35, 155-70.

Carroll, M. 2006. *Spirits of the Dead. Roman Funerary Commemoration in Western Europe*. Oxford.

Carroll, M. 2011. "'Memoria' and 'Damnatio Memoria'. Preserving and Erasing Identities in Roman Funerary Commemoration." In M. Carroll & J. Rempel, eds. *Living Through the Dead*. Oxford, 65-90.

Casella, E.C. 2006. "'Safe' Genders?" *Archaeological Dialogues* 13.1, 25-7.

Casella, E. & C. Fowler, eds. 2005. *The Archaeology of Plural and Changing Identities Beyond Identification*. Boston.

Cavalier, O. eds. 2005. *La collection d'inscriptions gallo-grecques et latines du Musèe Calvet*. Paris.

Centanni, M. 2006. "Malinconica Polimnia. La 'Musa pensosa' come figura del pathos dell' intellettuale." In A. Bottini, ed. *La Musa pensosa. L'immagine dell'intellettuale nell'antichità*. Milano, 151-61.

Chiarlo, C.R. 1976. "Sul significato dei sarcofagi a ληνος decorate con leoni." *Annali della Scuola Normale Superiore di Pisa,* ser. III, IV 1309-40.

Clark, G. 1998. "The Old Adam: the Fathers and the Unmaking of Masculinity." In L. Foxhall and J. Salmon, eds. *Thinking Men. Masculinity and its Self-Representation in the Classical Tradition*. London.

Clarke, J. 1998. *Looking at Lovemaking. Constructions of Sexuality in Roman Art, 100 B.C.-A.D. 250*. Berkeley.

Clarke, J. 2002. "Look Who's Laughing at Sex. Men and Women Viewers in the Apodyterium of the Suburban Baths at Pompeii." In D. Fredrick, ed. *The Roman Gaze. Vision, Power and the Body*. Baltimore, 149-81.

Clarke, J. 2003. *Art in the Lives of Ordinary Roman. Visual Representation and Non-Elite Viewers in Italy, 100 B.C.-A.D. 315*. Berkeley.

Cohen, A. & J.B. Rutter, eds. 2007. *Constructions of Childhood in Ancient Greece and Italy*. Princeton.

Cohon, R. 1992. "A Muse Sarcophagus in its Context." *AA*, 109-19.

Cumont, F. 1942. *Recherches sur le symbolisme funéraire des Romains*. Paris.

Cumont, F. 1949. *Lux perpetua*. Paris.

Cumont, F. 1959 [1922]. *Afterlife in Roman Paganism. Lectures Delivered at Yale University on the Silliman Foundation*. New York.

Cuomo, S. 2007. *Technology and Culture in Greek and Roman Antiquity*. Cambridge.

D'Ambra, E. 1988. "A Myth for a Smith: A Meleager Sarcophagus from a Tomb in Ostia." *AJA* 92, 85-99.

D'Ambra, E. 1996. "The Calculus of Venus. Nude Portraits of Roman Matrons." In N. Kampen, ed. *Sexuality in Ancient Art*. Cambridge, 219-32

D'Ambra, E. 2001. Review of Ewald 1999. *AJA* 105, 365-66.

D'Ambra, E. 2007. *Roman Women*. Cambridge.

Dachner, J. 2006. "Grenzen der Nacktheit, Studien zum nackten männlichen Körper in der griechischen Plastik des 5. und 4. Jahrhunderts v. Chr.". *JdI* 120, 155-300.

Danesi, A. & S. Gambardella 2008. "La conservazione delle sculture di Palazzo Lancellotti ai Coronari. Il restauro come mezzo di ricerca storica." In M. Barbanera & A. Freccero, eds. *Collezione di antichità di Palazzo Lancellotti ai Coronari. Archeologia, architettura, restauro*. Studi miscellanei 34, 117-34.

Davies, G. 2008. "Portrait Statues as Models for Gender Roles in Roman Society." In I.L. Hansen & S. Bell, eds. *Role Models in the Roman World. Identity and Assimilation*. Ann Arbor, 210-20.

Davies, G. 2011. "Before Sarcophagi." In J. Elsner & J. Huskinson, eds. *Life, Death and Representation. Some New Work on Roman Sarcophagi.* Berlin, 21-54.

Davies, J. 1999. *Death, Burial and Rebirth in the Religions of Antiquity*. London.

Davies, P. 2004. *Death and the Emperor: Roman imperial funerary monuments from Augustus to Marcus Aurelius*. Cambridge.

Deckard, B. 1975. *The Women's Movement. Political, Socio-Economic and Psychological Issues*. New York.

Denzey, N.F. 2007. *The Bone Gatherers. The Lost Worlds of Early Christian Women*. Boston.

Dey, H.W. 2009. "'Crisis' and Roman Historiography in the Third Century." *JRA* 22, 643-47.

Díaz-Andreu García, M. et al., eds. 2005. *The Archaeology of Identity. Approaches to Gender, Age, Status, Ethnicity and Religion*. London.

Dillon, S. 2010. *The Female Portrait Statue in the Greek World*. New York.

Dimas, S. 1998. *Untersuchungen zur Themenwahl und Bildgestaltung auf römischen Kindersarkophagen*. Münster.

Dimas, S. 1998a. "Untersuchungen zur Themenwahl und Bildgestaltung auf römischen Kindersarkophagen." In G. Koch, ed. *Sarkophag-Studien 1. Akten des Symposiums "125 Jahre Sarkophag-Corpus". Marburg 4.-7. Oktober 1995*. Mainz, 28-33.

Dixon, S. 1992. *The Roman Family*. Baltimore.

Dixon, S. 2001. *Reading Roman Women. Sources, Genres, and Real Life*. London.

Dobres, M.A. & J. Robb, eds. 2000. *Agency in Archaeology*. London.

Dolci, E. 1989. *Il Marmo nella civiltà romana: la produzione e il commercio. Mostra seminario. Carrara, maggio-giugno 1989, Museo del Marmot*. Carrara.

Dowling, M. 2006. *Clemency & Cruelty in the Roman World*. Ann Arbor.

Dölger, F.J. 1930. "Die antiken Köpfe mit dem stehenden und liegenden Kreuz." *AuChr* 2, 284-96.

Dresken-Weiland, J. 2003. *Sarkophagbestattungen des 4.-6. Jahrhunderts im Westen des römischen Reiches*. Rome.

Dresken-Weiland, J. 2007. "Vorstellungen von Tod und Jenseits in den früchchristlichen Grabinschriften der Oikumene." *Antiquité Tardive* 15, 285-302.

Dresken-Weiland, J. 2010. *Bild, Grab und Wort. Untersuchungen zu Jenseitsvorstellungen von Christen des 3. und 4. Jahrhunderts*. Regensburg.

Dufour Bozzo, G. 1967. *Sarcofagi romani a Genova*. Genoa.

Eberle, A.F. 1990. "Fragment d'un sarcophage avec monstres marins au J. Paul Getty Museum." In G. Koch & M. True, eds. *Roman Funerary Monuments in the J. Paul Getty Museum* 1. Malibu, 71-82.

Eberle, A.F. 1990a. "Un sarcophage d'enfant au J. Paul Gettu Museum." In G. Koch & M. True, eds. *Roman Funerary Monuments in the J. Paul Getty Museum* 1. Malibu, 47-58.

Eck, W. 1986. "Inschriften aus der vatikanischen Nekropole unter St. Peter." *ZPE* 65, 245-93.

Eck, W. 1989. "Inschriften und Graubbauten in der Nekropole unter St. Peter." In G. Alföldy, ed. *Vom frühen Griechentum bis zur Kaiserzeit. Gedenk- und Jubiläumsvorträge am Heidelberger Seminar für Alte Geschichte*. Stuttgart, 55-89.

Edmonds, R. 2004. *Myths of the Underworld Journey. Plato, Aristophanes, and the 'Orphic' gold Tablets*. New York.

Edwards, C. 2007. *Death in Ancient Rome*. New Haven.

Eichner, K. 1977. *Die Werkstatt des sogenannten Dogmatischen Sarkophags*. Diss. Heidelberg.

Elsner, J. 1995. *Art and the Roman Viewer. The Transformation of Art from the Pagan World to Christianity*. Cambridge.

Elsner, J. 1996. Review of Koortbojian 1995. *AJA* 100, 434.

Elsner, J. 1998. *Imperial Rome and Christian Triumph. The Art of the Roman Empire AD 100-450*. Oxford.

Elsner, J. 2000. "Making Myth Visual. The Horae of Philostratus and the Dance of the Text." *RM* 107, 254-67.

Elsner, J. 2007. *Roman Eyes. Visuality & Subjectivity in Art & Text*. Princeton.

Elsner, J. & J. Huskinson, eds. 2011. *Life, Death and Representation. Some New Work on Roman Sarcophagi*. Berlin.

Engemann, J. 1973. *Untersuchungen zur Sepulkralsymbolik der späteren römischen Kaiserzeit*, *JAC*, Ergh. 2. Münster.

Engemann, J. 1982. "Der Ehrenplatz bim antiken Sigmamahl." In T. Klauser, E. Dassmann & K. Thraede, eds. *Jenseitsvorstellungen in Antike und Christentum*. *JAC*, Ergh. 9, Aschendorff, 239-50.

Erasmo, M. 2008. *Reading Death in Ancient Rome*. Columbus.

Ewald, B.C. 1998. "Bildungswelt und Bürgerbild. Ikonographische Elemente magistratischer und bürgerlicher Repräsentation auf den römischen Musen-Philosophensarkophagen." In R. Amedick & G. Koch, eds. *Sarkophag-Studien 1, Akten des Symposiums "125 Jahre Sarkophag-Corpus". Marburg. 4-7. Oktober 1995*. Mainz, 39-51.

Ewald, B.C. 1998a. "Das Sirenenabenteuer des Odysseus, ein Tugendsymbol? Überlegungen zur Adaptabilität eines Mythos." *RM* 105, 227-58.

Ewald, B.C. 1999. *Der Philosoph als Leitbild. Ikonographische Untersuchungen an Römischen Sarkophagreliefs*. *RM*, Ergh. 34. Mainz.

Ewald, B.C. 1999a. "Review Article: Death and Myth. New Books on Roman Sarcophagi." *AJA* 103, 344-48.

Ewald, B.C. 1999b. "Κακομουσια. La virtù di Ulisse e il potere della musica." in F. De Angelis & S. Muth, eds. *Im Spiegel des Mythos. Bilderwelt und Lebenswelt. Symposium, Rom 19.-20. Februar 1998*. Palilia 6. Wiesbaden, 143-54.

Ewald, B.C. 1999c. Review of Huskinson 1996. *AJA* 103, 344-48.

Ewald, B.C. 2003. "Sarcophagi and Senators. The Social History of Roman Funerary Art and Its Limits" (Review of Wrede 2001). *JRA* 16, 561-71.

Ewald, B.C. 2004. "Men, Muscle, and Myth. Attic Sarcophagi in the Cultural Context of the Second Sophistic." In B. Borg, ed. *Paideia: the World of the Second Sophistic*. Berlin, 329-267.

Ewald, B.C. 2005. "Rollenbilder und Geschlechterverhältnis in der römischen Grabkunst. Archäologische Anmerkungen zur Geschichte der Sexualität." In N. Sojc, ed. *Neue Fragen, neue Antworten. Antike Kunst als Thema der Gender Studies*. Münster, 55-73.

Ewald, B.C. 2011. "Myth and Visual Narrative in the Second Sophistic – a Comparative Approach. Notes on an Attic Hippolytos Sarcophagus in Agrigento." In J. Elsner & J. Huskinson, eds. *Life, Death and Representation. Some New Work on Roman Sarcophagi*. Berlin, 261-308.

Fabricius, J. 2001. "Verweiblichung und Verweichlichung. Zu männlichen und weiblichen Körperkonzepten in der griechischen Kultur." In C. Franz & G. Schwibbe, eds. *Geschlecht weiblich: Körpererfahrungen – Körperkonzepte*. Berlin.

Fabricius, J. 2007. "Grenzziehungen. Zu Strategien somatischer Geschlechterdiskurse in der griechischen und römischen Kultur." In E. Hartmann, U. Hartmann, & K. Pietzner, eds. *Geschlechterdefinitionen und Geschlechtergrenzen in der Antike*. Stuttgart, 65-86.

Fant, J.C. 1995. Review of Ward-Perkins 1992. *AJA* 99, 554-55.

Fasciato, M. 1947. "Ad quadrigam fori vinarii, Autour du port au vin d'Ostia." *MEFRA* 65-81.

Felton, D. 1999. *Haunted Greece and Rome. Ghost Stories from Classical Antiquity*. Austin.

Fejfer, J. 2008. *Roman Portraits in Context*. Berlin.

Ferrari, G. 1966. *Il commercio dei sarcofagi asiatici*. Rome.

Fittschen, K. 1969. "Zu einem Sarkophag-fragment in Berlin." *AA*, 301-8.

Fittschen, K. 1970. "Zwei Römische Bildnisse in Kassel." *RM*, 132-43.

Fittschen, K. 1970a. "Zum Kleobis und Biton-Relief in Venedig." *JdI* 85, 171-93.

Fittschen, K. 1971. "Zum angeblichen Bildnis des Lucius Verus im Thermen Museum." *JdI*, 244-50.

Fittschen, K. 1971a. Hochzeitsarkophag San Lorenzo. *AA*, 117-9.

Fittschen, K. 1972. Review of Wegner 1966. *Gnomon* 44, 486-504.

Fittschen, K. 1973. Review of Inan & Rosenbaum 1966. *GGA* 225, 46-67.

Fittschen, K. 1975. *Meleager-Sarkophag*. Frankfurt.

Fittschen, K. 1975a. "Die Krise des 3. Jahrhunderts n. Chr. im Spiegel der Kunst." In G. Alföldy, F. Seibt & A. Timm, eds. *Krisen in der Antike Bewusstsein und Bewältigung. Geschichte und Gesellschaft*. Düsseldorf, 133-44.

Fittschen, K. 1979. "Sarkophage römischer Kaiser oder vom Nutzen der Porträtforschung." *JdI* 94, 578-93.

Fittschen, K. 1984. "Über Sarkophage mit Porträts verschiedener Personen." *MarbWPr*, 129-63.

Fittschen, K. 1992. "Mädchen, nicht Knaben, zwei Kinderbüsten in Cleveland und Wellesley." *RM* 99, 301-05.

Fittschen, K. 1992a. "Der Tod der Kreusa und der Niobiden. Überlegungen zur Deutung griechischer Mythen auf römischen Sarkophage." In *Giornate Pisane, Atti del IX Congresso delle F.I.E.C. 24-30 Augosto 1989* (=*StIt* 85), 1046-60.

Flower, H.I. 1996. *Ancestor Masks and Aristocratic Power in Roman Culture*. Oxford.

Forster, E.S & E.H. Hefner. 1959. *Lucius Junius Moderatus Columella on Agriculture and Trees* III. Cambridge, Mass.

Fowler, C. 2004. *The Archaeology of Personhood. An Anthropological Approach*. London.

Fowler, H.W. & F.G. Fowler. 1905. *The Work of Lucian of Samosata* I-III. Oxford.

Freccero, A. 2003. *Roman Marbles. The Art Collection of Axel Munthe at Villa San Michele,* Capri. Värnamo.

Freier, H. 1963. *Caput Velare*. Diss. Eberhard-Karls-Universitet zu Tübingen.

Froning, H. 1980. "Ikonographische Tradition mythologischer Sarkophagreliefs." *JdI* 95, 322-41.

Gabelmann, H. 1968. Review of Wegner 1966. *BJb* 168, 533-42.

García y Bellido, A. 1949. *Esculturas romanas de España y Portugal*. Madrid.

Gerke, F. 1940. *Die christlichen Sarkophage der vorkonstantinischen Zeit*. Berlin.

Gerke, F. 1948. *Christus in der spätantiken Plastik*. Mainz.

Gessert, G. 2004. "Myth as *Consolatio*: Medea on Roman Sarcophagi." *GaR* 51, 217-49.

Geyer, A. 1978. "Ikonographische Bemerkungen zum Neapler 'Brüdersarkophag'." *JdI* 93, 389-93.

Ghilardi, M. 1996. Review of Huskinson 1996. *ArchCl* 48, 386-87.

Giglioli, G.Q. 1942. "Epigrafi e sculture romane conservate alla Manziana." *BullGov*, 5-28.

Gilchrist, R. 1999. *Gender and Archaeology. Contesting the Past*. London.

Gilchrist, R. 2004. "Archaeology and the Life Course. A Time and Age for Gender." In L. Meskell & R.W. Preucel, eds. *A Companion to Social Archaeology*. Oxford, 142-60.

Giuliani, L. 1989. "Achill-Sarkophage in Ost und West. Genese einer Ikonographie." *JbBerlMus*, 31, 25-39.

Giuliani, L. 2003, *Bild und Mythos. Geschichte der Bilderzählung in der griechischen Kunst*. Munich.

Giuliano, A., ed. 1979. *Museo Nazionale Romano* I, *le sculture* 1. Rome.

Giuliano, A., ed. 1981. *Museo Nazionale Romano* I, *le sculture* 2. Rome.

Giuliano, A., ed. 1982. *Museo Nazionale Romano* I, *le sculture* 3. Rome.

Giuliano, A., ed. 1983. *Museo Nazionale Romano* I, *le sculture* 5. *I Marmi Ludovisi nel Museo Nazionale Romano*. Rome.

Giuliano, A., ed. 1984. *Museo Nazionale Romano* I, *le sculture* 7, 1. Rome.

Giuliano, A., ed. 1984. *Museo Nazionale Romano* I, *le sculture* 7, 2. Rome.

Giuliano, A., ed. 1985. *Museo Nazionale Romano* I, *le sculture* 8, 1. Rome.

Giuliano, A., ed. 1985. *Museo Nazionale Romano* I, *le sculture* 8, 2. Rome.

Giuliano, A., ed. 1986. *Museo Nazionale Romano*, 1, *le sculture* 6. *I marmi Ludovisi dispersi*. Rome.

Giuliano, A., ed. 1988. *Museo Nazionale Romano* I, *le sculture* 10. *Magazzini: I sarcofagi* 2. Rome.

Giuliano, A., ed. 1996. *Museo Nazionale Romano* I, *le sculture* 10. *Magazzini: I sarcofagi* 1. Rome.

Goldfarb, H. 1994. *Myth and Allusion. Meanings and Uses of Myth in Ancient Greek and Roman Society (Isabella Stewart Gardner Museum)*. Boston.

Gordon, R. 1990. "The Veil of Power. Emperors, sacrificers, and benefactors." In M. Beard, ed. *Pagan Priests. Religion and Power in the Ancient World*. London, 201-31.

Grassinger, D. 1994. "The Meaning of Myth on Roman Sarcophagi." In H. Goldfarb, ed. *Myth and Illusion. Meaning and Uses of Myth in Ancient Greek and Roman Society (Isabella Stewart Gardner Museum)*. Boston, 91-107.

Grassinger, D. 1998. "Mythen auf römischen Sarkophagen." *JRA* 11, 554-56.

Grassinger, D. 1999. *Die mythologischen Sarkophage – Achill bis Amazonen. ASR* XII 1. Berlin.

Greenhalgh, M. 1989. *The Survival of Roman Antiquities in the Middle Ages*. London.

Griffin, J. 1986. *The Mirror of Myth. Classical Themes & Variations*. London.

Guerrini, L. 1982. *Palazzo Mattei di Giove. Le antichità*. Rome.

Guerrini, L. et al. 1971-72. *Sculture di Palazzo Mattei*. Rome.

Gullini, G. 1960. *Maestri e botteghe in Roma da Gallieno alla Tetrarchia*. Turin.

Gütschow, M. 1938. *Das Museum der Prätexta-katakombe*, MemPontAcc III, IV. Rome.

Haarløv, B. 1977. *The Half-Open Door. A Common Symbolic Motif within Roman Sepulchral Sculpture*. Odense.

Hachlili, R. 2009. *Ancient Mosaic Pavements. Themes, Issues and Trends*. Leiden.

Hallett, C.H. 2005. Review of Zanker & Ewald 2004. *ArtB* 87, 157-61.

Hallett, C.H. 2005a. *The Roman Nude. Heroic Portrait Statuary 200 B.C.-A.D. 300*. Oxford.

Hanfmann, G.M. 1951. *The Season Sarcophagus in Dumbarton Oaks* I-II. *Dumbarton Oaks Studies* II. Cambridge, Mass.

Hannestad, N. 1988. *Roman Art and Imperial Policy*. Aarhus.

Hansen, I.L. 2007. "Gendered Identities and the Conformity of Male-Female Virtus on Roman Mythological Sarcophagi." In L.L. Lovén & A. Strömberg, eds. *Public Roles and Personal Status. Men and Women in Antiquity. Proceedings of the Third Nordic Symposium on Gender and Women's History in Antiquity. Copenhagen 3-5 October 2003*. Sävedalen, 107-21.

Hansen, I.L. 2008. "Muses as Models. Learning and the Complicity of Authority." In I.L. Hansen & S. Bell, eds. *Role Models in the Roman World. Identity and Assimilation*. Ann Arbor, 273-85.

Harlow, M. 1998. "In the Name of the Father. Procreation, Paternity and Patriarchy." In L. Foxhall & J. Salmon, eds. *Thinking Men. Masculinity and its Self-Representation in the Classical Tradition*. London, 155-69.

Harlow, M. & R. Laurence 2002. *Growing Up and Growing Old in Ancient Rome. A Life Course Approach*. London.

Harlow, M. & R. Laurence, eds. 2007. *Age and Ageing in the Roman Empire*. JRA Supplementary Series. Portsmouth, RI.

Haskell, H.J. 1964. *This was Cicero*. Greenwich.

Hänninen, M.-L. 2007. "How to be a Great Roman Lady. Images of Cornelia in Ancient Literary Tradition." In L.L. Lovén & A. Strömberg, eds. *Public Roles and Personal Status. Men and Women in Antiquity. Proceedings of the Third Nordic Symposium on Gender and Women's History in Antiquity. Copenhagen 3-5 October 2003*. Sävedalen, 73-88.

Heintze, H. von. 1957. "Studien zu den Porträts des 3. Jahrhunderts nach Christus." *RM* 64, 69-91.

Heintze, H. von. 1959. "Studien zu den Porträts des 3. Jahrhunderts nach Christus." *RM* 66, 175-95.

Heintze, H. von. 1974. *Römische Porträts*. Darmstadt.

Heinz, M. 2001. "Sarkophage der sogenannten kleinasiatischen Hauptgruppe und ihre Nachahmungen in Ephesos." *ÖJh* 70, 51-64.

Heinzelmann, M. 2000. *Die Nekropolen von Ostia. Untersuchungen zu den Gräberstraßen vor der Porta Romana und an der Via Laurentina*. Munich.

Helbig, W. 1963. *Führer durch die öffenlichen Sammlungen klassischer Altertümer in Rom* I. New edition by B. Andreae et al. Tübingen.

Helbig, W. 1969. *Führer durch die öffenlichen Sammlungen klassischer Altertümer in Rom* III. New edition by B. Andreae et al. Tübingen.

Hemelrijk, E.A. 1999. *Matrona docta. Educated Women in the Roman Elite from Cornelia to Julia Domna*. London.

Herdejürgen, H. 1984. "Sarkophage mit Darstellungen von Kultgeräten." In B. Andreae, ed. *Symposium über die antiken Sarkophage. Pisa 5.-12 September 1982. MarbWPr*, 7-25.

Herdejürgen, H. 1996. *Die dekorativen römischen Sarkophage. Stadtrömische und italische Girlandensarkophage. Die Sarkophage des ersten und zweiten Jahrhunderts. ASR* VI 2, 1. Berlin.

Herdejürgen, H. 1996a. "Girlandensarkophage des 3. Jahrhunderts nach Chr. Bemerkungen zur Chronologie." *AA*, 485-504.

Herdejürgen, H. 2000. "Sarkophage von der Via Latina. Folgerungen aus dem Fundkontext". *RM* 107, 209-34.

Herdt, G.H. 1994. *Third Sex, Third Gender. Beyond Sexual Dimorphism in Culture and History*. New York.

Hesberg, H. 1992. *Römische Grabbauten*. Darmstadt.

Hesberg, H. & P. Zanker, eds. 1987. *Römische Gräberstrassen. Selbstdarstellung, Status, Standard. Kolloquium in München vom 28. bis 30. Oktober 1985*. Munich.

Hill, T. 2004. *Ambitiosa mors. Suicide and Self in Roman Thought and Literature*. New York.

Hillert, A. 1990. *Antike Ärztedarstellungen*. Marburger Schriften zur Medizingeschichte 25. Frankfurt.

Himmelmann-Wildschütz, N. 1962. "Sarkophag eines gallienischen Konsul." In N. Himmelmann-Wildschütz & H. Beisantz, eds. *Festschrift für Friedrich Matz*. Mainz, 110-24.

Himmelmann-Wildschütz, N. 1973. *Typologische Untersuchungen an römischen Sarkophagreliefs des 3. und 4. Jahrhunderts nach Chr.* Mainz.

Himmelmann-Wildschütz, N. 1974. "Sarcofagi romani a rilievo. Problemi di cronologia e iconografia." *AnnPisa* 4, 139-77.

Himmelmann, N. 1980. *Uber Hirten-Genre in der antiken Kunst*. Abhandlungen der Rheinisch-Westfälischen Akademie der Wissenschaften 65. Opladen.

Himmelmann, N. 1990. *Ideale Nacktheit in der Griechischen Kunst*. JdI, Ergh. 26.

Hope, V. 1997. "Constructing Roman Identity. Funerary Monuments and Social Structure in the Roman World." *Mortality* 2, 2, 103-21.

Hope, V. 1997a. "A Roof over the dead: Communal Tombs and Family Structure." In R. Laurence & A. Wallace-Hadrill, eds. *Domestic Space in the Roman world. Pompeii and Beyond*. Ann Arbor, 69-88.

Hope, V. 1998. "Negotiating Identity and Status. The Gladiators of Roman Nimes." In R. Laurence, & J. Berry, eds. *Cultural Identity in the Roman Empire*. London, 179-95.

Hope, V. 2000. "Inscriptions and Sculpture: the Construction of Identity in the Military Tombstones of Roman Mainz." In G.J. Oliver, ed. *The Epigraphy of Death. Studies in History and Society of Greece and Rome*. Liverpool, 155-85.

Hope, V. 2003. "Remembering Rome. Memory, Funerary Monuments and the Roman Soldier." In H. Williams, ed. *Archaeologies of Remembrance. Death and the Memory in Past Societies*. New York, 113-40.

Hope, V. 2007. *Death in Ancient Rome. A Source Book*. London.

Hope, V. 2009. *Roman Death. Dying and the Dead in Ancient Rome*. London.

Hope, V. 2011. "Remembering to Mourn: Personal Mementos of the Dead in Ancient Rome." In V. Hope & J. Huskinson, eds. *Memory and Mourning. Studies on Roman Death*. Oxford, 176-95.

Hopkins, M.K. 1965. "The Age of Roman Girls at Marriage." *Population Studies* 18.3, 309-27.

Hopkins, A. & M. Wyke, eds. 2005. *Roman Bodies. Antiquity to the Eighteenth Century*. London.

Hölscher, T. 1992. "Bilderwelt, Formensystem, Lebenskultur. Zur Methode archäologischer Kulturanalyse." *StIt, Terza Serie* X, I-II, 460-84.

Hölscher, T. 2008. "The Concept of Roles and the Malaise of 'Identity'." In I.L. Hansen & S. Bell, eds. *Role Models in the Roman World. Identity and Assimilation*. Ann Arbor, 41-56.

Højte, J.M., ed. 2002. *Images of Ancestors*. Aarhus.

Huskinson, J. 1993. "The Decoration of Early Christian Children's Sarcophagi." *Studia Patristica* 24, 114-18.

Huskinson, J. 1996. *Roman Children's Sarcophagi. Their Decoration and its Social Significance*. Oxford.

Huskinson, J. 1998. "Unfinished Portrait Heads on Later Roman Sarcophagi: Some New Perspectives." *PBSR* 66, 129-158.

Huskinson, J. 1999. "Women and Learning. Gender and Identity in Scenes of Intellectual Life on Late Roman Sarcophagi." In R. Miles, ed. *Constructing Identities in Late Antiquity*. London, 190-213.

Huskinson, J. 2002. "Representing Women on Roman Sarcophagi." In A. McClanan & K.R. Encarnacion, eds. *Material Culture of Sex, Procreation and Marriage in Premodern Europe*. New York, 11-31.

Huskinson, J. 2005. "Disappearing Children? Children in Roman Funerary Art of the First to the Fourth Century AD." In K. Mustakallio et al., eds. *Hoping for Continuity. Childhood, Education and the Death in Antiquity and the Middle Ages*. Rome, 91-103.

Huskinson, J. 2005a. Review of Zanker & Ewald 2004. *JRS* 95, 303-4.

Huskinson, J. 2007. "Constructing Childhood on Roman Funerary Memorials." In A. Cohen & J. Rutter, eds. *Constructions of Childhood in Ancient Greece and Italy*. Princeton, 323-38.

Huskinson, J. 2007a. "Growing up in Ravenna. Evidence from the Decoration of Children's Sarcophagi." In M. Harlow, & R. Laurence, eds. *Age and Ageing in the Roman Empire*. JRA Supplementary Series. Portsmouth, RI, 55-79.

Huskinson, J. 2008. "Degrees of Differentiation. Role Models on Early Christian Sarcophagi." In S. Bell & I.L. Hansen, eds. *Role Models in the Roman World. Identity and Assimilation*. Ann Arbor, 287-99.

Ide, A.F. 1984. *Woman as Priest. Bishop and Laity in the Early Catholic Church to 440 A.D.* Mesquite.

Ide, A.F. 1986. *God's Girls. Ordination of Women in the Early Christian & Gnostic Churches*. Garland.

Inan, J. & E. Rosenbaum 1966. *Roman and Early Byzantine Portrait Sculpture in Asia Minor*. Oxford.

Irvin, D. 1980. "The Ministry of Women in the Early Christian Church. The Archaeological Evidence." *Duke Divinity School Review* 45, 76-86.

Irwin, K. 1984. "Archaeology Does not Support Women's Ordination; A Response to Dorothy Irvin." *Journal of Women and Religion* 3, 2, 39-40.

Işık, F. 2000. "Stadtrömisch oder Kleinasiatisch?" In T. Mattern & D. Korol, eds. *Festschrift für Hans Wiegartz*. Münster, 113-23.

Işık, F. 2007. *Girlanden-Sarkophage aus Aphrodisias*. Sarkophag-Studien 3. Mainz.

Jenkins, R. 2006. *Social identitet*. Aarhus.

Jensen, A. 2001. "Women in the Christianization of the West." In A. Kreider, ed. *The Origins of Christendom in the West*. Edinburgh, 205-26.

Jensen, R.M. 2008. "Dining with the Dead: From the Mensa to the Altar in Christian Late Antiquity." In L. Brink & D. Green, eds. *Commemorating the Dead. Texts and Artifacts in Context*. Berlin, 107-43.

Jucker, H. 1961. *Das Bildnis im Blätterkelch. Geschichte und Bedeutung einer römischen Porträtform*. Olten.

Jung, H. 1978. "Zum Reliefstil der Stadtrömischen Sarkophage des frühen 3. Jahrhunderts n. Chr." *JdI* 93, 328-68.

Junker, H. 1966. "Die Behauptung des Balbinus." *AA*, 501-14.

Junker, K. 2005/6. "Römische mythologische Sarkophage, Zur Entstehung eines Denkmaltypus." *RM* 112, 163-88.

Kampen, 1981. "Biographical Narration and Roman Funerary Art." *AJA* 85, 47-58.

Kampen, N. 1981a. *Image and Status: Roman Working Women in Ostia*. Berlin.

Kampen, N. 1996. *Sexuality in Ancient Art. Near East, Egypt, Greece, and Italy*. Cambridge.

Kampen, N. 1996a. "Omphale and the Instability of Gender." In N. Kampen, ed. *Sexuality in Ancient Art. Near East, Egypt, Greece and Italy*. Cambridge.

Kampen, N. 1996b. "Gender Theory in Roman Art." In D.E.E. Kleiner & S. Matheson, eds. *I, Claudia. Women in Ancient Rome*. New Haven, 14-25.

Kampen, N. 2007. "The Family in Late Antiquity." In L.L. Lovén & A. Strömberg, eds. *Public Roles and Personal Status. Men and Women in Antiquity. Proceedings of the Third Nordic Symposium on Gender and Women's History in Antiquity. Copenhagen 3-5 October 2003*. Sävedalen, 123-42.

Kaschnitz von Weinberg, G. 1937. *Sculture del magazzino del Museo Vaticano*. Vatican City.

King, M. 2000. "Commemoration of Infants on Roman Funerary Inscriptions." In G.J. Oliver, ed. *The Epigraphy of Death. Studies in History and Society of Greece and Rome*. Liverpool, 117-54.

King, K.L. 2003. *The Gospel of Mary of Magdala. Jesus and the First Woman Apostle*. Santa Rosa.

Kirchhainer, K. & G. Koch, eds. 2002. *Akten des Symposiums "Frühchristliche Sarkophage". Marburg, 30.6.-4.7.1999*. Sarkophag-Studien 2. Mainz.

Klauser, T. 1958. "Studien zur Entstehungsgeschichte der christlichen Kunst I." *JAC* 1, 20-51.

Klauser, T. 1959. "Studien zur Entstehungsgeschichte der christlichen Kunst II. Heidnische Vorläufer des christlichen Oransbildes." *JAC* 2, 115-45.

Klauser, T. 1960. "Studien zur Entstehungsgeschichte der christlichen Kunst III. Schafträger und Orans als Vergegenwärtigung einer populären Zweitugendethik auf Sarkophagen der Kaiserzeit." *JAC* 3, 112-33.

Klauser, T. 1963. "Studien zur Entstehungsgeschichte der christlichen Kunst VI. Das Sirenenabenteuer des Odysseus – ein Motiv der christlichen Grabkunst?" *JAC* 6, 71-100.

Klauser, T. 1964. "Studien zur Entstehungsgeschichte der christlichen Kunst VII. Noch einmal zur heidnischen Herkunft des Bildmotives der Orans und des Schafträgers." *JAC* 7, 67-76.

Klauser, T. 1965-66. "Studien zur Entstehungsgeschichte der christlichen Kunst VIII. Vorbemerkungen zu abschließenden Untersuchungen über das Schafträger-Motiv." *JAC* 8-9, 126-70.

Kleiner, D.E.E. 1987. *Roman Imperial Funerary Altars with Portraits*. Rome.

Kleiner, D.E.E. & S. Matheson, eds. 1996. *I, Claudia. Women in Ancient Rome*. New Haven.

Kleiner, D.E.E. & S. Matheson, eds. 2000. *I, Claudia II. Women in Roman Art and Society*. Austin.

Koch, G. 1975. *Die mythologischen Sarkophage – Apollon bis Grazien. ASR* XII 2. Berlin.

Koch, G. 1976. "Verschollene mythologische Sarkophage." *AA*, 101-10.

Koch, G. 1988. *Roman Funerary Sculpture: Catalogue of the Collections*. Malibu.

Koch, G. 1990. "Ein dekorativer Sarkophag mit Scherengitter in der Henry E. Huntington Library and Art Gallery, San Marino." In G. Koch & M. True, eds. *Roman Funerary Monuments in the J. Paul Getty Museum* 1. Occasional Papers in Antiquities. Malibu, 47-58.

Koch, G. 1993. *Sarkophage der römischen Kaiserzeit*. Darmstadt.

Koch, G. 1993a. *Grabeskunst der römischen Kaiserzeit*. Mainz.

Koch, G. 1993b. "Einige Fragmente figurengeschmückter Sarkophage." *AA*, 409-35.

Koch, G. 1997. Review of Huskinson 1996. *JRA* 10, 454-62.

Koch, G. 2000. *Frühchristliche Sarkophage*. Munich.

Koch, G. 2010. *Sarkophage der römischen Kaiserzeit in der Türkei*. Antalya.

Koch, G. & H. Sichtermann. 1982. *Römische Sarkophage*. Munich.

Koortbojian, M. 1995. *Myth, Meaning, and Memory on Roman Sarcophagi*. Berkeley.

Koortbojian, M. 1999. Review of Huskinson 1996. *Gnomon* 71, 639-42.

Koortbojian, M. 2006. "The Freedman's Voice. The Funerary Monument of Aurelius Hermia and Aurelia Philematio." In E. D'Ambra & G. Métraux, eds. *The Art of Citizens, Soldiers and Freedmen in the Roman World*. BAR. Oxford, 91-9.

Koortbojian, M. 2008. "The double Identity of Roman Portrait Statues. Costumes and their Symbolism at Rome." In J. Edmondson & A. Keith, eds. *Roman Dress and the Fabrics of Roman Culture*. Toronto, 71-93.

Köhler, J. 1995. "Zum Feldherrnsarkophag Belvedere." *RM* 102, 371-79.

Kragelund, P., M. Moltesen, & J.S. Østergaard. 2003. *The Licinian Tomb. Fact or Fiction?* Copenhagen.

Kranz, P. 1984. *Jahreszeiten-Sarkophage – Entwicklung und Ikonographie des Motivs der Vier Jahrzeiten auf kaiserzeitlichen Sarkophagen und Sarkophagdeckeln. ASR* V 4. Berlin.

Kranz, P. 1993. "Zur Ikonographie stadtrömischer Eroten-Komos-Sarkophage." In G. Koch, ed. *Grabeskunst der römischen Kaiserzeit*. Mainz.

Kranz, P. 1999. *Die stadtrömische Eroten-Sarkophage – Dionysische Themen. ASR* V 2, 1. Berlin.

Kranz, P. 2001. Review of Ewald 1999. *BJb* 201, 584-89.

Kristensen, T.M. 2012. "Miraculous Bodies: Christian Viewers and the

Transformation of 'Pagan' Sculpture in Late Antiquity." In S. Birk & B. Poulsen, eds. *Patrons and Viewers in Late Antiquity*. Aarhus, 31-66.

Künzl, E. 2010. *Ein Traum vom Imperium. Der Ludovisisarkophag. Grabmal eines Feldherren Roms*. Mainz.

La Rocca, E. & C.P. Presicce. 2010. *Musei Capitolini. Le sculture del Palazzo Nuovo*. Milan.

La Regina, A., ed. 1998. *Palazzo Massimo alle Terme*. Milan.

Lange, U. 1996. *Ikonographisches Register für das Repertorium der christlich-antiken Sarkophage 1 (Rom und Ostia)*. Dettelbach.

Lameere, W. 1939. "Un symbole pythagoricien dans l'art funéraire de Rome." *BCH* 63, 43-85.

Lattimore, R.B. 1942. *Themes in Greek and Latin Epitaphs*. Urbana, Ill.

Laurence, R. & J. Berry, eds. 1998. *Cultural Identity in the Roman Empire*. London.

Lawrence, M. 1976. "The Phaedra Sarcophagus in San Clemente." In H. Heintze & C. Lord, eds. *Essays in Archaeology and the Humanities. In memoriam Otto J. Brendel*. Mainz, 173-78.

Leach, E.W. 1999. "Reconstructing Discourse: Readings of Gender, Identity, and Ideology in Ancient Art." Review article. *CP* 94, 89-98.

Leach, E.W. 2006. "Freedmen and Immortality in the Tomb of the Haterii." In E. D'Ambra, G. Métraux eds. *The Art of Citizens, Soldiers and Freedmen in the Roman World*. Oxford, 1-18.

Lee, M. 2000. "Deciphering Gender in Minoan Dress." In A.E. Rautman, ed. *Reading the Body, Representations and Remains in the Archaeological Record*. Philadelphia, 111-23.

Lehmann-Hartleben, K. & E. Olsen. 1942. *Dionysiac Sarcophagi in Baltimore*. New York.

Lenzi, P. 1998. 'Sita in loco qui vocatur calcaria': attiviá di spoliazione e forni da calce a Ostia." *Archeologia Medievale* 25, 247-63.

Lewerentz, A. 1995. "Die Sepulkralsymbolik des Hippolytosmythos auf stadtrömischen Sarkophagen." *Boreas* 18, 111-30.

Lindner, R. 1984. *Der Raub der Persephone in der antiken Kunst*. Würzburg.

Liverani, P. & G. Spinola. 2006. *La necropoli vaticana lungo la via Trionfale*. Rome.

Liverani, P. & G. Spinola, eds. 2010. *The Vatican Necropoles. Rome's City of the Dead*. Turnhout.

L'Orange, H.P. 1953. *Studies on the Iconography of Cosmic Kingship in the Ancient World*. Oslo.

L'Orange, H.P. 1976. "The Apotropaic Lion Head and the Arena Lion on 3rd Century Sarcophagi." In K. Ascani, ed. *Studia romana in honorem Petri Krarup septuagenarii*. Odense.

L'Orange, H.P. & F. Gerke. 1939. *Der spätantike Bildschmuck des Konstantinbogens*. Berlin.

Lorenz, K. 2011. "Images in Distress? The Death of Meleager on Roman Sarcophagi." In J. Elsner & J. Huskinson, eds. *Life, Death and Representation. Some New Work on Roman Sarcophagi*. Berlin, 309-36.

Lovén, L.L. 1998. "LANAM FECIT – Wool Working and Female Virtue." In L.L. Lovén & A. Strömberg, eds. *Aspects of Women in Antiquity. Proceedings of the First Nordic Symposium on Women's Lives in Antiquity. Göteborg 12-15 June 1997*. Jonsered, 85-95.

Lovén, L.L. & A. Strömberg, eds. 1998. *Aspects of Women in Antiquity. Proceedings of the First Nordic Symposium on Women's Lives in Antiquity. Göteborg 12-15 June 1997*. Jonsered.

Lovén, L.L. 2010. "Coniugal Concordia: Marriage and Marital Ideals on Roman Funerary Monuments." In L.L. Lovén & A. Strömberg, eds. *Ancient Marriage in Myth and Reality*. Newcastle, 204-20.

Lücken, G.von 1956. "Zu römischen Hochzeitssarkophage." *Das Altertum* 2, 28-38.

Maischberger, M. 1997. *Marmor in Rom. Anlieferung, Lager- und Werkplätze in der Kaiserzeit*. Wiesbaden.

Marrou, H.I. 1938. *Mousikos aner. Étude sur les scènes de la vie intellectuelle figurant sur les monuments funéraires romains*. Rome.

Massner, A. 1982. *Bildnisangleichung. Untersuchungen zur Entstehungs- und Wirkungsgeschichte der Augustusporträts (43 v. Chr.-68 n. Chr.)*. Das Römische Herrscherbild IV. Berlin.

Matz, F. 1958. *Ein römisches Meisterwerk; der Jahreszeitensarkophag Badminton-New York*. Berlin.

Matz, F. 1968. *Die dionysischen Sarkophage. ASR* IV 1. Berlin.

Matz, F. 1968a. *Die dionysischen Sarkophage. ASR* IV 2. Berlin.

Matz, F. 1968b. "Das Problem der Orans und ein Sarkophag in Córdoba." *MM* 9, 300-10.

Matz, F. 1969. *Die dionysischen Sarkophage. ASR* IV 3. Berlin.

Matz, F. 1970. "Der Sarkophag eines Centurio der ersten Cohors Praetoria." *Saeculum* 21, 180-94.

Matz, F. 1975. *Die dionysischen Sarkophage. ASR* IV 4. Berlin.

McCann, A. 1978. *Roman Sarcophagi in the Metropolitan Museum of Art*. New York.

McClanan, A. & K.R. Encarnacion, eds. 2002. *The Material Culture of Sex, Procreation, and Marriage in Premodern Europe*. New York.

Meinecke, K. 2012. "Invisible Sarcophagi. Coffin and Viewer in the Late Imperial Age." In S. Birk & B. Poulsen, eds. *Patrons and Viewers in Late Antiquity*. Aarhus, 83-105.

Meskell, L. 1999. *Archaeologies of Social Life. Age, Sex, Class Etcetera in Ancient Egypt*. Malden.

Meskell, L. & R.W. Preucel, eds. 2004. *A Companion to Social Archaeology*. Malden.

Meyer, H. 1986. "Zu römischen Umbestattungen. Noch eine Behauptung des Balbinus." *BullComm*, 91, 279-98.

Meyer, H. 2002. "Vom Herold Odios und der schönwangigen Diomede. Neues zur Ikonographie der Briseïssage und dem Themenrepertoire römischer Sarkophagwerkstätten." *Boreas* 25, 159-65.

Michaelis, A. 1882. *Ancient Marbles in Great Britain*. Cambridge.

Micheli, M.E. & A. Santucci, eds. 2011. *Comae. Identitá femminili nelle acconciature di etá romana*. Pisa.

Mielsch, H. & H. von Hesberg 1995. *Die heidnische Nekropole unter St. Peter in Rom 1. Die Mausoleen E-I und Z-Psi*. Rome.

Mikocki, T. 1995. *Collection de la Princesse Radziwill. Les monuments antiques et antiquisants d'Arcadie et du Château de Nieborów*. Wrocław.

Mikocki, T. & J. Zeazowski. 2001. "A Strigil Sarcophagus Aquired Recently by the National Museum in Warsaw." *Swiatowit* 3, 203-15.

Miles, R., ed. 1999. *Constructing Identities in Late Antiquity*. London.

Miniero, P. & S. Zevi, eds. 2008. *Museo archeologico dei Campi Flegrei*. Naples.

Monteagudo, G. 1999. "The Triumph of Dionysus in Two Mosaics in Spain." *Assaph* 4, 35-60.

Montserrat, D., ed. 1998. *Changing Bodies, Changing Meanings. Studies on the Human Body in Antiquity*. London.

Montserrat, D. 2000. "Reading Gender in the Roman World." In J. Huskinson, ed. *Experiencing Rome, Culture Identity and Power in the Roman Empire*. London, 153-82.

Moore, H.L., ed. 1999. *Anthropological Theory Today*. Cambridge.

Moore, H.L. 1999a. "Gender and Other Crises in Anthropology." In H. L. Moore, ed. *Anthropological Theory Today*, 151-71.

Moretti, M. 1975. *Nuove scoperte e acquisizioni nell'Etruria Merdionale*. Rome.

Morris, I. 1992. *Death-ritual and Social Structure in Classical Antiquity*. Cambridge.

Mottahedeh, P.E. 1984. Review of Wrede 1981. *AJA* 88, 95-6.

Mucznik, S. 1999. *Devotion and Unfaithfulness. Alcestis and Phaedra in Roman Art*. Rome.

Mucznik, S. 1999a. "Roman Priestesses. The Case of Metilia Acte." *Assaph* 4, 61-78.

Mucznik, S. 2000. "Ariadne and Phaedra: Iconography and Symbolism on Roman Sarcophagi." In A. Ovadiah, ed. *Mediterranean Cultural Interaction* II. Tel Aviv, 131-46.

Murray, P. & L. Murray. 2004. *A Dictionary of Christian Art*. Oxford.

Muth, S. 1998. *Erleben von Raum, Leben im Raum. Zur Funktion mythologischer Mosaikbilder in der römisch-kaiserzeitlichen Wohnarchitektur*. Heidelberg.

Muth, S. 1999. "Hylas oder 'Der ergriffene Mann'. Zur Eigenständigkeit der Mythenrezeption in der Bildkunst." In F. de Angelis & S. Muth, eds. *Im Spiegel des Mythos. Bilderwelt und Lebenswelt*. Palilia 6. Wiesbaden, 109-29.

Müller, F.G.J.M. 1994. *The So-called Peleus and Thetis Sarcophagus in the Villa Albani*. Amsterdam.

Müller, R. 2002. *Sic hostes Ianua frangit. Spolien und Trophäen im mittelalterlichen Genua*. Weimar.

Nelson, S.M., ed. 2006. *Handbook of Gender in Archaeology*. Lanham.

Nelson, M.C., S.M. Nelson, & A. Wylie, eds. 1994. *Equity Issues for Women in Archaeology*. Arlington.

Newby, Z. 2007. "Art at the Crossroads? Themes and Styles in Severan Art." In S. Swain, S. Harrison, & J. Elsner, eds. *Severan Culture*. Cambridge, 201-49.

Newby, Z. 2011. "In the Guise of Gods and Heroes: Portrait Heads on Roman Mythological Sarcophagi." In J. Elsner & J. Huskinson, eds. *Life, Death and Representation. Some New Work on Roman Sarcophagi*. Berlin, 189-228.

Nock, A.D. 1932. "Cremation and Burial in the Roman Empire." *HTR* 25, 4, 321-59.

Nock, A.D. 1946. "Sarcophagi and Symbolism." *AJA* 50, 140-70.

Nock, A.D. 1972. *Essays on Religion and the Ancient World* (ed. Z. Stewart). Cambridge, Mass.

Nodelman, S. 1970. "Structural Analysis in Art and Anthropology." In J. Ehrmann, ed. *Structuralism*. New Haven, 79-93

Noguera, J.M. 2007. "Un sarcofago con Muse a Murcia e il suo contesto du reutilizzo." In G. Koch, ed. *Sarkophag-Studien 3*. Mainz, 43-7.

Nolte, S. 2005. *Steinbruch – Werkstatt – Skulptur. Untersuchungen zu Aufbau und Organisation griechischer Bildhauerwerkstätten*. Göttingen.

Noy, D. 2009. "Death." In A. Erskin, ed. *A Companion to Ancient History*. Oxford, 514-24.

Nuccio, M.D. & L. Ungaro. 2002. *I marmi colorati della Roma imperiale*. Venice.

Nuzzo, D. 2000. *Tipologia sepolcrale delle catacombe romane. I cimiteri ipogei delle vie Ostiense, Ardeatina e Appia*. Oxford.

Oakley, J.H. 2011. *Die attischen Sarkophage. Andere Mythen*. *ASR* IX 1, 3. Berlin.

Oehmke, S. 2004. *Das Weib im Manne: Hermaphroditos in der griechisch-römischen Antike*. Berlin.

Oehmke, S. 2007. "Halbmann oder Supermann? Bemerkungen zum effeminierten Priapos." In E. Hartmann, U. Hartmann, & K. Pietzner, eds. *Geschlechterdefinitionen und Geschlechtergrenzen in der Antike*. Stuttgart, 263-76.

Østergaard, J.S. 1996. *Romersk kejsertid. Katalog. Ny Carlsberg Glyptotek*. Copenhagen.

Østergaard, J.S. 1998. "Metropolitan Roman Sarcophagi in the Ny Carlsberg Glyptotek." In G. Koch & R. Amedick, eds. *Akten des Symposiums "125 Jahre Sarkophag-Corpus". Marburg 4.-7. Okt. 1995*. Mainz, 97-105.

Østergaard, J.S. 2011. "Tracking Colour. The Polychromy of Greek and Roman Sculpture in the Ny Carlsberg Glyptotek." *Preliminary Report* 3. (www.trackingcolour.com).

Olson, K. 2008. *Dress and the Roman Woman. Self-Presentation and Society*. Milton Park.

Otranto, G. 1989. "Note sul buon pastore e sull' orante nell' arte cristiana antica (II-III secolo)." *Vetera Christianorum* 26, 69-87.

Ousager, A. 2004. *Plotinus on Selfhood, Freedom and Politics*. Aarhus.

Paduano Faedo, L. 1970. "Contributo allo studio dei sarcofagi con Muse." *Studi classici e orientali* 19-20, 442-49.

Paduano Faedo, L. 1981. "I sarcofagi romani con Muse." *ANRW* 2. 12. 2, 65-155.

Panella, C. 1967. *Iconografia delle Muse sui sarcofagi romani*. Studi Miscellanei. Rome.

Panella, C. 1968. Review of Wegner 1966. *ArchCl* 20, 327-51.

Pantel, P.S. 1992. "Representations of Women." In P.S. Pantel, ed. *A History of Women in the West. From Ancient Goddess to Christian Saints*. Cambridge, Mass., 1-8.

Paroli, L. 1999. *Scavi di Ostia XII. La basilica cristiana di Pianabella*. Rome.

Peek, W. 1955. *Griechische Vers-Inschriften. Grab-Epigramme*. Berlin.

Peek, W. 1960. *Griechische Grabgedichte*. Darmstadt.

Pelikán, O. 1965. *Vom antiken Realismus zur spätantiken Expressivität*. Prague.

Pensabene, P. & C. Panella. 1993. "Reimpiego e progettazione architettonica nei monumneti trado-antichi." *RendPontAcc* 66, 111-283.

Pesce, G. 1957. *Sarcofagi romani di Sardegna*. Rome.

Pfanner, M. 1989. "Über das Herstellen von Porträts." *JdI* 104, 157-257.

Piacentini, P. 1961. "Un sarcofago strigillato già della Collectione Simonetti e altri sarcofagi con filosofi." *ArchCl* 13, 76-91.

Polaschek, K. 1972. "Studien zu einem Frauenkopf im Landesmuseum Trier und zur weiblichen Haartracht der julisch-claudischen Zeit." *Trierer Zeitschriften für Geschichte und Kunst des Trierer Landes und seiner Nachbargebiete* 35, 141-210.

Pomeroy, S.B. 1975. *Goddesses, Whores, Wives, and Slaves. Women in Classical Antiquity*. New York.

Pomeroy, S.B. 1991. "The Study of Women in Antiquity. Past, Present, and Future." *AJPh* 112, 263-68.

Poulsen, F. 1951. *Catalogue of Ancient Sculpture in the Ny Carlsberg Glyptotek*. Copenhagen.

Prusac, M. 2011. *From Face to Face. Recarving of Roman Portraits and the late-antique Portrait Arts*. Leiden.

Rabinowitz, N. & A. Richlin. 1993. *Feminist Theory and the Classics*. New York.

Raeck, W. 2002. Review of Ewald 1999. *Gnomon* 74, 62-6.

Rautman, A. E. 2000. *Reading the Body. Representations and Remains in the Archaeological Record*. Philadelphia.

Rawson, B. 1986. "Children in the Roman Familia." In B. Rawson, ed. *The Family in Ancient Rome. New Perspectives*. Ithaca, N.Y, 170-200.

Rawson, B. 2003. *Children and Childhood in Roman Italy*. Oxford.

Reekmans, L. 1958. "La *dextrarum iunctio* dans l'iconographie romain et paléochrétienne." *BIHBelge* 31, 23-95.

Reinsberg, C. 1983. "*Concordia*. Die Darstellung von Hochzeit und ehelicher Eintracht in der Spätantike." In Spätantike und frühes Christentum. Ausstellung im Liebieghaus, Museum alter Plastik, Frankfurt am Main. 16. Dezember bis 11. März 1984. Frankfurt, 312-17.

Reinsberg, C. 1985. "Der Balbinus-Sarkophag, Grablege eines Kaisers?" *MarbWPr*, 3-16.

Reinsberg, C. 1995. "Senatorensarkophage." *RM* 102, 353-70.

Reinsberg, C. 1996. "Die Repräsentation der Grabherrin auf den *Vita Romana*-Sarkophagen." In G. Koch, ed. *Grabeskunst der römischen Kaiserzeit*. Mainz, 141-42.

Reinsberg, C. 2006. *Die Sarkophage mit Darstellungen aus dem Menschenleben. ASR* I 3. Berlin.

Revell, L. 2005. "The Roman Life Course: A View from the Inscriptions." *EJA* 8, 43-63.

Revell, L. 2009. *Roman Imperialism and Local Identities*. Cambridge.

Richmond, I. 1950. *Archaeology and the After-Life in Pagan and Christian Imagery*. Oxford.

Pitts, M. 2007. "The Emperor's New Clothes? The Utility of Identity in Roman Archaeology." *AJA* 111, 693-713.

Robert, C. 1897. *Einzelmythen 1. Actaeon. ASR* III. Berlin.

Robert, C. 1904. *Einzelmythen – Niobiden bis Triptolemos. ASR* III 3. Rome.

Robert, C. 1919. *Einzelmythen – Hippolytos bis Meleagros. ASR* III 2. Rome.

Robinson, J.D. 2010. "Lethean Landscapes: Forgetting in Late Modern Commemorative Spaces." In E. Anderson & A. Maddrell, eds. *Memory, Mourning, Landscape*. Amsterdam, 79-97.

Rodenwaldt, G. 1921/22. "Eine spätantike Kunstströmnung." *RM* 36/37, 58-110.

Rodenwaldt, G. 1931. "Sitzung am 3. Februar." *AA* (*JdI* Beiblatt 46), 318-38.

Rodenwaldt, G. 1935. *Über den Stilwandel in der antoninischen Kunst*. Berlin.

Rodenwaldt, G. 1936. "Zur Kunstgeschichte der Jahre 220 bis 270." *JdI* 51, 82-113.

Rodenwaldt, G. 1943. "Sarkophagprobleme." *RM* 58, 1-26.

Rodenwaldt, G. 1944. "Jagdsarkophag in Reims." *RM* 59, 191-203.

Rogge, S. 1995. *Die attischen Sarkophage, Achill und Hippolytos. ASR* IX 1, 1. Berlin.

Ronke, J. 1987. *Magistratische Repräsentation im römischen Relief. Studien zu standes- und statusbezeichnenden Szenen*. BAR 307. Oxford.

Rossbach, A. 1973. *Römische Hochzeits- und Ehedenkmäler*. Aalen.

Rousseau, P. 1995. "Learned Women and the Development of a Christian Culture in Late Antiquity." *SymbOslo* 70, 116-47.

Rousselle, A. 1993. *Porneia. On Desire and the Body in Antiquity*. Cambridge.

Rössler, D. 1997. "Zum Problem der 'Gallienischen Renaissance' – Anmerkungen und Fragen." In J. Bouzek & I. Ondrejová, eds. *Roman Portraits, Artistic and Literary*. Mainz, 42-4.

Rudolf, E. 1981. "Typologische Untersuchungen zu den stadtrömischen Musensarkophagen des 3. Jh. n. Chr." *MarbWPr*, 33-44.

Rumpf, A. 1939. *Die Meerwesen auf den antiken Sarkophagreliefs. ASR* V 1. Berlin.

Rushforth, G.M. 1915. "Funeral Lights in Roman Sepulchral Monuments." *JRS* 5, 149-64.

Russell, B. 2011. "The Roman Sarcophagus 'Industry': a Reconsideration." In J. Elsner & J. Huskinson, eds. *Life, Death and Representation. Some New Work on Roman Sarcophagi*. Berlin, 119-48.

Salathé, J. 2000. "Venus and the Representation of Virtue on Third-Century Sarcophagi." *Latomus* 59, 873-88.

Saller, R. 1998. Review of Flower 1996. *AJA* 102, 448-49.

Sande, S. 2010. "The Female Hunter and other Examples of Change of Sex and Gender Context on Roman Sarcophagi." In S. Sande & T.K. Seim, eds. *Woman as Subject and Object* (=*ActaAArtHist* 22, n.s. 8), 56-86.

Sapelli, M. 1998. *Arte tardoantica in Palazzo Massimo alle Terme*. Rome.

Savarese, N. 2007. *In scæna. Il teatro di Roma antica*. Milan.

Saverkina, I.I. 1979. *Römische Sarkophage in der Ermitage*. Berlin.

Schackleton-Bailey, D.R. 2003. *Statius Silvae with an English translation*. Cambridge.

Schauenburg, K. 1963. "Zum Sarkophag der Avidia Agrippina." *JdI* 78, 294-317.

Schauenburg, K. 1972. "Ganymed und Hahnekämpfe auf römischen Sarkophagen." *AA*, 501-616.

Schauenburg, K. 1975. "Die Sphinx unter dem *Clipeus*." *AA*, 280-95.

Schauenburg, K. 1980. "Porträts auf römischen Sarkophagen." In *Eikones. Studien zum griechischen und römischen Bildnis. Hans Jucker zum sechzigsten Geburtstag gewidmet. AntK* Beihefte 12, 153-59.

Schauenburg, K. 1987. "Bockskämpfe und Verwandte Motive." *JdI* 102, 233-89.

Schauenburg, K. 1995. *Die stadtrömische Eroten-Sarkophage – Zirkusrennen und Verwandte Darstellungen. ASR* V 2, 3. Berlin.

Schmidt, T.M. 1993. "Ein römischer Sarkophag mit Lese- und Reiterszene." In G. Koch, ed. *Grabeskunst der römischen Kaiserzeit*. Mainz, 205-18.

Schoenbeck, H.V. 1936. "Die Christliche Sarkophagplastik unter Konstantin." *RM* 51, 238-336.

Schumacher, W.N. 1958. "Zum Sarkophag eines christlichen Konsul." *RM* 65, 100-20.

Schumacher, W.N. 1977. *Hirt und "Guter Hirt". Studien zum Hirtenbild in der römischen Kunst vom zweiten bis zum Anfang des vierten Jahrhunderts besonderer Berücksichtigung der Mosaiken in der Südhalle von Aquileja. RömQSchr* 34. Suppl. Rome.

Sharrock, A.R. 2002. "Looking at Looking. Can You Resist a Reading?" In D. Fredrick, ed. *The Roman Gaze. Vision, Power and the Body*. Baltimore, 265-95.

Shaw, B.D. 1987. "The Age of Roman Girls at Marriage: Some Reconsiderations." *JRS* 77, 30-46.

Shelton, J. 1988. *As the Romans Did. A Source Book in Roman Social History*. New York.

Sichtermann, H. 1966. *Späte Endymion-Sarkophage. Methodisches zur Interpretation*. Baden-Baden.

Sichtermann, H. 1970. "Beiträge zu den Meerwesensarkophagen." *AA*, 214-41.

Sichtermann, H. 1984. "Leda und Ganymed." *MarbWPr*, 43-57.

Sichtermann, H. 1992. *Die Mythologischen Sarkophage. Meleager. ASR* XII 6. Berlin.

Sichtermann, H. & G. Koch. 1975. *Griechische Mythen auf römischen Sarkophagen*. Tübingen.

Sigismund-Nielsen, H. 1997. "Interpreting Epithets in Roman Epitaphs." In B. Rawson, ed. *The Roman Family in Italy*. Oxford, 169-204.

Sigismund-Nielsen, H. 2006. "Collegia: A New Way for Understanding the Roman Family." *Hephaistos* 24, 201-13.

Sigismund-Nielsen, 2007. "Children for Profit and Pleasure." In M. Harlow & R. Laurence, eds. *Age and Ageing in the Roman Empire*. JRA Suppl. 65. Portsmouth, RI, 37-54.

Simon, E., 1970. "Ein spätgallienischer Kindersarkophag mit Eberjagd." *JdI* 85, 194-223.

Sinn, F., 1991. *Vatikanische Museen. Museo Gregoriano Profano ex Lateranense 1. Katalog der Skulpturen 1.* Mainz.

Sinn, F. 1996. *Vatikanische Museen. Museo Gregoriano Profano ex Lateranese I. Katalog der Skulpture 2. Die Ausstattung des Hateriergrabes.* Mainz.

Skinner, M. 2005. *Sexuality in Greek and Roman culture.* Malden, MA.

Smith, R.R.R. 1988. Review of Andreae 1985. *CR* 32, 362-63.

Sorabella, J. 2001. "A Roman Sarcophagus and Its Patron." *BMMA* 36, 67-81.

Sørensen, M.L.S. 2001. "Gender Agenda? Aspects of Women in Antiquity." *Antiquity* 75, 288, 440-42.

Sørensen, M.L.S., 2006. "Gender, Things, and Material Culture." In S.M. Nelson, ed. *Handbook of Gender in Archaeology.* Oxford, 105-35.

Sørensen, M.L.S. 2006a. "The 'Romanization' of Gender Archaeology." *Archaeological Dialogues* 13, 27-31.

Spera, L. 2000. "Un sarcofago con temi agro-pastorali dallo scavo dell'arenario centrale della catacomba di Priscilla." *RACr 76*, 243-84.

Steinby, E.M. 2001. "La necropoli della Via Triumphalis. Il rito funerario nel I secolo d. C." In M. Heinzelmann et al., eds. *Römischer Bestattungsbrauch und Beigabensitten in Rom, Norditalien und den Nordwestprovinzen von der späten Republik bis in die Kaiserzeit. Internationales Kolloquium, Rom 1.-3. April 1998.* Palilia 8. Wiesbaden, 31-4.

Stewart, P. 2003. *Statues in Roman Society. Representation and Response.* Oxford.

Stewart, P. 2008. *The Social History of Roman Art.* Cambridge.

Stirling, L.M. 2005. *The Learned Collector. Mythological Statuettes and Classical Taste in Late Antique Gaul.* Ann Arbor.

Strathern, M. 1992. *Reproducing the Future. Essays on Anthropology, Kinship, and the New Reproductive Technologies.* New York.

Strocka, V. 1968. "Zum neapler Konsulsarkophag." *JdI* 83, 221-39.

Strong, E. 1915. *Apotheosis and Afterlife. Three Lectures on Certain Phases of Art and Religion in the Roman Empire.* Freeport.

Stroszeck, J. 1998. *Löwen-Sarkophage – Sarkophage mit Löwenkopfen, schreitenden Löwen und Löwen-Kampfgruppen. ASR* VI 1. Berlin.

Stuart Jones, H. 1968. *A Catalogue of the Ancient Sculptures Preserved in the Municipal Collections of Rome. The Sculptures of the Palazzo dei Conservatori.* Rome.

Swain, S. 2006. "Minds and Bodies. The Culture of High Roman Empire." (Review of Borg 2004). *JRA* 19, 643-48.

Taccalite, F. 2009. *I colombari sotto la basilica di San Sebastiano fuori le mura.* Rome.

Tarlow, S. 1999. *Bereavement and Commemoration. An Archaeology of Mortality.* Oxford.

Tarlow, S. 2000. "Emotion in Archaeology." *Current Antropology* 41, 5, 713-46.

Taylor, R. 2008. *The Moral Mirror of Roman Art.* New York.

Toynbee, J.M.C. 1971. *Death and Burial in the Roman World.* London.

Toynbee, J. & J. Ward-Perkins. 1956. *The Shrine of St. Peter and the Vatican Excavations.* London.

Treggiari, S. 1991. "Divorce Roman Style: How Easy and how Frequent Was it?" In B. Rawson, ed. *Marriage, Divorce, and Children in Ancient Rome.* Ithaca, NY, 31-46.

Treggiari, S. 1991a. *Roman Marriage:* Iusti Coniuges *from the Time of Cicero to the Time of Ulpian.* Oxford.

Treggiari, S. 1996. "Women in Roman Society." In D.E.E. Kleiner & S. Matheson, eds. *I Claudia. Women in Ancient Rome.* Austin.

Trillmich, W. et al. 1993. *Hispania antiqua. Denkmäler der Römerzeit.* Mainz.

Trimble, J. 2002. "Understanding Muse and Philosopher Imagery." (Review of Ewald 1999). *JRA* 15, 507-10.

Tulloch, J.H. 2004. "Art and Archaeology as a Historical Resource for the Study of Women in Early Christianity: An Approach for Analyzing Visual Data (from Late Antiquity)." *Journal of Feminist Theology* 12, 277-305.

Turcan, R. 1966. *Les Sarcophages romains à représentations dionysiaques, essai de chronologie et d'histoire religieuse.* Paris.

Turcan, R. 1978. "Les sarcophages romains et le probleme du symbolisme funéraire." *ANRW* 16.1, 1700-35.

Turcan, R. 1992. "Bilan et perspectives." In *Giornate Pisane, Atti del IX Congresso delle F.I.E.C. 24-30 Augosto 1989* (=StIt 85), 1086-1102.

Turcan, R. 1999. *Messages d'outre-tombe. L'iconographie des sarcophages romains.* Paris.

Tusa, V. 1957. *I sarcofagi romani in Sicilia.* Palermo.

Tusa, V. 1995 [1957]. *I sarcofagi romani in Sicilia.* Rome.

Uggeri, G. 1967/68. "Sul sarcofago di Flavio Arabiano prefetto dell'Annona." *RendPontAcc* 40, ser. III, 113-22.

Vaccaro Melucco, A. 1963/64. *Sarcofagi romani di caccia al leone.* Studi Miscelanei 11. Rome.

Van Keuren, F. et al. 2011. "Multimethod Analysis of Roman Sarcophagi at the Museo Nazionale Romano, Rome." In J. Elsner & J. Huskinson, eds. *Life, Death and Representation. Some New Work on Roman Sarcophagi.* Berlin, 149-87.

Varner, E.R. 2008. "Transcending Gender: Assimilation, Identity, and Roman Imperial Portraits." In S. Bell & I.L. Hansen, eds. *Role Models in the Roman World. Identity and Assimilation.* Ann Arbor, 185-205.

Vermeule, C.C. 1960. *The Dal Pozzo-Albani Drawings of Classical Antiquities in the British Museum.* Philadelphia.

Vermeule, C.C. 1966. "The Dal Pozzo-Albani Drawings of Classical Antiquities in the Royal Library at Windsor Castle." *TAPS* 56, 1-170.

Veyne, P. 1987. *A History of Private Life 1. From Pagan Rome to Byzantium.* Cambridge, Mass.

Veyne, P. 1988. "Conduct Without Belief and Works of Art Without Viewers." *Diogenes* 36.1, 1-22.

Voss, B. 2000. "Feminisms, Queer Theories, and the Archaeological Study of Past Sexualities." *World Arcaheology* 32. 2, 180-92.

Voss, B. 2008. "Sexuality Studies in Archaeology." *Annual Review of Anthropology* 37, 317-35.

Walker, S. 1985. *Memorials to the Roman Dead.* London.

Walker, S. 1990. "The Sarcophagus of Maconiana Severiana." In G. Koch & M. True, eds. *Roman Funerary Monuments in the J. Paul Getty Museum* 1. Malibu, 83-94.

Wallace-Hadrill, A. 1996. "Engendering the Roman House." In D.E.E. Kleiner & S. Matheson, eds. *I, Claudia. Women in Ancient Rome.* New Haven, 104-15.

Wallace-Hadrill, A. 2008. *Rome's Cultural Revolution.* Cambridge.

Ward-Perkins, J.B. 1969. "The Imported Sarcophagi of Roman Tyre." *BMusBeyr* 22, 109-45.

Ward-Perkins, J.B. 1980. "Nicomedia and the Marble Trade." *PBSR* 48, 23-69.

Ward-Perkins, J.B.1992. *Marble in Antiquity. Collected Papers of J. B. Ward-Perkins.* London.

Ward-Perkins, J.B. & P. Throckmorton. 1965. "The San Pietro Wreck." *Archaeology* 18, 201-09.

Warrior, V. 2006. *Roman Religion.* Cambridge.

Weber, W. 1978. *Die Darstellung einer Wagenfahrt auf römischen Sarkophagdeckeln und Loculusplatten des 3. und 4. Jahrhunderts nach Chr.* Rome.

Wegner, M. 1966. *Die Musensarkophage. ASR* V 3. Berlin.
Wegner, M., ed. 1971. *Caracalla, Geta, Plautilla. Das römische Herrscherbild* III 1. Berlin.
Whitehead, J. 1984. *Biography and Formula in Roman Sarcophagi.* Diss. Yale University.
Wiedemann, T. 1989. *Adults and Children in the Roman Empire.* New Haven.
Wiegartz, H. 1965. *Kleinasiatische Säulensarkophage. Untersuchungen zum Sarkophagtypus und zu den figürlichen Darstellungen.* Berlin.
Wilpert, J. 1929-1932. *I sarcofagi cristiani antichi* I-III. Rome.
Wolf, U. 1977. *Die Nekropole "In Vaticano ad circum".* Rome.
Wood, S. 1978. "Alcestis on Roman Sarcophagi." *AJA* 82, 499-510.
Wood, S. 1986. *Roman Portrait Sculpture, 217-260 A.D. The Transformation of an Artistic Tradition.* Leiden.
Wood, S. 1993. "Alcestis on Roman Sarcophagi." In E. D'Ambra, ed. *Roman Art in Context. An Anthology.* Englewood Cliffs, 84-103.
Wood, S. 2004. Review of Zanker & Ewald 2004. *BMCR.* http://bmcr.brynmawr.edu/2004/2004-11-22.html.
Wrede, H. 1977. "Stadtrömische Monumente, Urnen und Sarkophage des Klinentypus in den beiden ersten Jahrhunderten nach Chr." *AA*, 395-431.
Wrede, H. 1981. *Consecratio in formam deorum. Vergöttlichte Privatpersonen in der römischen Kaiserzeit.* Mainz.
Wrede, H. 2001. *Senatorische Sarkophage Roms. Der Beitrag des Senatorenstandes zur römischen Kunst der hohen und späten Kaiserzeit.* Mainz.
Zanker, P. 1995. *The Mask of Socrates. The Image of the Intellectual in Antiquity.* Berkeley.
Zanker, P. 1995a. *Die Maske des Sokrates. Das Bild des Intellektuellen in der antiken Kunst.* Munich.
Zanker, P. 1999. "Phädras Trauer und Hippolytos' Bildung. Zu einem Sarkophag im Thermenmuseum." In F. de Angelis & S. Muth, eds. *Im Spiegel des Mythos. Bilderwelt und Lebenswelt.* Palilia 6. Wiesbaden, 131-42.
Zanker, P. 2000. *Die mythologischen Sarkophagreliefs und ihre Betrachter.* Munich.
Zanker, P. 2005. "Ikonographie und Mentalität. Zur Veränderung mythologischer Bildthemen auf den kaiserzeitlichen Sarkophagen aus der Stadt Rom." In R. Neudecker & P. Zanker, eds. *Lebenswelten. Bilder und Räume in der römischen Kaiserzeit. Symposium am 24. und 25. Januar 2002 zum Abschluss des von der Gerda Henkel Stiftung geförderten Forschungsprogramms "Stadtkultur in der Kaiserzeit."* Palilia 16. Wiesbaden, 243-51.
Zanker, P. & B.C. Ewald. 2004. *Mit Mythen Leben. Die Bildwerk der römischen Sarkophage.* Munich.
Zimmer, G. 1982. *Römische Berufsdarstellungen.* Berlin.

Sarcophagi Commemorating Women, Men, Children, and Couples[1]

Sarcophagi commemorating a woman:

Learned: 1, 2, 4, 6, 10, 11, 12, 13, 14, 16, 18, 20, 22, 23, 24, 26, 28, 29, 30, 34, 37, 38, 42, 47, 48, 49, 51, 64, 67, 74, 75, 76, 83, 89, 96, 97, 102, 103, 107, 109, 110, 112, 121, 122, 123, 126, 128, 131, 132, 134, 135, 136, 138, 139, 140, 142, 143, 144, 149, 150, 152, 153, 155, 157, 158, 162, 167, 168, 170, 171, 178, 182, 184, 185, 186, 189, 190, 191, 195, 196, 197, 200, 202, 205, 208, 210, 211, 215, 220, 223, 224, 225, 226, 228, 230, 232, 233, 234, 235, 236, 237, 239, 240, 242, 244, 245, 247, 250, 251, 252.
Bust or figure without a scroll: 256, 263, 265, 268, 272, 280, 291, 293, 295, 300, 308, 314, 317, 318, 319, 323, 325, 328, 331, 337, 342, 343, 345, 348, 352, 354, 360, 361, 362, 363, 364, 365, 370, 373, 374, 375, 376, 377, 379, 380, 382, 383, 387, 389, 394, 399, 401, 204, 404, 408, 409, 413, 414, 419, 420, 421, 425, 426, 427.
Hunt: 489, 496, 511.
Reclining: 530, 537, 538.
Carriage: 543, 544.
Myths: 551, 555, 556, 557, 558, 559, 560, 561, 563, 565, 566, 567, 585, 590, 607, 608, 609, 611, 613, 614. Ritual: 642.
Life course: 617.

Total: 199

Sarcophagi commemorating a man:

Learned: 8, 15, 21, 27, 35, 39, 41, 44, 46, 56, 60, 61, 65, 68, 69, 71, 79, 81, 84, 85, 86, 87, 95, 99, 101, 104, 105, 108, 113, 118, 124, 125, 127, 129, 130, 137, 141, 145, 146, 147, 148, 161, 166, 169, 172, 174, 176, 179, 187, 188, 193, 198, 199, 201, 203, 204, 207, 209, 212, 213, 214, 217, 218, 227, 231, 238, 243, 246, 249, 253.
Bust or figure without a scroll: 254, 255, 260, 262, 266, 267, 273, 274, 275, 276, 277, 278, 282, 285, 286, 288, 294, 296, 297, 298, 301, 307, 309, 310, 316, 320, 321, 322, 326, 327, 329, 330, 332, 333, 335, 336, 338, 341, 346, 347, 349, 350, 351, 353, 355, 356, 347, 358, 359, 367, 368, 372, 378, 385, 386, 388, 391, 392, 396, 397, 400, 405, 407, 412, 416, 422, 423, 424, 429.
Hunt: 477, 478, 480, 481, 482, 483, 484, 485, 486, 487, 488, 490, 491, 492, 493, 495, 497, 500, 501, 502, 503, 504, 505, 506, 510, 513, 516, 517, 518, 519, 521, 522.
Reclining: 531, 532, 533, 535, 536.
Carriage: 539, 540, 541.
Myths: 553, 568, 576, 577, 579, 581, 582, 583, 587, 588, 589, 597, 599, 601, 602, 603.
Battle: 624, 625, 627.
Profession?: 628, 629.
Ritual: 641, 656, 660, 661, 665, 667, 672.

Total 207

Sarcophagi with a dual commemoration

Learned: 7 (only women), 9, 32, 43, 45, 52, 54, 55, 57, 58, 59, 62 (two men), 66, 73, 78 (women & girl), 80, 82, 88, 90, 91, 92, 93, 94, 98, 100 (woman, boy & man), 106, 111, 114 (women & man), 116, 119, 120, 156, 163, 164, 165, 173, 177, 180, 181, 183, 241, 248
Bust or figure without a scroll: 258, 269, 299, 303, 304, 305, 324, 395, 428.
Clipeus bust of a woman and man: 430, 431, 432, 433, 434, 435, 436, 437, 438, 439, 440, 441, 442, 443, 444, 445, 446, 447, 448, 449, 450, 451, 452, 453, 454, 455, 456, 457, 458 (man, woman & boy), 459, 460, 461, 462, 463, 464, 465, 466, 467, 468, 469, 470, 471, 472, 473, 474, 475, 476.

764 All numbers in the appendices A-C refer to catalogue numbers.

Hunt: 479, 494, 498 (men), 499, 507, 508, 509, 512, 514, 515, 520, 523.
Reclining: 524, 525, 526, 527, 528, 529, 534.
Carriage: 542.
Myths: 545, 546, 547, 548, 549, 550, 552, 554, 562, 564, 573, 574, 575, 578, 580, 584, 586, 591, 592, 593, 594, 595, 596, 598, 600, 604, 606, 610, 612.
Battle: 626.
Ritual: 630, 632, 633, 634, 635, 636, 637, 638, 639, 640, 643, 644, 645 (man, woman & boy), 646, 647, 648, 649, 650, 651, 652, 653, 654, 655, 657, 658, 659 (man and boy), 662, 663, 664, 666, 668, 669, 670, 671, 673, 674, 675, 676.

Total 186

Sarcophagi commemorating a child:

Learned: 3, 5, 17, 25, 36, 31, 33, 40, 50, 53, 63, 70, 72, 77, 115, 117 (dual commemoration), 133, 151, 154, 159, 160, 175, 192, 194, 206, 216, 221, 229.
Bust or figure without a scroll: 257, 259, 261, 264, 270, 271, 279, 281, 283, 284, 287, 289, 290, 292, 302, 306, 311, 312, 313, 315, 334, 339, 340, 344, 366, 369, 371, 381, 384, 390, 393, 398, 403, 406, 411, 415, 417, 418. Myths: 569, 570, 571, 572, 605 (dual commemoration).
Ritual: 631.
Life course: 615 (family), 616, 618, 619, 620, 621 (family), 622, 623.

Total 80

Sarcophagi commemorating a person of unknown sex:

Learned: 19, 219, 222 (bust or figure without a scroll) 410.

Total 4

APPENDIX B

Sarcophagi with Blank Portraits

Sarcophagi commemorating women: 1, 4, 6, 10, 12, 13, 16, 34, 28, 30, 47, 83, 89, 96, 107, 123, 139, 143, 149, 153, 186, 191, 202, 211, 215, 220, 223, 224, 225, 228, 233, 234, 235, 236, 244, 251, 252, 256, 265, 272, 314, 328, 331, 343, 345, 373, 402, 404, 408, 419, 538, 558, 561,

Total 53

Sarcophagi commemorating men: 8, 15, 35, 41, 44, 69, 101, 104, 108, 125, 141, 146, 172, 193, 201, 212, 255, 274, 275, 276, 277, 297, 298, 307, 316, 321, 329, 347, 351, 353, 388, 396, 397, 400, 423, 478, 481, 485, 495, 504, 516, 531, 532, 535, 540, 541, 583, 597,628.

Total 49

Sarcophagi commemorating children: 3, 31, 33, 36, 50, 53, 151, 281, 313, 334, 371, 569, 570, 572, 618, 619.

Total 16

Sarcophagi commemorating couples: 52, 57, 66, 80, 88, 93,94, 100, 111, 117, 119, 120, 169, 173, 181, 183, 299, 303, 324, 395, 428, 433, 434, 435, 437, 441, 442, 443, 444, 445, 448, 450, 452, 453, 454, 457, 463, 464, 467, 468, 499, 512, 514, 523, 524, 526, 528,548, 562, 564, 578, 586, 592, 595, 596, 604, 605, 606, 610, 626, 630, 633, 634, 637, 643, 644, 646, 647, 651, 652, 655, 657, 659, 611, 662, 670, 673, 674, 676,

Total 79

Unknown sex: 19, 219, 222

Total 3

Learned Figures with Portraits on Sarcophagi

1: Learned female figures with portraits on sarcophagi

AD/Type	Learned woman	Muse	Educated woman (alone)	Orans	Couple/lyre	Couple/scroll	Muse to a philosopher	Other
150-200		200						
200-25	22, 128, 78	162		20		183		
225-50	18, 64, 60, 97, 102, 103, 150, 155, 170, 185, 226	168	190,			92, 114(x3), 177, 180, 183	91, 169	97 (phil.)
250-75	26, 49, 74, 76, 110, 114, 123, 126, 140, 143, 144, 178, 205, 210, 224, 232, 240, 245, 248, 252, 446, 512	42, 110	184, 189, 250	90	45, 88, 107, 157,	9, 43, 54 (x2), 66, 98, 119	91, 114(x3), 120,	
275-300	2, 3, 7, 11, 13, 24, 30, 34, 37, 47, 48, 83, 112, 131, 135, 136, 138, 139, 142, 149, 152, 153, 158, 182, 195, 196, 197, 200, 202, 208, 211, 215, 220, 225, 235, 236, 237, 244, 247, 544		121,162, 186,	2, 9	7 (x2), 122, 93, 94, 96, 165, 167, 251,	52, 111	116 (x2), 117	
300 →	1, 4, 6, 12, 16, 23, 28, 29, 38, 51, 64, 75, 89, 134, 191, 223, 233, 230, 234, 239, 242,	171		10, 14, 132, 642	164, 173	32, 82, 163, 181, 241, 639, 646		228 (phil.)

2: Learned male figures with portraits on sarcophagi

AD/Type	Learned man	Philosopher (alone)	Learned couple (scroll/ philosopher)	Single portrait on *dex. iunc.* scenes	Busts of a couple in a *clipeus* (the man holds a scroll)	Couple making a sacrifice/*dex. iunc.*
150-200			615 (x2)	665, 656, 658, 661, 672		657, 659, 668, 652, 664
200-25	65		57, 73, 640			648, 650, 640
225-50	39, 44, 56, 113, 148, 156, 172, 198, 231	113	55, 58, 562, 114 (x2), 177, 169, 180, 183			651
250-75	21, 35, 41, 46, 68, 71, 79, 101 (x2), 126, 130, 137, 141, 145, 214, 217, 249, 641 (x2)	84, 87, 118, 124, 125, 161, 641	9, 43, 45, 48, 66, 88, 90, 91, 92, 98, 106, 119, 120	667	439, 440, 441, 445, 455, 460, 466, 471, 474, 475	
275-300	27, 62 (x2), 81, 86, 146, 147, 179, 187, 193, 203, 204, 207, 209, 212, 213, 227, 243, 246, 253, 498, 541	85, 95, 105, 108, 109, 127, 129, 166, 176, 218	52, 59, 80, 93, 94, 111, 116, 117, 181, 647	54	434, 435, 438, 449, 452, 464	635, 647, 673, 674
300 →	8, 15, 60 (x2), 61, 188, 199, 201, 238, 495, 540	69, 99, 104	32, 82, 111, 163, 164, 173, 241, 542	644, 646,	431, 432, 433, 468	639

3: Learned children with portraits on sarcophagi

Learned boys	Learned girls	Unknown
5, 17, 25, 33, 53, 72, 77, 100 (x2), 115, 133, 154, 159, 160 (x2), 175, 192, 194, 206, 216, 221, 229, 615, 616, 620, 623, 645	36, 40, 50, 70, 78	31, 63, 151

4: Learned adults: sex unknown: 19, 151, 219, 222

Table of Contents

Hippolytus cat. nos. 590-593
Hylas cat. no. 594
Laodamia and Protesilaus cat. nos. 595
Liber and Venus cat. nos. 596-597
Mars and Rhea Silvia cat. nos. 598-600
Meleager cat. nos. 601-605
Pelops cat. no. 606
Proserpina cat. nos. 607-611
Theseus and Ariadne cat. no. 612
Venus cat. nos. 613-614

Children's Life Course
cat. nos. 615-623

Commanders (battle)
cat. nos. 624-627

Profession (?)
cat. nos. 628-629

Rituals (*dextrarum iunctio*, sacrifice, and prayer)
Bucolic cat. nos. 630-632
Cupids cat. no. 633
Death Door cat. no. 634
Decorative Scheme cat. nos. 635-636
Eros and Psyche cat. nos. at. no. 637
Learned Sphere cat. nos. 638-647
Myth cat. nos. 648-655
Adults' Life Course cat. nos. 656-661
Lion cat. no. 662
Procession cat. nos. 663-669
Ritual cat. nos. 670-672
Seasonal cat. nos. 673-674
Unknown cat. nos. 675-676

Addenda A1-6

How to Use the Catalogue

The common denominator for all of these sarcophagi is that one or more of the figures on each relief has been individualised through the application of a portrait. It was devised as a working-tool with the purpose of acquiring an overview of the different ways identity was expressed on as large a selection as possible of Roman sarcophagi with one or more portraits. The different forms of self-representation, as they can be found in the categories of the catalogue, supported my idea that sarcophagus images were more than merely decorative funerary pictures, and that the personal qualities of the deceased played a central role in the selection of a motif. The criteria for the inclusion of a sarcophagus in the catalogue were: the presence of at least one portrait or blank portrait; and a place of production in Rome. The time frame covers the entire period of production of Roman pagan sarcophagi, which means that sarcophagi featuring scenes from the Old and New Testament are not included. Furthermore, sarcophagi from which only the fragment with the portrait is preserved have as a general rule been omitted. They have only been included in cases in which it was possible to identify the original motif of the fragment. One example of such a case is the fragment of a hunt sarcophagus listed as cat. no. 481. I have also omitted some sarcophagi when it is clearly stated in their publication that the portrait on the relief is modern. However, since the restoration of sarcophagi is still an unsolved problem and an insufficiently studied issue, sarcophagi with modern portraits and restorations are occasionally included in the catalogue.

During my work on the book, new sarcophagi with portraits kept presenting themselves to me, especially on my wanderings in the catacomb and the streets of Rome, and identifying all of them would be a lifetime's task.[1] The catalogue is therefore not an exhaustive collection, but constitutes a sample of sarcophagi with portraits. My estimation is that it covers 90% of the preserved sarcophagi with one or more portrait figures, and my guess is that it is mostly strigillated and other kinds of non-narrative sarcophagi that make up the remaining 10%.[2] The high proportion of extant examples

1 For the purposes of making the catalogue, the corpus *Die antiken Sarkophagreliefs* has been my primary reference work. The usefulness of such catalogue-based volumes in obtaining a broad view of the content of the preserved material is inexpressible. Numerous visits to museums and churches have furthermore expanded the extent of the catalogue. Other publications, such as Ewald's *Der Philosoph als Leitbild*, *Roman Children's Sarcophagi* by Janet Huskinson, Susan Walker's catalogue of the sarcophagi from the British Museum, Repertorium I and museum catalogues, including those of the *MNR* volumes, together with the publication of the sarcophagi in the Louvre and Eugenio La Rocca and Claudio Parisi Presicce's publication of the sculptures form the Capitoline Museum, have also been useful sources (Metzger & Baratte 1985; Ewald 1999; Huskinson 1996; Walker 1990; Museo Nazionale Romano (*MNR*); La Rocca & Presicce 2010). I did not find it necessary to repeat all the bibliographical references that have been so comprehensively gathered by the authors of these publications.

2 Strigillated sarcophagi have until now never been published as a group or in a monograph. However, this catalogue contains around 217 strigillated sarcophagi, which can give us an idea about the nature of the group (the catalogue contains 629 coffins and 48, lids which means that one third of all the sarcophagi are of the strigillated type).

included, together with the fact that the sarcophagi have been collected to represent all the different motif types, makes this catalogue a representative sample of individualised sarcophagi that is suitable for quantitative analysis.

The focus on identity and individuality in this book means that the categorisation of the sarcophagi is determined by the roles of the individualised figures, meaning that sarcophagi are classified according to forms of self-representation, rather than in the traditional way of listing them according to the overall theme. The outcome of this categorisation was that the variations in possible forms of self-representation were shown to be limited, and considerable differences in the popularity of different figure types were revealed. Some of the categories are relatively large – *Learned Figures*, for example, contains 253 catalogue numbers – whereas other categories have only a few catalogue numbers. A secondary classification was made when each of the established groups was divided into secondary groups according to the theme of the scenes related to the portrait figure (what I call 'secondary motifs'). If both the lid and the coffin are preserved, it is the scene of the object on which that portrait is placed that is categorised as the secondary motif. In cases where either part is fragmented the portrait is sometimes associated with the motif on the other part (an example is cat. no. 5).

Some of the secondary groups were fairly easy to define. Others, such as the bucolic and seasonal groups, as well as cupids, were more difficult. The reason for this is that figures from these spheres were sometimes used together in the same scenes, and at other times they clearly characterised a special sphere. For example, the ram-bearer is a common denominator but since he belongs, at least in a pagan context, to the idyllic landscape, the ram-bearer has here been placed in the category labelled *bucolic*, despite the fact that he is often represented as the counterpart to a learned figure. Similarly, the *garlands* group is much smaller than the actual number of sarcophagi showing garlands would suggest; garlands are a fairly common decorative element on sarcophagi and are therefore often used with other motifs. Sarcophagi have been assigned to the *garlands* group only in cases where the garlands are the only decorative element on the coffin. Despite these difficulties in separating the motifs, the two main categories of the primary and secondary motif give a good overview of which motifs were popular alongside portraits and what combinations were possible.

The catalogue has been divided into eleven main categories: *learned figures*, *figures without scrolls or musical instruments*, *clipeus busts of a couple*, *hunters and Virtus*, *reclining figures*, *figures riding in a carriage*, *mythological figures*, *children's life course*, *commanders*, *profession(?)*, and *rituals*. The first main category (cat. nos. 1-253) contains the individualised figures on non-narrative scenes that are shown holding a scroll. I have chosen to call them *learned men, women, and children* according to the age and sex of the portrait subject. Figure types such as the philosopher, the Muse, the Orans, the magistrate, and figures playing a musical instrument have been included in this category.[3]

The second main category (cat. nos. 254-429) comprises individualised figures on non-narrative scenes without a scroll or a musical instrument. I have chosen to use scrolls and musical instruments as denominators since other attributes are very rarely found. In the cases in which the individualised figure holds an object other than a scroll or an instrument, they have been included in this category. Despite the fact that these figures often wear the same type of clothing as the figures that hold a scroll, I have chosen not to see the clothing as an explicit expression of *paideia*. I think that in this context, dress does not specifically connote learnedness; rather it became a convention in funerary reliefs.[4]

The third main category (cat. no. 330-476) is the group of sarcophagi with *clipeus* busts of a couple. Even though some of the figures hold scrolls and other do not, I have categorised them in one group because the composition is standardised and expresses the same values in a specific social relationship.

3 The instrument is included in this category because it most often is found in a context with a figure with a scroll; see chapter 3, "The Female Ideal", and chapter 2, "The Learned Figure". I have included figures with senators' or magistrates' costumes in this category, because they should be read metaphorically (alongside mythological figures).

4 For reflections on the meaning of the clothing, especially the *pallium/palla*, see Ewald 1999, 14, and on conventions in the use of the Roman toga and the Greek *pallium*, see Wallace-Hadrill 2008, 41-57.

The fourth to the tenth main categories, focus on individualised figures on what can be called narrative scenes (cat. nos. 477-629). A narrative scene is a scene in which the individualised figures interact as one of the protagonists. These groups sometimes contain sarcophagi with strigillated panels or other features that separate the figures from the surrounding scenes (an example is cat. no. 514). When these sarcophagi have been included in one of these groups, it is because these 'abbreviated' scenes originate in the same motif sphere as the narrative scenes in that group and therefore should not be separated out.

The last of major category contains all the sarcophagi showing a ritual, such as a *dextrarum iunctio* scene or the so-called biographical sarcophagi and other types of sarcophagi that represent sacrifices (cat. nos. 630-76). This category has again been divided into the same secondary categories that are used in the first two main groups, in an effort to highlight patterns in the use of these symbolic figures.

Non-Narrative Scenes with Learned Figures

Bucolic

1 *CLIPEUS* PORTRAIT OF A LEARNED WOMAN

Location/Inv.: Adore, Reggio Calabria.
Condition: The coffin is preserved.
Provenience: Adore.
Frontal relief: Divided into five panels. The second and fourth panels are strigillated. A ram bearer is represented on the first and fifth panel. A *clipeus* with a bust of a learned woman holding a scroll is represented on the central panel, and a bucolic scene with a herdsman and a sheep is placed beneath the *clipeus*. Two flowers are seen in the upper corners of the central panel.
Short ends: Griffin.
Portrait: Blank female portrait.
Dating: Late third or early fourth century (Sichtermann 1984, 48).

Bibliography: Schumacher 1977; Himmelmann 1980, 151; Sichtermann 1984.

2 LEARNED WOMAN AND *ORANS* (FIG. 17)

Location/Inv.: Copenhagen, Ny Carlsberg Glyptotek, inv. 2343.
Size (coffin): L: 2.16 H: 0.58 D: 0.84
Condition: The coffin is preserved.
Frontal relief: Divided into five panels. The second and fourth panels are strigillated. An *Orans* with scrolls at her feet is represented on the first panel. Her hands are raised and the palms are turned towards the viewer. A *parapetasma* is suspended behind her. A ram-bearer is depicted on the fifth panel, and a *clipeus* with a bust of a learned woman holding a scroll is shown on the central panel. Two *cornucopiae* are carved beneath the *clipeus*. The ornamented profiles on the panels and upper rim are an unusual feature on Roman sarcophagi.
Left short end: Two winged cupids working in the field.
Right short end: Two winged cupids pressing grapes.
Portrait: The bust and the *Orans* are carved with a portrait of a woman.
Dating: Late third century (Østergaard 1996, cat. 66).

Bibliography: Østergaard 1996, 153-55, cat. 66; Koch 1990.

3 BUST OF A LEARNED GIRL

Location/Inv.: Copenhagen, Ny Carlsberg Glyptotek, inv. 2468.
Size (coffin): L: 1.04 H: 1.80 D: 0.56
Condition: The coffin and lid are preserved.
Frontal relief: Three winged cupids carry rich garlands and theatrical masks. Birds and a hare are eating grapes from the ground. For a description, see Østergaard 1996, cat. 48.
Short ends: Without relief decoration.
Lid. A central inscription panel with a Greek inscription. There is a bucolic scene on the left side of the panel and a bust of a woman with a scroll on the right side. Behind her is a *parapetasma* held by two cupids.
Portrait: Blank portrait. Traces of paint are preserved on and around the portrait but no facial features seem to have been drawn.
Inscription: ΑΥΡ(ΗΛΙΑΝ) ΚΥ[ΡΙΛΛΑ[Ν] ΤΗΝ / ΚΑΙ ΥΠ[Ε] ΡΕΧΙΑΝ / ΤΗ[Ν] ΕΑΥΤΟΥ ΕΚΓΟ / ΝΗ[Ν] ΑΥΡ(ΗΛΙΟC) ΝΕΙΚΑΝΔΡΟC Ο Λ[Α]Μ / ΠΡΟ(ΤΑΤΟC) ΔΥCΤΥΧΗC ΠΑΠΠΟΣ
Dating: Around 300 (Østergaard 1996, cat. 48).
Comment: Child sarcophagus. Paint has been preserved on several places; see Østergaard, 2011.

Bibliography: Østergaard 1996, cat. 48; 2011.

4 LEARNED WOMAN

Location/Inv.: Rome, Catacombe di S. Callisto.
Size (coffin): L: 2.06 H: 0.55 D: 0.64
Condition: The coffin is preserved.

Frontal relief: Divided into five panels. The second and fourth panels are strigillated. A ram-bearer is represented on the first and fifth panels, and on the central panel, a woman with a scroll is depicted in front of a *parapetasma*.
Portrait: The woman with a scroll is shown with a blank portrait.
Dating: First quarter of the fourth century (*Rep.* I, cat. 396).

Bibliography: *Rep.* I, cat. 396.

5 BUST OF A LEARNED BOY

Location/Inv.: Rome, Musei Capitolini, inv. 2075.
Size (coffin): L: 1.40 H: 0.47
Condition: The coffin and part of the lid are preserved.
Frontal relief: Divided into four panels. The second and third panels are strigillated. A ram-bearer is represented on the first and fourth panels, and a *mandorla* with vertical lines is seen in the middle of the relief.
Lid: The corner is adorned with a theatrical mask. A bust of a boy with a scroll is shown in front of a *parapetasma* held by two cupids. An inscription panel held by two cupids is the central feature. The right end is lost.
Portrait: The bust is carved with a portrait of a boy.
Inscription: SEXTO ACERRE / VRSO SANTO / QVI VIXIT / ANNIS VI / MENSES VIII / DIEBVS VII / FILIO DVL/CISSIMO / VRBANVS / ET IVSTINA / PARENTES / S A N T O HISPIRITO / VRSO IN PACE
Dating: First part of the fourth century (*Rep.* I, cat. 823).
Comment: Child sarcophagus. Christian inscription.

Bibliography: *Rep.* I, cat. 823.

6 LEARNED WOMAN

Location/Inv.: Rome, Musei Vaticani, Museo Pio Crsitiano, inv. 21.
Size (coffin): L: 1.72 H: 0.60 D: 0.60
Condition: The coffin is preserved.
Provenience: Catacombe di Pretestato, Cripta di Passione.
Frontal relief: Divided into five panels. The second and fourth panels are strigillated. A ram-bearer is represented on the first and fifth panels. A woman with a scroll is depicted in front of a *parapetasma* on the central panel.
Short ends: Probably without relief decoration.
Portrait: The woman is carved with a blank portrait.
Dating: First quarter of the fourth century (*Rep.* I, cat. 74).

Bibliography: *Rep.* I, cat. 74.

7 EDUCATED WOMEN AND A BUST OF A LEARNED WOMAN (FIG. 71)

Location/Inv.: Rome, Musei Vaticani, Museo Pio Cristiano, inv. 128.
Size (coffin): L: 2.20 H: 0.65 D: 0.70
Condition: The coffin is preserved.
Frontal relief: The central panel shows a bust of a woman with a scroll, and on each end of the relief a woman playing an instrument is seated. The woman on the left plays a lyre and the woman on the right a *pandurium*. Seasonal representations and herdsmen are represented on each side of the central panel.
Short ends: Without relief decoration.
Portrait: The two seated women and the bust on the central panel have portrait features. All of the portraits seem to be of different woman.
Dating: From Tetrarchic time to the beginning of the fourth century. For discussion, see Ewald 1999, cat. E 14.

Bibliography: Wegner, *ASR* V 3 (1966) cat. 114; Kranz, *ASR* V 4 (1984) cat. 127; *Rep.* I, cat. 32; Marrou 1938, cat. 218; Gerke 1940, cat. II 1; Bovini 1949, cat. 48; Hanfmann 1951, cat. 484; Klauser 1958, cat. 60; Schumacher 1977; Ewald 1999, cat. E 14, pl. 57, 1.

8 LEARNED MAN

Location/Inv.: Rome, Musei Vaticani, Museo Pio Cristiano, inv. 150.
Size (coffin): L: 2.02 H: 0.55 D: 0.63; (lid): L: 2.09 H: 0.22 D: 0.63
Condition: The coffin and lid are preserved.
Provenience: Rome, Via Prensentina (Tenuta dei Massimi della Tor Sapienza).
Frontal relief: Bucolic landscape. A ram-bearer is represented on the left side of the relief and a female *Orans* in front of a *parapetasma* is shown on the right side.
Lid: From left to right there is a hunting scene, an empty inscription panel, and a bust of a man with a scroll in front of a *parapetasma* held by two seasonal personifications. A third *genius* is harvesting grapes (?).
Portrait: The male bust on the lid has a blank portrait.
Dating: End of the third or beginning of the fourth century (*Rep.* I, cat.2).

Bibliography: *Rep.* I, cat. 2.

9 PHILOSOPHER AND LEARNED WOMAN

Location/Inv.: Rome, Musei Vaticani, Museo Pio Cristiano, inv. 181.
Size (coffin): L: 2.40 H: 0.75
Condition: The coffin is preserved but extensively restored.
Provenience: Rome, Via Salaria.
Frontal relief: A seated philosopher and a seated woman with a scroll are placed opposite each other at each end of the relief. A herdsman, a ram-bearer, and an *Orans* are represented between them. A ram instead of a lion head is depicted on the rounded end of the relief. For a description, see Ewald 1999, cat. E 11.
Short ends: *Lenos*-shaped.
Portrait: Both the seated man and the seated woman have portrait features. They have been described as idealised portraits (*Rep.* I, cat. 66).
Dating: 270-280 (Ewald 1999, cat. E 11). Last third of the third century (*Rep.* I, cat. 66).

Bibliography: *Rep.* I, cat. 66; Schumacher 1980, 121-23; Himmelmann 1980, 132-33; Ewald 1999, cat. E 11; Bisconti 2004, 57.

10 FEMALE *ORANS*
Location/Inv.: Rome, Palazzo Farnese.
Size (coffin): L: 2.13 H: 0.57
Condition: The frontal relief is preserved.
Frontal relief: A female veiled *Orans* in a bucolic setting is represented in front of a *parapetasma*. Two ram-bearers frame the rural scenes.
Portrait: The *Orans* has a blank portrait.
Dating: Last quarter of the third century (*Rep.* I, cat. 961).

Bibliography: *Rep.* I, cat. 961.

11 *CLIPEUS* PORTRAIT OF A LEARNED WOMAN
Location/Inv.: Rome, Palazzo Senatorio (location information is uncertain).
Condition: The coffin is preserved.
Frontal relief: Divided into five panels. The second and fourth panels are strigillated. A herdsman is represented on the first and fifth panels. A *clipeus* with a bust of a woman with necklaces holding a scroll is represented on the central panel. Two *cornucopiae* are depicted beneath the *clipeus*.
Short ends: Unknown.
Portrait: The bust is carved with a female portrait.
Dating: Probably late third or early fourth century.

Bibliography: Arachne image no.: 147965 (http://arachne.unikoeln.de/item/objekt/147965).

12 LEARNED WOMAN
Location/Inv.: Rome, Rampa di Sebastianello. Today used as a fountain.
Size (coffin): L: 2.12 H: 0.66 D: 0.74
Condition: The coffin is preserved.
Frontal relief: Divided into five panels. The central panel depicts a woman holding a scroll and dressed in a *palla*. A *parapetasma* is suspended behind her. The second and fourth panels are strigillated. A ram-bearer is represented on the first and fifth panels.
Short ends: Fruit basket.
Portrait: The woman on the central panel has a blank portrait.
Dating: First quarter of the fourth century (Ewald 1999, cat. F 15).

Bibliography: Himmelmann 1980, pl. 59; Ewald 1999, cat. F 15.

13 LEARNED WOMAN
Location/Inv.: Rome, S. Lorenzo.
Size (coffin): L: 1.28 H: 0.45 D: 0.41
Condition: Fragment of the coffin.
Provenience: Excavation beneath the central nave, still *in situ*.
Frontal relief: Divided into five panels. The second and fourth panels are strigillated. A ram-bearer is represented on the first and fifth panels. The central panel depicts a woman holding a scroll represented between two Muses.
Right short end: A herdsman is represented between two trees (the left short end is not visible).
Portrait: The learned woman is carved with a blank portrait.
Dating: Last quarter of the third century (Ewald 1999, cat. H 14).

Bibliography: *Rep.* I, cat. 696, pl. 111; Ewald 1999, cat. H 14.

14 FEMALE *ORANS* (FIG. 72)
Location/Inv.: Rome, S. Prassede.
Size (coffin): L: 1.73 H: 0.63
Condition: The frontal relief is preserved.
Frontal relief: Divided into five panels (the first panel is lost). The second and fourth panels are strigillated. A ram-bearer is represented on the fifth panel and a veiled woman is represented in front of a *parapetasma* on the central panel.
Portrait: The *Orans* on the central panel has portrait features.
Dating: Beginning of the fourth century (*Rep.* I, cat. 757).

Bibliography: *Rep.* I, cat. 757.

Cupids

(see also addendum A2)

15 LEARNED MAN (FIG. 6)
Location/Inv.: Avignon, Musée Calvet, Lapidaire, inv. N2 and N4.
Condition: The lid is preserved, two fragments.
Lid: From left to right there is a scene with a *Sigma-Mahl*, an inscription panel, a male bust with a scroll in front of a *parapetasma* held by *victoriae*, and yet another inscription panel supported by another two *victoriae*.
Portrait: The bust is carved with a blank portrait.
Dating: Early fourth century.
Inscription: (first panel) ANTODONIV[S] / ANIMA DV[LCIS] / IN PACE QVI [VI] XIT ANN / XIV M VIII D [X] XVI; (second panel) GAVDENTIVS/ET PALLADI/VS FRATRI/INNOCENTIS/SIMO FECER

Bibliography: Cavalier 2005, 219-24.

16 BUST OF A LEARNED WOMAN
Location/Inv.: Berlin, Schloss Klein-Glienicke, inv. GI 43.
Size (coffin): L: 0.96 H: 0.32 D: 0.11
Condition: Fragment of a lid.
Lid: A centrally placed bust of a woman with a scroll is represented in front of a *parapetasma* held by two cupids. A cupid with a *kantharos* in his hand supported by another cupid is depicted to the left of this composition, and there is a sleeping cupid to the right.
Portrait: The bust is carved with a blank portrait.
Inscription: ANTODONIV[S] / ANIMA DV[LCIS] / IN PACE QVI [VI] XIT ANN / XIV M VIII D [X]XVI
Dating: 320s (*ASR* V 2, 1, cat. 3).

Bibliography: Kranz, *ASR* V 2, 1 (1999) cat. 3, pl. 65, 4.

17 *CLIPEUS* PORTRAIT OF A BOY AS A MUSE (FIG. 97)

Location/Inv.: Copenhagen, Ny Carlsberg Glyptotek, inv. 854.
Size (coffin): L: 1.68 H: 0.57 D: 0.60
Condition: The coffin is preserved.
Frontal relief: Divided into five panels. The second and fourth panels are strigillated. A sleeping cupid leaning against a torch is represented on the first and the fifth panels. A *clipeus* with a bust of a child is shown in the central panel. He has one naked shoulder and is playing a *pandurium*. Two masks are depicted beneath the *clipeus*. For a description, see Østergaard 1996, cat. 56.
Short ends: *Lenos*-shaped. Shield and spears.
Portrait: The bust is carved with a portrait of a boy. His hair is short but with locks. The bust is female and the right shoulder is exposed, an allusion to Venus. The breasts are visible beneath the sleeveless tunic.
Dating: Around 250-300 (Østergaard 1996, cat. 56, 132).
Comment: Child sarcophagus.

Bibliography: Østergaard 1996, cat. 56; Birk 2011, 238, fig. 7.4.

18 BUST OF A LEARNED WOMAN

Location/Inv.: Copenhagen; Ny Carlsberg Glyptotek, inv. 2302.
Size (coffin): L: 1.98 H: 0.59 D: 0.60
Condition: The coffin is preserved.
Frontal relief: A bust of a woman with a scroll is represented in front of a *parapetasma* held by two flying cupids. Two peacocks are shown beneath this scene. There is a cupid on each end of the relief. For a description, see Østergaard 1996, cat. 52.
Short ends: Deer, tree, and dog.
Reverse: Smooth band on the lower part, then a sharp edge and the surface rises into a rough surface made by a pick axe.
Portrait: The bust is carved with a female portrait.
Dating: 200-250 (Østergaard 1996, cat. 52).

Bibliography: Østergaard 1996, cat. 52

19 LEARNED BUST

Location/Inv.: Ostia, Museo Nazionale, inv. 36231.
Size (coffin): L: 1.65 H: 0.55 D: 0.59; (lid) H: 0.25
Condition: The coffin and lid are preserved.
Frontal relief: Hunting scene. For a description, see *ASR* I 2, cat. 61.
Short ends: *Lenos*-shaped.
Lid: In the centre is a bust with a scroll. Cupids are represented on the left end, and shepherds with sheep are seen on the right end. Originally made for a rectangular coffin but reworked to suit the *lenos*-shaped coffin.
Portrait: The bust on the lid is carved with a blank portrait.
Dating: Around 300 (*ASR* I 2, cat. 61).

Bibliography: Andreae, *ASR* I 2 (1980) cat. 61; Huskinson 1996, cat. I. 16.

20 *CLIPEUS* PORTRAIT OF A VEILED WOMAN (*ORANS*)

Location/Inv.: Ostia, Museo Nazionale, inv. 37843bis.
Size (coffin): L: 0.92 H: 0.48 D: 0.53
Condition: The coffin is preserved. Fragments are missing.
Provenience: Isola Sacra, Pianabella, Basilica.
Frontal relief: Divided into five panels. The second and fourth panels are strigillated. A *clipeus* with a female bust (*Orans*) with a veil is shown on the central panel, and a cupid with a torch is depicted on the first and fifth panels. Two *cornucopiae* are placed beneath the *clipeus*. For description, see Paroli 1999, no. B 28.
Short ends: Weapons.
Portrait: The woman in the *clipeus* has portrait features.
Dating: Dated to the late Severan period on the basis of the style of the cupids (Paroli 1999, 230).

Bibliography: Paroli 1999, no. B 28, pl. 97, 1.

21 *CLIPEUS* PORTRAIT OF A LEARNED MAN

Location/Inv.: Paris, Musèe du Louvre, inv. Ma 1628.
Size (coffin): L: 1.91 H: 0.49
Condition: The frontal relief is preserved.
Frontal relief: A centrally placed *clipeus* with a bust of a man with a scroll is held by flying cupids. Tellus, Oceanus, and Ganymede and the eagle are depicted beneath the *clipeus*. *Lenos*-shaped coffin.
Portrait: The bust is carved with a portrait of a youth or a boy.
Dating: Second half of the third century (Baratte & Metzger 1985, cat. 126).

Bibliography: Baratte & Metzger 1985, cat. 126

22 *CLIPEUS* PORTRAIT OF A LEARNED WOMAN

Location/Inv.: Paris, Musèe du Louvre, inv. Ma 2954.
Size (coffin): L: 1.63 H: 0.52 D: 0.53
Condition: The coffin is preserved.
Frontal relief: Divided into five panels. The second and fourth panels are strigillated. A sleeping cupid with a torch is shown on the first and fifth panels. A bust of a young woman with a scroll is represented on the central panel. Two *cornucopiae* are depicted beneath the bust.
Portrait: The portrait seems to be of a girl with an adult hair-style.
Dating: Around 225 (Baratte & Metzger 1985, cat. 129).

Bibliography: Baratte & Metzger 1985, cat. 129.

23 LEARNED WOMAN

Location/Inv.: Rome, Catacombe di S. Callisto.
Size (lid): L: 1.00 H: 0.30
Condition: Fragment of a lid.
Provenience: Rome, Catacombe di S. Callisto.
Lid: A bust of a woman with a scroll is represented in front of a *parapetasma* held by cupids. Two cupids holding an inscrip-

tion panel are depicted to the right of the female bust. For a description, see *Rep* I, cat. 475.
Portrait: The bust is carved with a female portrait wearing a necklace.
Inscription: AVR(ELIA) FIEDS / DEP(OSITA) KAL(ENDAS) IAN(VARIAS) / VERONICA / NVS FIL(IVS) FECIT
Dating: Second third of the fourth century (*Rep.* I, cat. 475).

Bibliography: *Rep.* I, cat. 475.

24 LEARNED WOMAN

Location/Inv.: Rome, Catacombe di Domitilla.
Condition: Fragment.
Frontal relief: Female bust with a scroll in front of a *parapetasma* held by a cupid.
Portrait: The bust is carved with a female portrait.
Dating: Late third century, based on the hairstyle.

Bibliography: Koch & Sichtermann 1982, 216.

25 LEARNED BOY

Location/Inv.: Rome, Catacombe di Pretestato.
Size (coffin): L: 1.50 H: 0.65 (including lid)
Condition: The coffin and lid are preserved.
Provenience: Rome, Catacombe di Prestestato.
Frontal relief: Divided into five panels. The second and fourth panels are strigillated. On the first and fifth panels, there is a sleeping cupid leaning against a torch. A boy is represented with a scroll in front of a *parapetasma* on the central panel. For a description, see *Rep.* I, cat. 564.
Lid: Swimming dolphins on each side of a central inscription.
Portrait: The boy has portrait features.
Inscription: FLAVIVS INSTEIVS CILO C(LARISSIMVS) P(VER) / FILIVS FLAVI IVLIANI / C(LARISSIMI) V(IRI) ET INSTEIAE / CILONIDIS C(LARISSIMAE) F(EMINAE / HIC DEPOSITVS / EST XI KAL(ENDAS) IANVA/RIAS
Dating: Early fourth century (Gütshow 1938; Huskinson 1996).
Comment: Child sarcophagus.

Bibliography: Gütschow 1938, 235-37; *Rep.* I, cat. 564, pl. 87; Huskinson 1996, cat. 9. 39.

26 BUST OF A LEARNED WOMAN

Location/Inv.: Rome, Catacombe di Pretestato.
Size (coffin): L: 1.83 H: 0.88 D: 0.58.
Condition: The coffin is preserved. The right end is missing.
Frontal relief: Two flying cupids hold a *parapetasma* that frames a bust of a woman with a scroll. A sleeping cupid with a torch and a garland is seen on the left end, and Oceanus and Tellus lay on the ground. For a description, see Gütschow 1938, 123-25.
Left short end: Seasonal personification.
Portrait: The bust is carved with a female portrait.
Dating: 260-265 (Gütschow 1938, 125).

Bibliography: Gütschow 1938, 123-25, pls. 19, 1 & 33, 1.

27 *CLIPEUS* BUST OF A LEARNED MAN

Location/Inv.: Rome, Catacombe di Pretestato.
Size (coffin): L: 1.63 H: 0.45
Condition: The frontal relief is preserved.
Frontal relief: Two flying cupids hold a *clipeus* with a bust of a man with a scroll. Seasonal personifications frame the composition, and Oceanus and Tellus lay on the ground. For a description, see Gütschow 1938, 125.
Portrait: The bust is carved with a male portrait.
Dating: 270-280s (Gütschow 1938, 126).

Bibliography: Gütschow 1938, 123-25, pl. 19, 2.

28 *CLIPEUS* PORTRAIT OF A LEARNED WOMAN

Location/Inv.: Rome, Musei Capitolini, staircase to the Galleria delle Congiunzione, inv. 2412.
Condition: The coffin is preserved.
Provenience: Rome, Via Prenestina.
Frontal relief: Divided into five panels. The second and fourth panels are strigillated with vertical grooves. A cupid with an up-turned torch is represented on the first and fifth panels. A *clipeus* with a bust of a woman with a scroll is depicted on the central panel. Leda and the swan are shown on a mythological scene beneath the *clipeus*.
Short ends: Without decoration.
Portrait: The bust is carved with a blank portrait.
Dating: Late third or early fourth century.

Bibliography: Koch & Sichtermann 1982, 157; Sichtermann 1984, fig. 15.

29 *CLIPEUS* PORTRAIT OF A LEARNED WOMAN

Location/Inv.: Rome, Musei Capitolini, Palazzo Nuovo (formerly Museo Mussolini, inv. 816).
Size (coffin with lid): L: 1.92 H: 0.65 D: 0.92
Condition: The coffin and lid are preserved.
Frontal relief: Divided into five panels. The second and fourth panels are strigillated. A sleeping cupid is represented on the first and fifth panels. A *clipeus* with a bust of a woman with scroll is depicted on the central panel. Two theatrical masks are placed beneath the *clipeus*.
Lid: Sea-monsters and an inscription panel.
Portrait: The learned bust is carved with female portrait features.
Inscription: MM / AVREL(IA) / EXTRICATAE
Dating: First half of the fourth century (*ASR* V 1, cat. 209).

Bibliography: Rumpf, *ASR* V 1 (1939) cat. 209, pl. 59, 2.

30 BUST OF A LEARNED WOMAN

Location/Inv.: Rome, Musei Vaticani, Museo Gregoriano Profano, Viale della Zitella, inv 68.
Size (coffin): L: 2.19 H: 0.63 D: 0.62
Condition: The coffin is preserved.
Provenience: Via Latina, Tomb of the Pancrati (Herdjürgen 2000, 224-25).

Frontal relief: Divided into five panels. The second and fourth panels are strigillated. A sleeping cupid is depicted on the first and fifth panels. A bust of a woman with a scroll is represented on the central panel. A *parapetasma* is suspended behind the bust. The bust seems to grov from acanthus leaves.
Portrait: The female bust on the central panel is carved with a blank portrait.
Dating: 270s (Herdjürgen 2000, 224).

Bibliography: Benndorf & Schöne 1867, cat. 197; Herdejürgen 2000, 223-24; Jucker 1961, 36-7. cat. S 7.

31 *CLIPEUS* PORTRAIT OF A LEARNED CHILD

Location/Inv.: Rome, Musei Vaticani, Museo Gregoriano Profano, inv. 5375.
Size (coffin): L: 0.90 H: 0.37 D: 0.38
Condition: The frontal relief is preserved.
Frontal relief: Divided into five panels. The second and fourth panels are strigillated. A sleeping cupid leaning on a torch is represented on the first and fifth panels. A *clipeus* with a bust of a child with a scroll is depicted on the central panel. Two theatrical masks are placed beneath the *clipeus.*
Portrait: The child bust is carved with a blank portrait.
Inscription: On the upper profile.
Comment: Child sarcophagus.

Bibliography: Arachne: http://arachne.uni-koeln.de/item/objekt/60021.

32 BUSTS OF A MALE *ORANS* AND A LEARNED WOMAN

Location/Inv.: Rome, Musei Vaticani, Museo Pio Cristiano, Galleria Lapidaria.
Size (lid): L: 1.08 H: 0.28
Condition: Fragment of a lid.
Lid: Half-length figures (a man and a veiled woman) are shown in front of a *parapetasma* held by two cupids. An inscription panel is placed on the right end of the relief.
Portrait: The male *orans* and the veiled woman are carved with portrait features.
Inscription: [M]νησθη ο θεος Ευγενιης / τελευτα ετων νζ′ δεσιου β′ / οικησασα μετα του συνβιου / αυτης παρθενεκου / ετη μα′ καταλειπουσα τεκνα δ′ / ενγονα θ′.
Dating: Beginning of the fourth century (*Rep.* I, cat. 120).

Bibliography: Wilpert I (1929), 75; *Rep.* I, cat. 120.

33 LEARNED BOY (PHILOSOPHER)

Location/Inv.: Rome, Musei Vaticani, magazine, inv. 4942.
Size (coffin): L: 0.41 H: 0.35
Condition: A fragment of the frontal relief is preserved.
Frontal relief: A seated philosopher is represented with a scroll. Two cupids stand on his right side. One of the cupids holds a lyre. For a description, see *ASR* V 2, 1, cat. 136.
Portrait: The seated figure is carved with a blank portrait.
Dating: 280-290 (*ASR* V 2, 1, cat. 136).
Comment: Child sarcophagus.

Bibliography: Kranz, *ASR* V 2, 1 (1999) cat. 136, pl. 52, 1; Ewald 1999, cat. D6.

34 LEARNED WOMAN

Location/Inv.: Rome, Museo Nazionale Romano, inv. 9167/9183.
Size (lid): L: 1.56 H: 0.025 D: 0.45
Condition: Lid. Preserved in two pieces.
Lid: A bust of a woman with a scroll is shown in front of a *parapetasma* held by two sea-monsters. Boats with fishing cupids are depicted on both sides of the bust. For a description, see *MNR* I 10, 2, cat. 2.
Portrait: The female bust is carved with a blank portrait.
Dating: The style of the relief indicates a dating around 270-280 (*MNR* I 10, 2, cat. 2).

Bibliography: *MNR* I 10, 2, cat. 2.

35 BUST OF A LEARNED MAN

Location/Inv.: Rome, Museo Nazionale Romano, inv. 11636.
Size (coffin): L: 0.34 H: 0.36 D: 0.06
Condition: Fragment of a frontal relief?
Provenience: Rome, Colosseum.
Frontal relief: A bust of a man with a scroll is placed in front of a *parapetasma* held by a cupid. For a description, see *MNR* I 10, 2, cat. 211.
Portrait: The bust is carved with a blank portrait.
Dating: Second half of the third century (*MNR* I 10, 2, cat. 211).

Bibliography: *MNR* I 10, 2, cat. 211.

36 LEARNED GIRL (FIG. 91)

Location/Inv.: Rome, Museo Nazionale Romano, inv. 65200.
Size (coffin): L: 0.95 H: 0.26 D: 0.33
Condition: The coffin and lid are preserved.
Frontal relief: Divided into three panels. Cupids engaged in a cockfight are represented on the first and third panels. A child with a scroll is shown standing in front of a *parapetasma* on the central panel. Palm trees are depicted on each end of the relief.
Short ends: Imitation of a wall (city wall?).
Lid: With a reclining figure – female blank portrait.
Portrait: The figure on the central panel is carved with a portrait of a girl. A reclining girl with a blank portrait is carved on the lid.
Dating: Fourth century (*MNR* I 10, 2, cat. 115).
Comment: Child sarcophagus.

Bibliography: *MNR* I 10, 2, cat. 115.

37 LEARNED WOMAN

Location/Inv.: Rome, Museo Nazionale Romano, inv. 106214.
Size (coffin): L: 1.56 H: 0.43 D: 0.36
Condition: The coffin is preserved, but fragmented.
Frontal relief: A woman with a scroll dressed in a tunic and a *palla* is represented on the central panel. A lion with cupids crawling on its back is depicted on each side of this composi-

tion. A ram- bearer is shown on the left and right ends of the relief. For a description, see *MNR* I 8, 1, cat. II, 18.
Left short end: Without relief decoration.
Right short end: Basket with fruit.
Portrait: The female figure is carved with portrait features.
Dating: 280-300 (*MNR* I 8, 1, cat. II, 18)
Comment: The size of the coffin, the portrait, and the playing cupids indicate that the sarcophagus commemorated a girl or a young woman.

Bibliography: *MNR* I 8, 1, cat. II, 18.

38 BUST OF A LEARNED WOMAN

Location/Inv.: Rome, Museo Nazionale Romano, inv. 106215.
Size (lid): L: 0.34 H: 0.22 D: 0.13
Condition: Fragment of a lid.
Provenience: Rome, Monteverde.
Lid: A bust of a woman with a scroll is shown in front of a *parapetasma* held by a cupid. For a description, see *MNR* I 10, 2, cat. 239.
Portrait: The bust is carved with female portrait features.
Dating: Second quarter of the fourth century (*MNR* I 10, 2, cat. 239).

Bibliography: *MNR* I 10, 2, cat. 239.

39 LEARNED MAN

Location/Inv.: Rome, Museo Nazionale Romano, inv. 124741.
Size (coffin): L: 2.02 H: 0.52 D: 0.55
Condition: The coffin is preserved.
Frontal relief: Divided into five panels. The second and fourth panels are strigillated. Cupids are depicted on the first and fifth panels. A man with a scroll is represented in front of a *parapetasma* on the central panel.
Short ends: Weapons.
Portrait: The man on the central panel is represented with portrait features.
Dating: First half of the third century (*MNR* I 7, 2, cat. XII, 13).

Bibliography: *MNR* I 7, 2, cat. XII, 13.

40 *CLIPEUS* PORTRAIT OF A LEARNED GIRL

Location/Inv.: Rome, Museo Nazionale Romano, inv. 475044.
Condition: The coffin is preserved.
Frontal relief: Divided into five panels. The second and fourth panels are *strigillated*. A learned girl with a scroll is represented in a *clipeus* on the third panel, and on the first and fifth, a cupid with a down-turned torch is seen. Two *cornucopias* are shown beneath the *clipeus*.
Short ends: Without relief decoration.
Portrait: The bust in the *clipeus* is carved with the portrait features of a girl.
Dating: Late third century or early fourth based on the hairstyle and the style of the portrait.
Comment: Child sarcophagus.

41 BUST OF A LEARNED MAN

Location/Inv.: Rome, Vatican, The necropolis beneath S. Pietro.
Size (coffin): L: 1.90 H: 0.58 D: 0.61; (lid): L: 1.92 H: 0.30 D: 0.59
Condition: The lid and coffin are preserved.
Provenience: The tomb of the Valerii (Mausoleum H). Found together with five other sarcophagi (Dresken-Weiland 2003, cat. A 110).
Frontal relief: The coffin is strigillated with a lion-horse group represented on each end of the relief.
Short ends: *Lenos*-shaped. The lion-horse group of the frontal relief continues on the short ends.
Lid: Central panel with an inscription. A scene with hunting cupids is shown on the right side of the panel, and on the left side there is a female bust with a scroll in front of a *parapetasma* held by two cupids.
Portrait: The bust on the lid is carved with a blank portrait.
Inscription: D M / T(ito) CAESENIO SEVERI / ANO BENEMERENTI / CAESENII / FAVSTINVS POMPE / IANVS ET RVFINVS / PATRI INCOMPARABI / LI
Dating: 260-270 (*ASR* VI 1, cat. 377).
Comment: The inscription mentions a man and his two sons, who buried him. The hairstyle of the roughly carved bust was prepared with a female coiffure but the bust shows no indications of breasts.

Bibliography: Stroszeck, *ASR* VI 1 (1998) cat. 377; Dresken-Weiland 2003, cat. A 110; Birk 2012, 112.

42 *CLIPEUS* PORTRAIT OF A WOMAN REPRESENTED AS A MUSE (FIG. 38)

Location/Inv.: Rome, Villa Doria Pamphilj.
Size (coffin): L: 2.12 H: 0.55
Condition: The coffin is preserved.
Frontal relief: The relief is divided into five panels. The second and fourth panels are strigillated. A sleeping cupid leaning against a torch is shown on the first and fifth panels. The central panel depicts a *clipeus* with a bust of a woman represented as a Muse. Two *cornucopiae* are placed beneath the *clipeus*. For a description, see Calza 1977, cat. 268.
Short ends: *Lenos*-shaped. The motif of the first panel continues on the short ends.
Portrait: The Muse in the *clipeus* is carved with a female portrait.
Dating: Around the middle of the third century (Calza 1977, cat. 268).

Bibliography: Calza 1977, cat. 286, pl. CLIII.

43 BUSTS OF A LEARNED WOMAN AND MAN

Location/Inv.: Rome, Villa Doria Pamphilj, Casino Belrespiro.
Condition: The front relief of the lid is preserved.
Lid: A central inscription panel is flanked by busts of a woman and a man. Both hold scrolls. A *parapetasma* held by two

cupids is suspended behind the busts. For a description, see Calza 1977, cat 260.
Portrait: The two busts are carved with respectively a female and a male portrait.
Inscription: M(ARCO) AVRELIO / SECVNDO / FILIO DVLCISSIMO QVI VIXIT AN/NIS XXXVIIII DIEBVS / XLVIII REFRIGE / RET ISPITITVS
Dating: 250-90 (Calza 1977, cat. 260).
Comment: Mother and son (?).

Bibliography: Calza 1977, cat. 260, pl. CIL; *CIL* VI 13224

44 *CLIPEUS* PORTRAIT OF A LEARNED MAN

Location/Inv.: Rome, Villa Doria Pamphilj.
Size (coffin): L: 1.74 H: 0.48 D: 0.46
Condition: The coffin is preserved.
Frontal relief: The relief is divided into five panels. The second and fourth panels are strigillated. A sleeping cupid leaning on a torch is shown on the first and fifth panels. The central panel depicts a *clipeus* with a portrait bust of a man with a scroll. Two *cornucopiae* are placed beneath the *clipeus*. For a description, see Calza 1977, cat. 269.
Short ends: The motif of the first panel continues on the short end.
Portrait: The *clipeus* bust i carved with a blank portrait.
Dating: The first half of the third century (Calza 1977, cat. 269).

Bibliography: Calza 1977, cat. 269, pl. CLIII.

45 EDUCATED WOMAN AND A LEARNED MAN (PHILOSOPHER)

Location/Inv.: Rome, lost. Previously on the art market.
Size (coffin): L: 1.05 H: 0.43
Condition: Various joint fragments (*ASR* V 2, 1, cat. 61).
Frontal relief: A man and a woman are seated opposite each other. Eight of the Nine Muses are depicted behind them. The woman is probably a substitute for the ninth Muse. The coffin was *lenos*-shaped. For a description, see *ASR* V 2, 1 cat. 62.
Portrait: The male and the female figures have portraits carved in modern times, probably from blank portraits.
Dating: 250-270 (*ASR* V 2, 1, cat. 62).

Bibliography: Kranz, *ASR* V 2, 1 (1999) cat. 62, pl. 51, 2.

46 BUST OF A LEARNED MAN

Location/Inv.: St. Petersburg, Hermitage, inv. A 1222.
Size (coffin): L: 1.96 H: 0.49 D: 0.50
Condition: The coffin is preserved.
Frontal relief: Divided into five panels. The second and fourth panels are strigillated. A sleeping cupid leaning against a torch is shown on the first and fifth panels. The central panel depicts a bust of a man on a small pedestal holding a scroll. He is surrounded by hanging garlands.
Short ends: Weapons.
Portrait: The bust is carved with the portrait features of a man or a boy.
Dating: Middle of the third century (Saverkina 1979, cat. 26).

Bibliography: Saverkina 1979, cat. 26, pl. 56.

Cupids Harvesting

47 BUST OF A LEARNED WOMAN

Location/Inv.: Berlin, Klein Glienicke.
Size (coffin): L: 0.98 H: 0.29
Condition: The lid is preserved.
Lid: A bust of a woman in front of a *parapetasma* held by cupids. Other cupids are harvesting on the left end of the lid. A cupid with a basket (a seasonal personification) is seen on the right end. For description, see *ASR* V 2, 2, cat. 10.
Portrait: The bust is carved with a blank portrait.
Dating: 290-300 (*ASR* V2, 2, cat. 10).

Bibliography: Bielefeld, *ASR* V 2, 2 (1997) cat. 10, pl. 51, 4.

48 BUST OF A LEARNED WOMAN

Location/Inv.: Nepi, S. Biagio. Built into the wall of the church.
Size (coffin): L: 2.20 H: 0.36
Condition: The lid is preserved. Minor fragments have been lost and the surface is damaged.
Lid: A central inscription panel. *Putti* harvesting grapes are represented on the left end, and on the right end a bust of a woman with a scroll is depicted in front of a *parapetasma*. For a description, see *ASR* V 2, 2, cat. 57.
Portrait: The female bust is carved with a portrait. The surface is damaged.
Inscription: D M / VELIAE PV / MIDIAE / MAXILLE / C(oniux) / F(ecit) AVRELI / VS PROPIN / QVS V(ixit) C(um) V / XORI KARISSI / MAE
Dating: 280-300 (ARS V 2, 2, cat. 57).

Bibliography: Bielefeld, *ASR* V 2, 2 (1997) cat. 57, pl. 49, 2.

49 BUST OF A VEILED LEARNED WOMAN (FIG. 41)

Location/Inv.: Rome, Catacombe di Pretestato, Museo, inv. 21.
Size (lid): L: 0.86 H: 0.38
Condition: Fragment of a lid.
Provenience: Rome, Le Catacombe di Pretestato.
Lid: A bust of a woman with a scroll is represented in front of a *parapetasma*. Cupids harvesting are depicted on the right side of the bust. For a description, see *ASR* V 2, 2, cat. 91.
Portrait: The bust is carved with a female portrait.
Dating: 260/270 (*ASR* V 2, 2, cat. 91).

Bibliography: Bielefeld, *ASR* V 2, 2 (1997) cat. 91, pl. 49, 4.

50 BUST OF A LEARNED GIRL (FIG. 87)
Location/Inv.: Rome, Musei Capitolini, Palazzo Conservatori, inv. MC 2428/S.
Size (coffin): L: 2.10 H: 0.25
Condition: Both the lid and the coffin are preserved.
Frontal relief: The coffin is decorated with cupids harvesting grapes.
Short ends: Lenos-shaped. The motif of the frontal relief continues on the short end.
Lid: A central inscription panel is held by two cupids. The left end is lost but on the right end, a bust of a girl with a scroll is represented in front of a *parapetasma.* For a description, see *ASR* V 2,2, cat. 140.
Portrait: The bust on the lid is carved with a blank portrait.
Inscription: VARENA / Q(uinta) FLAVIAE / SEVERINE / FILIAE DVL / CISSIME QVE / VIX(it) ANN(is) II / M.. D XVII
Dating: Around 280 (*ASR* V 2, 2, cat. 140).
Comment: The inscription commemorates a girl. The bust was prepared for a man/boy. Child sarcophagus.

Bibliography: Kranz, *ASR* V 4 (1984) cat. 546; Bielefeld, *ASR* V 2, 2 (1997) 124-25, cat. 140, pl. 19, 1; Koch & Sichtermann 1982, 258.

51 LEARNED WOMAN
Location/Inv.: Rome, Musei Capitolini, Palazzo Nuovo, Sala del Fauno 28, inv. Albani C 47.
Size (lid): L: 1.37 H: 0.37
Condition: The lid is preserved.
Lid: A scene with cupids harvesting grapes is depicted on the left side of a central inscription panel. On the right side of the panel a bust of a woman with a scroll is placed in front of a *parapetasma*.
Portrait: The bust is carved with a portrait of a young woman.
Inscription: AVRELIA / SVSILIA / MATER / FECIT / FILIA / R(equiescat) / MATERNE / IN PACE
Dating: 300 (*ASR* V 2, 2, cat. 118).

Bibliography: Bielefeld, *ASR* V 2, 2 (1997) cat. 118, pl. 49, 1.

52 BUSTS OF A LEARNED WOMAN AND LEARNED MAN
Location/Inv.: Rome, Muzeo Nazionale Romano, inv. 124711.
Size (coffin): L: 2.21 H: 0.37 D: 0.90
Condition: The coffin and lid are preserved.
Frontal relief: Dionysian *thiasoi* among vines. Dionysus himself is standing on the right end of the relief.
Lid: A central inscription panel. On the left side of the panel, cupids are depicted harvesting and pressing grapes. On the right side, a bust of a woman and a man, both with scrolls, are represented in front of a *parapetasma* held by two cupids. For a description, see *ASR* V 4, cat. 335.
Portrait: The busts are carved with blank portraits.
Dating: Tetrarchic period (*ASR* V 4, cat. 335).

Bibliography: Kranz, *ASR* V 4 (1984) cat. 335, pl. 95, 3; Zanker & Ewald 2004, 157; *MNR* I 8, I, cat. I, 3 (with description of the coffin).

53 BUST OF A LEARNED BOY
Location/Inv.: Ronchinne (Namur), built into the walls of the castle.
Size (lid): L: 0.83 H: 0.17
Condition: The lid is preserved.
Lid: A central inscription panel. On the right side, there is a bust with a scroll in front of a *parapetasma* held by cupids, and on the left side cupids are harvesting. For a description, see *ASR* V 2, 2, cat. 187.
Portrait: The bust is carved with a blank portrait.
Dating: Early fourth century (*ASR* V 2, 2, cat. 187).
Comment: Child sarcophagus.

Bibliography: Bielefeld, *ASR* V 2, 2 (1997) cat. 187, pl. 71, 5.

Death Door

54 LEARNED WOMAN, MUSE, AND LEARNED MAN (FIG. 68)
Location/Inv.: Córdoba, Alcázar de los Reyes Cristianos.
Size (coffin): L: 2.37 H: 1.08
Condition: The coffin is preserved.
Frontal relief: Divided into three niches framed by columns. Two women with scrolls are represented on the first panel. Behind them is a parapetasma, and a kantharos with fruit and a bird on top is placed on their right. Two men are represented on the third panel. The man in front is holding a scroll, and the other man is a philosopher with a generic head. The central panel depicts a door decorated with lion and ram heads. The gable is decorated with peacocks and another vase, and the acroteria are carved as palmettes and tritons.
Short ends: Pegasus and a lion.
Portrait: The two women on the first panel and the man with the scroll on the third panel have portrait features.
Dating: Around 270 (*ASR* I 3, cat. 11).

Bibliography: Reinsberg, *ASR* I 3 (2006) cat. 11, pl. 79, 1.

55 PIOUS WOMAN AND A LEARNED MAN (FIG. 67)
Location/Inv.: Firenze, Museo dell' Opera del Duomo.
Size (coffin): L: 2.46 H: 1.19 D: 1.27
Condition: The coffin is preserved.
Frontal relief: Divided into three niches framed by columns. A veiled woman is represented on the first panel. A *Kantharos* with fruit and a bird on top is placed to the right of her. A man with scrolls is represented on the third panel. On his right is a citula and additional scrolls, and a small scale boy is standing on his left. A *parapetasma* is suspended behind both of them. A door decorated with heads of Medusa and lions is depicted on the central panel, and flying *victeriae* are decorating the gable.
Short ends: Griffin.

Portrait: The woman on the first panel and the man on the third panel have portrait features.
Dating: 240-250 (*ASR* I 3, cat. 14).

Bibliography: Reinsberg, *ASR* I 3 (2006) cat. 14, pl. 74, 2.

56 LEARNED MAN

Location/Inv.: Genzano, Villa Riva.
Size (coffin): L: 2.29 H: 0.84 D: 0.86
Condition: The coffin is preserved.
Frontal relief: Divided into five panels. The second and fourth panels are strigillated. A woman is represented on the first panel (her hands and head are restored), and a man clad in a toga holding a scroll is represented on the fifth panel. A *parapetasma* is suspended behind both of them. A door decorated with heads of Medusa and lions are depicted on the central panel. For a description, see Ewald 1999, cat. A 10.
Short ends: A seated philosopher with a scroll.
Portrait: The man on the right panel has portrait features. The head of the woman and the hands of both figures are modern restorations (Ewald 1999, cat. A 10).
Dating: 240, because of similarities between the portrait of Maximinus Thrax and the man (Ewald 1999, cat. 10 A).

Bibliography: Ewald 1999, cat. A 10, pl. 7, 1.

57 WOMAN AND A LEARNED MAN

Location/Inv.: Pisa, Camposanto A 8 est.
Condition: The coffin is preserved.
Frontal relief: Divided into five panels. The second and the fourth panels are strigillated. A woman is represented on the first panel and a man with scrolls is represented on the fifth panel. Both the man and the woman stand on statue bases and a *parapetasma* is suspended behind them. A death door decorated with personifications of the four seasons is depicted on the central panel. For a description, see Arias 1977, A 8 est.
Left short end: Griffins flanking a candelabrum.
Right short end: Pegasus.
Portrait: The woman and the man are carved with blank portraits.
Dating: 210-220 (Arias 1977, 60).

Bibliography: Arias 1977, A 8 est, pl. 8, 1.

58 SACRIFICING WOMAN AND LEARNED MAN

Location/Inv.: Rome, Musei Vaticani, Cortile del Belvedere.
Size (coffin): L: 2.39 H: 1.20
Condition: The frontal relief is preserved.
Frontal relief: Four columns divide the relief into three niches. A woman is represented in the first niche and a man with a scroll is shown in the third niche. The central niche frames a death door.
Portrait: The woman in the first and the man in the third niche are carved with portraits.
Dating: 250 (*ASR* I 3, cat. 151).

Bibliography: Reinsberg, *ASR* I 3 (2006) cat. 151, pl. 78, 1.

Decorative Scheme

59 WOMAN AND LEARNED MAN

Location/Inv.: Paris, art market. Lost. 1943.
Size (coffin): L: 2.12 H: 1.00
Condition: Fragment of the frontal relief.
Frontal relief: Strigillated with a central panel representing a man and a woman together. The man holds a scroll, and a bird and a chest are depicted at the woman's feet. The woman turns her face towards the man.
Portrait: The man and the woman are both carved with portrait features.
Dating: 280 (*ASR* I 3, cat. 162).

Bibliography: Reinsberg, *ASR* I 3 (2006) cat. 162, pl. 115, 2.

60 LEARNED MEN

Location/Inv.: Rome, Catacombe de Pretestato, Museo.
Size (coffin): L: 2.00 H: 0.45
Condition: The frontal relief is preserved.
Frontal relief: Strigillated with two end panels and a *mandorla*. A man (*togatus*) with a diptych is represented on the left panel, and a magistrate with a scroll is represented on the right panel.
Portrait: The men on the first and fourth panels are carved with portrait features.
Dating: 330-40 (*ASR* I 3, cat. 74).

Bibliography: Reinsberg, *ASR* I 3 (2006) cat. 74, pl. 50, 3.

61 *CLIPEUS* PORTRAIT OF A LEARNED MAN

Location/Inv.: Rome, Catacombe di S. Sebastiano.
Size (coffin): L: 1.94 H: 0.52 D: 0.56
Condition: The coffin is preserved.
Frontal relief: Divided into five panels. Number two and four are strigillated. A column is represented on the first and fifth panels. A *clipeus* with a bust of a man holding a scroll is depicted on the central panel, and two *cornucopiae* are shown beneath the *clipeus*.
Lid: Dolphins and inscription.
Portrait: The man on the central panel is carved with a portrait.
Inscription: FL(avius) PATRICIVS VIR HONESTVS INNOCENTIS/SIMVS ET PVDENTISSIMVS QVI VIXIT ANNIS / XXVII MENSIBVS XI DIEBVS IIII DEPOSITVS IN / PACE XII KAL(endas) FEB(ruarii) D(ominis) N(osris) CONSTANTIO AUG(usto) / X et IVLIANO CAES(are) III CONS(ulibus). AVR(elia) REDEMP/TA MATER [F]ILIO BENE MENENTI F(ecit)
Dating: 360 (inscription) (*Rep.* I, cat. 238).

Bibliography: *Rep.* I, cat. 238.

62 BUSTS OF TWO LEARNED MEN

Location/Inv.: Rome, Musei Vaticani, Galleria Lapidaria. Inv. 9261.
Size (coffin): L: 2.06 H: 1.02 D: 0.76; (lid) H: 0.29

Condition: The coffin and lid are preserved.
Frontal relief: Strigillated sarcophagus with a portrait bust at each end: one of a man in *sagum* with a scroll and one of a bearded man in toga, also holding a scroll. Both are placed on plinths. The central *mandorla* does not show any figural decoration. For a description, see Amelung 1903, 285-6.
Short ends: Weapons.
Lid: Decorated with harvesting, dancing, and playing cupids. An empty inscription panel is placed in the middle of the composition.
Portrait: The two busts are carved with portraits of two different men, the left with a beard and the right without a beard.
Dating: Late third century (ASR V 2, 2, cat. 209).

Bibliography: Amelung 1903, 285, cat. 162; Kranz, *ASR* V 2, 1 (1999) cat. 139; Bielefeld, *ASR* V 2, 2 (1997) cat. 209; Baratta 2004, 194.

63 *CLIPEUS* PORTRAIT OF A LEARNED CHILD

Location/Inv.: Rome, Museo Nazionale Romano, inv. 115247.
Size (coffin): L: 1.47 H: 0.46 D: 0.64
Condition: The coffin is preserved.
Provenience: Via di Decima, Rome (Dresken-Weiland 2003, cat. A 86).
Frontal relief: Strigillated with a central *clipeus* showing a bust of a child holding a scroll. A cockfight is represented beneath the *clipeus* and a column is depicted on each end of the relief.
Short ends: Without relief decoration.
Reverse: Without relief decoration.
Portrait: The *clipeus* bust is carved with a portrait of a girl or boy.
Dating: First half of the fourth century (*MNR* I 3, cat. III, 11).
Comment: Child sarcophagus.

Bibliography: *MNR* I 3, cat. III, 11; Dresken-Weiland 2003, cat. A 86.

64 LEARNED WOMAN

Location/Inv.: Rome, Museo Nazionale Romano, inv. 135929.
Size (coffin): L: 1.21 H: 0.38 D: 0.45
Condition: The coffin is preserved.
Provenience: Via dei Marconisti, presso la Via Laurentina. Together with another Sarcophagus (*MNR* inv. 135930).
Frontal relief: Strigillated with a central panel showing a woman in front of a *parapetasma.* A small chest and scrolls are depicted at her feet. A column is depicted on each end of the relief.
Portrait: The woman on the central panel is carved with portrait features.
Dating: First quarter of the fourth century (*MNR* I 8, 2, cat. VII, 14).

Bibliography: *Rep.* I, cat. 780; *MNR* I 8, 2, cat. VII, 14.

65 *CLIPEUS* PORTRAIT OF A LEARNED MAN

Location/Inv.: Rome, Museo Nazionale Romano, inv. 172189.
Size (coffin): L: 2.23 H: 0.72 D: 0.72
Condition: The coffin is preserved.
Provenience: Fidena, Via S. Gimignano (Dresken-Weiland 2003, cat. A 10).
Frontal relief: Strigillated with a central *clipeus* showing a bust of a boy holding a scroll. A pilaster is depicted on each end of the relief. Two *cornucopiae* are placed beneath the *clipeus.*
Short ends: Roughly carved.
Reverse: Roughly carved.
Portrait: The *clipeus* bust is carved with male portrait features.
Dating: First quarter of the third century (*MNR* I 7, 2, cat. X, 9).
Comment: One skeleton was found in the coffin.

Bibliography: *MNR* I 7, 2, cat. X, 9; Dresken-Weiland 2003, cat. A 10.

66 LEARNED MAN AND LEARNED WOMAN

Location/Inv.: Rome, Ospedale di S. Giovanni, Oratorio di S. Andrea, portico.
Condition: The coffin is preserved.
Frontal relief: Divided into four panels with a central *mandorla* with a vase. The second and third panels are strigillated. A learned man is represented on the first panel and a learned woman is shown on the fourth.
Short ends: Strigillation continues onto the curved short ends.
Portrait: Both the man and the woman have blank portraits.
Dating: Third century.

67 *CLIPEUS* PORTRAIT OF A LEARNED WOMAN

Location/Inv.: Rome, Vatican, necropolis beneath S. Pietro, Mausoleum H, inv. SK12/inv. S6.
Size: L: 1.80 H: 0.74 D: 0.42
Condition: The lid and coffin are preserved.
Provenience: The tomb of the Valerii (Mausoleum H) (Dresken-Weiland 2003, cat. 110).
Frontal relief: Strigillated with a central *clipeus* showing a bust of a woman holding a scroll. The *clipeus* is placed on a plinth.
Lid: Dolphins and trident.
Portrait: The bust is carved with a portrait of a woman.
Inscription: DM / POMPEIAE MARITIM(a)E / MATRI / T(itus) OMO(eius) PROCVLVS SVCCES(sus) / B(ene) M(erenti) FECIT
Dating: 230 (Wolf 1977).

Bibliography: Wolf 1977, 86-86, sark S6; Eck 1986, 263, nr. 16; Dresken-Weiland 2003, cat. A 110.

Eros and Psyche

68 *CLIPEUS* PORTRAIT OF A LEARNED MAN (FIG. 3)

Location/Inv.: Copenhagen, Ny Carlsberg Glyptotek, inv. 1890.
Size (coffin): L: 1.95 H: 0.63 D: 0.60
Condition: The coffin is preserved, but extensively restored.

Frontal relief: A *clipeus* with a bust of a man holding a scroll is held by two flying cupids. An Eros and Psyche group is depicted on each end of the relief. Oceanus and Tellus are represented lying beneath the *clipeus*. For a description, see Østergaard 1996, cat. 50.
Short ends: Lenos-shaped. The motif of the frontal relief continues on the short ends.
Portrait: The bust is carved with a male portrait.
Dating: 250-270 (Østergaard 1996, cat. 50).

Bibliography: Østergaard 1996, cat. 50.

69 LEARNED MAN (PHILOSOPHER)

Location/Inv.: Genoa, S. Lorenzo.
Size (coffin): L: 2.00 H: 0.45
Condition: The frontal relief is preserved.
Frontal relief: Divide into five panels. The second and fourth panels are strigillated. Eros and Psyche are represented on the first and fifth panels. A seated philosopher is represented on the central panel. For a description, see Ewald 1999, cat. D 8.
Portrait: The seated philosopher is carved with a blank portrait.
Dating: The end of the third or the beginning of the fourth century (Ewald 1999, cat. D 8).

Bibliography: Ewald 1999, cat. D 8, pl. 47, 2.

70 *CLIPEUS* PORTRAIT OF A LEARNED GIRL

Location/Inv.: Rome, Catacombe di S. Callisto.
Size (coffin): L: 0.78 H: 0.38
Condition: The frontal is presented (fragmentary).
Frontal relief: Two cupids support a *clipeus* with a bust of a girl holding a scroll. A scene with Eros and Psyche embracing is depicted on the right side of the *clipeus*, and a ram-bearer is shown further to the right of this scene. A child with fruit baskets is placed beneath the *clipeus*. The left end is lost.
Portrait: The *clipeus* bust is carved with a portrait of a young girl.
Dating: Early fourth century (Huskinson 1996, cat. 10. 8).
Comment: Child sarcophagus.

Bibliography: *Rep.* I, cat. 381; Huskinson 1996, cat. 10. 8.

71 BUST OF A LEARNED MAN

Location/Inv.: Rome, Musei Vaticani; Galleria Lapidaria, inv. 8806.
Size (lid): L: 0.95 H: 0.36
Condition: A fragment of the lid is preserved.
Lid: Eros and Psyche hold a *parapetasma* suspended behind a bust of a man with a scroll. A man pouring wine from a cask is represented on the left. To the right, part of an inscription panel is preserved.
Portrait: The bust in front of the *parapetasma* has a portrait of a middle-aged man with a beard. It could be a re-carving because of the depth of the relief around the head.
Inscription: Illegible. It seems, however, to be a formulaic inscription, since fragments of a name and the number of lived years are still visible.
Dating: Gallienic (*ASR* I 4, cat. 259).

Bibliography: Amedick, *ASR* I 4 (1991) cat. 259, pl. 109, 4.

72 *CLIPEUS* PORTRAIT OF LEARNED BOY

Location/Inv.: Rome, S. Giovanni in Laterano, Museo della Basilica.
Size (coffin): L: 1.70 H: 0.46 D: 0.52
Condition: The coffin is preserved.
Frontal relief: A central *clipeus* with a bust of a boy held by two cupids. More cupids with arrows, *cithara*, *pedum*, and a mirror (?) are depicted on each side of the *clipeus* and another two cupids and a *kantharos* are placed beneath the *clipeus*.
Short ends: Lenos-shaped. Eros and Psyche.
Portrait: The *clipeus* bust is carved with a portrait of a boy.
Dating: 270-290 (*ASR* V 2, 1, cat. 94).
Comment: Child sarcophagus.

Bibliography: Kranz, *ASR* V 2, 1 (1999) cat. 94, pl. 55, 3.

73 BUST OF A WOMAN AND A LEARNED MAN

Location/Inv.: Rome, Vatican. The necropolis beneath S. Pietro.
Size (lid): L: 2.25 H: 0.98 D: 1.04
Condition: The coffin and lid are preserved.
Provenience: Rome, Vatican Necropolis, Mausoleum Phi, tomb of the Marcii. The sarcophagus was placed centrally in the room on an *opus sectile* floor (Dresken-Weiland 2003, cat. A 107).
Frontal relief: Divided into five panels. The second and fourth panels are strigillated. A maenad is represented on the first panel and a satyr with baby Dionysus are shown on the fifth panel. The central panel depicts Dionysus supported by a satyr.
Short ends: Without relief decoration.
Lid: Busts of a woman and of a man with a scroll in front of a *parapetasma* are placed on each side of a central inscription tablet. The *parapetasma* behind the woman is held by two Psyche figures and the *parapetasma* behind the man by two Eros figures. The tablet is supported by two satyrs.
Portrait: The two busts on the lid are carved with the portraits of a man and a woman.
Inscription: Q MARCIVS / HERMES SIBI / ET MARCIAE / THRASONIDI / DIGNISSIMAE / CONIVGI / POSVIT
Dating: Around the reign of Alexander Severus (*ASR* IV 4, cat. 306); 250-260 (Andreae 1984, 121-23).

Bibliography: Matz, *ASR* IV 4 (1975) cat. 306, pl. 323, 2; Andreae 1984, 121-23; Dresken-Weiland 2003, cat. A 107: Liverani & Spinola 2010, fig. 33.

74 *CLIPEUS* PORTRAIT OF A LEARNED WOMAN

Location/Inv.: Rome, Villa Doria Pamphilj.
Condition: The coffin is preserved.

Frontal relief: Two seasonal personifications hold a central *clipeus* with a bust of a woman with a scroll. Eros and Psyche are represented on each side of this composition. A lion killing a deer is depicted on each end of the relief. A scene showing children watching a cockfight is placed beneath the *clipeus*. For description, see *ASR* VI, 1, cat. 354.
Short ends: *Lenos*-shaped. The lion-deer group of the frontal relief continues on the short ends.
Portrait: The *clipeus* bust is carved with a female portrait.
Dating: 260-270 (*ASR* VI 1, cat. 354).

Bibliography: Calza 1977, Stroszeck, *ASR* VI 1(1998) cat. 354, pl. 67, 2.

75 LEARNED WOMAN

Location/Inv.: Sesto Fiorentino, Villa Guicciardini.
Size (coffin): L: 2.04 H: 0.54
Condition: The coffin is preserved.
Frontal relief: Divided into five panels. The second and fourth panels are strigillated. Eros and Psyche are represented on the first and fifth panels. A woman with a scroll and two Muses in front of a *parapetasma* are represented on the central panel. For a description, see Ewald 1999, cat. F 12.
Short ends: Without relief decoration.
Portrait: The woman with a *palla* has portrait features.
Dating: Around 300 (Ewald 1999, cat. F 12).

Bibliography: Wegner, *ASR* V 3 (1966) cat. 220; Ewald 1999, cat. F 12, pl. 74, 4.

Garlands

76 BUST OF A LEARNED WOMAN

Location/Inv.: Rome, Museo Torlonia.
Condition: The coffin is preserved.
Frontal relief: Garlands held by seasonal personifications frame a bust of a woman with a scroll. Two masks are depicted above the garlands. For a description, see Herdejürgen 1996a.
Portrait: The bust is carved with female portrait features.
Dating: 260 (Herdjürgen 1996a, 498).

Bibliography: Herdejürgen 1996a, fig. 29.

77 LEARNED BOY

Location/Inv.: Rome, Palazzo Mattei. Built into the wall in the courtyard.
Condition: The frontal relief is preserved.
Frontal relief: Garlands held by seasonal personifications frame a full-length figure of a boy in front of a *parapetasma*. Scrolls are placed at his feet. Two masks are shown above the garlands. For a description, see Herdejürgen 1996a.
Portrait: Boy.
Dating: Around 240 (Herdjürgen 1996a).
Comment: Child sarcophagus.

Bibliography: Herdejürgen 1996a, fig. 20.

78 BUSTS OF A WOMAN AND A LEARNED GIRL (FIG. 94)

Location/Inv.: Rome, S. Maria in Aracoeli.
Condition: The coffin is preserved.
Frontal relief: Two garlands are held by a dancing satyr. Above each garland is a bust. The left bust is female and the right bust, which is male, holds a scroll. Both busts are carved with female portraits. Baskets with fruit and children playing with animals are depicted beneath the garlands. For a description, see Herdejürgen 1996.
Short ends: *Lenos*-shaped. The motif of the frontal relief continues on the short ends.
Portrait: The female bust is carved with a female portrait and the male bust is carved with a portrait of a girl.
Dating: Beginning of the third century (Herdejürgen 1996a, 485).
Comment: Cross-gendered. A girl's portrait has been carved on a male bust.

Bibliography: Herdejürgen 1996a, fig. 1; Prusac 2011, 119.

79 BUST OF A LEARNED MAN

Location/Inv.: Rome, S. Paolo fuori le mura.
Condition: The coffin is preserved.
Frontal relief: Divided into three panels. A bust of a boy with a scroll is represented on the central panel. The bust is flanked by two burning torches and is supported by acanthus leaves. The right and left panels are adorned with garlands held by cupids. A mask is depicted above the garlands and two birds eating grapes from a basket are depicted beneath.
Portrait: The bust is carved with a portrait of a youth.
Dating: 270 (Herdejürgen 1996a, 500).

Bibliography: Herdejürgen 1996a, fig. 32.

80 BUSTS OF A WOMAN AND A LEARNED MAN

Location/Inv.: Rome, Villa Albani.
Condition: The coffin is preserved.
Frontal relief: Three seasonal personifications hold two garlands. A bust is depicted above each garland. The left bust is female and holds a piece of fruit. The right bust is male and holds a scroll. For a description, see Herdejürgen 1996a.
Short ends: *Lenos*-shaped. Garlands and fruit baskets.
Portrait: The busts are carved with blank portraits.
Dating: Tetrarchic period (Herdejürgen 1996a, 502).

Bibliography: Herdejürgen 1996a; Bielefeld 1998, pl. 4, 3.

Hunting

81 BUST OF A LEARNED MAN

Location/Inv.: Ferentillo, Abbazia S. Pietro in Valle.
Size (coffin): L: 2.01 H: 0.28 D: 0.54

Condition: The lid is preserved. It may have belonged to another sarcophagus found at the same place (*ASR* I 2, cat. 30).
Provenience: Ferentillo.
Lid: A *Sigma-Mahl* is represented on the left end of the relief and a hunting scene is represented on the right end. A bust of a man with a scroll dressed in a toga is depicted in a central panel. For a description, see *ASR* I 2, cat. 29.
Portrait: The bust is carved with a portrait of a man, apparently with a beard.
Dating: Late Tetrarchic period (*ASR* I 2, cat. 29).

Bibliography: Andreae, *ASR* I 2 (1980) cat. 29; Rodenwaldt 1921/22, 70; Himmelmann-Wildschütz 1973, 65, cat. 54.

82 LEARNED WOMAN AND LEARNED MAN (FIG. 37)

Location/Inv.: Rome, Musei Capitolini, Palazzo Nuovo, inv. MC 9/S (courtyard).
Size (coffin): L: 2.17 H: 1.42
Condition: The coffin and lid are preserved.
Provenience: Catacombs of S. Sebastiano (Dresken-Weiland 2003, cat. D 12).
Frontal relief: Divided into three panels. A man is represented on the first panel, and a woman on the third panel. Both figures are placed in front of a *parapetasma* and have scrolls at their feet. Beside the woman there is furthermore a chest with a lock. The second panel is strigillated with a central *mandorla* depicting a figure of Victoria writing on a shield.
Short ends: Without relief decoration.
Lid: Hunt scenes and a central inscription panel without an inscription.
Portrait: The man and the woman are carved with portrait features.
Dating: 320-330 (*ASR* I 2, cat. 105).

Bibliography: Andreae, *ASR* I 2 (1980) cat. 105; Dresken-Weiland 2003, cat. D 12; Brandenburg 2004, 11; La Rocca & Presicce 2010, 40-5 with a full bibliography.

Learned Sphere

(See also addendum A3)

83 LEARNED WOMAN

Location/Inv.: Amalfi, Cathedral.
Condition: Fragment of the left end of a coffin.
Frontal relief: A seated woman is represented dressed in a *palla* and holding a scroll. A lyre is placed in front of her on a pedestal (the lyre may be held by a Muse?). For a description, see Ewald 1999, cat. E 31.
Short ends: Lenos-shaped. Weapons.
Portrait: The seated woman is carved with a blank portrait.
Dating: Last third of the third century (Ewald 1999, cat. E 31).

Bibliography: Ewald 1999, cat. E 31, pl. 59, 1.

84 LEARNED MAN (PHILOSOPHER)

Location/Inv.: Berlin, Schloss Klein-Glienicke, inv. GI. 84.
Size (coffin): L: 0.41 H: 0.50
Condition: A fragment of the frontal relief is preserved.
Frontal relief: A philosopher (or magistrate?) clad in a toga is seated on a *cella curulis* and holds a scroll in his left hand. For a description, see *ASR* I 3, cat. 8.
Portrait: The seated man has portrait features.
Dating: 260-270 (*ASR* I 3, cat. 8).
Comment: Reinsberg (1995, 368) interprets him as a magistrate.

Bibliography: Reinsberg, *ASR* I 3 (2006) cat. 8, pl. 100, 1; Reinsberg 1995.

85 LEARNED MAN (PHILOSOPHER) AND HUNTER

Location/Inv.: Berlin, Staatliche Museen, inv. 6596.
Size (coffin): L: 2.10 H: 0.67 D: 0.81
Condition: The coffin is preserved.
Frontal relief: A seated philosopher with scrolls at his feet is represented in architectural surroundings. In front of him, there is a scene with grape harvest activities mixed with hunters departing for a hunt. One of the hunters is on horseback. For a description, see Schmidt 1993.
Short ends: Without relief decoration.
Portrait: The seated philosopher and horseman have portrait features.
Dating: Last quarter of the third century (Ewald 1999, cat. G 3).

Bibliography: Bielefeld, *ASR* V 2, 2 (1997) cat. 13; Schmidt 1993; Ewald 1999, cat. G 3, pl. 93, 2.

86 BUST OF A LEARNED MAN

Location/Inv.: Cagliari, Cathedral, cript.
Size (coffin): L: 2.05 H: 0.56; (lid) H: 0.27
Condition: The lid and coffin are preserved.
Frontal relief: Divided into five panels. The second and fourth are strigillated. A bust of a man with a scroll is represented on the central panel. The bust is placed on an acanthus leaf pedestal and is framed by garlands. A herm is placed on each end of the relief. For a description, see Pesce 1957, 74-9.
Short ends: Unknown.
Lid: Central inscription panel with a post-antique inscription. On both sides of the panel, there are scenes with representations of philosophers.
Portrait: The bust on the frontal relief is carved with male portrait features.
Inscription: MEMORIA ANTIOCHI PRAESBYTER. Post-antique inscription.
Dating: Late third century (Ewald 1999, cat. I 5); 270 based on the portrait (Pesce 1957, cat. 31).

Bibliography: Pesce 1957, cat. 31; Ewald 1999, cat I 5, pl. 98, 3.

87 PHILOSOPHER

Location/Inv.: Catania.

Size (coffin): L: 0.40 H: 0.30
Condition: Fragment of a frontal relief.
Frontal relief: A herm, a sage, and a seated philosopher with portrait features.
Portrait: The seated philosopher is represented with a male, bearded portrait.
Dating: Third quarter of the third century (Ewald 1999, cat. C 21).

Bibliography: Ewald 1999, cat C 21, pl. 35, 3.

88 EDUCATED WOMAN AND LEARNED MAN (PHILOSOPHER)

Location/Inv.: Civita Castellana, Bishop's Palace, inv. 490.
Size (coffin): L: 2.14 H: 0.50
Condition: The coffin is preserved.
Frontal relief: Divided into four panels. The second and third are strigillated. On the first panel, a seated woman is playing a lyre, and on the left panel there is a bare-chested philosopher. A *parapetasma* is suspended behind both of them. For a description, see *ASR* V 3, cat. 25.
Short ends: *Lenos*-shaped. The strigillation continues onto the short ends.
Portrait: The seated woman and the philosopher are carved with blank portraits.
Dating: Second half of the third century (Ewald 1999, cat. E 23).
Comment: "Lycian-motif"

Bibliography: Wegner, *ASR* V 3 (1966) cat. 25, pl. 112a-b; Ewald 1999, cat. E 23.

89 *CLIPEUS* PORTRAIT OF A LEARNED WOMAN

Location/Inv.: Copenhagen, Ny Carlsberg Glyptotek, inv. 853.
Size (coffin): L: 2.10 H: 0.54 D: 0.59
Provenience: Probably from a burial chamber in Vigna Jacabini, Rome (see Meinecke 2012, 95)
Condition: The coffin is preserved.
Frontal relief: The relief is divided into five panels. The second and fourth panels are strigillated. A Muse is represented on the first and fifth panels (Melpomene & Thaleia). A *clipeus* with a bust of a woman with a scroll is depicted on the central panel. Beneath the *clipeus,* there is a scene with a peasant milking a goat.
Short ends: Roughly carved.
Portrait: The bust is carved with a blank portrait.
Dating: 310-320 (Østergaard 1996, cat. 43).
Comment: Thought by Wegner (*ASR* V 3, cat. 35) to be a forgery which, however, was refuted by Gabelmann in his review of the same publication.

Bibliography: Wegner, *ASR* V 3 (1966) cat. 35, pl. 151, 1; Gabelmann 1968, 539-40; Østergaard 1996, cat. 43.

90 *ORANS* AND LEARNED MAN

Location/Inv.: Lyon, Musée des Beaux-Arts.
Condition: The coffin is preserved.
Frontal motif: Divided into four panels with a central *mandorla* showing an amphora. The second and third panels are strigillated. A semi-*Orans* is represented on the first panel and a man with scrolls at his feet is represented on the fourth.
Short ends: Weapons.
Portrait: The semi-*Orans* wears a portrait of a woman, and the learned man has a portrait of a man. Both heads have been damaged.
Dating: Second half of the third century (Ewald 1999, cat. F 19).

Bibliography: Matz 1968b, 300-10, cat. 8, pl. 111; Ewald 1999, cat. F 19.

91 MUSE AND LEARNED MAN (PHILOSOPHER)

Location/Inv.: Marseille, Musée d'Histoire de la ville de Marseille.
Size (coffin): L: 2.12 H: 0.72
Provenience: Found in the area around the cathedral (*ASR* V 3, cat. 35).
Condition: The coffin is preserved.
Frontal relief: Divided into five panels. The second and fourth panels are strigillated. A Muse with scrolls is represented on the first, and a philosopher is represented on the fifth panel. The central panel depicts a scene with a seated philosopher and a Muse (Polyhymnia). For a description, see *ASR* V 3, cat 53.
Portrait: The philosopher and the Muse on the central panel are represented with portrait features.
Dating: 250 (Ewald 1999, cat. C 7).

Bibliography: Wegner, *ASR* V 3 (1966) cat. 53; Ewald 1999, cat. C 7, pl. 35, 2.

92 LEARNED WOMAN AND LEARNED MAN

Location/Inv.: Massa, Villa Massoni.
Size (coffin): L: 2.22 H: 0.57
Condition: The coffin is preserved.
Frontal relief: Divided into five panels. The second and fourth panels are strigillated. A veiled woman (scroll now lost) is represented on the first panel, and a man in a toga is represented on the fifth panel. Both have scrolls at their feet, and a *parapetasma* is suspended behind them. The central panel depicts a scene with a seated philosopher and a Muse (Polyhymnia type). For a description, see Ewald 1999, cat. C 8.
Short ends: Without relief decoration.
Portrait: The woman on the first panel and the man on the fifth panel are carved with blank portraits.
Dating: Between the late second century to after the middle of the third century (Ewald 1999, cat. C 8).

Bibliography: Koch & Sichtermann 1982, 202, note 94; Ewald 1999, cat. C 8, pl. 26, 1.

93 EDUCATED WOMAN AND A LEARNED MAN (PHILOSOPHER) (FIG. 36)

Location/Inv.: Milan, Museo Castello Sforzesco.

Size (coffin): L: 0.37 H: 0.52 (left fragment); L: 0.49 H: 0.52 (right fragment).
Provenience: Two fragments of a frontal relief are preserved.
Frontal relief: A seated woman with naked shoulder playing a lyre is depicted on the left fragment. Part of a Muse is visible behind her. A seated man with a scroll is represented on the right fragment. A philosopher with naked chest is visible beside him. For a description, see *ASR* V 3, cat 47.
Portrait: The seated woman and man are carved with blank portraits.
Dating: Late third century (*ASR* V 3, cat. 47).

Bibliography: Wegner, *ASR* V 3 (1966) cat. 47, pl. 111b; Ewald 1999, cat. E 33.

94 EDUCATED WOMAN AND MAN (PHILOSOPHER)

Location/Inv.: Milan, privately owned.
Size (coffin): L: 2.35 H: 0.92
Condition: The coffin is preserved.
Frontal relief: Divided into four panels. The second and third panels are strigillated. A woman seated in a basket chair is represented on the first panel. She is playing a lyre and in front of her is a Muse (Polyhymnia). A man seated in a chair with lion feet-shaped legs is depicted on the fourth panel. In front of him is a Muse (Urania). A *parapetasma* is suspended behind both of the seated figures. The central decoration is a *mandorla* with an amphora. For a description, see Piacentini 1961.
Short ends: Strigillated.
Portrait: The seated woman and man are carved with blank portraits.
Dating: Late third century. For discussion, see Ewald 1999, cat. E 15.

Bibliography: Piacentini 1961; Wegner, *ASR* V 3 (1966) cat. 48; Ewald 1999, cat. E 15, pl. 60, 1.

95 LEARNED MAN (PHILOSOPHER)

Location/Inv.: New York, The Metropolitan Museum of Art, inv. 48.76.1.
Size (coffin): L: 2.14 H: 0.55 D: 0.58
Condition: The coffin is preserved.
Frontal relief: Divided into three panels. The first and third panels are strigillated. A philosopher reading a scroll is represented on the central panel. He is seated in a chair and dressed in a *pallius* and a tunic. Beside him there is a closet with scrolls and a vessel. On top of the closet, there is an object that looks like an open toolbox.
Short ends: Roughly carved.
Reverse: Roughly carved.
Portrait: The seated philosopher has portrait features.
Inscription: Greek inscription carved into the profile around the central panel and on the upper profile. See Ewald 1999, 114-15.
Dating: Tetrarchic period (Ewald 1999, C 34; Koch & Sichtermann 1982, 122); 300 (*ASR* I 4, cat. 81).
Comment: Interpreted as a doctor in front of a cabinet (Hillert 1990, cat. 29; Cuomo 2007, 93).

Bibliography: Amedick, *ASR* I 4 (1991) cat. 81; Koch & Sichtermann 1982, 122, note 16; Hillert 1990; Ewald 1999, cat. C 34; CUOMO 2007.

96 EDUCATED WOMAN

Location/Inv.: Ostia, Museo, inv. 1263.
Size (coffin): L: 1.42 H: 1.08
Condition: Part of the frontal relief is preserved.
Frontal relief: Originally divided into five panels. The second and fourth panels are strigillated. A woman seated in a chair is represented on the first panel. She plays a lyre and wears a chiton and a *palla*. Her right shoulder is naked. The central decoration is a column with a vase on top. For a description, see Ewald 1999, cat. E 30.
Portrait: The seated woman is carved with a blank portrait.
Dating: Late third century (Ewald 1999, cat. E 30).
Comment: "Lycian motif".

Bibliography: Ewald 1999, cat. E 30, pl. 65, 1.

97 LEARNED WOMAN AND FEMALE PHILOSOPHER (FIG. 42)

Location/Inv.: Ostia, Museo, inv. 48277.
Size (coffin): L: 2.12 H: 0.65 D: 0.64
Condition: The coffin is preserved.
Provenience: Isola Sacra, tomb 34. For further description, see Baldassarre 1991/92, 305-22; Dresken-Weiland 2003, cat. A 95.
Frontal relief: Divided into five panels. The second and fourth panels are strigillated. A woman with scrolls is represented on the first panel and a male figure with a cloak and a short tunic is represented on the fifth panel. The central panel depicts a scene with a seated philosopher and a Muse (Polyhymnia). A *parapetasma* behind the figures was at some point converted into trees with leaves. For a description, see Baldassarre 1991/92, 315-19.
Short ends: Without relief decoration.
Reverse: Smooth band on the lower part, then a sharp edge and a rough surface made by a pick axe. The upper band is smooth like the first.
Portrait: The seated philosopher on the central panel and the figure on the fifth panel have both been carved with female features.
Dating: Late Severan to early Tetrarchic period (Ewald 1999, cat. C 10). A stylistic comparison with cat. nos. 102, 103, 110, and 119 suggests a dating around 250-275.
Comment: The sarcophagus was re-worked but never finished. It is noteworthy that it seems to have been worth re-working, but not worth finishing the figural decoration. The pattern of the reverse indicated that the sarcophagus was carved from a previously used blok, probably an architrave (for this perspective, see Birk forthcoming). One skeleton was found in the coffin.

Bibliography: Baldassarre 1991/92, 305-22, fig. 8; Ewald 1999, cat. C 10; Dresken-Weiland 2003, cat. A 95.

98 LEARNED WOMAN AND LEARNED MAN

Location/Inv.: Ostia, Necropol at Porta Romana.
Size (coffin): L: 2.16 H: 0.66 D: 0.73
Condition: The coffin is preserved.
Frontal relief: Divided into five panels. The second and fourth panels are strigillated. A woman with a scroll is represented on the first panel and a philosopher is represented on the fifth panel. A *parapetasma* is suspended in the background. The central panel depicts a philosopher or magistrate in an *aedicula*. For a description, see Ewald 1999, cat. F 4.
Right short end: Lion and panther with wings.
Portrait: The woman on the first panel and the man in the central *aedicula* have portrait features.
Dating: Around the middle of the third century (Ewald 1999, cat. F 4).

Bibliography: Ewald 1999, cat. F 4, pl. 72, 1.

99 LEARNED MAN (PHILOSOPHER)

Location/Inv.: Palestrina, Villa Fiorini.
Condition: Fragment of the frontal relief (the fifth panel of a strigillated sarcophagus).
Frontal relief: Seated philosopher with a scroll. Two Muses are standing at his side. For a description, see *ASR* V 3, cat. 71.
Portrait: The seated philosopher is carved with portrait features.
Dating: Early fourth century (Ewald 1999, cat. E 34).

Bibliography: Wegner, *ASR* V 3 (1966) cat. 71, pl. 124,b; Ewald 1999, cat. E 34.

100 WOMAN, LEARNED BOYS, AND MILITARY MAN

Location/Inv.: Pisa, Camposanto B 1 EST.
Size (coffin): L: 2.28 L: 1.30 D: 1.54
Condition: The coffin is preserved.
Frontal relief: Divided into five panels. The second and fourth panels are strigillated. A woman is represented on the first and a man in a cuirass is represented on the fifth panel. Two young men with scrolls are represented on the central panel. For a description, see *ASR* I 3, cat. 54.
Short ends: *Lenos*-shaped.
Reverse: Reused sarcophagus; lion heads turned back to front.
Portrait: The two boys on the central panel have portrait features, and the woman and the man on the first and fifth panels are carved with blank portraits.
Inscription: S(e)P (ulcrum) FALCHONO(rum) and a cross. The inscription is placed on the left upper profile and can be dated to the 14th century. The Falconi were a merchant family from that time.
Dating: Around 230 (*ASR* I 3, cat. 54).
Comment: The sarcophagus is often referred to as the 'Tabernakel' or 'brother sarcophagus'.

Bibliography: Reinsberg, *ASR* I 3 (2006) cat. 54, pl. 31, 3; Andreae 1984.

101 SACRIFICING MAN AND LEARNED MEN

Location/Inv.: Pisa, Camposanto C 8 est.
Size (coffin): L: 2.11 H. 0.68 D: 0.63
Condition: The coffin is preserved.
Frontal relief: Divided into five panels. The second and fourth panels are strigillated. The central panel depicts a *togatus* with scrolls in an *aedicula*. A man dressed in a tunic and *paludamentum* making a sacrifice is represented on the first panel. A man in *pallium* with scrolls at his feet is represented on the fifth panel. A *parapetasma* is suspended in the background. All the figures are placed on statue bases. For a description, see Ewald 1999, cat. F 5.
Left short end: Griffins flanking a vase.
Right short end: Pegasus and a *krater*.
Portrait: The three men are carved with blank portraits. Today the heads are badly weathered.
Dating: Second half of the third century (Ewald 1999, cat. F 5). Reinsberg has, however, suggested a date around 160-170 (*ASR* I 3, cat. 55).

Bibliography: Reinsberg, *ASR* I 3 (2006) cat. 55; Arias et al. 1977, 133; Ewald 1999, cat. F 5, pl. 72, 2.

102 LEARNED WOMAN (FIG. 39)

Location/Inv.: Pisa, Camposanto C 10 est.
Size (coffin): L: 2.06 H: 0.68
Condition: The coffin is preserved.
Frontal relief: Divided into five panels. The second and fourth panels are strigillated. A woman with chiton and a bird at her feet is represented on the first panel. A philosopher (*pallium* without tunic) is represented on the fifth panel. A *parapetasma* is suspended behind both figures. The central panel depicts a seated philosopher and a veiled woman/Muse. All the figures are placed on statue bases. For a description, see Ewald 1999, cat. C 5.
Short ends: Griffin.
Portrait: The woman on the first panel has portrait features.
Dating: The sarcophagus has played a central role in the discussion of early strigillated sarcophagi because the female hairstyle covers the ears. The sarcophagus may therefore be dated before 250 (Ewald 1999, cat. C 5). Arias dated it to 260-270 (Arias et al. 1977).

Bibliography: Arias et al. 1977; Ewald 1999, cat. C 5, pl. 28, 1.

103 LEARNED WOMAN

Location/Inv.: Porto Torres (Sardinia), Basilica di S. Gavino, Cripta.
Size (coffin): L: 2.06 H: 0.55 D: 0.54
Condition: The coffin is preserved.
Frontal relief: Divided into five panels. The second and fourth panels are strigillated. The central panel depicts a scene with a seated philosopher and a Muse (Polyhymnia). A woman holding a scroll (now lost) is represented on the first panel, and a philosopher is represented on the fifth. A *parapetasma* is

suspended behind all the figures. For a description, see Ewald 1999, cat. C 9.
Short ends: Griffin.
Portrait: The woman on the first panel has portrait features.
Dating: Between 240-250 and the first part of the fourth century. For discussion, see Ewald 1999, cat. C 9.

Bibliography: Wegner, *ASR* V 3 (1966) cat. 81; Ewald 1999, cat. C 9, pl. 27, 1.

104 LEARNED MAN (PHILOSOPHER)

Location/Inv.: Ravenna, Museo Nazionale.
Size (coffin): L: 0.87 H: 0.31 D: 0.30
Condition: The coffin is preserved.
Frontal relief: A young girl with a chest, a veiled semi-*Orans*, and a philosopher are represented on the left part of the relief. The central group consists of a seated philosopher with scrolls at his feet and a Muse (Polyhymnia) placed in front of a *parapetasma*. Bucolic scenery with sheep and a ram-bearer is depicted on the right side of the relief. For a description, see Ewald 1999, cat. C 3.
Left short end: A cupid in a boat.
Right short end: A fisherman at sea.
Portrait: The seated philosopher on the central scene is carved with a blank portrait.
Dating: Around 300 (Ewald 1999, cat. C 3).

Bibliography: Wilpert I, pl. 2, 2; Ewald 1999, cat. C 3.

105 LEARNED MAN (PHILOSOPHER)

Location/Inv.: Rome, Catacombe di Domitilla, Basilica di Petronilla.
Condition: Fragmented. The left end of the coffin is lost.
Frontal relief: Divided into three panels with a central *mandorla* without decoration. The second panel is strigillated. A seated philosopher with scrolls is represented on the third panel. The first panel is lost. For a description, see Ewald 1999, cat. E 20.
Portrait: The seated philosopher has the portrait features of a young man (boy?).
Dating: Last quarter of the third century (Ewald 1999, cat. E 20).
Comment: "Lycian motif".

Bibliography: Wegner, *ASR* V 3 (1966) cat. 96; Wilpert I, 12, pl. 5, 7; Bovini 1949, 273, cat. 23; Ewald 1999, cat. E 20.

106 LEARNED MAN, WOMAN, AND *CLIPEUS* PORTRAIT OF A MAN

Location/Inv.: Rome, Catacombe di Domitilla.
Condition: The coffin is preserved.
Provenience: Catacomba di Domitilla together with two lion head/strigillated sarcophagi (Dresken-Weiland 2003, cat. D 22).
Frontal relief: Divided into five panels. The second and fourth panels are strigillated. A man with a scroll is represented on the first panel, and a woman is represented on the fifth panel. A *clipeus* with a bust of a man is depicted on the central panel and two *cornucopiae* are displayed below the *clipeus*.
Portrait: The man on the first panel, the woman on the fifth panel, and the male *clipeus* bust have portrait features.
Dating: 250/260 (*ASR* V 2, 2, p. 116, cat. 89).

Bibliography: Bielefeld, *ASR* V 2, 2 (1997) cat. 89; Nuzzo 2000, 47, fig. 60, Dresken-Weiland 2003, cat. D 22.

107 EDUCATED WOMAN

Location/Inv.: Rome, Catacombe Ebraica di Vigna Randanini.
Size (coffin): 2.03 H: 0.64 D: 0.69
Condition: Fragments of a coffin.
Provenience: From a *cubiculum* in the catacombs.
Frontal relief: Divided into four panels with a central *mandorla* with a vase. The second and third panels are strigillated. A seated woman in a basket chair is represented on the first panel. She is playing a lyre and in front of her is a Muse. Opposite her, on the third panel, a man seated in a chair with lion feet-shaped legs is depicted. In front of him is a philosopher. A *parapetasma* is suspended behind both of the seated figures. For a description, see Ewald 1999, cat. E 16.
Short sides: *Lenos*-shaped. The decoration of the frontal relief continues on the short ends.
Portrait: The seated woman is carved with a blank portrait.
Dating: Late Gallienic period (Ewald 1999, cat. E 16).

Bibliography: Ewald 1999, cat. E 16, 177.

108 LEARNED MAN (PHILOSOPHER)

Location/Inv.: Rome, Catacombe di Pretestato.
Size (coffin): L: 0.55 H: 0.40
Condition: Fragment of a frontal relief.
Provenience: Catacombe di Pretestato.
Frontal relief: Strigillated. A seated philosopher with a scroll and two Muses are represented on the preserved panel. For a description, see *ASR* V 3, cat. 108.
Portrait: The seated philosopher is carved with a blank portrait.
Dating: Late third century (Ewald 1999, cat. C 26).

Bibliography: Wegner, *ASR* V 3 (1966) cat. 108, pl. 122b; Ewald 1999, cat. C 26.

109 LEARNED WOMAN (PHILOSOPHER)

Location/Inv.: Rome, Catacombe di Pretestato.
Size (coffin): L: 0.48 H: 0.37
Condition: Fragment of a lid.
Lid: A bust of a woman with a scroll is placed in front of a *parapetasma*. A Muse with a lyre is depicted to the right of the bust.
Portrait: The bust is carved with a female portrait.
Dating: 283-285 on the basis of stylistic similarities with the portrait of Urbica, wife of Carinus (Ewald 1999, cat. I 29).

Bibliography: Ewald 1999, cat. I 29, fig. 12.

110 LEARNED WOMAN AND MUSE

Location/Inv.: Rome, Musei Capitoloni, Palazzo dei Conservatori, Galleria 20, inv. 966.
Size (coffin): L: 2.17 H: 0.63
Condition: The frontal relief is preserved.
Frontal relief: Divided into five panels. The second and fourth panels are strigillated. A philosopher is represented on the first panel and a veiled woman with a scroll is represented on the fifth panel. Her right hand was once raised but is now lost. The central panel depicts a seated philosopher and a Muse. For a description, see *ASR* V 3, cat. 121.
Portrait: The Muse on the central panel has portrait features. As noted by Ewald, the head seems slightly too small for the body and it is possible that the head was re-carved from a generic face into a portrait. The woman on the fifth panel has portrait features as well. Ewald sees them as portraits of two different women.
Dating: 250-275. For discussion, see Ewald 1999, cat. C 22.

Bibliography: Wegner, *ASR* V 3 (1966) cat. 121, pl. 76 b; Ewald 1999, cat. C 22.

111 LEARNED WOMAN AND A MAN (PHILOSOPHER) (FIG. 83)

Location/Inv.: Rome, Musei Capitolini, Palazzo dei Conservatori, Sala dei Monumenti Cristiani, inv. MC 1329/S.
Size (coffin): L: 1.90 H: 0.62 D: 0.59
Condition: The coffin is preserved.
Provenience: Discovered in 1957 at Via Salentini, Rome.
Frontal relief: Divided into five panels. The second and fourth panels are strigillated. A woman seated in a chair is represented on the first panel. She is veiled and wears a tunic and a *palla*. The fifth panel depicts a man seated in a chair with lion feet-shaped legs. He is dressed in a tunic and a *pallium*. Both figures hold scrolls and beside them is a Muse. A *parapetasma* is suspended behind both of them. The central panel depicts a ram-bearer (head restored). For a description, see Ewald 1999, cat. E 17.
Short sides: Without relief decoration.
Portrait: The seated woman and man on the first and fifth panels are carved with blank portraits.
Dating: Last third of the third century (Ewald 1999, cat. E 17).
Comment: "Lycian motif".

Bibliography: *Rep.* I, cat. 817; Ewald 1999, cat. E 17, pl. 63, 1-2.

112 LEARNED WOMAN

Location/Inv.: Rome, Musei Capitolini, Staircase II (beneath the Marcus Aurelius reliefs), inv. 819.
Size (coffin): L: 1.95 H: 0.60 D: 0.56
Condition: The coffin is preserved in its entirety. A minor breakage is found on the middle of the lower profile on the frontal relief. The lid is not preserved.
Frontal relief: Divided into four panels with a central *mandorla* with schematic decoration. The second and third panels are strigillated. A veiled woman with a scroll is represented on the first panel and a bare-chested philosopher with is represented on the fourth panel. For a description, see Ewald 1999, cat. F 17.
Short ends: Weapons carved in a very low relief.
Reverse: Roughly cut. The bottom 25 cm is smooth and polished.
Portrait: The woman on the first panel has portrait features. The face of the philosopher is lost, but the remains of the beard suggests that it was a generic figure.
Dating: Second third of the third century, on the basis of the woman's hairstyle (Ewald 1999, cat. F 17).

Bibliography: Ewald 1999, cat. F 17.

113 LEARNED MAN AND A PHILOSOPHER

Location/Inv.: Rome, Musei Capitolini, staircase II (beneath the Marcus Aurelius reliefs), inv. 821.
Size (coffin): L: 2.24 H: 0.60 D: 0.65
Condition: The coffin is preserved.
Frontal relief: Divided into four panels with a central *mandorla* with schematic decoration. The second and third panels are strigillated. A female figure with a scroll is represented on the first panel and a bare-chested philosopher is represented on the fourth panel. For a description, see Ewald 1999, cat. F 18.
Short ends: Weapons carved in a very low relief.
Reverse: Roughly cut. The bottom 25 cm is smooth and polished.
Portrait: On the panel to the right is a male portrait, which should probably be dated to the first part of the third century. The portrait on the left panel is likewise a male portrait but on a female body. The remains of either a female hairstyle or a *bosse* prepared for a female hairstyle are still traceable.
Dating: 225-250 (Ewald 1999, cat. F 18).
Comment: Ewald (1999) does not see the left figure as originally intended for a woman but explains the strange un-plastic body and drapery as a post-antique re carving. Jones, however, thought that the figure was originally female. In line with Jones, I think the figure was re-carved in antiquity from a female to a male figure by altering the clothes and the portrait features.

Bibliography: Stuart Jones 1968, cat. 15; Ewald 1999, cat F 18.

114 LEARNED WOMAN, MUSES, AND PHILOSOPHERS (FIG. 44)

Location/Inv.: Rome, Musei Vaticani, Cortei del Belvedere, inv. 871.
Size (coffin): L: 2.50 H: 1.36
Condition: The frontal relief and the two short end reliefs are preserved but separated from each other. The frontal relief has been extensively restored.
Frontal relief: A veiled woman with a *palla* and scroll is represented in the central *aedicula*. Holding on to her is a naked boy. A seated man dressed in a *pallium* and a standing woman (with a *palla*), both holding scrolls, are depicted in the left and right *aediculae*. In the background, there is a girl with a

dress tied beneath the breast, in the fashion of the Muses. The group has been interpreted as consisting of a father, a mother, and a daughter (Ewald 1999, cat. E 1). For a description, see *ASR* V 3, cat. 135.
Left short end: Three women /Muses.
Right short end: Three women /Muses.
Portrait: The woman in the central *aedicula* together with the three figures in the left and the right *aediculae* have portrait features. It is probably the same family portrayed twice. The three women on the short ends are supposed, on the basis of the hairstyle, to have portrait features as well (Ewald 1999, cat. E 2).
Dating: Around 240 because of stylistic similarities between the portrait of Pulpienus and the deceased man. For discussion, see Ewald 1999, cat. E2.
Comment: It is unusual that the figures on the short end reliefs have portrait features.

Bibliography: Wegner, *ASR* V 3 (1966) cat. 135; Wrede 1981, cat. 243; Koch & Sichtermann 1982, 201; Zanker 1995, 259-60; Ewald 1999, cat. E 1, pl. 48, 1.

115 LEARNED BOY (PHILOSOPHER) (FIG. 69)

Location/Inv.: Rome, Musei Vaticani, Galleria dei Candelabri I 20, inv. 2422.
Size (coffin): L: 1.16 H: 0.46; (lid): H: 0.44
Condition: The coffin and lid are preserved.
Frontal relief: A boy with scrolls is represented as an enthroned philosopher in front of a *parapetasma*. He is surrounded by children endowed with the attributes of the Muses.
Short ends: Lenos-shaped. The motif of the frontal relief continues on the short ends.
Lid: A three-dimensional sculpture of a reclining boy.
Portrait: The seated philosopher on the frontal relief and the reclining boy on the lid have portrait features. The portraits on the relief and lid are so similar that they probably depict the same boy.
Dating: 270-280 (*ASR* V 3, cat. 139; Huskinson 1996, cat. 5.5; Ewald 1999, cat. D 5; *ASR* V 3, cat. 139).
Comment: Child sarcophagus.

Bibliography: Wegner, *ASR* V 3 (1966) 58, cat. 139, pl. 59; Gabelmann 1968, 539; Paduano Faedo 1981, 92-3; Zanker 1995, 260-61; Huskinson 1996, 38-9; cat. 5. 5; Ewald 1999, 169, cat. D 5.

116 LEARNED MAN (PHILOSOPHER) AND MUSES (FIG. 46)

Location/Inv.: Rome, Musei Vaticani, Museo Gregoriano Profano, inv. 9504.
Size (coffin): L: 2.40 H: 1.50
Condition: Fragment of the central part of a frontal relief. For a discussion of its preservation, see Ewald 1999, cat. D 3.
Frontal motif: A seated philosopher reading a scroll is flanked by two Muses. The Muse on his right side holds a scroll. Both Muses are veiled. Behind the group are three philosophers, with a *parapetasma* suspended behind them. For a description, see Ewald 1999, cat. D 3.
Portrait: The seated philosopher and the two Muses at his side have portrait features.
Dating: Around 280 (Fittschen 1972, 491).
Comment: Rodenwaldt suggested in 1922 that this was the sarcophagus of Plotinus (Rodenwaldt 1922, 122; Rodenwaldt 1936, 102); this is not generally accepted today (Fittschen 1972; 1979). The philosopher on the right end of the relief was originally a female figure, as can be seen from its long dress.

Bibliography: Wegner, *ASR* V 3 (1966) cat. 116, pl. 71; Rodenwaldt 1921/22; 122; 1936, 102; Fittschen 1972, 491-92; 1979; Ewald 1999, cat. D 3.

117 LEARNED MAN (PHILOSOPHER) AND MUSE

Location/Inv.: Rome, Musei Vaticani, magazine, inv. 9516.
Size (coffin): L: 0.84 H: 0.26
Condition: The frontal relief is preserved.
Frontal relief: Strigillated (vertical) with a central panel representing a seated philosopher and a standing Muse (Polyhymnia). For a description, see *ASR* V 3, cat. 115.
Portrait: The Muse and the philosopher are carved with blank portraits.
Dating: Late third century (Ewald 1999, cat. C 38).
Comment: Child sarcophagus.

Bibliography: Wegner, *ASR* V 3 (1966) cat. 115, pl. 119b; Ewald 1999, cat. C 38.

118 LEARNED MAN (PHILOSOPHER) (FIG. 45)

Location/Inv.: Rome, Museo Nazionale Romano, inv. 12265.
Size (coffin): L: 0.14 H: 0.07
Condition: Fragment of a frontal relief.
Frontal relief: Head of a seated figure with a Muse by his side. A *parapetasma* is suspended behind them. For a description, see Ewald 1999, cat. K 10.
Portrait: The seated figure is carved with a portrait of a boy or a young man.
Dating: Middle to late third century (Ewald 1999, cat. K 10).

Bibliography: Ewald 1999, cat. K 10; *MNR* I 10, 1, cat. 37.

119 LEARNED WOMAN AND MAN (PHILOSOPHER)

Location/Inv.: Rome, Museo Nazionale Romano, inv. 112329.
Size (coffin): L: 2.13 H: 0.64 D: 0.65
Condition: The coffin is preserved.
Provenience: Rome, found in 1930 near the Portonaccio Station together with two other sarcophagi (Museo Nazionale Romano, inv. 112328 and inv. 112327). For further information on the location, see Ewald 1999, cat. C 32.
Frontal relief: Divided into five panels. The second and fourth panels are strigillated. A veiled woman with a scroll or, and more likely, a poppy is represented on the first panel. A philosopher (dressed in a *pallium* without a tunic) with a scroll is represented on the fifth panel. Both figures have a *parapetasma* suspended behind them. A seated philosopher and a male bust

on a column are depicted on the central panel. For a description, see Ewald 1999, cat. C 32.
Short ends: Roughly carved.
Reverse: Smooth but without relief decoration.
Portrait: The woman on the first and the man on the fifth panels are carved with blank portraits.
Dating: Gallienic (Ewald 1999; *MNR* I 8, cat V 9).

Bibliography: Ewald 1999, cat. C 32, pl. 26, 3; *MNR* I 8, cat. V 9, p. 238-39.

120 LEARNED MAN (PHILOSOPHER) AND MUSE

Location/Inv.: Rome, Museo Torlonia, inv. 424.
Size (coffin): L: 2.22 H: 1.33
Condition: The coffin and lid are preserved.
Provenience: Found five miles from Porta S. Giovanni, Rome, between Via Appia and Via Latina.
Frontal relief: A man reading a scroll and a woman are represented as a philosopher and his Muse. To their left and right are Muses and sages. For a description, see *ASR* V 3, cat. 133.
Short ends: Three satyrs with *pedum* are pressing grapes.
Lid: Panel with inscription flanked by peacocks and cupids.
Portrait: The seated philosopher has portrait features, and his veiled Muse has a blank portrait.
Inscription: L(vcio) PVLLIO PEREGRINO (centurioni) LEGION(is) / DEPVTATO QVI VIX(it) ANN(os) XXVIIII / MEN(es) III DIE(s) I HOR(as) I S(emis) / EQ(viti) R(omano)
Dating: 250 or slightly later (*ASR* V 3, cat. 133).
Comment: Traces of golden paint are preserved on both the hair and the beard.

Bibliography: Wegner, *ASR* V 3 (1966) cat. 133, pl. 60; Bielefeld *ASR* V 2, 2 (1997) cat. 142; Rodenwaldt 1936, 101; Himmelmann-Wildschütz 1962, 122-23; Andreae 1969; 1984, 119-20; Wrede 1981, cat. 246; Ewald 1999, 47, cat. C 1 (with full bibliography).

121 EDUCATED WOMAN

Location/Inv.: Rome, Palazzo Corsini.
Size (coffin): L: 2.12 H: 0.92 D: 0.87
Condition: The coffin and lid are preserved.
Frontal relief: Divided into five panels. The second and fourth panels are strigillated. A woman seated in a chair is represented on the first panel. She is playing a lyre and around her are three Muses. A man seated in a chair with lion feet-shaped legs is represented on the fifth panel. Three philosophers are depicted around him. The central decoration is a *mandorla* with a ram-bearer. For a description, see Ewald 1999, cat. E 22.
Short ends: Roughly carved.
Lid: The central panel is an empty inscription panel. When the sarcophagus was found traces of paint and gilt, probably from a painted inscription, were still visible. A race with wagons, cupids harvesting, and at the corners masks of Sol and Selene are depicted on the left and right side of the inscription panel.
Portrait: The seated woman has portrait features but they have been re-carved in modern times. The head of the man is not preserved.
Dating: 300 (Koch & Sichtermann 1982, 202; Ewald 1999, cat. E 22).
Comment: The head of the woman has been re-carved from a *bosse*. The plait on top of her head is roughly carved.

Bibliography: *Rep.* I, cat. 945; Koch & Sichtermann 1982, 202; Ewald 1999, cat. E 22, pl. 61, 3.

122 *ORANS*

Location/Inv.: Rome, Palazzo Sanseverino, Via del Corso 519.
Size (coffin): L: 1.05
Condition: The frontal relief is preserved.
Frontal relief: Divided into five panels. The central panel depicts a scene with a seated philosopher reading a scroll and a Muse leaning against a column. The second and fourth panels are strigillated. A veiled woman dressed in *palla* is represented on the first panel and a ram-bearer is represented on the fifth panel. For a description, see Ewald 1999, cat. C 15.
Portrait: The woman on the first panel has portrait features (probably re-worked in a post-antique period).
Dating: End of the third century (Ewald 1999, cat. C 15).

Bibliography: Ewald 1999, cat. C 15, pl. 29, 1. 22.

123 LEARNED WOMAN

Location/Inv.: Rome, S. Maria in Trastevere.
Size (coffin): L: 0.44 H: 0.58
Condition: A fragment of the frontal relief is preserved.
Frontal relief: A woman dressed in *palla* and with a scroll in her left hand is represented on the relief. Behind her is a mask on a pedestal. For a description, see Ewald 1999, cat. F 16.
Portrait: The woman is carved with a blank portrait.
Dating: Second half of the third century (Ewald 1999, cat. F 16).

Bibliography: Ewald 1999, cat. F 16, pl. 83, 4.

124 LEARNED MAN (PHILOSOPHER)

Location/Inv: Rome, Via del Corso.
Condition: A fragment of the frontal relief is preserved.
Frontal relief: Strigillated. The fragment shows a philosopher with a *pallium* and naked chest. He is placed on a statue base and a box for scrolls is depicted at his feet. A *parapetasma* is suspended behind him. For a description, see Ewald 1999, cat. F 35.
Portrait: The philosopher is carved with a male portrait. The portrait is damaged and the features are difficult to recognise.
Dating: Second half of the third century (Ewald 1999, cat. F 35).

Bibliography: Ewald 1999, cat. F 35, pl. 84, 4.

125 LEARNED MAN (PHILOSOPHER)

Location/Inv.: Rome, Villa Albani.
Size (coffin): L: 0.65 H: 0.87

Condition: A fragment of the frontal relief is preserved (left figure panel of a strigillated sarcophagus).
Frontal relief: A bare-chested philosopher with a scroll stands on a statue base. A *parapetasma* is suspended behind him. For a description, see Bol 1998, 837.
Portrait: The philosopher is carved with a blank portrait.
Dating: Second half of the third century (Ewald 1999, cat. F 36); 210-220 (Bol 1998, cat. 837).

Bibliography: Bol 1998, cat. 837, pl. 149; Ewald 1999, cat. F 36.

126 LEARNED WOMAN

Location/Inv.: Rome, Villa Albani.
Size (coffin): L: 0.36 H: 0.48
Condition: A fragment of the frontal relief is preserved (part of the left figure panel of a strigillated sarcophagus).
Frontal relief: Seated woman in front of a *parapetasma*. According to the repetitive decorative scheme of Roman sarcophagi she should be reconstructed with a lyre or a scroll. For a description, see Bol 1998, cat. 667.
Portrait: The seated woman has portrait features.
Dating: Second half of the third century (Ewald 1999, cat. E 36).

Bibliography: Bol 1998, cat. 667, pl. 63b; Ewald 1999, cat. E 36.

127 LEARNED MAN (PHILOSOPHER)

Location/Inv.: Rome, Villa Albani, built into the Coffee House.
Size (coffin): L: 0.51 H: 0.80
Condition: The two end panels of a strigillated sarcophagus have been separated from the rest of the coffin and built into a wall.
Frontal relief: A seated woman and a Muse are represented on one of the fragments. A seated philosopher with a scroll is depicted on the other fragment. Another Muse stands beside him. A *parapetasma* is suspended behind both of them. For a description, see Bol 1998, cat. 777 and 783.
Portrait: The philosopher is carved with a male portrait. The head of the seated woman has not been preserved.
Dating: Tetrarchic period (Ewald 1999, cat. E 32).
Comment: The surface is badly weathered.

Bibliography: Bol 1998, cat. 777 and 783, pl. 137; Ewald 1999, cat. E 32.

128 LEARNED WOMAN

Location/Inv.: Rome, Villa Doria Pamphilj.
Size (coffin): L: 0.90 H: 0.39 D: 0.35
Condition: The coffin is preserved.
Frontal relief: Divided into four panels. A learned woman or a Muse (Calliope?) with a scroll and a philosopher are represented on the first panel. Apollo and a Muse (Euterpe) are represented on the fourth panel. The two central panels are strigillated. For a description, see Calza 1977, cat. 267.
Short ends: Strigillated.
Portrait: The head of the learned woman is carved with a portrait. It can be compared to female portraits from the period of Julia Memea (Calza 1977, cat. 267).
Dating: 220-230s (Calza 1977, cat. 267). From the first to the third quarter of the third century. For discussion, see Ewald 1999, cat. H 15.

Bibliography: Wegner, *ASR* V 3 (1966) cat. 211; Fittschen 1972, 499; Calza 1977, 267; Koch & Sichtermann 1982, 202; Ewald 1999, cat. H 15, pl. 83, 1-2.

129 LEARNED MAN (PHILOSOPHER)

Location/Inv.: St. Petersburg, Hermitage, inv. A540.
Size (coffin): L: 0.37 H: 0.73
Condition: Fragment, probably the right end panel of a strigillated sarcophagus.
Frontal relief: A seated philosopher reading a scroll and two Muses.
Portrait: The seated philosopher is carved with a male portrait.
Dating: The last quarter of the third century (*ASR* V 3, cat. 40).

Bibliography: Wegner, *ASR* V 3 (1966) cat. 40, pl. 65b; Ewald 1999, cat. E 29.

130 *CLIPEUS* PORTRAIT OF A LEARNED MAN

Location/Inv.: Switzerland, privately owned.
Size (coffin): H: 0.55
Condition: A fragment of the frontal relief is preserved.
Frontal relief: Fragment of a strigillated relief. Only the *clipeus* with a bust of a man dressed in *pallium* with a scroll is preserved. A scene with a sage/philosopher and Muses with a sundial between them is depicted beneath the *clipeus*. For a description, see Ewald 1999, C 29.
Portrait: The *clipeus* bust is carved with a male portrait.
Dating: Around 270 (with Ewald 1999, cat. C 29).

Bibliography: Ewald 1999, cat. C 29, pl. 37, 5.

131 LEARNED WOMAN (FIG. 40)

Location/Inv.: Tarragona, Museu Nacional Arquelògic de Tarragona.
Size (coffin): L. 2.16 H: 0.70 D: 0.67
Condition: Preserved coffin and a fragmented lid.
Provenience: From the pagan/Christian necropolis at Tarragona. A skeleton and grave goods were found in the sarcophagus. For further information, see Ewald 1999, cat. C 6.
Frontal relief: Divided into five panels. The second and fourth panels are strigillated. A woman with tunic, *palla*, and scroll is represented on the first panel. A philosopher (in a *pallium* without a tunic) is represented on the fifth panel. Both stand on a statue base. A scene with a seated philosopher surrounded by two busts and a small figure (a boy?) is depicted on the central panel. For a description, see Ewald 1999, cat. C 6.
Short ends: Roughly carved.
Lid: Sea-*thiasos* and an inscription panel without inscription.
Portrait: The woman on the first panel is carved with a female portrait.

Dating: Late third century. For discussion, see Ewald 1999, cat. C 6. The woman's hairstyle belongs stylistically to the second century.

Bibliography: Ewald 1999, cat. C 6, pl. 28, 3.

132 FEMALE *ORANS* AND A *CLIPEUS* PORTRAIT OF A LEARNED FIGURE

Location/Inv.: Terni, Library.
Condition: The coffin is preserved.
Frontal relief: Divided into five panels. The second and fourth panels are strigillated. An *Orans* in front of a *parapetasma* is represented on the first panel and a philosopher is represented on the fifth panel. The central panel shows a *clipeus* with a bust. The bust holds a scroll but the head has been lost. A bucolic scene is depicted beneath the *clipeus*. For a description, see Ewald 1999, cat. F 25.
Short ends: Lenos-shaped. Without decoration.
Portrait: The portrait of the learned woman in the first panel is damaged but her hairstyle has survived. The portrait of the *clipeus* bust is lost.
Dating: Around 300 (Ewald 1999, cat. F 25).

Bibliography: Koch & Sichtermann 1982, 120; Ewald 1999, cat. F 25, pl. 79, 1.

133 LEARNED BOY (PHILOSOPHER)

Location/Inv.: Vitterbo, Museo Civico.
Condition: The coffin is preserved.
Frontal relief: Divided into five panels. The second and fourth panels are strigillated. A bare-chested philosopher with scrolls is represented on the first panel, and a *parapetasma* is suspended behind him. A ram-bearer is represented on the fifth panel. The central panel depicts a man with a *pallium* and naked chest in an *aedicula*. All the figures are placed on statue bases. For a description, see Ewald 1999, cat. F 6
Portrait: The man on the central panel has the portrait features of a boy.
Dating: Second quarter of the third century (Ewald 1999, cat. F 6).
Comment: Child sarcophagus.

Bibliography: Ewald 1999, cat. F 6, pl. 72, 3.

Lion

(See also Addendum A1)

134 LEARNED WOMAN

Location/Inv.: Arezzo, Duomo.
Condition: The coffin is preserved.
Frontal relief: Divided into five panels. The second and fourth panels are strigillated. A scene showing an attacking lion watched by two men is represented on the first and fifth panels. A woman between a philosopher and a Muse, all with scrolls, is depicted on the central panel. For a description, see Ewald 1999, cat. F 13.
Short ends: Lenos-shaped. The motif of the fifth panel continues on the short ends.
Portrait: The woman on the central panel is carved with a female portrait.
Dating: 300 (Fittschen 1972, 496, b). End of the third or early fourth century (*ASR* VI 1, cat. 204).
Comment: According to Fittschen, the sarcophagus has been extensively re-carved in modern times. Reused in 1810 as the tomb of a local martyr.

Bibliography: Stroszeck, *ASR* VI 1 (1998) cat 204, pl. 71, 1; Fittschen 1972, 496 b; Ewald 1999, cat. F 13.

135 LEARNED WOMAN

Location/Inv.: Cliveden, on display in the park.
Size (coffin): L: 1.36 H: 0.91 D: 0.97
Condition: The coffin is preserved.
Frontal relief: Strigillated with a *mandorla* with a woman dressed in *palla* and holding a scroll.
Short ends: Lenos-shaped. Lion killing an ox.
Portrait: The woman in the *mandorla* is carved with a portrait.
Dating: 290-300 (*ASR* VI 1, 212).

Bibliography: Stroszeck, *ASR* VI 1 (1998) cat. 212, pl. 47, 2; Ewald 1999, cat. F 34.

136 *CLIPEUS* PORTRAIT OF A LEARNED WOMAN

Location/Inv.: Diecimo, S. Maria Assunta.
Size (coffin): L: 2.10 H: 0.46 D: 0.58
Condition: The coffin is preserved.
Frontal relief: Strigillated with a central *clipeus* with a bust of a woman holding a scroll. The *clipeus* is supported by a fruit basket. A lion killing a deer is represented on each end of the relief. For a description, see *ASR* VI, cat. 213.
Short ends: Lenos-shaped.
Reverse: Roughly carved.
Portrait: The bust is carved with a female portrait.
Dating: 270-280 (*ASR* VI 1, cat. 213).

Bibliography: Stroszeck, *ASR* VI, 1 (1998) cat. 213, pl. 117, 5.

137 BUST OF A LEARNED MAN

Location/Inv.: Florence, Palazzo Pitti.
Condition: The coffin is preserved.
Frontal relief: Strigillated with a central bust of a man holding a scroll on a pedestal, dressed in a tunic and mantle. A lion is represented on each end of the relief. For description, see *ASR* VI 1, cat. 174.
Short ends: Lenos-shaped. The lion of the frontal relief continues on the short ends.
Portrait: The bust is carved with a male portrait.
Dating: 250-260 (*ASR* VI 1, cat. 174).

Bibliography: Stroszeck, *ASR* VI 1 (1998) cat. 174, pl. 22, 1.

138 *CLIPEUS* PORTRAIT OF A LEARNED WOMAN

Location/Inv.: Lucca, Palazzo Pfanner, entrance.
Size (coffin): L: 1.95 H: 0.71 D: 0.65
Frontal relief: Strigillated with a central *clipeus* showing a bust of a woman holding a scroll. A bucolic scene is depicted beneath the *clipeus*. A lion killing a deer or a boar is represented on each end of the relief. For a description, see *ASR* VI, 1, cat. 230.
Short ends: Lenos-shaped. The lion scene of the frontal relief continues on the short ends.
Reverse: Roughly carved.
Portrait: The bust is carved with a female portrait, but the surface is badly damaged.
Dating: 280-300 (*ASR* VI 1, cat. 230).

Bibliography: Stroszeck, *ASR* VI 1 (1998) cat. 230, pl. 69, 1.

139 *CLIPEUS* PORTRAIT OF A LEARNED WOMAN

Location/Inv.: Paris, Museé du Louvre, inv. MA 360.
Size (coffin): L: 2.15 H: 0.70 D: 0.60
Condition: The coffin is preserved.
Frontal relief: Strigillated with a central *clipeus* with a bust of a woman holding a scroll. Two *cornucopiae* are depicted beneath the *clipeus*. A lion killing an animal is depicted on each end of the relief. For a description, see *ASR* VI, 1, cat. 241.
Short ends: Lenos-shaped. The lion scene of the frontal relief continues on the short ends.
Portrait: The bust is carved with a blank portrait.
Dating: 280-300 (*ASR* VI, 1, cat. 241).

Bibliography: Stroszeck, *ASR* VI, 1 (1998) cat. 241, pl. 61, 4; Baratte & Metzger 1985, cat. 128.

140 *CLIPEUS* PORTRAIT OF A LEARNED WOMAN

Location/Inv.: Pisa, Camposanto, inv. A 8.
Size (coffin): L: 1.96 H: 0.52 D: 0.55
Condition: The coffin is preserved.
Frontal relief: Strigillated with a central *clipeus* showing a bust of a woman holding a scroll. Two *cornucopiae* are depicted beneath the *clipeus*. A lion killing a deer is represented on each end of the relief. For a description, see *ASR* VI, 1, cat. 246.
Short ends: Lenos-shaped. The lion scene of the frontal relief continues on the short ends.
Portrait: The bust is carved with a portrait of a girl.
Inscription: M(arco) VALERIO DOMITIO ET DOMITIAE PATER FILIIS PIENTISSIMIS (*CIL* XI 1, 291, nr. 1494). The inscription is placed on the upper profile.
Dating: 250-260 (*ASR* VI 1, cat. 246).
Comment: The inscription mentions two individuals but there is only one portrait (the girl).

Bibliography: Stroszeck, *ASR* VI, 1 (1998) cat. 246, pl. 34, 1.

141 *CLIPEUS* PORTRAIT OF A LEARNED MAN

Location/Inv.: Rome, Museo Nazionale Romano, inv. 121540.
Size (coffin): L: 2.24 H: 0.63 D: 0.64
Lid: L: 2.24 H: 0.15 D: 0.67
Condition: The coffin and lid are preserved.
Frontal relief: Strigillated with a central *clipeus* with a bust of a man holding a scroll. A chest with fruit and flowers is depicted beneath the *clipeus*. A lion killing a deer is represented on each end of the relief. For a description, see *ASR* VI, 1, cat. 296.
Short ends: Lenos-shaped. The lion scene of the frontal relief continues on the short ends.
Reverse: Roughly carved.
Lid: An empty inscription panel and an imitation of roof decoration with *acroteria*.
Portrait: The bust is carved with a blank portrait.
Dating: 260-270 (*ASR* VI 1, cat. 296):

Bibliography: Stroszeck, *ASR* VI 1 (1998) cat. 296, pl. 59, 1; *MNR* I 7, 2, cat. X, 38.

142 BUST OF A LEARNED WOMAN

Location/Inv.: Rome, Museo Nazionale Romano, inv. 124745.
Size (coffin): L: 1.70 H: 0.63 D: 0.60; *Lid:* H: 0.35
Provenience: Rome, found near Via Prenestina between Aqua Bullicante and Tor de'Schiavi in 1946.
Frontal relief: Strigillated with a central bust of a woman with a scroll. A lion killing a deer is represented on each end of the relief. For a description, see *MNR* I 8, 1, cat. 1,1.
Short ends: Lenos-shaped. The lion scene of the frontal relief continues on the short ends.
Reverse: Roughly carved.
Lid: Imitation of a tile roof with antefix. At the centre, there is an empty inscription panel.
Portrait: The portrait of a woman is carved on a male body (according to *MNR* I 8, 1, cat. 1,1).
Dating: Around 275-280 (*MNR* I 8, 1).
Comment: Another very similar sarcophagus is today at the archaeological museum in Tarragona. The female portrait is carved on a male bust and the sex of the bust is more obviously male than on this example (reference *ASR* VI 1, cat. 365). The lid is not of the same shape as the sarcophagus but they were discovered together.

Bibliography: Stroszeck, *ASR* VI 1 (1998) cat. 298; *MNR* I 8, 1, cat. 1,1, p. 1-5.

143 *CLIPEUS* PORTRAIT OF A LEARNED WOMAN

Location/Inv.: Rome, Palazzo Caetani, courtyard.
Size (coffin): L: 2.12 H: 0.50 D: 0.54
Condition: The coffin is preserved.
Frontal relief: Strigillated with a central *clipeus* showing a bust of a woman holding a scroll. Two *cornucopiae* are depicted beneath the *clipeus*. A lion killing a deer is represented on each end of the relief. For a description, see *ASR* VI, 1, cat. 311.
Short ends: Lenos-shaped. The lion scene of the frontal relief continues on the short ends.
Portrait: The *clipeus* bust is carved with a blank portrait.
Dating: 260-280 (*ASR* VI 1, cat. 311).

Bibliography: Stroszeck, *ASR* VI 1 (1998) cat. 311, pl. 43, 1.

144 SHELL WITH A PORTRAIT OF A LEARNED WOMAN

Location/Inv.: Rome, Palazzo Colonna.
Size (coffin): L: 1.82 H: 0.45 D: 0.53
Condition: The coffin is preserved but the surface is badly weathered.
Frontal relief: Strigillated with a central shell showing a bust of a woman holding a scroll. A scene with Psyche and Eros is shown beneath the shell. A lion killing a deer is represented on each end of the relief. For description, see *ASR* VI 1, cat. 312.
Short ends: Lenos-shaped. The lion scene of the frontal relief continues on the on the short ends.
Reverse: Roughly carved.
Portrait: The bust is carved with a female portrait. Part of her plait is still visible but the face is badly damaged.
Dating: 260-270 (*ASR* VI 1, cat. 312).

Bibliography: Stroszeck, *ASR* VI 1 (1998) cat. 312, pl. 59, 4.

145 *CLIPEUS* PORTRAIT OF A LEARNED MAN

Location/Inv.: Rome, S. Paolo fuori le mura, south side of the monastery.
Size (coffin): L: 1.72 H: 0.67 D: 0.66
Condition: The coffin is preserved but has been pieced together. The right end is lost.
Frontal relief: Strigillated with a central *clipeus* with a bust of a man holding a scroll. A scene with a sage/philosopher and Muses is depicted beneath the *clipeus*. A lion killing a deer is represented on the left end of the relief. For a description, see Ewald 1999, C 27.
Short ends: Lenos-shaped. The lion scene of the frontal relief continues on the short ends.
Portrait: The bust is carved with a portrait of a young man.
Dating: From the second quarter of the third to the first half of the fourth century. For discussion, see Ewald 1999, cat. C 27.

Bibliography: Stroszeck, *ASR* VI 1 (1998) cat. 333; Ewald 1999, cat. C 27, pl. 36, 2.

146 *CLIPEUS* PORTRAIT OF A LEARNED MAN

Location/Inv.: Rome, S. Saba, entrance hall.
Size (coffin): L: 1.55 H: 0.49 D: 0.49
Condition: The coffin is preserved.
Frontal relief: Strigillated with a central *clipeus* with a bust of a man holding a scroll. Two masks are depicted beneath the *clipeus*. A lion killing a deer is represented on each end of the relief. For a description, see *ASR* VI, 1, cat. 334.
Short ends: Lenos-shaped. The lion scene of the frontal relief continues on the short ends.
Portrait: The bust is carved with a blank portrait.
Dating: 280-290 (*ASR* VI 1, cat. 334).

Bibliography: Stroszeck, *ASR* VI 1 (1998) cat. 334, pl. 51, 1.

147 *CLIPEUS* PORTRAIT OF A LEARNED MAN

Location/Inv.: Rome, Villa Borghese, in front of the façade of the Galleria Borghese.
Size (coffin): L: 2.10 H: 0.55 D: 0.70
Condition: The coffin is preserved.
Frontal motif: Strigillated with a central *clipeus* with a bust of a man holding a scroll. Two masks are depicted beneath the *clipeus*. A lion killing a deer is represented on each end of the relief. For a description, see *ASR* VI, 1, cat. 352.
Short ends: Lenos-shaped. The lion scene of the frontal relief continues on the short ends.
Reverse: The lowest part of the relief is smoothly carved and the upper part is roughly carved. The transition between the two surfaces is sharp.
Portrait: The bust is carved with a male portrait. The face is badly damaged. The man had a long beard and a short hairstyle.
Dating: Tetrarchic period (*ASR* VI 1, cat. 352).

Bibliography: Stroszeck, *ASR* VI 1 (1998) cat. 352.

148 *CLIPEUS* PORTRAIT OF A LEARNED MAN

Location/Inv.: Rome, Villa Doria Pamphilj.
Size (coffin): L: 2.32 H: 0.73 D: 0.59
Condition: The coffin is preserved.
Frontal relief: Strigillated with a central *clipeus* with a *togatus* bust of a man holding a scroll. Two masks are depicted beneath the *clipeus*. A head of a lion is represented on each end on the relief. For a description, see *ASR* VI, 1, cat. 129.
Short ends: Lenos-shaped. The strigillation of the frontal relief continues on the short ends.
Portrait: The bust is carved with a male portrait.
Dating: 240-250 (*ASR* VI 1, cat. 129).

Bibliography: Stroszeck, *ASR* VI 1 (1998) cat. 129; Calza 1977, cat. 271.

149 *CLIPEUS* PORTRAIT OF A LEARNED WOMAN

Location/Inv.: Soriano nel Cimino, Palazzo Chigi-Albani.
Condition: The coffin is preserved.
Frontal relief: Strigillated with a central *clipeus* with a bust of a woman holding a scroll. Two *cornucopiae* are depicted beneath the *clipeus*. A lion drinking from a *krater* is represented on each end of the relief. An animal keeper is shown behind the lion. For a description, see *ASR* VI 1, cat. 196.
Short ends: Lenos-shaped. The lion scene of the frontal relief continues on the short ends.
Portrait: The bust is carved with a blank portrait.
Dating: 270-280 (*ASR* VI 1, cat. 196).

Bibliography: Stroszeck., *ASR* VI 1 (1998) cat. 196, pl. 25, 1.

150 BUST OF A LEARNED WOMAN

Location/Inv.: Tarragona, Museu Paleocristino, inv. 53.
Size (coffin): L: 2.08 H: 0.68 D: 0.75
Condition: The coffin is preserved.

Provenience: Tarragona. Reused for a burial in the Christian cemetery.
Frontal relief: Strigillated with a central bust of a woman on a pedestal. A lion killing a deer is represented on each end of the relief. For a description, see *ASR* VI, 1, cat. 365.
Short ends: Lenos-shaped. The lion scene of the frontal relief continues on the short ends.
Reverse: Roughly carved.
Portrait: The male bust has been carved with the portrait features of an elderly woman.
Dating: 240-250 (*ASR* VI 1, cat. 365).
Comment: Museo Nazionale Romano, inv. 124745 is of the same type (see cat. no. 142).

Bibliography: Stroszeck, *ASR* VI 1 (1998) cat. 365, pl. 28, 4.

151 *CLIPEUS* PORTRAIT OF A LEARNED CHILD

Location/Inv.: Vienna, Kunsthistorisches Museum, inv. 1128.
Size (coffin): L: 1.35 H: 0.36 D: 0.40
Condition: The coffin is preserved.
Provenience: Catajo.
Frontal relief: Strigillated with a central *clipeus* with a bust holding a scroll. Two cocks are depicted beneath the *clipeus*. A lion killing a deer or a boar is represented on each end of the relief. For a description, see *ASR* VI 1, cat. 406.
Short ends: Lenos-shaped. The lion scene of the frontal relief continues on the short ends.
Reverse: The lions from the short ends continue in a very low relief. Part of the relief is roughly carved.
Portrait: The bust is carved with a blank portrait.
Dating: 280-300 (*ASR* VI 1, cat. 406).
Comment: Child sarcophagus.

Bibliography: Stroszeck, *ASR* VI 1 (1998) cat. 406, pl. 68, 1.

152 *CLIPEUS* PORTRAIT OF A LEARNED WOMAN

Location/Inv.: Vienna, lost.
Condition: The coffin was preserved.
Frontal relief: Strigillated with a central *clipeus* with a bust of a woman holding a scroll. The three Graces are depicted beneath the *clipeus*. A lion killing a boar is represented on each end of the relief.
Short ends: Lenos-shaped. The lion scene of the frontal relief continues on the short ends.
Portrait: The bust is carved with female portrait features.
Dating: 270-280 (*ASR* VI 1, cat. 403).

Bibliography: Stroszeck, *ASR* VI 1 (1998) cat. 403, pl. 109, 1.

Nine Muses

153 LEARNED WOMAN

Location/Inv.: Berlin, Staatliche Museen, Antikensamlung, inv. 1967. 12.
Size (coffin): L: 0.68 H: 0.45
Condition: Fragment of the frontal relief.
Frontal relief: A woman is represented with a scroll. Four of the Nine Muses are represented on her right side. A *parapetasma* is depicted behind the figures. For a description, see Ewald 1999, cat. B 11.
Portrait: The woman with the scroll is carved with a blank portrait.
Dating: Last quarter of the third century (Ewald 1999, cat. B 11).

Bibliography: Fittschen 1972, 496, nr. C; Ewald 1999, cat. B 11, pl. 23, 2.

154 MUSE (BOY) (FIG. 34)

Location/Inv.: Civita Catsellana, Forte Sangallo, inv. 59646.
Size (coffin): L: 1.56 D: 0.56
Condition: The coffin is preserved.
Provenience: Cava Cacciano. Discovered in a ditch lined with blocks of tufa and concrete. Covered with tile "alla cappuccina" (Moretti 1975; Dresken-Weiland 2003, cat. A 3).
Frontal relief: The Nine Muses. For a description, see Ewald 1999, cat. H 2.
Left short end: Griffin.
Right short end: Apollo with lyre.
Portrait: The lyre-playing Muse has male portrait features.
Dating: Early Antonine. A Sesterce of Antoninus Pius from about 140-143 was found in the coffin (Ewald 1999, 208).
Comment: Inside the coffin was the skeleton of a 12-year-old boy and an Antoninus Pius sesterce. Child sarcophagus.

Bibliography: Moretti 1975, 259-63; Wrede 1981, cat. 139; Koch & Sichtermann 1982, 198; Huskinson 1996, cat. 5.1; 2002, 26; Ewald 1999, cat. H 2; Dresken-Weiland 2003, cat. A 3.

155 LEARNED WOMAN

Location/Inv.: Kansas City (Missouri), The Nelson Atkins Museum of Art, inv. 87-21.
Size (coffin): L: 2.39 H. 0.82 D: 0.81
Provenience: Discovered in a tomb at Vigna Casali together with cat. nos. 482 and 557 (Koch 888, 36, nr. 13) (Dresken-Weiland 2003, cat. A 58).
Frontal relief: A woman in a short tunic holding a scroll is represented next to Athena. The Nine Muses are depicted around these two central figures. For a description, see Cohon 1992.
Short ends: Lion griffin.
Portrait: The woman has female portrait figures but she wears the clothes of a man.
Dating: Between 240-255 (Ewald 1999, 149).

Bibliography: Wegner, *ASR* V 3 (1966) cat. 197; Koch 1988, 36, nr. 13; Cohon 1992; Ewald 1999, cat. B 3, pl. 21, 1-3; Dresken-Weiland 2003, cat. A 58.

156 LEARNED MAN AND A WOMAN

Location/Inv.: Lansdowne House, lost.
Size (coffin): L: 2.16
Condition: Frontal relief is preserved but it is much restored.
Frontal relief: A figure with a scroll is represented between Athena and Hermes. The group is surrounded by the Nine Muses. Between the third and fourth Muse from the right, a female portrait is shown. This portrait was probably carved at a later time, probably at a second burial of a wife or a daughter (?). The female portrait is placed in the background between two Muses, an unusual place for a portrait figure. On this place a mask or a philosopher's head would usually be seen. For a description, see *ASR* V 3, cat. 36. For a discussion of the female portrait, see Ewald 1999, cat. B 2.
Portrait: The figure between Hermes and Athena is carved with male portrait features but wears the clothes of a woman. The head of a woman with a period hairstyle is visible between the Muse with scroll and the Muse with a lyre on the right end.
Dating: Around 230 (*ASR* V 3, cat. 36) or 245 (Ewald 1999, cat. B 2).

Bibliography: Wegner, *ASR* V 3 (1966) cat. 36; Ewald 1999, cat. B 2, pl. 20, 1.

157 EDUCATED WOMAN

Location/Inv.: Malibu (California) The Getty Villa, inv. 72.AA.90.
Size (coffin): H: 1.20 D: 0.69
Condition: Fragments of the frontal relief and the right short end of a coffin are preserved.
Frontal relief: A seated woman is represented with a lyre. To her right are four Muses and fragments of a fifth. For a description, see Koch 1988, 50-57.
Right short end: Philosopher.
Portrait: The seated woman is carved with a female portrait. Only the lower part of her face is preserved.
Dating: 253-260 (Koch 1988, 56). I propose a dating in the fourth century because of similarity in style and technique with the face of the statuette of the seated Christ from Palazzo Massimo alle Terme. For the statuette, see Sapelli 1998, cat. 19.
Comment: This is the largest known sarcophagus produced in Rome.

Bibliography: Koch 1988, 50-7; Ewald 1999, cat. A 12.

158 LEARNED WOMAN

Location/Inv.: Murcia Cathedral.
Size (coffin): L: 1.73 H: 0.65
Condition: The frontal relief is preserved.
Frontal relief: The Nine Muses and sages. The deceased is depicted as the ninth Muse with a scroll. For a description, see *ASR* V 3, cat. 58.
Portrait: The fourth Muse from the left is carved with a female portrait.
Dating: Last quarter of the third century (*ASR* V 3, cat. 58).

Bibliography: Wegner, *ASR* V 3 (1966) cat. 58; Ewald 1999, cat. B 7; Noguera 2007.

159 MUSE (BOY) (FIG. 89)

Location/Inv.: Naples, Museo Archeologico Nazionale, inv. 205250. Once in Villa Mario Astarita.
Size (coffin): L: 1.20 H: 0.74
Condition: The coffin is preserved but has been damaged.
Provenience: Discovered at a Roman necropolis on the land belonging to Villa del Balzo, Naples.
Frontal relief: The Nine Muses. A boy is represented as a philosopher or as the Muse Thalia. For a description, see *ASR* V 3, cat. 23.
Short ends: Without relief decoration.
Portrait: The boy has portrait features but most of the face is damaged.
Dating: First quarter of the fourth century (*ASR* V 3, cat. 23).
Comment: Child sarcophagus.

Bibliography: Wegner, *ASR* V 3 (1966) cat. 23; Wrede 1981, cat. 256; Ewald 1999, cat. H 5; Huskinson 1999, 195.

160 EDUCATED BOY AND LEARNED BOY

Location/Inv.: Palermo, in the crypt of the cathedral.
Size (coffin): L: 2.21 H: 1.03
Condition: The coffin is preserved. The coffin and lid did not originally belong together.
Frontal relief: A seated person is represented on each end of the relief. The female figure to the left holds a lyre, and the male figure to the right holds a scroll. Eight Muses are standing between them. A ninth figure seems to have been removed behind the seated woman. The central Muse with the lyre is probably a representation of Apollo. For a description, see *ASR* V 3, cat. 68.
Short ends: Philosopher.
Portrait: Both of the seated figures are carved with the portrait of a boy.
Dating: Third quarter of the third century (*ASR* V 3, cat. 68) or 220-240 (Fittschen 1984, note 38).
Comment: Used as a child sarcophagus.

Bibliography: Wegner, *ASR* V 3 (1966) cat. 68; Fittschen 1972, 490, nr. 68; Fittschen 1984, note 38b; Ewald 1999, cat. A 13, pl. 51, 1.

161 LEARNED MAN (PHILOSOPHER)

Location/Inv.: Paris, Musée du Louvre, inv. MA.29.
Size (coffin): L: 1.15 H: 1.20
Condition: Fragment. Right end of the frontal relief.
Frontal relief: A seated philosopher with scrolls and three Muses. A *parapetasma* is suspended behind them. For a description, see *ASR* V 3, cat. 73.
Portrait: The seated figure is carved with a male portrait.

Dating: Around the middle of the third century (*ASR* V 3, cat. 73).

Bibliography: Wegner, *ASR* V 3 (1966) cat. 73, pl. 65a; Baratta & Metzger 1985, cat. 86.

162 *CLIPEUS* PORTRAIT OF A WOMAN REPRESENTED AS A MUSE

Location/Inv.: Pisa, Camposanto A 3 est.
Size (coffin): L: 1.95 H: 0.72
Condition: Fragment of the frontal relief.
Frontal relief: The deceased is represented in a *clipeus*. A herdsman with his herd is depicted on the left side of the *clipeus* and on the right side, there are eight Muses. The deceased is represented as the ninth Muse.
Left short end: Bull.
Right short end: Cypress.
Portrait: The bust shows a female hairstyle, but the portrait is damaged.
Dating: 200 (Ewald 1999, cat. G 10).

Bibliography: Arias et al. 1977, 53, pl. 2; Ewald 1999, cat. G 10; Zanker & Ewald 2004, 172, ill. 158.

163 LEARNED WOMAN AND LEARNED MAN

Location/Inv.: Pisa, Camposanto.
Size (coffin) H: 1.44
Condition: The coffin and lid are preserved.
Frontal relief: Divided into five niches. A Muse is represented in the first, fourth, and fifth niches. The second niche shows a woman, and a man holding a scroll is depicted in the third niche.
Short ends: Two niches with Muses.
Lid: Kline-Deckel – the reclining figures are lost.
Portrait: The woman in the second and the man in the third niche are represented with portraits.
Dating: End of the third or beginning of the fourth century (*ASR* V 3, cat. 78).

Bibliography: Wegner, *ASR* V 3 (1999) cat. 78, pl. 96.

164 EDUCATED WOMAN AND LEARNED MAN (PHILOSOPHER)

Location/Inv.: Porto Torres, Basilica di S. Gavino, cripta.
Size (coffin): L: 2.13 H: 0.71
Condition: The frontal relief is preserved.
Frontal relief: The Nine Muses and Apollo are represented in front of a *parapetasma*. A seated woman and man are depicted on each end of the relief (the so-called Lycian motif). The woman plays the lyre and the man holds a scroll. For a description, see *ASR* V 3, cat. 80.
Portrait: The seated man and woman are represented with portraits.
Dating: Beginning of the fourth century. For discussion, see Ewald 1999, cat. E 10.

Bibliography: Wegner, *ASR* V 3 (1966) cat. 80, pl. 128a; Ewald 1999, cat. E 10.

165 EDUCATED WOMAN AND LEARNED MAN (PHILOSOPHER)

Location/Inv.: Rome, Musei Vaticani, Cortile del Belvedere.
Size (coffin): L: 2.36 H: 1.16
Condition: The frontal relief is preserved but has been significantly restored. The head of the deceased man is modern and numerous other modern restorations are visible (See *ASR* V 3, cat. 138).
Frontal relief: A man and a woman are seated opposite each other. Eight of the Nine Muses are represented behind them. Since only eight of the Muses are represented beside her and her husband, the deceased woman is probably a substitute for the ninth Muse. The woman holds a lyre and the man a scroll. For a description, see *ASR* V 3, cat. 138.
Portrait: The seated woman has portrait features. The man was also carved with a portrait, but the head is modern. A drawing from the Dal-Pozzo Collection shows the original portrait heads.
Dating: 270-280 (*ASR* V 3, cat. 138).

Bibliography: Wegner, *ASR* V 3 (1966) cat. 138; Vermeule 1966, 48, cat. 48; Wrede 1981, cat. 250; Ewald 1999, cat. E 6.

166 LEARNED MAN (PHILOSOPHER)

Location/Inv.: Rome, Palazzo Balestra, via Veneto.
Size (coffin): L: 1.15 H: 0.57
Condition: Two fragments (of the same relief) have been fitted together. A section is missing between the piece with the seated man and the piece with the two Muses.
Frontal relief: A seated man is represented between five Muses. A *parapetasma* is suspended behind them. For a description, see *ASR* V 3, cat. 196.
Portrait: The seated man is carved with a portrait.
Dating: End of the third century (*ASR* V 3, cat. 196); post-Gallienic (Fittschen 1972).

Bibliography: Wegner, *ASR* V 3 (1966) cat. 196, pl. 72; Ewald 1999, cat. D 4.

167 EDUCATED WOMAN

Location/Inv.: Rome, Palazzo Borghese.
Size (coffin): L: 2.22 H: 0.87
Condition: The coffin is preserved.
Frontal relief: Strigillated relief divided into four panels. A seated woman with a lyre is represented on the left end. Two Muses stand behind her. A seated man (head lost) is represented on the right end. A philosopher stands behind him.
Short ends: Lenos-shaped. Strigillation (?).
Portrait: The woman has a female hairstyle. The carving of the face is worn.
Dating: Late third century (*ASR* V 3, cat. 160).

Bibliography: Wegner, *ASR* V 3 (1966) cat. 160, pl. 111a.

168 LEARNED WOMAN (MUSE)

Location/Inv.: Rome, Palazzo Giustiniani. Grouted into the wall in the courtyard.
Size (coffin): L: 2.50 H: 2.60
Condition: Two fragments from two different (?) frontal reliefs have been pieced together.
Frontal relief: The Nine Muses and a seated philosopher. A Muse/learned woman is standing on the right side of a seated philosopher, who holds a scroll. On each side of them two Muses are represented. These figures belong to the same relief. Additional Muses are shown on the left and right ends; they are however part of a different relief. For a description, see *ASR* V 3, cat. 165.
Portrait: The Muse on the right side of the seated figure is carved with female portrait features. It has been questioned whether the female portrait of the seated philosopher is antique or modern. Ewald has summarised the discussion (Ewald 1999, 166-67).
Dating: Around 240 (Ewald 1999, 167), or the third quarter of the third century (*ASR* V 3, cat. 165).

Bibliography: Wegner, *ASR* V 3 (1966) cat. 165; Wrede 1981, cat. 247; Ewald 1999, cat. D 1, pl. 40.

169 LEARNED MAN (PHILOSOPHER) AND MUSE

Location/Inv.: Rome, Palazzo Mattei. Grouted into the wall in the courtyard.
Size (coffin): L: 1.56 H: 0.50
Condition: The frontal relief is preserved.
Frontal relief: A seated philosopher with scrolls is represented surrounded by Muses. For a description, see *ASR* V 3, cat. 167.
Short ends: *Lenos*-shaped. The representation of the Muses continues on the short ends.
Portrait: The philosopher has a blank portrait. It is a possibility that the Muse on the left end has portrait features as well (Ewald 1999, 38).
Dating: Between 220-250. For discussion, see Ewald 1999, D 2.

Bibliography: Wegner, *ASR* V 3 (1966) cat. 167; Guerrini 1982, cat. 91; Wrede 1981, cat. 242; Ewald 1999, D 2.

170 LEARNED WOMAN

Location/Inv.: Rome, Palazzo Rospigliosi. Grouted into the façade of the Casino.
Condition: The frontal relief is preserved.
Frontal relief: A female poet dressed in a *palla* accompanied by Athena is represented on the centre of the relief. They are surrounded by the Nine Muses. For a description, see *ASR* V 3, cat. 170.
Portrait: The poet is carved with a female portrait.
Dating: Around 240-250 (*ASR* V 3, cat. 179).

Bibliography: Wegner, *ASR* V 3 (1966) cat. 170, pl. 37a; Ewald 1999, 134.

171 LEARNED WOMAN (MUSE)

Location/Inv.: Rome, Piazza Margana 24. In the courtyard, used as a fountain.
Size (coffin): L: 2.18 H: 0.60
Condition: The coffin is preserved.
Frontal relief: The Nine Muses and a woman depicted as a Muse (Calliope type). For a description, see *ASR* V 3, cat. 176.
Left short end: Without relief decoration. Roughly carved.
Right short end: Grouted into a wall.
Portrait: The central Muse has portrait features.
Dating: 310-320 (*ASR* V 3, cat. 176).

Bibliography: Wegner, *ASR* V 3 (1966) cat. 176, pl. 125a; Ewald 1999, cat. B 9.

172 LEARNED MAN

Location/Inv.: Rome, S. Maria del Priorato, Aventino. Today the tomb of Bishop Spinellis.
Size (coffin): L: 2.09 H: 0.70
Condition: The coffin is preserved.
Frontal relief: A man with a scroll is accompanied by Athena and the Nine Muses. For a description, see *ASR* V 3, cat. 183.
Short ends: Philosopher with a beard.
Portrait: The man beside Athena is carved with a blank portrait.
Dating: 240s (*ASR* V 3, cat. 183).

Bibliography: Wegner, *ASR* V 3 (1966) cat. 183, pl. 36a; Ewald 1999, cat. A 7.

173 EDUCATED WOMAN AND LEARNED MAN (PHILOSOPHER)

Location/Inv.: Rome, S. Saba, museum.
Size (coffin): L: 2.09 H: 0.54
Condition: Fragmented coffin.
Frontal relief: A seated woman and a man are represented on the left and right ends of the relief. She holds a lyre and he holds a scroll. Between them are the Nine Muses and Apollo. A third man in low relief is depicted standing behind Apollo. For a description, see *ASR* V 3, cat. 188.
Short ends: Roughly carved.
Portrait: The seated woman has portrait features. The seated man seems to have a blank portrait.
Dating: Beginning of the fourth century (Ewald 1999, cat. E 9).

Bibliography: Wegner, *ASR* V 3 (1966) cat. 188; Ewald 1999, cat. E 9, pl. 55, 1-3.

174 LEARNED MAN (MUSE)

Location/Inv.: Rome, now lost. Recorded by Cassiano del Pozzo, Museum Chartaceum, London, British Museum I fol. 12.
Frontal relief: The Nine Muses are represented in a colonnade. The portrait figure is depicted between the central columns

as the Ninth Muse, holding a scroll. For a description, see Vermuele 1960, cat. 14.
Portrait: The man or a boy depicted as a poet or Muse in the central niche is carved with portrait features.
Dating: Third century.

Bibliography: Wegner, *ASR* V 3 (1966) cat. 232; Vermuele 1960, cat. 14, ill. 14; Wrede 1981, cat. 257; Huskinson 1996, 195; Koch 1993b, 428.

175 MUSE (BOY)

Location/Inv.: Verona, Museo Maffeiano.
Size (coffin): L: 1.27 H: 0.39
Condition: The frontal relief is preserved.
Frontal relief: The deceased is represented as a Muse (Calliope?) with a scroll among the eight other Muses; behind them a *parapetasma* is suspended. For a description, see *ASR* V 3, cat. 227.
Portrait: The portrait features of a boy have been applied to the central Muse. It has been debated whether it is a roughly carved head or a portrait (see Ewald 1999, 210).
Dating: Last quarter of the third century (*ASR* V 3, cat. 227).
Comment: Child sarcophagus (*ASR* V 3, cat. 227).

Bibliography: Wegner, *ASR* V 3 (1966) cat. 227, pl. 127b; Wrede 1981, 255; Huskinson 1996, cat. 5. 6; 1999, 195; Ewald 1999, cat. H 16.

176 LEARNED MAN (PHILOSOPHER)

Location/Inv.: Vienna, Antikensammlung, inv. I 1117.
Size (coffin): L: 0.72 H: 0.38
Condition: Fragment of the frontal relief. The relief is probably much restored. The four Muses on the left end of the relief are modern.
Frontal relief: A seated man with a scroll is represented on the right end of the relief. Muses are standing around him. For a description, see *ASR* V 3, cat. 230.
Portrait: The seated figure is carved with a portrait of a young man.
Dating: Last quarter of the third century (ARS V 3, cat. 230).

Bibliography: Wegner, *ASR* V 3 (1966) cat. 230, pl. 127a; Ewald 1999, cat. E 8.

Myths

177 LEARNED WOMAN AND LEARNED MAN (FIG. 19)

Location/Inv: Ostia, Museo, inv. 1202.
Size (coffin): L: 1.98 H: 0.58
Condition: The coffin is preserved.
Frontal relief: Divided into five panels. The second and fourth panels are strigillated. A woman with a *palla* and a scroll is represented on the first panel and a philosopher is represented on the fifth panel. A *parapetasma* is suspended behind both of them. The central panel depicts Orpheus playing his lyre. For a description, see Ewald 1999, cat. F 10.
Portrait: The woman on the first and the Philosopher on the fifth panel are carved with portrait features.
Dating: Either the second quarter or the middle of the third century. The male portrait is similar to the portrait of Gordian III (Ewald 1999, cat. F 19).

Bibliography: *Rep.* I, cat. 1022, pl. 164, Ewald 1999, cat. F 10.

178 *CLIPEUS* PORTRAIT OF A LEARNED WOMAN

Location/Inv.: Ostia, Museo, inv. 36136.
Condition: A fragment of the frontal relief is preserved.
Provenience: Isola Sacra, Pianabella, Basilica.
Frontal relief: Strigillated sarcophagus with a central *clipeus* with a bust of woman holding a scroll. A scene showing Romulus, Remus, and the she-wolf is placed beneath the *clipeus*. For a description, see Paroli 1999, B 101.
Portrait: The bust is carved with a female portrait.
Dating: Third quarter of the third century (Paroli 1999, B 101).

Bibliography: Paroli 1999, b 101, pl. 117, 1.

179 BUST OF A LEARNED MAN

Location/Inv.: Pisa, Camposanto, C 4 est.
Size (coffin): L: 2.15 H: 0.67 D: 0.71
Condition: The coffin is preserved.
Frontal relief: A bust of a man with a scroll is placed in front of a *parapetasma* held by two flying cupids. There is a representation of Minerva on the left end of the relief, and there is one of Orpheus on the right end. Tellus and Oceanus are depicted beneath the bust. For a description, see Arias 1977, C 4 est.
Short ends: Probably without relief decoration.
Reverse: Inscriptions from the fourteenth century.
Portrait: The bust is carved with a male portrait.
Dating: The portrait has been dated to 270-275 (Arias 1977, 127).

Bibliography: Arias et al. 1977, C 4 est.

180 LEARNED WOMAN AND MAN (PHILOSOPHER)

Location/Inv.: Porto Torres (Sardinia), Basilica di S. Gavino, Cripta.
Size (coffin): L: 2.16 H: 0.58 D: 0.55
Condition: The coffin is preserved.
Provenience: Discovered at the necropolis in Porto Torres.
Frontal relief: Divided into five panels. The second and fourth panels are strigillated. A woman dressed in a *palla* is represented on the first panel. The object in her hand is probably a scroll. A philosopher with a naked chest is represented on the fifth panel. A *parapetasma* is suspended behind both of them. The central panel depicts Orpheus playing his lyre. For a description, see Ewald 1999, cat. F 9.
Portrait: The woman on the first and the man on the fifth panel are shown with portrait features.

Dating: 244-249 (with Ewald 1999, cat. F 9). The style of the male portrait can be compared to the portrait of Philip the Arab.

Bibliography: Pesce 1957, cat. 56; Ewald 1999, cat. F 9, pl. 72, 4.

181 LEARNED WOMAN AND LEARNED MAN

Location/Inv.: Rome, Muzeo Nazionale Romano, inv. 113226.
Size (coffin): L: 2.32 H: 0.90 D: 0.88
Condition: The coffin is preserved.
Frontal relief: The relief is divided into five panels. The second ad fourth panels are strigillated. A woman with veil and a scroll is represented on the first panel and a man with scrolls is represented on the fifth panel. A *parapetasma* is suspended behind both of them. On the central panel, there is a column showing the three Graces. For a description, see *MNR* I 8, 1, cat. I, 2.
Short ends: Bucolic scene.
Portrait: The woman on the first and the man on the fifth panel are carved with blank portraits.
Dating: Late third century (*MNR* I 8, cat. I, 2).

Bibliography: *MNR* I 8, 1, cat. I, 2, p. 6.

182 *CLIPEUS* PORTRAIT OF A LEARNED WOMAN

Location/Inv.: Rome, Vatican cemetery beneath S. Pietro.
Size (coffin): L: 2.10; (lid): L: 2.10 H: 0.30
Condition: Both the coffin and the lid are preserved.
Provenience: The Vatican cemetery. Standing in the street against the north wall of tomb X, where it was placed by Constantin's workmen (Toynbee & Ward-Perkins 1956, 92).
Frontal relief: Divided into five panels. The second and fourth panels are strigillated. One of the Dioscuroi with a horse is represented on the first and fifth panels. The central panel depicts a *clipeus* with a bust of a woman holding a scroll. Two masks are placed beneath the *clipeus*.
Short ends: *Lenos*-shaped. The Dioscuros scenes continue onto the short ends.
Lid: A central inscription panel framed on each side by cupids and a *krater* filled with grapes. For a description, see *ASR* V 4, cat. 519.
Portrait: The *clipeus* bust is carved with a female portrait.
Inscription: D M S / MARCIAE FELI / CITATI MARCIA / VRBICA SORORI / CARISSIMAE
Dating: Post-Gallienic to Tetrarchic period (*ASR* V 4, cat. 519).

Bibliography: Kranz, *ASR* V 4 (1984) cat. 519, pl. 109, 1; Toynbee & Ward-Perkins 1956, 92.

183 LEARNED WOMAN AND LEARNED MAN (FIG. 29)

Location/Inv.: Withington Hall (Chelford).
Condition: The coffin is preserved.
Frontal relief: Divided into five panels. The second and fourth panels are strigillated. A learned woman and a small female figure with an incense box are represented on the first panel, and a learned man is represented on the fifth panel. A *parapetasma* is suspended behind them. The central panel depicts the three Graces. For a description, see *ASR* I 3, cat. 169.
Short end: Weapons.
Portrait: The woman and the man on the first and fifth panels are carved with blank portraits.
Dating: 220-230 (*ASR* I 3, cat. 169).

Bibliography: Sichtermann, *ASR* XII 2 (1992) cat. 168; Reinsberg, *ASR* I 3 (2006) cat. 169, pl. 74, 1.

Sea-Monsters and Nymphs

184 SHELL WITH A PORTRAIT OF AN EDUCATED WOMAN

Location/Inv.: Cagliari, Sardinia (museum).
Condition: The coffin is preserved.
Frontal relief: A central shell with a bust of a woman playing the lute is surrounded by groups of sea-monsters and nymphs, some with instruments. A cupid supports the shell.
Short ends: Unknown.
Portrait: The bust is carved with a female portrait. Her chiton has slipped from her right shoulder and a veil blows around her shoulders.
Dating: Middle of the third century (*ASR* V 1, cat. 76).

Bibliography: Rumpf, *ASR* V 1 (1939) cat. 76, pl. 19, 2.

185 SHELL WITH A PORTRAIT OF A LEARNED WOMAN

Location/Inv.: Hever Castle.
Frontal relief: A bust of a woman with a scroll is framed by a shell. On both sides are sea-centaurs and nymphs, some of which are playing instruments (lyre and lute). A cupid in a boat is depicted beneath the shell.
Portrait: The bust is carved with a female portrait.
Dating: 230s.

Bibliography: Arachne image no. http://arachne.uni-koeln.de/item/objekt/7337.

186 *CLIPEUS* PORTRAIT OF AN EDUCATED WOMAN

Location/Inv.: Naples, Museo Nazionale, inv. 6598.
Size (coffin): L: 1.86 H: 0.65 D: 0.47
Condition: The coffin is preserved.
Frontal relief: A central *clipeus* with a bust of a woman playing an instrument (lute) is flanked by sea-centaurs and nymphs. Two of the nymphs are playing an instrument (lute). Cupids and sea-monsters are depicted beneath the *clipeus*.
Short ends: *Lenos*-shaped. The motif of the frontal relief continues on the short ends.

Portrait: The female bust is carved with a blank portrait. The chiton has slipped from the right shoulder and a veil blows around the shoulders.
Dating: End of the third century (*ASR* V 1, cat. 66).
Comment: Venus iconography.

Bibliography: Rumpf, *ASR* V 1 (1939) cat. 66, pl. 17, 5.

187 PORTRAIT BUST OF A LEARNED MAN ENCLOSED BY A SHELL

Location/Inv.: Malibu, J. Paul Getty Museum, inv. 73.AA.48.
Size (coffin): L: 0.45 H: 0.44 D: 0.09
Condition: Fragment of the frontal relief.
Frontal relief: A shell with a bust of a man holding a scroll is shown with cupids placed on either side of him. The head of a sea-creature can be seen below the shell.
Portrait: Male portrait, arguably carved from a female head, with short hair and a beard.
Dating: The relief is dated to the late third century and the portrait to the beginning of the fourth century (Eberle 1990).

Bibliography: Koch 1988, 48-9; Eberle 1990.

188 *CLIPEUS* PORTRAIT OF A LEARNED MAN

Location/Inv.: Rome, Musei Capitolini, Palazzo Conservatori.
Size (coffin): L 0.51 H: 0.33 D: 0.03
Condition: Fragment of a frontal relief. The part with the *clipeus* is lost today.
Provenience: Rome, Verano.
Frontal relief: A central *clipeus* with a bust of a man holding a scroll is flanked by sea-centaurs and nymphs. On the lower register three boats are depicted, each with a rowing man.
Portrait: The bust is carved with a male portrait.
Dating: Around the middle of the fourth century (*ASR* V 1, cat. 62).

Bibliography: Rumpf, *ASR* V 1 (1939) cat. 62, fig. 33, p.22.

189 SHELL WITH A PORTRAIT OF AN EDUCATED WOMAN

Location/Inv.: Rome, Ospedale di S. Giovanni.
Condition: The coffin is preserved.
Frontal relief: A shell with a bust of a woman playing the lute is surrounded by groups of sea-monsters and nymphs, some with instruments. A hole has been made beneath the shell in a post-antique period.
Short ends: Sea-panthers.
Portrait: The bust is carved with a female portrait. Her chiton has slipped from her right shoulder and a veil blows around her.
Dating: Middle of the third century (*ASR* V 1, cat. 78).

Bibliography: Rumpf, *ASR* V 1 (1939) cat. 78, pl. 24, 2.

190 SHELL WITH A PORTRAIT OF AN EDUCATED WOMAN

Location/Inv.: Rome, Villa Doria Pamphilj.
Size (coffin): L: 1.10 H: 0.31
Condition: Fragment of the frontal relief.
Frontal relief: A shell with a bust of a woman playing the lute is surrounded by groups of sea-monsters and nymphs.
Portrait: The bust is carved with a female portrait. A veil blows around her shoulders.
Dating: Second quarter of the third century (*ASR* V 1, cat. 80).

Bibliography: Rumpf, *ASR* V 1 (1939) cat. 80, fig. 48, p.32.

Seasonal

191 LEARNED WOMAN

Location/Inv.: Acilia, Via di Acilia/Via C. Beschi.
Size (coffin): L: 2.08 H: 0.71
Condition: The frontal relief is preserved.
Frontal relief: Divided into five panels. The second and fourth panels are strigillated. A seasonal personification is represented on the first and fifth panels, and a standing woman with a scroll is depicted on the central panel. A *parapetasma* is suspended behind her. The relief is unfinished. For a description, see *ASR* V 4, cat. 175.
Portrait: The woman on the central panel is carved with a blank portrait.
Dating: Constantinian period (*ASR* V 4, cat. 175).

Bibliography: Kranz, *ASR* V 4 (1984) cat. 175, pl. 75, 3.

192 *CLIPEUS* PORTRAIT OF A LEARNED BOY

Location/Inv.: Agrigento, Museo Regionale.
Size (coffin): L: 1.44 H: 0.49 D: 0.47
Condition: The coffin is preserved.
Frontal relief: Personifications of the four seasons flank a *clipeus* with a bust of a boy holding a scroll. Two girls, engaged in the production of garlands, are depicted beneath the *clipeus*. A lion killing a deer is represented on each end of the relief. For a description, see *ASR* VI, 1, cat. 200.
Short ends: *Lenos*-shaped. The lion scene of the frontal relief continues on the short ends.
Portrait: Boy. The hair is carved with uneven and very coarse strokes.
Dating: 280-300 (*ASR* VI 1, cat. 200).
Comment: The bust is a good example of the generic learned man/woman type. Child sarcophagus.

Bibliography: Amedick, *ASR* I 4 (1991) cat. 3; Kranz, *ASR* V 4 (1984) cat. 27; Bielefeld, *ASR* V 2, 2 (1997) cat. 1; Stroszeck, *ASR* VI 1 (1998) cat. 200, pl. 67, 1; Huskinson 1996, 8, 2.

193 LEARNED MAN IN FRONT OF A *PARAPETASMA*

Location/Inv.: Ajaccio, Prefecture de la Région Corse.
Size (coffin): L: 1.89 H: 0.54 D: 0.56
Frontal relief: A man with a scroll is represented in front of a *parapetasma* held by two seasonal personifications. More seasonal personifications are placed on both sides. For a description, see *ASR* V 4, cat. 75.
Short ends: Without relief decoration.
Portrait: The standing man is carved with a blank portrait.
Dating: Late Tetrarchic or early Constantinian (*ASR* V 4, cat. 75).
Comment: According to Koch & Sichtermann the sarcophagus was not produced in Rome but is a local "copy" (1982, 295).

Bibliography: Kranz, *ASR* V 4 (1984) cat. 75, pl. 50, 4; Koch & Sichtermann 1982, 295.

194 *CLIPEUS* PORTRAIT OF A LEARNED BOY

Location/Inv.: Berkeley, University of California, Lowie Museum of Anthropology, inv. 8/4278.
Size (coffin): L: 0.69 H: 0.31
Condition: Fragment of frontal relief.
Frontal relief: Standing cupids hold a *clipeus* with a bust of a boy holding a scroll. A *scrinium* and a mask are depicted below the *clipeus*. For a description, see *ASR* V 4, cat. 29.
Portrait: The bust is carved with a boy's portrait.
Dating: Around 310 (Huskinson 1996, 8.11).
Comment: Child sarcophagus.

Bibliography: Kranz, *ASR* V 4 (1984) cat. 29, pl. 40, 2; Huskinson 1996, 8.11.

195 *CLIPEUS* PORTRAIT OF A LEARNED WOMAN

Location/Inv.: Cagliari, Cathedral.
Size (coffin): L: 1.82 H: 0.58
Condition: The frontal relief is preserved.
Frontal relief: A central *clipeus* with a bust of a woman holding a scroll is placed above two theatre masks. Three seasonal personifications are represented on each side of the *clipeus* and Tellus and Oceanus are shown between their feet. For a description, see *ASR* V 4, cat. 32.
Portrait: The *clipeus* bust is carved with a female portrait.
Dating: 270-280 (*ASR* V 4, cat. 32).

Bibliography: Kranz, *ASR* V 4 (1984) cat. 32, pl. 33, 3.

196 *CLIPEUS* PORTRAIT OF A LEARNED WOMAN

Location/Inv.: Cagliari, Museo Archeologico Nazionale, inv. 5936.
Size (coffin): L: 2.03 H: 0.77 D: 0.66
Condition: The coffin is preserved.
Frontal relief: A central *clipeus* with a bust of a woman holding a scroll is held up by two *victoriae*; seasonal personifications are represented on each side of this composition. A scene with cupids pressing grapes is depicted beneath the *clipeus*. For a description, see *ASR* V 4, cat. 63.
Left short end: Pine.
Right short end: Laurel.
Portrait: The bust is carved with a female portrait.
Inscription: (a)NNO VNO MENS(ibus) VIII DIEB(us) XVI (*CIL* X nr. 7737).
Dating: Late Tetrarchic period to the early fourth century (*ASR* V 4, cat. 63).
Comment: The inscription on the upper profile is probably secondary. It mentions a child of one year and eight months, but the portrait wears an adult hairstyle. This sarcophagus is included in the statistics on learned women.

Bibliography: Kranz, *ASR* V 4 (1984) cat. 63, pl. 44, 4.

197 BUST OF A LEARNED WOMAN

Location/Inv.: Castellamare di Stabia, Antiquarium.
Size (coffin): L: 1.86 H: 0.23
Condition: The lid is preserved.
Lid: Cupids, empty inscription panel, and a bust of a woman with a scroll.
Portrait: The bust is carved with a female portrait.
Dating: Tetrarchic or early Constantinian (*ASR* V 4, cat. 522).

Bibliography: Kranz, *ASR* V 4 (1984) cat. 522.

198 *CLIPEUS* PORTRAIT OF A LEARNED MAN

Location/Inv.: Copenhagen, Ny Carlsberg Glyptotek, inv. 2631.
Size (coffin): L: 2.09 H: 0.74 D: 0.73
Condition: The central relief is preserved but fragmented.
Frontal relief: The relief shows a central *clipeus* with a bust of a man holding a scroll. Two *victoriae* hold the *clipeus* and two seasonal personifications are represented on each side of the composition. Beneath are two satyrs with panthers. For a description, see *ASR* V 4, cat. 65.
Short ends: *Lenos*-shaped. The motif of the frontal relief continues on the short ends.
Portrait: The bust is carved with a male portrait.
Dating: First half of the 260s (*ASR* V 4, cat. 65).

Bibliography: Kranz, *ASR* V 4 (1984) cat. 65, pl. 42, 4; Østergaard 1996, cat. 47; Ewald 1999, cat. B 4.

199 LEARNED MAN

Location/Inv.: Frascati, Mueo Tuscolano, Palazzo Vescovile.
Size (coffin): L: 1.97 H: 0.60 D: 0.59
Condition: The frontal relief is preserved.
Frontal relief: A man with a scroll is represented in front of a *parapetasma* held by two *Genii*. Seasonal personifications are represented on both sides of the man. A lion killing a deer or a horse is depicted on each end of the relief. For a description, see *ASR* V 4, cat. 76.
Short ends: *Lenos*-shaped. The motif of the frontal relief continues on the short ends.
Reverse: Roughly carved.
Portrait: The central man is carved with a male portrait.
Dating: 300-320 (*ASR* VI 1, cat. 214).

Bibliography: Stroszeck, *ASR* VI 1 (1998) cat. 214, pl. 71, 4.

200 LEARNED WOMAN

Location/Inv.: Genoa, S. Matteo (facade). The frontal relief is grouted in the façade of the church.
Condition: The frontal relief is preserved.
Frontal relief: Eight seasonal personifications are grouped around a learned woman, who is placed in front of a *parapetasma* held by two personifications.
Portrait: The woman is carved with a female portrait. The portrait has been re-carved.
Dating: Around 290.
Comment: Reused for a tomb in the fourteenth century.

Bibliography: Kranz, *ASR* V 4 (1984) 207, cat. 77, pl. 50, 3; Dufour Bozzo 1967, cat. 24; Müller 2002, 116-22, figs. 56-7.

201 SHELL WITH PORTRAIT OF A LEARNED MAN

Location/Inv.: Girona, Museo Archeologico Provinciale, inv. 1056.1057.
Size (coffin): L: 2.08 H: 0.55 D. 0.64; (lid): L: 2.12 H: 0.27 D: 0.65
Condition: The coffin and lid are preserved.
Frontal relief: A central shell with a bust of a man holding a scroll is held by two cupids. A scene of Selene and the sleeping Endymion is depicted beneath the shell. Seasonal personifications are represented on each side of the central group. Between the seasons on the left side of the relief, a ram-bearer is depicted. For a description, see *ASR* V 4, cat. 35.
Short ends: Without relief decoration.
Lid: Harvesting scenes and an empty inscription panel.
Portrait: The bust is carved with a blank portrait.
Dating: Beginning of the fourth century (*ASR* V 4, cat. 35).

Bibliography: Kranz, *ASR* V 4 (1984) cat. 35, pl. 41, 1; Trillmich et al., 1993, cat 222b.

202 LEARNED WOMAN

Location/Inv.: Gloucester, Hammond Museum.
Condition: The coffin is preserved.
Provenience: Rome, Vigna Sassi (Pomponias Hylas' tomb).
Frontal relief: A woman with a scroll is standing in front of a *parapetasma* held by two seasonal personifications. Other seasonal personifications are represented on either side of her. For a description, see *ASR* V 4, cat. 78.
Short ends: Without relief decoration.
Portrait: The central woman is carved with a blank portrait.
Dating: Early Tetrarchic period (*ASR* V 4, cat. 78).

Bibliography: Kranz, *ASR* V 4 (1984) cat. 78, pl. 50, 2; Hanfmann 1951, cat. A-16.

203 *CLIPEUS* POTRAITT OF A LEARNED MAN

Location/Inv.: Gubbio, Palazzo dei Consoli.
Size (coffin): L: 2.06 H: 0.57 D: 0.53
Condition: The coffin is preserved.
Frontal relief: A central *clipeus* with a bust of a man holding a scroll is shown with three seasonal personifications represented on either side; two figures pressing grapes are depicted beneath the *clipeus*. For a description, see *ASR* V 4, cat. 36.
Short ends: Griffin.
Portrait: The bust is carved with a male portrait.
Dating: 270-280 (*ASR* V 4, note 288, cat. 36).

Bibliography: Kranz, *ASR* V 4 (1984) cat. 36, pl. 33, 4.

204 *CLIPEUS* PORTRAIT OF A LEARNED MAN

Location/Inv.: Naples, S. Restituta.
Size (coffin): L: 2.05 H:0.60 D:0.67
Condition: The coffin is preserved.
Frontal relief: A central *clipeus* with a bust of a man holding a scroll is shown with two seasonal personifications represented on either side; between their feet, Tellus and Oceanus are depicted. Two peacocks and a flower basket are placed beneath the *clipeus*. For a description, see *ASR* V 4, cat. 39.
Short ends: Re-worked. Fourteenth-century relief.
Reverse: Re-worked. Fourteenth-century relief.
Portrait: The bust was carved with portrait features. Today it is very damaged.
Dating: 270-280 (*ASR* V 4, cat. 39).
Comment: Reused in the fourteenth century for a new burial.

Bibliography: Kranz, *ASR* V 4 (1984) cat. 39, pl. 39, 1; Schauenburg 1972.

205 *CLIPEUS* PORTRAIT OF A LEARNED WOMAN

Location/Inv.: Ostia, Museo, inv. 1163.
Size (coffin): L: 2.15 H: 0.54 D: 0.56
Condition: The coffin is preserved.
Frontal relief: Divided into five panels. The second and fourth panels are strigillated. A seasonal personification is represented on the first and fifth panels. The central panel depicts a *clipeus* with a bust of a woman holding a scroll. A bucolic scene is depicted beneath the *clipeus*. For a description, see *ASR* V 4, cat. 154.
Short ends: Griffin.
Portrait: The bust is carved with a female portrait.
Dating: 270s (*ASR* V 4, cat. 154).

Bibliography: Kranz, *ASR* V 4 (1984) cat. 154, pl. 70, 1.

206 *CLIPEUS* PORTRAIT OF A LEARNED BOY

Location/Inv.: Oxford, Ashmolean Museum, inv. 114 or VI 1668.
Size (coffin): L: 1.56 H: 0.48 D: 0.50
Condition: The coffin is preserved.
Frontal relief: Seasonal personifications hold a *clipeus* with a bust of a young boy holding a scroll. Two more seasonal personifications are represented on each side of this composition, and two theatrical masks are shown beneath the *clipeus*. A lion-horse group is depicted on each end of the relief. For a description, see *ASR* V 4, cat. 42.

Short ends: Lenos-shaped. The lion-horse group continues on the short ends.
Portrait: The bust is carved with a portrait of a boy (Huskinson 1996, cat. 8, 4).
Dating: Around 270 (Huskinson 1996, cat. 8, 4); 290-310 (*ASR* VI 1, cat. 238).
Comment: Child sarcophagus.

Bibliography: Kranz, *ASR* V 4 (1984) cat. 42, pl. 67, 3; Stroszeck, *ASR* VI 1 (1998) cat. 238; Huskinson 1996, cat. 8, 4.

207 LEARNED MAN

Location/Inv: Oxford, Ashmolean Museum.
Size (coffin): L: 1.24 H: 0.41 D: 0.41
Condition: The coffin is preserved.
Frontal relief: Divided into five panels. The second and fourth panels are strigillated. A cupid with a torch is represented on the first and fifth panels. A man with a scroll is depicted on the central panel.
Short ends: Playing cupids.
Portrait: The man on the central panel is carved with portrait features.
Dating: Third century (Huskinson 1996, cat. 6. 19).
Comment: Huskinson categorises it as a child sarcophagus.

Bibliography: Amedick, *ASR* I 4 (1991) cat. 110; Huskinson 1996, cat. 6. 19, pl. 12, 1-3.

208 LEARNED WOMAN

Location/Inv.: Palermo, Museo Archeologico Nazionale, inv. 1063.
Size (coffin): L: 2.12 H: 0.55 D: 0.53
Condition: The coffin and lid are preserved. The lid was re-worked in medieval times.
Provenience: The monastery of S. Agostino, Palermo.
Frontal relief: Divided into five panels. The second and fourth panels are strigillated. A seasonal representation is depicted in the first and fifth panels. Two Muses and a woman with a scroll are represented in the central panel.
Short ends: Without relief decoration.
Lid: Medieval re-working.
Portrait: The central woman on the central panel has portrait features. The faces of all three figures were re-worked in the medieval period.
Inscription: Medieval.
Dating: Late third century (*ASR* V 3, cat. 70).

Bibliography: Wegner, *ASR* V 3 (1966) cat. 70; Kranz, *ASR* V 4 (1984) cat. 148; Tusa 1957, cat. 72; Fittschen 1972, cat. 70; Ewald 1999, cat. F 11, pl. 74, 3.

209 *CLIPEUS* PORTRAIT OF A LEARNED MAN

Location/Inv.: Porto, Museu Nacional de Soares dos Reis.
Size (coffin): L: 1.95 H: 0.59 D: 0.63
Condition: The frontal relief is preserved.
Provenience: Portugal.
Frontal relief: A *clipeus* held by two *victoriae* with a bust of a man holding a scroll is shown with seasonal personifications represented on either side. A scene of a peasant ploughing is depicted beneath the *clipeus*. For a description, see *ASR* V 4, cat. 68.
Portrait: The bust is carved with a male portrait.
Dating: Late 280s (*ASR* V 4, cat. 68).

Bibliography: Kranz, *ASR* V 4 (1984) cat. 68, pl. 44, 2.

210 *CLIPEUS* PORTRAIT OF A LEARNED WOMAN

Location/Inv.: Porto Torres, Basilica S. Gavino, crypt.
Size (coffin): L: 1.94 H: 0.59 D: 0.60
Condition: The coffin is preserved.
Frontal relief: Divided into five panels. The second and fourth panels are strigillated. A seasonal personification is represented on the first and fifth panels. A *clipeus* with a bust of a woman is depicted on the central panel and two *cornucopiae* are shown beneath the *clipeus*. For a description, see *ASR* V 4, cat. 158.
Short ends: Without relief decoration.
Portrait: The bust is carved with a female portrait.
Dating: Late Gallienic to early Tetrarchic period (*ASR* V 4, cat. 158).

Bibliography: Kranz, *ASR* V 4 (1984) cat. 158, pl. 72, 3.

211 LEARNED WOMAN

Location/Inv.: Rome, Catacombe di S. Callisto, museum.
Size (coffin): L: 0.91 H: 0.37
Condition: Fragments of a frontal relief.
Frontal relief: A bust of a woman with a scroll on a pedestal is placed in front of a *parapetasma* held by flying *victoriae*. Only the figure to the right is preserved. For a description, see *ASR* V 4, cat. 101.
Portrait: The bust is carved with a blank portrait and a roughly carved female hairstyle
Dating: Tetrarchic (*ASR* V 4, cat. 101).

Bibliography: Kranz, *ASR* V 4, (1984) cat. 101, pl. 63, 8; Wilpert I 1929, 101; Hanfmann 1951, cat. 458.

212 *CLIPEUS* PORTRAIT OF A LEARNED MAN

Location/Inv.: Rome, Catacombe di Domitilla, Basilica S. Petronilla.
Size (coffin): L: 1.50 H: 0.43 D: 0.44
Condition: The coffin is preserved.
Frontal relief: Divided into five panels. The second and fourth panels are strigillated. A seasonal personification is represented on the first and fifth panels. A *clipeus* with a bust of a man is shown on the central panel, and two masks and scrolls are depicted beneath the *clipeus*. For a description, see *ASR* V 4, cat. 159.
Portrait: The bust is carved with a blank portrait.
Dating: Late Tetrarchic (*ASR* V 4, cat. 159).
Comment: This could be the sarcophagus of a boy rather than a man, as the size of the coffin is no longer than 1.50 m.

Bibliography: Kranz, *ASR* V 4 (1984) cat. 159, pl. 72, 2.

213 BUST OF A LEARNED MAN

Location/Inv.: Rome, Catacombe di Pretestato.
Size (coffin): L: 1.13 H: 0.39
Condition: Fragment of a lid.
Provenience: Rome, Catacombe di Pretestato.
Lid: Seasonal personifications, a ram-bearer, and a bust of a man in front of a *parapetasma* holding a scroll.
Portrait: The bust is carved with a male portrait.
Inscription: DIDO(rus). Roughly carved on upper profile.
Dating: Late third century (*Rep.* I, cat. 593).

Bibliography: *Rep.* I, cat. 593.

214 *CLIPEUS* PORTRAIT OF A LEARNED MAN

Location/Inv.: Rome, Colosseum (close by).
Size (coffin): L: 2.11 H: 0.67 D: 0.72
Frontal relief: Two flying cupids hold a central *clipeus* with a bust of a man holding a scroll. A scene with Oceanus and Tellus flanking two cupids in a boat is depicted beneath the *clipeus*. A seasonal personification is represented on each end of the relief. For a description, see *ASR* V 4, cat. 102.
Short ends: Flying *Genius*.
Portrait: The bust was carved with a portrait (roughly carved?). Today the head is badly damaged.
Dating: 250s (*ASR* V 4, cat. 102).

Bibliography: Kranz, *ASR* V 4 (1984) cat. 102, pl. 60, 3.

215 *CLIPEUS* PORTRAIT OF A LEARNED WOMAN

Location/Inv.: Rome, Musei Capitolini, Palazzo dei Conservatori, inv. 839.
Size (coffin): L: 2.01 H: 0.59 D: 0.65; (lid): L: 2.05 H: 0.37 D: 0.67
Condition: The coffin and lid are preserved.
Provenience: Rome, Prati di Castello (Dresken-Weiland 2003, cat. 104).
Frontal relief: Two flying cupids hold a *clipeus* with a bust of a woman holding a scroll. Two masks flanked by Tellus and Oceanus are depicted beneath the *clipeus*. A seasonal personification and animals are represented on each end of the relief. For a description, see *ASR* V 4, cat. 104.
Short ends: Without relief decoration.
Lid: Cupids harvesting and pressing grapes. An empty inscription panel is placed on the centre of the lid.
Portrait: The bust is carved with a blank portrait.
Dating: Before 290s (*ASR* V 4, cat. 104).
Comment: One skeleton. Plundered in antiquity through a hole in one end of the coffin.

Bibliography: Kranz, *ASR* V 4 (1984) cat. 104, pl. 62, 1; Dresken-Weiland 2003, cat. 104.

216 LEARNED BOY

Location/Inv.: Rome, Musei Vaticani, Cortile Ottagono del belvedere, inv. 879.
Size (coffin): L: 2.12 H: 0.74 D: 0.74
Condition: The coffin is preserved.
Frontal relief: A female figure with a scroll is placed in front of a *parapetasma* held by two naked seasonal personifications. Two other seasonal personifications are represented on each side of this group. They wear short tunica and are holding hunted game and fruit baskets.
Short ends: *Lenos*-shaped. A lion killing a deer.
Portrait: The learned female figure is carved with a portrait of a boy.
Inscription: Post-antique inscription on the upper profile.
Dating: Second quarter of the third century.
Comment: Cross-gendered. The central figure was intended for a woman (the clothes are female), but the head was carved with male portrait features. Child sarcophagus.

Bibliography: Kranz, *ASR* V 4 (1984) cat. 90, pls. 48, 4; 49, Koch 1990, 65-7.

217 *CLIPEUS* PORTRAIT OF A LEARNED MAN

Location/Inv.: Rome, Musei Vaticani, Cortile Ottagono del Belvedere, inv. 1081.
Size (coffin): L: 1.97 H: 0.60
Condition: The frontal relief is preserved.
Frontal relief: Two seasonal personifications hold a central *clipeus* with a bust of a man holding a scroll. Another four seasonal personifications are represented on either side of the *clipeus*. A man ploughing with two oxen is depicted beneath the *clipeus*.
Portrait: The bust is carved with a male portrait, heavily restored.
Dating: 260s (*ASR* V 4, cat. 61).

Bibliography: Kranz, *ASR* V 4 (1984) cat. 61, pl. 33, 1.

218 LEARNED MAN (PHILOSOPHER)

Location/Inv.: Rome, Musei Vaticani, Cortile delle Pigna, inv. 5171.
Size (coffin): L: 2.14 H: 0.62 D: 0.64
Condition: The coffin is preserved.
Frontal relief: Divided into five panels. The second and fourth panels are strigillated. A seasonal personification is represented on the first and fifth panels. A seated philosopher with a scroll is depicted on the central panel. Behind him, there is a *parapetasma*. For a description, see *ASR* V 4, cat. 183.
Portrait: The seated philosopher is carved with a portrait of a young man.
Dating: The end of the third century (Ewald 1999, cat. C 37).

Bibliography: Kranz, *ASR* V 4 (1984) cat. 183, pl. 74, 6; Ewald 1999, cat. C 37.

219 BUST OF A LEARNED FIGURE

Location/Inv.: Rome, Musei Vaticani, Museo Pio Cristiano, inv. 37.
Size (coffin): L: 1.48 H: 0.39 D: 0.47
Condition: The coffin and lid are preserved.

Frontal relief: A bust on a plinth of a figure holding a scroll is depicted in front of a *parapetasma* held by two flying *Genii.* Two seasonal personifications are represented on either side of this composition. For a description, see *ASR* V 4, cat. 93.
Lid: Acroter.
Portrait: The bust is carved with a blank portrait.
Dating: 270-280 (*ASR* V 4, cat. 93).
Comment: The bust seems to be feminine, but the outline of the head looks as if it could have been carved with a portrait of a man. It was probably designed so it could be carved into either a man or a woman.

Bibliography: Kranz, *ASR* V 4 (1984) cat. 93, pl. 48, 5; Wilpert 1936, 12-4; Gütschow 1938, 155-57; Huskinson 1996, cat. 8. 14.

220 *CLIPEUS* PORTRAIT OF AN EDUCATED WOMAN

Location/Inv.: Rome, Musei Vaticani, Museo Pio Cristiano, inv. 203.
Size (coffin): L: 1.00 H: 0.30
Condition: The frontal relief is preserved.
Frontal relief: Divided into five panels. The second and fourth panels are strigillated. A seasonal personification is represented on the first and fifth panels. A *clipeus* with a bust of a woman is represented on the central panel. A personification and a deer are depicted beneath the *clipeus.* For a description, see *ASR* V 4, cat. 171.
Portrait: The bust is carved with a blank portrait.
Dating: Late Tetrarchic period (*ASR* V 4, cat. 171).
Comment: Possibly from a child sarcophagus because of its length. Could be a *loculus* plate (*ASR* V 4, cat. 171).

Bibliography: Kranz, *ASR* V 4 (1984) cat. 171, pl. 73, 3; Sichtermann 1984.

221 *CLIPEUS* PORTRAIT OF A LEARNED BOY

Location/Inv.: Rome, Musei Vaticani, Museo Pio Cristiano, inv. 214.
Size (coffin): L: 0.90 H: 0.27
Condition: The frontal relief is preserved.
Frontal relief: Divided into five panels. The second and fourth panels are strigillated. A seasonal personification is represented on the first and fifth panels. A *clipeus* with a bust of a boy holding a scroll is shown on the central panel, and two masks are placed beneath it. For a description, see *ASR* V 4, cat. 172.
Portrait: The bust is carved with a portrait of a boy.
Inscription: QVI BISIS ANIS DOBVS MESIB(us) VI.
Dating: Around 300 (Huskinson 1996, 8. 25). Late Tetrarchic period (*ASR* V 4, cat. 172).
Comment: The sarcophagus is included in the statistics on learned boys. Child sarcophagus. Could be a *loculus* plate (*ASR* V 4, cat. 172).

Bibliography: Kranz, *ASR* V 4 (1984) cat. 172, pl. 73, 2; Huskinson 1996, 8. 25.

222 LEARNED FIGURE

Location/Inv.: Rome, Musei Vaticani, Magazzino sculture, inv. 4754.
Size (coffin): L: 0.33 H: 0.25 D: 0.05
Condition: A fragment of the frontal relief is preserved.
Provenience: From Rome, Giardino delle Pigna.
Frontal relief: From the left, a seasonal personification, a learned figure, and a flying cupid are represented. For a description, see *ASR* V 4, cat. 121.
Portrait: The learned figure is carved with a blank portrait.
Dating: Between the Tetrarchic and Constantinian periods (*ASR* V 4, cat. 121).
Comment: The portrait figure could be turned into either a man or a woman.

Bibliography: Kranz, *ASR* V 4 (1984) cat. 121, pl. 52, 8.

223 BUST OF A LEARNED WOMAN

Location/Inv.: Rome, Museo Nazionale Romano, inv. 385/407.
Size (coffin): L: 1.93 H: 0.65 D: 0.63; (lid): L: 1.93 H: 0.21 D: 0.63
Condition: The coffin and lid are preserved.
Frontal relief: Seasonal personifications, ram-bearer, Dionysus, and a small satyr.
Short ends: Without relief decoration.
Lid: Bust of a woman with a scroll, an empty inscription panel, and cupids.
Portrait: The bust on the lid is carved with a blank portrait.
Dating: Between 320-400. For discussion, see *ASR* IV 4, cat. 256.

Bibliography: Matz, *ASR* IV 4 (1975) cat. 256; Kranz, *ASR* V 4 (1984) cat. 133; Bielefeld, *ASR* V 2, 2 (1997) cat. 119 (lid).

224 LEARNED WOMAN

Location/Inv.: Rome, Museo Nazionale Romano, inv. 57289.
Size (coffin): L: 0.39 H: 0.35 D: 0.06
Condition: Fragment of a lid?
Lid: A woman with a scroll is represented in front a *parapetasma* held by seasonal personifications. A rabbit is seated at her feet. For a description, see *MNR* I 10, 2, cat. 174.
Portrait: The woman is carved with a blank portrait.
Dating: Second half of the third century (*MNR* I 10, 2, cat. 174).

Bibliography: *MNR* I 10, 2, cat. 174.

225 BUST OF A LEARNED WOMAN

Location/Inv.: Rome, Museo Nazionale Romano, inv. 115172.
Size (coffin): L: 2.16 H: 0.57 D: 0.62
Condition: The coffin and lid are preserved.
Provenience: Rome, Foro Italico 1934.
Frontal relief: Cupids in a Dionysian procession. For a description, see *MNR* I 8, 1, cat. V, 7.
Short ends: Large fruit baskets flanked by winged cupids and two lambs.

Lid: An empty inscription panel is placed in the centre. Five of the Nine Muses (a theatre play?) are represented to the left of the panel and to the right, a bust of a woman with a scroll is depicted in front of a *parapetasma* held by two seasonal personifications. For a description, see *ASR* V 4, cat. 547.
Portrait: The bust on the lid is carved with a blank portrait.
Dating: Early Tetrarchic (*ASR* V 4, cat. 547).

Bibliography: Wegner, *ASR* V 3 (1966) cat. 130; Kranz, *ASR* V 4 (1984) cat. 547, pl. 113, 6; 1993; *MNR* I 8, 1, cat. V, 7; Huskinson 1996, 31, 52, 72, 102, 107-8, 114, cat. A 10.

226 *CLIPEUS* PORTRAIT OF A LEARNED WOMAN

Location/Inv.: Rome, Museo Nazionale Romano, inv. 135926.
Size (coffin): L: 1.94 H: 0.54 D: 0.56; (lid): H: 0.22
Condition: The coffin and lid are preserved.
Provenience: Via Ostiense (Dresken-Weiland 2003, cat. A 89).
Frontal relief: Divided into five panels. The second and fourth panels are strigillated. A seasonal personification is represented on the first and fifth panels. A *clipeus* with a bust of a woman holding a scroll is represented on the central panel. Three theatre masks are depicted beneath the *clipeus*. For a description, see *ASR* V 4, cat. 162.
Short ends: Griffin.
Lid: Sea-*thiasos* and an empty inscription panel.
Portrait: The bust on the frontal relief is carved with a female portrait.
Dating: 220-230s (*ASR* V 4, cat. 162).
Comment: Contained the skeleton of a woman.

Bibliography: Kranz, *ASR* V 4 (1984) cat. 162, pl. 68, 5; Dresken-Weiland 2003, cat. A 89.

227 *CLIPEUS* PORTRAIT OF A LEARNED MAN

Location/Inv.: Rome, Palazzo della Cancelleria (staircase).
Size (coffin): L: 2.06 H: 0.56 D: 0.61
Condition: The coffin is preserved.
Frontal relief: Two flying cupids support a central *clipeus* with a bust of a man holding a scroll. A cockfight flanked by Tellus and Oceanus is depicted beneath the *clipeus*. A seasonal personification with a basket, dog, and animal is represented on each end of the relief. For description, see *ASR* V 4, cat. 105.
Short ends: Without relief decoration.
Portrait: It is debatable whether the man has a portrait or simply a roughly carved head. The face is today damaged.
Dating: Tetrarchic period (*ASR* V 4, cat. 105).

Bibliography: Kranz, *ASR* V 4 (1984) cat. 105, pl. 62, 3.

228 LEARNED WOMAN (PHILOSOPHER) (FIG. 43)

Location/Inv.: Rome, Palazzo Lazzaroni.
Size (coffin): L: 2.08 H: 0.60
Condition: The coffin is preserved.
Frontal relief: Divided into five panels. The second and fourth panels are strigillated. A seasonal personification is represented on the first and fifth panels. A seated woman with a scroll is depicted on the central panel, and a *parapetasma* is suspended behind her. For a description, see *ASR* V 4, cat. 181.
Short ends: Fruit baskets. Today not visible.
Portrait: The seated woman on the central panel is carved with a blank portrait.
Dating: First half of the fourth century (Ewald 1999, C 13), or Constantinian period (*ASR* V 4, cat. 181).

Bibliography: Kranz, *ASR* V 4 (1984) cat. 181. pl. 74, 7; Ewald 1999, cat. C 36.

229 LEARNED BOY

Location/Inv.: Rome, Palazzo Mattei.
Size (coffin): L: 1.15 H: 0.37
Condition: The frontal relief is preserved.
Frontal relief: A standing figure in a *pallium* holds a scroll. Three seasonal personifications are represented on each side of the figure. For a description, see *ASR* V 4, cat. 120.
Portrait: The standing figure is carved with a portrait of a boy.
Dating: Around 300 (Huskinson 1996, 8. 17).
Comment: Child sarcophagus. The portrait is likely to be modern.

Bibliography: Kranz, *ASR* V 4 (1984) 120; Guerrini 1982, cat. 96, pl. 72, b; Huskinson 1996, 8. 17.

230 LEARNED WOMAN

Location/Inv.: Rome, Palazzo Mattei.
Size (coffin): L: 0.59 H: 0.53
Condition: Several fragments of a frontal relief.
Frontal relief: A woman/girl stands between two seasonal personifications holding a *parapetasma*. Two more seasonal personifications are preserved on the right end of the relief.
Portrait: The woman/girl is carved with a portrait.
Dating: Constantinian period (*ASR* V 4, cat. 82).

Bibliography: Kranz, *ASR* V 4 (1984) cat. 82, pl. 51, 1; Guerrini 1982, cat. 97.

231 *CLIPEUS* PORTRAIT OF A LEARNED MAN

Location/Inv.: Rome, Palazzo Sacchetti.
Size (coffin): L: 2.03 H: 0.61 D: 0.67
Condition: The coffin is preserved.
Frontal relief: Two flying cupids hold a central *clipeus* with a bust of a man holding a scroll. A cockfight flanked by Oceanus and Tellus is depicted beneath the *clipeus*. A seasonal personification with a basket is represented on each end of the relief. For a description, see *ASR* V 4, cat. 107.
Short ends: Seasonal personifications.
Portrait: The head of the bust is now lost.
Dating: 240s (*ASR* V 4, cat. 107).

Bibliography: Kranz, *ASR* V 4 (1984) cat. 107, pl. 60, 4.

232 *CLIPEUS* PORTRAIT OF A LEARNED WOMAN

Location/Inv.: Rome, Palazzo Sacchetti (staircase).
Size (coffin): L: 1.98 H: 0.43 D: 0.51
Condition: The coffin is preserved.

Frontal relief: Divided into five panels. The second and fourth panels are strigillated. A seasonal personification is represented on the first and fifth panels. A *clipeus* with a bust of a woman with a scroll is depicted on the central panel. A bucolic scene is depicted beneath the *clipeus*. For a description, see *ASR* V 4, cat. 164.
Short ends: Without relief decoration.
Portrait: The bust is carved with a female portrait, but the facial features are damaged.
Dating: Post-Gallienic period (*ASR* V 4, cat. 164).

Bibliography: Kranz, *ASR* V 4 (1984) cat. 164, pl. 70, 4.

233 SHELL WITH BUST OF A LEARNED WOMAN

Location/Inv.: Rome, S. Andrea, Oratorio.
Size (coffin): L: 0.93 H: 0.35 D: 0.43
Condition: The coffin is preserved.
Frontal relief: Unfinished relief. A shell with a bust of a woman holding a scroll is held by seasonal personifications. More seasonal personifications are represented on each side of this group. For a description, see *ASR* V 4, cat. 48.
Short ends: Without relief decoration.
Portrait: The bust in the shell has been prepared for a portrait but the relief was never finished.
Dating: Early fourth century (Huskinson 1996, 8. 6); the Constantinian period (*ASR* V 4, cat. 48).

Bibliography: Kranz, *ASR* V 4 (1984) cat. 48, pl. 39, 4; Huskinson 1996, 8. 6.

234 *CLIPEUS* PORTRAIT OF A LEARNED WOMAN

Location/Inv.: Rome, S. Sebastiano, Museo.
Size (coffin): L: 1.75 H: 0.42 D: 0.57; (lid): L: 1.71 H: 0.26 D: 0.54
Condition: The coffin and lid are preserved.
Provenience: Rome, S. Sebastiano.
Frontal relief: Divided into five panels. The second and fourth panels are strigillated. A seasonal personification is shown on the first and fifth panels. A *clipeus* with a bust of a woman holding a scroll is depicted on the central panel. Two cocks are depicted beneath the *clipeus*. For a description, see *ASR* V 4, cat. 168.
Short ends: Without relief decoration.
Lid: Scenes with cupids harvesting, loading, and pressing grapes flank an empty inscription panel.
Portrait: The bust is carved with a blank portrait. The roughly carved hair seems to be prepared for a Constantinian hairstyle (*ASR* V 4, cat. 168).
Dating: Late Constantinian period (*ASR* V 4, cat. 168).

Bibliography: Kranz, *ASR* V 4 (1984) cat. 168, pl. 73, 1.

235 LEARNED WOMAN

Location/Inv.: Rome, Vatican, in the garden, Fontana Aquilone.
Size (coffin): L: 0.87 H: 0.40 D: 0.40
Condition: The coffin is preserved.
Frontal relief: Unfinished. Seasonal personifications flank a woman with a scroll.
Short ends: Without relief decoration.
Portrait: The woman is carved with a blank portrait.
Dating: Late third century (*ASR* V 4, cat. 89).

Bibliography: Kranz, *ASR* V 4 (1984) cat. 89, pl. 51, 4.

236 LEARNED WOMAN (FIG. 35)

Location/Inv.: Rome, Vatican, S. Pietro.
Condition: The coffin is preserved.
Frontal relief: Divided into five panels. The second and fourth panels are strigillated. A seasonal personification is represented on the first and fifth panels. A standing woman in chiton and mantle with a scroll is depicted on the central panel. A *parapetasma* is suspended behind her. For a description, see *ASR* V 4, cat. 185.
Short ends: Without relief decoration.
Portrait: The woman is carved with a blank portrait.
Dating: Late Tetrarchic (*ASR* V 4, cat. 185).

Bibliography: Kranz, *ASR* V 4 (1984) cat. 185, pl. 75, 2.

237 LEARNED WOMAN

Location/Inv: Rome, Via Bocca di Leone.
Size (coffin): L: 0.56 H: 0.55
Condition: A fragment of the frontal relief is preserved.
Frontal relief: A woman is standing in front of a *parapetasma* held by two seasonal personifications (the figure to the right is lost). For a description, see *ASR* V 4, cat. 84.
Portrait: The portrait is lost but the hairstyle of a woman is preserved.
Dating: Tetrarchic period (*ASR* V 4, cat. 84).

Bibliography: Kranz, *ASR* V 4 (1984) cat. 84, pl. 52, 2.

238 LEARNED *EQUITUS*

Location/Inv.: Rome, Viale Regina Margherita, Cimitero anonimo, S. Lorenzo di Novazione, Cripta principale.
Size (coffin): L: 1.43 H: 0.91 (with lid)
Condition: The coffin and lid are preserved.
Provenience: Cemetery of Novatian. Preserved *in situ* (Dresken-Weiland 2003, cat. D 2).
Frontal relief: A young man in a cuirass with a scroll is represented in front of a *parapetasma* held by two flying cupids. Playing children, Tellus, and Oceanus are depicted on either side of the young man/boy. A *Genius* with a basket, fruit, and animals is represented on each end of the relief. For a description, see *ASR* V 4, cat. 112.
Short ends: Unknown (grouted into the wall).
Lid: An inscription tablet is held by two cupids. A group with seasonal personifications flanking a *krater* is represented on each side of the tablet.
Portrait: The learned *equitus* is carved with the portrait of a boy.

Inscription: FLORENTIO DOMITIO MARINIANO EQ(viti) R(omano) QVI VIXIT ANN(is) VIIII MENS(ibus) DVOBVS DEFVNCTVS III NON(as) AVG(ustas) DEPOSITVS VIII IDVS AVGVSTAS TVLLIANVS ET ARISTIA PAREN(tes) FILIO DVLCISSIMO
Dating: Around 320 (Huskinson 1996, 8. 12); early Constantinian period (*ASR* V 4, cat. 112, cat. 504).

Bibliography: Kranz, *ASR* V 4 (1984) cat. 112, cat. 504; *Rep.* I, cat. 663; Huskinson 1993, 117; 1996, 8. 12, pl. XVI, 3; Dresken-Weiland 2003, cat. D 2.

239 *CLIPEUS* PORTRAIT OF A LEARNED WOMAN

Location/Inv.: Rome, Villa Doria Pamphilj.
Size (coffin): L: 1.85 H: 0.74
Condition: The frontal relief is preserved.
Frontal relief: Two *victoriae* hold a central *clipeus* with a bust of a woman. Two seasonal personifications are represented on either side of this group. A scene with Selene visiting the sleeping Endymion is depicted beneath the *clipeus*. For a description, see *ASR* V 4, cat. 71.
Portrait: The bust is carved with a female portrait.
Dating: Late Constantinian period (*ASR* V 4, cat. 71).
Comment: The woman probably held a scroll, but it is lost today. This sarcophagus is included in the statistics on learned women.

Bibliography: Kranz, *ASR* V 4 (1984) cat. 71, pl. 45, 3; Calza 1977, cat. 257.

240 *CLIPEUS* PORTRAIT OF A LEARNED WOMAN

Location/Inv.: Rome, Villa Doria Pamphili, Casino Belrespiro.
Condition: The frontal relief is preserved.
Frontal relief: Two flying cupids hold a *clipeus* with a bust of a woman holding a scroll. Oceanus and Tellus are represented beneath the *clipeus*. A *Genius* with a dog and a hare is depicted on either end of the relief. For a description, see *ASR* V 4, cat. 113.
Portrait: The bust is carved with a portrait of a girl, which has been partially restored.
Dating: 270s (*ASR* V 4, cat. 113).

Bibliography: Kranz, *ASR* V 4 (1984) cat. 113, pl. 61, 1; Hanfmann 1951, cat. 455; Schumacher 1977, 51, 54; Calza 1977, cat. 254.

241 LEARNED WOMAN AND LEARNED MAN

Location/Inv.: Rome, Villa Doria Pamphili, Coffee House.
Size (coffin): L: 1.75 H: 0.77
Condition: The frontal relief is preserved.
Frontal relief: Two cupids hold a *parapetasma* in front of which are placed a female and a male bust (both with scrolls). Two plinths support the two busts. For a description, see *ASR* V 4, cat. 86.
Portrait: The busts are carved with a female and a male portrait.
Dating: Around 330 (*ASR* V 4, cat. 86).

Bibliography: Kranz, *ASR* V 4 (1984) cat. 86, pl. 48, 1.

242 LEARNED WOMAN

Location/Inv.: Rome, Villa Doria Pamphili (lost).
Condition: A fragment of the frontal relief was preserved.
Frontal relief: A woman with a scroll is represented standing in front of a *parapetasma* held by two seasonal personifications (the figure to the left is lost). For a description, see *ASR* V 4, cat. 88.
Portrait: The woman is carved with a portrait.
Dating: Constantinian period (*ASR* V 4, cat. 88).

Bibliography: Kranz, *ASR* V 4 (1984) cat. 88, pl. 52, 3; Calza 1977, cat. 255.

243 BUST OF A LEARNED MAN

Location/Inv.: Rome, Villa Giustiniani Massimo, Casino.
Condition: Fragment of a lid.
Lid: A central bust of a figure holding a scroll is represented in front of a *parapetasma* held by two Genii. Seasonal personifications are depicted on either end of the relief. For a description, see *ASR* V 4, cat. 538.
Portrait: The bust is carved with a portrait of a young man (or boy). The head seems to be too small for the shoulders.
Dating: Late Gallienic or early Tetrarchic period (*ASR* V 4, cat. 538).
Comment: The size of the head compared to the bust makes it likely that the portrait is a later addition or a re-carving.

Bibliography: Kranz, *ASR* V 4 (1984) cat. 538, pl. 113, 5; Hanfmann 1951, cat. A-8.

244 LEARNED WOMAN

Location/Inv.: Rome, lost. Previously on the art market (Barsanti).
Condition: The coffin was preserved.
Frontal relief: Four seasonal personifications frame a figure with scrolls standing in front of a *parapetasma*. A lion killing a deer or a horse is represented on either end of the relief. The relief is unfinished. For a description, see *ASR* V 4, cat. 79.
Short ends: Lenos-shaped. The lion scene of the frontal relief continues on the short ends.
Portrait: The standing figure and its portrait are unfinished.
Dating: 280-300 (*ASR* VI 1, cat. 378).

Bibliography: Kranz, *ASR* V 4 (1984) cat. 79; Stroszeck, *ASR* VI 1 (1998) cat. 378, pl. 71, 3.

245 *CLIPEUS* PORTRAIT OF A LEARNED WOMAN

Location/Inv.: San Francisco, M. H. de Young Memorial Museum, inv. 54662.
Size (coffin): L: 1.78 H: 0.51 D: 0.51
Condition: The coffin is preserved.
Frontal relief: Two seasonal personifications hold a central *clipeus* with a bust of a woman holding a scroll. Another two seasonal personifications are represented on each side of this scene and cupids are playing in between them. Cupids playing with a mask are depicted beneath the *clipeus*. For a description, see *ASR* V 4, cat. 58.

Short ends: Lenos-shaped. The motif from the frontal relief continues on the short end.
Lid: Modern carving.
Portrait: The *clipeus* bust is carved with a female portrait.
Dating: 270s (*ASR* V 4, cat. 58),

Bibliography: Kranz, *ASR* V 4 (1984) cat. 58, pl. 34, 4.

246 LEARNED MAN (FIG. 74)

Location/Inv.: San Marino, California, Henry E. Huntington Library and Art Gallery, inv. 22.6.
Size (coffin): L: 2.01 H: 0.74 D: 0.69
Condition: The coffin is preserved.
Frontal relief: The relief is divided into five panels. The second and fourth panels are carved as an imitation of a fence. Seasonal personifications are represented on the first and fifth panels. The central panel depicts a figure with a scroll. The figure was re-carved from a woman into a man; the dress has been shortened and the head was carved either from a roughly carved head or from a female portrait. The outline of the female hairstyle is visible on the back of the relief.
Left short end: Unfinished lion griffin.
Right short end: Without decoration; roughly carved.
Reverse: Without decoration. Cutting marks indicated a previous use as an architectural block (?).
Portrait: The figure on the central panel is carved with a male portrait.
Dating: Late 280s or early 290s (*ASR* V 4, cat. 182).
Comment: Re-carved. The figure is carved from a female figure into a male.

Bibliography: Kranz, *ASR* V 4 (1984) cat. 182; Koch 1990; Huskinson 2002, 25-26; Birk forthcoming.

247 *CLIPEUS* PORTRAIT OF A LEARNED WOMAN

Location/Inv.: Toronto, Royal Ontario Museum, inv. 923.4.54.
Size (coffin): L: 0.88 H: 0.53
Condition: A fragment of the relief is preserved.
Frontal relief: A central *clipeus* with a bust of a woman holding a scroll is held by two seasonal personifications. On each side of the *clipeus*, there are fragments of more seasonal personifications. Young children playing are depicted beneath the *clipeus*. For a description, see *ASR* V 4, cat. 59.
Portrait: The bust is carved with a female portrait.
Inscription: Placed in the *clipeus*. QV(a)E VIXIT AN(nos) XXV DORMIT IN PACE.
Dating: Early Tetrarchic period (*ASR* V 4, 59).

Bibliography: Kranz, *ASR* V 4 (1984) cat. 59, pl. 40, 3.

Vita Romana

248 LEARNED WOMAN AND COMMANDER

Location/Inv.: Mainz, Römisch-Germanisches Zentralmuseum. Once in Rome, The Collection.
Size (lid): L: 2.76 H: 0.76
Condition: The lid is preserved but has been broken several places (it is probably the lid of the Ggreat Ludovisi sarcophagus, cat. no. 625).
Provenience: Found 1621 in Rome, Vigna Bernusconi, near Porta San Lorenzo.
Lid: A central *tabula ansata* without an inscription. A woman with a scroll in front of a *parapetasma* is represented to the right of the inscription. To the left side, there is a military scene with a seated commander. For a description, see *ASR* I 3, cat. 31.
Portrait: Both the seated commander and the female bust with a scroll are carved with portrait features.
Dating: 260 (*ASR* I 3, cat. 31). According to Fittschen, the female bust should be dated to the early Severian period because of the hairstyle (Fittschen 1984, 149).

Bibliography: Reinsberg, *ASR* I 3 (2006) cat. 31, pl. 46, 5; Fittschen 1984; Wrede 2001; Künzl 2010, 103-7.

249 LEARNED MAN AND TWO MEN (FIG. 62)

Location/Inv.: Rome, Musei Vaticani, Museo Gregoriano Profano, inv. 9517.
Size (lid): L: 0.68 H: 0.26
Condition: The relief is well preserved.
Provenience: Probably discovered near the Tiber in Ostia in 1801.
Lid: The relief is divided into three panels. A seated man with a scroll (?) in his left hand is represented on the first panel. He stretches his right hand forward and grasps the hand of another man, who stands in front of him. Both men are dressed in tunics with sleeves. The standing man wears a *stola* around his left arm. Two mirrors and a curtain hang from a rod behind them. It seems as if the seated man is holding one of the mirrors, maybe to put it into the hand of the other man. A portrait bust of a man with a scroll is depicted on the second panel. Despite his rather large hands (holding a scroll) and his beard, he is depicted with drapery that has slipped from his shoulder. Furthermore, the outline of breasts are visible beneath the cloth. The griffin on the third panel was probably never finished.
Reverse: Reused architectural element with carved profiles (Sinn 1991, cat. 21, with illustration).
Portrait: The seated salesman (?) and the standing customer (?) on the first panel have male portrait features, but the face of the latter was re-carved from a figure of a woman with long hair. The female locks are still visible on the back of the head. The bust on the central panel is carved with a portrait of a

bearded middle-aged man. The portrait is carved deeper into the relief than the bust.
Dating: Third quarter of the third century (*ASR* I 4, cat. 285).
Comment: Thought to be a sarcophagus lid (Benndorf & Schöne 1867, 3, cat. 7), but could also be a *loculus* plate.

Bibliography: Amedick, *ASR* I 4 (1991) cat. 285; Benndorf & Schöne 1867, 3, cat. 7; Sinn 1991, cat. 21; Birk 2011, 242.

250 EDUCATED WOMAN

Location/Inv.: Rome, Villa Albani.
Size (coffin): L: 1.10
Condition: Fragment of a frontal relief.
Frontal relief: A seated woman playing a *pendurium*. For a description, see *ASR* I 4, cat. 230.
Portrait: The seated figure is carved with a female portrait.
Dating: Around 250 (*ASR* I 4, cat. 230).

Bibliography: Amedick, *ASR* I 4 (1991) cat. 230, pl. 8, 3; Bol 1998, cat. 614, 128-130.

251 EDUCATED WOMAN

Location/Inv.: Sassari, Museo Nazionale.
Size (coffin): L: 0.75 H: 0.73
Condition: Fragment of a frontal relief.
Frontal relief: A seated woman playing a *pendurium*. For a description, see *ASR* I 4, cat. 243.
Portrait: The woman is carved with a blank portrait.
Dating: Severan period (Pesce 1957, no. 53) or around 300 (*ASR* I 4, cat. 243. On page 18 in the same publication the dating is estimated to the time of Gallienus or shortly after).

Bibliography: Amedick, *ASR* I 4 (1991) cat. 243, pl. 10, 1; Pesce 1957, no. 53; Himmelmann 1973, no. 5.

Unknown

252 SHELL WITH WOMAN AND LEARNED WOMAN (FIG. 84)

Location/Inv.: Rome, Museo Nazionale Romano, inv. 196637.
Size (coffin): L: 0.60 H: 0.73 D: 0.13
Condition: Fragment of a frontal relief.
Provenience: Rome, near Via Appia. Once built into the Tomb of the Sons of Sesto Pompeo.
Frontal relief: Strigillated sarcophagus with a central shell with two busts. A female figure places her hand on the male figure, which is holding a scroll. Two *cornucopiae* are depicted beneath the shell. For a description, see *MNR* I 2, 244.
Portrait: The head of the female portrait bust with one naked shoulder has a blank portrait. The male bust has been carved with female portrait features.
Dating: Middle of the third century (*MNR* I 2, 244).

Bibliography: *MNR* I 2, 244, cat. 38.

253 LEARNED MAN

Location/Inv.: Rome, Museo Nazionale Romano (unknown inv.).
Size (coffin): L: 0.24 H. 0.61 D. 0.31
Condition: Fragment of the frontal relief.
Frontal relief: The right figural panel of a strigillated sarcophagus. A man with a scroll is represented in front of a *parapetasma*.
Portrait: The standing figure is carved with a male portrait.
Dating: Late third century (*MNR* I 3, cat. III, 5).

Bibliography: *MNR* I 3, cat. III, 5.

Non-Narrative Scenes with Figures without Scrolls or Musical Instruments

Bucolic

254 *CLIPEUS* PORTRAIT OF A MAN
Location/Inv.: Florence, Giardino Boboli.
Condition: The coffin is preserved.
Frontal relief: Divided into five panels. The second and fourth panels are strigillated. A veiled woman is represented on the first panel and a herdsman stands on the fifth panel. A *clipeus* with a bust of a man is shown on the central panel, and a bucolic scene with a herdsman and sheep is depicted beneath the *clipeus*. Two flowers are seen in the upper corners of the central panel.
Short ends: Without decoration.
Portrait: The bust is carved with a portrait of a man.
Dating: Third century (Sichtermann 1984, 50, note 44).
Bibliography: Sichtermann 1984.

255 *CLIPEUS* PORTRAIT OF A MAN
Location/Inv.: Rome, Catacombe di Priscilla, Basilica di S. Silvestro.
Condition: The coffin is preserved but damaged.
Provenience: Rome, Catacombe di Priscilla, regione dell'arenario.
Frontal relief: Clipeus with a bust of a man. The *clipeus* is supported by two *cornucopiae* and is surrounded by bucolic scenes.
Short ends: Fruit baskets.
Portrait: The bust is carved with a blank portrait.
Dating: Fourth century.
Bibliography: Bisconti 2004, 57, fig. 23; Spera 2000, 243-84.

256 BUST OF A WOMAN (GIRL?)
Location/Inv.: Rome, Palazzo Corsetti, now lost.
Condition: The lid is preserved.
Lid: From the left: a mask, cupids, a bust of a woman in front of a *parapetasma*, an inscription panel, a bucolic scene, and a mask.
Portrait: The bust is carved with a blank portrait.
Inscription: AVRIEI (probably Aurelia) MENISE / VIXIT ANN(os) LXXXI / AMENSES CII DEPOSITA PRIIDVS M(artis) / AT PARENTES FECE / RVNT
Dating: First part of the fourth century (*Rep.* I, cat. 939).
Bibliography: *Rep.* I, cat. 939; Hanfmann 1951, cat. 523.

Cupids

257 *CLIPEUS* PORTRAIT OF A BOY
Location/inv.: California, Malibu, J. P. Getty Museum, inv. 74. AA. 25.
Size (coffin): L: 1.16 H: 0.32 D: 0.41
Condition: The coffin and lid are preserved.
Frontal relief: Two cupids support a *clipeus* bust of a young boy.
Short ends: Cupid giving a drink to an eagle-griffin.
Lid: Central pillar flanked by acanthus scrolls emerging from cupids and griffins on the end of the relief.
Portrait: The bust is carved with a portrait of a boy.
Dating: Around 120 (Huskinson 1996, cat. 9. 13).
Comment: Child sarcophagus.
Bibliography: Eberle 1990a, fig. 1a; Huskinson 1996, cat. 9. 13.

258 BUSTS OF A WOMAN AND A MAN
Location/Inv.: Copenhagen, Ny Carlsberg Glyptotek, inv. 2349.
Size (coffin): L: 2.20 H: 0.61 D. 0.82

Condition: The coffin is preserved.
Frontal relief: Two busts, one of a woman and one of a man, are flanked by two flying cupids. Torches are placed beneath the busts.
Short ends: Weapons.
Portrait: The busts are carved with female and male portrait features.
Dating: After 250 (Østergaard 1996, cat. 53).

Bibliography: Østergaard 1996, cat. 53, p. 125.

259 *CLIPEUS* PORTRAIT OF A CHILD

Location/Inv.: Liverpool Museum.
Size (coffin): L: 1.22 H: 0.28
Condition: Two fragments of a frontal relief.
Frontal relief: A central *clipeus* with a bust of a child is shown above depictions of snakes confronting panthers. A cupid with garlands is represented on either end of the relief.
Portrait: The bust is carved with the portrait of a boy (?).
Dating: Third century (Huskinson 1996, cat. 9. 32).
Comment: Child sarcophagus.

Bibliography: Huskinson 1996, cat. 9. 32.

260 *CLIPEUS* PORTRAIT OF A MAN

Location/Inv.: London, British Museum, inv. GR 1805.7-3.155.
Size (coffin): L: 2.00 H: 0.50 D: 0.55
Condition: The coffin is preserved.
Provenience: Found near Rome. Purchased by Charles Townley from the heirs of the Burioni family in 1779 (Walker 1999, cat. 35).
Frontal relief: Two flying cupids hold a *clipeus* with a bust of man. Three masks are depicted beneath the *clipeus*: two of satyrs and one of a goat. A goat and a lion griffin (?) flank the masks. A cupid with a garland is represented on either end of the relief. For a description, see Walker 1990, cat. 35.
Short ends: Griffin.
Portrait: The bust is carved with portrait features, a full moustache, and a short beard.
Dating: Around the middle of the third century (Walker 1990, cat. 35).

Bibliography: Bergmann 1977, pl. 5, 5; Walker 1990, cat. 35, pl. 13.

261 *CLIPEUS* PORTRAIT OF A BOY

Location/Inv.: London, British Museum, inv. GR 1896.6-19.5.
Size (coffin): L: 1.00 H: 0.36 D: 0.46
Condition: Only the frontal relief is preserved, and it has been broken at both ends. It is diagonally cracked across the right side and the cupid's genitals are damaged.
Frontal relief: Two female figures hold a central *clipeus* with a bust of a boy. The *clipeus* rests on an inscription panel. A cupid with a torch is represented on either end of the relief.
Portrait: Portrait of a boy possibly re-cut from that of a woman (Huskinson 1996, 9. 36).
Inscription: D M / OCTAVIO ISOCRHY / SO FILIO DVLCISSIM / Q V AN I D XXX / CRHYSEROS ET F / PRIMITIBA PA REN (*CIL* VI 23287).
Dating: The style of the portrait and the hair cropped straight across the top of the forehead suggests a date towards the end of the third century or the early fourth century. This date is supported by the the drilling of the hair and of the fruit flanking the *clipeus* (Walker, 1990, cat. 36).
Comment: The sarcophagus was made for a woman, but was used for the burial of a boy. Child sarcophagus.

Bibliography: Walker 1990, cat. 36; Huskinson 1996, cat. 9. 36; 2007, 335.

262 *CLIPEUS* PORTRAIT OF A MAN

Location/Inv.: Madison, Wisconsin (USA). University of Wisconsin, Chazen Museum of Art, inv. 69.13.1.
Size (coffin): L: 1.82 H: 0.71 D: 0.67
Condition: The coffin is preserved.
Frontal relief: Two cupids with wings hold a central *clipeus* with a bust of a man. Another two cupids with arrows, *chitara*, *pedum*, and a mirror (?) are represented to the left and right of this scene. A cockfight is depicted beneath the *clipeus.*
Short ends: Without relief decoration.
Portrait: The bust is carved with a male portrait.
Dating: 270-290 (*ASR* V 2, 1, cat. 23).

Bibliography: Kranz, *ASR* V 2, 1 (1999) cat. 23, pl. 55, 2.

263 BUST OF A WOMAN

Location/Inv.: Ostia, Museo Nazionale, magazine. Inv. 1560.
Size (lid): L: 1.03 H: 0.32 D: 0.26
Condition: Fragment of a lid.
Provenience: From the harbour?
Lid: A inscription tablet supported by two Psyche figures. A circus scene with a cupid is represented on the left side of the relief. Another cupid holding a *parapetasma* is represented on the right side. A bust of a woman is depicted in front of the *parapetasma*. The relief is broken on both ends. For a description, see *ASR* I 4, cat. 96.
Portrait: The bust is carved with female portrait features.
Inscription: AELIAE / SABINE / NEVIA / FORTUNA/TA FILIAE/DULCISSI/ME IN PACE (*CIL* XIV nr. 1952).
Dating: Tetrarchic period (*ASR* I 4, cat. 96).

Bibliography: Amedick, *ASR* I 4 (1991) cat. 96, pl. 100, 1.

264 BUST OF A GIRL

Location/Inv.: Paris, Musèe du Louvre, inv. Ma 302.
Size (lid): L: 1.63 H: 0.30
Condition: The lid is preserved.
Lid: Divided into seven niches. A bust of a girl flanked by two figures of Hermes is placed in the central niche. A garland is suspended above the bust. The scenes in the other niches are all cupids carrying out activities related to the Dionysian sphere.
Portrait: The bust is carved with the portrait of a girl.
Dating: around 240 (Barette & Metzger 1985, cat. 140).

Comment: Child sarcophagus.

Bibliography: Barette & Metzger 1985, cat. 140.

265 WOMAN

Location/Inv.: Rome, Antiquario Comunale, inv. 4981.
Size (coffin): L: 2.13 H: 0.57
Condition: The coffin and lid are preserved.
Provenience: Prati di Castello (Dresken-Weiland 2003, cat. A 105).
Frontal relief: Divided into five panels. The second and fourth panels are strigillated. The first panel is lost. A cupid is depicted on the fifth panel. A woman in front of a *parapetasma* is represented on the central panel.
Left short end: Lost.
Right short end: Without relief decoration.
Lid: Travertine plate without any relief decoration.
Portrait: The woman is carved with a blank portrait.
Dating: Post-Gallenic (*ASR* V 4, cat. 177).
Comment: Contained a 1.80 m-long skeleton, probably of a man.

Bibliography: Kranz, *ASR* V 4 (1984) cat. 177; Dresken-Weiland 2003, cat. A 105.

266 *CLIPEUS* PORTRAIT OF A MAN

Location/Inv.: Rome, Colosseum.
Condition: The coffin is preserved.
Frontal relief: Divided into five panels. The second and fourth panels are strigillated. A cupid leaning against a torch is represented on the first and fifth panels. A *clipeus* with a bust of a man is represented on the central panel. A scene with cupids pressing grapes is depicted beneath the *clipeus*. For a description, see *ASR* V 2, 2, cat. 116.
Portrait: The bust is carved with a male portrait. The head is too damaged for the facial features to be recognisable.
Dating: Last third of the third century (*ASR* V 2, 2, cat. 116).

Bibliography: Bielefeld, *ASR* V 2, 2 (1997) cat. 116, pl. 85, 3.

267 *CLIPEUS* PORTRAIT OF A MAN

Location/Inv.: Rome, Musei Capitolini, Palazzo dei Conservatori.
Size (coffin): L: 1.67 H: 0.47 D: 0.47
Condition: The coffin and lid are preserved.
Provenience: From Rome, Porta Salaria (Huskinson 1996, 9. 48).
Frontal relief: Divided into five panels. The second and fourth panels are strigillated. A cupid leaning against a torch is represented on the first and fifth panels. A *clipeus* with a bust of a young man is represented on the central panel. Two *cornucopiae* are depicted beneath the *clipeus*. For a description, see Stuart Jones 1968, cat. 2.
Short ends: Griffin.
Lid: Roof-shaped with antefixes and an inscription panel.
Portrait: The bust is carved with a portrait of a young man.
Inscription: Hellenius Optatinus. *CIL* VI. 31854.
Dating: Late third century (Huskinson 1996, 9. 47).

Bibliography: Stuart Jones 1968, 21, cat. 2, pl. 10; Huskinson 1996, 9. 47.

268 *CLIPEUS* PORTRAIT OF A WOMAN

Location/Inv.: Rome, Musei Capitolini, Palazzo Nuovo (atrio), inv. S 1894.
Condition: The frontal relief is preserved.
Frontal relief: Flying cupids holding a *clipeus* with a bust of a woman. Two cupids leaning towards torches are flanking the scene, and three theatrical masks are displayed beneath the *clipeus*. Oceanus and Tellus are lying beneath the flying cupids.
Short ends: Griffin.
Portrait: The bust is carved with a female portrait.
Dating: Dated around the middle of the third century (Rocca & Presicce 2010).
Comment: Paint is still visible on the portrait and on some of the other figures.

Bibliography: La Rocca & Presicce 2010, 178-81 with full bibliography.

269 BUSTS OF A WOMAN AND A MAN (FIG. 9)

Location/Inv.: Rome, Musei Vaticani, Cortile del Belvedere.
Condition: The lid is preserved. It is grouped today with a Achilles and Penthesilea sarcophagus.
Lid: A female bust is represented on the left side of an inscription panel and a male bust is represented on the right side. A *parapetasma* is suspended behind both of them. A sleeping cupid is depicted on each corner of the lid.
Portrait: The two busts are carved with a female and a male portrait.
Inscription: PAEVS MYRON AVRELIAE AGRIPPI / NAE COIVGI SANCTISSIMAE ET AE / LIS ARRIAE CRESCENTI FILIS DVL / CISSIMIS AEDEM A SO FECIT (CIL VI 10742).
Dating: Third century.
Comment: P. Aelius Myron bought the sarcophagus for Aurelia Agrippina (his wife), Aelia Arria (his daughter), and Crescens (his son). Dresken-Weiland 2003, 246.

Bibliography: Dresken-Weiland 2003, 246; Zanker & Ewald 2004, ill. p. 286.

270 *CLIPEUS* PORTRAIT OF A BOY

Location/Inv.: Rome, Musei Vaticani, Galleria Lapidaria, inv. 9262.
Size (coffin): L: 0.59 H: 0.36 D: 0.30
Condition: The coffin is preserved.
Frontal relief: Cupids hold a central *clipeus* with a bust of a boy. Baskets with flowers are depicted beneath the *clipeus*. Sleeping cupids are represented on either end of the relief.
Portrait: The bust is carved with a portrait of a boy.
Dating: Second half of the third century.
Comment: Child sarcophagus.

Bibliography: Schaeuenburg 1987, fig. 12, p. 243; Huskinson 1996, 9.30.

271 *CLIPEUS* PORTRAIT OF A GIRL

Location/Inv.: Rome, Musei Vaticani, repository.
Size (coffin): L: 1.11 H: 0.34
Condition: The coffin is preserved.
Frontal relief: Two cupids with torches hold a central *clipeus* with a bust of a girl. Playing and dancing cupids are represented on each side of this composition.
Portrait: The bust is carved with a portrait of a girl.
Dating: Around 250 (Huskinson 1996, 9. 31).
Comment: The sex of the portrait is difficult to determine. It could be another cross-gendered image, but judging from the bust type the sarcophagus commemorates a girl.Child sarcophagus.

Bibliography: Kaschnitz-Weinberg 1937, no. 504, pl. 85, 2; Huskinson 1996, 9. 31.

272 BUST OF A WOMAN

Location/Inv.: Rome, Museo Nazionale Romano, inv. 12826.
Size (coffin): L: 0.49 H: 0.30 D: 0.09
Condition: Fragment of a frontal relief.
Frontal relief: A bust of a woman in front of a *parapetasma* held by a cupid (the right figure is lost). For a description, see *MNR* I 10, 2, cat. 217.
Portrait: The bust is carved with a blank portrait.
Dating: Tetrarchic period (*MNR* I 10, 2, cat. 217).

Bibliography: *MNR* I 10, 2, cat. 217.

273 BUST OF A MAN

Location/Inv.: Rome, Museo Nazionale Romano, inv. 61311.
Size (coffin): L: 0.45 H: 0.59 D: 0.08
Condition: Fragment of a frontal relief.
Frontal relief: A bust of a man on a plinth. A *parapetasma* held by two cupids is shown behind the bust. Two birds are depicted on either side of the plinth. For a description, see *MNR* I 10, 2, cat. 233.
Portrait: The bust is carved with a male portrait.
Dating: Tetrarchic period (*MNR* I 10, 2, cat. 233).
Comment: Re-carved from a female portrait or *bosse*.

Bibliography: *MNR* I 10, 2, cat. 233.

274 BUST OF A MAN

Location/Inv.: Rome, Museo Nazionale Romano, inv. 67625.
Size (lid): L: 0.55 H: 0.41
Condition: Fragment of a lid?
Provenience: Rome, Via Latina.
Lid: A bust of a man is placed in front of a *parapetasma* held by a cupid (the right figure is lost). For a description, see *MNR* I, 10, 2, cat. 235.
Portrait: The man is carved with a blank portrait.
Dating: Second half of the fourth century (*MNR* I 10, 2, cat. 235).

Bibliography: *MNR* I 10, 2, cat. 235.

275 *CLIPEUS* PORTRAIT OF A MAN

Location/Inv.: Rome, Museo Nazionale Romano, inv. 23894.
Size (coffin): L. 2.16 H: 0.65 D: 0.50
Condition: The coffin and lid are preserved.
Provenience: Via della Lungara (Dresken-Weiland 2003, cat. A 85).
Frontal relief: Two *victoriae* hold a *clipeus* with a bust of a man. Two *cornucopiae* are depicted beneath the *clipeus*. Cupids with spears making offerings on a burning altar are depicted on either side of the *clipeus*. For a description, see *MNR* I 8, 1 cat. V, 5.
Short ends: Roughly carved.
Reverse: Roughly carved.
Lid: A inscription panel. Hunting scenes are depicted on both sides of the panel.
Portrait: The bust on the frontal relief is carved with a blank portrait.
Dating: 250-260 (*MNR* I 8, 1, cat. V, 5).
Comment: Contained a skeleton of an elderly woman. The head seems to have been embalmed. Gold thread was found among the skeletal remains.

Bibliography: *MNR* I 8, 1, 228, cat. V, 5; Dresken-Weiland 2003, cat. A 85.

276 BUST OF A MAN

Location/Inv.: Rome, Museo Nazionale Romano, inv. 115878.
Size (coffin): L: 0.33 H: 0.31
Condition: Fragments of the lid are preserved.
Lid: A bust of a man in front of a *parapetasma* held by cupids.
Portrait: The bust is carved with a blank portrait.
Dating: 250-275 (*MNR* I 10, 2, cat. 243).

Bibliography: *MNR* I 10, 2, cat. 243.

277 *CLIPEUS* PORTRAIT OF A MAN

Location/Inv.: Rome, Museo Nazionale Romano, inv. 124121.
Size (coffin): L: 1.99 H: 0.46 D: 0.52 (lid): H: 0.25
Condition: The coffin and fragments of the lid are preserved.
Frontal relief: Divided into five panels. The second and fourth panels are strigillated. A sleeping cupid is represented on the first and fifth panels. The central panel depicts a *clipeus* with a bust of a man. Two *cornucopiae* are placed beneath the *clipeus*. For a description, see *MNR* I 7, 2, cat. X 5.
Lid: Dolphins and an inscription panel (lost).
Portrait: The bust on the frontal relief is carved with a blank portrait.
Dating: Just after the middle of the third century (*MNR* I 7, 2, cat. X, 5).

Bibliography: *MNR* I 7, 2, cat. X 5.

278 *CLIPEUS* PORTRAIT OF A MAN

Location/Inv.: Rome, Museo Nazionale Romano, inv. 128083.
Size (coffin): L: 2.28 H: 0.45 D: 0.49
Condition: The coffin is preserved, but very weathered.
Provenience: Sutri.

Frontal relief: Two cupids hold a central *clipeus* with a bust of a man. Lions drinking from a *kantharos* are represented on each end of the relief. Two peacocks are depicted beneath the *clipeus*. For a description, see *ASR* VI 1, cat. 182.
Portrait: The bust is carved with a male portrait.
Dating: Around 260 (Huskinson 1996, 9. 28) or 270-290 (*ASR* VI 1, cat. 182).

Bibiography: Stroszeck, *ASR* VI, 1 (1998) cat. 182, pl. 27, 1; Huskinson 1996, 9. 28.

279 *CLIPEUS* PORTRAIT OF A BOY (FIG. 88)

Location/Inv.: Rome, Museo Nazionale Romano, inv. 135741.
Size (coffin): L: 1.42 H: 0.50 D: 0.41
Condition: The coffin and lid are preserved.
Provenience: Rome, Via Laurentina.
Frontal relief: Divided into five panels. The second and fourth panels are strigillated. Cupids with raised torches are represented on the first and fifth panels. A *clipeus* with a bust of a boy is depicted on the central panel. For a description, see *MNR* I 8, 2, 384.
Short ends: Roughly carved.
Lid: Dolphins.
Portrait: The bust is carved with a portrait of a boy with *Horus* lock.
Dating: Late third century (Huskinson 1996, 9. 45).
Comment: Child sarcophagus.

Bibliography: *MNR* I 8, 2, cat. VIII, 18; Huskinson 1996, 9. 45.

280 *CLIPEUS* PORTRAIT OF A WOMAN

Location/Inv.: Rome, Museo Nazionale Romano, inv. 198745.
Size (coffin): L: 2.00 H: 0.56 D: 0.46
Condition: The coffin is preserved.
Frontal relief: A central *clipeus* with a bust of a woman is held by two flying cupids. A winged cupid with a torch is represented on either side of the *clipeus*. Two *cornucopiae* are depicted beneath the *clipeus*.
Short ends: Weapons.
Portrait: The bust is carved with a female portrait wearing earrings.
Dating: Late second or early third century (*MNR* I 8, 2, cat. MP, 3).

Bibliography: *MNR* I 8, 2, cat. MP, 3.

281 *CLIPEUS* PORTRAIT OF A CHILD (FIG. 90)

Location/Inv.: Rome, Museo Nazionale Romano, inv. 229694.
Size (coffin): L: 1.53 H: 0.69 D: 0.43
Condition: The coffin and lid are preserved.
Provenience: Rome, Rignano Flaminio.
Frontal relief: Cupids support a central *clipeus* with a bust. The *clipeus* rests on a base of acanthus leaves. More cupids and hunters between trees are represented on either side of the *clipeus*. For a description, see *ASR* I 4, cat. 184.
Short ends: Without relief-decoration.
Lid: An empty inscription panel is flanked on either side by cupids hunting and playing.
Portrait: The bust on the frontal relief is carved with a blank portrait.
Dating: Third quarter of the third century (*ASR* I 4, cat. 184).
Comment: Child sarcophagus.

Bibliography: Amedick, *ASR* I 4 (1991) cat. 184, pl. 99, 3; Huskinson 1996, cat. 6. 33.

282 *CLIPEUS PORTRAIT* OF A MAN

Location/Inv.: Rome, Palazzo Volpi.
Size (coffin): L: 1.36 H: 0.23 D: 0.45
Condition: The coffin is preserved.
Frontal relief: Two flying cupids hold a central *clipeus* with a bust of a man. Cupids and birds are depicted beneath the *clipeus*.
Short ends: Lenos-shaped. Scene from a circus with cupids.
Portrait: The bust is carved with a male portrait.
Dating: First quarter to the middle of the third century (*ASR* V 2, 3, cat. 140).

Bibliography: Schauenburg, *ASR* V 2, 3 (1995) cat. 140; Kranz, *ASR* V 4 (1984) 74, note 439.

283 BUST OF A BOY

Location/Inv.: Rome, S. Sebastiano, Museo.
Size (coffin): L: 0.58
Condition: Fragment of the frontal relief.
Frontal relief: A bust of a boy is supported by two cupids.
Portrait: The bust is carved with a portrait of a boy.
Dating: Late Tetrarchic period (*ASR* V 4, cat. 126).
Comment: Child sarcophagus.

Bibliography: Kranz, *ASR* V 4 (1984) cat. 126, pl. 63, 11; Huskinson 1996, cat. 9. 25.

284 *CLIPEUS* PORTRAIT OF A GIRL

Location/Inv.: Rome, Santi Quatro Coronati, court.
Condition: The frontal relief is preserved.
Frontal relief: Divided into five panels. The second and fourth are strigillated. A *clipeus* portrait of a girl is represented on the third panel. The *clipeus* is carried by a dancing cupid. The first panel is lost but a sleeping cupid with a down-turned torch is shown on the fifth panel.
Portrait: The bust is carved with a portrait of a girl.
Dating: Beginning of the third century, based on the style of the portrait and the hairstyle.
Comment: The lower profile has been removed. Child sarcophagus.

285 *CLIPEUS* PORTRAIT OF A MAN

Location/Inv.: Rome, Villa Ada.
Size (coffin): L: 2.10 H: 0.70 D: 0.70
Condition: The coffin is preserved.

Frontal relief: Divided into five panels. The second and fourth panels are strigillated. A sleeping cupid is represented on the first and fifth panels. A *clipeus* with a bust of a man is depicted on the central panel. Two *cornucopiae* are placed beneath the *clipeus*.
Portrait: The bust is carved with a portrait of a man or youth.
Dating: Middle of the third century (*MNR* I 6, cat. VII, 7).

Bibliography: *MNR* I 6, cat. VII, 7.

286 *CLIPEUS* PORTRAIT OF A MAN

Location/Inv.: Rome, Villa Albani, inv. 324.
Size (coffin): L: 1.16 H: 0.40 D: 0.42
Condition: The coffin is preserved.
Frontal relief: Two flying cupids hold a *clipeus* with a bust of a man. A scroll flanked by theatre masks, Oceanus, and Tellus are depicted beneath the *clipeus*. Mourning cupids are represented on each end of the relief. For a description, see Bol 1992, cat. 402.
Short ends: Without relief decoration.
Portrait: The bust is carved with a portrait of a youth.
Dating: Later third century (Huskinson 1996, cat. 2. 22).

Bibliography: Bol 1992, cat. 402, pl. 299; Huskinson 1996, cat. 2. 22.

287 *CLIPEUS* PORTRAIT OF A BOY

Location/Inv.: Rome, lost. Formerly in Palazzo Vaccari-Bacchetti.
Condition: The fontal relief is preserved.
Frontal relief: Boats with fishing cupids and Psyche figures. A *clipeus* with a bust of a boy is depicted in the upper right corner. A panel with an inscription to a 7-year-old Julius Filocyrius is placed beneath the *clipeus*.
Portrait: The bust is carved with a portrait of a boy.
Inscription: D M / JVLIO FILOCYRIO FILIO BENE MERENTI DVLCISSIMO Q B ANN VII D V JVLIVS FILOCY/RIVS PATER FECIT
Dating: Around 250 (Lawrence 1962, 291).
Comment: Child sarcophagus.

Bibliography: Lawrence 1962, 290-91; Huskinson 1996, cat. 6. 40, pl. 11. 3.

288 *CLIPEUS* PORTRAIT OF A MAN

Location/Inv.: Salerno, Cathedral, Atrium.
Condition: The frontal relief and the coffin (?) are preserved.
Frontal relief: Four winged cupids carrying garlands frame a *clipeus* bust.
Portrait: The bust is carved with a portrait of a man.
Dating: Probably second half of the third century.

Bibliography: Photo: Marburg 2018/Arachne image no. 18362 (http://arachne.uni-koeln.de/item/marbilder/312566)

289 *CLIPEUS* PORTRAIT OF A GIRL

Location/Inv.: Toronto, Royal Ontario Museum, inv. 923.4.53.
Condition: A fragment of the frontal relief is preserved.
Frontal relief: Two cupids hold a *clipeus* with a bust of a girl. Two children watching a cockfight are depicted beneath the *clipeus*. A hare is eating grapes between the feet of the cupids. For a description, see Schauenburg 1972.
Portrait: The bust is carved with a portrait of a girl.
Dating: Late Severan period (Bielefeld, 1998 10).
Comment: Child sarcophagus.

Bibliography: Schauenburg 1972; Bielefeld 1998.

290 *CLIPEUS* PORTRAIT OF A BOY

Location/Inv.: Toronto, Royal Ontario Museum, inv. 925.23.21.
Size (coffin): L: 1.50 H: 0.36 D: 0.45
Condition: The coffin is preserved.
Frontal relief: Two cupids hold a *clipeus* with a bust of a boy. A cupid with a garland is depicted on either side of the *clipeus*.
Short ends: Weapons.
Portrait: The bust is carved with a portrait of a boy.
Dating: Around 160 (*ASR* VI 2, 1, cat. 144).
Comment: Child sarcophagus.

Bibliography: Herdejürgen, *ASR* VI 2, 1 (1996) cat. 144, pl. 97, 1.

Cupids Harvesting

291 BUST OF A YOUNG WOMAN

Location/Inv.: Baltimore, Walters Art Gallery, inv. 23.37.
Size (lid): L: 2.10 H: 0.25
Condition: The coffin and lid are preserved. The coffin was originally found without the lid (Østergaard 2003, 113, cat. 23).
Provenience: The coffin was found on Via Salaria (*NS* 1885, 76-77).
Frontal relief: Dionysian procession and the sleeping Ariadne.
Lid: Cupids harvesting are represented on either side of a bust of a young woman.
Portrait: The bust on the lid is carved with a female portrait.
Dating: 180-200 (*ASR* V 2, 2, cat. 4).

Bibliography: Bielefeld, *ASR* V 2, 2 (1997) cat. 4, pl. 11, 1; Lehmann & Olsen 1941, 14-15; Kragelund, Moltesen & Østergaard 2003.

292 GIRL WITH BIRD

Location/Inv.: Berlin, Staatliche Museum, Antikensammlung, inv. Sk 855.
Size (coffin): L: 1.10 H: 0.28 D: 0.39
Condition: The coffin is preserved.
Frontal relief: A girl holding a bird is represented. Playing cupids are depicted on either side of her. Some of the cupids are collecting fruit and one cupid offers grapes to the girl.
Short ends: Vertical strigillation.
Portrait: The girl is carved with a portrait of a young child.
Dating: 140-150 (*ASR* V 2, 1, cat. 5).
Comment: Child sarcophagus.

Bibliography: Kranz, *ASR* V 2, 1 (1999) cat. 5, pl. 1, 1; Beschreibung der antiken Skulpturen 1891, 340-41, no. 855 Huskinson 1996, cat. 6, 1.

293 BUST OF A WOMAN

Location/Inv.: Rome, Musei Vaticani, Museo Pio Crostiano, inv. 31502.
Size (lid): L: 1.30 H: 0.22
Condition: Fragment of a lid.
Provenience: Rome, Catacombe di S. Callisto.
Lid: A central inscription panel. Cupids harvesting grapes are depicted on the left side of the inscription panel and a bust of a woman in front of a *parapetasma* is represented on the right side of the panel. For a description, see *ASR* V 2, 2, cat. 213.
Portrait: The bust is carved with a female portrait.
Inscription: ANNIA / ΘΑΥCΤΕΙΝΑ
Dating: 300-310 (*ASR* V 2, 2, cat. 213).

Bibliography: Bielefeld, *ASR* V 2, 2 (1997) cat. 213, pl. 49, 3.

294 BUST OF A MAN

Location/Inv.: Rome, Palazzo Borghese.
Size (coffin): L: 2.17 H: 0.64 D: 0.65
Condition: The lid is preserved.
Provenience: Rome, Via Labicana, Torre Nova (*ASR* IV 4, 332).
Lid: The relief is divided into eight niches and a central square inscription panel. They are all decorated with Dionysian *thiasoi* and cupids harvesting except for the first two on the right side of the inscription. The first of these once contained a Dionysian figure, but it was erased and an inscription was added instead. The other shows a bust.
Portrait: The bust is carved with a portrait of a bearded man.
Inscription: POMPEIA FVLCI/NIA CANDIDA C F / Q POMPE(10) CALL/ISTRATO DARE/NO ALVMNO / BENEMERENTI (*CIL* VI 37072a) DS M / TERENTIUS / VALENTINVS / IN PACE / VIXIT ANNOS / XXIII DIES XVI / MERENTI FI / L /// BC (*CIL* 72072b)
Dating: Third quarter of the third century (*ASR* IV 4, cat. 332).

Bibliography: Matz, *ASR* IV 4 (1975) cat. 332, pl. 333; *NS* 2, 1905, 418-19.

Decorative Scheme

295 *CLIPEUS* PORTRAIT OF A WOMAN

Location/Inv.: Barcelona, Museu d'Arqueologia de Catalunya.
Size (coffin): L: 2.20 H: 0.60 D: 0.58
Condition: The frontal relief is preserved.
Frontal relief: Divided into five panels. The second and fourth panels are strigillated. A pilastre is represented on the first and fifth panels. A *clipeus* with a bust of a woman is represented in the central panel. Two *cornucopiae* are depicted beneath the *clipeus*.
Portrait: The bust is carved with a portrait of a young woman or girl.
Dating: Middle of the third century (Garcia & Bellido 1949).

Bibliography: García & Bellido 1949, 277-78, cat. 275; Arachne image no.: INMadD875.

296 *CLIPEUS* PORTRAIT OF A MAN

Location/Inv.: Ferentillo, Abbazia, S. Peitro in Valle.
Size (coffin): L: 2.01 H: 0.25 D: 0.54
Condition: The coffin is preserved.
Frontal relief: Divided into three panels. The first and third panels are strigillated. The central panel depicts a *clipeus* with a bust of a man. Two *cornucopiae* are placed beneath the *clipeus*.
Portrait: The bust is carved with a portrait of a bearded man.
Dating: Late second or third century.
Comment: A lid with hunting scenes and a bust (*ASR* I 2, cat. 29, here cat. no. 81) is today placed on this sarcophagus, but they did not originally belong together.

Bibliography: Arachne image no.: D-DAI-ROM-79.1535 (http://arachne.uni-koeln.de/item/objekt/132101).

297 *CLIPEUS* PORTRAIT OF A MAN

Location/Inv.: Grottaferrata, Museo Abbazia inv. 1175.
Size (coffin): L: 0.63 H: 0.27
Condition: Fragment of a frontal relief.
Frontal relief: Vertical strigillation and a *clipeus* with a male portrait bust.
Portrait: The bust is carved with a blank portrait.
Dating: Third century.

Bibliography: Ambrogi in Ambrogi et al. 2008, 190-1.

298 *CLIPEUS* PORTRAIT OF A MAN

Location/Inv.: Ostia, Museo Nazionale, inv. 18625.
Size (coffin): L: 0.79 H: 0.35 D: 0.05
Condition: The frontal relief is preserved.
Provenience: Ostia, Isola Sacra, Pianabella.
Frontal relief: Divided into five panels. The second and fourth panels are strigillated. A column is depicted on the first and fifth panels. The central panel shows a *clipeus* with a bust of a man. Two *cornucopiae* are placed beneath the *clipeus*. For a description, see Paroli 1999 B 100.
Portrait: The bust is carved with a blank smooth surface.
Dating: Third quarter of the third century (Paroli 1999, B 100).

Bibliography: Paroli 1999, cat. B 100.

299 BUSTS OF A WOMAN AND A MAN

Location/Inv.: Pisa, Camposanto, C 1 est.
Size (coffin): L: 2.35 H: 1.06 D: 1.20
Condition: The coffin is preserved.
Frontal relief: Strigillated with a vessel in the central *mandorla*. A woman with a naked shoulder and a wind-blown veil is represented on the left end and a man in a toga holding a sceptre

with a bust of Mercury on top is represented on the right end. Both figures seem to grow from an acanthus. For description, see Arias 1977, C 1 est.
Short ends: Vertical strigillation.
Portrait: The woman has portrait features and the man has a blank portrait.
Dating: First half of the third century (Arias 1977, C 1 est).
Comment: The figures are carved from roughly carved lion heads (I am grateful to Janet Huskinson for making me aware of this re-use).

Bibliography: Jucker 1961, cat. S3; Arias et al. 1977, cat. C 1 est; Wrede 2001, cat. 14.

300 *CLIPEUS* PORTRAIT OF A WOMAN

Location/Inv.: Rome, Catacombs of S. Teclo, hyogeum D, Basilica.
Size (coffin): L: 2.00 H: 0.56 D: 0.58
Lid: Lost (see Fasola 1970, 211).
Provenience: Rome, Catacomb of S. Tecla, hyogeum D. Placed in a niche in the northern wall of the underground basilica (Nuzzo 2000, 18, fig. 19). Part of the lid that probably belonged to the sarcophagus was found and then stolen during the excavation (Dresken-Weiland 2003, cat. D 25).
Frontal relief: Strigillated (vertical) with a central *clipeus* showing a bust of a girl. The panel below the *clipeus* is undecorated. Two flowers are depicted in the corners above the *clipeus*.
Short ends: Lenos-shaped. Without relief decoration.
Lid: Inscription tablet supported by two winged cupids. A bust of a girl with a scroll.
Portrait: The bust on the frontal relief is carved with a portrait of a young woman dressed in a tunic and a *palla*.
Inscription: AVRELIA / THEODO/RA PVEL/LA INNO/CENTISSI/MA
Dating: Middle of the fourth century (Nuzzo 2000, 18).
Comment: Placed in the niche on top of three "tombe a fossa". The sarcophagus was placed on the floor and was visible to the people entering the basilica.

Bibliography: Fasola 1970, 210-11; Nuzzo 2000, 18, fig. 15; Dresken-Weiland 2003, cat. D 25.

301 *CLIPEUS* PORTRAIT OF A MAN

Location/Inv.: Rome, Musei Capitolini, Palazzo Nuovo/formerly Museo Mussolini, inv. 818.
Size (coffin): L: 1.80 D: 0.84; (lid): L: 1.81 H: 0.24 D: 0.04
Condition: The coffin and lid are preserved.
Frontal relief: Strigillated with a central *clipeus* showing a bust of a man.
Short ends: Unknown.
Lid: Sea-*thiasoi* and an inscription panel.
Portrait: The bust is carved with a portrait of a man.
Dating: Late second to early third century (*ASR* V 1, cat. 212).

Bibliography: Stroszeck, *ASR* V 1 (1998) cat. 212, pl. 59, 3; Koch & Sichtermann 1982, 118.

302 *CLIPEUS* PORTRAIT OF A GIRL

Location/Inv.: Rome, Musei Vaticani, Museo Pio Cristiano (unknown inv.).
Size (coffin): L: 0.75 H: 0.32
Condition: The frontal relief is preserved.
Frontal relief: Divided into three panels. The first and third panels are strigillated. A *clipeus* with a bust of a girl is shown on the central panel. An inscription panel is placed beneath the *clipeus*. For a description, see *Rep.* I, cat. 84.
Portrait: The bust is carved with a portrait of a girl.
Inscription: καταθεσις · Οχταβιλλης · προ θ χαλ σεπ · Ρωμουλι
Dating: 343. Date is given by the inscription.
Comment: Child sarcophagus.

Bibliography: *Rep.* I, cat. 84, pl. 24; Huskinson 1996, 9. 49.

303 BUSTS OF A WOMAN AND A MAN

Location/Inv.: Rome. Museo Nazionale Romano, inv. 112121/124710.
Size (coffin): L: 2.13 H. 0.71 D: 0.86
Condition: The coffin is preserved.
Frontal relief: Strigillated with busts of a woman and a man, both on statue bases. A column is depicted on either end of the relief.
Short ends: Weapons.
Reverse: Roughly carved.
Portrait: Both busts are carved with blank portraits.
Dating: Third century (*MNR* I 8, 1, cat. VI, 15).

Bibliography: *MNR* I 8, 1, cat. VI, 15.

304 BUSTS OF A WOMAN AND A MAN (FIG. 7)

Location/Inv.: Rome, Museo Nazionale Romano, inv. 115175.
Size (coffin): L: 2.01 H: 0.70 D: 0.69
Condition: The coffin is preserved.
Provenience: Ostia, Isola Sacra.
Frontal relief: Strigillated with a central panel containing busts of a woman and a man. An inscription panel is placed beneath the busts. A column is depicted on either end of the relief.
Short ends: Weapons.
Portrait: The busts are carved with a female and a male portrait.
Inscription: MASCVLINIO TITIANO / AEMILIA AFRODITE / MARITO / INCOMPARABILI/ QVI BIXIT/ ANNIS XXXXIIII / MENS(ibus) XI / DIEB(us) XVII
Dating: 260s (*MNR* I 8, 1, cat. VI, 19).

Bibliography: *MNR* I 8, 1, cat. VI, 19.

305 *CLIPEUS* PORTRAITS OF A WOMAN AND A MAN

Location/Inv.: Rome, Museo Nazionale Romano (unknown inv.).
Size (coffin): L: 2.30 H. 0.86 D: 0.85
Condition: The coffin is preserved.

Frontal relief: Strigillated with two *clipei*, one with a bust of a woman on the left side of the relief and the other with a bust of a man on the right side.
Short ends: Lenos- shaped, strigillation continues onto the short ends.
Portrait: The busts are carved with a female and a male portrait.
Dating: First part of the third century (*MNR* I 7, 2, cat. XI, 18).

Bibliography: *MNR* I 7, 2, cat. XI, 18.

306 *CLIPEUS* PORTRAIT OF A GIRL

Location/Inv.: Rome, Palazzo dei Conservatori.
Size (coffin): L: 1.15 H: 0.40 D: 0.33
Condition: The coffin and lid are preserved.
Provenience: Rome, Porta Salaria (Huskinson 1996, 9. 47).
Frontal relief: Divided into five panels. The second and fourth panels are strigillated. A column is depicted on the first and fifth panels. The central panel contains a *clipeus* with a bust. An inscription panel is placed beneath the *clipeus*.
Short ends: Without decoration.
Lid: Low gable on either end with plain *acroteria* in front. Inscription on the profile.
Portrait: The bust is carved with a portrait of a young girl.
Inscription: PVBLIAE AILIAE PROBAE FILIAE / PAELVS PROBVS ET CLODIA PLAVTIA PARENTES VIIII / FILIAE INNOCENTISSIMAE. *CIL* VI. 34263. On the *lid:* Petro Lilluti Paulo.
Dating: Late third century (Huskinson 1996, 9. 48).
Comment: Child sarcophagus.

Bibliography: *NS* 1885, 189; Stuart Jones 1968, 78, no. 4, pl. 29, fig. 4; Huskinson 1996, 9. 48.

307 *CLIPEUS* PORTRAIT OF A MAN

Location/Inv.: Rome, Santi Quattro Coronati, court.
Condition: Fragment of a frontal relief.
Frontal relief: Strigillated relief with a *clipeus* portrait. There is no decoration beneath the *clipeus*.
Portrait: The bust is carved with a blank portrait.
Dating: Third century.

308 BUST OF A WOMAN

Location/Inv.: Soriano, once in the ownership of the Albani family now lost.
Condition: The frontal relief is preserved.
Frontal relief: Divided into three panels. The first and the third are strigillated. On the central panel an acanthus leaf bust of a woman is displayed. A *parapetasma* is suspended behind her. For a description, see Schauenburg 1963.
Portrait: The bust is carved with a portrait of an elderly woman.
Inscription: θ K ·Κεῖτε ὡδε ʽΑβιδία ʽΑγριππῖνα, ἐκδημήσασα δύσιν καὶ ἀνατολήν, καλῶς βιώσασα μηδενὶ μηδέν ὀφείλονσα, κελεύω τοὺς ἀπελευθέρους μου καί εἴ τις ἕτερος ἄλλος, μὴ ἐζὸν αὐτῷ εἶναι μήτε.
Dating: Around 225-250 (Schauenburg 1963, 300).
Comment: The inscription is unusual since it mentions the personal experiences of the woman, namely that she had travelled both to the east and the west.

Bibliography: Schauenburg 1963.

309 *CLIPEUS* PORTRAIT OF A MAN

Location/Inv.: Wilton House, Inner Courtyard, inv. 1963,26.2.
Condition: The coffin is preserved.
Provenience: Rome, Via Appia, outside Porta S. Sebastiano, Columbarium (1726). Later on display in the Badminton House, Duke of Beaufort (c. 1730).
Frontal relief: Strigillated with a central *clipeus* with a bust of a man. Two *cornucopiae* are depicted beneath the *clipeus*.
Short ends: Weapons.
Portrait: The bust is carved with a male portrait.
Dating: Third century.

Bibliography: Michaelis 1882, 702, cat. 143; Arachne image no.: FA 2543-02 (http://arachne.uni-koeln.de/item/objekt/23095).

Eros and Psyche

310 PORTRAIT OF A YOUNG MAN ENCLOSED BY A WREATH

Location/Inv.: Copenhagen, Ny Carlsberg Glyptotek, inv. 852.
Size (coffin): L: 1.82 H: 0.44 D: 0.52
Condition: The coffin is preserved.
Frontal relief: Two flying cupids hold a central wreath with a bust of a man. Two overturned vases with flowers are depicted beneath the wreath. Eros and Psyche are represented on either end of the relief. For a description, see Østergaard 1996, cat. 49.
Short ends: Griffin.
Portrait: The bust is carved with a portrait of a young man.
Dating: Beginning of the third century.

Bibliography: Østergaard 1996, cat. 49.

311 *CLIPEUS* PORTRAIT OF A BOY

Location/Inv.: Ostia, Museo, inv. 25583 and 35584.
Size (coffin): L: 1.20 H. 0.35 D: 0.43
Condition: The coffin and lid are preserved.
Provenience: Isola Sacra, columbarium 1, Pinanabella. Placed towards the back wall in the first room (Dresken-Weiland 2003, cat. A 93).
Frontal relief: Two cupids hold a central *clipeus* with a bust. Eros and Psyche are represented on both ends of the relief. For a description, see Paroli 1999, B 7.
Short ends: Griffin.
Lid: Without relief decoration. Roughly carved.
Portrait: The bust is carved with a portrait of a boy.

Dating: Between the late second and the middle of the third century (Paroli 1999, 219).
Comment: Child sarcophagus. Bones and an Antoninus Pius coin were found in the coffin.

Bibliography: Paroli 1999, B 7; Dresken-Weiland 2003, cat. A 93.

312 *CLIPEUS* PORTRAIT OF A GIRL

Location/Inv.: Palermo, Museo Nazionale, inv. 993.
Condition: The coffin and lid are preserved.
Frontal relief: Two flying *victoriae* support a *clipeus* with a bust. A cockfight is depicted beneath the *clipeus*. Eros and Psyche are represented on either end of the relief. For a description, see Tusa 1957, cat. 67.
Short ends: Weapons.
Lid: Flying cupids and garlands on both sides of an inscription panel.
Portrait: The bust on the frontal relief is carved with a portrait of a girl with short hair, like a boy's.
Inscription: DM / VOLVSIA LONGINA Q ET / DIONYSIODORA QV E ANN V / M IIII D XVIII FEC DIONYSIODO / RVS LONGINVS PATER FIL DVLC
Dating: End of the second to the beginning of the third century (Fittschen 1992).
Comment: Child sarcophagus.

Bibliography: Tusa 1957, cat. 67; Fittschen 1992, 303.

313 *CLIPEUS* PORTRAIT OF A GIRL

Location/Inv.: Rome, Catacombe di Pretestato, Museo.
Size (coffin): L: 0.78 H: 0.33
Condition: Fragments. The central and right part of the frontal relief are preserved.
Provenience: Rome, Catacombe di Pretastato?
Frontal relief: Two cupids hold a *clipeus* with a bust. A nurse breastfeeding a baby is depicted beneath the *clipeus*. A scene with Eros bringing Psyche a bird is shown to the right of the *clipeus*. For a description, see *ASR* I 4, cat. 141.
Portrait: The bust is carved with a blank portrait. It was probably intended for a girl, because of the exposed right shoulder.
Dating: Last quarter of the fourth century (*ASR* I 4, cat. 141).
Comment: Child sarcophagus.

Bibliography: Amedick, *ASR* I 4 (1991) cat. 141, pl. 61, 4; Huskinson 1996, 7. 5.

314 PORTRAIT OF A WOMAN ENCLOSED BY A WREATH

Location/Inv.: Rome, Musei Vaticani, Museo Gregoriano Profano, inv. 10397.
Condition: The coffin is preserved.
Provenience: Discovered in 1999.
Frontal relief: Two winged cupids hold a wreath with a bust of a woman. Eros and Psyche are represented on both ends of the relief.
Short ends: Griffin.
Portrait: The bust is carved with a blank portrait.
Dating: Third century.

Bibliography: Arachne image no.: FA 6005-10 (http://arachne.uni-koeln.de/item/objekt/63211).

315 PORTRAIT OF A GIRL ENCLOSED BY A WREATH

Location/Inv.: Rome, Museo Nazionale Romano (unknown inv.).
Size (coffin): L: 1.57 H: 0.40 D: 0.43
Condition: The coffin is preserved.
Frontal relief: Bust in a wreath held by flying cupids. Eros and Psyche are represented on both ends of the relief. For a description, see *MNR* I 2, cat. 9.
Short ends: Without relief decoration.
Portrait: The bust is carved with a portrait of a girl.
Dating: Around 200 (Huskinson 1996, 7. 6).
Comment: Child sarcophagus.

Bibliography: *MNR* I 2, cat. 9, p. 99; Huskinson 1996, 7. 6.

316 *CLIPEUS* PORTRAIT OF A MAN

Location/Inv.: St. Petersburg, Hermitage, inv. A 546.
Size (coffin): L: 2.13 H: 0.55 D: 0.52
Condition: The coffin is preserved.
Frontal relief: Two flying cupids hold a *clipeus* with a male bust. Tellus and Oceanus are depicted beneath the *clipeus*. Eros and Psyche are represented on both ends of the relief.
Short ends: Griffins.
Portrait: The bust is carved with a blank portrait.
Dating: Second half of the third century (Saverkina 1979, 27).

Bibliography: Saverkina 1979, 27, pl. 57, 1.

317 *CLIPEUS* PORTRAIT OF A WOMAN

Location/Inv.: Vienna, Kunsthistorisches Museum, inv. I.1125.
Size (coffin): L: 1.34 H: 0.42
Condition: The frontal relief is preserved.
Frontal relief: Flying *victoriae* hold a central *clipeus* with a bust. Two kneeling youths watching a cockfight are depicted beneath the *clipeus*. Eros and Psyche are represented on both ends of the relief.
Portrait: The bust is carved with a portrait of a woman
Dating: Third century.

Bibliography: Schauenberg 1975; Huskinson 1996, cat. 7. 11.

Garlands

318 *CLIPEUS* PORTRAIT OF A WOMAN

Location/Inv.: Paris, Musée du Louvre.
Size (coffin): L: 1.95 H. 0.53

Condition: The frontal relief is preserved.
Frontal relief: Garlands held by cupids frame a *clipeus* with a bust. The sleeping Ariadne is represented beneath the *clipeus*. Two theatre masks are depicted above the garlands. For a description, see Herdejürgen 1996.
Portrait: The bust is carved with a portrait of a woman.
Dating: 220 (Herdjürgen 1996, 490).

Bibliography: Baratte & Metzger 1985, cat. 120; Herdjürgen 1996, fig. 11.

319 *CLIPEUS* PORTRAIT OF A WOMAN

Location/Inv.: Rome, Musei Vaticani, magazine.
Condition: Fragment of the frontal relief.
Frontal relief: A *clipeus* with a bust is framed by two torches and garlands.
Portrait: The bust is carved with a portrait of an elderly woman.
Dating: 260 (Herdjürgen 1996, 498).

Bibliography: Herdjürgen 1996, fig. 30.

Hunting

320 *CLIPEUS* PORTRAIT OF A MAN

Location/Inv: Civitavecchia, Museo Nazionale.
*Size (*coffin): L: 2.04 H: 0.58 D: 0.58 ca.
Condition: Fragments of the coffin is preserved.
Frontal relief: A *clipeus* with a bust held by *victoriae* is framed by hunt motifs. A scene with a sacrifice to Diana is furthermore represented on the left side of the relief. For description, see *ASR* I 2, cat. 24.
Portrait: The bust is carved with a male portrait.
Dating: Around 220 (*ASR* I 2, cat. 24).

Bibliography: Andreae, *ASR* I 2 (1980) cat. 24, pl. 6, 1.

321 BUST OF A MAN

Location/Inv.: Rome, Studio Canova.
Size (lid): L: 0.85 H: 0.28
Condition: Fragment of a lid.
Lid: Preparations for a meal (probably the meal that took place after a hunt). The meal was represented on the right end of the relief but is lost today. A bust of a man is shown on the right end of the fragment. Two flying cupids holding a garland are depicted behind the bust.
Portrait: The bust is carved with a blank portrait.
Dating: First part of the third century (*ASR* XII 6, cat. 132).

Bibliography: Koch, *ASR* XII 6 (1975) cat. 132.

Learned Sphere

322 BUST OF A MAN

Location/Inv.: London, British Museum, inv. GR 1805.7-3.152.
Size (lid): L: 1.17
Condition: Lid. The right end is lost.
Provenience: Discovered "in vinea fratum".
Lid: Central inscription panel with an inscription that refers to the deceased's skills in poetry and music. A scene with a philosopher and a Muse is represented on both sides of the panel. A bust of a man is depicted on the right end of the relief. For a description, see Ewald 1999, I 7.
Portrait: The bust is carved with a male portrait.
Inscription: Μ. (Σ) [εμπρώνιος Νεικοκράτης] · ἤμην ποτὲ μουσικὸς ἀνήρ · ποιητὴς καὶ κιθαριστὴς · μὰλιστα δὲ καὶ συνοδείτης · πολλὰ βυθοισι καμὼν · ὁδηπορίες (sic) δ΄ ἀτονήσας · ἒνπορος εὐμόρφων Υενόμην · φίλοι μετέπειτα Υυναικων · πνευμα λαβὼν δάνος ὑρανόθεν · τελέσας χρύνυν αὒτ' ἀπέδωκα καί μετὰ τὸν θάνατον · Μουσαί μου τὸ σωμα κρατουσιν
Dating: Late third or early fourth century. For discussion, see Ewald 1999, 112-13, cat. I 7.

Bibliography: Wegner, *ASR* V 3 (1966) cat. 45; Fittschen 1972, 490; Walker 1990, cat. 25; Ewald 1999, cat. I 7.

323 *CLIPEUS* PORTRAIT OF A WOMAN (FIG. 18)

Location/Inv.: Ostia, Ufficio dell' Opera Nazionale Combattenti.
Size (coffin): L: 2.17 H: 0.54 D: 0.55
Condition: The coffin is preserved. A large fragment is missing on the right end of the frontal relief.
Provenience: Ostia, Isola Sacra (1925).
Frontal relief: Divided into five panels. The second and fourth panels are strigillated. A veiled woman with one hand raised and a scroll in her other hand is shown on the first panel and a philosopher with a scroll is pictured on the fifth panel. The central panel depicts a *clipeus* with a bust of a woman wearing a necklace and earrings. A scene with a sleeping shepherd, a capricorn, and a dog is depicted beneath the *clipeus*. For a description, see Ewald 1999, cat. F 23.
Portrait: The woman is carved with a portrait.
Dating: 235-240 (Calza 1964-65); second half of the third century (Ewald 1999, cat. F 23).

Bibliography: Calza 1964/65, cat. 14; Ewald 1999, cat. F 23, pl. 78, 3.

324 BUSTS OF A WOMAN AND A MAN

Location/Inv: Rome, Antiquarium Comunale.
Condition: Fragment of a coffin.
Frontal relief: Strigillated with half-length busts of a man and a woman. A Muse and a philosopher are shown in the *mandorla*.
Portrait: The woman is carved with a portrait and the man with a blank portrait.
Dating: The middle of the third century (Ewald 1999, C 31).

Bibliography: Fittschen 1972, 446, no. e; Ewald 1999, C 31.

325 BUST OF A WOMAN

Location/Inv.: Rome, Musei Vaticani, magazine, inv. 4750.
Size (coffin): L: 0.33 H: 0.24
Condition: Fragment of the frontal relief.
Frontal relief: The upper part of the body and head of a woman are pictured; on her left side, the upper part of the body and head of a Muse (Polyhymnia) are visible. For a description, see *ASR* V 3, cat. 141.
Portrait: The woman is carved with a portrait.
Dating: Late third century (*ASR* V 3, cat. 141).

Bibliography: Wegner, *ASR* V 3 (1966) cat. 141, pl. 80d; Ewald 1999, cat. B 10.

326 BUST OF A MAN

Location/Inv.: Rome, Museo Nazionale Romano, inv. 113227.
Size (lid): L: 2.16 H: 0.32
Condition: The lid seems to be preserved in its full length.
Provenience: Discovered in 1932 in a secondary context at Via Tiburtina no. 5, Rome.
Lid: The lid has a central inscription panel, to the left of which is a scene from the tale of Odysseus; to the right, there is a bust in front of a *parapetasma* flanked by philosophers. For a description, see *MNR* I 8,1, 234-37.
Portrait: The portrait is of a man but the bust is female. The inscription mentions a 17-years-old man. Stylistically, his portrait features are similar to the portrait features of Gordian III.
Inscription: DM / M AVRELIO / ROMANO EQ(viti) R(omano / FILIO DVLCISSIMO / QVI VIX(it) ANN(is) XVII / M AVR(elius) IVLIANVS / PATER
Dating: To the reign of Gordian III (238-244) (*MNR* I 8, 1, 234-37).
Comment: Cross-gendered image.

Bibliography: *MNR* I 8, 1, 234-37; Klauser 1963, cat. 12; Ewald 1999, cat. I 1.

327 *CLIPEUS* PORTRAIT OF A MAN

Location/Inv.: Rome, Museo Nazionale Romano (unknown inv.).
Size (coffin): L. 2.16 H: 0.66 D: 0.73
Condition: The coffin and the lower part of the relief on the lid are preserved.
Frontal relief: Divided into five panels. The second and fourth panels are strigillated. A veiled woman with a scroll is represented on the first panel, and a bare-chested philosopher with naked chest is represented on the fifth panel. A *parapetasma* is suspended behind both figures. The central panel depicts a *clipeus* with a bust of a man in a *pallium*. A scene with a shepherd, a capricorn, and a dog is depicted beneath the *clipeus*. For a description, see Ewald 1999, cat. F 24.
Lid: An empty inscription panel flanked by reclining figures.
Portrait: The bust is carved with a male portrait.
Dating: Early Tetrarchic period (Ewald 1999, cat. F 24).

Bibliography: Ewald 1999, cat. F 24.

328 BUST OF A WOMAN

Location/Inv.: Rome, Museo Nazionale degli Strumenti Musicali.
Size (lid): L: 0.79 H: 0.35
Condition: Fragment of a lid.
Lid: Three Muses and a bust of a woman are partially preserved.
Portrait: The bust is carved with a blank portrait.
Dating: Third quarter of the third century (Ewald 1999, cat. I 28).

Bibliography: Ewald 1999, cat. I 28, pl. 103, 1.

329 *CLIPEUS* PORTRAIT OF A MAN

Location/Inv.: Rome, Ospedale di S. Giovanni, Oratorio di S. Andrea.
Condition: The coffin is preserved.
Frontal relief: Divided into five panels. The second and fourth panels are strigillated. A veiled woman with a scroll is represented on the first panel, and a bare-chested philosopher is represented on the fifth panel. The central panel depicts a *clipeus* with a bust in a *pallium*. A scene with a shepherd, a capricorn, and a dog is depicted beneath the *clipeus*. For a description, see Ewald 1999, cat. F 22.
Short ends: Weapons.
Portrait: The bust is carved with a blank portrait.
Dating: Last third of the third century (Ewald 1999, cat. F 22).

Bibliography: Ewald 1999, cat. F 22.

330 *CLIPEUS* PORTRAIT OF A MAN

Location/Inv.: Rome, S. Crisogono.
Size (coffin): L: 2.12 H: 0.50 D: 0.51
Condition: The coffin is preserved. The relief has been damaged, and the surface is weathered.
Frontal relief: Divided into five panels. The second and fourth panels are strigillated. A ram-bearer is represented on the first panel, and a philosopher with a naked chest is represented on the fifth panel. The central panel depicts a *clipeus* with a bust in a *pallium*. Two rams are depicted beneath the *clipeus*. For a description, see Ewald 1999, cat. F 21.
Short ends: Pegasus, roughly carved.
Portrait: The bust is carved with a portrait of a bearded male. The features have been erased by weathering.
Dating: End of the third century (Ewald 1999, cat. F 21).

Bibliography: *Rep.* I, cat. 744; Sichtermann, *ASR* XII 2 (1992) 21 cat. 4 (motif on the short end reliefs); Ewald 1999, cat. F 21.

331 BUST OF A WOMAN

Location/Inv.: Rome, lost, formerly Woodyat Collection.
Size (coffin): L: 0.79 H: 0.26
Condition: Fragment of a lid.
Lid: A bust of a woman is pictured between two scenes with philosophers. A mask is depicted on the right end of the lid.
Portrait: The bust is carved with a blank portrait.

Dating: Around the middle of the third century (Ewald 1999, 219).

Bibliography: Ewald 1999, cat. I 11, fig. 10.

332 *CLIPEUS* PORTRAIT OF A MAN

Location/Inv.: Salerno, Duomo.
Size (coffin): L: 2.03 H: 0.61 L: 0.60
Condition: The coffin is preserved. The lid did not belong to the coffin originally.
Frontal relief: Divided into five panels. The second and fourth panels are strigillated. A philosopher with a naked chest is represented on the first panel, and a veiled woman (Fortuna? see Ewald 1999) is represented on the fifth panel. The central panel depicts a *clipeus* with a bust in a *pallium*. Two *cornucopiae* are shown beneath the *clipeus*. For a description, see Ewald 1999, cat. F 26.
Short ends: Griffin.
Portrait: The bust is carved with a male portrait.
Dating: Last quarter of the third century (Ewald 1999, cat. F 26).

Bibliography: Ewald 1999, cat. F 26.

333 *CLIPEUS* PORTRAIT OF A MAN

Location/Inv.: Salerno, Duomo.
Size (coffin): L: 2.18 H. 0.58
Condition: The coffin is preserved.
Frontal relief: Divided into five panels. The second and fourth panels are strigillated. A philosopher with a naked chest is represented on the first panel, and a veiled woman is represented on the fifth panel. A *parapetasma* is suspended behind both figures. The central panel depicts a *clipeus* with a bust in a *pallium*. For a description, see Ewald 1999, cat. F 27.
Portrait: The bust was carved with male portrait features.
Dating: End of the third century (Ewald 1999, cat. F 27).
Comment: The portrait is lost today but is documented by photos (Ewald 1999, Inst. Neg. Rom. 28.104).

Bibliography: Ewald 1999, cat. F 27.

Life Course

334 *CLIPEUS* PORTRAIT OF A CHILD

Location/Inv.: Rome, Catacombe di Pretestato, Museo, inv. 315.
Size (coffin): L: 1.65 H: 0.15
Condition: Fragments of the frontal relief.
Frontal relief: One fragment depicts a *clipeus* with a bust of a child, and the other a scene with a woman bathing a baby. For a description, see *ASR* I 4, cat. 142.
Portrait: The bust is carved with a blank portrait of unknown sex.
Dating: End of the third century (*ASR* I 4, cat. 142).
Comment: Child sarcophagus.

Bibliography: Amedick, *ASR* I 4 (1991) cat. 142, pl. 61, 8.

Lion

335 *CLIPEUS* PORTRAIT OF A MAN

Location/Inv.: Anzio, Villa Spigarelli.
Condition: The coffin is preserved; it may have been pieced together from fragments of different sarcophagi, see *ASR* VI 1, cat. 203.
Frontal relief: Strigillated with a *clipeus* with a bust of a man. A lion killing a boar is represented on the left end of the relief. For a description, see *ASR* VI 1, cat. 203.
Left short end: *Lenos*-shaped. The lion of the frontal relief continues on the short end.
Right short end: Smooth surface but without relief decoration.
Portrait: The bust is carved with a male portrait.
Dating: 270-280 (*ASR* VI 1, cat. 203).

Bibliography: Stroszeck *ASR* VI 1 (1998) cat. 203, pl. 106, 9.

336 *CLIPEUS* PORTRAIT OF A MAN

Location/Inv.: Copenhagen, Ny Carlsberg Glyptoteket, inv. 855.
Size (coffin): L: 2.07 H: 0.66 D: 0.70
Condition: The coffin is preserved.
Frontal relief: Strigillated with vertical lines and a central *clipeus* with a male bust. Two masks are depicted beneath the *clipeus*. A lion is represented on either end of the relief. For a description, see *ASR* VI 1, cat. 175.
Short ends: *Lenos*-shaped. The lion of the frontal relief continues on the short ends.
Portrait: The bust is carved with a male portrait.
Dating: 250-270 (*ASR* VI 1, cat. 175).

Bibliography: Stroszeck, *ASR* VI 1 (1998) cat. 175; Østergaard 1996, cat. 57.

337 *CLIPEUS* PORTRAIT OF A WOMAN

Location/Inv.: Malibu, The J. Paul Getty Villa, inv. 77.AA.65.
Size (coffin): L: 1.70 H: 0.55 D: 0.40
Condition: The coffin is preserved but fragmented.
Frontal relief: Strigillated with vertical lines and a central *clipeus* with a bust of a woman. Two masks are depicted beneath the *clipeus*. A lion killing a boar is represented on either end of the relief. For a description, see *ASR* VI, 1, cat. 231.
Short ends: *Lenos*-shaped. The lion of the frontal relief continues on the short ends.
Portrait: The bust is carved with a female portrait.
Dating: 280-300 (*ASR* VI 1, cat. 231).
Comment: The bust could be male or female. The portrait is female.

Bibliography: Stroszeck, *ASR* VI 1 (1998) cat. 231, pl. 65, 3; Koch 1988, 58-9.

338 *CLIPEUS* PORTRAIT OF A MAN

Location/Inv.: Rochester, N.Y. Memorial Art Gallery of the University of Rochester.
Size (coffin): L: 1.83 H: 0.48
Condition: The coffin is preserved.
Frontal relief: Strigillated with a central *clipeus* with a bust. A bucolic scene is depicted beneath the *clipeus*. A head of a lion with a ring in its mouth is represented on either end on the relief. For a description, see *ASR* VI 1, cat. 56.
Short ends: Lenos-shaped. The strigillated frontal relief continues on the short ends.
Reverse: Roughly carved.
Portrait: The bust is carved with a male portrait.
Dating: 240-250 (*ASR* VI 1, cat. 56).

Bibliography: Stroszeck, *ASR* VI 1 (1998) cat. 56, pl. 10, 2.

339 *CLIPEUS* PORTRAIT OF A BOY

Location/Inv.: Rome, Catacombe di Calepodio, cubiculum B a.
Condition: The coffin is preserved but fragmented.
Provenience: Rome, the catacombs on Via Aurelia (Galleria no. A 17).
Frontal relief: Strigillated with a central *clipeus* with a bust. Two *cornucopiae* are depicted beneath the *clipeus*. A lion killing a boar is represented on either end of the relief. For a description, see *ASR* VI 1, cat. 266.
Left short end: Not preserved.
Right short end: Lenos-shaped. The lion of the frontal relief continues onto this short end.
Portrait: The bust is carved with a portrait of a boy.
Dating: 260-270 (*ASR* VI 1, cat. 266).
Comment: Child sarcophagus.

Bibliography: Stroszeck, *ASR* VI 1 (1998) cat. 266, pl. 43, 4.

340 *CLIPEUS* PORTRAIT OF A BOY

Location/Inv.: Rome, Museo Nazionale Romano, inv. 326135.
Size (coffin): L: 1.18 H: 0.35 D: 0.39
Condition: The coffin is preserved.
Provenience: Once in Rome, S. Stefano.
Frontal relief: Strigillated with a central *clipeus* with a bust in a *pallium*. Two *cornucopiae* are depicted beneath the *clipeus*. A lion killing an animal is represented on either end of the relief.
Short ends: Lenos-shaped. The lion of the frontal relief continues on the short ends.
Portrait: The bust is carved with a portrait of a boy.
Dating: Around 250 (Huskinson 1996, 9. 46).
Comment: Child sarcophagus.

Bibliography: Caronna 1983, pl. 6, 1; Huskinson 1996, cat. 9. 46.

341 *CLIPEUS* PORTRAIT OF A MAN

Location/Inv.: Rome, Ospedale di S. Spirito, Cortile della scuola.
Size (coffin): L: 2.08 H. 0.47 D: 0.54
Condition: The coffin is preserved.
Frontal relief: Strigillated with a central *clipeus* with a bust in a *pallium*. Two *cornucopiae* are depicted beneath the *clipeus*. A lion killing a horse is represented on either end of the relief.
Short ends: Lenos-shaped. The lion of the frontal relief continues on the short ends.
Reverse: Roughly carved.
Portrait: The bust is carved with a male portrait.
Dating: Around 260 (*ASR* VI 1, cat. 307).

Bibliography: Stroszeck, *ASR* VI 1 (1998) cat. 307, pl. 45, 1.

342 *CLIPEUS* PORTRAIT OF A WOMAN

Location/Inv.: Rome, Palazzo Farnese.
Condition: The coffin is preserved.
Frontal relief: Strigillated with vertical lines and a central *clipeus* with a bust. Two *cornucopiae* are depicted beneath the *clipeus*. A lion killing a boar is represented on either end of the relief. For description, see *ASR* VI 1, cat. 315.
Short ends: Lenos-shaped. The lion of the frontal relief continues on the short ends.
Portrait: The bust is carved with a female portrait.
Dating: 260-270 (*ASR* VI 1, cat. 315)

Bibliography: Stroszeck, *ASR* VI 1 (1998) cat. 315, pl. 61, 2.

343 *CLIPEUS* PORTRAIT OF A WOMAN

Location/Inv.: Rome, Palazzo Lazzaroni.
Condition: The coffin is preserved.
Frontal relief: Strigillated with a central *clipeus* with a bust. Two *corncopiae* are depicted beneath the *clipeus*. A lion killing a horse is represented on either end of the relief.
Short ends: Lenos-shaped. The lion of the frontal relief continues on the short ends.
Portrait: The bust is carved with a blank portrait prepared for a female hairstyle.
Dating: 280-300 (*ASR* VI 1, cat. 318).

Bibliography: Stroszeck, *ASR* VI 1 (1998) cat. 318, pl. 43, 2.

344) *CLIPEUS* PORTRAIT OF A CHILD

Location/Inv.: Rome, Palazzo Spada, galleria, inv. 383 (429).
Size (coffin): L: 1.47 H: 0.41 D: 0.45
Condition: The coffin is preserved.
Frontal relief: Strigillated with a central *clipeus* with a bust of a child. Two masks are depicted beneath the *clipeus*. A lion killing a deer is represented on either end of the relief. For a description, see *ASR* VI 1, cat. 321.
Short ends: Lenos-shaped. The lion of the frontal relief continues on the short ends.
Portrait: The bust is carved with a portrait of a child, probably a boy.
Dating: Around 250 (*ASR* VI 1, cat. 321).
Comment: Child sarcophagus.

Bibliography: Stroszeck, *ASR* VI 1 (1998) cat. 321, pl. 45, 4.

345 *CLIPEUS* PORTRAIT OF A WOMAN

Location/Inv.: Rome, S. Clemente, Basilica.
Size (coffin): L: 1.95 H: 0.66 D: 0.56
Condition: The coffin is preserved.
Frontal relief: A central *clipeus* containing a bust of a woman is framed by garlands. Two *cornucopiae* are depicted beneath the *clipeus*. A lion killing a boar is represented on either end of the relief. For a description, see *ASR* VI 1, cat. 325.
Short ends: Lenos-shaped. The lion of the frontal relief continues on the short ends.
Reverse: Roughly carved.
Portrait: The bust is carved with a blank portrait
Dating: 260-270 (*ASR* VI 1, cat. 235).

Bibliography: Stroszeck, *ASR* VI 1 (1998) cat. 325, pl. 34, 2.

346 *CLIPEUS* PORTRAIT OF A MAN

Location/Inv.: Rome, Vatican, the Santa Rosa necropolis, Via Triumphalis.
Condition: The coffin is preserved.
Provenience: The Santa Rosa necropolis.
Frontal relief: Strigillated with vertical lines and a central *clipeus* with a bust of a man. Two peasants and an ox are depicted beneath the *clipeus*. A lion drinking from a *kantharos* is pictured on either end of the relief.
Short ends: Lenos-shaped. Lion eating from *kantharos*.
Portrait. The bust is carved with a male portrait.
Dating: 260-280.

Bibliography: Liverano & Spinola 2006, 93, fig. 108; 2010, 273, 284, figs. 117-18.

347 *CLIPEUS* PORTRAIT OF A MAN

Location/Inv.: Rome, Via di S. Gregorio. Once used as a well.
Size (coffin): L: 1.95
Condition: The frontal relief is preserved.
Frontal relief: Strigillated with a central *clipeus* with a bust of a man. Two *cornucopiae* are depicted beneath the *clipeus*. A lion killing a deer is represented on either end of the relief. For a description, see *ASR* VI 1, cat. 307.
Short ends: Lenos-shaped. The lion of the frontal relief continues on the short ends.
Reverse: Roughly carved.
Portrait: The bust is carved with a blank portrait.
Dating: 270-280 (*ASR* VI 1, cat. 307).

Bibliography: Stroszeck, *ASR* VI 1 (1998) cat. 307, pl. 55, 3.

348 *CLIPEUS* PORTRAIT OF A WOMAN

Location/Inv.: San Simeon, Hearst Castle, California.
Size (coffin): L: 1.58 H: 0.61 D: 0.59
Condition: The coffin is preserved.
Frontal relief: Strigillated with vertical lines and a central *clipeus* with a bust of a woman. Two *cornucopiae* are depicted beneath the *clipeus*. A lion drinking from a *krater* is represented on either end of the relief. For description, *ASR* VI, 1, cat. 195.
Short ends: Lenos-shaped. The lion of the frontal relief continues on the short ends.
Reverse: Roughly carved.
Portrait: The bust is carved with a portrait of a girl.
Dating: 280-300 (*ASR* VI 1, cat. 195).

Bibliography: Stroszeck, *ASR* VI 1 (1998) cat. 195.

349 *CLIPEUS* PORTRAIT OF A MAN

Location/Inv.: Stockholm, Medelhavsmusset.
Size (coffin): L: 2.14 H: 0.62 D. 0.64
Condition: The coffin is preserved.
Provenience: Once in Villa Rondinini, Rome.
Frontal relief: Strigillated with a central *clipeus* with a bust of a man in a *pallium*. A scene with a philosopher and Muses is depicted beneath the *clipeus*. A lion attacking a boar is represented on either end of the relief. For a description, see Ewald 1999, C 28.
Short ends: Lenos-shaped. The lion-boar group of the frontal relief continues on the short ends.
Portrait: The bust is carved with a male portrait.
Dating: 270-280 (Ewald 1999, cat. C 28).

Bibliography: Stroszeck, *ASR* VI 1 (1998) cat. 363; Ewald 1999, cat. C 28, pl. 36, 1.

Myths

350 BUST OF A MAN

Location/Inv.: Copenhagen, Ny Carlsberg Glyptotek, inv. 844.
Size (coffin): L. 2.10 H: 0.63; (lid): L: 2.10
Condition: The front reliefs of the coffin and lid are preserved.
Provenience: Sidon, Lebanon.
Frontal relief: Marsyas sarcophagus. For a description, see Østergaard 1996, cat. 35.
Lid: In the centre, a bust of a man is framed by garlands. Apollo and Artemis flank the bust. Muses are represented on either end of the relief.
Portrait: The bust is carved with a portrait of a bearded man.
Inscription: ΕΡΜΟΓΕΝΗ ΧΡΗϹΤΕ ΚΑΙ ΑΛΥΠΕ ΧΑΙΡΕ /ΥΗϹΑϹ ΕΤΗ Ν
Dating: 200-210 (Østergaard 1996, cat. 35).

Bibliography: Wegner, *ASR* V 3 (1966) 20; Poulsen 1951, cat. 782; Østergaard 1996, cat. 35.

351 *CLIPEUS* PORTRAIT OF A MAN

Location/Inv.: Genoa, Cornigliano, Abbazia di S. Andreae.
Size (coffin): L: 2.10 H: 0.70 D. 0.60
Condition: The coffin is preserved.
Frontal relief: Divided into five panels. The second and fourth panels are strigillated. Meleager is represented on the first relief, and Oineus from the myth of Meleager is represented on

the fifth panel. The central panel depicts a *clipeus* with a bust of a man. The *clipeus* is supported by a plinth.
Short ends: Unknown.
Portrait: The bust is carved with a blank portrait.
Dating: 180-190 (*ASR* XII 6, cat. 145).

Bibliography: Koch, *ASR* XII 6 (1975) cat. 145, pl. 120, 2.

352 *CLIPEUS* PORTRAIT OF A WOMAN

Location/Inv.: Genzano, Villa Cesarini.
Size (coffin): L: 01.86 H: 0.57 D: 0.55
Condition: The coffin is preserved.
Frontal relief: A satyr supports a central *clipeus* with a bust of a woman. Marsyas is represented on one side of the *clipeus*, and Apollo is represented on the other. Both are accompanied by other figures from the myth.
Short ends: Lion griffin.
Portrait: The bust is carved with a female portrait.
Dating: Late second century (*ASR* III 2, cat. 209).

Bibliography: Robert, *ASR* III 2 (1904) cat. 209.

353 *CLIPEUS* PORTRAIT OF A MAN

Location/Inv.: Florence, Villa la Pietra.
Size (coffin): L: 2.07 H: 0.61 D. 0.52
Condition: The coffin is preserved.
Frontal relief: Dionysian procession. Two centaurs hold a central *clipeus* with a bust of a man. A representation of Dionysus standing in his wagon is depicted on either end of the relief.
Portrait: The bust is carved with a blank portrait.
Dating: Between the Gallienic and Tetrarchic periods (*ASR* IV 4, cat. 271).

Bibliography: Matz, *ASR* IV 4 (1975) cat. 271, pl. 292, 1.

354 BUST OF A WOMAN

Location/Inv.: New York, Metropolitan Museum of Art, inv. 47.100. 4a,b.
Size (coffin): L: 1.60/1.89 H: 0.54 D: 0.46/0.69
Condition: The coffin and lid were found together and both are preserved.
Provenience: Ostia, found in 1947 (Sorabella 2001).
Frontal relief: The sleeping Endymion and Selene who comes to him in her wagon. A head of a lion is represented on either end of the relief. For a description, see *ASR* XII 2, cat. 80.
Short ends: *Lenos*-shaped. The frontal relief continues on the short ends.
Reverse: Bucolic setting in which the myth takes place.
Lid: Small niches with representations of different mythological figures. The central niche is shaped as a *tabula ansata* with an inscription. The niche to the right of the *tabula ansata* shows a bust of a woman.
Portrait: The bust is carved with a female portrait. The portrait bust is placed on the lid in one of the small niches to the right of the inscription.
Inscription: ANINIA HILARA / CL ARRIAE MARI / INCONPARABILE / FECIT VIXIT / ANN L MEN / X (*CIL* 14.565).
Dating: 220 (Sorabella 2001).

Bibliography: Robert, *ASR* III 1 (1897) cat. 83; Sichtermann, *ASR* XII 2 (1992) cat. 80; Walker 1990; Sorabella 2001.

355 *CLIPEUS* PORTRAIT OF A MAN

Location/Inv.: Oxford, Ashmolean Museum, inv. 1947.279.
Size (coffin): L: 2.13 H: 0.72 D: 0.67
Condition: The coffin is preserved.
Frontal relief: Dionysian procession. Two centaurs hold a central *clipeus* with a bust. Representationsof Dionysus standing in his wagon are placed on either end of the relief. Cupids harvesting grapes are shown beneath the *clipeus.*
Short ends: Weapons.
Portrait: The bust is carved with a male portrait.
Dating: 240-250 (*ASR* IV 4, cat. 269).

Bibliography: Matz, *ASR* IV 4 (1975) cat. 269.

356 *CLIPEUS* PORTRAIT OF A MAN

Location/Inv.: Philippeville, Algeria.
Size (coffin): L: 2.20 H: 0.60 D: 0.26
Condition: The coffin and lid are preserved.
Frontal relief: Dionysian procession. Two centaurs hold a *clipeus* with a bust. Representations of Dionysus standing in his wagon are placed on either end of the relief.
Portrait: The bust is carved with a portrait of a man.
Dating: First half of the third century (*ASR* IV 4, cat. 270).

Bibliography: Matz, *ASR* IV 4 (1975) cat. 270, pl. 290, 1.

357 *CLIPEUS* PORTRAIT OF A MAN

Location/Inv: Poggio a Caiano, Villa Medicea.
Size (coffin): L: 2.13 H. 0.70 D: 0.62
Condition: The coffin is preserved.
Frontal relief: Two winged cupids hold a central *clipeus* with a bust. Venus is represented to the left of this group, and Mars is represented on the right. A woman with a cupid standing at her feet is depicted beneath the *clipeus*. A Victoria is represented on both ends of the relief.
Portrait: The bust is carved with a portrait of a bearded man.
Dating: First half of the third century (*ASR* XII 2, cat. 7).

Bibliography: Sichertmann, *ASR* XII 2 (1992) cat. 7, pl. 10, 2.

358 *CLIPEUS* PORTRAIT OF A MAN

Location/Inv.: Rome, Museo Nazionale Romano, inv. 124735.
Size (coffin). L: 2.10 H. 0.47 D. 0.50
Condition: The coffin and lid are preserved.
Provenience: Via Casilina, Dresken-Weiland 2003, cat. A 47.
Frontal relief: Two flying cupids hold a *clipeus* with a bust. An eagle flanked by Oceanus and Tellus are depicted beneath the

clipeus. Achilles and Chiron are represented on each end of the relief. For a description, see *MNR* I 2, cat. II, 6.
Short ends: Griffin.
Lid: Without relief decoration.
Portrait: The bust is carved with a portrait of a man.
Dating: Within the reign of Gallienus (*MNR* I 2, cat. II, 6).

Bibliography: *MNR* I 2, 90, cat. II, 6; Grassinger, *ASR* XII 1 (1999) cat. 3; Dresken-Weiland 2003, cat. A 47.

359 *CLIPEUS* PORTRAIT OF A MAN

Location/Inv.: Rome, S. Maria Sopra Minerva (lost).
Condition: A coffin was preserved.
Frontal relief: Two flying cupids hold a *clipeus* with a bust. Hippolytus is represented sacrificing to Diana to the left of this group, and Hippolytus in a hunt is represented to the right.
Short ends: Weapons.
Portrait: The bust has the portrait of a youth.

Bibliography: Robert, *ASR* III 2 (1904) cat. 177; Huskinson 1996, cat. 2. 9.

360 BUST OF A WOMAN

Location/Inv.: Rome, Vatican Cemetery, Mausoleum C.
Size (coffin): L: 1.90 H: 0.59 D: 0.56
Condition: The coffin and lid are preserved.
Frontal relief: Strigillated with a sleeping cupid on either end of the relief.
Lid: Bucolic setting with the sleeping Endymion, an inscription tablet, and a bust of a woman in front of a *parapetasma* held by sleeping cupids.
Portrait: The bust on the lid is carved with a female portrait.
Inscription: D M / T CAESENNIO SEVERI/ANO BENEMERENTI / CAESENII / FAVSTINVS POMPE/IANVS ET RVFINVS PATRI INCOMPARABI/LI
Dating: Late third century.

Bibliography: Wolf 1977, cat. S9; Eck 1989, pl. II.

361 *CLIPEUS* PORTRAIT OF A WOMAN

Location/Inv.: Rome, Villa Borghese, Uccelleria.
Size (Coffin): L: 2.14 H: 0.68 D: 0.63
Condition: The coffin is preserved.
Frontal relief: Dionysian procession. Two centaurs hold a *clipeus* with a bust. Representations of Dionysus standing in his wagon are placed on either end of the relief.
Short ends: Without relief decoration.
Portrait: The bust is carved with a portrait of a woman.
Dating: The Aurelian period (*ASR* IV 4, cat. 272).

Bibliography: Matz, *ASR* IV 4 (1975) cat. 272, pl. 290, 2.

Sea-Monsters and Nymphs (see also Addendum 6)

362 SHELL WITH A BUST OF A WOMAN

Location/Inv.: Florence, Palazzo de'Martelli (lost).
Condition: Fragment of the frontal relief.
Frontal relief: A shell with a bust of a woman is surrounded by groups of sea-monsters and nymphs. A sleeping figure is represented beneath the shell.
Portrait: The bust is carved with a female portrait.
Dating: Middle of the third century (*ASR* V 1, cat. 76).

Bibliography: Rumpf, *ASR* V 1 (1939) cat. 76, fig. 47, p. 31.

363 SHELL WITH A BUST OF A WOMAN

Location/Inv.: Herver Castle, UK.
Condition: The coffin is preserved.
Frontal relief: A shell with a bust is surrounded by groups of sea-monsters and nymphs.
Short ends: Cupid riding a sea-monster.
Portrait: The bust is carved with a portrait of a woman.
Dating: Late second or early third century.

Bibliography:Andreae & Jung 1977, 338-41, figs. 6-7. Arachne image no.: FA1082-05 (http://arachne.uni-koeln.de/item/objekt/7338).

364 *CLIPEUS* PORTRAIT OF A WOMAN

Location/Inv.: Naples, Museo Nazionale, inv. 11800.
Size (coffin): L: 2.06 H. 0.50 D: 0.64
Condition: The coffin and lid are preserved.
Frontal relief: A central *clipeus* with a bust of a woman is held by two sea-centaurs. Flying cupids with conch horns and cupids riding dolphins are represented on either side of this group. For a description, see *ASR* V 1, cat. 65.
Short ends: *Lenos*-shaped.
Lid: Inscription tablet, sea-horses, and griffins.
Portrait: The bust is carved with a portrait of an elderly lady with a short veil.
Inscription: DM / C IVLIVS MARINV/S IVLIA AELIAS / CODIVGI SV/AE FECIT
Dating: First half of the fourth century (*ASR* V 1, cat. 65).
Comment: This coffin belonged to Julia Aelias, who was commemorated by her husband C. Julius Marinus.

Bibliography: Rumpf, *ASR* V 1 (1939) cat. 65, pl. 38, 1.

365 SHELLL WITH A BUST OF A WOMAN

Location/Inv.: Paris, Musée du Louvre.
Size (coffin): L: 2.10 H: 0.56 D: 0.06
Condition: The frontal relief is preserved.
Frontal relief: A shell with a bust of a woman is surrounded by groups of swimming sea-centaurs, sea-bulls, and nymphs. A young Triton flanked by a sea-sheep and a sea-bull supports the shell. For description, see *ASR* V 1, cat. 72.
Portrait: The bust is carved with a female portrait.

Dating: 220 based on the similarity between the hairstyle of the woman and the wife of Elagabalus (*ASR* V 1, cat. 72).

Bibliography: Rumpf, *ASR* V 1 (1939) cat. 72, pl. 25; Baratte & Metzger 1985, cat. 78.

366 SHELL WITH A BUST OF A BOY

Location/Inv.: Paris, Musée du Louvre.
Size (coffin): L: 1.80 H: 0.56 D: 0.65
Condition: The coffin is preserved.
Frontal relief: A central shell with a bust of a boy is surrounded by groups of swimming sea-centaurs, nymphs, and cupids. A cupid supports the shell.
Left short end: Sea-panther.
Right short end: Modern carving.
Portrait: The bust is carved with a portrait of a boy in *paludamentum*.
Dating: 220-250 based on the style of the portrait of the boy (*ASR* V 1, cat. 69).
Comment: Child sarcophagus.

Bibliography: Rumpf, *ASR* V 1 (1939) cat. 69, pl. 21, 3: Baratte & Metzger 1985, cat. 77.

367 SHELL WITH A BUST OF A MAN

Location/Inv.: Pisa, Camposanto.
Size (coffin): L: 1.77 H: 0.65 D: 0.64
Condition: The coffin is preserved.
Frontal relief: A shell with a bust of a man (?) is surrounded by sea-monsters and nymphs. Swimming cupids are depicted beneath the shell.
Short ends: Cupid riding on three sea-horses.
Portrait: According to Rumpf, the portrait is of a man and the hairstyle corresponds with that of the young Marcus Aurelius.
Dating: Last quarter of the second century (*ASR* V 1, cat. 68).

Bibliography: Rumpf, *ASR* V 1 (1939) cat. 68, pl. 26, 1.

368 SHELL WITH A BUST OF A MAN

Location/Inv.: Pisa, Camposanto.
Size (coffin): L: 2.00 H. 0.50 D. 0.54
Condition: The coffin is preserved.
Frontal relief: A shell with a bust of a man is surrounded by sea-monsters, nymphs, and cupids. Swimming dolphins are depicted beneath these scenes.
Short ends: Sea-griffin.
Portrait: According to Rumpf, this is a portrait of a man whose stylistic features bear some similarities to the portrait of Traianus Decius.
Dating: Second third of the third century (*ASR* V 1, cat. 86).

Bibliography: Rumpf, *ASR* V 1 (1939) cat. 86, pl. 23, 4.

369 *CLIPEUS* PORTRAIT OF A CHILD

Location/Inv.: Rome, Catacombe di Pretestato, inv. 01458.
Size (coffin): L: 1.17 ca.; (lid): L: 1.17 H: 0.16
Condition: The coffin and lid are preserved.
Provenience: Rome, Catacombe di Pretestato, placed in a niche in a cubiculum. Found together with other sarcophagi (Dresken-Weiland 2003, cat. D 9).
Frontal relief: A *clipeus* with a bust of a child is held by two sea-centaurs. More sea-centaurs and Nereids are represented on either side of this group. A boat with two figures is depicted beneath the *clipeus*.
Lid: Sigma-Mahl and *palaestra* scenes.
Portrait: The bust is carved with a portrait of a boy.
Inscription: CURTIAE / CANTIANAE / C(larissima) q (puella) IN PACE. (*ICUR* V, nr. 14155).
Dating: Tetrarchic period (*ASR* I 4, cat. 145).
Comment: Child sarcophagus.

Bibliography: Rumpf, *ASR* V 1 (1939) cat. 61; Amedick, *ASR* I 4 (1991) cat. 145, pl. 88, 5; Gütschow 1938, 234-37.

370 SHELL WITH A BUST OF A WOMAN

Location/Inv.: Rome, Galleria Borghese.
Size (coffin): L: 2.07 H: 0.57 D: 0.66
Condition: The frontal relief is preserved.
Frontal relief: A shell with a bust is held by two sea-centaurs and surrounded by sea-monsters and nymphs. A cupid supports the shell.
Portrait: The bust is carved with a portrait of a woman.
Dating: Third century (*ASR* V 1, cat. 74).

Bibliography: Rumpf, *ASR* V 1 (1939) cat. 74, pl. 24, 1.

371 *CLIPEUS* PORTRAIT OF A GIRL

Location/Inv.: Rome, Musei Vaticani, inv. 2312.
Size (coffin): L: 1.27 H: 0.46 D: 0.38; (lid): L: 1.28 H: 0.10
Condition: The coffin and lid are preserved.
Frontal relief: A *clipeus* with a bust of a girl with a naked shoulder is held by two sea-centaurs and surrounded by sea-monsters and nymphs. A nymph is represented on both ends of the relief with her arms around a sea-bull.
Short ends: Sea-horse.
Lid: Dolphins and trident.
Portrait: The bust of the girl is carved with a blank portrait.
Dating: Late second century (*ASR* V 1, cat. 57).
Comment: Venus iconography. Child sarcophagus.

Bibliography: Rumpf, *ASR* V 1 (1939) cat. 57, pl. 20, 3.

372 *CLIPEUS* PORTRAIT OF A MAN

Location/Inv.: Rome, Museo Nazionale Romano, inv. 56966.
Size (coffin): L: 0.59 H: 0.39 D: 0.09
Condition: Fragment of the frontal relief.
Frontal relief: A *clipeus* with a bust is held by a sea-centaur. A Nereid is riding on the back of the sea-centaur.
Portrait: The bust is carved with a portrait of a man.
Dating: 230-260 (*MNR* I 10, 2, cat. 18).

Bibliography: *MNR* I 10, 2, cat. 18.

373 SHELL WITH A BUST OF A WOMAN

Location/Inv.: Rome, Museo Nazionale Romano, inv. 104478.
Size (coffin): L: 2.02 H: 0.47 D: 0.60
Condition: The coffin and lid are preserved.
Provenience: Rome, Via Trumphalis, hypogeum of the gens Octavia or Octavia Paulina (Dresken-Weiland 2003, cat. A 116). For another sarcophagus with a portrait from this tomb, see *MNR*, inv. 104479 (here cat. no. 374).
Frontal relief: A shell with a bust of a woman is held by sea-centaurs and surrounded by groups of sea-monsters, sea-bulls, and nymphs. A cupid supports the shell.
Short ends: Cupid riding a sea-horse.
Lid: Sea-animals and swimming cupids. Empty inscription tablet.
Portrait: The bust is carved with a blank portrait.
Dating: Beginning of the third century (*ASR* V 1, cat. 70).

Bibliography: Rumpf, *ASR* V 1 (1939) cat. 70, pl. 20, 1.

374 *CLIPEUS* PORTRAIT OF A WOMAN

Location/Inv.: Rome, Museo Nazionale Romano, inv. 104479.
Size (coffin): L: 1.80 H: 0.48 D: 0.53; (lid): L: 1.80 H: 0.14
Condition: The coffin and lid are preserved.
Provenience: Rome, Via Trumphalis, hypogeum of the gens Octavia or Octavia Paulina (Dresken-Weiland 2003, cat. A 116). For another sarcophagus with a portrait from this tomb, see Nazionale Romano, inv. 104478 (here cat. no. 373).
Frontal relief: A *clipeus* with a bust of a woman is held by two sea-centaurs and surrounded by sea-monsters and nymphs.
Short ends: Sea-horses and cupid.
Lid: Sea-monsters being ridden by hunting cupids. An empty inscription tablet.
Portrait: The bust is carved with a portrait of a young woman.
Dating: Late second to early third century (*MNR* I 8, 1, cat. VI, 9).

Bibliography: Rumpf, *ASR* V 1 (1939) cat. 56; *MNR* I 8, 1, cat. VI, 9.

375 SHELL WITH A BUST OF A WOMAN

Location/Inv.: Rome, Palazzo Giustiniani.
Condition: The coffin is preserved.
Frontal relief: A shell with a bust of a woman is held by two sea-centaurs and surrounded by groups of sea-monsters and nymphs (some of which are swimming). A cupid supports the shell.
Short ends: Sea-panther and sea-horse.
Portrait: The bust is carved with a portrait of a woman.
Dating: Beginning of the third century (*ASR* V 1, cat. 71).

Bibliography: Rumpf, *ASR* V 1 (1939) cat. 71, pl. 20, 2.

376 SHELL WITH A BUST OF A WOMAN

Location/Inv: Rome, Palazzo Lancelotti
Condition: The coffin is preserved.
Frontal relief: A central shell with a bust of a woman is surrounded by groups of sea-monsters and nymphs. Cupids in boats are depicted between the figures and a nymph supports the *clipeus*.
Short ends: Sea-centaur and nymph.
Portrait: The portrait is lost but the female bust has been preserved.
Dating: Third quarter of the third century (*ASR* V 1, cat. 84).

Bibliography: Rumpf, *ASR* V 1 (1939) cat. 84, figs. 50-1.

377 SHELL WITH A BUST OF A WOMAN

Location/Inv.: Rome, Palazzo Mattei.
Size (coffin): L: 1.85 H. 0.52
Condition: The frontal relief is preserved.
Frontal relief: A shell with a bust is held by two sea-centaurs and surrounded by groups of sea-monsters and nymphs. A cupid supports the shell.
Portrait: The bust is carved with a portrait of a woman.
Dating: 220-250, based on the hairstyle (*ASR* V 1, cat. 73).

Bibliography: Rumpf, *ASR* V 1 (1939) cat. 73, pl. 24, 4.

378 SHELL WITH A BUST OF A MAN

Location/Inv.: Rome, S. Crisogono.
Size (coffin): L: 2.16 H: 0.68 D: 0.61
Condition: The coffin is preserved.
Frontal relief: A shell with a bust is held by sea-centaurs and surrounded by groups of sea-monsters and nymphs. Cupids, one in a boat, are depicted beneath the shell.
Portrait: The bust is carved with a portrait of a man.
Dating: Second third of the third century (*ASR* V 1, cat. 87).

Bibliography: Rumpf, *ASR* V 1 (1939) cat. 87, pl. 26, 4.

379 *CLIPEUS* PORTRAIT OF A WOMAN

Location/Inv.: Rome, Via Bocca di Leoni 17.
Size (coffin): L: 2.06 H: 0.49 D: 0.68
Condition: The coffin is preserved.
Frontal relief: A *clipeus* with a bust of a woman is held by sea-centaurs and surrounded by groups of more sea-centaurs and nymphs. A cupid is depicted on both ends of the relief.
Short ends: Young Triton.
Portrait: The bust is carved with a portrait of a young woman or girl.
Dating: Second half of the second century (*ASR* V 1, cat. 55).

Bibliography: Rumpf, *ASR* V 1 (1939) cat. 55, pl. 17, 1.

380 SHELL WITH A BUST OF A WOMAN

Location/Inv.: Rome, Vigna S. Ambrosio im Padiglione.
Condition: Small fragment of a frontal relief.
Frontal relief: Part of a shell with a fragmented portrait. Part of a sea-centaur is preserved on her right.
Portrait: The bust in the shell is carved with a female portrait.
Dating: Last quarter of the second century (*ASR* V 1, cat. 88)

Bibliography: Rumpf, *ASR* V 1 (1939) cat. 88, pl. 32, 3.

381 *CLIPEUS* PORTRAIT OF A BOY

Location/Inv.: Rome, art market.
Condition: Only the frontal relief is preserved?
Frontal relief: A central *clipeus* with a bust of a boy is held by two sea-centaurs, each with a nymph riding on their backs.
Portrait: Boy wearing a toga.
Dating: First half of the fourth century (*ASR* V 1, cat. 60).
Comment: Child sarcophagus.

Bibliography: Rumpf, *ASR* V 1 (1939) cat. 60, pl. 6, 1.

382 SHELL WITH A BUST OF A WOMAN

Location/Inv.: Siena, Museo dell'Opera, inv. 136.
Size (coffin): L: 1.73 H. 0.51
Condition: The frontal relief is preserved.
Frontal relief: A shell with a bust is held by two nymphs and surrounded by groups of sea-monsters and more nymphs. Cupids on either side support the shell.
Portrait: The bust is carved with a portrait of a woman or a girl.
Dating: Late second to early third century (*ASR* V 1, cat. 67).

Bibliography: Rumpf, *ASR* V 1 (1939) cat. 67, pl. 21, 1.

383 SHELL WITH A BUST OF A WOMAN

Location/Inv.: Verona, Museo Maffeiano, inv. no. 28764.
Size (coffin): L: 1.95 H: 0.45 D: 0.53
Condition: The frontal relief is preserved.
Frontal relief: A shell with a bust is held by sea-centaurs and surrounded by groups of sea-monsters and nymphs, some with musical instruments. A cupid supports the shell.
Lid: Two flying cupids hold an empty inscription tablet. Sea-creatures are depicted on each side of this group.
Portrait: The bust on the frontal relief is carved with a portrait of a woman.
Dating: Middle of third century (*ASR* V 1, cat. 75).

Bibliography: Rumpf, *ASR* V 1 (1939) cat. 75, pl. 19, 1.

Seasonal

384 *CLIPEUS* PORTRAIT OF A CHILD

Location/Inv.: Bellocq, France, St. Clemens.
Size (coffin): L: 1.75 H. 0.53 D: 0.66; (lid): L: 1.78 H: 0.38
Condition: Coffin and lid are preserved.
Frontal relief: Six seasonal personifications are shown, with the attributes of the seasons. Two of them, wearing cloaks, hold a *clipeus* with a bust of a child. Two small boys wearing cloaks (seasonal personifications?) support the *clipeus*.
Left short end: Two cupids harvesting grapes.
Right short end: Two cupids carrying a basket with fruit.
Lid: Empty inscription tablet framed by boys playing with wheels.
Portrait: The bust is carved with a portrait of a child.
Dating: 300 (*ASR* I 4, cat. 13).
Comment: Child sarcophagus.

Bibliography: Kranz, *ASR* V 4 (1984) cat. 577; Amedick, *ASR* I 4 (1991) cat. 13 (lid), pl. 101, 1; Bielefeld, *ASR* V 2, 2 (1997) cat. 6; Hanfmann 1951, cat. 534.

385 MAN WITH TUNIC AND CLOAK

Location/Inv.: Boston, Museum of Fine Arts, inv. 1892.2583.
Size (coffin): L. 2.29 H: 0.58 D: 0.59
Condition: The coffin is preserved.
Frontal relief: A man dressed in a tunic and *pallium* is represented between seasonal personifications. A *parapetasma* is suspended behind him. For a description, see *ASR* V 2, cat. 8.
Short ends: A peasant ploughing.
Portrait: The man in a tunic and *pallium* is carved with a portrait.
Dating: 270-290 (*ASR* V 2, cat. 8).

Bibliography: Kranz, *ASR* V 2, 1 (1999) cat. 8; Kranz, *ASR* V 4 (1984) pl. 53, 3.

386 *CLIPEUS* PORTRAIT OF A MAN

Location/Inv.: Brussels, Musée Cinquantenarire, inv. A 3680.
Size (coffin): L: 1.56 H: 0.55
Condition: The frontal relief is preserved.
Frontal relief: A *clipeus* with a bust is held by two winged cupids. Two seasonal personifications with flower baskets are represented on either side of the group. Tellus is represented on the left side of the *clipeus*, and Oceanus is seen on the right. Beneath the *clipeus* is another fruit or flower basket and two peacocks. For a description, see *ASR* V 4, cat. 30.
Portrait: The bust is carved with a portrait of a man. The portrait has been extensively re-carved in modern times.
Dating: Around 270 (Huskinson 1996, 8.3).

Bibliography: Kranz, *ASR* V 4 (1984) cat. 30, pl. 32, 2; Huskinson 1996, 8. 3.

387 *CLIPEUS* PORTRAIT OF A WOMAN

Location/Inv.: Buffalo, Albright-Knox Art Gallery.
Size (coffin): L: 2.15 H. 0.711 D: 0.622
Condition: The coffin is preserved.
Frontal relief: A *clipeus* with a bust is held by two cupids. Two seasonal personifications and large vases are represented on either side of the group. Tellus and the four seasons are depicted beneath the *clipeus*.
Short ends: Probably undecorated.
Portrait: The bust is carved with a portrait of a woman.
Dating: 250-260 (Kleiner 1996, cat. 164).

Bibliography: Kleiner & Matheson 1996, cat. 164.

388 *CLIPEUS* PORTRAIT OF A MAN

Location/Inv.: Camaiore (Lucca) Pieve.
Size (coffin): L: 1.48 H: 0.40 D: 0.34
Condition: The coffin is preserved.

Frontal relief: A *clipeus* with a bust of a man is held by two *victoriae*. Seasonal personifications are represented on either side of the group. For a description, see *ASR* V 4, cat. 64.
Short ends: Eros.
Portrait: The bust is carved with a blank portrait.
Dating: Late third century (*ASR* V 4, cat. 64).
Comment: Possibly a child sarcophagus, due to its size.

Bibliography: Kranz, *ASR* V 4 (1984) cat. 64, pl. 43, 2.

389 *CLIPEUS* PORTRAIT OF A WOMAN

Location/Inv.: Florence, Villa la Pietra.
Size (coffin): L: 2.06 H. 0.55 D: 0.59
Condition: The coffin is preserved.
Frontal relief: A *clipeus* with a bust is held by two flying cupids. A *Genius* with a *pedum* is represented on either end of the relief. The Roman she-wolf flanked by Oceanus and Tellus is depicted beneath the *clipeus*. For a description, see *ASR* V 4, cat. 96.
Short ends: Pegasus.
Portrait: The bust is carved with a portrait of a woman.
Dating: 230-240 (*ASR* V 4, cat. 96).

Bibliography: Kranz, *ASR* V 4 (1984) cat. 96, pl. 60, 1.

390 BUST OF A BOY FRAMED BY GARLANDS

Location/Inv.: Liverpool Museum, inv. 343.
Size (coffin): L: 0.84 H. 0.32
Condition: The frontal relief is preserved. Restored.
Frontal relief: A bust is framed by garlands and flanked by winged cupids/seasonal figures. One of the Dioscuroi with a horse is represented on both ends of the relief. For description, see *ASR* V 4, cat. 124.
Portrait: The bust is carved with a portrait of a boy.
Dating: Around 270 (Huskinson 1996, 8. 16).
Comment: Child sarcophagus.

Bibliography: Kranz, *ASR* V 4 (1984) cat. 124, pl. 53, 1; Huskinson 1996, 8. 16.

391 *CLIPEUS* PORTRAIT OF A MAN

Location/Inv.: Ostia, Castello Chigi, Piazza della Rocca 13.
Condition: The frontal relief is preserved.
Frontal relief: A *clipeus* with a bust is held by two flying cupids. A *Genius* with a basket and a *pedum* is represented on either end of the relief. A basket and two peacocks are depicted beneath the *clipeus*. For a description, see *ASR* V 4, cat. 97.
Portrait: The bust is carved with a portrait of a man.
Dating: Late Gallienic period or just after (*ASR* V 4, cat. 97).

Bibliography: Kranz, *ASR* V 4 (1984) cat. 97, pl. 61, 6.

392 *CLIPEUS* PORTRAIT OF A MAN

Location/Inv.: Ostia, Palazzo Vescovile.
Size (coffin): L: 2.04 H. 0.61 D. 0.84
Condition: The coffin is preserved.
Frontal relief: A *clipeus* with a bust held by two *victoriae*. Seasonal personifications are represented on either end of the relief. A scene with cupids pressing grapes is depicted beneath the *clipeus*. For a description, see *ASR* V 4, cat. 66.
Short ends: Unknown.
Portrait: The bust is carved with a male portrait.
Dating: 270-280 (*ASR* V 4, cat. 66).

Bibliography: Kranz, *ASR* V 4 (1984) cat. 66, pl. 42, 5.

393 *CLIPEUS* PORTRAIT OF A CHILD

Location/Inv.: Paris, Musée du Louvre, inv. Ma 952.
Size (coffin): L: 2.12 H. 0.74 D. 0.74
Condition: The frontal relief is preserved.
Frontal relief: Divided into five panels. The second and fourth panels are strigillated. A seasonal personification is represented on the first and fifth panels. The central panel depicts a *clipeus* with a bust of a child holding a bird, to which he is offering grapes. Two *cornucopiae* are depicted beneath the *clipeus*. For a description, see *ASR* V 4, cat. 155.
Portrait: The child on the central panel is carved with portrait features. Sex unknown.
Dating: 280s (*ASR* V 4, cat. 155).
Comment: Child sarcophagus.

Bibliography: Kranz, *ASR* V 4 (1984) cat. 155, pl. 72, 1; Baratte & Metzger 1985, cat. 130; Huskinson 1996, 8. 23.

394 *CLIPEUS* PORTRAIT OF A WOMAN

Location/Inv.: Paris, Musée du Louvre, inv. Ma 1627.
Size (coffin): L. 2.04 H. 0.58
Condition: The frontal relief is preserved.
Frontal relief: Two flying *victoriae* hold a *clipeus* with a bust. One of the *Horae* is represented on either end of the relief. Tellus and Oceanus and a cupid in a boat are depicted beneath the *clipeus*.
Portrait: The bust is carved with a portrait of a young woman.
Dating: Third quarter of the third century (Baratte & Metzger 1985, cat. 127).

Bibliography: Baratte & Metzger 1985, cat. 127.

395 BUST OF A WOMAN AND A MAN

Location/Inv.: Paris, Musée du Louvre, inv. 3570.
Size (coffin): L: 2.30 H. 1.08 d. 0.80; (lid): L: 2.30 H. 0.28 D: 0.87
Condition: The coffin and lid are preserved.
Frontal relief: Achilles motif.
Lid: A bust of a woman and a man framed by garlands are represented on a central panel. A cupid with a torch is depicted behind the busts. Cupids offering grapes to reclining women (*Hora*) are represented on either side of the panel. For a description, see *ASR* V 4, cat. 363.
Portrait: The busts are carved with blank portraits.
Dating: 220s (*ASR* V 4, cat. 363).

Bibliography: Kranz, *ASR* V 4 (1984) cat. 363, pl. 103, 1; Baratte & Metzger 1985, cat. 13.

396 *CLIPEUS* PORTRAIT OF A MAN
Location/Inv.: Pisa, Camposanto, inv. 62.
Size (coffin): L: 2.19 H. 0.57 D. 0.63
Condition: The coffin is preserved.
Frontal relief: Divided into five panels. The second and fourth panels are strigillated. Seasonal personifications are represented on the first and fifth panels. The central panel depicts a *clipeus* with a bust of a man. Two masks are placed beneath the *clipeus*. For a description, see *ASR* V 4, cat. 157.
Short ends: Without relief decoration.
Portrait: The bust is carved with a blank portrait.
Dating: 270s (*ASR* V 4, cat. 157).

Bibliography: Kranz, *ASR* V 4 (1984) cat. 157, pl. 70, 3.

397 BUST OF A MAN
Location/Inv.: Rome, Catacombe di Marcellino e S. Pietro.
Size (coffin): L: 2.03 H: 0.91
Condition: The coffin and lid are preserved.
Frontal relief: Strigillated with a *mandorla* and cupid. An *Orans* with a scroll at her feet is represented on the left end of the relief and a ram-bearer is represented on the right end.
Lid: Seasonal personifications, cupids, an empty inscription panel, and a bust of a man in front of a *parapetasma* held by cupids.
Portrait: The bust on the lid is carved with a blank portrait.
Dating: First quarter of the fourth century (*Rep.* I, cat. 646).

Bibliography: *Rep.* I, cat. 646.

398 *CLIPEUS* PORTRAIT OF A BOY
Location/Inv.: Rome, Catacombe di Pretestato.
Size (coffin): L: 1.65 H. 0.26
Condition: Fragments of the frontal relief are preserved.
Frontal relief: A *clipeus* with a bust is held by two cupids. Oceanus and Tellus are represented beneath the *clipeus* and between them a basket of flowers is visible. Seasonal personifications are represented on either end of the relief.
Portrait: The bust is carved with a portrait of a boy.
Dating: Around 280 (Huskinson 1996, cat. 2. 21)
Comment: Child sarcophagus.

Bibliography: Kranz, *ASR* V 4 (1984) cat. 100, pl. 63, 4; Huskinson 1996, cat. 2. 21.

399 *CLIPEUS* PORTRAIT OF A WOMAN
Location/Inv.: Rome, Catacombe di Pretestato, inv. 905.
Size (coffin): L: 2.18 H: 0.55 D: 0.59
Condition: The coffin is preserved.
Provenience: Hypogeum in the Catacombs of S. Croce (Via Appia Antica, 109) (Dresken-Weiland 2003, cat. A 64).
Frontal relief: Divided into five panels. The second and fourth panels are strigillated. A seasonal personification is represented on the first and fifth panels. The central panel depicts a *clipeus* with a bust. Two *cornucopiae* are depicted beneath the *clipeus*. For a description, see *ASR* V 4, cat. 160.
Short ends: Griffin.
Portrait: The bust is carved with a portrait of a woman.
Dating: 260s (*ASR* V 4, cat. 160).

Bibliography: Kranz, *ASR* V 4 (1984) cat. 160, pl. 69, 1.

400 BUST OF A MAN
Location/Inv: Rome, Catacombe di Priscila, basilica.
Condition: A fragment of the frontal relief is preserved.
Frontal relief: Divided into five panels. The second and fourth panels are strigillated. A bust of a man is represented in front of a *parapetasma* on the third panel, and a seasonal personification is represented on the fifth panel. The first panel is lost. For a description, see *ASR* V 4, cat. 178.
Portrait: The bust is carved with a blank portrait.
Dating: 240s (*ASR* V 4, cat. 178).

Bibliography: Kranz, *ASR* V 4 (1984) cat. 178, pl. 74, 4.

401 *CLIPEUS* PORTRAIT OF A WOMAN
Location/Inv.: Rome, Catacombe di S. Croce (lost).
Size (coffin): L: 1.52 H: 0.32
Condition: The frontal relief. The lid did not originally belong to the coffin.
Frontal relief: Divided into five panels. The second and fourth panels are strigillated. A seasonal personification is represented on the first and fifth panels. The central panel depicts a *clipeus* with a bust. Two *cornucopiae* are depicted beneath the *clipeus*. For a description, see *ASR* V 4, cat 319.
Lid: The lid has an empty inscription panel and seasonal personifications in wagons drawn by capricorn or panthers. The left end is lost.
Portrait: The bust is carved with a portrait of a woman.
Dating: Gallienic (ASR V 4, cat. 319).

Bibliography: Kranz, *ASR* V 4 (1984) cat. 319, pl. 91, 2.

402 *CLIPEUS* PORTRAIT OF A WOMAN
Location/Inv.: Rome, Collegio Romano, courtyard.
Size (coffin): L. 2.05 H: 0.54 D: 0.59
Condition: The coffin is preserved.
Frontal relief: Divided into five panels. The second and fourth panels are strigillated. A seasonal personification is represented on the first and fifth panels. The central panel depicts a *clipeus* with a bust of a woman. Two *cornucopiae* are depicted beneath the *clipeus*. For a description, see *ASR* V 4, cat. 161.
Short ends: Without relief decoration.
Portrait: The bust is carved with a blank portrait.
Dating: Tetrarchic period (*ASR* V 4, cat. 161).

Bibliography: Kranz, *ASR* V 4 (1984) cat. 161, pl. 73, 4.

403 BOY WITH BIRD
Location/Inv.: Rome, Musei Vaticani, Galleria Lapidaria, inv. 9256.
Size (coffin): L: 1.09 H: 0.36

Condition: The frontal relief is preserved.
Frontal relief: Divided into five panels. The second and fourth panels are strigillated with vertical lines. A seasonal personification is represented on the first and fifth panels. The central panel depicts a standing boy with a bird. For a description, see *ASR* V 4, cat. 191.
Portrait: The boy with the bird is carved with a portrait with short hair.
Dating: 280s (*ASR* V 4, cat. 191).
Comment: Child sarcophagus.

Bibliography: Kranz, *ASR* V 4 (1984) cat. 191, pl. 75, 4.

404 *CLIPEUS* PORTRAIT OF A WOMAN

Location/Inv.: Rome, Musei Vaticani, Museo Gregoriano Profano, inv. 10411 and 10411A.
Size (coffin): L: 2.17 H: 0.63 D: 0.66; (lid): L: 1.89 H: 0.33 D: 0.37
Condition: The coffin and lid are preserved, but the lid is fragmentary.
Provenience: Rome, Via Latina. Tomb of the Pancrati (Dresken-Weiland 2003, cat. A55; Herdejürgen 2000, 223).
Frontal relief: A *clipeus* with a bust of a woman is held by two seasonal personifications. Another two seasonal personifications and Victoria with a garland are represented on either side of this composition. A scene with *putti* playing with a mask is depicted beneath the *clipeus*. For a description, see *ASR* V 4, cat. 62.
Lid: A bucolic motif and an empty inscription panel.
Portrait: The bust on the frontal relief is carved with a blank portrait.
Dating: Late Gallienic period or just after (*ASR* V 4, cat. 62).
Comment: The lid may not belong to the coffin.

Bibliography: Kranz, *ASR* V 4 (1984) cat. 62, pl. 34, 3.

405 FIGURE OF A MAN

Location/Inv.: Rome, Museo Nazionale Romano, inv. 108677.
Size (coffin): L: 0.75 H: 0.47
Condition: Fragment of the frontal relief.
Frontal relief: A *krater* with a seasonal representation depicted on its left and the deceased represented on its right. For a description, see *MNR* I 10, 2, cat. 181.
Portrait: The man on the right of the *krater* is carved with portrait features.
Dating: After the reign of Gallienus (*MNR* I 10, 2, cat. 182).

Bibliography: Kranz, *ASR* V 4 (1984) cat. 119, pl. 21, 1; *MNR* I 10, 2, cat. 182.

406 *CLIPEUS* PORTRAIT OF A BOY

Location/Inv.: Rome, Museo Nazionale Romano, inv. 113406.
Size (coffin): L: 0.62 H: 0.25 D: 0.29
Condition: The frontal relief is preserved.
Provenience: Orticoli.
Frontal relief: A *clipeus* with a bust of a child is held by seasonal personifications. Two overturned baskets are depicted beneath the *clipeus*. For a description, see *MNR* I 10, 2, cat. 182.
Portrait: The bust is carved with a portrait of a boy.
Dating: Early Tetrarchic period (*ASR* V 4, cat. 47).
Comment: Child sarcophagus.

Bibliography: Kranz, *ASR* V 4 (1984) cat. 47, pl. 53, 2; *MNR* I 10, 2, cat. 182; Huskinson 1996, 8. 5.

407 *CLIPEUS* PORTRAIT OF A MAN

Location/Inv.: Rome, Museo Nazionale Romano, inv. 128086.
Size (coffin): L: 1.00 H: 0.35 D: 0.39
Condition: The coffin is preserved.
Provenience: Ostia.
Frontal relief: A *clipeus* with a bust is held by two cupids. A seasonal personification is represented on either end of the relief. A cockfight and masks are depicted beneath the *clipeus*. For a description, see *ASR* V 4, cat. 46.
Short ends: Roughly carved.
Portrait: The bust is carved with a portrait of a man, which has been re-worked from a portrait of a boy with a *Horus* lock.
Dating: 280-300 (Huskinson 1996, 9. 29).

Bibliography: Kranz, *ASR* V 4 (1984) cat. 46, pl. 38, 2; Koch 1990, 65-6; Huskinson 1996, 9. 29.

408 BUST OF A WOMAN

Location/Inv.: Rome, Museo Nazionale di Villa Giulia, Ninfeo.
Size (lid): L: 2.09 H: 0.24 D: 0.65
Condition: The coffin and lid are preserved.
Frontal relief: Divided into five panels. The second and fourth panels are strigillated. Dionysian scenes are represented on the first, third, and fifth panels.
Lid: A central empty inscription tablet with seasonal personifications represented on both sides. On the left end of the relief, a bust of a woman is depicted in front of a *parapetasma* held by two of the personifications. For a description, see *ASR* V 4, cat. 532.
Portrait: The bust on the lid is carved with a blank portrait.
Dating: Tetrarchic or Constantinian period (*ASR* V 4, cat. 532).

Bibliography: Kranz, *ASR* V 4 (1984) cat. 532, pl. 113, 4.

409 *CLIPEUS* PORTRAIT OF A WOMAN

Location/Inv.: Rome, Palazzo Mattei.
Condition: The coffin is preserved.
Frontal relief: A *clipeus* with a bust is held by two flying *victoriae*. A seasonal personification is represented on each end of the relief.
Portrait: The bust is carved with a portrait of a young woman.
Dating: Late second or first half of the third century.

Bibliography: Arachne no.: http://arachne.uni-koeln.de/item/objekt/51940.

410 *CLIPEUS* PORTRAIT

Location/Inv.: Rome, Palazzo Ruspoli.
Size (coffin): L: 1.26 H: 0.47 D: 0.50
Frontal relief: A *clipeus* with a bust is held by two cupids. Two seasonal personifications are represented on either side of this composition. A scene with cupids harvesting grapes is depicted beneath the *clipeus*. For a description, see *ASR* V 4, cat. 53.
Short ends: Without relief decoration.
Portrait: The bust was carved with, or perhaps just prepared for, a portrait. The portrait is not preserved.
Dating: 270-280 (Huskinson 1996, cat. 8. 7).

Bibliography: Kranz, *ASR* V 4 (1984) cat. 53, pl. 40, 5; Huskinson 1996, cat. 8. 7.

411 *CLIPEUS* PORTRAIT OF A BOY

Location/Inv.: Rome, Palazzo Venezia.
Size (coffin): L: 1.39 H. 0.55
Condition: The frontal relief is preserved.
Frontal relief: A *clipeus* with a bust is held by two *victoriae*. Two seasonal personifications are represented on either side of this composition. A scene with Ganymede and the eagle is depicted beneath the *clipeus*. For a description, see *ASR* V 4, cat. 70.
Portrait: The bust is carved with a portrait of a boy.
Dating: Late Gallienic period (*ASR* V 4, cat. 70).
Comment: Child sarcophagus.

Bibliography: Kranz, *ASR* V 4 (1984) cat 70, pl. 42; Sichtermann, *ASR* XII 2 (1992) cat. 140; L'Orange 1953, 101; Huskinson 1996, 2. 7.

412 *CLIPEUS* PORTRAIT OF A MAN

Location/Inv.: Rome, Piazza del Popolo. Used as a fountain.
Condition: The coffin is preserved.
Frontal relief: Strigillated sarcophagus divided into five panels. The second and fourth are strigillated and the central panel shows a *clipeus* with a bust. The *clipeus* is supported by *cornucopiae*. A seasonal personification/cupid is represented on the first and fifth panel.
Short ends: No decoration.
Portrait: The bust is carved with a portrait of a man.
Dating: Second half of the third century, based on the style of the portrait.

413 *CLIPEUS* PORTRAIT OF A WOMAN

Location/Inv.: Rome, S. Maria Antiqua, Forum Romanum.
Size (coffin): L: 2.04 H: 0.55 D: 0.53
Condition: The coffin is preserved.
Frontal relief: A *clipeus* with a bust is held by two flying cupids. A seasonal personification is represented on either end of the relief. Oceanus and Tellus are depicted beneath the *clipeus*. For a description, see *ASR* V 4, cat. 108.
Left short end: Seasonal personification with basket and *pedum*.
Right short end: Olive harvesting.
Portrait: The bust is carved with a portrait of a woman.
Dating: 250s (*ASR* V 4, cat. 108).

Bibliography: Kranz, *ASR* V 4 (1984) cat. 108, pl. 61, 2.

414 *CLIPEUS* PORTRAIT OF A WOMAN

Location/Inv.: Rome, S. Maria in Cosmedin.
Condition: The coffin is preserved.
Frontal relief: Divided into five panels. The second and fourth panels are strigillated. A seasonal personification is represented on the first and fifth panels. The central panel depicts a *clipeus* supported by a pedestal with a bust. Rosettes are placed around the *clipeus*. For a description, see *ASR* V 4, cat. 165.
Short ends: Without relief decoration.
Portrait: The bust is carved with a portrait of a woman.
Dating: Early Gallienic period (*ASR* V 4, cat. 165).

Bibliography: Kranz, *ASR* V 4 (1984) cat. 165, pl. 69, 5.

415 *CLIPEUS* PORTRAIT OF A CHILD

Location/Inv.: Rome, S. Paolo fuori le mura.
Size (coffin): L: 1.46 H: 0.39 D. 0.42
Condition: The coffin is preserved.
Provenience: Ponticello, in a "grotta" (Dresken-Weiland 2003, cat. A 82).
Frontal relief: Divided into five panels. The second and fourth panels are strigillated. A seasonal personification is represented on the first and fifth panels. The central panel shows a *clipeus* with a bust. A cockfight is depicted beneath the *clipeus*. For a description, see *ASR* V 4, cat. 166.
Short ends: Without relief decoration.
Portrait: The bust is carved with a portrait of a child. Sex unknown.
Dating: Around 260 (Huskinson 1996, 8. 23).

Bibliography: Kranz, *ASR* V 4 (1984) cat. 166, pl. 70, 2; Huskinson 1996, 8. 23; Dresken-Weiland 2003, cat. A 82.

416 *CLIPEUS* PORTRAIT OF A MAN

Location/Inv.: Rome, S. Sabina, Atrium.
Size (coffin): L: 2.22 H: 0.65 D: 0.64
Condition: The coffin is preserved.
Frontal relief: Divided into five panels. The second and fourth panels are strigillated. A seasonal personification is represented on the first and fifth panels. The central panel depicts a *clipeus* with a bust. An *aedicula* framing a bucolic scene with a tree and a deer is depicted beneath the *clipeus*. A *parapetasma* is suspended behind the scene in the *aedicula*. For a description, see *ASR* V 4, cat. 167.
Short ends: Seasonal personification.
Portrait: The bust is carved with a portrait of a man. The surface is damaged.
Dating: Gallienic period or just after (*ASR* V 4, cat. 156).

Bibliography: Kranz, *ASR* V 4 (1984) cat. 167, pl. 71, 4.

417 *CLIPEUS* PORTRAIT OF A BOY

Location/Inv.: Rome, Santi Quattro Coronati.
Size (coffin): L: 0.76 H: 0.36
Condition: Fragmentary frontal relief.
Frontal relief: A *clipeus* with a bust is held by two flying cupids. Seasonal personifications are represented on either side of this composition. Cupids riding a peacock and a basket are depicted beneath the *clipeus*.
Portrait: The bust is carved with a portrait of a boy.
Dating: Around 310 (Huskinson 1996, 9. 26). First quarter of the fourth century (*ASR* V 4, cat. 110).
Comment: Child sarcophagus.

Bibliography: Kranz, *ASR* V 4 (1984) cat. 110, pl. 63, 6; Huskinson 1996, 9. 26.

418 *CLIPEUS* PORTRAIT OF A BOY

Location/Inv.: Rome, Vatican, Campo Santo Teoutonico, inv. A. 30.
Size (coffin): L: 0.95 H: 0.28 D: 0.34
Condition: The coffin is preserved.
Frontal relief: A *clipeus* with a bust is held by two flying cupids. A seasonal personification is represented on either end of the relief. Two peacocks are depicted beneath the *clipeus*.
Short ends: Without relief decoration.
Portrait: The bust is carved with a portrait of a boy.
Dating: Early fourth century (Huskinson 1996, 8. 15; *ASR* V 4, cat. 114).
Comment: Child sarcophagus.

Bibliography: Kranz, *ASR* V 4 (1984) cat. 114, pl. 63, 10; Huskinson 1996, 8. 15.

419 *CLIPEUS* PORTRAIT OF A WOMAN

Location/Inv.: Rome, Vatican, the Santa Rosa necropolis, Via Triumphalis.
Condition: The coffin is preserved.
Provenience: Tomb VIII (Liverani & Spinola 2006, fig. 105).
Frontal relief: A *clipeus* with a bust of a woman is held by two flying *victoriae*. A seasonal personification is placed on either end of the relief. Tellus and Oceanus and cupids in a boat are depicted beneath the *clipeus*.
Lid: See Liverani & Spinola 2010
Portrait: The bust is carved with a blank portrait prepared for a female hairstyle.
Dating: Second half of the third century.

Bibliography: Liverani & Spinola 2006, fig. 105; 2010, 265-73, figs. 109-11.

420 *CLIPEUS* PORTRAIT OF A WOMAN

Location/Inv.: Rome, Via del Seminario 113, courtyard.
Size (coffin): L: 2.18 H: 0.55 D: 0.62
Condition: The coffin is preserved.
Frontal relief: Divided into five panels. The second and fourth panels are strigillated. A seasonal personification is represented on the first and fifth panels. The central panel depicts a *clipeus* with a bust. Two *cornucopiae* are depicted beneath the *clipeus*. For a description, see *ASR* V 4, cat. 169.
Short end: Weapons.
Portrait: The bust is carved with a portrait of a woman.
Dating: Late Tetrarchic period (*ASR* V 4, cat. 169).

Bibliogrphy: Kranz, *ASR* V 4 (1984) cat. 169, pl. 72, 4.

421 *CLIPEUS* PORTRAIT OF A WOMAN

Location/Inv.: Rome, Villa Doria Pamphilj.
Condition: The frontal relief is preserved.
Frontal relief: A *clipeus* with a bust is held by two cupids. Two seasonal personifications are represented on either side of this composition. Two *cornucopiae* are depicted beneath the *clipeus*. For a description, see *ASR* V 4, cat. 55.
Portrait: The bust is carved with a portrait of a woman.
Dating: Early Tetrarchic period (*ASR* V 4, cat. 55).

Bibliography: Kranz, *ASR* V 4 (1984) cat. 55, pl. 40, 1, Calza 1977, cat. 256.

422 BUST OF A MAN

Location/Inv: Rome, Villa Doria Pamphilj (lost).
Condition: The coffin and lid are preserved.
Provenience: Lorium.
Frontal relief: Divided into five panels. The second and fifth panels are strigillated. The first, third, and fifth panels are made as projecting *aediculae*. A seasonal personification is represented in the first and fifth *aediculae* and a bust is represented in the central *aedicula*.
Short ends: Fruit basket.
Lid: Shaped as a roof with statuary figures above each *aediculae*. Furthermore an inscription is shown above the central *aedicula*.
Portrait: The bust is carved with a portrait of a man.
Inscription: (above the central *aedicula*) Οσ πάσας Χάριτας καὶ τὰς θρένας ἐνφάδ᾽ ἔκλεισε κεῖται Καρονἐντις πολὺ Φίλτατος οἷσι τοκευσι.
(on the lower profile) Τρὶς μάκαρος δὲ λίθος τόσσν ἔχων ἀγαθόν (*IG* XIV 2258).
Dating: 280 (*ASR* V 4, cat. 189).

Bibliography: Kranz, *ASR* V 4 (1984) cat. 189, pl. 77, 1; Calza 1977, cat. 266.

423 *CLIPEUS* PORTRAIT OF A MAN

Location/Inv.: Rome, Villa Wolkonsky.
Size (coffin): L: 0.98 H. 0.33
Condition: The frontal relief is preserved.
Frontal relief: A *clipeus* with a bust of a man is held by two seasonal personifications. Two more seasonal personifications are represented on either side of this composition. Two peacocks and a flower basket are depicted beneath the *clipeus*. For a description, see *ASR* V 4, cat. 57.
Portrait: The bust is carved with a blank portrait.
Dating: Late Gallienic period or just after (*ASR* V 4, cat. 57).

Comment: Possibly a child sarcophagus, due to the length of the coffin.

Bibliography: Kranz, *ASR* V 4 (1984) cat. 57, pl. 26, 3; Huskinson 1996, 8. 8.

424 BUST OF A MAN

Location/Inv.: Rome, once on the art market (Pollak).
Condition: The coffin is preserved.
Frontal relief: Divided into five panels. The second and fourth panels are strigillated. A seasonal personification is represented on the first and fifth panels. The central panel depicts a bust supported by acanthus leafs. A *parapetasma* is suspended behind the bust. For a description, see *ASR* V 4, cat. 179-180.
Short ends: Without relief decoration.
Portrait: The bust is carved with a portrait of a man.
Dating: 270s (*ASR* V 4, cat. 179).

Bibliography: Kranz, *ASR* V 4 (1984) cat. 179-80, pl. 74, 1.

425 *CLIPEUS* PORTRAIT OF A WOMAN

Location/Inv.: Sassari, Mueo Nazionale G. A. Sanna.
Size (coffin): L: 1.33 H: 0.72
Condition: Part of the frontal relief is preserved.
Provenience: Near Sassari.
Frontal relief: A bust enclosed in a *clipeus* adorned with symbols from the zodiac wheel is held by two *victoriae*. Seasonal personifications are represented on the left end of the relief; the right end is lost. A scene with Selene visiting the sleeping Endymion is depicted beneath the *clipeus*. For a description, see *ASR* V 4, cat. 72.
Portrait: The bust is carved with a portrait of a woman.
Dating: Early Constantinian period (*ASR* V 4, cat. 72).

Bibliography: Kranz, *ASR* V 4 (1984) cat. 72, pl. 45, 2.

426 *CLIPEUS* PORTRAIT OF A WOMAN

Location/Inv.: Tutzing, Evangelieche Akademie.
Size (coffin): L: 1.62 H: 0.52 D: 0.59
Condition: The coffin is preserved.
Frontal relief: A *clipeus* with a bust wearing a toga is held by two seasonal personifications. Two more seasonal personifications are represented on either side of this composition. Ganymede and the eagle are depicted beneath the *clipeus*.
Short ends: Lenos-shaped. Lion.
Portrait: The male bust is carved with a female portrait.
Dating: 270-280 (Huskinson 1996, 8. 9); 290-310 (*ASR* V I 1, cat. 368).
Comment: Cross-gendered.

Bibliography: Kranz, *ASR* V 4 (1984) cat. 60; Stroszeck, *ASR* VI 1 (1998) cat. 368, pl. 67, 4; Huskinson 1996, 8. 9.

Vita Romana

427 BUST OF A WOMAN

Location/Inv.: Florence, Baptisterium.
Size (coffin): L: 2.23 H: 0.73 D: 0.61
Condition: The coffin is preserved.
Frontal relief: A bust is placed in front of a *parapetasma*. A basket is depicted beneath the bust. A scene showing the making of garlands appears to the left of the bust, and on the right is a scene with a cupid showing a garland to a seated woman. The scenes are flanked by two sleeping cupids. For a description, *ASR* I 4, cat. 45.
Short ends: Without relief decoration.
Portrait: The bust in front of the *parapetasma* has portrait features. The seated woman on the right may have portrait features as well.
Dating: Last third of the third century (*ASR* I 4, cat. 45).

Bibliography: Amedick, *ASR* I 4 (1991) cat. 45, pl. 104, 2.

428 BUST OF A MAN, FIGURES ON A NARRATIVE SCENE

Location/Inv.: Rome, Catacombe di Pretestato, Museo.
Size (coffin): L: 1.78 H: 0.38
Condition: Fragments of a lid are preserved.
Lid: There is a central inscription panel, to the right of which is a male bust in front of a *parapetasma*; on the left side a scene with a *lupercus* is depicted.
Portrait: The male bust has a blank portrait. The woman, who is being punished, is represented with a female portrait hairstyle. The flogging man on the same scene has a blank portrait as well.
Inscription: ELIA AFANA / CIA POS(u)I(t) SA(r)/COFACVM / NE SVIS DO/M(esticis) ELPIDIO/NIDO RVF(o) (H. Fuhrmann in Gütschow 1938, 206).
Dating: 265-289 (Gütschow 1938, 187).

Bibliography: Gütschow 1938, 181, 207; Andreae 1984, fig. 2.

429 *CLIPEUS* PORTRAIT OF A MAN

Location/Inv.: Rome, Musei Vaticani, Museo Gregoriano Profano, inv. 3262.
Size (coffin): L: 0.45 H: 0.45
Condition: The central part of a frontal relief is preserved.
Frontal relief: Clipeus with a bust. A scene from a workshop with two men making table legs is depicted beneath the *clipeus*. For a description, see *ASR* I 4, cat. 283.
Portrait: The bust is carved with a portrait of a man.
Dating: Last quarter of the fourth century (*ASR* I 4, cat. 283).

Bibliography: Amedick, *ASR* I 4 (1991) cat. 283, pl. 112, 2.

Clipeus Busts of a Couple

Bucolic

430 *CLIPEUS* PORTRAITS REPRESENTING A COUPLE (FIG. 2)

Location/Inv.: Cefalù, Chiesa di S. Francesco.
Size (coffin): L: 2.18 H. 0.55 D: 0.40
Condition: The coffin is preserved.
Frontal relief: Divided into five panels. The second and fourth panels are strigillated. A ram-bearer is represented on the first panel and another herdsman is represented on the fifth panel. The central panel depicts a *clipeus* with busts of a couple. A bucolic scene is depicted beneath the *clipeus*. For a description, see *ASR* V 2, 2, cat. 21.
Portrait: The two busts are carved with female and male portrait features (post antique reworking?).
Dating: Last third of the third century (*ASR* V 2, 2, cat. 21).

Bibliography: Bielefeld, *ASR* V 2, 2 (1997) cat. 21, pl. 85, 4; Tusa 1995, 27-8.

431 *CLIPEUS* PORTRAITS REPRESENTING A COUPLE

Location/Inv.: Covarrubias, Burgos, Spain. Church.
Size (coffin): L: 2.04 H: 0.54 D: 0.63
Condition: The coffin is preserved.
Frontal relief: Divided into five panels. The second and fourth panels are strigillated. A herdsman is represented on the first and fifth panels. The central panel depicts a *clipeus* with busts of a couple. The woman wears a necklace and the man holds a scroll. A personification of the sky is depicted beneath the *clipeus*.
Portrait: The two busts are carved with female and male portrait features.
Dating: First part of the fourth century (Trillmich et al 1996, 418).
Comment: The lid is from the 10th century.

Bibliography: Trillmich et al. 1996, 418, pl. 222a.

432 *CLIPEUS* PORTRAITS REPRESENTING A COUPLE (FIG. 76)

Location/Inv.: Rome, Catacombe di S. Sebastiano.
Size (coffin): L: 2.07 H: 0.72 D: 0.96
Condition: The coffin is preserved.
Frontal relief: Divided into five panels. The second and fourth panels are strigillated. A ram-bearer is represented on the first and fifth panels. The central panel depicts a *clipeus* with busts of a couple. The woman wears a necklace. A scene with a shepherd and his sheep is depicted beneath the *clipeus*.
Portrait: The two busts are carved with female and male portrait features.
Dating: Second third of the fourth century (*Rep.* I, cat. 239).

Bibliography: *Rep.* I, cat. 239.

433 *CLIPEUS* PORTRAITS REPRESENTING A COUPLE

Location/Inv.: Rome, Musei Vaticani, Museo Pio Cristiano.
Size (coffin): L: 1.97 H. 0.64 D: 0.72
Condition: The coffin and lid are preserved.
Provenience: Rome, Catacombe di Pretestato.
Frontal relief: Divided into five panels. The second and fourth panels are strigillated. A ram-bearer is represented on the first and fifth panels. The central panel depicts a *clipeus* with busts of a couple. The man holds a scroll, and the woman wears a necklace. A scene with a shepherd and his sheep is depicted beneath the *clipeus*.
Lid: Dolphins and an inscription. Lower part carved with a pick.
Portrait: The busts are carved with blank portraits.
Inscription: FAVSTINVS III IDVS AVG(osto) CONST/ANTIO AVG(usto) G CIC.NSTANTIO II CON/SS IN PACE
Dating: 353, based on the inscription (*Rep.* I, cat. 87).

Bibliography: *Rep.* I, cat. 87; Gütschow 1938, 238; Liverani, & Spinola 2010, 35.

434 *CLIPEUS* PORTRAITS REPRESENTING A COUPLE

Location/Inv.: Rome, Museo Nazionle Romano, inv. 59672.
Size (coffin): L: 2.15; (lid): L: 2.15 H: 0.35 D: 0.94
Condition: The coffin and lid are preserved.
Provenience: Via Tiburtina (1912).
Frontal relief: Divided into five panels. The second and fourth panels are strigillated. Columns are present on the first and fifth panels. The central panel shows a *clipeus* with busts of a couple. The man holds a scroll. A scene with a shepherd and his sheep is depicted beneath the *clipeus*.
Lid: Divided into three panels. A scene with two fishermen in a boat and Jonah and the sea- monster is represented on the first panel. An inscription is depicted on the central panel, and a *Sigma-Mahl* is represented on the third panel.
Portrait: The busts on the frontal relief are carved with blank portraits.
Inscription: CAENABI CONS[T]AN[T]I/ MARC(iae) IUL (iae) BAEBIAE HERMO/FILE H(onestae) M(emorie) F(eminae) VNICE CASTI/TATIS ORORI ET COMITI/ SVPER FINEM AMORIS/ DILIGENS MARITVM/ CONIVG(I) BENIGNISS(imae) ET IN/COPARAB(ili) MATRONE VALERI/VS VALENTINIANVS B(ene) F(iciarius) PREF(ecti) P(raetorio)/ CVM COHEREDIBVS SVIS (*CIL* VI nr. 37231)
Dating: End of the third century (*ASR* I 4, cat. 186).
Comment: Found without the lid.

Bibliography: Amedick, *ASR* I 4 (1991) cat. 186, pl. 28, 2; *Rep* I, cat. 778; Dresken-Weiland 2003, 304, cat. A 27.

435 *CLIPEUS* PORTRAITS REPRESENTING A COUPLE

Location/Inv.: Rome, Plazzo Franese.
Size (coffin): L. 2.22 H. 1.02 D: 0.97
Condition: The coffin is preserved.
Frontal relief: Divided into five panels. The second and fourth panels are strigillated with vertical lines. A sleeping cupid is represented on the first and fifth panels. The central panel depicts a *clipeus* with busts of a couple. The man holds a scroll. A scene with a shepherd/ram-bearer and his sheep is depicted beneath the *clipeus*.
Short end reliefs: Shield and spear.
Portrait: The busts are carved with blank portraits.
Dating: Last third of the third century (*Rep.* I, cat. 962).

Bibliography: *Rep.* I, cat. 962.

Cupids

436 *CLIPEUS* PORTRAITS REPRESENTING A COUPLE

Location/Inv.: Rome, Musei Vaticani, Museo Gregoriano Profano, inv. 10465.
Size (coffin): L: 2.32 H: 0.86 D: 0.18; (lid): L: 2.36 H: 0.23
Condition: The coffin and lid are preserved but both are heavily restored. The lid may not belong to the coffin.
Frontal relief: Two flying *victoriae* hold a *clipeus* with busts of a couple. A sleeping cupid leaning on a torch is represented on either end of the relief. Fruit baskets are depicted beneath the *clipeus*.
Lid: A central inscription tablet is flanked by scenes with the *Horae*, cupids, and fruit baskets.
Portrait: The busts are carved with female and male portrait features.
Inscription: D M / GLADIAE PRIMITIVAE CONIVGI SANTISSIMAE CVM / QVA VIXI ANNIS XXXIII SINE / VLLA QVAERELLA M MANLIVS EGLECTVS / FECIT ET SIBI
Dating: Middle to late Antonine period (*ASR* V 4, cat. 406).

Bibliography: Kranz, *ASR* V 4 (1984) cat. 406, pl. 101, 5.

437 *CLIPEUS* PORTRAITS REPRESENTING A COUPLE

Location/Inv.: Rome, Palazzo Farnese, placed in the courtyard.
Condition: The coffin is preserved.
Frontal relief: Divided into five panels. The second and fourth are strigillated with vertical lines, and on the first and fifth a sleeping cupid is shown. The central panel depicts a *clipeus* with two busts (a female and a male), and underneath there is a bucolic scene.
Short ends: Without relief decoration.
Portrait: The busts are carved with blank portraits.
Dating: Late third century.

Bibliography: Buranelli 2010, figure on p. 12.

Cupids Harvesting

438 *CLIPEUS* PORTRAITS REPRESENTING A COUPLE

Location/Inv: Rome, Palazzo Farnese.
Condition: The coffin is preserved.
Frontal relief: Strigillated. A central *clipeus* shows busts of a couple; the man holds a scroll. There is a scene showing cupids pressing grapes beneath the *clipeus* and a pilaster is depicted on either end of the relief. For a description, see *ASR* V 2, 2, cat. 151.
Short ends: Roughly carved.
Portrait: Both the female and the male busts probably had portrait features. The face of the woman is damaged.
Dating: Second half of the third century (*ASR* V 2, 2, cat. 151).

Bibliography: Bielefeld, *ASR* V 2, 2 (1997) cat. 151, pl. 85, 1.

439 *CLIPEUS* PORTRAITS REPRESENTING A COUPLE

Location/Inv.: Rome, Via dei Portoghesi 18, in the courtyard.
Size (coffin): L: 2.28 H: 0.68 D. 0.75
Condition: The coffin is preserved.
Frontal relief: Strigillated with a *clipeus* with busts of a couple; the man holds a scroll. There is a scene showing cupids pressing grapes beneath the *clipeus* and a pilaster is depicted on either end of the relief. For a description, see *ASR* V 2, 2, cat. 176.
Portrait: Both the female and the male busts probably had portrait features. Today the faces are damaged.
Dating: Around the middle of the third century (*ASR* V 2, 2, cat. 176).

Bibliography: Bielefeld, *ASR* V 2, 2 (1997) cat. 176, pl. 85, 2.

Decorative Scheme

440 *CLIPEUS* PORTRAITS REPRESENTING A COUPLE

Location/Inv.: Rome, Museo Nazionale Romano, inv. 77264.
Size (coffin): L: 1.24 H. 0.20 D: 0.13
Condition: Fragment of a frontal relief.
Frontal relief: Strigillated in two levels. A central *clipeus* shows busts of a couple; the man holds a scroll.
Portrait: Both the female and the male busts are carved with portrait features, but they are heavily worn.
Dating: Middle of the fourth century (*MNR* I 3, cat. IV, 10).

Bibliography: *MNR* I 3, cat. IV, 10.

441 *CLIPEUS* PORTRAITS REPRESENTING A COUPLE

Location/Inv.: Rome, Museo Nazionale Romano, inv. 124709.
Size (coffin): L: 2.19 H. 0.82 D: 0.80
Condition: The coffin is preserved.
Frontal relief: Strigillated with a central *clipeus* with two busts; the man holds a scroll. Two masks are depicted beneath the *clipeus* and a pilaster appears on either end of the relief. For a description, see *MNR* I 8, 1, cat. VI, 20.
Portrait: Both the female and the male busts are carved with blank portraits.
Dating: Middle of the third century (*MNR* I 8, 1, cat. VI, 20).

Bibliography: *MNR* I 8, 1, cat. VI, 20.

442 *CLIPEUS* PORTRAITS REPRESENTING A COUPLE

Location/Inv.: Rome, Museo Nazionale Romano, inv. 2001498.
Size (coffin): L: 1.99 H: 0.65 D: 0.84
Condition: The coffin is preserved.
Frontal relief: Strigillated with a central *clipeus* with two busts. The man may hold a scroll, but the relief is roughly carved here and it is difficult to tell. Two cupids are depicted beneath the *clipeus*. The relief was never fully finished.
Short ends: Roughly carved.
Reverse: Roughly carved.
Portrait: Both the female and the male busts are carved with blank portraits.
Dating: 330-340 (*MNR* I 8, 2, cat. VII, 13).

Bibliography: *MNR* I 8, 2, cat. VII, 13,

443 *CLIPEUS* PORTRAITS REPRESENTING A COUPLE

Location/Inv.: Rome. Santi Quatro Coronati, court.
Condition: Fragment of a frontal relief.
Frontal relief: Strigillated relief with a *clipeus* with two busts. The hands of the man are not preserved; the woman has her arms around him.
Portrait: Both the female and the male busts are carved with blank portraits.
Dating: Third century.

444 *CLIPEUS* PORTRAITS REPRESENTING A COUPLE

Location/Inv.: Rome, Vatican Cemetery, the necropolis beneath S. Pietro, Mausoleum H (Valerii).
Condition: The coffin and a lid without decoration are preserved.
Provenience: Rome, Tomb of the Valerii, (Mausoleum H).
Frontal relief: Strigillated with a central *clipeus* enclosing busts of a couple. The busts are supported by acanthus leaves. A pilaster appears on either end of the frontal relief.
Portrait: Both the female and the male busts are carved with blank portraits.
Dating: Tetrachic.

Bibliography: Wolf 1977, no. 54; Mielsch & Hesberg 1995, 156, figs. 160-61; Dresken-Weiland 2003, cat. A 110.

445 *CLIPEUS* PORTRAITS REPRESENTING A COUPLE (FIG. 15)

Location/Inv.: Rome, Via Latina, Tomb of the Pancrati.
Condition: The coffin and lid are preserved.
Provenience: Rome, Via Latina, Tomb of the Pancrati.
Frontal relief: Strigillated with a *clipeus* enclosing busts of a couple. The man holds a scroll while the woman exposes one shoulder, placing one hand on the chest of the man and the other on his shoulder. A panel with an inscription appears beneath the *clipeus*. A pilaster is depicted on either end of the relief.
Lid: Bucolic scenes.
Portrait: Both the female and the male busts are carved with blank portraits.
Inscription: C SERVIENIVS DEMETRIVS / MAR F VIVAE SEVERAE / VXORI SANTISSIMAE ET / MIHI Q BIXIT MECVM AN/NIS XXII MENS VIIII DIES V INQVIBVS SEM-

PER MIHI / BENE FVIT CVMILLA / PANCRATI HIC (*CIL* VI 2, no. 10281)
Dating: Around 270 (Herdjürgen 2000, 224).
Comment: The sarcophagus is built into the wall.

Bibliography: Herdjürgen 2000, 224.

446 *CLIPEUS* PORTRAITS OF A WOMAN AND A LEARNED WOMAN (FIG. 89)

Location/Inv.: Rome, Via Veneto 56, Palazzo Balestra, courtyard.
Frontal relief: Vertically strigillated with a *clipeus* with two female busts. The woman to the right holds a scroll. Two *cornucopiae* are depicted beneath the *clipeus*.
Portrait: Both busts are carved with a female portrait.
Dating: 250-275.
Comment: I am grateful to Björn Christian Ewald for bringing this sarcophagus to my attention.

Learned Sphere

447 *CLIPEUS* PORTRAITS REPRESENTING A COUPLE, AN *ORANS*, AND A PHILOSOPHER

Location/Inv.: Basel, Antikenmuseum Basel und Sammlung Ludwig, inv. 256.
Size (coffin): L: 2.32 H: 1.07 D: 1.03
Condition: Several fragments of a coffin.
Provenience: Probably from the vicinity of Rome.
Frontal relief: A *clipeus* with busts of a couple is shown, to the left of which are a fisherman and an *Orans*; on the right are a herdsman with a ram on his shoulder and a seated philosopher. A bucolic scene is depicted beneath the *clipeus*. For a description, see Ewald 1999, cat. A 11.
Left short end: Herdsman and sheep.
Right short end: Two philosophers: one with a scroll and one gesticulating, which probably illustrates that he is teaching.
Portrait: The man in the *clipeus* has portrait features but the surface is weathered. The head of the woman is lost. The *Orans* and the seated philosopher might have had portrait features as well.
Dating: Middle of the third century (Ewald 1999, cat A 11).

Bibliography: Zanker 1995, 267; Ewald 1999, cat. A 11, pl. 8, 1.

448 *CLIPEUS* PORTRAITS REPRESENTING A COUPLE

Location/Inv.: Berlin, Staatliche Museum, inv. 2785
Size (coffin): L: 2.15 H: 0.94
Condition: The frontal relief and the lid are preserved.
Frontal relief: Divided into five panels. The second and fourth panels are strigillated. A woman dressed in a *palla* is represented on the first panel and a bare-chested philosopher is represented on the fifth panel. A *parapetasma* is suspended behind both figures. The central panel depicts a *clipeus* with busts of a couple. Two peacocks are shown beneath the *clipeus*. For a description, see Ewald 1999, cat. F 30.
Lid: An empty inscription panel and sea-*thiasoi*.
Portrait: Both the female and the male busts are carved with blank portraits.
Dating: Tetrarchic (Ewald 1999, cat. F 30).

Bibliography: Ewald 1999, cat. F 30, pl. 80, 2.

449 *CLIPEUS* PORTRAITS REPRESENTING A COUPLE

Location/Inv.: Pisa, Camposanto, C 19 est.
Size (coffin): L: 2.15 H: 0.75 D: 0.76
Condition: The coffin is preserved. The lid placed on the coffin today does not belong to the sarcophagus.
Frontal relief: Divided into five panels. The second and fourth panels are strigillated. A veiled woman with a scroll is represented on the first panel and a bare-chested philosopher is represented on the fifth panel. The central panel depicts a *clipeus* with busts of a couple; the man is holding a scroll. A bucolic scene appears beneath the *clipeus*. For a description, see Ewald 1999, cat. F 29.
Short ends: Griffin.
Portrait: Both the female and the male busts are carved with portrait features, but the heads are much damaged.
Dating: Late third century (Ewald 1999, cat. F 29).

Bibliography: Arias et al. 1977, 148-49, pl. 89; Ewald 1999, cat. F 29.

450 *CLIPEUS* PORTRAITS REPRESENTING A COUPLE

Location/Inv.: Rome, Musei Capitolini, Palazzo dei Conservatori, Inv. 813.
Size (coffin): L: 2.17 H: 0.65 D. 0.72
Condition: The coffin is preserved.
Provenience: Found 1891 in Rome, between Porta Salaria and Porta Pinciana.
Frontal relief: Divided into five panels. The second and fourth panels are strigillated. A woman dressed in a *palla* is represented on the first panel, and a bare-chested philosopher is represented on the fifth panel. The third panel depicts a *clipeus* with two busts. A bucolic scene appears beneath the *clipeus*. For a description, see Ewald 1999, cat. F 28.
Short ends: Griffin.
Portrait: Both the female and the male busts are carved with blank portraits.
Dating: From 250 to the end of the third century. For discussion, see Ewald 1999, cat. F 28.

Bibliography: Gerke 1940, 346 III B no. 3, Ewald 1999, cat. F 28, pl. 80, 1.

451 *CLIPEUS* PORTRAITS REPRESENTING A COUPLE

Location/Inv.: Rome, Palazzo Koch.

Size (coffin): L 2.06 H: 0.56 D: 0.57
Condition: The coffin is preserved.
Frontal relief: A *clipeus* with two busts. The woman places her right hand on the chest of the man. A ram-bearer appears on either side of the *clipeus*, and two peacocks are depicted beneath it. A veiled woman (*Orans*) is represented on the left end of the relief and there is a philosopher in front of a *parapetasma* on the right end. For a description, see Ewald 1999, cat. G 20.
Portrait: Both the female and the male busts are carved with portrait features.
Dating: First half of the fourth century (Ewald 1999, cat. G 20).
Comment: Included in the statistics on learned figures.

Bibliography: Ewald 1999, cat. G 20, pl. 93, 3.

452 *CLIPEUS* PORTRAITS REPRESENTING A COUPLE

Location/Inv.: Rome, Palazzo Nuono della Propaganda, now lost (?).
Condition: The coffin is preserved.
Frontal relief: Divided into five panels. The second and fourth panels are strigillated. A philosopher with a tunic and *pallium* is represented on the first panel and a Muse with feathers in her hair is represented on the fifth panel. A *parapetasma* is suspended behind both figures. The central panel depicts a *clipeus* with two busts. The woman has placed her right arm on the chest of the man, who is holding a scroll. A bucolic scene appears beneath the *clipeus*. For a description, see Ewald 1999, cat. F 31.
Portrait: Both the female and the male busts are carved with blank portraits.
Dating: Last third of the third century (Ewald 1999, cat. F 31).
Comment: Ewald mentions that the sarcophagus could not be located in 1997.

Bibliography: Bielefeld, *ASR* V 2, 2 (1997) cat. 197; Koch & Sichtermann 1982, 202; Ewald 1999, cat. F 31, pl. 80, 3.

453 *CLIPEUS* PORTRAITS REPRESENTING A COUPLE

Location/Inv.: Rome, Vatican, The necropolis beneath S. Pietro.
Size (coffin): L: 2.10 H: 0.87
Condition: The coffin is preserved.
Provenience: Rome, the Vatican Necropolis beneath S. Pietro, Mausoleum R.
Frontal relief: Divided into five panels. The second and fourth panels are strigillated. A learned man is represented on the first and fifth panels. The central panel depicts a *clipeus* with two busts. A bucolic scene appears beneath the *clipeus*.
Shorte ends: Roughly carved.
Portrait: Both the female and the male busts are carved with blank portraits.
Dating: Late third century (?).
Comment: Never finished which in this case may explain the blank portraits.

Bibliography: Apolllonj-Ghetti et al. 1951, 81, pl. XXVIIb (XXVIII); Liverani & Spinola 2010, 137-39.

454 *CLIPEUS* PORTRAITS REPRESENTING A COUPLE, A WOMAN IN *PALLA,* AND A LEARNED MAN (FIG. 66)

Location/Inv.: Rome, Villa Medici, inv. 87.
Size (Coffin): L: 2.10 H. 1.01 D: 1.02
Condition: The coffin is preserved but the relief is weathered.
Frontal relief: Divided into five panels. The second and fourth panels are strigillated. On the first panel is a female figure with a scroll in front of a *parapetasma*, and a man with a scroll is represented on the fifth panel. The central panel depicts a *clipeus* with busts of a couple. A scene from a bakery appears beneath the *clipeus*. For a description, see *ASR* I 4, cat. 240.
Portrait: Both the female and the male busts are carved with blank portraits.
Dating: Severan (*ASR* I 4, cat. 240).

Bibliography: Amedick, *ASR* I 4 (1984) cat. 240; Ewald 1999, cat. F 32, pl. 82, 1.

Lion

455 *CLIPEUS* PORTRAITS REPRESENTING A COUPLE

Location/Inv.: Rome, Musei Vaticani, Cortile della Pigna, inv. 5155.
Size (coffin): L: 2.15 H: 0.94 D. 0.91
Condition: The coffin is preserved.
Frontal relief: Strigillated with a central *clipeus* with two busts. The man wears a toga. The *clipeus* is supported by a pedestal with a Corinthian capital. A lion head with a ring in its mouth is depicted on either end of the relief. For a description, see *ASR* VI, 1, cat. 149.
Short ends: Weapons.
Reverse: Roughly carved.
Portrait: Both the female and the male busts are carved with portrait features.
Dating: 250-260 (*ASR* VI 1, cat. 149).

Bibliography: Stroszeck *ASR* VI 1 (1998) cat. 149, pl. 14, 2.

456 *CLIPEUS* PORTRAITS OF A GIRL AND A MAN

Location/Inv.: Rome, Palazzo Corsetti-Podocatari. Current location unknown.
Size (coffin): L: 1.79 H: 0.57 D: 0.57
Condition: The upper part of the relief is preserved.
Frontal relief: Strigillated with a central *clipeus* with two busts, one male and one female. The man wears a toga. A lion head with a ring in its mouth is depicted on each end of the relief. For a description, see *ASR* VI 1, cat. 97.

Portrait: The female bust is carved with the portrait of a girl and the male bust with the portrait of a man.
Dating: 250-260 (*ASR* VI 1, cat. 97).

Bibliography: Stroszeck, *ASR* VI 1 (1998) cat. 97, pl. 14, 3.

457 *CLIPEUS* PORTRAITS REPRESENTING A COUPLE

Location/Inv.: Rome, Palazzo di Spagna.
Size (coffin): L: 1.98 H. 0.71 D: 0.84
Condition: The coffin is preserved.
Frontal relief: Strigillated with a central *clipeus* with two busts. Two *corncopiae* are depicted beneath the *clipeus*. A lion killing a boar is represented on either end of the relief. For a description, see *ASR* VI 1, cat. 322.
Short ends: Lenos-shaped. The lion-boar group of the frontal relief continues on the short ends.
Portrait: Both the female and the male busts are carved with blank portraits.
Dating: 280-300 (*ASR* VI 1, cat. 322).

Bibliography: Stroszeck, *ASR* VI 1 (1998) cat. 322, pl. 65, 2.

458 *CLIPEUS* PORTRAITS REPRESENTING A COUPLE AND A BOY

Location/Inv.: Rome, now lost.
Size (coffin): L: 2.15 H: 0.70 D. 0.75
Condition: The coffin was preserved.
Frontal relief: Strigillated with a *clipeus* with busts of a couple and a child. Two theatre masks are depicted beneath the *clipeus*. A lion and a *krater* are represented on either end of the relief.
Short ends: Lenos-shaped.
Portrait: All the busts are carved with portrait features. They are either late antique or much re-worked portraits (*ASR* VI 1, cat. 199).
Dating: 270-280 (*ASR* VI 1, cat. 199).

Bibliography: Stroszeck, *ASR* VI 1 (1998) cat. 199, pl. 126, 2.

459 SHELL WITH BUSTS OF A WOMAN AND A MAN

Location/Inv.: San Simeon, Hearst Castle, California.
Size (coffin): L: 2.29 H: 1.03 D: 0.94
Frontal relief: A central shell with a bust of a woman and a man is held by two flying cupids. The shell is supported by an inscription panel. A lion killing a deer is represented on either end of the relief. For a description, see *ASR* VI 1, cat. 419.
Short ends: Lenos-shaped. The lion-deer group of the frontal relief continues on the short ends.
Portrait: Both the female and the male busts are carved with portrait features.
Comment: May be modern (notes from the Hearst Castle archives).

Bibliography: Stroszeck, *ASR* VI 1 (1998) cat. 419.

460 *CLIPEUS* PORTRAITS REPRESENTING A COUPLE

Location/Inv.: Wilton House, Salisbury (Wiltshire).
Size (coffin): L: 2.05 H: 0.75
Condition: The coffin is preserved.
Provenience: Rome, Via Appia in a columbarium (in an *arcoso lium*) originally belonging to a freed person by Livia (Dresken-Weiland 2003, cat. A 65). (Found together with Meleager and Atalante, Wilton House, here cat. no. 604).
Frontal relief: Strigillated with a central *clipeus* with two busts. The man is holding a scroll. Two theatre masks are depicted beneath the *clipeus*. A lion killing a deer or a boar is represented on either end of the relief. For a description, see *ASR* VI 1, cat. 408.
Short ends: Lenos-shaped. The lion-boar group of the frontal relief continues on the short ends.
Portrait: Both the female and the male busts are carved with portrait features.
Dating: 250-260 (*ASR* VI 1, cat. 408).

Bibliography: Stroszeck, *ASR* VI 1 (1998) cat. 408, pl. 65, 1.

Myths and Dionysian Processions

461 *CLIPEUS* PORTRAITS OF A YOUNG WOMAN AND A BOY (FIG. 52)

Location/Inv.: Paris, Musèe du Louvre, inv. F 243.
Condition: The frontal relief is preserved.
Frontal relief: Dionysian procession. A *clipeus* with busts of a woman and a child is held by two centaurs.
Portrait: The busts are carved with the portraits of a young woman and a boy.
Dating: 230-240 (*ASR* IV 4, cat. 268).

Bibliography: Matz, *ASR* IV 4 (1975) cat. 268; Baratte & Metzger 1985, cat. 71; Zanker & Ewald 2004, 187.

462 *CLIPEUS* PORTRAITS REPRESENTING A COUPLE

Location/Inv.: Salerno, Cathedral S. Matteo.
Size (coffin): L: 2.20 H: 1.00 D. 0.98
Condition: The coffin is preserved.
Frontal relief: Dionysian procession. A central *clipeus* with busts of a couple is held by two centaurs. Dionysius standing in his wagon is represented on either end of the relief.
Short ends: Pilaster, garland, and disc.
Portrait: The busts are carved with male and female portraits.
Dating: Early to late Severan period (*ASR* IV 4, cat. 273).

Bibliography: Matz, *ASR* IV 4 (1975) cat. 273, pl. 291, 2.

Sea-Monsters and Nymphs

463 SHELL WITH BUSTS OF A WOMAN AND A MAN

Location/Inv.: Rome, Palazzo Altieri.
Condition: The frontal relief is preserved.
Frontal relief: A shell with busts of a woman and a man is framed by sea-monsters and nymphs. The man wears a toga. A cupid in a boat is depicted beneath the shell.
Portrait: The female and male busts are carved with blank portraits.
Dating: Third quarter of the third century (*ASR* V 1, cat. 81).

Bibliography: Rumpf, *ASR* V 1 (1939) cat. 81, pl. 24, 3.

464 SHELL WITH BUSTS OF A WOMAN AND A LEARNED MAN

Location/Inv.: Rome, S. Agnese fuori le mura.
Size (coffin): L: 1.10 H. 0.66 D: 0.66
Condition: Fragment of the frontal relief.
Frontal relief: A shell encloses two busts: one of a woman with an exposed shoulder and one of a man with a scroll. The shell is framed by sea-monsters and nymphs.
Portrait: The female and male busts are carved with blank portraits.
Dating: Third quarter of the third century (*ASR* V 1, cat. 82).

Bibliography: Rumpf, *ASR* V 1 (1939) cat. 82, pl. 27, 1.

465 *CLIPEUS* PORTRAITS REPRESENTING A COUPLE

Location/Inv.: Salerno, Cathedral S. Matteo.
Size (coffin): L: 2.04 H: 0.38 D: 0.49
Condition: The coffin and lid are preserved.
Frontal relief: A *clipeus* with two busts is surrounded by sea-centaurs and nymphs. A sleeping cupid is represented on either end of the relief. The figures are carved in very low relief.
Short ends: Unknown.
Portrait: The *clipeus* busts are carved with respectively a female and a male portrait.
Inscription: Inscription from the $15^{th}/16^{th}$ century is placed on the lower profile.
Dating: Late third or early fourth century.

Bibliography: Rumpf, *ASR* V 1 (1939) cat. 58, pl. 20, 4.

Seasonal

466 *CLIPEUS* PORTRAITS REPRESENTING A COUPLE

Location/Inv.: Agrigento, Museo Civico.
Condition: A fragment of the frontal relief is preserved.
Frontal relief: Divided into five panels. The second and fourth panels are strigillated. A seasonal personification (now lost) was represented on the first and fifth panels. The central panel depicts a *clipeus* with two busts; the man holds a scroll. Two masks appear beneath the *clipeus*. For a description, see *ASR* V 4, cat. 152.
Portrait: The busts are carved with female and male portraits.
Dating: Late Gallenic period or just after (*ASR* V 4, cat. 156).

Bibliography: Kranz, *ASR* V 4 (1984) cat. 156, pl. 71, 3; Tusa 1957, cat. 5.

467 *CLIPEUS* PORTRAITS REPRESENTING A COUPLE

Location/Inv.: Cologne-Weiden, Aachener Str. 328.
Size (coffin): L: 2.09 H: 0.84 D. 0.87
Condition: The coffin is preserved but fragmented.
Provenience: Roman tomb in Weiden (still *in situ*).
Frontal relief: A *clipeus* with two busts is held by two *victoriae*. Seasonal personifications with baskets are represented on either end of the relief. Cupids pressing grapes are seen beneath the *clipeus*. For a description, see *ASR* V 4, cat. 74.
Left short end: Genius with apples.
Right short end: Genius with flowers.
Portrait: The bust of the man is lost but the head of the female bust is carved as a blank portrait.
Dating: Not later than the beginning of the fourth century (*ASR* V 4, cat. 74).

Bibliography: Kranz, *ASR* V 4 (1984) cat. 74, pl. 44, 3.

468 *CLIPEUS* PORTRAITS REPRESENTING A COUPLE

Location/Inv.: Georgetown, Dumbarton Oaks College of Harvard University, inv. 36.65.
Size (coffin): L: 2: 24 H: 1.09 D: 1.16
Condition: The coffin is preserved.
Provenience: Rome, Palazzo Barberini, until 1693.
Frontal relief: A *clipeus* with two busts. The man holds a scroll. Two seasonal personifications are represented on either side of the *clipeus*. A bucolic scene is depicted between them. Cupids harvesting grapes are seen beneath the *clipeus*. The profile frame of the *clipeus* is adorned with symbols of the zodiac. For a description, see *ASR* V 4, cat. 34.
Short ends: Without relief decoration.
Portrait: The male and female busts are carved with blank portraits.
Dating: Later part of the Constantinian period. For discussion, see *ASR* V 4, cat. 34, note 263.

Bibliography: Kranz, *ASR* V 4 (1984) cat. 34, pl. 39, 3; Bielefeld, *ASR* V 2, 2 (1997) cat. 226; Zanker & Ewald 2004, 257.

469 *CLIPEUS* PORTRAITS REPRESENTING A COUPLE

Location/Inv.: Pisa, Camposanto, inv. 31.
Size (coffin): L: 2.15 H: 0.98 D: 0.29

Condition: The frontal relief is preserved. Parts of it have been restored, such as the second personification from the left.
Frontal relief: A *clipeus* with two busts. Two seasonal personifications with Tellus and Oceanus between them are represented on either side of the *clipeus*. Two peasants ploughing are depicted beneath the *clipeus*. The profile frame of the *clipeus* is adorned with the zodiac. For a description, see *ASR* V 4, cat. 44.
Portrait: The busts are carved with a female and a male portrait.
Dating: 220-230 (*ASR* V 4, cat. 44; *ASR* V 2, 2, cat. 78).

Bibliography: Kranz, *ASR* V 4 (1984) cat. 44, pl. 32, 2; Bielefeld, *ASR* V 2, 2 (1997) cat. 78; Hanfmann 1951, cat. 464.

470 *CLIPEUS* PORTRAITS REPRESENTING A COUPLE (FIG. 85)

Location/Inv.: Pisa, Camposanto, inv. 12.
Size (coffin): L: 2.16 H: 0.80 D: 0.84
Condition: The coffin is preserved.
Frontal relief: A *clipeus* with two busts. Two seasonal personifications are represented on either side of the *clipeus*, and theatre masks are depicted beneath. For a description, see *ASR* V 4, cat. 43.
Left short end: Sphinx.
Right short end: Sphinx. Part of the relief is not finished.
Portrait: The female bust is carved with a male portrait, and the male bust is carved with a female portrait. The surface of both portraits is badly damaged. The hairstyles are fairly well preserved.
Dating: Around 200 (*ASR* V 4, 41). Previously dated half a century later. For discussion, see *ASR* V 4, cat. 43.

Bibliography: Kranz, *ASR* V 4 (1984) cat. 43, pl. 24, 4.

471 *CLIPEUS* PORTRAITS REPRESENTING A COUPLE

Location/Inv.: Pisa, Camposanto, inv. 44 (old inv. 36).
Size (coffin): L: 2.20 H: 0.92 D. 1.04
Condition: The coffin is preserved.
Frontal relief: Divided into five panels. The second and fourth panels are strigillated. A seasonal personification is represented on the first and fifth panels. The central panel depicts a *clipeus* with busts of a couple; the man holds a scroll. Two *cornucopiae* are depicted beneath the *clipeus*. For a description, see *ASR* V 4, cat. 156.
Portrait: The busts are carved with the portraits of an elderly man and a woman. The heads of the busts are badly weathered.
Inscription: Post-antique.
Dating: Late Gallienic period or just after (*ASR* V 4, cat. 156).

Bibliography: Kranz, *ASR* V 4 (1984) cat. 156, pl. 71, 1; Arias et al. 1977, cat. A 14 est.

472 *CLIPEUS* PORTRAITS REPRESENTING A COUPLE

Location/Inv.: Rome, Museo Nazionale Romano, inv. 80666.
Size (coffin): L: 1.98 H. 0.75 D. 0.70
Condition: The coffin is preserved.
Frontal relief: A *clipeus* with two busts is held by two *victoriae*. A cupid with garlands is represented on either side of this composition. A bearded and bare-chested man is depicted beneath the *clipeus*. For a description, see *MNR* I 8, cat. VII, 6.
Portrait: The busts are carved with female and male portrait features respectively. Both portraits are badly weathered.
Dating: 230-240 (*MNR* I 8, 2, cat. VII, 6).

Bibliography: *MNR* I 8, 2, cat. VII, 6, p. 338.

473 *CLIPEUS* PORTRAITS REPRESENTING A COUPLE

Location/Inv.: Rome, Palazzo Giustiniani (Palazzo Madama).
Condition: Fragments of the frontal relief. Heavily restored. Parts of the relief are today in Boston, see *ASR* V 4, cat. 50.
Frontal relief: A *clipeus* with two busts is held by two seasonal personifications. Another four seasonal personifications are grouped around the *clipeus*. A man ploughing with two oxen is depicted beneath the *clipeus*.
Portrait: The two busts have been restored and both portraits have been re-worked in modern times.
Dating: 270-280 (*ASR* V 2, 2 cat. 152).

Bibliography: Kranz, *ASR* V 4 (1984) cat. 50, pl. 34, 1; Bielefeld, *ASR* V 2, 2 (1997) cat. 152; Hanfmann 1951, 477.

474 *CLIPEUS* PORTRAITS REPRESENTING A COUPLE

Location/Inv.: Rome, Palazzo Mattei (loggia).
Size (coffin): L: 2.30 H: 1.15
Condition: The frontal relief is preserved.
Frontal relief: A *clipeus* with two busts is held by two seasonal personifications. The man holds a scroll. More seasonal personifications are represented on either side of this composition. Cupids harvesting and pressing grapes are depicted beneath the *clipeus*. For a description, see *ASR* V 4, cat. 52.
Portrait: The busts are carved with a male and a female portrait. According to Kranz, the portraits are a late addition to the relief (*ASR* V 4, cat. 52).
Dating: The relief is dated to the early years of the 250s, and the portraits are dated between the late third and early fourth century (*ASR* V 4, cat. 52); 250-260 (*ASR* V 2, 2, cat. 155).

Bibliography: Kranz, *ASR* V 4 (1984) cat. 52, pl. 26, 1; *ASR* V 2, 2, cat. 155; Hanfmann 1951, cat. 528; Guerrini 1982, cat. 95.

475 *CLIPEUS* PORTRAITS REPRESENTING A COUPLE

Location/Inv.: Rome, Piazza del Popolo. Used as a fountain.
Condition: The coffin is preserved
Frontal relief: Strigillated sarcophagus divided into three panels. The first and the third are strigillated, and the second contains a *clipeus* with two busts. Lotus flowers are seen in the corners. The man holds a scroll and the woman has one naked shoulder. The *clipeus* is supported by *cornucopiae.*
Short ends: No decoration.
Reverse: Not visible.
Portrait: The busts are carved with a male and a female portrait.
Dating: Middle or second half of the third century, based on the portraits and the female hairstyle.

476 *CLIPEUS* PORTRAITS REPRESENTING A COUPLE

Location/Inv.: Rome, Villa Albani.
Size (coffin): L: 2.37 H: 0.83 D. 0.79
Condition: The coffin is preserved.
Frontal relief: A *clipeus* with two busts is held by two seasonal personifications. Another two seasonal personifications are represented on either side of this composition. Two figures pressing grapes are depicted beneath the *clipeus*. For a description, see *ASR* V 4, cat. 54.
Short ends: Griffin.
Portrait: The *clipeus* busts are carved with respectively a female and a male portrait.
Dating: 250s (*ASR* V 4, cat. 54, note 232).

Bibliography: Kranz, *ASR* V 4 (1984) cat. 54, pl. 32, 3. Bol 1998, 526-29, cat. 881 (Bielefeld, D.).

Hunters and Virtus

477 HUNTER
Location/Inv.: Avignon, Musée Calvet, Lapidaire.
Size (coffin): L: 1.03 H: 0.55
Condition: A fragment of the frontal relief is preserved.
Provenience: Arles.
Frontal relief: A central hunter and a huntsman. For a description, see *ASR* I 2, cat. 5.
Portrait: The central hunter is carved with a portrait.
Dating: 300 (*ASR* I 2, cat. 5).

Bibliography: Andreae, *ASR* I 2 (2980) cat. 5; Rodenwaldt 1921/22, 62;.

478 HUNTER
Location/Inv.: Avignon, Musée Calvet, Lapidaire.
Size (coffin): L: 0.56 H: 0.45
Condition: Fragment of the frontal relief.
Provenience: Orange.
Frontal relief: Hunting scene with a central hunter on horseback.
Portrait: The hunter on horseback has a blank portrait.
Dating: Around 300 (*ASR* I 2, cat. 6).

Bibliography: Andreae, *ASR* I 2 (1980) cat. 6 (with further references).

479 LION HUNTER, DIANA, AND COMMANDER (FIG. 57)
Location/Inv.: Barcelona, Museo Archeológico, inv. 870.
Size (coffin): L: 1.40 H: 0.76 D: 0.81
Condition: The coffin is preserved.
Frontal relief: The relief is divided into two scenes. A departure scene with Diana and the deceased are represented on the left end. The hunting scene with a central huntsman on horseback is represented on the right end.
Left short end: Two huntsmen with donkey and hunting trophy.
Right short end: A huntsman on horseback and a dog. Beside them is a column with an image of Diana.
Reverse: No decoration.
Portrait: Three portraits. The hunter and Diana on the left end of the relief and the central huntsman on the hunting scene are carved with portrait features. In all probability the two male portraits represent the same man.
Dating: Around 230 (*ASR* I 2, cat. 8, Andreae 1995, 29).

Bibliography: Andreae, *ASR* I 2 (1980) cat. 8, pl. 1, 2; Vaccaro Melucco 1963/64, cat. 21; Andreae 1977, 20; Fittschen 1984, note 47b; Andreae 1995, 29.

480 LION HUNTER AND COMMANDER
Location/Inv.: Basel, Sammlung Ludwig, inv. LU 267.
Size (coffin): L: 2.47 H: 1.27
Condition: Fragments of the frontal relief are preserved.
Frontal relief: Lion hunt with two scenes. A commander accompanied by Virtus is represented on the left and a lion hunt is shown on the right end of the relief. For a description, see Blome 1998.
Portrait: Both the commander and the lion hunter are carved with portrait features.
Dating: 260s (Blome 1998, 6).

Bibliography: Blome 1998, 6, pl. 1, 1.

481 HUNTER
Location/Inv.: Berlin, Schloss Glienicke, inv. GL 308.
Size (coffin): L: 0.25 H: 0.20
Condition: Fragment of the frontal relief.
Frontal relief: Head and shoulders of a huntsman.
Portrait: Blank portrait.
Dating: Around 270 (*ASR* I 2, cat. 18).

Bibliography: Andreae, *ASR* I 2 (1980) cat. 18, pl. 83, 1.

482 LION HUNTER (FIG. 20)
Location/Inv.: Copenhagen, Ny Carlsberg Glyptotek, IN 849.
Size (coffin): L: 2.10 H. 0.92 D: 1.06
Condition: The coffin is preserved. The relief is intact except for minor breakages.
Provenience: A tomb at Vigna Casali together with cat. nos. 155 and 577 (Koch 888, 36, nr. 13; Dresk-Weiland 2006, cat. A 58).
Frontal relief: Lion hunt scene with a central hunter on horseback accompanied by Virtus and more huntsmen. For a description see Østergaard 1998, 67-9.
Left short end: Lion griffin.

Right short end: Two griffins with candelabra.
Portrait: The central hunter is carved with a portrait.
Dating: 240 (*ASR* I 2, cat. 41).
Comment: Previously thought to be the sarcophagus of the emperor Balbinus because of the similarity of the man's portrait with that of Balbinus. It is described as being the only lion hunt sarcophagus with a detailed representation of the landscape.

Bibliography: Andreae, *ASR* I 2 (1980) cat. 41, pl. 22, 1; Vaccaro Melucco 1963/64, cat.3; Cohon 1992; Østergaard 1998.

483 HUNTER

Location/Inv.: Dresden, Skulpturensammlung, Staatliche Kunstsammlungen, inv. Hm 309.
Size (coffin): L: 2.33 H. 0.85 D: 0.95
Condition: The frontal relief is preserved.
Provenience: Rome.
Frontal relief: Lion hunt scene with a central hunter on horseback accompanied by Virtus and more huntsmen. For description see *ASR* I 2, cat. 28.
Portrait: The central hunter is carved with a portrait.
Dating: Middle of the third century (*ASR* I 2, cat. 28).
Comment: Entered the sculpture collection in 1790; purchased by Count Marcolini in Rome.

Bibliography: Andreae, *ASR* I 2 (1980) cat. 28.

484 LION HUNTER

Location/Inv.: Girona, S. Felix, Presbetyrium.
Size (coffin): L: 2.19 H: 0.61
Condition: The frontal relief is preserved.
Frontal relief: Lion hunt scene. A central huntsman attacks a lion and other hunters fight a lioness. For a description, see *ASR* I 2, cat. 32.
Portrait: The central hunter is carved with a portrait.
Dating. 315-320 (*ASR* I 2, cat. 32).

Bibliography: Andreae, *ASR* I 2 (1980) cat. 32, pl. 55, 2.

485 HUNTER

Location/Inv.: Grottaferrata, Abbazia, Museo.
Size (coffin): L: 0.47 H: 0.49
Condition: Fragment of a frontal relief.
Frontal relief: A hunter on horseback accompanied by Virtus.
Portrait: The hunter has a blank portrait.
Dating: Beginning of the fourth century (*ASR* I 2, cat. 33).

Bibliography: Andreae, *ASR* I 2 (1980) cat. 33, pl. 82, 12; Ambrogi in Ambrogi et al. 2008, 135-36.

486 HUNTER

Location/Inv: Grottaferrata, Abbazia, Museo.
Condition: The lid is preserved.
Lid: A central hunter in a cuirass stands between the two Dioscuroi. A lion hunt scene is represented on their left side, and a scene with the hunt of Meleager on the boar is represented on their right side.
Portrait: The central hunter is represented with the portrait features of a youth.
Dating: Last third of the third century (*ASR* XII 6, cat. 64).

Bibliography: Koch, *ASR* XII 6 (1975) cat. 64, pl. 54, 1; Huskinson 1996, cat. A 1.

487 HUNTER

Location/Inv.: Munich, Glyptothek.
Condition: Fragments of a frontal relief.
Frontal relief: Lion hunt with two scenes. For a description, see *ASR* I 2, cat. 50.
Short ends: Dioscuros?
Portrait: The central hunter is carved with a portrait.
Dating: 270-280 (*ASR* I 2, cat. 50).

Bibliography: Andreae, *ASR* I 2 (1980) cat. 50, pls. 34, 1-4; 1995, 35-9, 45-6.

488 LION HUNTER

Location/Inv.: Naples, Museo Nazionale, inv. 6766.
Size (coffin): L: 2.08 H. 0.64
Condition: The coffin is preserved.
Frontal relief: A lion hunt is represented on the left end of the relief and a battue appears on the right.
Portrait: The hunter on horseback is carved with a portrait.
Dating: 320-330 (*ASR* I 2, cat. 57).

Bibliography: Andreae, *ASR* I 2 (1980) cat. 57, pl. 93, 5; Koch & Sichtermann 1982, 96.

489 LION HUNTRESS (FIG. 73)

Location/Inv.: Nieborow Schloss (Poland), Arcadia, inv. Nb 2723 MNW.
Condition: Fragments of the frontal relief are preserved.
Frontal relief: A central horseman is hunting a lion with a spear. Virtus and another huntsman are represented behind him. Another two huntsmen are represented on the right end of the relief. A boar, a deer, and a dog are part of the scenery. For a description, see Mikocki 1995, 118-19.
Portrait: The hunter on horseback is carved with female portrait features.
Dating: Late third century.

Bibliography: Mikocki 1995, cat. 58; Mikocki & Zelazowski 2001.

490 HUNTER (FIG. 61)

Location/Inv.: Osimo, Cathedral, cript.
Size (coffin): L: 2.22 H: 0.79 D: 0.85; (lid): L: 2.31 H: 0.38 D: 0.96
Condition: The coffin and lid are preserved.
Frontal relief: Hunt scene. For a description, see *ASR* I 2, cat. 59.

Lid: Mary with the child, the three Magi, and Moses are represented on the left side of an inscription panel, and Noah, Jonah, and the sea-monster are represented on the right side.
Portrait: The central hunter is carved with a portrait.
Inscription: Inscription from the 17th century.
Dating: 320 (*ASR* I 2, cat. 59).

Bibliography: Andreae, *ASR* I 2 (1980) cat. 59, pl. 94, 1.

491 LION HUNTERS

Location/Inv: Ostia, Museo, inv. 1141.
Size (coffin): L: 1.76 H: 0.42 D: 0.52; (lid): L: 1.76 H: 0.18 D: 0.49
Condition: The coffin and lid are preserved.
Provenience: Ostia, Isola Sacra, tomb C (Dresken-Weland 2006, cat. A 99).
Frontal relief: Lion hunt scene. Two central lion hunters are pursuing a lion and a lioness. For a description, see *ASR* I 2, cat. 60.
Portrait: The two central hunters on horseback are carved with blank portraits.
Inscription: Post-antique inscription on the lid.
Dating: 280-290 (*ASR* I 2, cat. 60).

Bibliography: Andreae, *ASR* I 2 (1980) cat. 60, pl. 37, 5; Huskinson 1996, cat. 1. 15.

492 LION HUNTERS

Location/Inv.: Paris, Musée du Louvre, inv. 1808.
Size (coffin): L: 2.28 H. 0.88
Condition: The frontal relief is preserved with minor damage.
Provenience: Rome? From the Borghese Collection.
Frontal relief: Lion hunt with two scenes. On the left, preparations for hunting are shown; the hunt itself is represented on the right part. Virtus is depicted where the two scenes meet. For a description, see *ASR* I 2, cat. 65.
Portrait: Both the hunter on the left end of the relief and the hunter on horseback have portrait features.
Dating: Around the reign of Balbinus. Middle of the 230s (*ASR* I 2, cat. 65).

Bibliography: Andreae, *ASR* I 2 (1980) cat. 65, pl. 1, 3; Vaccaro Melucco 1963/64, cat. 9; Baratte & Metzger 1985, cat. 1.

493 LION HUNTER

Location/Inv.: Pisa, Camposanto, B 2 INT.
Size (coffin): L: 2.47 H: 0.83 D: 0.23
Condition: The coffin is preserved but fragmented.
Frontal relief: Lion hunt with two scenes. A central lion hunter attacks a lion on the left end of the relief and on the right there is a scene with a lioness being hunted.
Portrait: The central hunter is carved with male portrait features.
Dating: Last decade of the third century (*ASR* I 2, cat. 69).

Bibliography: Andreae, *ASR* I 2 (1980) cat. 69, pl. 55, 1.

494 LION HUNTER, COMMANDER, AND VIRTUS.

Location/Inv.: Reims, Musée des Beaux Arts, Sct. Nicaise.
Size (coffin): L: 2.83 H: 1.49 D: 1.31
Condition: The coffin is preserved. For restorations, see Vaccaro Melucco 1963-64, cat.7.
Frontal relief: Lion hunt with two scenes. A man and Virtus in full armour are represented on the left part of the relief. The hunt itself appears on the right. For a description, see *ASR* I 2, cat. 75.
Left short end: A huntsman and the rear part of the body of the horse from the frontal relief.
Right short end: Two huntsmen.
Reverse: Without relief decoration.
Portrait: The man on the left scene, Virtus, and the central huntsman on the right scene all have portrait features.
Dating: The relief is dated to 250-260, but the male portraits can be dated to the time of Constantine (*ASR* I 2, cat. 75).
Comment: The face of Virtus has been re-carved form a generic figure into a portrait.

Bibliography: Andreae, *ASR* I 2 (1980) cat. 75; Rodenwaldt 1944; Andreae 1981, 123.

495 LION HUNTER (FIG. 47)

Location/Inv.: Rome, Catacombe di S. Callisto.
Size (coffin): L: 1.75 H: 0.52
Condition: The frontal relief and part of the coffin are preserved.
Frontal relief: Lion hunt with two scenes. The man on the departure scene holds a scroll. For a description, see *ASR* I 2, cat. 101.
Short ends: Lenos-shaped. The motif of the frontal relief continues on the short ends.
Portrait: The central hunter is carved with a blank portrait.
Dating: Around 300 (*ASR* I 2, cat. 101).

Bibliography: Andreae, *ASR* I 2 (1980) cat. 101, pl. 74, 3.

496 VIRTUS

Location/Inv.: Rome, Catacombe di Pretestato, Museo.
Size (coffin): L: 2.62 H: 1.28 D: 1.12; (lid): L: 2,67 H: 0,57 (does not originally belong to this sarcophagus)
Condition: Consists of more fragments. For a description of condition and restorations, see Gütschow 1938, 66-8.
Provenience: Rome, Catabombe di Pretestato. Found in Region Scala Maggiore. Fell into the catacombs from the Roman necropolis above.
Frontal relief: The central huntsman is represented as a naked hero on foot with a stone as his only weapon. Virtus is standing behind him. Two huntsmen on horseback and an attacking lion are represented on the right part of the relief. The scene is framed by the Dioscuroi. For a description, see *ASR* I 2, 57-9.
Left short end: Two huntsmen with spear.
Right short end: Two huntsmen and a dog.
Lid: An empty inscription panel with hunt motifs on both sides.

Portrait: Virtus has female portrait features. The head of the central hunter is not preserved.
Dating: Beginning of the 260s (Andreae-Oehlschlegel-Weber 1972, 425).

Bibliography: Andreae, *ASR* I 2 (1980) cat. 86, pl. 23, 1; Gütschow 1938, 66-77; Vaccaro Melucco 1963/64, cat. 4; Hansen 2007, 108-10.

497 HUNTER

Location/Inv.: Rome, Catacombe Torlonia (lost).
Size (coffin): L: 0.52 H: 0.43
Frontal relief: Fragment showing a hunter with a spear. He is not on horseback but a fallen hunter is depicted between his legs.
Portrait: The hunter is carved with male portrait features.
Dating: Last quarter of the third century (*ASR* I 2, cat. 102).

Bibliography: Andreae, *ASR* I 2 (1980) cat. 102, pl. 90, 2.

498 LION HUNTER AND A LEARNED MAN (FIG. 60)

Location/Inv.: Rome, Cimitero Maggiore, Regione delle Cattedre, Cubiculum K.
Size (coffin): L: 2.10 H: 1.10 D. 0.63
Condition: The coffin and lid are preserved.
Provenience: Rome, still *in situ*.
Frontal relief: Lion hunt scene with a central huntsman on horseback. Many of the huntsmen have shields and Virtus holds a bow. For a description of the entire sarcophagus, see *ASR* I 2, cat. 78.
Lid: A portrait bust in front of a *parapetasma* held by two *putti* is represented on the left side of a central inscription panel; a hunting scene appears on the right. The inscription panel has been reused twice.
Inscription: 2) AVR TABVLA SER/VVS DEI QVI DORVM/IT IN PACE VIXIT / ANNIS XXIIII / PATER FECIT.
3) VAL SABBINO FILIO DVLCISSIMO QVI VIXIT / ANN(os) XIIII M(enses) X D(ies) / XXII DEP(ositus) XV KAL(endas) NOB(embres) / IOBIANO ET VARRONIANO CONN(ulibus) / IN PACE
The first inscription was erased. The next inscription mentions a 24-year-old man (*servus dei*) commemorated by his father. A third inscription is carved on the upper profile of the lid. This inscription mentions a 14-year-old son and a consul year (364). Both the preserved inscriptions are Christian.
Portrait: The bust on the lid is carved with a male portrait with a beard; the central huntsman on the frontal relief also has male portrait features.
Dating: 290-300 (*ASR* I 2, cat. 78).
Comment: Reused twice.

Bibliography: Andreae, *ASR* I 2 (1980) cat. 78, pl. 53, 1; Vaccaro Melucco 1963/64, 51.

499 LION HUNTER AND VIRTUS (FIG. 58)

Location/Inv.: Rome, Musei Capitolini, Palazzo Nuovo, Inv. MC 221/S.
Size (coffin): L: 2.08 H: 1.08
Condition: The frontal relief of a *lenos*-shaped coffin is preserved.
Provenience: Rome, Via Appia near Vigna Moroni in 1817.
Frontal relief: Lion hunt scene. Only the most important characters of the formulaic hunt scene are represented: Virtus, the central huntsman, the fallen huntsman and one accompanying huntsman on horseback. The scene is framed by two lion heads. For a description, see *ASR* I 2, cat. 104.
Portrait: The central huntsman has a male portrait and Virtus is carved with a blank portrait.
Dating: Around 250 (*ASR* I 2, cat. 44).

Bibliography: Andreae, *ASR* I 2 (1980) cat. 104; Vaccaro Melucco 1963/64, cat. 10; Rocca & Presicce 2010, 402-7 (with a full bibliography).

500 HUNTER

Location/Inv.: Rome, Musei Capitolini, Palazzo dei Conservatori, fasti moderni I 13.
Size (coffin): L: 2.08 H: 0.98 D: 0.55
Condition: The coffin and lid are preserved.
Frontal relief: Hunt scene with two central hunters on horseback surrounded by more hunters, also on horseback. For a description, see *ASR* I 2, cat. 112.
Lid: Unfinished hunt scenes and a blank inscription panel.
Portrait: The central hunters is carved with portrait features.
Dating: 270-280 (*ASR* I 2, cat. 112).
Comment: The latest known lion hunt sarcophagus.

Bibliography: Andreae, *ASR* I 2 (1980) cat. 112, pl. 95, 4.

501 HUNTERS

Location/Inv.: Rome, Museo Nazionale Romano, inv. 372546/2005906.
Size (coffin): L: 2.46 H: 0.92
Provenience: Rome, Località Torre Matura, near a Roman villa.
Frontal relief: Hunt scene with two central hunters on horseback surrounded by more hunters, also on horseback. For a description, see *MNR* I 10, 1, cat. 18.
Short ends: Scenes related to the hunt.
Portrait: The two central hunters on horseback are carved with portrait features.
Dating: 310-330 (*MNR* I 10, 1, cat. 18).

Bibliography: Andreae, *ASR* I 2 (1980) cat. 180; *MNR* I 10, 1, cat. 18.

502 HUNTER

Location/Inv: Rome, Museo Nazionale Romano, inv. 2003522.
Condition: Fragment of the frontal relief.
Frontal relief: Probably a fragment of a hunt sarcophagus. For a description, see *MNR* I 10, 1 cat. 98.
Portrait: Male.
Dating: Around the reign of Balbinus.

Bibliography: *MNR* I 10, 1, cat. 98.

503 HUNTER

Location/Inv.: Rome, Musei Vaticani, Cortile del Belvedere, inv. 1011.
Size (coffin): L: 1.85 H: 1.25
Condition: A fragment of the frontal relief is preserved. A large part of the relief as it is seen today is the result of modern restorations.
Frontal relief: The central huntsman, Virtus, and part of a third huntsman from the canonical hunt scene (probably a lion hunt) are preserved.
Portrait: The central hunter is carved with a portrait.
Dating: 220-230 (*ASR* I 2, cat. 213).

Bibliography: Andreae, *ASR* I 2 (1980) cat. 213; Vaccaro Melucco 1963/64, cat. 2.

504 HUNTER

Location/Inv.: Rome, Musei Vaticani, Museo Gregoriano Profano, inv.4968.
Size (coffin): L: 1.04 H: 0.70
Condition: A fragment of the frontal relief is preserved.
Frontal relief: A hunter on foot spears a boar. A naked male figure has taken Virtus' place behind the hunter. Virtus is represented in front of the hunter with a stone in her hand. For a description, see *ASR* I 2, cat. 235.
Portrait: A modern male portrait has been carved on the hunter from what was probably a blank portrait.
Dating: 260-270 (*ASR* I 2, cat. 235).

Bibliography: Andreae, *ASR* I 2 (1980) cat. 235, pl. 90, 1.

505 HUNTER

Location/Inv.: Rome, Musei Vaticani, magazine, inv. 543.
Size (coffin): L: 0.59 H: 0.25
Condition: Fragment of the frontal relief.
Frontal relief: The head of a huntsman and a man with helmet.
Portrait: The huntsman is carved with portrait features.
Dating: 230 (*ASR* I 2, cat. 217).

Bibliography: Andreae, *ASR* I 2 (1980) cat. 217, pl. 7, 5.

506 HUNTERS

Location/Inv.: Rome, Palazzo Massimi alle Colonne, built into the wall.
Condition: The frontal relief is preserved.
Frontal relief: Two hunt scenes. On the left, preparation for a hunt are shown; the hunt itself is represented on the right part of the relief. For a description, see *ASR* I 2, cat. 125.
Portrait: The man on the left end of the relief and the central hunter are carved with male portrait features.
Dating: 230 (*ASR* I 2, cat. 125).

Bibliography: Andreae, *ASR* I 2 (1980) cat. 125, pl. 86, 1.

607 LION HUNTER, COMMANDER, AND VIRTUS

Location/Inv.: Rome, Palazzo Mattei, built into the wall along the stairway.
Size (coffin): L: 2.25 H: 1.33
Condition: The frontal relief is preserved but has been extensively restored.
Frontal relief: Lion hunt with two scenes. A military man with a horse is represented on the left part of the relief, and the hunting scene itself appears on the right part. Virtus is depicted where the two scenes meet. For a description, see Vaccaro Melucco 1963-64, cat. 6.
Portrait: Both the military man and the central huntsman have portrait features, probably of the same man.
Dating: Around 250 (*ASR* I 2, cat. 128); 240-250 (Andreae-Oehlschlegel-Weber 1972, 431).
Comment: Often referred to as 'Mattei II'.

Bibliography: Andreae, *ASR* I 2 (1980) cat. 128; Vaccaro Melucco 1963/64, cat. 6; Andreae, Oehlschlegel & Weber 1972, 431; Guerrini 1982, 189-91; Birk 2010/11, 20 and note 105.

508 LION HUNTER AND VIRTUS

Location/Inv.: Rome, Palazzo Mattei, built into the wall along the stairway.
Size (coffin): L: 2.56 H: 1.37
Condition: The frontal relief is preserved but has been extensively restored.
Frontal relief: Formulaic lion hunt scene. For a description, see Vaccaro Melucco 1963/64, cat. 1.
Right short end: A man with an ox wagon, which contains the quarry from the hunt. The relief is placed in another part of the courtyard.
Portrait: The central huntsman has portrait features. It seems that the portrait has not been as extensively restored as the rest of the relief.
Dating: 220 (Rodenwaldt 1936, 82-113); 280 (*ASR* I 2, cat. 126).
Comment: Often referred to as 'Mattei I'.

Bibliography: Andreae, *ASR* I 2 (1980) cat. 126; Rodenwaldt 1936, 82-113; Vaccaro Melucco 1963/64, cat.1; Fittschen 1972, 503; Guerrini 1982, 184-88; Birk 2010/11.

509 LION HUNTER, COMMANDER, AND VIRTUS

Location/Inv.: Rome, Palazzo Rospigliosi Pallavicini, built into the wall of the palace.
Size (coffin): L: 2.90 H: 1.40
Condition: The frontal relief is preserved.
Frontal relief: Lion hunt with two scenes. A military man with his horse is represented on the left part of the relief; the hunt itself appears on the right part. Virtus is depicted where the two scenes meet. For a description, see *ASR* I 2, cat. 131.
Portrait: Both the military man and the central huntsman have portrait features, probably of the same man.
Dating: 240-250 (*ASR* I 2, cat. 131).

Bibliography: Andreae, *ASR* I 2 (1980) cat.131, pl. 12, 1; Vaccaro Melucco 1963/64, cat. 15.

510 HUNTER

Location/Inv.: Rome, S. Lorenzo, chistro.
Size (coffin): L: 0.35 H: 0.26
Condition: Fragment of the frontal relief.
Frontal relief: The upper part and the head of a man on horseback are preserved.
Portrait: The horseman is carved with portrait features. Surface damaged.
Dating: 230-240 (*ASR* I 2, cat. 137).

Bibliography: Andreae, *ASR* I 2 (1980) cat. 137, pl. 82, 4.

511 HUNTRESS (FIG. 60)

Location/Inv.: Rome, S. Sebastiano, Museo II.
Size (coffin): H. 0.58; (lid): L: 1.21 H: 0.225 Approximate length 2.09 m.
Condition: Fragments of the frontal relief and lid.
Provenience: Rome, found in 1929 at cubiculum 47d to the left of the museum at S. Sebastiano (Dresken-Weiland 2003, cat. A 67).
Frontal relief: Lion hunt with two scenes. A man with a horse and a scroll is represented on the left part of the relief. He is attended by a servant. The lion hunt itself appears on the right part. For a description, see *ASR* I 2, cat. 150.
Lid: Sigma-Mahl and inscription.
Portrait: The central horseman on the frontal relief has female portrait features.
Inscription: DEP(osito) BERA / V KAL(endas) MART(ias).
Dating: 290-300 (*ASR* I 2, cat. 150). The portrait indicates a date in the early fourth century (Prusac 2011, 119).
Comment: Her name was Bera and she was a Christian (the inscription).

Bibliography: Andreae, *ASR* I 2 (1980) cat. 150, pl. 74, 2; Amedick, *ASR* I 4 (1991) cat. 167; Huskinson 2002, 26, 28.

512 LION HUNTER AND BUST OF A LEARNED WOMAN (FIG. 10)

Location/Inv.: Rome, Vatican, The necropolis beneath S. Pietro.
Size (coffin): L: 2.28 H: 0.64 D: 0.66; (lid): L: 1.13 H: 0.24 D: 0.71
Condition: The coffin and the lid are preserved with only minor damage.
Provenience: Tomb of Valerii, (Mausoleum H) in 1943 (Dresken-Weiland 2003, cat. A 110).
Frontal relief: Lion hunt scene with a central huntsman accompanied by Virtus and more huntsmen. Two huntsmen killing a lioness are shown on the left part of the relief. For a description, see *ASR* I 2, cat. 240.
Left short end: Huntsman with shield and dog. The huntsman seems to have portrait features.
Lid: A procession with wagons drawn by oxen, an inscription tablet supported by two cupids, and a female bust.
Portrait: The central hunter is carved with male portrait features. The female bust on the lid has a blank portrait.
Inscription: D M / VALERINVS / VASATVLVS / VIXIT ANNIS / XXI M IIII D X H III VALERIA FLO/RENTIA COIVS=CONIVNX / FECIT MARITO / SVO ANIME / BENEMERENTI DP EIVS VII IDVS SEP M
Dating: Between 268 and 282 (Vaccaro Melucco 1963-64).
Comment: Given by Valeria Florentina to her 32-year-old husband (inscription). The word "deposito" suggests that they were Christians.

Bibliography: Andreae, *ASR* I 2 (1980) 77-8, cat. 240; Vaccaro Melucco 1963/64, cat. 14; Andreae 1984, 123.

513 LION HUNTER

Location/Inv.: Rome, Vatican, Via Fondamenta.
Size (coffin): L: 2.15 H: 0.52 D: 0.48
Condition: The coffin is preserved but the relief is damaged in several places.
Frontal relief: Lion hunt with a central huntsman on horseback accompanied by Virtus and more huntsmen. A scene with a wild boar hunt is represented on the left part of the relief.
Left short end: Huntsman with shield and spear.
Right short end: Huntsman.
Portrait: The central hunter is carved with a portrait.
Dating: 270-280 (*ASR* I 2, cat. 241).

Bibliography: Andreae, *ASR* I 2 (1980) 77-8, cat. 241, pl. 44, 3; Vaccaro Melucco 1963/64, cat. 22.

514 LION HUNTER AND VIRTUS

Location/Inv.: Rome, Via dei Condotti 47, Palazzo Mancano.
Size (coffin): L: 2.03 H. 0.58 D: 0.61
Condition: The frontal relief is preserved.
Frontal relief: Lion hunt scenes with a central lion hunter who, accompanied by Virtus, fights a lion.
Portrait: Both the central hunter and Virtus have blank portraits.
Dating: Late third century (*ASR* I 2, cat. 162).

Bibliography: Andreae, *ASR* I 2 (1980) cat. 162, pl. 80, 1.

515 LION HUNTER AND VIRTUS

Location/Inv.: Rome, Villa Borghese, Viale Pietro Canonoca/ Via del Aqua felix.
Size (coffin): L: 2.37 H. 1.03
Condition: A fragment of the frontal relief is preserved but the relief has been destroyed by weathering.
Frontal relief: The central part of a lion hunt scene. Virtus, the central hunter, a fallen huntsman, the lion and another huntsman on horseback are represented.
Portrait: The central hunter is carved with male portrait features.
Dating: 270-280 (*ASR* I 2, cat. 179).

Bibliography: Andreae, *ASR* I 2 (1980) 77-8, cat. 179; Vaccaro Melucco 1963/64, cat. 18.

516 LION HUNTER

Location/Inv.: Rome, Villa Doria Pamphilj.
Condition: The frontal relief is preserved but has been extensively restored. Both ends of the frontal relief are new additions.
Frontal relief: Formulaic lion hunt. For a description, see Calza 1977, cat. 225.
Portrait: The central hunter is carved with a blank portrait.
Dating: End of the third century or early fourth century (Calza 1977, 195).

Bibliography: Andreae, *ASR* I 2 (1980) cat. 181; Calza 1977, cat. 225, pl. 134, 2.

517 HUNTER

Location/Inv.: Rome, Villa Doria Pamphilj (lost).
Condition: Fragment of the frontal relief.
Frontal relief: A huntsman on horseback and an accompanying huntsman. For a description, see *ASR* I 2, cat. 188.
Portrait: The central hunter is carved with a portrait.
Dating: Around the middle of the third century (*ASR* I 2, cat. 188).

Bibliography: Andreae, *ASR* I 2 (1980) cat. 188, pl. 82, 6.

518 LION HUNTER

Location/Inv.: Rome, Villa Medici, built into the east façade.
Size (coffin): L: 2.10 H. 0.80
Condition: The frontal relief is preserved but the surfaced has been destroyed by weathering.
Frontal relief: Formulaic lion hunt. For a description, see Vaccaro Melucco 1963/64, cat. 11.
Portrait: The central hunter is carved with a portrait.
Dating: 260-280 (*ASR* I 2, cat. 192).

Bibliography: Andreae, *ASR* I 2 (1980) cat.192, pl. 22, 3; Vaccaro Melucco 1963/64, cat.11.

519 LION HUNTER

Location/Inv.: Rome, Villa Medici, built into the east façade.
Size (coffin): L: 2.30 H: 0.62
Condition: The frontal relief is preserved.
Frontal relief: Lion hunt with two scenes. A group of huntsmen about to kill a boar appear on the left part of the relief, and the lion hunter on horseback spearing a lion is represented on the right. For a description, see *ASR* I 2, cat. 193.
Portrait: The central hunter is carved with a portrait.
Dating: Around 280 (*ASR* I 2, cat. 193).

Bibliography: Andreae, *ASR* I 2 (1980) 77-8, cat. 193, pl. 45, 3.

520 LION HUNTER, COMMANDER, AND VIRTUS

Location/Inv.: S. Elpido a Mare, Chiesa Colleggiata.
Size (coffin): L: 2.18 H: 0.91 D: 0.92
Condition: The coffin is preserved.
Frontal relief: Lion hunt with two scenes. A commander with his horse is represented on the left part of the relief, and the lion hunt itself appearson the right. The central hunter on horseback is accompanied by Virtus. For a description, see *ASR* I 2, cat. 204.
Portrait: The lion hunter, the commander, and Virtus all have portrait features.
Dating: 315-320 (*ASR* I 2, cat. 204).

Bibliography: Andreae, *ASR* I 2 (1980) cat. 204, pl. 54, 3.

521 LION HUNTER AND COMMANDER

Location/Inv: Spoleto, Piazza del Duomo.
Size (coffin): L: 2.34 H: 0.71 D.0.79
Condition: The coffin is preserved.
Frontal relief: Lion hunt with two scenes. A commander with his horse is represented on the left part of the relief, and the lion hunt itself appears on the right. The central hunter on horseback is accompanied by Virtus.
Portrait: Both the lion hunter and the commander have male portrait features.
Dating: First decade of the fourth century (*ASR* I 2, cat. 208).

Bibliography: Andreae, *ASR* I 2 (1980) cat. 208, pl. 54, 2.

522 LION HUNTER

Location/Inv.: Viterbo, Piazza del Comune, built into Sct. Angelo.
Size (coffin): L: 2.17 H: 0.75 D: 0.69
Condition: The frontal relief and the short ends are preserved but separated. The surface has been significantly damaged by weathering.
Frontal relief: The scene is different from other lion hunt scenes because the lion is not attacking the central huntsman; instead it is shown attacking a wild boar. Another fight between two animals is depicted on the far right of the scene.
Left short end: Huntsman with dog.
Right short end: Seated huntsman. At his feet lays a dead lion.
Portrait: The central hunter is carved with a portrait.
Dating: 270-280 (*ASR* I 2, cat. 246).
Comment: Today the sarcophagus on the piazza has been replaced with a modern replica. The sarcophagus itself has been moved to the museum.

Bibliography: Andreae, *ASR* I 2 (1980) cat. 246, pl. 37, 1; Vaccaro Melucco 1963/64, cat. 16.

523 LION HUNTER AND VIRTUS

Location/Inv.: Vienna, Kunsthistorisches Museum, Antikensammlung, inv. 1133.
Size (coffin): L: 2.12 H: 0.74 D: 0.74
Condition: The coffin is preserved. The relief is well-preserved except for minor damage.
Frontal relief: A formulaic lion hunt sarcophagus. For a description, see *ASR* I 2, cat. 247.
Portrait: The central huntsman and Virtus have blank portraits.
Dating: 260-270 (*ASR* I 2, cat. 247).

Bibliography: Andreae, *ASR* I 2 (1980) cat. 247, pl. 36, 1; Vaccaro Melucco 1963/64, cat. 15.

Reclining Figures

Reclining Couples and Banquets

524 RECLINING WOMAN AND MAN
Location/Inv.: Paris, Musée du Louvre, Reserve epigraphique, salle F.
Size (lid): L: 0.34 H: 0.24 D: 0.32; Fragment b: L: 0.33 H: 0.23 D: 0.32
Condition: Two fragments of the lid are preserved.
Lid: A man and a woman are represented reclining on a bed. A flying cupid with a garland is depicted above them and two servants with long hair approach them from behind. Fragment b shows servants and musicians.
Portrait: The reclining man and woman have blank portraits.
Dating: Last quarter of the third century (*ASR* I 4, cat. 113).

Bibliography: Amedick, *ASR* I 4 (1991) cat. 113, pl. 9, 4.

525 RECLINING WOMAN AND MAN
Location/Inv.: Rome, Catacombe di Pretestato, Museo.
Size (lid): L: 2.30 H: 0.34 D: 0.10
Condition: Fragments of the lid are preserved.
Lid: A woman and a man are represented reclining on a bed. A seated woman playing a *pandurium* is depicted beside the bed. Servants are engaged with serving the couple.
Portrait: The two reclining figures have portrait features.
Dating: Around 290 (*ASR* I 4, cat. 138).

Bibliography: Andreae, *ASR* I 2 (1980) cat. 88; Amedick, *ASR* I 4 (1991) cat. 138, pl. 11, 2.

526 RECLINING WOMAN AND MAN
Location/Inv.: Rome, Musei Vaticani, Museo Chiaramonti, inv. 116.
Size (lid): L: 0.46 H: 0.25
Condition: A fragment of a lid is preserved.
Lid: A woman and a man are represented reclining on a bed. A servant and a flying cupid with a garland are depicted behind them.
Portrait: The reclining man and woman have blank portraits.
Dating: Last quarter of the third century (*ASR* I 4, cat. 271).

Bibliography: Amedick, *ASR* I 4 (1991) cat. 271, pl. 10, 3.

527 RECLINING WOMAN AND MAN
Location/Inv.: Rome, Musei Vaticani, Museo Gregoriano Profano, inv. 9546.
Size (lid): L: 0.80 H: 0.36
Condition: A fragment of the lid is preserved.
Lid: A woman and a man are reclining on a bed. Two flying cupids with a garland are depicted above them. A third cupid is placed behind the woman, and a small servant is depicted to the right of the bed. A theatre mask appears in the right corner.
Portrait: The reclining man and woman have portrait features. The woman wears a wreath.
Dating: Beginning of the fourth century (*ASR* I 4, cat. 287).

Bibliography: Amedick, *ASR* I 4 (1991) cat. 287, pl. 11, 3.

528 RECLINING WOMAN AND MAN
Location/Inv.: Rome, Museo Nazionale Romano, inv. 2003215.
Size (lid): L: 0.56 H. 0.38
Condition: A fragment of a lid is preserved.
Lid: A woman and a man are represented reclining on a bed. Three men (one with a jug and one with a tassel) and a boy with a *patera* are depicted behind them.
Portrait: The reclining man and woman have blank portraits.
Dating: Beginning of the fourth century.

Bibliography: Amedick, *ASR* I 4 (1991) cat. 174, pl. 11, 1; *MNR* I 10, 1, cat. 97.

529 RECLINING WOMAN AND MAN

Location/Inv.: Rome, previously on the art market.
Size (coffin): L: 0.60 H: 0.75
Condition: A fragment of the frontal relief is preserved, but it is badly damaged.
Frontal relief: A woman and a man are reclining on a bed. A garland is suspended behind them.
Portrait: The reclining man and woman have portrait features.
Dating: Around 270 (*ASR* I 4, cat. 170).

Bibliography: Amedick, *ASR* I 4 (1991) cat. 170, pl. 8, 1.

Reclining Individuals and Banquets

530 RECLINING WOMAN

Location/Inv.: Berlin, Schloss Klein-Glienicke, Gardenhof Wand III E, inv. Gl. 139.
Condition: A fragment of the frontal relief is preserved.
Frontal relief: A woman with a naked shoulder is reclining on a bed. Another woman playing a *pandurium* is represented beside the bed. A flying cupid with a garland appears above the reclining woman.
Portrait: The reclining woman has portrait features.
Dating: Gallienic (*ASR* I 4, cat. 16).

Bibliography: Amedick, *ASR* I 4 (1991) cat. 16, pl. 8, 4.

531 RECLINING MAN

Location/Inv.: Berlin, Staatliche Museen, Frühchr.-Sammlung.
Condition: A fragment of the lid is preserved.
Lid: A representation of a *Sigma-Mahl.* The central figure at the table is lifting his right arm above his head in a gesture similar to that of the sleeping Endymion. Another person is seated at his left side. A servant brings food to the diners, and a *parapetasma* is suspended behind the scene. Part of an inscription tablet is visible on the left side of the scene.
Portrait: The central figure at the table has a blank portrait.
Dating: Late third or early fourth century.

Bibliography: Engemann 1982, 241, pl. 14, 2.

532 RECLINING MAN

Location/Inv.: Berlin, Staatliche Museen, Pergamonmuseum, inv. Sk. 838.
Size (lid): L: 0.79 H: 0.36
Condition: A fragment of the lid is preserved. The surface is badly damaged.
Provenience: Rome, the Vescovali Collection.
Lid: A man is reclining on a bed, and a seated woman playing a *pandurium* is represented next to him. A young woman and a servant pouring wine from a jug are depicted to the left of the scene.
Portrait: The reclining man has a blank portrait.
Dating: The last third of the third century (*ASR* I 4, cat. 26).

Bibliography: Amedick, *ASR* I 4 (1991) cat. 26, pl. 14, 3.

533 RECLINING MAN

Location/Inv.: Carrara, Villa Dervillé (to the left of the entrance).
Size (coffin): L: 2.04 H: 0.57
Condition: The coffin is preserved.
Provenience: From Carrara. The marble is probably from the local quarry (Dolci 1980, 210).
Frontal relief: A reclining figure is attended by three servants bringing food. A flying cupid with a garland is depicted above the figure, and a *parapetasma* is depicted behind him.
Short ends: Palm tree.
Portrait: The reclining figure is carved with a male portrait. The figure appears to have a female body and male portrait features.
Comment: Cross-gendered.

Bibliography: Amedick, *ASR* I 4 (1991) pl. 4, 5; Dolci 1989, 210, 235-36.

534 RECLINING MAN AND SERVING WOMAN (FIG. 63)

Location/Inv.: Malibu, California, The Getty Villa, inv. 86.AA.701.
Size (coffin): L: 1.75 H: 0.47 D: 0.09
Condition: The frontal relief is preserved.
Frontal relief: Banquet scene with a reclining man attended by a woman. Wool-working activities are being carried out on either side of the reclining scene, and a cultic (?) scene is seen in the background. For a description, see Koch 1988.
Portrait: The reclining man and the female servant are carved with portraits. The two wool-working men might also have portraits.
Inscription: FVERIT POST ME ET POST GAVDENIA NICENE / VETO ALIVM QVISQVIS HVNC TITVLVM LEGERIT / MI ET ILLEI FECI T AELIO EVANGELO / HOMINI PATIENTI MERVM PROFVNDAT
Dating: 180-190 (*ASR* I 4, cat. 86).
Comment: The relief could also be a *loculus* plate. Probably produced in Ostia (Koch 1988, 25).

Bibliography: Amedick, *ASR* I 4 (1991) cat. 68; Koch 1988, cat. 9.

535 RECLINING MAN

Location/Inv.: Rome, Antiquarium Communale.
Condition: A fragment of the lid is preserved.
Lid: Banquet scene with a reclining man attended by a seated woman playing a lyre. Two flying cupids carrying garlands are depicted behind this scene, and a *putto* playing with a hare is depicted beneath the *kline.*
Portrait: The man is carved with a blank portrait.
Dating: Last quarter of the fourth century (*ASR* I 4, cat. 127).

Bibliography: Amedick, *ASR* I 4 (1991) cat. 127, pl. 14, 1.

536 RECLINING MAN (AND HUNTER (?)) (FIG. 81)

Location/Inv.: Rome, Musei Vaticani, Museo Gregoriano profano, inv. 9538/9539.
Size (coffin): L: 2.11 H: 0.93 D: 0.73
Condition: The coffin and the lid are preserved. The lid is fragmented.
Provenience: Discovered between Formello and Sacrofano, Rome.
Frontal relief: Banquet scene with a reclining man attended by a seated woman playing a *pandurium*. Several servants are attending the man, carrying plates of food. Flying cupids and garlands are shown behind this scene, and children playing with a dog are depicted beneath the bed.
Short ends: Lenos-shaped. The motif of the frontal relief continues on the short ends.
Reverse: Lion hunt scene. The face of the central hunter is probably meant to be a portrait. The hairstyle and the way of carving the beard show that this man had a fairly long beard, similarly to the portrait of the man on the frontal relief. However, this relief is in contrast to the frontal relief very low. The scene could be a later addition, in this case probably contemporary with the portrait of the frontal relief
Lid: Market scenes and an inscription panel.
Portrait: The reclining person has a female body but the head is carved with male portrait features. According to Amedick (*ASR* I 4), it could be a re-carving. The beard is carved with some plasticity and the long coarse strokes indicate that it is not a short beard. Also the hair is carved with plasticity.
Inscription: D M S/P CAECILI/VALLIANI/A MILITIS/VIXIT ANN/LXIII
Dating: Around 270 (*ASR* I 4, cat. 268).

Bibliography: Andreae, *ASR* I 2 (1980) cat. 232, pl. 41, 1-2; Amedick, *ASR* I 4 (1991) cat. 286, pl. 15, 2; Koch & Sichtermann 1982, 111; Huskinson 2002, 26.

537 RECLINING WOMAN (DEATHBED) (FIG. 70)

Location/Inv.: Rome, Palazzo Pallavicini-Rospigliosi, Terrasse del Casino.
Size (coffin): L: 1.88 H: 0.40 D: 0.52
Condition: The coffin is preserved.
Frontal relief: A woman is represented on her deathbed with an eagle at her shoulder. The scene is flanked by cupids holding a garland.
Short ends: Without relief decoration.
Portrait: The woman on the bed has portrait features.
Dating: 150-160 (*ASR* VI 2, 1 cat. 127).

Bibliography: Herdejürgen, *ASR* VI 2, 1 (1996) cat. 127, pl. 91, 1.

538 RECLINING WOMAN

Location/Inv.: Rome, Vatican, Loggia Scoperta, inv. 13.
Size (lid): L: 0.33 H: 0.23
Condition: A fragment of the lid is preserved.
Lid: A woman is reclining on a bed. Servants are serving food to her.
Portrait: The woman on the bed has portrait features.
Dating: End of the third century (*ASR* I 4, cat. 262).

Bibliography: Amedick, *ASR* I 4 (1991) cat. 262, pl. 30, 2.

Figures Riding in a Carriage

539 LEARNED MAN RIDING IN A CARRIAGE

Location/Inv.: Aquileia, Museo Archeologica, inv. 225.
Size (coffin): L: 0.76 H: 0.35 D: 0.11
Condition: Fragment of the frontal relief.
Frontal relief: Procession with a figure in a vehicle. The seated man is a magistrate, symbolised by what is probably a sceptre with a bust. For a description, see Ronke 1987, cat. 204.
Portrait: The man with the sceptre has portrait features.
Dating: Fourth century (Ronke 1987, cat. 204); 360-370 (*ASR* I 3, 2).

Bibliography: Amedick, *ASR* I 4 (1991) 2; Ronke 1987, 186, cat. 204, pl. 102, 5.

540 LEARNED MAN RIDING IN A CARRIAGE

Location/Inv.: Rome, Catacombe di Pretestato, Museo.
Size (coffin): L: 0.64 H: 0.43 D: 0.3 – 0.8
Condition: Five fragments of a lid are preserved.
Provenience: Rome, Catacombe di Pretestato?
Lid: A woman and a man are riding in a carriage. The carriage is driven by a servant and drawn by two horses. The man holds a scroll. For a description, see *ASR* I 4, cat. 149.
Portrait: The man has a blank portrait. The head of the woman is not preserved.
Dating: Around 300 (*ASR* I 4, cat. 149).

Bibliography: Amedick, *ASR* I 4 (1991) cat. 149, pl. 44, 1.

541 MAN RIDING IN A CARRIAGE

Location/Inv.: Rome, Catacombe di Pretestato, Museo.
Size (lid): L: 0.29 H: 0.24
Condition: A fragment of the lid is preserved.
Provenience: Rome, Catacombe di Pretestato.
Lid: A man holding a scroll is riding in a carriage drawn by a horse and driven by a servant. For a description, see *ASR* I 4, cat. 148.
Portrait: The man in the carriage is carved with a blank portrait.
Dating: Tetrarchic period (*ASR* I 4, cat. 148).

Bibliography: Amedick, *ASR* I 4 (1991) cat. 148, pl. 42, 1.

542 WOMAN AND MAN RIDING IN A CARRIAGE

Location/Inv.: Rome, Musei Capitolini, Antiquarium Communale, mag. sculture 857.
Size (lid): L: 0.53 H. 0.30 D. 0.05
Condition: A fragment of the lid is preserved.
Lid: A woman and a man are riding in a carriage in a city. The man holds a scroll. The carriage is driven by a servant, and part of a horse is visible. A servant with long hair and a jug is depicted behind the carriage. For a description, see *ASR* I 4, cat. 128.
Portrait: The man and the woman in the carriage are carved with portrait features.
Dating: Around 300 (*ASR* I 4, cat. 128)

Bibliography: Amedick, *ASR* I 4 (1991) cat. 128.

543 WOMAN RIDING IN A CARRIAGE (FIG. 48)

Location/Inv.: Rome, Museo Nazionale Romano, inv. 8942.
Size (coffin): L: 0.92 H. 0.35
Condition: The frontal relief is preserved but fragmented.
Frontal relief: A woman and a man with a scroll are riding in a carriage through a city. For a description, see *MNR* I 8, 1, cat. III, 4.
Portrait: The woman is carved with female portrait features.
Dating: Around 280 (*MNR* I 8, 1, cat. III, 4).

Bibliography: *MNR* I 8, 1, 127-28, cat. III, 4.

544 LEARNED WOMAN AND WOMAN RIDING IN A CARRIAGE (FIG. 75)

Location/Inv.: Stockholm, Medelhavsmuseet.
Size (coffin): L: 0.53 H: 0.58
Condition: A fragment of the frontal relief is preserved.

Frontal relief: Two women, one holding a scroll, are sitting in a carriage drawn by two horses. They are driving through an arch with an equestrian statue on top. Servants are depicted around the carriage, and an old woman is shown wringing clothes from a window.
Portrait: The two women in the carriage have portrait features.
Dating: Around 300 (*ASR* I 4, cat. 247).

Comment: A composition that we assume was normally used for a married couple is here chosen by two women. Another sarcophagus with the same motif but with representations of a woman and a man is *ASR* I 4, cat. 128 (here cat. no. 542).

Bibliography: Amedick, *ASR* I 4 (1991) cat. 247, pl. 39, 2; Antonsson 1958, 141-43; Himmelmann-Wildschütz 1973, 31-4; Sande 2010, 70.

Mythological Figures

Achilles and Penthesilea/Briseis

545 ACHILLES AND PENTHESILEA

Location/Inv.: Rome, Musei Capitolini, Antiquario Comunale.
Size (coffin): L: 1.27 H: 0.88
Condition: A fragment of the frontal relief is preserved.
Frontal relief: Achilles and Penthesilea are represented in a battle scene; Achilles supports the dying Penthesilea. For a description, see *ASR* XII 1, cat. 131.
Portrait: Achilles and Penthesilea are carved with portrait features.
Dating: 250-260 because of similarities between the portrait of Achilles and Gallienus (*ASR* XII 1, cat. 131).

Bibliography: Grassinger, *ASR* XII 1 (1999) cat. 131, pl. 113, 1.

546 ACHILLES AND PENTHESILEA

Location/Inv.: Rome, Musei Vaticani, Cortile del Belvedere, inv. 900.
Size (coffin): L: 2.27 H: 0.88
Motif: The frontal relief is preserved but has been significantly restored.
Frontal relief: Achilles and Penthesilea are represented in a battle scene; Achilles supports the dying Penthesilea. For a description, see *ASR* XII 1, cat. 125.
Portrait: Achilles is carved with male portrait features. Penthesilea's head is modern.
Dating: 220-230 (*ASR* XII 1, cat. 125).

Bibliography: Grassinger, *ASR* XII 1 (1999) cat. 125, pl. 111, 2.

547 ACHILLES AND PENTHESILEA

Location/Inv.: Rome, Musei Vaticani, Cortile del Belvedere, inv. 933.
Size (coffin): L: 2.52 H: 1.19 D: 1.02
Condition: The coffin is preserved.
Frontal relief: Achilles and Penthesilea are represented in a battle scene; Achilles supports the dying Penthesilea. For a description, see Sichtermann & Koch 1975, cat. 12.
Left short end: An Amazon on a rearing horse.
Right short end: An Amazon and a subjugated barbarian. Another Amazon is seen behind a city wall.
Portrait: Achilles and Penthesilea are carved with portrait features.
Dating: 230-240, because of the stylistic similarities between the portrait of Achilles and the portrait of Maximus or Maximinius Thraks, and between the portrait of Penthesilea and the portrait of Julia Mamea (*ASR* XII 1, 180).

Bibliography: Grassinger, *ASR* XII 1 (1999) cat. 127; Sichtermann & Koch 1975, cat. 12.

548 ACHILLES AND PENTHESILA

Location/Inv.: Rome, Palazzo Borghese.
Size (coffin): L: 2.18 H: 0.80
Condition: The frontal relief is preserved.
Frontal relief: Achilles and Penthesilea are represented in a battle scene; Achilles supports the dying Penthesilea. The scene is depicted in one register. For a description, see *ASR* XII 1, cat. 119.
Portrait: Achilles and Penthesilea are carved with blank portraits.
Dating: Early third century (*ASR* XII, cat. 119).

Bibliography: Grassinger, *ASR* XII 1 (1999) cat. 119, pl. 110, 2.

549 ACHILLES AND BRISEÏS

Location/Inv.: Rome, lost. Previously in the magazines by the Forum of Trajan.
Condition: Fragment of the frontal relief.

Frontal relief: A man with a beard, a woman, and two other figures are placed side by side. More figures appear behind these four. A tree is depicted on either end of the relief.
Portrait: The woman and the man on her right are carved with portrait features.
Dating: 253-260 (Meyer 2002, 163).
Comment: The identification of the scene is uncertain.

Bibliography: Meyer 2002, 159-65, pl. 27, 1.

Adonis and Venus

550 ADONIS AND VENUS (FIG. 55)

Location/Inv.: Rome, Musei Vaticani, Museo Gregoriano Profano, inv. 10409.
Size (coffin): L: 2.15 H: 0.72 D: 0.71
Condition: The coffin is preserved. The lid does not belong to the coffin (Dresken-Weiland 2003, A 55).
Provenience: Found in 1857 in the main chamber of the tomb of the Pancrati on Via Latina together with at least seven other sarcophagi (Dresken-Weiland 2003, A55).
Frontal relief: A farewell scene is represented on the left end of the relief. Venus and Adonis are seated in front of a *parapetasma* on the second scene. The third scene shows the hunt of the boar, separated from the other scenes by an architectural arch. For a description, see Wrede 1981, cat. 2.
Short ends: Huntsman with spear and a dog.
Lid: Scenes from the tale of Oedipus.
Portrait: The seated Venus and Adonis are carved with portrait features.
Dating: Around 220 (*ASR* XII 1, cat. 65).
Comment: Traces of paint are preserved.

Bibliography: Robert, *ASR* III 1 (1897) cat. 21; Grassinger, *ASR* XII 1 (1999) cat. 65, pl. 47, 2; Koch & Sichtermann 1975, cat. 7; Wrede 1981, 139, cat. 2; Fittschen 1984, 138; Dresken-Weiland 2003, cat. A 55.

Alcestis

551 ALCESTIS?

Location/Inv.: Rome, Musei Capitolini, Palazzo dei Conservatori.
Condition: Fragment of a frontal relief.
Frontal relief: Mythological representation (Protesilaus and Alcestis?). Woman on a *kline* surrounded by other figures.
Portrait: Alcestis is carved with a portrait with a wavy hairstyle which covers her ears.
Dating: Around 220. Based on the portrait.

Bibliography: Arachne: http://arachne.uni-koeln.de/item/objekt/52264.

552 ALCESTIS AND ADMETUS (FIG. 11)

Location/Inv.: Rome, Musei Vaticani, Museo Chiaramonti, inv. 1195.
Size (offin): L: 2.40 H: 0.54 D: 0.92
Condition: Both coffin and lid are very well preserved.
Provenience: Ostia.
Frontal relief: The tale of Alcestis' death, represented biographically.
Lid: An inscription is held by two flying *victoriae*. A mask of Attis and some objects connected with Cybele/Magna Mater are depicted on each corner of the lid.
Portrait: The king Admetus is displayed three times with portrait features. The reclining Alcestis has portrait features. An old woman and probably an elderly man behind the central scene have portrait features as well. The two young men on the left part of the sarcophagus may also show portrait features.
Inscription: C IVNIVS PAL EVTHODVS MAGISTER QQ / COLLEGI – FABR TIGN OSTIS LVSTRI XX FECIT SIBI ET METILIAE ACTE SACERDO / TI M D M COLON OST COIVGSANCTISSIM (*CIL* XIV, 371)
Dating: Around 160 (Wood 1993, 86).

Bibliography: Wegner, *ASR* V 3 (1966) 31-3, cat. 26; Matz, *ASR* III 1 (1897) cat. 27; Grassinger, *ASR* XII 1 (1999) cat. 76; Amelung 1903, 429-30, no. 179; Cumont 1942, 30, no. 4; Lehmann-Hartleben & Olsen 1942, 57; Giglioli 1953, 222-23; Helbig 1963, 229-30, no. 291; Pelikàn 1965, 42-3; Turcan 1966, index p. 653; Andreae 1968/69, 147-48; 1984, 120; Andreae et al. 1995, 846-51; Sichtermann & Koch 1975, 20-1, no. 8; Wood 1993; Muzcnik 1999a.

Apollo

553 APOLLO (FIG. 82)

Location/Inv.: San Simion, California, Hearst Castle, inv. P.C 6256.
Condition: The frontal relief and the right short end are preserved.
Frontal relief: Representation of Athena and the lyre-playing Apollo among the Nine Muses. For a description, see *ASR* V 3, cat. 219.
Right short end: Odysseus in his boat, tied to the mast to help him resist the song of the sirens.
Portrait: Apollo is carved with male portrait features.
Dating: 230 (*ASR* V 3, cat. 219); 240 because of similarities between the portrait and that of Gordian III (Fittschen 1984, 132).

Bibliography: Wegner, *ASR* V 3 (1966) cat. 219; Fittschen 1974, 494; 1984, 132; Wrede 1981, cat. 40; Ewald 1999, 35, cat. B1.

554 APOLLO AND DIONYSUS

Location/Inv.: Venice, Museo Archeologico, inv. 260 & inv. 110.
Condition: Two short ends of one sarcophagus are preserved.

Right short end: A boy with cloak, arch, and a griffin. Hermes is represented beside him.
Left short end: Boy represented with *thyrsus*, *kantharos*, and panther. A maenad is depicted beside him.
Portrait: The two boys with the attributes of Apollo and Dionysus are carved with portrait features.
Dating: Second quarter of the third century (Wrede 1981, cat. 39 & cat. 180).
Comment: Child sarcophagus.

Bibliography: Wrede 1981, cat. 39, pl. 6, 1-2.

Ariadne

555 ARIADNE

Location/Inv.: Bolsena, Municipio.
Size (coffin): L: 2.21 H: 0.95
Condition: The coffin is preserved.
Frontal relief: The sleeping Ariadne is found by Dionysus. For a description, see *ASR* IV 1, cat. 46.
Short ends: Lenos-shaped. The motif of the frontal relief continues on the short ends.
Reverse: Dionysian motifs and Medusa heads (low relief).
Portrait: The sleeping Ariadne is carved with portrait features.
Dating: 190-200 (Wrede 1981, 139, cat. 45).

Bibliography: Matz, *ASR* IV 1 (1968a) cat. 46, pl. 48; Wrede 1981, 139, cat. 45.

556 ARIADNE (FIG. 21)

Location/Inv.: Copenhagen, Ny Carlsberg Glyptoteket, inv. IN 849.
Size (coffin): L: 1.76 H: 0.65
Condition: The coffin is preserved.
Frontal relief: A figure represented in the manner of the sleeping Ariadne, with three cupids holding garlands. For a description, see *ASR* IV 3, cat. 229.
Short ends: Lenos-shaped. The motif of the frontal relief continues on the short ends.
Portrait: The reclining figure is carved with female portrait features.
Dating: 220-230 (Wrede 1981, 139, cat. 54).

Bibliography: Matz, *ASR* IV 3 (1969), cat. 229; Wrede 1981, 139, cat. 54, pl. 7, 1.

557 ARIADNE (FIG. 77)

Location/Inv: Malibu, California, The J. Paul Getty Museum, inv. 83. AA 275.
Size (coffin): L: 1.17 H: 0.53 D: 0.50; (lid): L: 1.17
Condition: The coffin and lid are preserved.
Provenience: A tomb at Vigna Casali, together with cat. nos. 155 and 482 (Koch 1988, 36, nr. 13; Dresken-Weiland 2003, cat. A 58).
Frontal relief: The sleeping Ariadne is found by Dionysus. For a description, see Wrede 1981, 139.
Left short end: A satyr pressing grapes.
Right short end: Satyr.
Reverse: A satyr pressing grapes.
Lid: Panels with Dionysian figures and an inscription panel.
Portrait: The sleeping Ariadne is carved with a blank portrait.
Inscription: D M / MACONIANAE SEVERIANAE / FILIAE DVLCISSIMAE / M SEMPRONIVS PROCVLVS / FAVSTINIANVS VC ET / PRAECILIA SEVERINA CF / PARENTES
Dating: Late third century (*ASR* IV 3, cat. 214) or 210-220 (Koch 1988, 40).

Bibliography: Matz, *ASR* IV 3 (1969) cat. 214; Wrede 1981, 139, cat. 47; Andreae 1984, 114; Koch 1988, 36-42; Walker 1990; Dresken-Weiland 2003, cat. A 58.

558 ARIADNE

Location/Inv.: Moscow, Puschkin- Museum.
Size (coffin): L: 2.20 H: 0.82
Condition: The coffin is preserved.
Frontal relief: The sleeping Ariadne is found by Dionysus. For a description, see *ASR* IV 1, cat. 47.
Short ends: Lenos-shaped. The motif of the frontal relief continues on the short ends.
Reverse: Dionysian scene, carved in high relief.
Portrait: The sleeping Ariadne is carved with a blank portrait.
Dating: 200-210 (*ASR* IV 1, cat. 47).

Bibliography: Matz, *ASR* IV 1 (1968) cat. 47, pl. 56 a-b; Wrede 1981, 139, cat. 49; Newby 2011, 203-4

559 ARIADNE

Location/Inv.: Naples, Museo Nazionale, inv. 144995.
Size (coffin): L: 2.34 H: 0.93 D: 0.95
Condition: The coffin is preserved.
Frontal relief: A figure represented in the manner of the sleeping Ariadne surrounded by cupids. For a description, see *ASR* I 4, cat. 76.
Left short end: Lenos-shaped. Grape harvest.
Right short end: Lenos-shaped. Cupids pressing grapes.
Portrait: The Ariadne figure is carved with female portrait features.
Dating: Around 270 (*ASR* I 4, cat. 76; *ASR* V 2, 2, cat. 56).

Bibliography: Matz, *ASR* IV 3 (1969) cat. 229; Amedick, *ASR* I 4 (1991) cat. 76, pl. 103, 1; Bielefeld, *ASR* V 2, 2 (1997) cat. 56; Wrede 1981, 139, cat. 56.

560 ARIADNE

Location/Inv.: Oslo, Nationalgalerie.
Size (coffin): L: 0.60 H: 0.61
Condition: Fragment of the right end of a *lenos*-shaped coffin.
Frontal relief: Hercules, a satyr, and the sleeping Ariadne.

Portrait: The sleeping Ariadne is carved with portrait features.
Dating: 200-210 (Wrede 1981, cat. 46).

Bibliography: Matz, *ASR* IV 1 (1968) cat. 46A, pl. 49, 1; Wrede 1981, cat. 46; Newby 2011, 202.

561 ARIADNE

Location/Inv.: Paris, Musée du Louvre, inv. Fr242.
Size (coffin): L: 0.63 H: 0.85
Condition: Fragment of the frontal relief.
Frontal relief: The sleeping Ariadne. For a description, see *ASR* IV 1, cat. 49.
Portrait: Ariadne is carved with a blank portrait.
Dating: First quarter of the third century (*ASR* IV, cat. 49).

Bibliography: Matz, *ASR* IV 1 (1968) cat. 49; Wrede 1981, 139, cat. 52; Baratte & Metzger 1985, cat. 53; Newby 2011, 202.

562 ARIADNE AND LEARNED MAN

Location/Inv.: Paris, Musée du Louvre, inv. 1346.
Size (coffin): L: 2.10 H: 0.63
Condition: The coffin and lid are preserved.
Provenience: St. Médard-d'Eyran near Bordeaux, together with an Endymion sarcophagus now in the Louvre (cat. no. 578). The burial context is secondary (Zanker & Ewald 2004, 108, 321).
Frontal relief: The sleeping Ariadne is found by Dionysus. For a description, see *ASR* IV 3, cat. 222.
Left short end: Pan playing a double flute.
Right short end: A satyr with *pedum* and a boy.
Lid: Dionysian scenes, an empty inscription panel, and a male bust in front of *a parapetasma.*
Portrait: Ariadne and the bust on the lid have blank portraits.
Dating: 230 (Wrede 1981, 139 cat.50).

Bibliography: Matz, *ASR* IV 3 (1969) cat. 222, pl. 234; Wrede 1981, 139, cat. 50; Baratte & Metzger 1985, cat. 67; Zanker & Ewald 2004, 109, abb.92; Newby 2011, 204-5.

563 ARIADNE

Location/Inv.: Paris, art market.
Size (coffin): L: 2.17 H: 0.65
Condition: The coffin is preserved.
Provenience: Mirabella-Eclano (Campania).
Frontal relief: The sleeping Ariadne is found by Dionysus. For a description, see Wrede 1981, 140, cat. 44.
Short end reliefs: *Lenos*-shaped. The motif of the frontal relief continues on the short ends.
Portrait: The sleeping Ariadne is carved with portrait features. The hairstyle belongs to the late Antonine period.
Dating: 170-190 (Wrede 1981, 140, cat. 44).

Bibliography: Matz, *ASR* IV 3 (1969) cat. 217, pl. 233, 3; Wrede 1981, 140, cat. 44; Newby 2011, 201.

564 ARIADNE AND DIONYSUS

Location/Inv.: Rom, Museo Nazionale Romano delle Terme, inv. 124682.
Size (coffin): L: 2.29 H: 0.94
Condition: The coffin and lid are preserved.
Frontal relief: Dionysus and Ariadne are seated on a rock. Gods and *thiasoi* are standing around them. For a description, see Wrede 1981, 139, cat. 48.
Portrait: Ariadne and Dionysus have blank portraits.
Dating: 210-220 (Wrede 1981, 139, cat. 48).

Bibliography: Matz, *ASR* IV 2 (1968a) cat. 76, pl. 89 a-b; Wrede 1981, 139, cat. 48.

565 ARIADNE

Location/Inv.: Rome, Palazzo Borghese.
Size (coffin): L: 2.29 H: 0.65
Condition: The frontal relief is preserved.
Provenience: Rome, Via Labicana, near Torre Nova.
Frontal relief: The sleeping Ariadne is found by Dionysus. For a description, see Wrede 1981, cat. 53.
Portrait: Ariadne is carved with with female portrait features.
Dating: Around 230 (Wrede 1981, 139, cat. 53).

Bibliography: Matz, *ASR* IV 3 (1969) cat. 223, pl. 232, 1; Wrede 1981, 139, cat. 53.

566 ARIADNE

Location/Inv.: St. Petersburg, Hermitage, inv. A 182.
Size (coffin): L: 2.11 H: 0.56
Condition: The frontal relief is preserved.
Frontal relief: The sleeping Ariadne is found by Dionysus. For a description, see *ASR* IV 3, cat. 212.
Portrait: Ariadne is carved with portrait features. The hairstyle seems to date to the late Severan period.
Dating: 220-235 (Wrede 1981, 139, cat. 51).

Bibliography: Matz, *ASR* IV 3 (1969) cat. 212, pl. 220, 1; Wrede 1981, 139, cat. 51.

Ceres

567 CERES

Location/Inv.: Ostia Antica, Museo, inv. 1101.
Condition: Fragment of the frontal (?) relief.
Provenience: Ostia, Cardo Maximus.
Frontal relief: Ceres in her wagon, searching for Persephone. Behind her is a female personification with a torch.
Portrait: Ceres is carved with portrait features.
Dating: 140-150, based on the similarity of the hairstyle to that of Faustina (Zanker & Ewald 2004, 94).

Bibliography: Calza 1964/65, cat. 160, pl. 94; Wrede 1981, cat. 77; Koch & Sichtermann 1982, 176; Zanker & Ewald 2004, 94, ill. 78.

Dionysus

568 DIONYSUS (FIG. 93)

Location/Inv.: Rome, Catacombe di Pretestato.
Size (coffin): L: 2.13 H: 0.80 D: 0.88
Condition: The coffin is preserved.
Provenience: Catacombe di Pretestato.
Frontal relief: Divided into five panels. The second and fourth are strigillated. The deceased is represented as a drunk Dionysus supported by a satyr on the third panel, and a maenad is shown on the first and fifth panels. A *parapetasma* is suspended behind Dionysus. For a description, see Gütschow 1928, 110-13.
Portrait: Dionysus is carved with portrait features.
Dating: 250 (Wrede 1981, cat. 181).

Bibliography: Matz, *ASR* IV 4 (1975) cat. 299; Gütschow 1938, 110-13; Wrede 1981, cat. 181, 25, 2; Zanker & Ewald 2004, 160, ill. 145.

Dionysian Cupids

569 CUPID

Location/Inv.: Florence, Galleria degli Uffizi, inv. 374.
Size (coffin): L: 1.10 H: 0.47 D: 0.43
Condition: The coffin is preserved.
Frontal relief: The boy is surrounded by cupids dancing, drinking, and playing. He is represented as a cupid with a cloak and a *cithara* in his right hand.
Short ends: Lenos-shaped. The motif of the frontal relief continues on the short ends.
Portrait: The cupid with the *cithara* is carved with a blank portrait.
Dating: 280-290 (*ASR* V 2, 1, cat. 12).
Comment: Child sarcophagus.

Bibliography: Kranz, *ASR* V 2, 1 (1999) cat. 12, 25, pl. 37, 1; Kranz 2001, 53.

570 CUPID (FIG. 92)

Location/Inv.: Rome, Musei Vaticani, Cortile del Belvedere, inv. 892.
Size (coffin): L: 1.53 H: 0.49 D: 0.50
Condition: The coffin is preserved.
Frontal relief: A boy wearing a cloak is surrounded by cupids dancing, drinking, and playing. He is represented as a drunk, supported by two of the cupids.
Short ends: Seated griffin.
Portrait: The boy-cupid is carved with a blank portrait.
Dating: 260-280 (*ASR* V 2, cat. 12) or 250-260 (Wrede 1981, 139, cat. 14).
Comment: Child sarcophagus.

Bibliography: Kranz, *ASR* V 2, 1 (1999) cat. 12; Amelung 1908, 180, nr. 73; Wrede 1981, 139, cat. 14.

571 CUPID

Location/Inv.: Rome, Museo Nazionale Romano, inv. 121593.
Size (coffin): L: 2.85 H: 0.89 D: 0.35
Condition: Fragments of a frontal relief.
Provenience: Rome, Via Imperiale, 1939.
Frontal relief: The boy is surrounded by cupids dancing, drinking, and playing. He is represented as a drunk cupid, supported by the other cupids.
Portrait: The boy-cupid is carved with portrait features.
Dating: 250-270 (*ASR* V 2, cat. 73).
Comment: Child sarcophagus.

Bibliography: Kranz, *ASR* V 2, 1 (1999) cat. 73, pl. 50, 2.

572 CUPID

Location/Inv.: Rome, Palazzo Barberini.
Size (coffin): Coffin: L: 1.83 H: 0.59/46 D: 0.78/74
Condition: The coffin is preserved.
Frontal relief: The boy is surrounded by cupids dancing and playing. For a description, see *ASR* V 2, 1 cat. 76.
Left short end: Lenos-shaped. Cupids harvesting grapes. A lion head *protom* separates the frontal relief from the short end relief.
Right short end: Lenos-shaped. Cupids with *pallium* and *pedum*. A lion head *protom* separates the frontal relief from the short end relief.
Portrait: The boy-cupid of the frontal relief is carved with a blank portrait.
Dating: 250-260 (*ASR* V 2 1, cat. 76); 220-230 (Wrede 1981, cat. 12).
Comment: Child sarcophagus.

Bibliography: Kranz *ASR* V 2, 1 (1999) cat. 76, pl. 45, 1; Wrede 1981, 139, cat. 12.

Endymion

573 (ENDYMION) AND SELENE

Location/Inv.: Assisi, S. Rufino.
Size (coffin): L: 2.12 H: 0.74 D: 0.74
Condition: The coffin is preserved.
Frontal relief: Selene comes in her chariot to the sleeping Endymion. For a description, see *ASR* XII 2, cat. 76.
Left short end: Herdsman with a stick and a tree.
Right short end: Selene in her chariot drawn by two bulls.
Portrait: Selene is carved with portrait features. The faces of Selene and Endymion are both damaged; Endymion may have had a portrait as well. For discussion, see *ASR* XII 2, cat. 76.
Dating: 220-240 (*ASR* XII 2, cat. 76).

Bibliography: Sichtermann, *ASR* XII 2 (1992) cat. 76, pl. 75, 3; Wrede 1981, cat. 187; Newby 2011, 205-9.

574 ENDYMION AND SELENE

Location/Inv.: Cliveden. Previously Rome, Villa Borghese.
Size (coffin): L: 2.37 H: 1.19
Condition: The frontal relief is preserved (restored).
Frontal relief: Selene comes in her chariot to the sleeping Endymion. For a description, see *ASR* XII 2, cat. 95.
Portrait: Selene and Endymion are carved with portrait features. It has been questioned whether they are portraits or generic heads (*ASR* XII 2, cat. 95).
Dating: The dating spans from the Antonine period to 270. For discussion, see *ASR* XII 2, cat. 95.

Bibliography: Sichtermann, *ASR* XII 2 (1992) cat. 95, pl. 86, 2; Newby 2011, 205-9.

575 (ENDYMION) AND SELENE

Location/Inv.: Frascati, Villa Aldobrandini.
Size (coffin): L: 2.08 H: 0.71 D: 0.64
Condition: The coffin is preserved but the surface is damaged.
Frontal relief: Selene comes in her chariot to the sleeping Endymion. For a description, see *ASR* XII 2, cat. 73.
Left short end: Herdsman with syrinx.
Right short end: Herdsman by a cottage.
Portrait: Selene is carved with portrait features. Endymion may have portrait features as well, but the face is too damaged to tell.
Dating: Between 200-270 (*ASR* XII 2, cat. 73).

Bibliography: Sichtermann, *ASR* XII (1992) cat. 73, pl. 75, 2; Newby 2011, 205-9.

576 ENDYMION (FIG. 80)

Location/Inv.: London, British Museum, inv. GR 1947.7-14.8.
Size (coffin): L: 2.20 H: 0.62 D: 0.64
Condition: The coffin is preserved. At some point in antiquity the breasts of the sleeping figure were diminished and a hole was made for the addition of male genitalia.
Frontal relief: The sleeping is Endymion surrounded by cupids with garlands, torches, and baskets of fruit. For a description, see *ASR* III 1, cat. 92.
Short ends: Lenos-shaped. The motif of the frontal relief continues on the short ends.
Portrait: The reclining figure (Endymion) is carved with a male portrait.
Dating: First half of the third century (*ASR* III 1, cat. 92).
Comment: It is possible that Endymion was re-carved from an Ariadne figure. For discussion, see *ASR* XII 2, cat. 54-55.

Bibliography: Robert, *ASR* III 1 (1897) cat. 92; Walker 1990, cat. 43, pl. 16; Huskinson 2002, 26; Elsner 1998, 152-53; Wrede 1981, 211, cat. 54; Newby 2011, 205-9; Prusac 2011, 119 (who dates the sarcophagus to the first century AD without further explanation).

577 ENDYMION

Location/Inv.: Ostia, Museo, depot, inv. 1304.
Condition: Fragment of a frontal relief.
Frontal relief: Selene comes in her chariot to the sleeping Endymion.
Portrait: The sleeping Endymion is carved with a portrait of a man with a beard.
Dating: 200 with Sichtermann (*ASR* XII 2, cat. 49). It has, however, also been dated to the late Gallienic or Tetrachic period based on the ornamentation of the chariot (L'Orange and Gerke 1939, 209).

Bibliography: Sichtermann, *ASR* XII 2 (1992) cat. 49, pl. 49, 2; L'Orange and Gerke 1939; Newby 2011, 205-9.

578 ENDYMION AND SELENE

Location/Inv.: Paris, Musée du Louvre, inv. MA 1335.
Size (coffin): L: 2.09 H: 0.95 D: 0.32; (lid): L: 2.09 H: 0.32
Condition: The coffin and lid are preserved.
Provenience: Found in Saint-Médard-d'Eyrans in 1804-05, together with a Ariadne sarcophagus (cat. no. 562). For a description of the context, see *ASR* II, 19, cat. 16; Zanker & Ewald 2004, 321.
Frontal relief: Selene comes in her chariot to the sleeping Endymion. For a description, see *ASR* XII 2, cat. 72.
Left short end: Shepherd with goats, sheep, a bull, and a dog.
Right short end: Selene in her chariot drawn by two bulls.
Lid: From the left, there is a scene representing the judgment of Paris, an empty inscription panel, and a scene showing garland production.
Portrait: Both Endymion and Selene are carved with blank portraits.
Dating: Between 220-260 (*ASR* XII 2, 127, cat. 72).

Bibliography: Robert, *ASR* II (1968) 19, cat. 16; Sichtermann, *ASR* XII 2 (1992) cat. 72, pl. 86, 1; Wrede 1981, 139, cat. 185; Baratte & Metzger 1985, cat. 25; Zanker & Ewald 2004, 319-21; Newby 2011, 205-9.

579 ENDYMION

Location/Inv.: Rome, Museo Nazionale Romano, inv. 113059.
Size (coffin): L: 1.10 H: 0.45
Condition: Fragment of the frontal relief.
Frontal relief: The sleeping Endymion. Part of Selene's clothing and horse are visible at his left side. For a description, see *ASR* XII 2, cat. 85.
Portrait: Endymion is carved with a portrait.
Dating: 220-230 (*ASR* VII 2, cat. 85).

Bibliography: Sichtermann, *ASR* XII 2 (1992) cat. 85, pl. 81, 3; Newby 2011, 205-9.

580 ENDYMION AND SELENE

Location/Inv.: Rome, Museo Nazionale Romano, inv. 2001492.
Size (coffin): L: 2.15 H: 0.63 D: 0.55
Condition: The coffin is preserved.
Provenience: Found in Monte S. Andrea, Cesano in 1934 in a Christian chapel, where it had been reused for a new burial.
Frontal relief: Selene comes in her chariot to the sleeping Endymion. For a description, see *ASR* XII 2, cat. 77.
Left short end: Herdsman with horse.

Right short end: Selene in her chariot drawn by two horses.
Portrait: Both Endymion and Selene are carved with portrait features. The poor condition of the relief has caused some uncertainty about their identification as portraits. For the discussion, see *ASR* XII 2, cat. 77.
Dating: First half of the third century. For discussion, see *ASR* XII 2, cat. 77.

Bibliography: Sichtermann, *ASR* XII 2 (1992) cat. 77, pl. 75, 1; *MNR* I 8, II, cat. MP 1; Newby 2011, 205-9.

581 ENDYMION

Location/Inv.: Rome, Palazzo Borghese.
Size (coffin): L: 2.17 H: 0.64 D: 0.65
Condition: The coffin is preserved.
Provenience: Rome, Near Via Labicana in the vicinity of Torre Nova. A lid was found with the coffin, but is now lost.
Frontal relief: Selene comes in her chariot to the sleeping Endymion. For a description, see *ASR* XII 2, cat. 56.
Short ends: Griffin.
Portrait: Endymion is carved with portrait features. The head of Selene is not preserved.
Dating: Around 230 (*ASR* XII 2, cat. 56).

Bibliography: Robert, *ASR* III 3 (1919) cat. 65; Sichtermann, *ASR* XII 2 (1992) cat. 56, pl. 52, 4; Wrede 1981, cat. 186; Newby 2011, 205-9.

582 ENDYMION

Location/Inv.: Rome, Palazzo Braschi.
Size (coffin): L: 2.14 H: 0.63 D: 0.57
Condition: The coffin is preserved.
Frontal relief: An Endymion-like figure is lying on the ground. A Dionysian scene is depicted at his feet, and Mars and Rhea Silvia are represented behind his head. A cupid with garlands flies above the Endymion figure. For a description, see *ASR* XII 2, cat. 102.
Short ends: Weapons.
Portrait: Endymion is carved with portrait features.
Dating: First third of the third century (*ASR* XII 2, 155, cat. 102).

Bibliography: Sichtermann, *ASR* XII 2 (1992) cat. 102, pl. 108, 3; Sichtermann 1966.

583 ENDYMION

Location/Inv.: Rome, Palazzo Corsetti.
Condition: Fragment of the frontal relief
Frontal relief: Fragment with the sleeping Endymion and Hypnos.
Portrait: Endymion is carved with a blank portrait.
Dating: Uncertain; possibly third century.

Bibliography: Sichtermann, *ASR* XII 2 (1992) cat. 90; Newby 2011, 206.

584 ENDYMION AND SELENE

Location/Inv.: Rome, Palazzo Doria, inv. 71.1497.
Size (coffin): L: 2.52 H: 1.32 D: 1.20
Condition: The coffin is preserved.
Frontal relief: Selene comes in her chariot to the sleeping Endymion. For a description, see *ASR* XII 2, cat. 93.
Left short end: Seated Oceanus with *cornucopia*. At his side is a young god.
Right short end: Herdsman with ram and dog.
Portrait: Both Selene and Endymion are carved with portrait features. It has been debated whether they are actually portraits or whether both heads are generic in style. For discussion, see *ASR* XII 2, cat. 93.
Dating: 220-260. (*ASR* XII 2, cat. 93). Fittschen dates Endymion's portrait to the late Gallienic period, Selene's to the late Antonine or early Severan period, and the style of the relief to 250 (Fittschen 1984, 151).

Bibliography: Sichtermann, *ASR* XII 2 (1992) cat. 93; Sichtermann & Koch 1975, cat. 18; Wrede 1981, cat. 188; Fittschen 1984.

585 SELENE

Location/Inv.: Rome, now lost, previously in Villa Pacca.
Condition: The frontal relief was preserved.
Provenience: Probably from Ostia.
Frontal relief: Selene comes in her chariot to the sleeping Endymion. For a description, see *ASR* XII 2, cat. 92.
Portrait: Selene is carved with portrait features. It has been debated whether it is a portrait or a generic head (Wrede 1981, cat. 19). The head of Endymion is not preserved.

Bibliography: Sichtermann, *ASR* XII 2 (1992) cat. 92; Wrede 1981, cat. 191.

586 ENDYMION AND SELENE

Location/Inv.: Woburn Abbey, Bedfordshire.
Size (coffin): L: 2.39 H: 1.17
Condition: The frontal relief is preserved.
Frontal relief: Selene comes in her chariot to the sleeping Endymion. For a description, see *ASR* XII 2, cat. 94.
Portrait: Selene is carved with portrait features whilst Endymion has a blank portrait.
Dating: 220-260 (*ASR* XII 2, cat. 94).

Bibliography: Sichtermann, *ASR* XII 2 (1992) cat. 94, pl. 87, 2; Wrede 1981, cat. 189; Newby 2011, 207.

Hercules

587 HERCULES

Location/Inv.: Florence. Now lost, but previously in Giardino Boboli.
Size (coffin): L: 2.12 H: 0.74 D: 0.74
Frontal relief: The twelve labours of Hercules. For a description, see Wrede 1981, cat. 136.
Portrait: The figure of Hercules capturing the golden hind of Artemis has portrait features.

Dating: 210-225 (Wrede 1981, cat. 136).

Bibliography: Robert, *ASR* III 1 (1897) cat. 107; Wrede 1981, 139, cat. 136.

588 HERCULES

Location/Inv.: Rome, Museo Nazionale Romano, Palazzo Altems, inv. 8642.
Size (coffin): L: 2.22 H: 0.74
Condition: The frontal relief is preserved.
Frontal relief: The twelve labours of Hercules. For a description, see *ASR* III 1, cat. 103.
Portrait: The figure of Hercules slaying the Stymphalian birds has portrait features.
Dating: 240-250.

Bibliography: Robert, *ASR* III 1 (1897) cat. 103; Wrede 1981, cat. 137.

589 HERCULES

Location/Inv.: Woburn Abbey.
Size (coffin): L: 2.43 H: 1.12
Condition: The coffin is preserved.
Provenience: Rome.
Frontal relief: Dionysian procession. Hercules is represented in a wagon. For a description, see *ASR* IV, cat. 100.
Portrait: Hercules is carved with portrait features.
Dating: 210-220 (Wrede 1981, 139, cat. 134).

Bibliography: Matz, *ASR* IV 2 (1968a) cat. 100, pl. 126; Wrede 1981, 139, cat. 134; Zanker & Ewald 2004, 162, ill. 146.

Hippolytus

590 MYTHOLOGICAL WOMAN

Location/Inv.: Rome, Museo Nazionale Romano, inv. 8644.
Size (coffin): L: 1.20 H: 0.72
Condition: Fragment of the frontal relief.
Frontal relief: A group of mythological women are represented behind the throne of Phaidra (this part is lost). A statue of Priapus is depicted between them.
Portrait: The woman on the left end of the relief has a portrait with a Severan hairstyle.
Dating: 180-200 (*MNR* I 5, cat. 82).

Bibliography: *MNR* I 5, cat. 82.

591 HIPPOLYTUS AND DIANA

Location/Inv.: Rome, Museo Nazionale Romano, inv. 1044.
Size (coffin): L: 2.12 H: 0.74 D: 0.74
Condition: A fragment of the frontal relief is preserved.
Frontal relief: The left part of the relief, representing Diana and the Venator of a mythological hunt scene, is preserved.
Portrait: Hippolytus and Diana are carved with portrait features.
Dating: 217-238 (*ASR* III 2, cat. 179).
Comment: Thought to have been produced at the same workshop as the so-called Venator sarcophagus (cat. no. 593).

Bibliography: Robert, *ASR* III 2 (1904) cat. 179, 1.

592 HIPPOLYTUS AND PHAIDRA (FIG. 53)

Location/Inv.: Rome, Museo Nazionale Romano, inv. 112444.
Size (coffin): L: 2.10 H: 0.77 D: 0.72; (lid): L: 2.16 H: 0.49 B: 0.76
Condition: The coffin and lid are preserved.
Provenience: Rome, near Via Muzio Attendolo.
Frontal relief: Two scenes. Phaidra is represented on the left scene receiving notes about Hippolytus' refusal, and Theseus is represented on the right scene receiving the message about the death of Hippolytus and the suicide of Phaidra.
Short ends: Without relief decoration.
Lid: Double-pitched roof with Attis masks at the corners.
Portrait: Phaidra and Hippolytus are carved with blank portraits.
Dating: End of the third century (Sichtermann & Koch 1975, cat. 30).

Bibliography: Sichtermann & Koch 1975, cat. 30, pl. 65; *MNR* I 8, 1, 12-7; Zanker 1999.

593 HIPPOLYTUS AND DIANA

Location/Inv.: Rome, Via delle Croce 78, in the courtyard of the palazzo that previously belonged to the Lepri family and later to the Gallo family.
Size (coffin): L: 2.027 H: 0.75 D: 0.96
Condition: The coffin is preserved.
Frontal relief: Two scenes. The left scene shows Diana and the Venator bidding farewell, and the hunt of Hippolytus is represented on the right. For a description, see *ASR* I 2, cat. 164.
Left short end: Bull and hut.
Right short end: Deer and bull.
Portrait: Both Diana and Hippolytus have portrait features. Neither of the portraits are very well preserved.
Dating: 220-230 (*ASR* I 2, cat. 164).
Comment: The dress of the Venator may have been re-worked (Koch & Sichtermann 1982, 152-53). Often referred to as the 'Venator sarcophagus Lepri-Gallo'.

Bibliography: Robert, *ASR* III 2 (1904) cat. 179; Andreae, *ASR* I 2 (1980) cat. 164, pl. 1, 1; Koch & Sichtermann 1982, 152-53; Andreae 1995, 29-30.

Hylas

594 HYLAS AND NYMPH (FIG. 79)

Location/Inv.: Rome, Palazzo Mattei, inserted in a decorative panel above a door in the portico.
Size (coffin): L: 1.81 H: 0.70

Condition: Only the frontal relief is preserved. Several breakages can be seen in the relief and it has been significantly restored. It seems that the faces of several of the figures are modern restorations.
Frontal relief: Hylas is the central figure, with a nymph on each side trying to grab hold of him. Heracles and Polyphemos have come to look for Hylas. Four winged cupids with torches are represented, and a woman is depicted between Hylas and the nymph on his left. For a description, see Wrede 1981, cat. 140.
Portrait: Hylas and the boy-nymph have portraits. The women to the left of Hylas, Heracles, and Polyphemos have modern heads.
Dating: Gallienic period (Fittschen 1984, note 47d).

Bibliography: Wrede 1981, cat. 140; Guerrini 1982, cat. 55; Fittschen 1984, note 47d; Zanker & Ewald 2004, 96-8; Birk 2011, 236-37.

Laodamia and Protesilaus

595 LAODAMIA AND PROTESILAUS (FIG. 49)

Location/Inv.: Rome, Musei Vaticani, Galleria dei Candelabri, inv. 2465.
Size (coffin): L: 2.05 H: 0.67 D: 0.70
Provenience: Via Appia Nuova. Probably in an underground chamber (Dresken-Weiland 2003, cat. A 59).
Frontal relief: Scenes from Troy and the death of Protesilaus, a temple door, and the two protagonists. The last scene represents the pain of Laodamia.
Left short end: Farewell scene.
Right short end: Figures from Hades: Sisyphus, Ixion, and Tantalus.
Portrait: Protesilaus and Laodamia are carved with blank portraits.
Dating: Around 170 (Zanker and Ewald 2004, 377).

Bibliography: Robert, *ASR* III 3 (1919) 498-500; Sichtermann & Koch 1975, cat. 69; Zanker & Ewald 2004, 101-2, 375-77; Dresken-Weiland 2003, cat. A 59; Newby 2011, 197-99.

Liber and Venus

596 LIBER AND VENUS

Location/Inv.: Rome, Musei Vaticani, Cortile del Belvedere, inv. 973.
Size (coffin): L: 2.52 H: 1.32
Condition: The frontal relief is preserved.
Provenience: Rome, Vigna Moiraga outside Porta Latina.
Frontal relief: Depiction of a harbour and the religious and everyday activities going on there. Two oversized characters dominate the central part of the relief. The figures are probably Liber and Venus. For a description, see Amelung 1908 II 1, 49-63.
Portrait: Both the so-called Liber and Venus are carved with blank portraits.
Dating: 250-260 (*ASR* I 4, cat. 256).
Comment: The relief is unfinished in several places.

Bibliography: Amedick, *ASR* I 4 (1991) cat. 256 pl. 57; Amelung 1908 II1, 49-63; Fasciato 1947, 74-8; Andreae 1963, 153-58.

597 RECLINING MAN (LIBER?)

Location/Inv.: Rome, Musei Vaticani, Museo Chiaramonti/Museo Gregoriano Etrusco, Antiquarium, inv. 1501.
Size (coffin): L: 1.19 H: 0.38 D: 0.37
Condition: The coffin is preserved.
Provenience: Rome, Vatican, Necropoli della Fonte della Galera, tomb 2.
Frontal relief: A harbour scene with cupids in boats. A person is reclining with Venus, who receives an offering from a figure (Fortuna?).
Short ends: Boat.
Portrait: The reclining man is carved with a blank portrait.
Dating: Around 300 (Dresken-Weiland 2003, cat. A 114).
Comment: Isola dei Beati (Liverani & Spinola 2006, fig. 8).

Bibliography: Andreae et al. 1995, pl. 886; Liverani & Spinola 2006; 2010, 154, fig 9; Dresken-Weiland 2003, cat. A 114; Liverani & Spinola 2010, 152, fig. 9.

Mars and Rhea Silvia

598 MARS AND RHEA SILVIA

Location/Inv.: Rome, Musei Vaticani, Museo Gregoriano profano, inv. 9558.
Size (coffin): L: 2.25 H: 0.82
Condition: The frontal relief is preserved.
Frontal relief: Two scenes. Mars is represented on the left scene visiting the sleeping Rhea Silvia, and Selene is represented on the right scene visiting the sleeping Endymion. For a description, see *ASR* XII 2, cat. 99.
Portrait: Both Mars and Rhea Silvia have portrait features.
Dating: Between 210 and the middle of the third century (*ASR* XII 2, 151, cat. 99).

Bibliography: Robert, *ASR* III 1 (1897) cat. 88; *ASR* III 2 (1904) cat. 191; Sichtermann, *ASR* XII 2 (1992) cat. 99, pl. 62, 3; Wrede 1981, cat. 200; Fittschen 1984, note 47a; Newby 2011, 209-13.

599 MARS

Location/Inv.: Rome, Palazzo Mattei, built into the east facade of the courtyard.
Size (coffin): L: 2.40 H: 0.95
Condition: The frontal relief is preserved but has been significantly restored.

Frontal relief: Mars visiting the sleeping Rhea Silvia. For a description, see Wrede 1981, cat. 201.
Portrait: Mars is carved with a portrait.
Dating: 220-230 (Wrede 1981, cat. 201).

Bibliography: Robert, *ASR* III 2 (1904), cat. 190; Wrede 1981, cat. 201; Guerrini 1982, 60.

600 MARS AND RHEA SILVIA (FIG. 22)

Location/Inv.: Rome, Palazzo Mattei. Built into the staircase. The short ends are at Musei Vaticani, Cortile del Belvedere.
Size (coffin): L: 2.36 H: 1.28 D: 1.06
Condition: The frontal relief and the short ends are preserved separately.
Frontal relief: Mars visiting the sleeping Rhea Silvia. For a description, see Wrede 1981, cat. 202.
Left short end: Rhea Silvia is led to the Tiber.
Right short end: Romulus, Remus, and the she-wolf. Two herdsmen are depicted beside them.
Portrait: Mars and Rhea Silvia are carved with portrait features.
Dating: Around 250 (Wrede 1981). The portrait of Rhea Silvia bears similarities to the portrait of Julia Domna. The portrait of Mars is dated to 240-250 (Fittschen 1984, 149). This means that there is a gap of 30 years between the two portraits.

Bibliography: Robert, *ASR* III 2 (19604) cat. 188; Sichtermann & Koch 1975, cat. 71; Wrede 1981, cat. 202; Guerrini 1982, cat. 61; Fittschen 1984, 149; Newby 2011, 210-3.

Meleager

601 MELEAGER

Location/Inv.: Cava dei Tirreni, Abbazia della Trinità.
Size (coffin): L: 2.23 H: 0.90 D: 1.00
Condition: The coffin is preserved.
Frontal relief: The hunting of the Calydonian boar.
Short ends: Weapons.
Portrait: Meleager is carved with portrait features.
Dating: Around 300 (*ASR* XII 6, cat. 152).

Bibliography: Koch, *ASR* XII 6 (1975) cat. 152, pl. 124, 3.

602 MELEAGER

Location/Inv.: Firenze, Galleria degli Uffizi, inv. 93.
Size (coffin): L: 1.50 H: 0.42 D: 0.40
Condition: The coffin is preserved.
Frontal relief: The hunting of the Calydonian boar. For a description, see *ASR* XII 6, cat. 26.
Left short end: Two huntsmen.
Right short end: Huntsman with a dog. The relief is unfinished.
Portrait: Meleager is carved with portrait features.
Dating: 220-230 (*ASR* XII 6, cat. 26).

Bibliography: Robert, *ASR* III 2 (1904) cat. 246; Sichtermann, *ASR* XII 2 (1992) cat. 26; Huskinson 1996, cat. 2.13; Koch, *ASR* XII 6 (1975) cat. 26, pl. 39, 1.

603 MELEAGER

Location/Inv.: Kassel, Staatliche Kunstsammlungen, inv. Sk 118.
Size (coffin): L: 1.90 H: 0.93
Condition: A fragment of the frontal relief is preserved.
Frontal relief: Hunter (probably from a Meleager relief). For a description, see *ASR* XII6, cat. 30.
Portrait: The hunter is carved with a male portrait.
Dating: 270-280, based on the portrait. For discussion, see *ASR* XII 6, cat. 30.
Comment: The fragment with the portrait figure was once thought to belong with fragments from a Meleager hunt relief. It has today been acknowledged that they come from two different reliefs.

Bibliography: Koch, *ASR* XII 6 (1975) cat. 30, pl. 44, 2; Fittschen 1975; Koch & Sichtermann 1982, 253; Bol 1983, cat. 94.

604 MELEAGER AND ATALANTE (FIG. 54)

Location/Inv.: Wilton House, Wiltshire.
Size (coffin): L: 2.08 H: 0.64 D: 0.58
Condition: The coffin is preserved.
Provenience: Rome, Via Appia in a columbarium originally belonging to one of Livia's freed men (Dresken-Weiland 2003, cat. A 65). Found together with a *clipeus* with a couple, today in Wilton House, see cat. no. 460.
Frontal relief: Divided into five panels. The second and fourth panels are strigillated. One of the Dioscuroi is represented on the first and fifth panels. Three figures are depicted on the central panel: Meleager sacrificing at an altar, Atalante, and a third huntsman. All of the figures are placed on plinths.
Short ends: Weapons.
Portrait: Meleager and Atalante are carved with blank portraits.
Dating: Around the middle of the third century (*ASR* XII 6, cat. 147).

Bibliography: Koch, *ASR* XII 6 (1975) cat. 147, pl. 120, 4.

605 MELEAGER AND VIRTUS/ATALANTE

Location/Inv.: Würzburg, Martin von Wagner-Museum, inv. Z 756.
Size (coffin): L: 1.48 H: 0.55 D: 0.59
Condition: The coffin is preserved.
Frontal relief: The hunting of the Calydonian boar. For a description, see *ASR* XII 6, cat. 72.
Short ends: *Lenos*-shaped. The motif of the frontal relief continues on the short ends.
Portrait: Meleager has portrait features and Atalante has a blank portrait.
Dating: The end of the third century (*ASR* XII 6, cat. 72).
Comment: Child sarcophagus.

Bibliography: Koch, *ASR* XII 6 (1975) cat. 72, pl. 64, 1; Simon 1970; Andreae 1984, 115.

Pelops

606 PELOPS AND HIPPODAMIA
Location/Inv.: Rome, Villa Albani, inv. 254.
Size (coffin): L: 2.17 H: 0.79 D: 0.91
Condition: The coffin is preserved.
Frontal relief: Oinomaus and Pelops are represented together on the left end of the relief. The next scene depicts the race between the two men, and the scene on the far right shows the wedding of Pelops and Hipodameia.
Short ends: Three huntsmen or soldiers.
Portrait: The figures of Pelops racing on the *dextrarum iunctio* scene have portrait features, whilst Hippodamia has a blank portrait.
Dating: 250 (Bol 1998, 269).

Bibliography: Robert, *ASR* III 3 (1919) cat. 325; Bol 1998, cat. 746, pl. 108.

Proserpina

607 PROSERPINA
Location/Inv.: Messina, Museo Nazionale, inv. A 24.
Size (coffin): L: 2.08 H: 0.73
Condition: The coffin is preserved.
Frontal relief: Pluto surprises Proserpina while she is picking flowers. For a description, see *ASR* III 3, cat. 399.
Short ends: Weapons.
Portrait: Proserpina is carved with a portrait. The hairstyle is Severan (Wrede 1981, cat. 266).

Bibliography: Robert, *ASR* III 3 (1919) cat. 399; Tusa 1957, 81-3; Wrede 1981, cat. 266.

608 PROSERPINA (FIG. 50)
Location/Inv.: Rome, Musei Capitolini, galleria 56, inv. 249. (Fig. 53)
Size (coffin): L: 2.18 H: 0.62
Condition: The coffin is preserved.
Frontal relief: Pluto takes Proserpina a way in his wagon. A scene with the flowe picking Peoserpina (with a generic face) is shown on the left side of the wagon scene. For description, see Wrede 1981, cat. 269.
Left short end: Two women with a *situla*.
Right short end: A veiled woman, Hermes, and Hades/Dies Pater.
Portrait: Proserpina is carved with a portrait.
Dating: 230 (Wrede 1981, cat. 269).

Bibliography: Robert, *ASR* III 3 (1919) cat. 392; Sichtermann & Koch 1975, 57-8, cat. 61; Wrede 1981, cat. 269; Koch & Sichtermann 1982, 177; Zanker & Ewald 2004, 92-4, 370-72.

609 PROSERPINA (FIG. 51)
Location/Inv.: Rome, Museo Nazionale Romano, inv. 255953.
Size (coffin): L: 2.19 H: 0.61
Condition: The frontal relief is preserved.
Frontal relief: The relief shows Proserpina in a wagon driven by snake, and the abduction of Proserpina by Pluto.
Portrait: Proserpina in the wagon is carved with a portrait.
Dating: 150-160 (*MNR* I 8, I, cat. II, 20).

Bibliography: *MNR* I 8, I, cat. II, 20.

610 PROSERPINA AND PLUTO
Location/Inv.: Rome, Palazzo Giustiniani.
Size (coffin): L: 2.20 H: 0.65
Condition: The frontal relief is preserved.
Frontal relief: Pluto surprises Proserpina while she is picking flowers and takes her away in his wagon. For a description, see Wrede 1981, cat. 265.
Portrait: The flower picking Proserpina has a blank portrait; Pluto is carved with male portrait features.
Dating: Around 240 (Wrede 1981, cat. 265).

Bibliography: Robert, *ASR* III 3 (1919) cat. 390, pl. 125, 1; Wrede 1981, cat. 265.

611 PROSERPINA
Location/Inv.: Rome, Villa Gentili, today lost.
Condition: Fragment of the frontal relief.
Frontal relief: Pluto abducts Proserpina. For a description, see Wrede 1981, cat. 267.
Portrait: Proserpina is carved with a portrait. The hairstyle is characteristic of the late Severan period (Wrede 1981, cat. 267).
Dating: 210-230 (Wrede 1981, cat. 267).

Bibliography: Robert, *ASR* III 3 (1919) cat. 380; Koch 1976, 110, pl. 24; Wrede 1981, cat. 267.

Theseus and Ariadne

612 THESEUS AND ARIADNE (FIG. 12)
Location/Inv.: Cliveden, Buckinghamshire, in the garden.
Size (coffin): L: 2.50 H: 1.25 D: 1.10
Condition: The coffin is preserved. The figures between Theseus and Ariadne at the ship are modern.
Provenience: Found in Rome, Via Salaria, Necropoli delle Fidene Romana, in 1883 (Notizie degli Scavi 1883, 372-73).
Frontal relief: On the left side of the relief Theseus bids Aigeus farewell; next follows a scene with Theseus in his ship; and on the right end of the relief, Theseus is depicted abandoning the sleeping Ariadne. For a description, see Zanker & Ewald 2004, 378-81.
Portrait: Theseus is portrayed three times as the same young man, and Ariadne has the portrait features of an elderly

woman. They probably represent the mother and the son mentioned in the inscription.
Left short end: Two men with sword, spear and shield.
Right short end: A veiled woman and two men with spears.
Reverse: Divided into three levels: the lower leve is smooth and polished, the next is only some 10 cm high and consists of a band carved into the marble with rough strokes, and the upper level is roughly carved.
Inscription: D M / ARTEMIDORI / AVG LIB ADLECTO / A MEMORIA / Q V ANN XVII / D XVII VALERIA / PHILO.. NE / FILIO DVL/CISSIMO (*CIL* XV 4062). It has been questioned whether the lid and coffin belong together. See Zanker & Ewald 2004, 45-8.
Dating: 240 (Zanker & Ewald 2004, 45, 381).

Bibliography: Robert, *ASR* III 3 (1919) cat. 430; Blome 1992; Wrede 1981, cat. 55; Zanker & Ewald 2004, 45-8, 378-81.

Venus

613 VENUS

Location/Inv.: Rome, Galleria Borghese LXXXI.
Size (coffin): L: 1.40 H: 0.67
Condition: The central part of the frontal relief is preserved.
Frontal relief: The birth of Venus. Venus is seen in a shell surrounded by sea-*thiasoi*. For a description, see *ASR* V 1, cat. 92.
Portrait: Venus is carved with a female portrait.
Dating: Beginning of the third century (*ASR* V 1, cat. 92; Wrede 1981, cat. 313).
Comment: ASR V 1, cat. 95 is the same type of sarcophagus and may have a portrait as well.

Bibliography: Rumpf, *ASR* V 1 (1939) cat.92; Jung 1978, 337-38; Wrede 1981, cat. 313; Fittschen 1984, 132; Zanker & Ewald 2004, fig. 110.

614 VENUS

Location/Inv.: Zürich, Rehalp Cemetery, once Rome, Villa Pacca.
Size (coffin): L: 2.20 H: 0.85
Condition: The coffin is preserved.
Frontal relief: Five niches. Venus is represented in the central niche. Seasonal personifications are represented in the other niches.
Portrait: Venus is carved with the portrait of a young woman or girl. The portrait features and hairstyle resemble those of Faustina the Younger.
Dating: Last part of the fourth century (Wrede 1981, cat. 312).

Bibliography: Wrede 1981, cat. 312, *RM* 84, 1977, pl. 157, 2.

Children's Life Course

615 LIFE COURSE: WOMAN, LEARNED MEN, AND CHILD (FIG. 14)

Location/Inv.: Paris, Musée du Louvre, inv. MA 659.
Size (coffin): L: 1.49 H: 0.48 D: 0.18-23
Condition: The coffin is preserved.
Frontal relief: Four scenes from a child's life. First a woman is shown nursing a child while a learned man watches; in the next scene, the man holds the child. The third scene depicts a child driving a wagon drawn by a ram, and the final one is a teaching scene with a boy and a philosopher.
Short ends: Griffin.
Portrait: The woman and the man in the nursing scene, the man with the child, the boy in the ram-wagon, and the man and the child on the teaching scene all show portrait features.
Inscription: M CORNELIO M F PAL STATIO .... FECER
Dating: Around 150 (*ASR* I 4, cat. 114).
Comment: Child sarcophagus.

Bibliography: Amedick, *ASR* I 4 (1991) cat. 114, pl. 53, 4; Baratte & Metzger 1985, cat. 3; Dimas 1998, 67, cat. 386.

616 LIFE COURSE: BOY IN A WAGON, PHILOSOPHER, AND RECLINING BOY (FIG. 95)

Location/Inv.: Paris, Musée du Louvre, inv. Ma 1520.
Size (coffin): L: 1.10 H: 0.33 D: 0.32
Condition: The coffin is preserved.
Frontal relief: A seated woman with a scroll is represented on the left end of the relief. Next follows a boy driving a ram-drawn wagon, a young man enthroned as a philosopher surrounded by Muses, and finally a young man reclining on a bed. For a description, see *ASR* I 4, cat. 112.
Left short end: Two boys by a tree.
Right short end: Two naked boys, one with a basket and one with a *tibiae.*
Portrait: The boy-philosopher and the reclining boy both have portrait features. It is possible that the girl/woman seated in the chair on the far left has a portrait as well.
Dating: There is great uncertainty about the dating of this sarcophagus. The dates proposed range from 150 to 280. For discussion, see Fittschen 1972, 491.
Comment: The sarcophagus may come from a "local" workshop (Fittschen 1972, 491). Traces of red and blue paint are preserved. Child sarcophagus.

Bibliography: Wegner, *ASR* V 3 (1966) cat. 77; Amedick, *ASR* I 4 (1991) cat. 112; Fittschen 1972, 491; Baratte & Metzger 1985, cat. 4; Ewald 1999, cat. D 7.

617 LIFE COURSE: WOMAN WITH A CHILD

Location/Inv.: Rome, Catacombe di Pretestato, Museo, inv. 105.
Size (coffin): L: 0.13 H: 0.28
Condition: A fragment is preserved, probably from a *lenos.*
Provenience: Rome, Catecombe di Pretestato?
Left short end: Woman with a child.
Portrait: The woman is carved with a portrait.
Dating: End of the third century (*ASR* I 4, cat. 140).

Bibliography: Amedick, *ASR* I 4 (1991) cat. 140, pl. 61, 1.

618 LIFE COURSE: INFANT

Location/Inv.: Rome, Catacombe di S. Sebastiano.
Condition: A fragment of the frontal relief is preserved.
Frontal relief: Woman breastfeeding a child. A herdsman stands behind them.
Portrait: The baby is carved with a blank portrait.
Dating: Tetrarchic period (*ASR* I 4, cat. 165).
Comment: Child sarcophagus.

Bibliography: Amedick, *ASR* I 4 (1999) cat. 165, pl. 61, 3; Huskinson 1996, cat. A 8.

619 LIFE COURSE: BOY DRIVING A WAGON

Location/Inv.: Rome, Musei Vaticani, Museo Chiaramonti, inv. 1632.
Size (coffin): L: 0.53 H: 0.27
Condition: A fragment of a frontal relief is preserved.

Frontal relief: A child's first bath is represented on the left scene, and a child driving a ram-drawn chariot is shown on the right.
Portrait: The child in the ram-drawn wagon has a blank portrait.
Dating: Last quarter of the third century (*ASR* I 4, cat. 273).
Comment: Child sarcophagus.

Bibliography: Amedick, *ASR* I 4 (1991) cat. 273, pl. 64, 1.

620 LIFE COURSE: RECLINING BOY (FIG. 96)

Location/Inv.: Rome, Museo Nazionale Romano, inv. 535.
Size (coffin): L: 0.97 H: 0.34 D: 0.31
Condition: The coffin and lid are well preserved.
Provenience: Via Latina in the tomb of the Fortunati. Having been in the possession of P. E. Visconti, it was handed over to "La Sapienza" (*ASR* I 4, cat. 177; Fittschen 172, 492).
Frontal relief: The deceased with a female body and a boy's portrait (?) is reclining on a bed surrounded by Muses. A dead naked boy – probably a representation of the lifeless body of the deceased – is represented beneath the bed. A lion head is carved on either end of the frontal relief. Romulus and Remus are represented with the she-wolf beneath the lion head on the left.
Left short end: Lenos-shaped. Two women, one seated and one standing, perhaps part of a biographical cycle.
Right short end: Lenos-shaped. A boy is being taught by a seated man. The boy stands with a book scroll, and the elderly man is seated.
Reverse: Four dancing cupids with wings and torches are depicted between two *gorgoneia*. The scene is carved in low relief.
Lid: Carved with panels adorned with *gorgoneia* and reclining naked figures. The central inscription panel is blank.
Portrait: The reclining figure has a portrait of a boy.
Dating: 210-220 (*ASR* I 4, cat. 177; Fittschen 1972, 492; Wrede 1981, cat. 241) or 175-300 (*ASR* V 3, cat. 126).
Comment: Child sarcophagus.

Bibliography: Wegner, *ASR* V 3 (1966) cat. 126; Amedick, *ASR* I 4 (1991) cat. 177, pl. 73, 2; *MNR* I 10, 1, cat. 28; Fittschen 1972, 492; Wrede 1981, cat. 241; Amedick 1993, 147; Dimas 1998, cat. 391.

621 LIFE COURSE: FAMILY RIDING IN A WAGON (FIG. 1)

Location/Inv.: Rome, Museo Nazionale Romano, inv. 65199.
Size (coffin): L: 1.06 H: 0.41 D: 0.39
Condition: The coffin and the lid are preserved.
Provenience: Found in Rome in 1723.
Frontal relief: Two families are riding in wagons drawn by horses. On the first scene the man and the woman (both with portrait features) are shown with a newborn child, and in the next wagon scene the child has grown older. It is probably the same family in two different periods of the life of the child. Between the two wagons, a small boy is learning how to walk by using a toy wagon, and an older boy, now capable of working, plays with a goose.
Short ends: No decoration.
Lid: Palmettos.
Portrait: The man and the woman in the wagons show portrait features, and the faces of the two children playing on the ground should probably be read as portrait as well.
Dating: Around 100 (*ASR* I 4, cat. 190).
Comment: Child sarcophagus

Bibliography: Amedick *ASR* I 4 (1991) cat. 190; Dimas 1998, cat. 405.

622 LIFE COURSE: RECLINING BOY

Location/Inv.: Rome, Museo Torlonia, inv. 414.
Size (coffin): L: 1.57 H: 0.36
Condition: The frontal relief is preserved.
Provenience: Rome, near Via Portuensis.
Frontal relief: Four scenes from a child's life. From the left are shown: a child having his first bath; next an educational scene; a mourning scene with the deceased laid out on a bed (*conclamatio*); and finally an *apotheosis*.
Portrait: The man on the *kline* has portrait features (the figure was originally intended for a boy). Some consider it to be a modern portrait carved from an antique *bosse* (*ASR* I 4, cat. 198). Other see the portrait as ancient (Huskinson 1996, 1.31). The surface of the head is much better preserved than the surface of the surrounding figures, suggesting that it may be modern. The same goes for the surface of the head of the woman beside the *kline*, and the philosopher in the teaching scene.
Dating: Around 200 (*ASR* I 4, cat. 198).
Comment: Child sarcophagus.

Bibliography: Amedick, *ASR* I 4 (1991) cat. 198, pl. 54, 3; Dimas 1998, 48-50, cat. 392.

623 LIFE COURSE: RECLINING BOY

Location/Inv.: Stuttgart, Württembergisches Landesmuseum, inv. Arch 6318.
Size (coffin): L: 1.05 H: 0.32 D: 0.41
Condition: The coffin and the lid are preserved.
Frontal relief: A reclining figure is surrounded by Muses and Hermes. Two lion heads flank the scene. For a description, see *ASR* I 4, cat. 248.
Left short end: Lenos-shaped. An education scene with a seated man and a boy with a scroll, behind which is a statue base with a bust of Athena (?).
Right short end: A seated woman and two women giving a child a bath.
Reverse: Smooth. With two holes for staples.
Lid: A reclining figure with a cupid leaning against his left shoulder. The head of the reclining figure is lost.
Portrait: The reclining figure on the relief has the portrait features of a boy.
Dating: 220 (*ASR* I 4, cat. 248).
Comment: Child sarcophagus.

Bibliography: Amedick, *ASR* I 4 (1991) cat. 248, pl. 73, 1.

Commanders (battle)

624 BUST OF A MAN AS COMMANDER

Location/Inv.: Rome, Museo Nazionale Romano, inv. 39400.
Size (coffin): L: 1.86 H: 0.48 D: 0.58
Condition: The coffin and lid are preserved.
Frontal relief: Battle scenes.
Left short end: Pegasus and weapons.
Right short end: Warrior killing a barbarian man.
Lid: Wreath carried by *victoriae* and trophies.
Portrait: The wreath on the lid shows a portrait of a bearded man in a cuirass.
Dating: 150-170 (*MNR* I 8, I, cat. VI, 7).

Bibliography: *MNR* I 8, I, cat. VI, 7.

625 COMMANDER

Location/Inv.: Rome, Museo Nazionale Romano, Palazzo Altems, inv. 8574. From the Ludovisi collection.
Size (coffin): L: 2.73 H: 1.53 D: 1.37
Condition: The coffin and the lid are preserved.
Provenience: Rome, near Porta S. Lorenzo in 1621.
Frontal relief: Battle scene in several levels. The central horseman makes a gesture with his right hand that indicates victory. Soldiers are fighting around him against barbarians. Some of the barbarians have fallen already but others are still fighting. For a description, see Künzl 2010.
Short ends: Battle scene.
Lid: See cat. no. 248.
Portrait: The central horseman has portrait features.
Dating: 235 (Rodenwaldt 1936, 90); around 251 (Heintze 1957-58, 91); around 260 (Fittschen 1979, 582).
Comment: Also called the Great Ludovisi battle sarcophagus.

Bibliography: Rodenwaldt 1936, 90-2; Helbig III 4, 276-83, no. 2354; Andreae 1956, 16 A II nr. 17, 85-6; Heintze 1957, 69-91; Andreae 1968; 1968/69, 153-64; Koch & Sichtermann 1982, 92; Fittschen 1979, 581-84; Fittschen 1984, 149; Zanker & Ewald 2004, 230; Künzl 2010 (an extensive study of the history, preservation and meaning of the sarcophagus).

626 COMMANDERS, WOMAN, GIRL (?), AND *DEXTRARUM IUNCTIO* (FIG. 23)

Location/Inv.: Rome, Museo Nazionale Romano, Palazzo Massimo, inv. 112327.
Size (coffin): L: 2.39 H: 1.50 D: 1.16 (lid): L: 2.39 H: 37 D: 1.16
Condition: The coffin and lid are preserved.
Provenience: Rome, found in 1931 at Via delle Cave di Pietralata, località Portonaccio.
Frontal relief: Battle scene with a victorious commander on horseback in the centre.
Lid: A mother seated while a small child reaching for a nurse are represented on the left end of the lid. Next follows a scene showing a young girl being taught by a Muse (?). In the centre is a *dextrarum iunctio* scene, and finally there is a representation of a commander showing *clementia.*
Left short end: Military scene with soldiers, captives and ships in a harbour.
Right short end: Clementia scene.
Portrait: The commander on the frontal relief has a blank portrait. On the lid, the mother, the couple in the marital scene, and the commander all have blank portraits. The girl on the teaching scene may have portrait features, though they are somewhat generic. Her hairstyle (*Melonenfrisur*) is used for both generic figures and representation of young girls.
Dating: Late Antonine period (*ASR* I 4, cat. 179).

Bibliography: Amedick, *ASR* I 4 (1991) cat. 179; Andreae 1956, cat. A II 13; Koch & Sichtermann 1982, 92, 255, 260; *MNR* I 8, 1, cat. IV, 4; Huskinson 1999, 15-7; Dowling 2009, 265-66; Künzl 2011, 49-50.

627 *CLIPEUS* PORTRAIT OF A MAN

Location/Inv.: Rome, Palazzo Farnese, used in the "Trofeo Farnese".
Condition: Fragment of a frontal relief.
Frontal relief: A *clipeus* portrait of a bearded man with a wreath on his head and a sword around his chest is carried by two captives. The man himself is bare-chested and wears a military cloak. Victoria stands on the left side of the *clipeus*, and next to her is a heroic figure with a military cloak. The right side is lost.
Portrait: The bust is carved with a portrait of a bearded man.

Bibliography: Buranelli 2010 (the fragment is illustrated on p. 13).

Profession (?)

628 SAILOR AND MAN IN A CARRIAGE

Location/Inv.: Rome, Galleria Colonna (Palazzo) in the garden.
Frontal relief: A ship with cargo, sail, and a captain is represented on the left part of the relief. The ship is entering a harbour. A man riding a horse-drawn carriage is shown on the right part of the relief, and a personification of a road is depicted beneath him. For a description, see *ASR* I 4, cat. 204.
Left short end: Lighthouse.
Right short end: Without relief decoration.
Portrait: The man in the ship and the man driving the horse-drawn carriage have blank portraits.
Dating: 250-260 (*ASR* I 4, cat. 204).

Bibliography: Amedick, *ASR* I 4 (1991) 58-9, cat. 204, pl. 51, 1.

629 CHARIOTEER

Location/Inv.: Rome, Villa Albani, inv. 493.
Size (coffin): H: 1.32 D: 0.95
Condition: A fragment, probably the left short end of a *lenos*-shaped sarcophagus, is preserved.
Left short end: *Lenos*-shaped. A *quadriga* is shown with a man who seems too large for the chariot. For a description, see Bol 1998, cat. 944, 465-68.
Portrait: The man in the *quadriga* has portrait features.
Dating: Around 240 (Bol 1998, cat. 944).
Comment: The motif is unique on sarcophagi, and is mostly known from mosaics (Bol 1998, cat. 944).

Bibliography: Schauenburg, *ASR* V 2, 3 (1995) cat. 108; Bol 1998, cat. 944, 465-68.

Rituals (*dextrarum iunctio*, sacrifice, and prayer)

Bucolic

630 RITUAL: *DEXTRARUM IUNCTIO*
Location/Inv.: Rome, Campo Santo Teutonico (formerly in Villa Ada).
Size (coffin): L: 1.94 H: 0.58
Condition: Fragment of the frontal relief.
Frontal relief: Divided into five panels. The second and fourth panels are strigillated. The head of a ram is preserved on the first panel, and a ram-bearer is represented on the fifth panel. The central panel depicts a *dextrarum iunctio* scene.
Portrait: Both the man and the woman on the marital scene have blank portraits.
Dating: 180-190 (*ASR* I 3, cat. 71).

Bibliography: Reinsberg, *ASR* I 3 (2006) cat. 71, pl. 128, 6.

631 RITUAL: PRAYING GIRL
Location/Inv.: Rome, Museo Nazionale Romano, inv. 79985.
Size (coffin): L: 1.28 H: 0.35 D: 0.47 (lid): L: 1.28 H: 0.23 D: 0.47
Condition: The coffin and lid are preserved.
Provenience: Rome, found in the Cimitero di S. Ciriaco near Mezzocammino on Via Ostiense in 1916 (Dresken-Weiland 2003, cat. A 88).
Frontal relief: The central motif is an *Orans* in front of a *parapetasma* held by two flying cupids. The scene is framed by ram-bearers. For a description, see *MNR* I 8, 1, cat. II, 19.
Short ends: Without relief decoration.
Reverse: Without relief decoration.
Lid: Dolphins and an inscription panel.
Portrait: The *Orans* is carved with the portrait features of a girl.
Inscription: HIC OPTATA SITA EST QVAM / TIRTIA RAPVIT AESTAS / LINGVA MANV NVNQVAM / DVLCIOR VLLA FVIT / IN PACE
Dating: Around 320 (*MNR* I 8, 1, cat. II, 19).
Comment: The sex of the portrait is difficult to determine, but the dress is female and the inscription commemorates a girl called Optata, who was three years old. Child sarcophagus.

Bibliography: *MNR* I 8, 1, cat. II, 19; *Rep* I, cat. 769; Huskinson 1996, cat. 70; Rawson 2003, 291-92; Dresken-Weiland 2003, cat. A 88; Backe-Dahmen 2006.

632 RITUAL: *DEXTRARUM IUNCTIO*
Location/Inv.: Vescovio, S. Salvatoe.
Condition: Fragment of the frontal relief.
Frontal relief: Divided into five panels. The second and fourth panels are strigillated (in two levels). The first panel is lost. A ram-bearer is represented on the fifth panel. A *dextrarum iunctio* scene appears on the central panel.
Portrait: Both the man and the woman in the marital scene have portraits.
Dating: 320-330 (*ASR* I 3, cat. 164).

Bibliography: Reinsberg, *ASR* I 3 (2006) cat. 164, pl. 116, 5.

Cupids

633 RITUAL: *DEXTRARUM IUNCTIO* (FIG. 28)
Location/Inv.: Rome, S. Cecilia in Trastevere, Museo.
Size (coffin): L: 0.50 /1.27 H: 0.48/0.48
Condition: Fragments of the frontal relief.
Frontal relief: Divided into five panels. The first and second panels are lost. The fourth panel is strigillated. A sleeping cupid is represented on the fifth panel. The central panel frames a *dextrarum iunctio* scene. A small child/cupid stands between the two figures and holds on to the folds of the woman's clothes.

Portrait: The female figure has a blank portrait. The head of the man is lost.
Dating: 220-240 (*ASR* I 3, cat. 110).
Bibliography: Reinsberg, *ASR* I 3 (2006) cat. 110, pl. 117, 4.

Portrait: Both the man and the woman on the central panel have portraits.
Dating: Around 280 (*ASR* I 3, cat. 56).
Comment: The woman's dress has been re-carved around the feet, for unknown reasons. It has also been suggested that the portraits are secondary (*ASR* I 3, 56).
Bibliography: Reinsberg, *ASR* I 3 (2006) cat. 56.

Death Door

634 RITUAL: WOMAN AND MAN MAKING A SACRIFICE (FIG. 33)

Location/Inv.: St. Petersburg, Hermitage, inv. Gr-9630.
Size (coffin): L: 2.09 H: 0.97
Frontal relief: Divided into three panels. A half-open death door with a person looking through it is represented on the central panel. A woman making a sacrifice appears on the first panel, and the third panel shows a man in a cuirass, also sacrificing. A *parapetasma* is suspended behind both of them. For a description, see *ASR* I 3, cat. 138.
Portrait: Both the man and the woman on the first and third panels have blank portraits.
Dating: 220-230 (*ASR* I 3, cat. 138).
Bibliography: Reinsberg, *ASR* I 3 (2006) cat. 138, pl. 31, 2; Saverkina 1979, cat. 19.

Decorative Scheme

635 RITUAL: *DEXTRARUM IUNCTIO*

Location/Inv.: London, art market, Sotheby's London 3.12.1991, 108 Nr. 188.
Size (coffin): L: 2.18 H: 0.99
Condition: The frontal relief is preserved.
Frontal relief: Divided into five panels. The second and fourth are strigillated. A column is depicted on the first and fifth panels. The central panel shows a couple making the *dextrarum iunctio* gesture. The woman is veiled and the man holds a scroll. For a description, see *ASR* I 3, cat. 23.
Portrait: Both the man and the woman have portraits.
Dating: 280-290 (*ASR* I 3, cat. 23).
Bibliography: Reinsberg, *ASR* I 3 (2006) 23, pl. 117, 6.

636 RITUAL: *DEXTRARUM IUNCTIO*

Location/Inv.: Pisa, Camposanto, C 11 EST.
Size (coffin): L: 2.09 H: 0.86 D: 0.89
Condition: The coffin is preserved.
Frontal relief: Divided into five panels. The second and fourth are strigillated. A column is depicted on the first and fifth panels. The central panel shows a couple making the *dextrarum iunctio* gesture.

Eros and Psyche

637 RITUAL: WOMAN AND MAN MAKING A SACRIFICE

Location/Inv.: Pisa, Camposanto, 6 A INT.
Size (coffin): L: 1.92 H: 0.52 D: 0.52
Condition: The coffin is preserved.
Frontal relief: Divided into five panels. The second and fourth panels are strigillated. A woman is represented on the first panel and a man making a sacrifice appears on the fifth panel. The central panel depicts Amor and Psyche.
Short ends: Griffin.
Portrait: Both the man and the woman have portraits (the head of the woman may be a blank portrait).
Dating: 190-200 (*ASR* I 3, cat. 51).
Bibliography: Reinsberg, *ASR* I 3 (2006) cat. 51, pl. 56, 4.

Learned Sphere

638 RITUAL: *DEXTRARUM IUNCTIO*

Location/Inv.: Copenhagen, Ny Carlsberg Glyptotek, inv. 1300.
Size (coffin): L: 1.68 H: 0.98
Condition: Part of the frontal relief is preserved.
Frontal relief: Two niches are flanked by columns. A couple making the *dextrarum iunctio* gesture are shown in the left niche, and a Greek philosopher is represented in the right niche. A *parapetasma* is suspended behind the figures. For a description see *ASR* I 3, cat. 22.
Portrait: Both the man and the woman have portraits.
Dating: 240-250 (*ASR* I 3, cat. 22).
Bibliography: Reinsberg, *ASR* I 3 (2006) 22, pl. 104, 3; Ewald 1999, cat. G5.

639 RITUAL: *ORANS* AND LEARNED MAN (BOY?) (FIG. 30)

Location/Inv.: Ince Blundell Hall. Once at Liverpool, Merseyside Country Museum, inv. 1959.148.229.
Size (coffin): L: 0.95 H: 0.91
Condition: The coffin is preserved.

Frontal relief: From left to right, there is an *Orans*, a woman with a scroll (the head, left shoulder and parts of the scroll are modern, and also the letters ANVS are inscribed on a joined-on piece); a man of which only the legs from the knees downwards and the lower half of the scrolls near his feet are preserved (the rest is a new restauration); a man with a cup; a man/boy clad in a toga and with a scroll, and behind him a herdsman. An animal group with a lion attacking a horse appears on either end of the relief.
Short ends: Lenos-shaped. The lion-horse group of the frontal relief continues on the short ends.
Portrait: The *Orans* and the boy have portrait features, and most probably the learned woman and the man making the sacrifice had portrait features as well.
Inscription: EMIL (ia) on the woman's scroll. CANTENI/VS is written on the scroll of the right *togatus*.
Dating: Around 300 (*ASR* I 3, cat. 25).
Comment: Heavily restored, see *ASR* I 3, 199.

Bibliography: Reinsberg, *ASR* I 3 (2006) cat. 25, pl. 95, 1; Michaelis, 1882, 377-78.

640 RITUAL: *DEXTRARUM IUNCTIO* AND MUSE (FIG. 31)

Location/Inv.: Munich, Glyptothek inv. Gl 533.
Size (coffin): L: 2.26 H: 0.99 D: 1.02
Condition: The coffin is preserved.
Frontal relief: Divided into five panels. The second and fourth panels are strigillated. A woman is represented on the first panel, and a bare-chested philosopher with a scroll is represented on the fifth panel. A *parapetasma* is suspended behind both of them and they are both standing on a plinth. The central panel depicts a couple making the *dextrarum iunctio* gesture in an architectonic frame. The woman and the man are veiled and the man holds a scroll.
Short ends: Weapons.
Portrait: The central couple and the woman and the man on the first and fifth panels have portrait features.
Dating: 210-220 (*ASR* I 3, cat. 35).

Bibliography: Reinsberg, *ASR* I 3 (2006) cat. 35, pl. 104, 1; Ewald 1999, cat. F 1.

641 RITUAL: MAGISTRATE, PHILOSOPHER, *DEXTRARUM IUNCTIO* (FIG. 4 & 78)

Location/Inv.: Naples. Museo Nazionale, inv. 6603.
Size (coffin): L: 2.55 H: 1.17 D: 0.36-8
Condition: The frontal relief is preserved except for the lower part of the relief and part of the upper left and right corners. Fragments of the short end relief are preserved as well.
Frontal relief: The relief is divided into four scenes. From the left, there is a scene with magistrates, a philosopher with a scroll, a learned man, and finally a *dextrarum iunctio* scene. For a description, see Himmelmann 1962.
Left short end: Fragment with part of a standing figure.
Right short end: Fragment with dancing children.
Portrait: The central man on all four scenes has portrait features. It is probably the same person depicted in four different roles.
Dating: 260 (Andreae 1969, 12); Gallienic (Fittschen 1972, 501).

Bibliography: Reinsberg, *ASR* I 3 (2006), cat. 36; Himmelmann 1962; Strocka 1968, 221-39; Andreae 1969; Geyer 1978; Fittschen 1979, 589-92; Ewald 1999, 54-62 cat. G9; Wrede 2001.

642 RITUAL: *DEXTRARUM IUNCTIO* AND *ORANS*

Location/Inv.: Ostia, Museo, inv. 1655; Mentana, Sammlung F. Zeri.
Size (coffin): L: 0.42 H: 0.72
Condition: Two fragments of the frontal relief are preserved.
Provenience: Ostia.
Frontal relief: The fragment in Ostia depicts a woman in a *dextrarum iunctio* scene. The fragment in Mentana depicts an *Orans* and a learned man with a scroll. For a description, see *ASR* I 3, cat. 40.
Portrait: The woman in the *dextrarum iunctio* scene and the *Orans* both have portrait features.
Dating: 310-320 (*ASR* I 3, cat. 40).

Bibliography: Reinsberg, *ASR* I 3 (2006) cat. 40, pl. 116, 1-2.

643 RITUAL: *DEXTRARUM IUNCTIO*, WOMAN, AND LEARNED MAN (FIG. 65)

Location/Inv.: Ostia, Museo.
Size (coffin): L: 2.16 H: 0.94 D: 0.81
Condition: The coffin and lid are preserved.
Frontal relief: Four columns divide the relief into three niches. A woman accompanied by another woman with a naked shoulder and holding a box with incense are represented in the first niche. Two learned men are represented in the third niche. The central niche depicts a couple in a *dextrarum iunctio* scene. A girl grasps the woman's garment, and a boy holds the man's. A cupid is standing between them. For a description, see *ASR* I 3, cat. 41.
Lid: A reclining couple.
Portrait: The woman in the first scene and the man in the third scene have blank portraits. The man on the *dextrarum iunctio* scene has a blank portrait as well; the woman is carved with a generic face.
Dating: 300-310 (*ASR* I 3, cat. 41).

Bibliography: Reinsberg, *ASR* I 3 (2006) cat. 41, pl. 96, 2.

644 RITUAL: *DEXTRARUM IUNCTIO*

Location/Inv.: Portogruaro, Museo Nazionale, inv. 222.
Size (coffin): L: 1.85 H: 0.93 D: 0.75
Condition: Fragments of the frontal relief.
Frontal relief: Four columns divide the relief into three niches. A servant is represented in the first niche. A *dextrarum iunctio* scene is depicted in the second, and two learned men are shown in the third.

Portrait: The couple in the *dextrarum iunctio* scene are carved with blank portraits.
Dating: 310 (*ASR* I 3, cat. 62).

Bibliography: Reinsberg, *ASR* I 3 (2006) cat. 62, pl. 96, 3.

645 RITUAL: *DEXTRARUM IUNCTIO* AND LEARNED BOY (FIG. 5 & 32)

Location/Inv.: Rome, Museo Nazionale Romano, Palazzo Massimo, inv.126372.
Size (coffin): L: 2.48 H: 1.49 D: 1.28
Condition: Several fragments of the coffin and some fragments of the lid are preserved.
Provenience: Acilia, located between Ostia and Rome.
Frontal relief: The central motif shows a *dextrarum iunctio* scene (the couple have alternatively been interpreted as a female praying figure and a male magistrate, see Reinsberg 1995, 360; *ASR* I 3, 145). Men in toga are represented on the left side of the couple, and women wearing long dresses are represented on the right. Only the feet of the female figures are preserved, except for a fragment of a female head. For a description, see Sapelli 1998.
Left short end: Lenos-shaped. The motif of the frontal relief continues on the short end. A figure of a man has been recarved to depict a boy with portrait features.
Right short end: Lenos-shaped. The motif of the frontal relief continues on the short end.
Lid: Cupids.
Portrait: The man on the *dextrarum iunctio* scene has portrait features. Only the lower part of the head is preserved, but the treatment of the beard and skin show us that it is a portrait. A male figure on the left short end has the portrait features of a boy.
Dating: 270-280 (Andreae & Jung 1977); 250 (Koch & Sichtermann 1982, 102-3).
Comment: Traces of reddish brown and golden paint are visible on the drapery and hair.

Bibliography: Reinsberg, *ASR* I 3 (2006) cat. 88; Bianchi-Bandinelli 1954; Heinze 1959, 188; Lücken 1956; Andreae 1969; Himmelmann-Wildschütz 1973, 6-11; *MNR* I 1, 298-304 with a bibliography until 1979; Koch & Sichtermann 1982, 102-3; Fittschen 1984, note 38; Reinsberg 1995; Sapelli 1998, 30-3; La Regina 1998; Birk 2010/11.

646 RITUAL: *DEXTRARUM IUNCTIO* AND LEARNED WOMAN (FIG. 16)

Location/Inv.: Rome, S. Saba.
Size (coffin): L: 2.55 H: 1.28 D: 1.27
Condition: The coffin is preserved.
Frontal relief: Divided into five panels. The second and fourth panels are strigillated. A veiled woman is represented on the first panel, and a philosopher is represented on the fifth panel. A *parapetasma* is suspended behind them. The central panel depicts a *dextrarum iunctio* scene. The woman is veiled and the man holds a scroll. For a description, see Ewald 1999, cat. F 2.
Short ends: Lion griffin.
Portrait: The *dextrarum iunctio* couple have blank portraits; the woman in the left scene has portrait features.
Dating: Late third or early fourth century (Ewald 1999, cat. F 2).

Bibliography: Ewald 1999, cat. F 2, pl. 67, 2.

647 RITUAL: *DEXTRARUM IUNCTIO*, WOMAN, AND PHILOSOPHER (FIG. 13)

Location/Inv.: Rome, S. Sabina.
Size (coffin): L: 2.00 H: 0.78
Condition: The frontal relief is preserved.
Frontal relief: Divided into five panels. The second and fourth panels are strigillated. A veiled woman is represented on the first panel and a bare-chested philosopher appears on the fifth panel. A *parapetasma* is suspended behind both of them. The central panel depicts a *dextrarum iunctio* scene. The woman is veiled and the man holds a scroll. For a description, see Ewald 1999, cat. F 3.
Portrait: The four figures all have blank portraits.
Inscription: OFILIA MARCELLA SIBI ET AVR(elio) VICTORI QVONDAM MARITO B(ene) M(erenti) (publised by Ewald 1999).
Dating: Late third century (Ewald 1999, cat. F 3).
Comment: Female patron. Commissioned for herself and her husband. Reused as a tomb relief by Ildebrando da Chiusi (1309).

Bibliography: Ewald 1999, cat. F 2, pl. 67, 1.

Myth

648 RITUAL: *DEXTRARUM IUNCTIO* AND COMMANDER (FIG. 26)

Location/Inv.: Berlin, Staatliche Museen, Antikensammlung, inv. 1987,2. Once in Villa Rinuccini, near Florence.
Size (Coffin): L: 2.15 H: 1.01 D: 0.99
Condition: The coffin is preserved.
Provenience: Probably from the vicinity of Empoli.
Frontal relief: From left to right are shown a *dextrarum iunctio* scene, a military sacrifice, and Meleager and the boar. For a description, see *ASR* I 3, cat. 6.
Left short end: Victimarius, a bull, and a man in toga.
Right short end: A hunter about to kill a boar.
Portrait: The man and woman in the *dextrarum iunctio* scene and the sacrificing military man all have portrait features.
Dating: Around 200 (Wrede 2001, 23); 200-210 (*ASR* I 3, cat. 6).

Bibliography: Reinsberg, *ASR* I 3 (2006) cat. 6, pl. 21, 1; Brilliant 1992; Wrede 2001; Zanker & Ewald 2004, 292-94.

649 RITUAL: SACRIFICING WOMAN, COMMANDER, AND *DEXTRARUM IUNCTIO* (?) (FIG. 27)

Location/Inv.: Florence, Museo dell' Opera del Duomo.
Size (coffin): L: 2.38 H: 1.17 D: 1.24
Condition: The coffin is preserved.
Frontal relief: Six columns divide the relief into five niches. A Dioscuros is represented in the first and fifth niches. The second niche represents a woman making a sacrifice, and a commander appears in the fourth. The central niche depicts a *dextrarum iunctio* scene.
Left short end: Commander/*clementia* scene.
Right short end: *Victimarius* with a bull.
Portrait: The woman making a sacrifice, the commander, and the man (and perhaps also the woman) in the *dextrarum iunctio* scene all have portrait features.
Dating: 190-200 (Wrede 2001, 117); Around 220 (*ASR* I 3, cat. 13).

Bibliography: Reinsberg, *ASR* I 3 (2006) cat. 13, pl. 31, 1; Wrede 2001.

650 RITUAL: PRAYING WOMAN, LEARNED MAN, AND *DEXTRARUM IUNCTIO*

Location/Inv.: Pisa, Camposanto, C 14 EST.
Size (coffin): L: 2.19 H: 0.97 D: 1.01
Condition: The coffin is preserved.
Frontal relief: Six columns divide the relief into five niches. A Dioscuros is represented in the first and fifth niches. The second niche contains a woman making a sacrifice, and a learned man is represented in the fourth. The central niche depicts a *dextrarum iunctio* scene.
Short ends: Sacrifice scene.
Portrait: The woman in the second, the man in the fourth and the couple in the central niche all have portrait features.
Dating: 200-210 (*ASR* I 3, cat. 57).

Bibliography: Reinsberg, *ASR* I 3 (2006) cat. 57, pl. 71, 2.

651 RITUAL: *DEXTRARUM IUNCTIO*

Location/Inv.: Rome, Musei Vaticani, Museo Chiaramonti, Galleria Lapidaria, inv. 169.
Size (coffin): L: 2.11 H: 0.80 D: 0.83
Condition: The coffin is preserved.
Frontal relief: Divided into five panels. The second and fourth panels are strigillated. Narcissus is represented on the first and fifth panels. The central panel depicts a *dextrarum iunctio* scene. The woman is veiled and the man holds a scroll; a cupid with a torch stands between them. For a description, see *ASR* I 3, cat. 150.
Short ends: Griffin.
Portrait: The man and the woman have blank portraits.
Dating: 220-230 (*ASR* I 3, cat. 150).
Comment: Narcissus is placed on a plinth, and as such the figure should probably be understood as a representation of a statue.

Bibliography: Reinsberg, *ASR* I 3 (2006) cat. 150, pl.11, 3.

652 RITUAL: SACRIFICE AND *DEXTRARUM IUNCTIO*

Location/Inv.: Rome, Museo Nazionale Romano, inv. 124712.
Size (coffin): L: 2.40 H: 0.79; (lid): L: 2.40 H: 0.39
Condition: The coffin and lid are preserved.
Provenience: Via Aurelia.
Frontal relief: Five columns divide the relief into four niches. A Dioscuros is represented in the first and fourth niches. A *dextrarum iunctio* scene is depicted in the second (the man holds a scroll), and a sacrifice scene is represented in the third.
Left short end: The outline of Sol in his wagon is incised. Unfinished.
Right short end: The outline of Selene in her wagon is visible. Unfinished.
Lid: Unfinished. Hunt scenes and a central *tabula ansata* with an inscription.
Portrait: The man and the woman have blank portraits.
Dating: 180 (*ASR* I 3, cat. 87).

Bibliography: Reinsberg, *ASR* I 3 (2006) cat. 87, pl. 56, 2.

653 RITUAL: *DEXTRARUM IUNCTIO*

Location/Inv.: Rome, Museo Nazionale Romano, Palazzo Massimo, inv. 203.
Size (coffin): L: 2.35 H: 1.05
Condition: The frontal relief is preserved.
Provenience: Rome, Via Appia.
Frontal relief: Four columns divide the relief into three niches. The Dioscuroi with their horses are represented in the first and third niches. The central niche depicts a *dextrarum iunctio* scene.
Portrait: Both man and woman had portraits judging from their hairstyles, but only the face of the man is preserved, and it is damaged.
Dating: 260-270 (*ASR* I 3, cat. 80).

Bibliography: Reinsberg, *ASR* I 3 (2006) cat. 80, pl. 114, 1.

654 RITUAL: WOMAN AND MAN MAKING A SACRIFICE

Location/Inv.: Rome, Villa Albani, Galleria delle Leda, inv. 435.
Size (coffin): L: 2.24 H: 1.07
Condition: The frontal relief is preserved.
Frontal relief: Five columns divide the relief into four niches. The Dioscuroi are represented in the first and fourth niches. The second niche depicts a woman, and a commander appears in the third. Both are crowned by Victoria. Together the two figures are making a sacrifice.
Portrait: The man and the woman in the second and third niches have portrait features.
Dating: 250 (*ASR* I 3, cat. 123).

Bibliography: Reinsberg, *ASR* I 3 (2006) cat. 123, pl. 39, 2.

655 RITUAL: *DEXTRARUM IUNCTIO*

Location/Inv.: Tipasa, Musée Nazional, Parc Trémaux.

Size (coffin): L: 2.04 H: 0.85 D: 0.92
Condition: The coffin is preserved, but damaged.
Provenience: Caesarea, near the city gate.
Frontal relief: Five columns divide the relief into four niches. A Dioscuros is represented in the first and fourth. The second niche depicts a sacrifice scene (heads lost), and a *dextrarum iunctio* scene appears in the third.
Short ends: Victimarius.
Portrait: The man and the woman on the marital scene have blank portraits.
Dating: Around 200 (Wrede 2001, 23); 180-190 (*ASR* I 3, cat. 40).

Bibliography: Reinsberg, *ASR* I 3 (2006) cat. 140, pl. 28, 4; Wrede 2001, appendix A 1.

Adults' Life Course

656 RITUAL: COMMANDER, SACRIFICE, AND *DEXTRARUM IUNCTIO*

Location/Inv.: Florence, Galleria degli Uffizi, inv. 82 (once Villa Medici at Rome).
Size (coffin): L: 2.43 H: 0.94 D: 1.10
Condition: The coffin is preserved.
Frontal relief: The relief is divided into three main scenes. From left to right, a commander is represented on a plinth with a barbarian family at his feet, followed by a sacrifice scene, and finally a *dextrarum iunctio* scene.
Left short end: Commander preparing for battle.
Right short end: A child's first bath, a veiled woman, and a nurse. The *Moirai* stand behind the scenery.
Portrait: The three male protagonists have portrait features. All can be dated to the Severan period (*ASR* I 3, cat. 12).
Dating: Around 170 (Wrede 2001, 23); 180 (*ASR* I 3, cat. 12).

Bibliography: Reinsberg, *ASR* I 3 (2006) cat. 12, pl. 1, 4; Wrede 2001, 23.

657 RITUAL: *DEXTRARUM IUNCTIO*

Location/Inv.: Frascati, Villa Borghese (once Taverna).
Size (coffin): L: 2.40 H: 1.25 D: 1.08
Condition: The coffin is preserved, but damaged.
Frontal relief: From left to right: a commander is represented on a plinth with a barbarian family at his feet, followed by a sacrifice scene, and finally a *dextrarum iunctio* scene.
Left short end: Victorious commander and barbarians.
Right short end: Three women with chest and garlands.
Portrait: The man in the *dextrarum iunctio* scene has portrait features, while the woman has a blank portrait. The heads of the other figures are not preserved.
Dating: 180 (Wrede 2001, 23) 190 (*ASR* I 3, cat. 15).

Bibliography: Reinsberg, *ASR* I 3 (2006) cat. 15, pl. 13, 2; Wrede 1981, chap. 2; Wrede 2001, 23.

658 RITUAL: COMMANDER, SACRIFICE, AND *DEXTRARUM IUNCTIO*

Location/Inv.: Mantua, Palazzo Ducale, inv. 186.
Size (coffin): L: 2.51 H: 0.77 D: 0.86-91; (lid): L. 2.38 H: 0.29
Condition: The coffin and the lid are preserved.
Frontal relief: From left to right: a commander is represented on a plinth with a barbarian family at his feet, followed by a sacrifice scene, and finally a *dextrarum iunctio* scene.
Lid: Sol in his wagon, Oceanus, Dioscuroi, Jupiter, Iuno, Fortuna, Minerva, and Selene in her wagon.
Left short end: A woman with a box and another with fruit. A young man with a short tunic, a jug and a box turns his head towards them.
Right short end: A bul and a *victimarius.*
Portrait: The commander and the man in the *dextrarum iunctio* scene have portrait features. The figure making the sacrifice has a boy's portrait.
Dating: Around 170 (Wrede 2001, 23).

Bibliography: Reinsberg, *ASR* I 3 (2006) cat. 33, pl. 1, 2; Wrede 2001; Hölscher 2008. 51-2.

659 RITUAL: COMMANDER, SACRIFICE, AND *DEXTRARUM IUNCTIO* (FIG. 64)

Location/Inv.: Los Angeles, County Museum, inv. 47.8.9.
Size (coffin): L: 2.35 H: 1.00 D: 0.74
Condition: The coffin is preserved.
Frontal relief: From left to right: a commander is represented on a plinth with a barbarian family at his feet, followed by a sacrifice scene, and finally a *dextrarum iunctio* scene.
Left short end: Commander preparing for battle.
Right short end: A child's first bath, a veiled woman, and a nurse. The *Moirai* stand behind the scenery.
Portrait: The commander and the man making a sacrifice have portrait features. The *dextrarum iunctio* couple have blank portraits.
Dating: 170 (Wrede 2001, 23); 170-180 (*ASR* I 3, cat. 29).

Bibliography: Reinsberg, *ASR* I 3 (2006) cat. 29, pl. 1, 3; Wrede 2001.

660 RITUAL: COMMANDER, SACRIFICE, AND *DEXTRARUM IUNCTIO*

Location/Inv.: Poggio a Caiano, Villa Medicea.
Size (coffin): L: 2.48 H: 0.76 D: 0.96
Condition: The coffin is preserved.
Frontal relief: From left to right: a commander is represented on a plinth with a barbarian family at his feet, followed by a sacrifice scene, and finally a *dextrarum iunctio* scene.
Left short end: A child's first bath.
Right short end: Battle.
Portrait: The commander, the man making a sacrifice, and the man in the *dextrarum iunctio* scene all have portrait features.
Dating: Around 200 (Wrede 2001, 23); 160-170 (*ASR* I 3, cat. 61).

Bibliography: Reinsberg, *ASR* I 3 (2006) cat. 61, pl. 1, 1; Wrede 2001.

661 RITUAL: MAN MAKING A SACRIFICE AND *DEXTRARUM IUNCTIO*

Location/Inv.: Rome, Musei Capitolini, Museo Nuovo, inv. 2785.
Size (coffin): L: 1.06 H: 0.88
Condition: Fragment of the frontal relief.
Frontal relief: Part of a sacrifice scene and part of a *dextrarum iunctio* scene.
Portrait: The man on the sacrifice scene and the man making the *dextrarum iunctio* gesture both have blank portraits.
Dating: 190 (*ASR* I 3, cat. 79).

Bibliography: Reinsberg, *ASR* I 3 (2006) cat. 79, pl. 13, 1.

Lion

662 RITUAL: *DEXTRARUM IUNCTIO*

Location/Inv.: Pisa, S. Paolo a Ripa d' Arno inv. XIII bis.
Size (coffin): L: 2.40 H: 1.12 D: 1.33
Condition: The coffin is preserved.
Frontal relief: Strigillated *lenos* with lion heads and a *mandorla* with a *dextrarum iunctio* scene.
Short ends: Lenos- shaped. Lion head.
Portrait: Both the man and the woman have blank portraits.
Dating: 250-260 (*ASR* VI 1, cat. 51).

Bibliography: Stroszeck, *ASR* VI 1 (1998) cat. 51.

Procession

663 RITUAL: *DEXTRARUM IUNCTIO*

Location/Inv.: Orvieto, Palazzo Comunale.
Size (coffin): L: 1.94 H: 0.71
Condition: The frontal relief is preserved.
Frontal relief: A procession of men and women surrounds a couple making the *dextrarum iunctio* gesture.
Portrait: The man and the woman on the marital scene have portrait features.
Dating: 160-170 (*ASR* I 3, cat. 39).

Bibliography: Reinsberg, *ASR* I 3 (2006) cat. 39, pl. 53, 2.

664 RITUAL: SACRIFICING MAN AND *DEXTRARUM IUNCTIO*

Location/Inv.: Rome, Musei Vaticani, Cortile del Belvedere, inv. 1089.
Size (coffin): L: 2.05 H: 1.00 D: 1.05
Condition: The coffin is preserved.
Frontal relief: Sacrificial procession.
Left short end: Dextrarum iunctio scene with the deceased couple (portraits). The man holds a scroll. Behind them a *parapetasma* is suspended.
Right short end: A hunter makes a farewell gesture.
Portrait: The man making a sacrifice and the marital couple on the left short end are carved with portrait features.
Dating: 190 (*ASR* I 3, cat. 153).

Bibliography: Reinsberg, *ASR* I 3 (2006) cat. 153, pl. 57, 3.

665 RITUAL: *DEXTRARUM IUNCTIO*

Location/Inv.: Rome, Musei Vaticani, Muse Pio Clementino, Sala delle Muse.
Size (coffin): L: 2.04 H: 0.42
Condition: The lid is preserved.
Lid: Sacrificial/funerary procession and *dextrarum iunctio*.
Portrait: The man on the marital scene has portrait features.
Dating: 160 (*ASR* I 3, cat. 156); 160-170 (Wrede 2001, 48).

Bibliography: Reinsberg, *ASR* I 3 (2006) cat. 156, pl. 53, 1; Wrede, 2001, 48.

666 RITUAL: *DEXTRARUM IUNCTIO*

Location/Inv.: Rome, Museo Nazionale Romano, Palazzo Massimo, inv. 40799.
Size (coffin): L: 2.08 H: 0.86 D: 0.89
Condition: The coffin is preserved.
Provenience: Rome, on the first part of Via Latina (exavated in 1877). For a discussion of the physical context and its significance for the interpretation of the iconography, see Meinecke 2012, 96-9.
Frontal relief: A *dextrarum iunctio* scene with Concordia and a candelabrum is shown at the centre. Personifications appear on both sides of the couple. For a description, see Giuliano 1985, 50.
Short ends: Roughly carved.
Reverse: Roughly carved.
Portrait: The man and the woman in the *dextrarum iunctio* scene have portrait features.
Inscription: An inscription of the upper profile has been erased. Some of the letters are still visible.
Dating: 270s (Giuliano 1985, 50); the male portrait has been dated to 253-268 and the female portrait to 270-275. For a description of the female portrait, see Sapelli 1998, 15.
Comment: The so-called 'Annona sarcophagus'

Bibliography: Reinsberg, *ASR* I 3 (2006) cat. 82, 124-25; Uggeri 1967/68; Andreae 1970, 83; *MNR* I 8, 1, 47-51; Sapelli 1998, 37-9; Meinecke 2012, 96-9.

667 RITUAL: *DEXTRARUM IUNCTIO*/MAGISTRAT

Location/Inv.: Rome, Museo Torlonia, inv. 395.
Size (coffin): L: 2.64 H: 1.48 D: 1.53
Condition: The frontal relief is preserved but heavily restored. For the extent of the restoration, see Wrede 2001, pl. 16,1.
Frontal relief: The central motif is a *dextrarum iunctio* or a magistrate (?) scene. Men and women are flanking the central couple. For a description, see Ewald 1999, cat. G 16.

Short ends: Lenos-shaped. The motif of the frontal relief continues on the short ends.
Portrait: The man with a scroll has portrait features.
Dating: 250 (Andreae 1969, 12).

Bibliography: Reinsberg, *ASR* I 3 (2006) cat. 94; Bianchi-Bandinelli 1954, 200-3; Andreae 1969; Himmelmann-Wildschütz 1973, pl. 10, 2; Koch & Sichtermann 1982, 103; Ewald 1999, G16; Wrede 2001.

668 RITUAL: MAN MAKING A SACRIFICE AND *DEXTRARUM IUNCTIO* (FIG. 24)

Location/Inv: Rome, S. Lorenzo fuori le Mura.
Size (coffin): L: 2.35 H: 1.02 D: 1.20; (lid): L: 2.37 H: 0.35 D: 1.18
Condition: The coffin and lid are preserved.
Frontal relief: Sacrifice procession and a *dextrarum iunctio* scene in front of a *parapetasma*.
Left short end: Sacrificial procession with pig.
Right short end: Three women with a mirror, shrine, and chest.
Lid: Sol, Oceanus, Dioscuros, Persephone, Dis Pater, Ceres, Dioscuros, and Selene. Masks are depicted on each corner.
Portrait: The man making a sacrifice (*velatus*) and the couple on the marital scene have portrait features. The head of the woman may have been re-worked in a post-antique period.
Inscription: Medieval inscription, see *ASR* I 3, cat. 113.
Dating: 180-190 (*ASR* I 3, cat. 113).

Bibliography: Reinsberg, *ASR* I 3 (2006) cat. 113.

669 RITUAL: WOMAN AND MAN MAKING A SACRIFICE (FIG. 25)

Location/Inv.: St. Petersburg, Hermitage, inv. Gr-4222.
Size (coffin): L: 2.09 H: 0.97
Condition: The coffin and lid are preserved.
Frontal relief: Sacrificial procession.
Left short end: Bucolic scene.
Right short end: Hunting scene.
Lid: Sol, Oceanus, three Moirae, Juno, Jupiter, Minerva, and Selene.
Portrait: The man and the woman on the sacrifice scene have portrait features.
Dating: 180 (*ASR* I 3, cat. 137).

Bibliography: Reinsberg, *ASR* I 3 (2006) cat. 137, pl. 57, 2.

Ritual

670 RITUAL: SACRIFICE AND *DEXTRARUM IUNCTIO*

Location/Inv.: Rignano, Via Flaminia.
Size (coffin): L: 2.10 H: 0.80 D: 0.97
Condition: The coffin is preserved.
Frontal relief: Divided into five panels. The second and fourth panels are strigillated. A man making a sacrifice is represented in front of a *parapetasma* on the first panel, and a praying woman is represented on the fifth panel. Both figures stand on statue plinths. The central panel depicts a *dextrarum iunctio* scene. An empty inscription panel appears beneath this composition.
Short ends: Griffin.
Portrait: The man on the sacrifice scene and the couple on the marital scene show blank portraits.
Dating: 180-190 (*ASR* I 3, cat. 67).

Bibliography: Reinsberg, *ASR* I 3 (2006) cat. 67, pl. 29, 1.

671 RITUAL: SACRIFICE (VENUS AND MILITARY MAN) AND *DEXTRARUM IUNCTIO*

Location/Inv.: Rome, Catacombe di Pretestato, Museo.
Size (coffin): L: 2.32 H: 1.17 D: 1.31; (lid): L: 2.32 H: 0.83 D: 1.17
Condition: The coffin and lid are preserved but have been pieced together from several fragments.
Provenience: Rome, Catacombe di Pretestato.
Frontal relief: The central motif is a sacrifice scene. A generic figure with *cornucopia* is represented to the left of this composition, and a *dextrarum iunctio* scene is represented to the right. For a description, see Gütschow 1938, 91-104.
Left short end: Three women with objects used in connection with cultic acts or sacrifices.
Right short end: Dancing woman and a flute player.
Lid: A reclining couple.
Portrait: The woman (Venus) and the military man on the central scene, the man in the marital scene, and the couple on the lid all have portrait features.
Dating: 238. The sarcophagus has been attributed to the Emperor Balbinus on the evidence of the portrait features of the man. This is questionable; the date should probably be given as after 238, probably around 240 (ASR I 3, 32).

Bibliography: Reinsberg, *ASR* I 3 (2006) 31-2, cat. 73, Gütschow 1938, 77-109; Junker 1966, 501-14; Reinsberg 1985, 3-16; Meyer 1986, 279-89; Wrede 2001, 60, 64, 65, pl. 15, 1.

672 RITUAL: SACRIFICE AND *DEXTRARUM IUNCTIO*

Location/Inv.: Rome, Palazzo Verospi (lost).
Size (coffin): L: 2.33 H: 0.78
Condition: The frontal relief is preserved.
Frontal relief: Divided into five panels. The second and fourth panels are strigillated. A man making a sacrifice is represented in front of a *parapetasma* on the first panel, and a praying woman is represented on the fifth panel. Both figures stand on statue plinths. The central panel depicts a *dextrarum iunctio* scene, also displayed on a plinth decorated with garlands.
Portrait: The man on the first and third panels has portrait features.
Dating: 180-190 (*ASR* I 3, cat. 109).

Bibliography: Reinsberg, *ASR* I 3 (2006) cat. 109, pl. 29, 2.

Seasonal

673 RITUAL: *DEXTRARUM IUNCTIO*
Location/Inv.: Pisa, Camposanto, inv. 81.
Size (coffin): L: 2.07 H: 0.91 D: 0.86
Condition: The coffin is preserved.
Frontal relief: Six columns divide the relief into five niches. A *dextrarum iunctio* scene is represented in the central niche. The woman is veiled. A seasonal personification is depicted in each of the other niches. A *parapetasma* is suspended behind the figures. For a description, see Arias 1977, cat. A 17.
Left short end: A panther with one paw on a *krater.*
Right short end: A panther with one paw on a *krater.*
Portrait: The woman and the man on the marital scene have blank portraits.
Dating: 270-280 (*ASR* V 4, cat. 11).

Bibliography: Kranz, *ASR* V 4 (1984) cat. 11, pl. 5, 2; Reinsberg, *ASR* I 3 (2006) cat. 52; Arias et al. 1977, cat. A 17.

674 RITUAL: *DEXTRARUM IUNCTIO*
Location/Inv.: Pisa, S. Pierino.
Size (coffin): L: 2.18/23 H: 0.71/76 D: 0.71
Condition: The coffin is preserved.
Frontal relief: Six columns divide the relief into five niches. A *dextrarum iunctio* scene is represented in the central niche. The woman is veiled and the man holds a scroll. Concordia is depicted behind the couple and a cupid stands between them. Seasonal personifications are represented in the remaining niches. For a description, see *ASR* V 4, cat. 12.
Portrait: The woman and man in the central niche have portrait features.
Dating: The portrait of the man on the marital scene can be dated to the Tetrarchic period (*ASR* V 4, cat. 12). The head of the woman is carved with a blank portrait.

Bibliography: Kranz, *ASR* V 4 (1984) cat. 12, pl. 5, 2.

Unknown

675 RITUAL: *DEXTRARUM IUNCTIO*
Location/Inv.: New York, Metropolitan Museum of Art, inv. 18.145.52.
Size (coffin): L: 0.40 H: 0.48
Condition: A fragment of the frontal relief is preserved.
Frontal relief: A couple are shown in a *dextrarum iunctio* scene. A cupid is depicted between them and Concordia appears behind them. For a description, see *ASR* I 3, cat. 38.
Portrait: The faces of the man and the woman are damaged, but the man at least has a portrait hairstyle.
Dating: 220-230 (*ASR* I 3, cat. 38).

Bibliography: Reinsberg, *ASR* I 3 (2006) cat. 38, pl. 110, 7.

676 RITUAL: *DEXTRARUM IUNCTIO*
Location/Inv.: Rome, Villa Doria Pamphilj, Villino della Servitù, northern wall.
Size (coffin): L: 0.42 H: 0.51
Condition: A fragment of the frontal relief is preserved.
Frontal relief: A couple in a *dextrarum iunctio* scene are represented between columns. For a description, see *ASR* I 3, cat. 128.
Portrait: The couple are carved with blank portraits.
Dating: 220-230 (*ASR* I 3, cat. 128).

Bibliography: Reinsberg, *ASR* I 3 (2006) cat. 128, pl. 110, 8.

Addenda

A1 LEARNED MAN

Location/Inv.: Rome, Musei Vaticani, Cortile del Belvedere inv. 1111
Size (coffin): L: 2.05 H: 0.76 D: 0.80
Condition: The coffin is preserved.
Frontal relief: Strigillated coffin with a lion head at each end. A learned man (*palliatus*) with a scroll is shown in the *mandorla*.
Portrait: The man in the *mandorla* has a blank portrait.
Dating: 260-270 (ASR VI 1, cat. 148).

Bibliography: Stroszeck, *ASR* VI 1 (1998) cat. 148, pl. 16, 2; Ewald 1999, cat. F 33.

A2 LEARNED MAN

Location/Inv.: Rome, Musei Vaticani, Museo Gregoriano Profano.
Condition: The coffin is preserved.
Frontal relief: Two sacrificing cupids placing fruit on an altar are shown on each end of the relif. A third cupid is placed beside them. The central motif is a *clipeus* with a portrait bust held by two *victoriae* with standarts.
Lid: a marble slab.
Portrait: The bust is carved with a blank portrait.

A3 EDUCATED WOMAN

Location/Inv.: Rome, Vatican, The necropolis beneath S. Pietro.
Provenience: Tomb R.
Condition: The coffin is preserved.
Frontal relief: Strigillated *lenos*-shaped coffin. A woman seated in a basket chair is represented on the first panel. She is playing a lyre and in front of her is a Muse (?). A man seated in a chair with lion feet-shaped legs is depicted on the fourth panel. Beside him is a column with a sundial and a philosopher (?) is standing behind him.
Short ends: Weapons.
Portrait: The woman is carved with a portrait. The head of the man is lost.
Dating: Late third century.
Comment: Lycian-motif.

Bibliography: Liverani & Spinola 2010, 136, figs. 84-5.

A4 *CLIPEUS* PORTRAIT OF A MAN

Location/Inv.: Rome, Vatican, the Santa Rosa necropolis.
Provenience: The Santa Rosa necropolis, tomb IX. Placed in a *forma*.
Condition: Fragments of the coffin and the lid are preserved.
Frontal relief: Strigillated. A column is represented at each end, and a bust of a man in toga is showen in a *clipeus* as the central motif. An inscription is placed beneath the *clipeus*.
Short ends: Unknown.
Lid: A marble slab without decoration.
Portrait: The man is carved with a blank portrait.
Inscription: VLPIA M../CELLA V../..VIII......
Dating: First half of the third century.
Comment: A male bust used for the commemoration of a woman.

Bibliography: Liverani & Spinola 2010, 263, fig. 106.

A5 *CLIPEUS* BUST OF A WOMAN AND A MAN

Location/Inv.: Rome, Museo Capitolini, Antiquarium.
Condition: The lid is preserved.
Lid: On each side of an empty inscription panel are placed a *clipeus* bust of a woman (to the left) and a man (to the right) held by flying cupids. Cornucopiae are placed beneath the *clipei*. A theatrical mask is placed at each end of the relief.
Portrait: Both the woman and the man are carved with a portrait.
Dating: Severan.

Bibliography: Unknown; DAI-Rom-Neg. 77.120 (file no. 2416_A04)

A6 SHELL WITH A BUST OF A WOMAN

Location/Inv.: Capri, the Art Collection of Axel Munthe at Villla San Michele.
Provenience: Unknown.
Condition: The coffin is preserved (used as a flower pot).
Frontal relief: The relief is unfinished. A central shell with a bust of a woman is carried by group of sea-monsters and nymphs. Swimming dolphins are shown beneath the shell. For a description, see Freccero 2003, 138-39.
Short ends: Without relief decoration.
Reverse: Roughly carved.
Portrait: The female bust is carved with a blank portrait.
Dating: Antonine period (Freccero 2003, 139)

Bibliography: Andrén 1965, 140, no. 38, pl. XII; Freccero 2003, 138-39.

Index

Q

R

S

T